(Continued on back endsheets)

Dictionary of Literary Biography® • Volume One Hundred Forty One

British Children's Writers, 1880–1914

Dictionary of Literary Biography® • Volume One Hundred Forty One

British Children's Writers, 1880–1914

Edited by
Laura M. Zaidman
University of South Carolina at Sumter

Editorial Adviser for the
British Children's Writers Series
Caroline C. Hunt
College of Charleston

A Bruccoli Clark Layman Book
Gale Research Inc.
Detroit, Washington, D.C., London

Printed in the United States of America

Published simultaneously in the United Kingdom
by Gale Research International Limited
(An affiliated company of Gale Research Inc.)

The paper used in this publication meets the minimum requirements
of American National Standard for Information Sciences—Permanence
Paper for Printed Library Materials, ANSI Z39.48-1984. ∞ ™

Library of Congress Catalog Card Number 94-076443
ISBN 0-8103-5555-8

I(T)P™

The trademark ITP is used under license.

10 9 8 7 6 5 4 3 2 1

To my daughter, Debbie,
and in loving memory of my parents,
Rose and Ben Mandell

Contents

Plan of the Series

The advisory board, the editors, and the publisher of the *Dictionary of Literary Biography* are joined in endorsing Mark Twain's declaration. The literature of a nation provides an inexhaustible resource of permanent worth. We intend to make literature and its creators better understood and more accessible to students and the reading public, while satisfying the standards of teachers and scholars.

To meet these requirements, *literary biography* has been construed in terms of the author's achievement. The most important thing about a writer is his writing. Accordingly, the entries in *DLB* are career biographies, tracing the development of the author's canon and the evolution of his reputation.

The purpose of *DLB* is not only to provide reliable information in a convenient format but also to place the figures in the larger perspective of literary history and to offer appraisals of their accomplishments by qualified scholars.

The publication plan for *DLB* resulted from two years of preparation. The project was proposed to Bruccoli Clark by Frederick C. Ruffner, president of the Gale Research Company, in November 1975. After specimen entries were prepared and typeset, an advisory board was formed to refine the entry format and develop the series rationale. In meetings held during 1976, the publisher, series editors, and advisory board approved the scheme for a comprehensive biographical dictionary of persons who contributed to North American literature. Editorial work on the first volume began in January 1977, and it was published in 1978. In order to make *DLB* more than a reference tool and to compile volumes that individually have claim to status as literary history, it was decided to organize volumes by topic, period, or genre. Each of these free-

*From an unpublished section of Mark Twain's autobiography, copyright by the Mark Twain Company

standing volumes provides a biographical-bibliographical guide and overview for a particular area of literature. We are convinced that this organization — as opposed to a single alphabet method — constitutes a valuable innovation in the presentation of reference material. The volume plan necessarily requires many decisions for the placement and treatment of authors who might properly be included in two or three volumes. In some instances a major figure will be included in separate volumes, but with different entries emphasizing the aspect of his career appropriate to each volume. Ernest Hemingway, for example, is represented in *American Writers in Paris, 1920-1939* by an entry focusing on his expatriate apprenticeship; he is also in *American Novelists, 1910-1945* with an entry surveying his entire career. Each volume includes a cumulative index of the subject authors and articles. Comprehensive indexes to the entire series are planned.

With volume ten in 1982 it was decided to enlarge the scope of *DLB*. By the end of 1986 twenty-one volumes treating British literature had been published, and volumes for Commonwealth and Modern European literature were in progress. The series has been further augmented by the *DLB Yearbooks* (since 1981) which update published entries and add new entries to keep the *DLB* current with contemporary activity. There have also been *DLB Documentary Series* volumes which provide biographical and critical source materials for figures whose work is judged to have particular interest for students. One of these companion volumes is entirely devoted to Tennessee Williams.

We define literature as the *intellectual commerce of a nation:* not merely as belles lettres but as that ample and complex process by which ideas are generated, shaped, and transmitted. *DLB* entries are not limited to "creative writers" but extend to other figures who in their time and in their way influenced the mind of a people. Thus the series encompasses historians, journalists, publishers, and screenwriters. By this means readers of *DLB* may be aided to perceive literature not as cult scripture in the keeping of intellectual high priests but firmly positioned at the center of a nation's life.

DLB includes the major writers appropriate to each volume and those standing in the ranks immediately behind them. Scholarly and critical counsel has been sought in deciding which minor figures to include and how full their entries should be. Wherever possible, useful references are made to figures who do not warrant separate entries.

Each *DLB* volume has a volume editor responsible for planning the volume, selecting the figures for inclusion, and assigning the entries. Volume editors are also responsible for preparing, where appropriate, appendices surveying the major periodicals and literary and intellectual movements for their volumes, as well as lists of further readings. Work on the series as a whole is coordinated at the Bruccoli Clark Layman editorial center in Columbia, South Carolina, where the editorial staff is responsible for accuracy of the published volumes.

One feature that distinguishes *DLB* is the illustration policy – its concern with the iconography of literature. Just as an author is influenced by his surroundings, so is the reader's understanding of the author enhanced by a knowledge of his environment. Therefore *DLB* volumes include not only drawings, paintings, and photographs of authors, often depicting them at various stages in their careers, but also illustrations of their families and places where they lived. Title pages are regularly reproduced in facsimile along with dust jackets for modern authors. The dust jackets are a special feature of *DLB* because they often document better than anything else the way in which an author's work was perceived in its own time. Specimens of the writers' manuscripts are included when feasible.

Samuel Johnson rightly decreed that "The chief glory of every people arises from its authors." The purpose of the *Dictionary of Literary Biography* is to compile literary history in the surest way available to us – by accurate and comprehensive treatment of the lives and work of those who contributed to it.

The *DLB* Advisory Board

Introduction

"When I am dead, I hope it may be said: / His sins were scarlet, but his books were read." Hilaire Belloc, writer of mock cautionary tales for children as well as books for adults, reminds his readers in this verse that good books outlast their authors. Indeed, some of the books enjoyed by children during the late Victorian and Edwardian eras have become classics and are still read. To acquaint readers with this dynamic period of literature and illustration for children, the essays in *British Children's Writers, 1880–1914* analyze the period's dominant figures and important works for juvenile readers.

The political, social, and cultural changes which shaped British society's attitudes about children created a receptive environment for children's books and periodicals during the last decades of the nineteenth century. Reform legislation improved children's status by protecting their welfare and enhancing the quality of living conditions and family life; with Queen Victoria's support Prime Minister Benjamin Disraeli initiated during the 1870s advances in public health, housing, recreation, and workers' rights. Reforms continued into the 1880s, and children benefited from many of the newly passed laws. Legislation in 1875 protected boys doing dangerous chimney sweeping. Both the National Society for the Prevention of Cruelty to Children, established in 1885, and the Prevention of Cruelty to Children Act of 1894 sought to protect children from abuse. Various other reform legislation included an 1886 law that forbade parents' selling their children into prostitution; the Children's Charter of 1889, which protected children from abuse; the Adoption Act of 1889; and the Custody of Children Act of 1891. These social reforms not only benefited Great Britain's youth but also created a climate more receptive to a child-centered literary period.

Even before the late Victorian period, though, various literary influences increased society's nurturing attitude toward children. Jean-Jacques Rousseau's *Émile* (1762) and William Wordsworth's *The Prelude* (1850), which romanticized childhood by glorifying the free-spirited child of nature, are familiar examples. New attitudes in early childhood education also became popular in the mid nineteenth century. In Germany Friedrich Froebel introduced the system of the kindergarten (children's garden) to reform early childhood education. Two of his books, *System of Infant Gar-*

dens (1855, English translation) and *Child and Child-Nature* (1879, English translation), inspired educators in England to form more liberal attitudes. Just as kindergarten encourages the child to begin a lifelong process of intellectual growth, garden images represent the pleasurable learning experience of reading children's books, and the garden motif abounds in children's literature of this period.

On the other hand, restrictions at home, school, and church during this time often limited the child's playtime freedom with the demands of manners, lessons, and morals. Didacticism dominated the books, magazines, and tracts produced for Sunday schools during the decades preceding 1880 as a result of the evangelical movement. The widely disseminated publications of the Religious Tract Society had an especially strong influence on early-nineteenth-century children's literature. In 1799 several religious leaders, including the Reverend George Burder, a Congregational minister and author of *Early Piety* (1776), established this society, which published sentimental, pious books with the explicit message of religious conversion, such as Leigh Richmond's *The Dairyman's Daughter* (1810). The Society for the Propagation of Christian Knowledge also distributed religious reading materials for youth. Though evangelical writers throughout the Victorian period captured many young readers' minds and souls and though didactic literature never disappeared, its influence was decreasing perceptibly in the last decades of the century.

By 1880 public education had created more readers eager for secular books and magazines. The government's child-labor and welfare laws protected children's physical well-being, and other legislation assured children's literacy. The Public Libraries Act of 1850 had made books more accessible to the public, and during the following years the public education system produced a nation of readers. A series of education acts of the 1870s provided publicly supported schools; by 1880 England had compulsory school attendance for all children under twelve. The University Tests Act of 1871 allowed more middle-class students at Oxford and Cambridge. These and other educational reforms led to greater social mobility and a more literate populace; by 1900 England's literacy rates were greatly increased.

In this better-educated society more parents bought books and magazines to read to their children. People wanted entertaining children's literature, and the book trade met this consumer demand. Publishers developed less expensive printing methods, more effective advertising, and innovations in illustration with color lithography to produce a higher-quality art. The thriving publishing industry supplied the demands of a receptive children's book market. Indicative of the increased popularity of entertaining, high-quality picture books is the fact that Kate Greenaway's *Under the Window* quickly sold over twenty thousand copies during the 1879 Christmas season. Many other writers enjoyed similar success in the following years as secular literature replaced the didactic books in homes and schools.

Adventure fiction and nonfiction also attracted a mass readership in the 1880s. One reason for the phenomenal success of these exciting tales by such writers as Rudyard Kipling, G. A. Henty, and Robert Louis Stevenson is that they supported the British government's policy of imperial expansion. The adventure genre became especially popular after Disraeli's death in 1881 when the Primrose League, named after the prime minister's favorite flower, published juvenile literature advocating the imperial cause. In the next two decades other writers reflected this spirit of adventurous militarism in line with the government's political views. Adventure books, with their tales of heroic adventures in faraway lands, produced a generation who emulated these heroes glorified as empire builders. Although defeats in the Second Boer War in South Africa (1899–1902) demoralized the British, books and magazines continued to idealize what society perceived as the masculine virtues: patriotism, self-sacrifice, and honor. These heroic models encouraged boys to accept the ideology of an imperialistic government determined to spread its doctrines both at home and abroad.

Complementing this tradition of establishing ideals of behavior through adventure fiction, the Boy Scouts organization became an important social and literary phenomenon. Scouting, rooted in values lauded by adventure fiction, was founded in 1908 by Robert Stephenson Smyth Baden-Powell, whose *Scouting for Boys* (1908) and other Scouting materials reflect the influence of Kipling's *Kim* (1901), *The Jungle Book* (1894), and *The Second Jungle Book* (1895). *Scouting for Boys* includes an outline of *Kim,* and Baden-Powell stated that Kim's title of "little friend to all the world" should serve as the model for all scouts. Kipling, in turn, wrote "A Boy Scout's Patrol Song" (1913). The group celebrated the virtues of individualism and patriotism, preparing boys to serve the expanding empire. Scouting reflected adventure novels' popular appeal, and Boy Scout readers increased the books' popularity.

Another social institution that mirrored the rise of a progressive society and the fall of the evangelical movement is the religious school. Although Sunday schools still awarded didactic prize books such as John Bunyan's *The Pilgrim's Progress* (1678) and James Janeway's *A Token for Children* (1671), they also selected as prizes popular contemporary works such as Lewis Carroll's Alice books (*Alice's Adventures in Wonderland,* 1865, and *Through the Looking-Glass and What Alice Found There,* 1872) and Henty's adventure novels. Adding to the decline of evangelicalism's influence on children's literature was the decrease in Sunday school attendance. It dropped after 1880 because compulsory elementary education and various youth organizations offered the educational, social, and moral instruction that had once been the exclusive domain of Sunday schools.

Further evidence of this distancing from didactic children's literature in Great Britain is found in the type of books given as prizes in public schools and the books approved by school libraries by the 1880s. Students who excelled in academic achievement, school attendance, and conduct no longer received Bibles, prayer books, and outdated classics such as Thomas Day's *Sandford and Merton* (1783–1789). Books with a heavily didactic religious purpose were eschewed as "old-fashioned moral tales," according to J. S. Bratton's *The Impact of Victorian Children's Fiction* (1981). Instead, schools awarded recent works of juvenile and some adult fiction. The London school board's prize and reward books in the late 1870s included contemporary writers' collections of fairy tales, Harriet Beecher Stowe's *Uncle Tom's Cabin* (1851), and Ennis Graham's (Mary Louisa Molesworth) *The Cuckoo Clock* (1877). By 1890 school prize committees virtually ignored religious books as rewards. School-approved library books also influenced children's reading habits. By 1880 the London school board's list of approved library books reflected the wider range of literary tastes: novels by Henty and Molesworth, fairy tales, and fantasies – especially the popular Alice books. Just as Alice followed a rabbit down a hole, most children's authors and illustrators followed Carroll's aim: to delight, not to instruct.

Thus both the receptive market for children's books and the success of other writers motivated many to enter the child's world, since one author's success led to another's trying to duplicate that feat. For instance, Stevenson began *A Child's Garden of*

Verses (1885) in 1881 when his mother gave him the popular *Kate Greenaway's Birthday Book for Children* (1880; text written by Mrs. Sale Barker). In late Victorian children's literature allusions to other books emphasize the interrelationships, such as when E. Nesbit pays homage to her contemporary Kenneth Grahame: her narrator Oswald Bastable in *The WouldbeGoods* (1901) says that Grahame's *The Golden Age* (1895) " 'is A.1., except where it gets mixed up with grown-up nonsense.' "

Indeed, childhood has a separate place in this era's literature. Many factors set children apart from adults. Whether physically apart (being in boarding school) or psychologically removed (being ignored by adults), children are free from adult responsibilities. Children's writers, by returning to the rich store of youth's golden days, create a magical realm of childhood through books and illustrations. Youngsters' playfulness and modes of recreation inspire writers' re-creation of childhood's sights, sounds, and feelings. Successful children's writers of the period could tune in children's inner feelings. Grahame, certainly a major figure because of his classic *The Wind in the Willows* (1908), presents the delights and sounds of childhood. He shares in his essay "The Inner Ear" his secret for being able to portray the inner voices that beckon the reader to experience childhood's adventures; Grahame explains that hearing children's thoughts requires listening to an "inner silence, in which 'the very rush of sap, the thrust . . . of germination, will join in the din, and go far to deafen us.' "

Critics of children's literature often attribute writers' success to their being able to know intuitively what being a child is like. E. Nesbit, for instance, created interesting characters who display the directness and honesty of real children. A case in point is this passage from "The Cockatoucan" (*Nine Unlikely Tales,* 1901) in which the young narrator expresses her annoyance with adults' rudeness:

> I can't think why grown-up people don't see how impertinent these questions are. Suppose you were to answer, "I'm top of my class, Auntie, thank you, and I'm very good. And now let's have a little talk about you. Aunt, dear, how much money have you got, and have you been scolding the servants again, or have you tried to be good and patient as a properly brought up aunt should be, eh, dear?"

A contemporary of Nesbit's, J. M. Barrie also successfully depicts the world from a child's imaginative viewpoint. In one of the most famous scenes of *Peter Pan* (1904), the title character represents childlike innocence when he asks the audience to clap if

they believe in fairies to save the dying Tinker Bell. This magic (or, rather, the willing suspension of disbelief) keeps alive the element of wonder in children's literature. Most of the authors and illustrators during this period depict childhood as an idyllic time of enchantment and separateness from the adult world.

The longest entries in this volume focus on the period's seven major writers for children: Barrie, Francis Hodgson Burnett, Grahame, Henty, Kipling, Nesbit, and Beatrix Potter. Seventeen other essays deal with important writers and illustrators who once enjoyed great popularity, though some may not be familiar to readers today. The appendix essay discusses popular minor illustrators. The twenty-five entries collectively represent a varied group of people whose divergent cultural experiences encompassed England, the United States, and far-off parts of the British Empire. For instance, at sixteen, Burnett moved from Manchester, England, to Knoxville, Tennessee, but often returned to England. Just before he was six, Kipling was taken to England from India and returned to India several times. Joseph Jacobs, born in Australia, lived in England and then migrated to New York. Bertha Upton moved to America while her daughter Florence remained in England. Besides revealing in their work this multiplicity of cultural backgrounds, these writers and artists expressed their creativity in richly diverse literary and artistic forms: magazine short stories and nonfiction, novels (from realistic fiction to fantasy), fairy tales, poetry, and illustrations for a juvenile audience.

Boys' magazines published many varieties of fiction, nonfiction, and art. Of the many boys' weeklies competing for the large working-class audience, the most successful was the *Boy's Own Paper* (1879–1967), published by the Religious Tract Society. It successfully merged Sunday school reading with mass-market reading tastes to appeal to a wide audience; it provided wholesome writing, Christian in tone, but not evangelical. Because contemporary young readers considered didactic literature outdated, this magazine gave them what they wanted. Whether exploring the worlds of adventure, survival, war, hobbies, or school, the periodical emphasized the imperialist ideology of aggressive, competitive, yet gentlemanly behavior. The *Boy's Own Paper* appealed to the boys who read and bought it, the parents who approved it, and the society that accepted its values. By 1884 it had a quarter of a million readers; in 1914 it shifted from weekly to monthly publication and ran more than fifty years. Profiting from the technological advances in printing, the *Boy's Own Paper* had high-quality engraved, color illustrations, text, paper, and printing. The first issue on 18 January 1879 included articles about the British navy, natural history, swimming the English Channel, and outdoor sports as well as puzzles and competitions; the front page featured "My First Football Match," with the byline "By an Old Boy" – Talbot Baines Reed, perhaps the most successful boys' school story writer of the period. After three months the magazine proved so popular that the *Boy's World* and many other rival quality magazines soon appeared in the same format, but none matched the popularity of the *Boy's Own Paper*.

Penny dreadfuls, with their crime and adventure tales, offered less literary quality but competed for the same audience of middle-class boys. Some critics ridiculed these "bloods" (for "blood and thunder" magazines) as trashy and sensationalized. For example, stories in *Gem* and *Magnet* featuring "London hooligans" were deemed "scurrilous" and came under additional fire for their repetitious style and predictable plots. Despite the lack of literary merit, these undeniably popular "bloods" had loyal young readers and even had the support of some adults. In 1906 W. T. Stead observed that "boys take penny dreadfuls as children take measles, and they usually recover." Others saw them as a stepping-stone to more serious literature and lifelong reading habits. Undeniably, these less "literary" magazines enjoyed phenomenal success. Alfred Harmsworth's empire of boys' juvenile papers grew rapidly in the 1890s with a succession of newly established magazines: *Marvel* (1893), *Union Jack* (1894), *Pluck* (1894), *Boys' Friend* (1895), and *Magnet* (1908). *Gem* (1907) was a school-story magazine, beginning with adventure stories, then shifting to "Tom Merry's Schooldays" stories by Charles Hamilton, under the pseudonym of Frank Richards, author of over seven thousand stories – in fact, the *Guinness Book of World Records* names him as the world's most prolific author, with more than 72 million words to his credit.

Girls' magazines also thrived in the late Victorian age. The *Girl's Own Paper* included in its premier issue on 3 January 1880 articles about Queen Victoria's girlhood (with a full-page, ready-for-framing portrait), ladies' fashion, cooking, and sewing – subjects obviously focusing on domestic skills and proper behavior suitable for young women. Its audience was not strictly juvenile readers: competitions had an age limit of twenty-five (in contrast to age sixteen for the *Boy's Own Paper*). Like other girls' magazines *Girls' Realms* (1890–1914) conformed to the social mores by encouraging do-

mesticity and discouraging radical causes, such as woman suffrage. Other magazines for working-class girls included *Girls' Friend* (1899–1931), *Girls' Reader* (1908–1915), and *Girls' Home* (1910–1915).

Often serialized in these successful girls' and boys' magazines, the school story genre soared in popularity. Writers refined the formula originated by Thomas Hughes's *Tom Brown's Schooldays* (1857), acknowledged as the first school story. Published a year after the Crimean War, the novel transforms the battlefield into the school playing field. The boys' school story both entertained and shaped boys into men by celebrating the virtues of team spirit, fair play, competition, mental stamina, and physical strength. Reed built his considerable reputation with stories such as *The Fifth Form at St. Dominic's* (1887), serialized beginning in 1881 in the *Boy's Own Paper;* they serve as the genre's model of excellence. The most popular and prolific author of girls' school stories is L. T. Meade (Elizabeth Thomasina Smith). Writing over two hundred and fifty books and contributing to collections of stories, Meade set the standard for the girls' school story in novels such as *A World of Girls* (1886). She also edited *Atalanta,* a periodical for girls. Others who promoted proper feminine virtues in their girls' school stories during this period include Evelyn Sharp, Ethel C. Kenyon, and Angela Brazil.

Just as the school stories present life at school, realistic fiction of the period focuses on the real world of the home. Burnett's *Little Lord Fauntleroy* (1885) and *A Little Princess* (1905; shorter version as *Sara Crewe,* 1887), as well as Nesbit's *The Story of the Treasure Seekers* (1899) and *The Railway Children* (1906), ranked among the period's most popular novels. Critics, however, have challenged the wisdom of their optimistic plot endings and saccharine, ideal characterizations of children. Some detractors blame sentimental fiction for inspiring a generation of little boys dressed in velvet suits with lace collars. Despite stereotyped characters and clichéd ideas, realistic fiction's largely optimistic worldview offered Victorian and Edwardian readers extremely popular entertainment.

Fantasy, a relatively new genre of children's literature, contrasts with the verisimilitude of the school story and other realistic fiction. Introducing magic into the contemporary realistic world, fantasies allow children to explore their wildest dreams. F. Anstey's (Thomas Anstey Guthrie) *Vice Versâ* (1882) combines two genres, the realistic school story and fantasy, as father and son switch bodies. Other notable fantasies include Anstey's *The Brass Bottle* (1900), Nesbit's *Five Children and It* (1900) and

The Phoenix and the Carpet (1904), Kipling's *Puck of Pook's Hill* (1906) and its sequel *Rewards and Fairies* (1910), Bertha and Florence K. Upton's Golliwogg series (thirteen books, 1895–1909), and Barrie's *Peter and Wendy* (1911). Fantasy allowed children's writers to satirize contemporary society gently and set the tradition for the following decades of books that soared beyond the here-and-now real world.

Fairy tales, another "new" type of children's book on the scene, enjoyed a revival from previous generations. The collected tales celebrate past traditions of Charles Perrault, the Brothers Grimm, and *Arabian Nights*. Andrew Lang's famous series of twelve anthologies (1889–1910) titled with different colors begins with *The Blue Fairy Book*. Lang, however, credits his wife Leonora with doing most of the work: "The Fairy Books have been almost wholly the work of Mrs. Lang . . . My part has been that of Adam, according to Mark Twain, in the Garden of Eden. Eve worked, Adam superintended." Joseph Jacobs, another important folklorist of the era, published *English Fairy Tales* (1890), stories of ogres, giants, and clever humans from chapbooks as early as the 1500s.

Literary fairy tales contrast with the traditional fairy tales passed from generation to generation. Most notably, Oscar Wilde and Lucy Clifford created original works that differ from folktales in that they offer more commentary on social attitudes. These late Victorians wrote for both children and adults, perhaps allowing them a larger forum to comment upon contemporary values and attitudes about materialism, class structure, and family duty. For example, Wilde's tales "The Happy Prince" and "The Selfish Giant" (1888) subtly show how the drive for materialism can lead to the neglect of spirituality. Clifford's "The New Mother," collected in *Anyhow Stories, Moral and Otherwise* (1882), portrays a mother who reluctantly abandons her two disobedient daughters and is replaced by a terrifying creature. Children's literature critic F. J. Harvey Darton comments in his *Children's Books in England: Five Centuries of Social Life* (1932; revised edition, 1982) that, even fifty years after reading this tale, he could still see in his mind the horrifying new mother, her glass eyes shining and her wooden tail thumping, coming to get the misbehaving children. The many varieties of fairy tales of the period transmit past traditions and introduce new twists on familiar themes, running the gamut from moralizing to entertaining to thrilling.

Animal tales offer still another type of children's fiction – as well as a quite different perspective from the earlier fables and bestiaries. By 1890 stories no longer employed animals to comment overtly on proper human behavior but rather engaged and entertained children with humanlike situations. Kipling's jungle books and *Just So Stories* (1902), Grahame's *The Wind in the Willows,* and Potter's many animal books such as *The Tale of Peter Rabbit* (1901) delighted younger readers. Older readers enjoyed animal stories such as Richard Jefferies's *Wood Magic* (1881) and Sir John Fortescue's *The Story of a Red Deer* (1897). These animal tales focus either on human interaction with animals or on animals behaving as humans. Adapting human behavior to the animal kingdom, the animal tales do not overtly preach proper conduct, yet some critics still find didacticism. John Rowe Townsend, for example, calls Kipling "as didactic as any Victorian moralist" in the way the jungle books establish a code of behavior in the jungle as a metaphor for human society.

Adventure stories and historical romances offer still more diverse reading. These books gained wide popularity by taking readers all over the empire and through different historical periods. Novels by Henty, Stevenson, Jefferies, Kipling, H. Rider Haggard, Stanley J. Weyman, and S. R. Crockett sold well. Henty, the most prolific writer of historical adventure novels, had annual sales of approximately 150,000 books in the 1890s, coinciding with the peak of enthusiasm for British imperialism. Certainly the shift away from evangelical reward books to adventure novels as school prizes enhanced his reputation even more. Proposing "to inculcate patriotism," Henty affirms the values of unselfish heroism, honesty, and responsibility in his over one hundred novels. Henty's books support the British imperialist policies by stressing personal virtues required by an English gentleman: courage, honesty, mercy, and kindness. Most adventure writing of the period supports British imperialism, and the newly literate masses bought books and magazines with stories glorifying England's political ideology. Though not heavily didactic tales, the stories instilled values, morals, and manners. Among the most popular were Henty's *With Clive in India; or, The Beginnings of an Empire* (1884), Haggard's *King Solomon's Mines* (1885; originally issued as a juvenile title but subsequently marketed as an adult book), and Stevenson's *Treasure Island* (1883) and *Kidnapped* (1886). Writing his friend W. E. Henley, Stevenson comments that writing *Treasure Island* was "awful fun . . . You just indulge the pleasure of your heart, that's all; no trouble, no strain . . . just drive along as the words come!" This carefree attitude about writing seems to parallel the imaginative spirit of adventuresome young heroes in late Victorian literature. Honest, manly, self-reliant, and noble, these dynamic young men epitomized the imperial spirit of the British Empire.

Poetry from 1880 to 1914 offers still another avenue to adventure by reflecting both the external realities and the internal fantasies of children. Stevenson's classic *A Child's Garden of Verses* poignantly recalls childhood pleasures. In the concluding poem the narrator relives fond memories of his own childhood, wistfully reflecting on the child who "has grown up and gone away," leaving but a memory – "a child of air / That lingers in the garden there." Belloc, however, offers less nostalgic views of childhood by parodying earlier tales warning children of the danger of foolish behavior. Some of his popular books of mock cautionary verse include *Bad Child's Book of Beasts* (1896), *More Beasts for Worse Children* (1897), and *Cautionary Tales for Children* (1907). Thus, whether realistic or satiric, poetry of the late Victorian and Edwardian periods creates different perspectives through which to see childhood.

Drama is perhaps the least noticed genre in children's literature of the period. Jan Susina observes in the 1993 issue of *Children's Literature,* "In celebrating the Victorian period as one of the zeniths of children's literature, literary critics have tended to value fiction more highly than poetry, drama, and nonfiction." Yet children's literature was written and adapted for the stage. Children's pantomime often based productions on fairy tales, and Carroll's Alice books were popular subjects, as in an 1886 version with Henry Savile Clarke's script. According to Susina, Sir John Tenniel's pictures for the books transfer readily to the stage as costumed actors and Carroll's text as the play's ready-made dialogue. However, with the exception of the immensely popular *Peter Pan,* children's literature from 1880 to 1914 does not immediately call to mind theatrical forms, despite the fact that so many well-known children's texts of this period have dramatic possibilities.

Illustration enhances all forms of children's literature. The art in books and magazines benefited from technological advances in color lithography, photography, and engraving. The era's leading engraver, Edmund Evans, produced the highest-quality children's books by hiring the brilliant triumvirate of Randolph Caldecott, Walter Crane, and Greenaway. Caldecott and Crane published many of their children's books before 1880, but Greenaway's major work came after 1880. Her popular books boosted the trade industry while her children's costumes influenced fashion. Similar to the way the Caldecott Medal has honored since 1938 the illustrator of the best picture book published in the United States, the Greenaway Medal has been awarded since 1955 to the best children's picture book published in the United Kingdom. Among the important illustrators who met the public's demand for quality books were L. Leslie Brooke, Potter, William Nicholson, Arthur Rackham, H. R. Millar, Gordon Browne, and Hugh Thomson.

The era's wealth of beautifully illustrated books signals the tremendous growth of children's literature during the nineteenth century. The shift from moral tales to entertaining stories introduced more freedom and fun into the child's world. Grahame's *The Golden Age* (1895) expresses this joyous new spirit as "a new world to be explored, a new species to be observed and described, a precious experience to be recaptured out of the past and presented truly and lovingly for its own sake." In children's literature enchantment, happy endings, and hopeful tomorrows reign supreme. Even adults can return to this arcadian world. Barrie affirms this sentiment in *Peter and Wendy* by mapping a child's mind as a magic island. Although Barrie's map of childhood has its rocky terrain, the Never Land for adults represents both sweetness and sadness. Barrie writes of this feeling of nostalgia that children's books afford their readers: "We too have been there; we can still hear the sound of the surf, though we shall land no more."

With all these classics that survive today, children's literature from 1880 to 1914 is rightly called a Golden Age. The large number of books still in print confirms the era's tremendous impact on the canon of children's literature in the English-speaking world. The very fact that these popular works have been passed from generation to generation is the best indication of their lasting quality and universal values. Breaking with Victorian didacticism, the era's writers and illustrators established the tradition of reading for pleasure, thus becoming the precursors of modern children's literature.

– *Laura M. Zaidman*

Acknowledgments

This book was produced by Bruccoli Clark Layman, Inc. Karen L. Rood is senior editor for the *Dictionary of Literary Biography* series. Sam Bruce was the in-house editor.

Production coordinator is George F. Dodge. Photography editors are Edward Scott, Dennis Lynch, and Robert S. McConnell. Layout and graphics supervisor is Penney L. Haughton. Copy-editing supervisor is Bill Adams. Typesetting supervisor is Kathleen M. Flanagan. Julie E. Frick is editorial associate. The production staff includes Phyllis A. Avant, Joseph Matthew Bruccoli, Ann M. Cheschi, Melody W. Clegg, Patricia Coate, Wilma Weant Dague, Brigitte B. de Guzman, Denise W. Edwards, Sarah A. Estes, Joyce Fowler, Laurel M. Gladden, Stephanie C. Hatchell, Rebecca Mayo, Kathy Lawler Merlette, Pamela D. Norton, Delores I. Plastow, Patricia F. Salisbury, and William L. Thomas, Jr.

Walter W. Ross and Deborah M. Chasteen did library research. They were assisted by the following librarians at the Thomas Cooper Library of the University of South Carolina: Linda Holderfield and the inter-library-loan staff; reference librarians Gwen Baxter, Daniel Boice, Faye Chadwell, Cathy Eckman, Gary Geer, Qun "Gerry" Jiao, Jean Rhyne, Carol Tobin, Carolyn Tyler, Virginia Weathers, Elizabeth Whiznant, and Connie Widney; circulation-department head Thomas Marcil; and acquisitions-searching supervisor David Haggard. Special thanks are due to Roger Mortimer and the Staff of Special Collections at the Thomas Cooper Library. The following librarians generously provided material: William Cagle and Joel Silver of the Lilly Library, Indiana University, and Ann Freudenberg, Kendon Stubbs, and Edmund Berkeley, Jr., of the University of Virginia Library.

The editor is indebted to colleagues and friends who supported this work: Caroline C. Hunt (editorial adviser for the *DLB* series on British children's writers) organized the volume, guided each stage, and assisted with the introduction and bibliography. Lois Rauch Gibson, Michael Joseph, William B. Thesing, Donna R. White, Harriet Williams, Ronda Dabbs Feinstein, Ginny Safford, Bonnie Disney, Pat Celley, and Christine Simonson provided help in various ways. The editor especially appreciates the generous support of many people at the University of South Carolina at Sumter: colleagues in the Division of Arts and Letters, particularly Ellen Arl, Lee Craig, Kwame Dawes, and Carol Reynolds; librarians Jane Ferguson, Martha Oliver Alston, Susan James, and Susan Towery; Computer Center staff; Les Carpenter, Tom Lisk, and the Faculty of the Rights and Responsibilities Committees, who awarded partial release time from teaching in 1993 and 1994. Above all, the editor wishes to thank all the scholars who contributed the essays in *British Children's Writers, 1880–1914*.

Dictionary of Literary Biography® • Volume One Hundred Forty One

British Children's Writers, 1880–1914

Dictionary of Literary Biography

F. Anstey
(Thomas Anstey Guthrie)

(8 August 1856 – 10 March 1934)

Jacqueline L. Gmuca
Coastal Carolina University

BOOKS: *Vice Versâ, or A Lesson to Fathers* (London: Smith, Elder, 1882; New York: Appleton, 1882; revised edition, London: Smith, Elder, 1883; revised, 1884; revised and corrected edition, London: Newnes, 1901);

The Black Poodle and Other Tales (London: Longmans, Green, 1884; New York: Appleton, 1884);

The Giant's Robe (London: Smith, Elder, 1884; New York: Appleton, 1884);

The Tinted Venus: A Farcical Romance (Bristol: Arrowsmith / London: Simpkin, Marshall, 1885; New York: Lovell, 1885);

A Fallen Idol (London: Smith, Elder, 1886; New York: Munro, 1886);

Burglar Bill, and Other Pieces for the Use of the Young Reciter (London: Bradbury, Agnew, 1888);

The Pariah (London: Smith, Elder, 1889; Philadelphia: Lippincott, 1889);

Voces Populi, Reprinted from "Punch," 2 volumes (London & New York: Longmans, Green, 1890–1892);

The Talking Horse, and Other Tales (New York: Lovell, 1891; London: Smith, Elder, 1892);

Tourmalin's Time Cheques (Bristol: Arrowsmith, 1891; New York: Appleton, 1891); republished as *The Time Bargain; or, Tourmalin's Cheque Book* (Bristol: Arrowsmith, 1905);

Mr. Punch's Model Music-Hall Songs and Dramas (London: Bradbury, Agnew, 1892; New York: National Book Company, 1892);

Mr. Punch's Young Reciter: Burglar Bill and Other Pieces (London: Bradbury, Agnew, 1892; enlarged, 1897);

F. Anstey (Thomas Anstey Guthrie) in the 1890s (photograph by Bassano, Ltd.)

The Travelling Companions; A Story in Scenes (London & New York: Longmans, Green, 1892);

The Man from Blankley's and Other Sketches (London & New York: Longmans, Green, 1893);

Mr. Punch's Pocket Ibsen; A Collection of Some of the Master's Best-Known Dramas Condensed, Revised,

3

and Slightly Re-arranged for the Benefit of the Earnest Student (London: Heinemann, 1893; New York & London: Macmillan, 1893); enlarged as *The Pocket Ibsen* (London: Heinemann, 1895);

Under the Rose: A Story in Scenes (London: Bradbury, Agnew, 1894);

Lyre and Lancet: A Story in Scenes (London: Smith, Elder, 1895; New York & London: Macmillan, 1895);

The Statement of Stella Maberly, Written by Herself (London: Unwin, 1896; New York: Appleton, 1896);

Baboo Jabberjee, B.A. (London: Dent, 1897); republished as *Baboo Hurry Bungsho Jabberjee, B.A.* (New York: Appleton, 1897);

Puppets at Large: Scenes and Subjects from Mr. Punch's Show (London: Bradbury, Agnew, 1897);

Paleface and Redskin, and Other Stories for Boys and Girls (London: Richards, 1898; New York: Appleton, 1912);

Love Among the Lions: A Matrimonial Experience (London: Dent, 1898; New York: Appleton, 1899);

The Brass Bottle (London: Smith, Elder, 1900; New York: Appleton, 1900);

A Bayard from Bengal (London: Methuen, 1902; New York: Appleton, 1902);

Only Toys! (London: Richards, 1903);

Salted Almonds (London: Smith, Elder, 1906);

Vice Versa: A Farcical Fantastic Play in Three Acts (London: Smith, Elder/Boston: Baker, 1910);

The Brass Bottle: A Farcical Fantastic Play in Four Acts (London: Heinemann, 1911);

In Brief Authority (London: Smith, Elder, 1915; New York: Doran, 1916);

Percy and Others: Sketches Mainly Reprinted from "Punch" (London: Methuen, 1915);

The Last Load: Stories and Essays (London: Methuen, 1925);

The Man from Blankley's: A Comedy of the Early Nineties (London: Hodder & Stoughton, 1927);

Humour & Fantasy (London: Murray, 1931; New York: Dutton, 1931);

A Long Retrospect (London & New York: Oxford University Press, 1936).

OTHER: "A Very Bad Quarter of an Hour," in *In a Good Cause*, edited by Margaret Susan Tyson-Amherst (London: Wells Gardner, Darton, 1885), pp. 137–146;

"Some Detached Thoughts on Omnibuses," in *Alma Mater's Mirror*, edited by Thomas Spencer Baynes and Lewis Campbell (Edinburgh: Edinburgh University Press, 1887), pp. 167–172;

"Three Wishes," in *With My Friends*, edited by Brander Matthews (Freeport, N.Y.: Books for Libraries Press, 1891), pp. 233–284;

"Some Fellow Passengers of Mine," in *Souvenir of the Charing Cross Hospital Bazaar*, edited by Herbert Beerbohm Tree (London: Nassau, 1899), pp. 11–15;

"Two Anecdotes Concerning Pictures," in *The Press Album*, edited by Thomas Catling (London: John Murray, 1909), pp. 175–176;

Molière, *The Would-Be Gentleman*, adapted by Anstey (London: Secker, 1926);

Molière, *The Imaginary Invalid*, adapted by Anstey (London: Hodder & Stoughton, 1929);

Four Molière Comedies, adapted by Anstey (London: Hodder & Stoughton, 1931);

Three Molière Plays: Tartuf, Scapin the Trickster, The School for Wives, adapted by Anstey (London: Oxford University Press, 1933);

"The Game of Adverbs," in *Another Book of Miniature Plays*, edited by Theodore Johnson (Boston: Baker, 1934), pp. 97–108.

SELECTED PERIODICAL PUBLICATIONS – UNCOLLECTED: "In the Snake-House at Feeding Time," *Time*, no. 3 (September 1880): 610–617.

The impact of F. Anstey, a leading humorist of the late nineteenth and early twentieth centuries, on children's literature is twofold. First, his short stories for children, collected in *Paleface and Redskin, and Other Stories for Boys and Girls* (1898), and his novel for children, *Only Toys!* (1903), follow the moralistic trend of much of children's literature in the late nineteenth century to instruct children in good behavior. Anstey achieves this goal through parodies of the "good" child as well as through fantasy situations. Anstey's second impact on the field comes from his two humorous fantasy novels, *Vice Versâ, or A Lesson to Fathers* (1882) and *The Brass Bottle* (1900). These works became popular with both children and adults and influenced other children's authors such as E. Nesbit. Indeed, Anstey's place in the development of children's literature comes primarily from his ability to blend humor and parody with the creation of realistic fantasy.

Anstey's autobiography, *A Long Retrospect* (1936), clearly shows how his childhood prepared him for a career as a humorist. Born in London on 8 August 1856, he was named for his father, Thomas Anstey Guthrie. His early years were happy ones. His father was a successful military tailor whose upper-class clients often became his friends and accepted his invitations to dinner. Anstey's mother, née Augusta Amherst Austen, was a pianist and organist before her marriage and was, in Anstey's words, "unmistakably a gentlewoman." Both parents possessed a strong sense of humor – certainly a quality which would have affected Anstey early in life. His childhood was replete with toys and children's parties, theatricals and exhibitions. In short, he and his two brothers and one sister enjoyed their childhood immensely. Anstey was introduced to humor and satire early on, studying Edward Lear's *A Book of Nonsense* (1846) "with profound interest" at the age of seven and laughing over the articles and cartoons in such periodicals as *Punch* and *Fun*.

Anstey approached his first year at a private boarding school with understandable trepidation as well as excitement. His experiences from 1867 to 1872 in Surbiton formed the basis for the scenes of school life in *Vice Versâ*. In his autobiography Anstey describes Crichton House, also the name given to the school in *Vice Versâ*, as an institution devoid of fights and bullies but full of backbiting, meals that were ample but not appealing, and instruction from conscientious yet poorly prepared instructors. Although Anstey was never reprimanded, he lived in fear of the headmaster, Mr. Grimstone, and his "row[s]," where the whole school was brought together, the culprits punished, and other undiscovered offenders badgered to confess. Small in size, Anstey was never proficient in sports, but he was fairly popular, known as a storyteller and a leader in charades.

His preparation at Crichton House was followed by three years as a day boarder at King's College School and then enrollment in Trinity Hall at Cambridge to study law. During these years Anstey began the *Home Journal*, an unsuccessful attempt at a humorous periodical, and then wrote several comic stories and poems which were published in the *Undergraduates' Journal* at Cambridge. It was on the basis of these contributions that Anstey was invited in 1877 to submit a series to a new weekly paper, the *Cambridge Tatler*. Inspired by W. S. Gilbert's *Fifty "Bab" Ballads: Much Sound and Little Sense* (1869), Anstey decided on the basic premise of his series, "Turned Tables," later to become *Vice Versâ*, in which a father and son exchange bodies and the father is whisked off to boarding school. As Anstey's autobiography relates, "It would not be difficult to arrange the machinery of the story, and as it was not many years since the Crichton House days, the local colour and details did not need to be invented – they were ready to hand."

Yet only a quarter of "Turned Tables" was completed when the *Cambridge Tatler* ceased publication. Despite the periodical's demise, Anstey was encouraged by his mother's praise and his father's offer to publish "Turned Tables" privately. He spent July 1877 reading law and revising his manuscript. However, his grief over his mother's death in August caused Anstey to lay the story aside for three years. Meanwhile, he continued to study law while writing stories and essays. It was with the publication of one of these stories, "Accompanied on the Flute," in the new humor weekly *Mirth* that Anstey acquired his pen name. The story had been submitted with T. Anstey as the author, but the typesetter inserted an *F* instead of a *T*, and Anstey never attempted to change the spelling. Encouraged by the acceptance of three more stories as well as an essay titled "In the Snake-House at Feeding Time" (1880), Anstey finally finished "Turned Tables."

The period of 1881–1882 was to be a decisive one in Anstey's ultimate career choice. In 1881 he passed the bar examination, albeit without distinction, and submitted *Vice Versâ* to two separate journals; each rejected it for publication, the second on the grounds that it was more fit for children as an audience. But in March 1882 the work was accepted by the publishing company of Smith, Elder. Based upon this acceptance as well as the advice of James Payn, the chief reader and advisor for Smith, Elder, who read other of Anstey's stories, Anstey made a critical decision: writing, not law, was to become his lifelong profession.

The critical reception of *Vice Versâ* was overwhelmingly favorable. As Roger Lancelyn Green recounts in a 1957 article for *English*, influential critics like Andrew Lang and George Saintsbury rolled with laughter upon reading the book. Sir John Squire, editor of the *London Mercury*, reminisces about the work's humor in his 1934 article on Anstey's career, praising the excellence of its prose style and the universality of its theme. C. S. Lewis, in *Surprised By Joy* (1955), adamantly agrees, finding *Vice Versâ* "the only truthful school story in existence." Twenty-one separate editions in England and the United States between 1882 and 1954, a published three-act-play version (1910), and several stage performances and film versions of the novel attest to its popularity with British and American audiences.

Unlike a realistic account of the hardships of a schoolboy's life which might have been dismissed by many as exaggeration, Anstey makes his points through the humorous exchange of bodies between Mr. Bultitude and his son, Dick. A magical "Garudâ

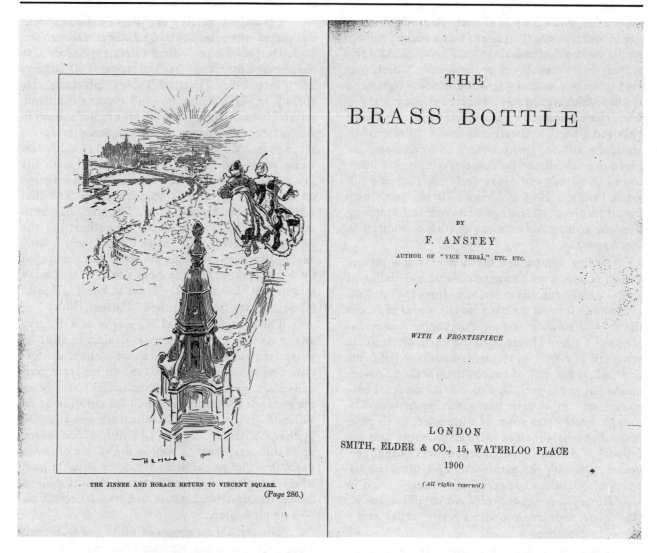

THE

BRASS BOTTLE

BY

F. ANSTEY

AUTHOR OF "VICE VERSÂ," ETC. ETC.

WITH A FRONTISPIECE

LONDON
SMITH, ELDER & CO., 15, WATERLOO PLACE
1900

(All rights reserved)

THE JINNEE AND HORACE RETURN TO VINCENT SQUARE.
(Page 286.)

Frontispiece and title page for one of Anstey's humorous fantasy novels, popular with both adults and children

stone" and the father's unfortunate wish to trade places with his son are the mechanisms by which the pompous, aloof Mr. Bultitude comes to understand what his son endures at Crichton House. From the unappetizing breakfast meat of sardines to the boredom of lessons poorly taught to forced games, Mr. Bultitude further complicates his life as his son by an obstinate refusal to adapt to his new environment. Speaking and thinking as an adult in his son's body, Mr. Bultitude becomes a tattletale; loses most of his son's friends; insults Dick's sweetheart, Dulcie; and nearly meets with a public flogging. But Mr. Bultitude also comes closer to understanding his son's vulnerability and need for affection. He too quakes under the authoritative reign of Mr. Grimstone and his relentless search for boys who have committed even the most minor of transgressions. By the novel's end, when Mr. Bultitude

and Dick are wished back to their former selves by the father's youngest son, the father has indeed learned the lessons indicated by the novel's subtitle. Mr. Bultitude "felt something spring up in his heart" – an unnamed affection and love toward Dick which he can now share with his other children as well. Truly, the child has become a father to the man in this comic story of role reversal.

In his autobiography Anstey relates that he was encouraged to follow up this early success with another story of role reversal, this time revolving around a girl and her mother exchanging places at home and boarding school. But lacking a knowledge of girls' schools and resolving to write only on topics that "interested or amused me enough to make work a pleasure," he abandoned the project.

The years between the unexpected success of *Vice Versâ* and the 1900 publication of *The Brass Bot-*

6

tle, the next of Anstey's novels to be popular with children, were extremely busy and fruitful. Invited to write for *Punch*, Anstey became a regular contributor, assuming in 1887 a seat at the prestigious *Punch* table, where staff members discussed their contributions; they also etched their names into the wood. His association with this leading weekly continued into the 1900s. Indeed, as Beth D. Fleischman's dissertation on Anstey documents, from 1887 until his death, Anstey created more than five hundred parodies, sketches, and dialogues for *Punch*. Many of these were collected and published in book form, with such titles as *The Man from Blankley's and Other Sketches* (1893) and *Mr. Punch's Pocket Ibsen* (1893), the latter of which contains parodies of four of Ibsen's plays, adding an original fifth satirizing Ibsen's typical subject matter and style.

For his second novel, *The Giant's Robe* (1884), Anstey attempted to break away from fantasy into the realm of the serious novel. This work of "ordinary middle-class life," as Anstey characterized the novel in his autobiography, details the fortunes and misfortunes of a plagiarist named Mark Ashburn. Reviewers found the early installments in the *Cornhill* magazine disappointingly obvious in plot, and when additional installments appeared, two of the major weekly papers accused Anstey himself of plagiarizing a work by W. W. Follett Synge titled *Tom Singleton, Dragoon and Dramatist* (1879). Despite Anstey's denial of these charges when the story appeared in book form, he failed to clear his name, and the novel met with only moderate financial success.

In Anstey's next novel, *The Tinted Venus* (1885), he returned to the exploration of the consequences of the supernatural entering the life of a middle-class man. This time the fantasy element takes the form of Aphrodite's spirit summoned to Victorian England when a ring is placed on the finger of a statue sculpted in her honor. Leander Tweddle, a successful hairdresser, is the unlucky man who places the ring there. Much to his dismay, Tweddle finds himself the object of Aphrodite's desire. The plot revolves around his attempts to discourage her advances, while protecting his fiancée's life from the goddess's wrath. Favorably reviewed, the work brought Anstey over five hundred pounds in royalties but failed to restore his lost reputation. Nor did the work ever equal the popularity of *Vice Versâ*. A reviewer in the 15 October 1885 issue of the *Nation* commented that the plot of *The Tinted Venus* was more tightly constructed than that of *Vice Versâ* but lacked a comparable "serious undercurrent" and originality of idea; he predicted that it would quickly be forgotten.

Four more adult novels rapidly followed. *A Fallen Idol* (1886) was Anstey's third humorous fantasy. Based upon an idea of Mrs. Panton, a friend and fellow writer, the novel positions a young painter named Ronald Campion in the malevolent grip of a Jain idol. The idol's spirit plagues Campion with one disaster after another until the stone is finally destroyed, and the work ends with a definite upswing in Campion's personal and professional life. With *A Fallen Idol* completed, Anstey turned once more to a serious novel, writing the opening chapters of *The Pariah* (1889) during the summer of 1887, and subsequently using his spare time after weekly contributions to *Punch* for finishing the novel by the spring of 1889. As in *Vice Versâ*, the plot revolves around transformation and whether or not changed circumstances can truly alter a person's basic personality. In the novel Allen Chadwick, an unattractive cockney youth, is reunited with his estranged father. When the father marries a wealthy widow, he hopes that Allen will emerge from his ignorance and awkwardness as an educated gentleman. But the opposite occurs. Allen becomes a pariah despite his conscientious attempts to become what his father wants him to be. Critics' unfavorable reception coupled with the fact that writing *The Pariah* had been surprisingly stressful and devoid of Anstey's usual pleasure of creation prompted him to leave the world of the serious novel for a time.

Articles for *Punch* filled the interval before Anstey's next fantasy, *Tourmalin's Time Cheques* (1891). With his typical joy of creation restored, Anstey centered this story around the possibility of time travel, not from one era to another, but within the limits of a young man's journey from Australia to London. At the suggestion of another passenger, Peter Tourmalin banks his time on board ship so that he can later redeem these checks when bored with his new life in England as a recently married man. The complications begin when the time checks are not redeemable in chronological order, and Tourmalin finds himself in awkward and highly compromising situations.

Anstey made his final attempt at more serious writing with *The Statement of Stella Maberly Written by Herself* (1896), which was to be his only tragic fantasy, a first-person narrative of an insecure and violent young woman. Stella Maberly firmly believes that Hugh, the man with whom she is desperately in love, is in love with her employer, Evelyn. Nothing could be further from the truth, however. Hugh loves Stella, and Evelyn has been attempting to bring the two of them together. Ironically, the same night that she clears up the misunderstanding with Stella, Evelyn dies of heart failure. Stella attempts to resurrect her by invoking any spirit of heaven or hell to bring her body back to life. This plea succeeds, and Evelyn, imbued by an evil spirit, returns to health and marries Hugh. The novel ends tragically when Stella strangles Evelyn and Hugh commits suicide. In *A Long Retrospect* Anstey is candid about the novel's failure: "It may be that I had not skill or power enough to treat the idea. . . . At all events it had very few readers." But he refused to be daunted by the reviewers' criticisms and shortly afterward began a humorous series for *Punch* on an Indian gentleman. These contributions, collected in the volume *Baboo Jabberjee, B.A.* (1897), pleased the critics and reading public alike.

During the years between *Vice Versâ* and *The Statement of Stella Maberly,* Anstey created several stories specifically for children. "The Story of a Sugar Prince," "A Toy Tragedy," and "A Farewell Appearance" were first published in the short-story collection *The Black Poodle and Other Tales* (1884), while "The Good Little Girl," "Don: The Story of a Greedy Dog," "Paleface and Redskin," and "Tommy's Hero" were included in *The Talking Horse, and Other Tales* (1891). All seven were later printed in a separate collection, *Paleface and Redskin, and Other Stories for Boys and Girls.*

Clearly, the purpose of each tale is twofold — to entertain and to instruct. "Don: The Story of a Greedy Dog" illustrates the obesity, lack of energy, and humiliation that result from avarice. "Paleface and Redskin" unmasks a boastful boy's cowardice, and "Tommy's Hero" depicts how hurtful humor at the expense of others can be. Anstey's most prominent topic of instruction, however, deals with the perils of overblown pride and vanity. Indeed, the main character of "A Toy Tragedy" is the embodiment of conceit. Ethelinda, the newest doll in Winifred's nursery, is a hateful character, scorning all around her, from the lowly jester to the helpful fairy to Winifred herself. In a fantasy concocted by Winifred's cousin, Archie, Ethelinda is accused of poisoning "Queen" Winifred. Archie, determined to carry out his fantasy, moves to execute Ethelinda, but the jester, hopelessly in love with her, wishes himself in Ethelinda's place and is beheaded instead. In contrast, the Sugar Prince in "The Story of the Sugar Prince," Dandy in "A Farewell Appearance," and Priscilla in "The Good Little Girl" are treated much more sympathetically, yet their vanity and pride are just as evident. The Sugar Prince, not realizing he is a mere cookie, is convinced that he will someday have a kingdom. Dandy, the dog, de-

tests playing with his owner's doll and runs out the gate in defiance, and Priscilla desperately yearns to reform her family just as all "good" heroines do.

Unlike Ethelinda, who chatters selfishly about her great adventure at the end of the story, blissfully unaware that such a romance has cost the jester's life, the other three characters learn bitter lessons. The Sugar Prince begins to suspect that he has no kingdom, for no one honors him at the party for which he was bought. Dandy, kidnapped by a dog thief, is forced to become the Toby dog character in a Punch and Judy show, unwillingly trading his pampered life for one of hunger and beatings. And Priscilla finds out that her goodness has been far from genuine as she discovers that the jewels dropping from her mouth when she corrects others are all fakes. For two of these characters, Dandy and Priscilla, the stories end positively. Dandy is found by his mistress and dies happily in her arms. Priscilla, resolving to be a prig no longer, gradually breaks her habit of trying to reform others. She emerges a humble, affectionate little girl by the story's end.

Interestingly enough, the Sugar Prince forgets all about his kingdom when he falls in love with Mabel, one of the little girls at the party. He feels their difference in size to be of no consequence and is delighted when she takes him home with her, foolishly believing she will one day come to love him. But when he is dunked into a cup of tea by Baby and his fine appearance is ruined, Mabel, being very hungry, decides to eat him, since, without his handsome curls and features, he is not worth saving. With this event, the story turns to a slightly different message, alluded to in Anstey's final sentence: "There is a beautiful moral belonging to this story, but it is of no use to print it here, because it only applies to sugar princes — until Mabel is quite grown up." On one level Anstey appears to be commenting on the destructiveness of women toward the men who are no longer worthy of or suitable for them. But when this moral is juxtaposed with the portrayal of a greedy young boy at the party, who devours everything in sight, a second meaning appears. Mabel, or any young girl, is being warned of her own destruction when her good looks fade. Hence, the word *beautiful* in Anstey's moral is appropriate, for the story ultimately enjoins men and women alike against too much reliance on their own pleasing appearances.

In the same year that these children's stories were published in a collected volume, Anstey began his second most popular novel, *The Brass Bottle.* His autobiography relates the genesis of this tale. Reading poetry as he searched for inspiration, Anstey stumbled upon Dante Gabriel Rossetti's "Rose Mary" with its mystic stone in which spirits are imprisoned. At first he thought of constructing a humorous novel based upon a similar object. But finding the idea unworkable, he found additional inspiration in the *Arabian Nights* story of the Fisherman and the Djinn. Quickly at work on a plot outline, Anstey finished a lengthy scenario by the spring of 1889. When the *Strand* magazine accepted the work for serial publication, Anstey spent his summer months busily writing. He would recall that this period was "among the happiest of my life; it was an unspeakable relief to feel that the literary instinct had revived, and that I was writing with keener zest than I had done for years."

The novel's protagonist, Horace Ventimore, a struggling young architect, unknowingly releases a "Jinnee" from a brass vase he had bought at an auction. The genie, Fakrash-el-Aamash, is determined to reward Ventimore handsomely for his rescue, and the fun begins as centuries-old notions of gratitude invade turn-of-the-century London. Perhaps the funniest episode surrounds what was to have been a simple dinner at Horace's bachelor quarters for his fiancée and her parents. Expecting modest lodgings, the Futvoyes enter high-ceilinged rooms of magnificent splendor to be greeted by Horace dressed in jewel-studded robes. All this has been the work of Fakrash. The humor continues as Ventimore tries to supply rational explanations for the multiple courses of Persian food and the exquisitely beautiful dancing girl. When Fakrash turns dangerous, Ventimore, like the fisherman in the *Arabian Nights,* succeeds in tricking the genie back into the bottle. The novel ends happily with Ventimore and his fiancée celebrating their engagement in the first home Horace has been commissioned to design. He is finally rewarded with financial prosperity and personal happiness.

A monetary success for Anstey, *The Brass Bottle* brought him over eight thousand pounds as it was serialized, published as a novel, and then adapted for the stage and motion pictures. Critical reaction was generally positive. David Hodge, a critic for *Living Age,* a magazine that anthologized essays from leading publications, praised the work as the best Anstey had written since *Vice Versâ. The Brass Bottle* was also influential in children's literature, for E. Nesbit not only directly refers to Anstey's genie in her novel, *Five Children and It* (1902), but may have, as John Rowe Townsend maintains in *Written for Children* (1965), taken her basic plot from his work.

Anstey in 1930 (photograph by Whitlock)

The novel is clearly a study of gratitude, rightly and wrongly expressed, rightly and wrongly motivated. While Ventimore is amazed at the extravagance of Fakrash's gifts, he embodies appreciation in his respectful politeness to the genie. Professor Futvoye is quite the opposite. He first fails to appreciate Horace's effort to bid on items at an antique auction. Then he upbraids Horace for undue extravagance at the ill-fated dinner. When the genie transforms the professor into a one-eyed mule to prove the truth of his existence and later reverses the spell, Futvoye is characteristically angry at his wife and daughter instead of glad to be human once again.

Just as important as these portrayals of gratitude and ingratitude is Anstey's unveiling of the genie's true motives for giving such magnificent gifts. At first Fakrash seems to be sincerely motivated by a wish to reward Ventimore for freeing him. Yet these gifts are actually part of a clever strategy to win Ventimore's loyalty and his ultimate compliance in a scheme for revenge. According to Fakrash, he had offered his kinswoman to the great ruler Suleyman; however, through this marriage, he was secretly planning the ruler's demise. This plan was overturned when Jarjarees, who was in love with the woman, revealed Fakrash's treachery, and as punishment, Fakrash was imprisoned in the brass bottle. Now free, Fakrash seeks revenge by enlisting Ventimore to kill Jarjarees. Unaware of Fakrash's ulterior motive throughout most of the novel, Ventimore only finds out the truth at the end. Clearly, Anstey's work warns against the conniving motives which may be behind excessive gratitude.

Shortly after the success of *The Brass Bottle,* Anstey wrote *Only Toys!,* his longest story for children, which was serialized in the *Strand* magazine in 1903. The work was scheduled to appear in book form near the end of that same year, but the publisher went bankrupt, and the copies had to be sold at a lower price. As a further consequence, *Only Toys!* received little advertising and scant attention from the critics. Such ill timing led to the book's quick demise.

Like his shorter tales for children, *Only Toys!* employs fantasy and fun to convey a serious moral. Its two main characters are parodies of a didactic writer's dreams come true. Torquil and Irene begin their adventures as two knowledgeable children, aged ten and nine respectively. Irene is busily writing an instructive essay for the *Girls' Own Garland* while Torquil is constructing a picture puzzle of the counties in England when they are interrupted by a visit from Santa Claus. Finding that they neither believe in his existence nor play with their toys, Santa literally and figuratively begins to put the two children in their place by reducing them to the size of dolls and enjoining them to play in the nursery. There Torquil and Irene wreak havoc by continually challenging this unrealistic world. They point out to the toy queen that the train conductor, for example, has no tickets to sell and that the farmer and his wife mistakenly believe that pigs lay eggs and cows' horns give milk. Santa Claus then transforms the toys into their more-than-realistic counterparts. Torquil and Irene are fired upon by the sentry when they cannot give the correct password, are unable to buy food or find shelter with their toy beads, and are put on trial at the end of the story for their failure to pay these debts. They subsequently yearn for their old toys, and Santa's lesson is complete. Torquil and Irene awake from their dreams of animated toys not only ready to play but, more important, content to enjoy their own childhood. Just as Anstey had overturned the literary image of a child priggishly devoted to the reform of others in "The Good Little Girl," in *Only Toys!* he overturns the portrait of the preco-

cious child common to much children's literature throughout the nineteenth century.

Anstey devoted the next decade of his literary career to articles for *Punch* as well as play adaptations of his own works. He wrote one last novel between 1910 and 1915. *In Brief Authority* (1915) transports a middle-class family to the fairy world of the Brothers Grimm. Indeed, the Wibberley-Stimpsons are mistakenly recognized as rulers of this peaceful, prosperous land and come close to ruining its economy. Despite the novel's favorable reviews, the work added little to Anstey's income or to his popularity as a writer. As he explains in his autobiography, however, its lack of popularity did not dismay him, for winning World War I concerned him more. During the war years Anstey served as a volunteer in the Inns of Court Reserve Corps, digging trenches and taking his turn at guard duty. After the war he wrote comparatively little, with the exception of his acclaimed adaptations of Molière's comedies and his autobiography, published posthumously.

In recognition of his influence and achievement, the Book Society published an anthology of his works titled *Humour & Fantasy* (1931), which included *Vice Versâ, The Tinted Venus, A Fallen Idol, The Talking Horse, Salted Almonds* (1906), and *The Brass Bottle.* As reported in the 15 August 1931 issue of the *Literary Digest,* critics from the *London News Chronicle, Sunday Times,* and *Morning Post* were unanimous in their praise of Anstey's humor. Anstey was gratified by this attention and undaunted by the volume's limited sales. As he admitted, "I have always recognized that there is something about my particular brand of humour that fails to appeal to more than a few." In the closing pages of *A Long Retrospect* he cites several reasons for this lack of popularity, such as long lapses of time between the publication of his different novels as well as his shy reluctance to be interviewed. His introduction to *Humour & Fantasy* provides the more compelling explanation that tastes in humor change.

On 10 March 1934 Anstey died of pneumonia after a brief illness. He was cremated, and his ashes were buried in the grave of his brother-in-law, George Millar. Anstey's epitaph was the final line from *The Giant's Robe:* "A nature whose love was unselfish and chivalrous." Anstey made his greatest contribution in the realm of humor. Through his aptly chosen dialogue and realistic portrayal of characters he brought to life the foibles of the English middle and upper classes. More often than not, feelings of superiority derived from good looks, a higher station, self-acclaimed goodness, or an overblown image of intellect are the focus of his humor. He influenced the development of children's fantasy through his carefully constructed, verisimilar plots that detailed the consequences of a single fantastic event, whether it be caused by a Garudâ stone, a released genie, or Santa Claus. In the evaluation of critic E. V. Lucas, Anstey was "the best novelist of the tight place," delighting his readers with accounts of characters caught by an "ironical and mischievous fate." Anstey's works were frequently praised by contemporary critics, although he was never as successful with the public. Without a doubt, *Vice Versâ* and *The Brass Bottle* are important components in the historical development of children's literature.

Bibliography:

Martin John Turner, *A Bibliography of the Works of F. Anstey* (London: Stockwell, 1931).

References:

Beth D. Fleischman, "F. Anstey (Thomas Anstey Guthrie), Late Victorian Humorist," Ph.D. dissertation, University of South Carolina, 1981;

Roger Lancelyn Green, *Tellers of Tales* (Leicester, U.K.: Ward, 1946);

Green, "A Neglected Novelist: 'F. Anstey,' " *English*, 11 (Summer 1957): 178–181;

David Hodge, "F. Anstey," *Living Age*, 293 (28 April 1917): 204–209;

C. S. Lewis, *Surprised By Joy* (London: Bles, 1955);

E. V. Lucas, "F. Anstey (Thomas Anstey Guthrie)," *English Illustrated Magazine*, 29 (August 1903): 544–545;

Patrick Scott, "The Private School in the Eighteen-Sixties: Anstey's *Vice Versa*," *History of Education Society Bulletin*, 8 (Autumn 1971): 13–25;

Sir John Squire, "F. Anstey," *London Mercury*, 29 (April 1934): 517–521;

Brian M. Stableford, "F. Anstey," in *Supernatural Fiction Writers: Fantasy and Horror*, volume 1, edited by E. F. Bleiler (New York: Scribners, 1985), pp. 287–292;

Nicholas Tucker, "*Vice Versa:* The First Subversive Novel for Children," *Children's Literature in Education*, 18 (1987): 139–147.

Papers:

The major collection of Anstey's correspondence, journals, notebooks, and manuscripts is at the British Library in London.

Helen Bannerman

(25 February 1862 – 13 October 1946)

Ruth K. MacDonald

BOOKS: *The Story of Little Black Sambo* (London: Richards, 1899; New York: Stokes, 1900); revised as *The Little Black Sambo Story Book,* by Bannerman and Frank Ver Beck (Philadelphia: Altemus, 1930);

The Story of Little Black Mingo (London: Nisbet, 1901; New York: Stokes, 1902);

The Story of Little Black Quibba (London: Nisbet, 1902; New York: Stokes, 1903);

Little Dechie-Head: An Awful Warning to Bad Babas (London: Nisbet, 1903); republished as *The Story of Little Kettle-head: An Awful Warning to Bad Babas* (New York: Stokes, 1904);

Pat and the Spider: The Biter Bit (London: Nisbet, 1904; New York: Stokes, 1905);

The Story of the Teasing Monkey (London: Nisbet, 1906; New York: Stokes, 1907);

The Story of Little Black Quasha (London: Nisbet, 1908; New York: Stokes, 1908);

The Story of Little Black Bobtail (New York: Stokes, 1909);

Sambo and the Twins: A New Adventure of Little Black Sambo (New York: Stokes, 1936; London: Nisbet, 1937);

The Story of Little White Squibba (London: Chatto & Windus, 1966).

Edition: *The Jumbo Sambo* (New York & Philadelphia: Stokes, 1942) – includes *The Story of Little Black Sambo; The Story of Sambo and the Twins; The Story of Little Black Quasha; The Story of Little Black Bobtail; The Story of the Teasing Monkey; The Story of Little Kettle-head.*

Helen Bannerman in 1889 (painting by Margaret Dempster, Bannerman Family Collection)

Helen Bannerman is an author of her own time, of historical interest primarily due to the controversy which continues to swirl around her most famous creation, *The Story of Little Black Sambo* (1899). Preceding Beatrix Potter by two years, she created a publishing phenomenon with her little book, of the same size as the ones Potter would make famous. The story is set in some indeterminate place, at times resembling Africa, at others imperial India. While the plot is harmless enough, the characterization of the African/Indians continues to

inspire controversy. The characters are all named with an emphasis on their non-Caucasian origins – Black Quasha, Black Bobtail – and their given names are equally offensive to the cosmopolitan ear. Black Mumbo and Black Jumbo, Sambo's parents, have names chosen for their alliterative qualities rather than any dignified values. The fact that their names together connote voodoo or confusion, rather than some other more honorable qualities, further distresses the book's later critics. Even the name Sambo, originally bearing the connotation of a rogue or rascal, has taken on derogatory racial connotations.

When Bannerman's books were originally published, their small size and bright, colorful illustrations, as well as their author's ability to craft a story with high narrative tension, were all remarkable. With many readers lacking a greater general knowledge of the actual conditions and culture of India during the British Empire, the books also served, however inappropriately, the native British thirst for information about life in that strange, faraway place which had lately become the home of so many British transplants. Bannerman's books, especially *Little Black Sambo,* continued to be popular long after the author's death, as a heritage passed down from original readers to their children. However, with the rise of the civil rights movement in the United States and its repercussions and raising of consciousness abroad, her books fell into disfavor, republished today for their historical interest rather than their lasting literary quality.

Helen Brodie Cowan Watson was born on 25 February 1862 in Edinburgh, Scotland, to Robert Boog Watson, an army chaplain, and his wife. The Watson family was prominent for its ownership of Thomas Constable and Son, a publishing company, and for its clerical leadership in the Church of Scotland. While the family lost its publishing fortune and therefore its comfortable cushion against poverty in Helen's childhood, funds remained for her to pursue higher education. Through correspondence courses she earned her LL.A. degree from the University of Saint Andrews, Fife, before her marriage on 26 June 1889 to William Burney Bannerman, a surgeon who entered the Indian Medical Service, a branch of the army. Soon after their marriage Helen Bannerman left Scotland, to return only for visits until her husband retired from the service some twenty-nine years later.

Although Bannerman had attained a higher level of education than was usual for a married woman of her day, she became a dutiful memsahib, wife of an officer in India, with a large household full of native Indian servants to oversee. With the birth of her children, two boys and two girls, she found her life's purpose in their care and in dutiful attention to her husband. She single-handedly managed the family while William Bannerman worked long, selfless hours, especially after the outbreak of the plague in India, when he oversaw the lab which produced the vaccine for the disease's prevention. As much as Scottish society transplanted to India tried to mimic life back home, there were significant climatic and cultural differences that could not be ignored: one was the influence of the long, tropical summer on the

health of Scottish children, who languished in the heat and humidity.

The solution for the Scots was to move with the children during the most unbearable part of the season to the mountains, where cooler, drier air restored them to health. Of course, such a move involved a temporary separation of families, since most fathers could not leave their posts in the army or some other government office for such extended periods. Many families, the Bannermans included, owned separate mountain homes and moved children, servants, and even furniture for periods of months at a time. Journeys to the mountains sometimes took several days, given the primitive railway and road conditions; parts of some trips even included elephant riding.

A common attitude at that time was that a husband needed his wife more than her children did; thus Helen frequently left her children for several weeks at a time in the healthful altitude, to rejoin her husband and provide companionship and care for him. These separations were not easy for Bannerman, who knew her duty but also missed her children. It was on such a trip that she wrote and illustrated *Little Black Sambo* for the two daughters she left behind. She bound the book herself and sent it to them; when Alice M. E. Bond, a friend who was returning to Scotland, saw the book, she offered to take it with her to London to see if there was any interest in publishing it. Bannerman consented, with the proviso that her explicit consent be obtained before any arrangements with a publisher were final.

What followed presents a legal quagmire. Bannerman's friend, taking Bannerman's desire for publication as primary, sold the rights to the book for five pounds to publisher Grant Richards when he pressed her for a commitment. Because mails from London to India took so long, the friend dared not wait until consent could be given. Of course, the sale of the copyright meant that Bannerman derived no economic benefit from the sales of *Little Black Sambo* beyond the few pounds offered in the original deal. Whether the author's consent had actually been obtained remained a distasteful legal matter between Bannerman and her publisher until Chatto and Windus, successors to Richards, finally made an outright gift of money, ex gratia, to settle the case in the late 1930s.

The book was a success, bringing much financial gain to Richards and some embarrassment to Bannerman, whose name appeared on the front cover against her wishes. Such notoriety was uncomfortable to a woman who had learned humility

Cover for Bannerman's best-known book. The title character was originally a native of India, but illustrations in later editions of the book, especially in the United States, portrayed him as African.

from its similarity to "Little Red Riding Hood." But, rather than a wolf, Sambo meets a series of four tigers, each of whom threatens to eat the boy until appeased by a piece of Sambo's new clothing. Gradually Sambo is reduced to his loincloth, while the tigers parade their finery, each convinced he is the finest in the jungle. The four meet in a boasting match, which gradually turns into tail chasing. Having abandoned Sambo's clothes in order to confront each other, the tigers chase each other in circles, tail in mouth, until they turn into a blur and then gradually into butter; Sambo, meanwhile, collects his clothes, his father collects the butter, and the story ends in a feast of pancakes with tiger butter.

While the story has an archetypal pattern in the quest structure and in the recurring confrontations with each of the four tigers, it is otherwise unremarkable in its language, except for the names of the characters and the Indian word *ghi,* which receives the parenthetical translation "clarified butter." The language has a simple style and therefore is accessible, though the pages are laid out with text-dense paragraphs that a child used to modern picture books would find difficult to penetrate. The use of the native Indian word was a trademark that Bannerman continued in other books, sometimes to the consternation of her publishers, who thought that the words should be either translated into English or explained. Bannerman insisted that her Indian words could be understood by her English-reading audience from context and did not need the slavish explication that her publishers thought necessary. Her assertion usually proved correct.

The names of the characters, on the other hand, are not so easily tolerated or explained away. Certainly Bannerman lived and wrote in an era when patronizing attitudes toward nonwhites were more acceptable than today. Such racial bigotry was encouraged in the British Empire as an extension of "the white man's burden"; the superior Caucasians had an obligation to other races, who seemed less fully human, to bring them the benefits of northern European ways of life no matter where they lived in the British Empire. The patronizing nature of the diminutive *little* in Sambo's name could imply the superiority of the larger narrator, larger in knowledge as well as size. The word *black* attached to the names denies personhood apart from race. Certainly Mumbo and Jumbo suggest nicknames rather than real names, and the lack of a last name for the family gives them no heritage, just as the lack of a last name among American slaves was a way to deny full humanity and to maintain the slaves' status as property. It is interesting to note that the crit-

and deference to her husband and who might otherwise have preferred anonymous publication. Her later books frequently appeared with the ascription "By the author of Little Black Sambo" rather than naming the author outright, at least until Bannerman was assured that the resulting fame would not be an intrusion into her life. Certainly her embarrassment did not occur because of the critical reception of the book; the critics found it lively, colorful, well paced, charming, and, for all they knew, authentic to India. While there were voices criticizing the inaccuracies of the depiction of Indian life, they were in the minority; Bannerman herself countered that the book is set in an imaginary place and so need not be held to standards of veracity.

The story of the little boy, given attractive new clothes by his parents and then permitted to roam in the wilderness, where he is threatened by predatory animals, derives some of its resonance

Bannerman's drawing of the title character in The Story of Little Black Sambo

icism of the book for its racism is a phenomenon in the United States, where the book seldom finds its way to the children's shelf today. Commentary in Great Britain has been much less concerned with the racial attitudes than with the veracity to Indian life.

The book's illustrations bear some resemblance to children's puppet theaters of the nineteenth century, with the characters resembling the cutout silhouette shapes of Punch and Judy in their awkward poses and bright colors. The primary colors used by Bannerman are also reminiscent of the puppet theaters; they are clearly chemically produced. Their lack of resemblance to natural tones emphasizes the fantastic nature of the story, and the exaggerated poses suggest caricatures of humans, further offending those who perceive racism in the text. As Phyllis J. Yuill has noted in *Little Black Sambo: A Closer Look* (1976), the figure of Sambo is sometimes posed like the one and only black character in Heinrich Hoffman's *Struwwelpeter* (1845), the widely read collection of cautionary but humorous

poems about various misbehaved children. In the book there is one hapless African victim, whose physique resembles that of Sambo, with leg outstretched in jointless straightness from a side view. Certainly Bannerman's writing elsewhere suggests a familiarity with the earlier book, as in her use of the cautionary tale in *Little Dechie-Head: An Awful Warning to Bad Babas* (1903). Even the opening picture of Sambo suggests the character of Johnnie Suck-a-Thumb in *Struwwelpeter,* who is shown in full frontal pose, with his fingers outstretched. The resemblance of Sambo and family to the traditional British comic figure of the golliwog, with its black minstrel heritage and caricatured African features, does nothing to elevate the dignity of the non-Caucasians, whether Indian or African, in this story.

With a critical and financial success on his hands, Richards quickly asked Bannerman for another book; the success of *Little Black Sambo* led the author to produce seven more books by 1909, though all but her first book are now largely forgotten. Her willingness to continue publishing with

Bannerman's illustration for the climax of The Story of Little Black Mingo

Richards was due at least in part to her reticence in pursuing the copyright issue legally and to her feeling flattered by the request for another book. In any case, so soon after the publication of *Little Black Sambo,* she could not have forseen the vast fortune that would pass by her with the copyright out of her control. Bannerman's second book, *The Story of Little Black Mingo* (1901), is a companion story to *Little Black Sambo,* this time concerned with a girl. Mingo is an orphan cared for by Black Noggy, a woman who treats her as a slave, and she undergoes a trial similar to Sambo's in that she is threatened with death from being eaten by a wild animal. Here the beast is called a "mugger," clearly identified in the picture as a crocodile and well known by the Indian name in Britain at the time.

As a slave Mingo is forced, on pain of beating and humiliation, to draw water in large pots that she carries balanced on her head. The abusive nature of her relationship with her mistress is made clear not only by the beatings, but also by the size of the pots she is forced to balance. By her own estimation they are too heavy for her to handle when they are filled with water; in such a case she is expected to make two trips with the pot half full. The first pot she carries is broken by the menacing crocodile, for which she is beaten; she nevertheless feels forced to fill a second pot, despite the danger of the crocodile, for fear of another beating. The second time the crocodile carries Mingo off to an island where its eggs have been laid, with a promise that it will return and eat her the next day, when the eggs hatch. Left alone, she sees a mongoose in the water, clinging to a floating branch, and she rescues him. When the mongoose reaches dry land, he begins to eat the crocodile eggs. The crocodile returns and tries to protect the eggs, first by surrounding them, then by covering them with Mingo's water pot, but the mongoose manages to eat them all. He then uses the pot to help himself and little Mingo escape to Mingo's home, where they bar the door. Enraged, the pursuing crocodile eats up Mingo's evil mistress, complete with a can of kerosene and matches. Unharmed inside the crocodile, the mistress lights a match and explodes both herself and the crocodile, and Mingo and the mongoose live happily ever after.

The improbable, lengthy plot, with its circuitous direction, repetitions that do not add to tension, and the somewhat contrived circumstances of the ending point to a lack of design in this story. The kerosene and matches introduced at the end of this fantasy allow for an interesting explosion and some satisfaction at eliminating the two biggest menaces in this fictional universe. The accompanying pictures, first of Black Noggy in the Mugger's belly, hunched over and lighting her matches, and then of Black Noggy's and the Mugger's body parts strewn in bloodless, nonconcentric circles away from the explosion, bring a certain smug satisfaction and gory fascination to the story. But the plot up to that point is loose, and the pictures less interesting and certainly less colorful than in *Little Black Sambo.* Sometimes the details in the picture, especially of Mingo running away in the distance and the mongoose floating in the water, are so small as to be difficult to distinguish. Finally, the house to which Mingo and the mongoose retreat is amazingly unexotic, given a landscape otherwise filled with crocodiles full of expression and occasional palm trees. In fact, their refuge looks like a thatched English cottage, with stout mud walls, more fitting for the three little pigs than for Mingo.

In *Little Black Mingo* Bannerman first succeeded in keeping the Anglicized Indian dialect that she had been so familiar with in India. The words are defined only by the context of the facing illustration, not at all by the author's intrusion. But the pe-

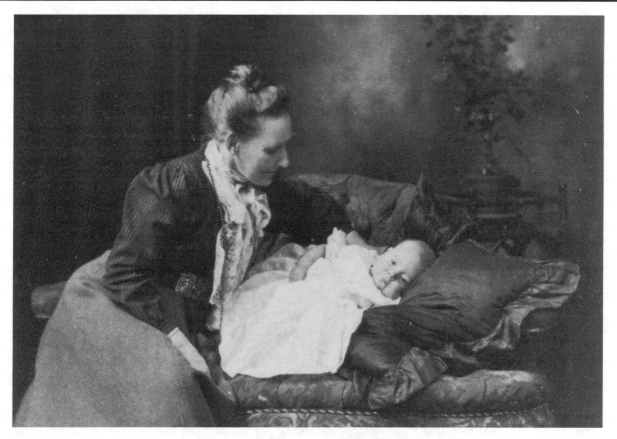

Bannerman with her son Rob in Edinburgh in 1902

culiar, attenuated quality of this story makes it less successful literarily than *Little Black Sambo,* though it attained some success as a companion piece to the earlier book. The companion design is clear from the beginning, with the cover picture of Mingo, who stands facing forward as if on exhibit, paralleling that of Sambo on his book. Yet, that she is a pitiful thing is clear from the slump of her shoulders and the dour expression on her face. In contrast, Sambo does not look directly at the viewer, but rather off to the side. His outstretched hands and arms are full of energy, whereas Mingo's hang limply.

In her next book, *The Story of Little Black Quibba* (1902), Bannerman again traces the activities of a lone child, this one a boy in spite of his name's feminine ending. Quibba leaves his mother's sickbed to find the mangoes that will help her recover. Once out of her presence, the child absentmindedly forgets about the mother until he returns home, triumphant, with mangoes luckily in hand. Along the way there are the usual adventures with odd animals, this time the most noteworthy of which is a snake who eats three frogs, after whose demise the frogs reemerge, unharmed, a reminiscence of Little Red Riding Hood in Wilhelm and Jacob Grimm's ver-

sion, who emerges whole after having been eaten by the wolf. As with Bannerman's earlier books, the Indian dialect – here the featured word is *mangoes* – concerned the publisher but not the readers, who found this otherwise unexceptional Bannerman book a likely purchase in the Christmas trade, where Bannerman's books had become a tradition.

Little Dechie-Head: An Awful Warning to Bad Babas signals a shift in genre for Bannerman, who clearly undertook a cautionary tale in this book. Unlike Sambo and Mingo, Dechie is a white child, blond and blue-eyed with ruffled bonnet and pinafore. Her name is Mary, and while the opening line states that she lives in India, nothing much about her existence is Indian except for her caretaker Domingo, who is clearly not Caucasian and appears dressed in something like pajamas. The name Dechie-Head derives from the peculiarly Indian pot depicted in the story. Against her wishes Bannerman found the tale depicted as "Little Kettlehead" in other editions, though the kettle looks more like a solid cooking pot than the rounder, clay shape of a dechie. Mary plays with fire against her mother's express prohibitions, setting her head on fire, by which it is completely consumed. In fairy-tale fash-

Page from one of Bannerman's illustrated letters to her daughters, relating how her son Rob summoned help with his screams when one of the Bannermans' servants fell into a well (Bannerman Family Collection)

ion Domingo finds her lying on the floor, showing no signs of pain or gore, and the servant rescues her and attaches the dechie in place of her head, covering it with her frilly bonnet. Mary is quite repaired at this point, though her parents do notice that she is peculiarly expressionless and has a limited vocabulary: "clip-clap-clapper-apper-apper," the onomatopoeia of her kettle's lid hitting the pot. Her parents do nothing to confront her except to note that she is rude when they talk to her. By managing to keep her sunbonnet in place and not letting them see her face, she eludes detection. Finally Christmas Eve comes, and Father Christmas sees her face as she

sleeps. In casting about in his bag for a gift, he finds the head of a broken doll, lovely and blond, which he leaves behind. When Dechie-Head awakes, she glues the head back on. Her parents are glad to see her, still frozen in expression, but this time at least a happy one. Their only comment is about the way her hair has grown long and blond in only one night.

Bannerman resorts here to a kind of story she tells nowhere else. This example claims an Indian setting, but the only Indian elements in it are the servant Domingo and the dechie; even the stove, which might have been given enough detail to make it more than a source of flame, is undistinguished. Except for these two details, the beginning of the story comes right out of the *Struwwelpeter* tradition of the cautionary tale. Because of its preposterousness and because Mary is not subjected to public humiliation, the cautionary nature of the story is severely undercut. The appearance of Father Christmas perhaps makes the point that even to those far away in India, the spirit of the season comes. But his presence might just as well be explained by extraliterary reasons: the biggest season for children's book sales, then as now, was Christmas, and Bannerman made the story into a Christmas piece by replacing the more traditional supernatural agency of the fairy godmother with the person of Father Christmas.

Mary's full frontal pose, at the beginning and end of the book, was a signature for Bannerman at this point, but in this book it does more than just introduce the character and exotic clothing, as it had with Mingo and Sambo. From the beginning it is clear that Mary is a doll, in her frilly clothes, lovely blue dress, and wooden, exhibitionary stance. At the end the only difference in her appearance is that she has long hair and a more obvious smile. She is a showpiece easily mended and absurd in her bloodless adventures. The story of a toy doll masquerades as a caution against playing with matches; one genre undercuts the other.

The next book Bannerman wrote was inspired by events closer to home. *Pat and the Spider: The Biter Bit* (1904) resulted from Bannerman's attempts to amuse her son Pat while he was suffering an unspecified but uncomfortable and debilitating contagious disease. A cautionary tale against biting, it is not the child but a superfluous, menacing tiger who receives the retaliation promised in the subtitle. Pat befriends the spider of the title, and when a tiger comes out of the jungle and pursues Pat, the spider intervenes and is eaten instead, thereby poisoning the tiger. The cover of the book bears an illustration of Bannerman's son, wearing a jaunty sailor suit and looking as much like a doll as does Dechie-Head. The story is set in a more active, fantastic landscape than Dechie's: brambles, or blackberries, coexist with bamboo; and Pat, like the title character in Lewis Carroll's *Alice's Adventures in Wonderland* (1865), changes size almost without reason. The book's evolution from a story told to Pat during his illness reveals Bannerman's preoccupation with her children and what pleased them in her published work. There is otherwise little of note in this book.

The Story of the Teasing Monkey (1906) returns Bannerman to a fictional, exotic setting where she had earlier found success and inspiration. The characters, a capuchin monkey named Jacko and a nameless lion, lioness, and bear, are not stuffed animals of the nursery, but animals in the wild. While the illustrations of the lions and bear are generic enough to be animal crackers, the monkey's deep-set eyes and gray coloring give him a realistic appearance rather than that of something created to be cute and suitable. This monkey lives in a banyan tree and climbs down the banyan's roots – which grow from the tree's branches in spidery vines extending to the ground – to tug the tails of passing animals. The lion and lioness find this naughty trick unpleasant and resolve to catch the monkey, with the help of the bear, by gnawing at the roots so that when the monkey climbs down them, they will break. They capture the monkey and imprison him in a rock larder, where they begin to fatten him in preparation for eating. The lions use enticing food, but, knowing that he is being fattened for slaughter, the monkey eats only one banana a day, giving the rest to the rats who visit him. The lions are confounded, but, overhearing the monkey talking to the rats and pining for a coconut, they oblige, though not without getting hit on their heads by the falling fruit. This time Jacko indulges, getting fat and making himself appear even fatter by applying to his own skin the fur of the coconut and fashioning a coat from the coconut fronds, all of which swell his proportions. The bear is invited back for a feast, and the lions make preparations. Recognizing his mistake, Jacko tries to slim down by taking off the fur and fronds and greasing himself, but to no avail. However, the bear, returning before the lions, finds himself unable to resist and invades the rock stronghold, which collapses on him and allows Jacko to escape. He climbs the coconut tree, and the three predators follow him, only to have their heads hit by falling coconuts. They all have headaches and eat bananas for supper, while Jacko lives happily ever after.

Because the characters in this tale are not human, Bannerman's sometimes awkward posing of them is less conspicuous. In fact, her illustration of the monkey is carefully delineated and anatomically correct. While the monkey's large eyes, especially when looking directly at the viewer, make him more soulful, he is elsewhere in such motion and commotion that the high jinks are enjoyable. The bear, on the other hand, is somewhat misshapen and undefined, sometimes looking more like an overgrown mole. Though this is a slight story, it is engaging, with no elements of Indian culture to slow the reader down and no particular moral message to

One of Bannerman's illustrations for Pat and the Spider. *Her son served as the model for the story's protagonist.*

give it undue weight or attention. Of all Bannerman's books, this is the most appropriate for small children, with its clear line drawings, colorful pictures, and lack of racism.

In *The Story of Little Black Quasha* (1908) Bannerman returns to the traditions and style of *Little Black Sambo* and *Little Black Mingo,* yet she shows some slender development in her characterization and plotting. The picture of Quasha on the front cover is not exhibitionist in stance; instead she is shown slightly bent over, walking toward the right corner of the picture, hand in hand with a frog, the magical agent in the story. Quasha has no particular family or home. The story starts off with her finding a strand of yarn, rolling it into a ball, and following it for a mile until she finds its owner, a woman who is knitting a sock. The first picture of this woman shows her in an unexplained, angry outburst, as menacing as Black Noggy, but she soon calms down and rewards Quasha with a coin. The girl proceeds to a bazaar to spend her pittance, choosing a book with green covers (the color of the first edition of *Little Black Sambo*), though the title is not shown and the only other details are a splotch of red and blue on the cover. Quasha sits down to read but is rapidly and quietly surrounded by a mob of tigers who want to eat her. A frog magically appears and offers to save her in exchange for her

book. He gets the tigers to agree, with surprising rationality, that Quasha cannot be shared among them. They begin to battle, and the field is quickly strewn with bloody bodies – the last two contenders are disposed of through frog trickery. Quasha willingly hands over the book, but since the frog finds it too big, he happily hands it back.

Like *Little Black Sambo,* this story features bloodthirsty tigers that self-destruct; like *Little Black Mingo,* it is a story of a lone black girl who needs the intervention of a magical agent. The threat of the Black Noggy–like villainess rapidly deflates into the role of the signaler, if not the causal agent, of good fortune. The frog, like the frog in the Grimms' "Frog Prince," is the rescuer, but he asks no unpleasant favors and his wish, when granted, is returned.

This is one story where Bannerman provides some kind of background in her illustrations: shrubbery, roads, trees, rocks, and landscape are found, if at all, in less abundance elsewhere. The smiling figure of Quasha is fleet of foot and more realistic in stance than Sambo, with elbows and ankles that work as they should. Green tones, as well as the red of blood, predominate, giving a freshness that is as lively and vibrant as Quasha herself. If there were an appropriate heir to the literary success of Bannerman's first book, *Little Black Quasha* would be it.

Her following book, *The Story of Little Black Bobtail* (1909), is really the story of three boys: Little Black Tag; Little Black Rag; and their baby brother, Little Black Bobtail. They live together at the edge of a river in a round thatched hut, with no parents in sight. The river floods, the house collapses, and the boys sail away on a ladder, later rescuing a basket and ample food. They continue their ocean trip until a storm upsets them, and the two older brothers part company with Bobtail, who drifts off in the basket. The two older boys find an abandoned ship, which rapidly collides, without harm, with an iceberg, whereupon the ship is boarded by a boy-eating polar bear, whom they blast to bits with the ship's cannon. Finally, Little Black Bobtail reappears at ship's side, having slept through the other adventures, and they all sail on happily ever after.

Obviously Bannerman has chosen a series of names similar to Winken, Blinken, and Nod, who are also known for their youthful, unlikely voyage. While the initial setting in some primitive place seems to suggest a real locale for the story, the appearance of the sturdy ladder, basket, and food, the lack of human evidence on the abandoned ship, and the rapid appearance of iceberg and polar bear mark this story as happening out of time. This is the last of the books from the productive decade that Bannerman spent creating such stories on demand. The story's rapid, improbable succession of major catastrophes points to a literary output that had overrun its course and to the strain on her creative resources from the demands of both public and publisher for another book resembling *Little Black Sambo*. The story is even misnamed, for it is not about Bobtail – who disappears for a good part of the story and who is mostly present only as a squeaking voice full of advice to his less wise older brothers, who are nevertheless resourceful in their baby brother's absence – it is really the story of all three. Once again Bannerman resorts to an explosion to resolve the story's action, perhaps even planning for it as one of the events she knew that her readers had enjoyed earlier. The children have nicknames, though it is explained in this case that they had real names earlier, but, after the death of their parents, no one remembered what they were. While an exciting story, it does not contain much of literary or artistic merit; in fact, this must have been one of the easier books to illustrate, given that a series of waves serves as background throughout.

After the publication of *Little Black Bobtail,* Bannerman turned away from her writing career. The strain of producing so many books in so short a

Cover for Bannerman's last book, completed by her daughter and published twenty years after the author's death

time, especially during periods when some of her children were extremely ill, and the final departure of the last of her children for Edinburgh schools left her without inspiration or desire. Her interest in writing had never been financial, but rather artistic and expressive of her love for her family. In fact, after *Little Black Sambo* the profits were modest, given that royalties were based upon a modest purchase price befitting such small books. Bannerman returned to her life as supportive spouse, entertaining more frequently than she had when her children and her publishing had taken more of her time. Her husband was promoted several times, she found herself more in the social scene as official functions increased, and her health, sometimes fragile, became even more so. World War I postponed her husband's retirement. While he saw no service, there were no other doctors to replace him at his post, and limited passages out of India stranded the whole family, including Bannerman's daughters who at the war's outbreak had returned to India only for a visit. Finally, at the war's conclusion Dr. Bannerman was mustered out, and the household returned, once and for all, to Edinburgh, where the other children and the rest of their extended families had remained during most of the Bannermans' adult lives.

Bannerman published only one other book in her lifetime, after the death of her husband and at the fervent request of her daughter Day. *Sambo and the Twins* (1936) is a highly derivative, weakly plotted piece that perpetuates the unconscious racism of its predecessor. Sambo is a bit more grown-up, though not yet adult, when his mother presents him with twin babies, whose origin is not clear. They are his to care for, and as they grow to be toddlers, he bathes them and celebrates their first birthday with gifts. He leaves the twins to his mother's care while he runs an errand for her, and, unattended at the doorway of their hut, they are carried off by monkeys, to the grief of Black Mumbo. Black Sambo finds them, and he attempts their rescue by climbing the palm tree where the monkeys have hidden them, only to find that the last few feet are too difficult. A passing eagle also offers to try, but the babies are scared of him. At last, with Black Sambo on his back, the eagle rescues the babies and returns all three children to Black Mumbo, who rewards him with two legs of mutton. The celebratory dinner among the humans predictably features pancakes.

Sambo has not changed his clothes from the first book, though he puts them aside when he goes into the forest, to keep from damaging them, a lesson he obviously learned from his first such journey. In only shorts he looks like an enlarged version of the twins. The two babies look like dolls rather than real children, and Black Mumbo and Black Jumbo look like black minstrels as they are depicted in their joy at the return of the babies, when they jump about in high leg kicks, wearing pajamas and bandanas – clothing that does not look at all like Sambo's. At the end it is still not clear whose children the twins are, given the obvious parental joy of Mumbo and Jumbo and Sambo's lack of parental emotion at their rescue. The story deemphasizes Sambo's own ability to solve problems, since the eagle must intervene – though even with this solution there is an initial false start. The identical twins are never really characterized; their passivity makes them doll-like and objectified. Also, there is not enough story or motivation to develop the character of Sambo. The book is simply a nostalgic attempt to resurrect the original Sambo, who at least had a more colorful world where his cleverness had a more significant reward.

Bannerman died on 13 October 1946, and her last book was published posthumously; the story was pieced together by Day Bannerman from materials left behind. Her daughter provided illustrations for the book, but they were of a lesser quality than Bannerman's work typically had been. *The Story of Little White Squibba* (1966) disappointed reviewers, readers, and publishers.

Bannerman's books offer little beyond historical interest for most current readers; many find her life to be more interesting, including her efforts to support the work of her husband in dealing with the plague in India during his long service there. Elizabeth Hay's biography, *Sambo Sahib: The Story of Little Black Sambo and Helen Bannerman* (1981), is an extended demonstration of Bannerman's modeling of ideal womanhood in Victorian terms, even though her education might have suggested another path. Her books may not be weighty in meaning or major accomplishment, though *Little Black Sambo,* despite its racist overtones, was certainly a change from earlier long, dreary didactic works for children. Ironically, the controversy over the book's racism has kept it alive, long after its accomplishment has been surpassed by other writers of small books about small creatures.

Biography:
Elizabeth Hay, *Sambo Sahib: The Story of Little Black Sambo and Helen Bannerman* (New York: Barnes & Noble, 1981).

References:
Selma G. Lanes, *Down the Rabbit Hole: Adventures and Misadventures in the Realm of Children's Literature* (Boston: Atheneum, 1971), pp. 158–178;

Nicholas Tucker, ed., *Suitable for Children? Controversies in Children's Literature* (Los Angeles & Berkeley: University of California Press, 1976), pp. 184–196;

Phyllis J. Yuill, *Little Black Sambo: A Closer Look* (Chicago: Racism and Sexism Resource Center for Educators, 1976).

Papers:
While Helen Bannerman's papers remain the property of her family, the largest collection of her works and related materials is available at the libraries of the University of Illinois at Urbana-Champaign.

J. M. Barrie

(9 May 1860 – 19 June 1937)

Donna R. White
Clemson University

See also the Barrie entry in *DLB 10: Modern British Dramatists, 1900–1945.*

BOOKS: *Better Dead* (London: Swan, Sonnenschein, Lowrie, 1888);

Auld Licht Idylls (London: Hodder & Stoughton, 1888; New York: Cassell, 1891);

When a Man's Single (London: Hodder & Stoughton, 1888; New York: Harper, 1889; first authorized American edition, New York: Scribners, 1896);

A Window in Thrums (London: Hodder & Stoughton, 1889; New York: Lovell, Coryell, 1890; first authorized American edition, New York: Scribners, 1897);

My Lady Nicotine (London: Hodder & Stoughton, 1890; New York: Rand, McNally, 1891; first authorized American edition, New York: Scribners, 1896);

Richard Savage (London: Privately printed, 1891);

The Little Minister (London: Cassell, 1891; Boston: Estes, 1891);

A Holiday in Bed and Other Sketches (New York: New York Publishing Company, 1892);

An Auld Licht Manse and Other Sketches (New York: John Knox, 1893);

Jane Annie, by Barrie and Arthur Conan Doyle (London: Chapell, 1893);

A Powerful Drug and Other Stories (New York: Ogilvie, 1893);

A Tillyloss Scandal (New York: Lovell, Coryell, 1893);

Two of Them (New York: Lovell, Coryell, 1893);

A Lady's Shoe (London: Chapman & Hall, 1894; New York: Brentano's, 1898);

Life in a Country Manse (New York: Ogilvie, 1894);

Scotland's Lament: A Poem on the Death of Robert Louis Stevenson (London: Privately printed for T. J. Wise, 1895);

Sentimental Tommy (London: Cassell, 1896; New York: Scribners, 1896);

Margaret Ogilvy (New York: Scribners, 1896; London: Hodder & Stoughton, 1896);

Tommy and Grizel (London: Cassell, 1900; New York: Scribners, 1900);

The Wedding Guest (London: Chapman & Hall, 1900; New York: Scribners, 1900);

The Boy Castaways of Black Lake Island (N.p.: Privately printed, 1901);

The Little White Bird, or Adventures in Kensington Gardens (London: Hodder & Stoughton, 1902; New York: Scribners, 1902);

Peter Pan in Kensington Gardens (London: Hodder & Stoughton, 1906; New York: Scribners, 1906);

Walker, London (London & New York: French, 1907);

Peter and Wendy (London: Hodder & Stoughton, 1911; New York: Scribners, 1911); republished as *Peter Pan and Wendy* (London: Hodder & Stoughton, 1921; New York: Scribners, 1921); republished as *The Blampied Edition of Peter Pan* (New York: Scribners, 1940); republished as *Peter Pan* (London: Hodder & Stoughton, 1949; New York: Scribners, 1950);

Quality Street (London: Hodder & Stoughton, 1913; New York: Scribners, 1918);

The Admirable Crichton (London & New York: Hodder & Stoughton, 1914);

Half Hours (New York: Scribners, 1914; London: Hodder & Stoughton, 1914)—includes *Pantaloon, The Twelve-Pound Look, Rosalind,* and *The Will;*

Der Tag, A Play (London & New York: Hodder & Stoughton, 1914); published in America as *Der Tag; or, The Tragic Man* (New York: Scribners, 1914);

Charles Frohman: A Tribute (London: Privately printed by Clement Shorter, 1915);

Shakespeare's Legacy (London: Privately printed by Clement Shorter, 1916);

Alice-Sit-by-the-Fire (London & New York: Hodder & Stoughton, 1918);

Echoes of the War (London & New York: Hodder & Stoughton, 1918)—includes *The New Word, The Old Lady Shows Her Medals, A Well-Remembered Voice,* and *Barbara's Wedding;*

J. M. Barrie

Mary Rose (London & New York: Hodder & Stoughton, 1918);

What Every Woman Knows (London: Hodder & Stoughton, 1918; New York: Scribners, 1918);

A Kiss for Cinderella (London: Hodder & Stoughton, 1920; New York: Scribners, 1921);

Dear Brutus (London: Hodder & Stoughton, 1922; New York: Scribners, 1922);

The Author (Cincinnati: Privately printed, 1925);

Cricket (London: Privately printed by Clement Shorter, 1926);

Representative Plays, edited by W. L. Phelps (New York: Scribners, 1926)–includes *Quality Street, The Admirable Crichton, What Every Woman Knows, Dear Brutus, The Twelve-Pound Look,* and *The Old Lady Shows Her Medals;*

Peter Pan; or, The Boy Who Would Not Grow Up (London: Hodder & Stoughton, 1928; New York: Scribners, 1928);

The Plays of J. M. Barrie in One Volume: The Definitive Edition, edited by A. E. Wilson (London: Hodder & Stoughton, 1928; revised edition, 1942);

Shall We Join the Ladies? (New York: Scribners, 1928; London: Hodder & Stoughton, 1929)–includes *Shall We Join the Ladies?, Half an Hour, Seven Women,* and *Old Friends;*

The Works of J. M. Barrie, 16 volumes (New York: Scribners, 1929–1940);

The Plays of James M. Barrie (New York: Scribners, 1930);

The Greenwood Hat (Edinburgh: A&T Constable, 1930);

Farewell, Miss Julie Logan (New York: Scribners, 1932; London: Hodder & Stoughton, 1932);

The Boy David (London: Davies, 1938; New York: Scribners, 1938);

M'Connachie and J. M. B. (London: Davies, 1938; New York: Scribners, 1939);

When Wendy Grew Up: An Afterthought (New York: Dutton, 1957);

Ibsen's Ghost; or, Toole Up-to-Date (London: Cecil Woolf, 1975).

PLAY PRODUCTIONS: *Bandelero, the Bandit,* Dumfries, Scotland, Dumfries Academy, 1877;

Richard Savage, by Barrie and H. B. Marriott Watson, London, Criterion Theatre, 16 April 1891;

Ibsen's Ghost; or, Toole Up-to-Date, London, Toole's Theatre, 30 May 1891;

Walker, London, London, Toole's Theatre, 25 February 1892;

Jane Annie; or, The Good Conduct Prize, by Barrie and Arthur Conan Doyle, with music by Ernest Ford, London, Savoy Theatre, 13 May 1893;

Becky Sharp, London, Terry's Theatre, 3 June 1893;

The Professor's Love Story, New York, Star Theatre, 13 December 1893;

The Little Minister, London, Haymarket Theatre, 13 July 1897;

A Platonic Friendship, London, Theatre Royal (Drury Lane), 17 March 1898;

The Wedding Guest, London, Garrick Theatre, 27 September 1900;

Quality Street, Toledo (Ohio), 14 October 1901;

The Admirable Crichton, London, Duke of York's Theatre, 4 November 1902;

Little Mary, London, Wyndham's Theatre, 24 September 1903;

Peter Pan; or, The Boy Who Wouldn't Grow Up, London, Duke of York's Theatre, 27 December 1904;

Pantaloon; or, A Plea for an Ancient Family, with music by John Crook, London, Duke of York's Theatre, 5 April 1905;

Alice-Sit-by-the-Fire: A Page from a Daughter's Diary, London, Duke of York's Theatre, 5 April 1905;

Josephine, London, Comedy Theatre, 5 April 1906;

Punch: A Toy Tragedy, London, Comedy Theatre, 5 April 1906;

"When Wendy Grew Up (An Afterthought)," London, Duke of York's Theatre, 22 February 1908 (one performance);

What Every Woman Knows, London, Duke of York's Theatre, 3 September 1908;

Old Friends, London, Duke of York's Theatre, 1 March 1910;

The Twelve-Pound Look, London, Duke of York's Theatre, 1 March 1910;

A Slice of Life: An Advanced Drama, London, Duke of York's Theatre, 7 June 1910;

Rosalind, London, Duke of York's Theatre, 14 October 1912;

The Dramatists Get What They Want, London, Hippodrome, 23 December 1912;

The Adored One: A Legend of the Old Bailey, London, Duke of York's Theatre, 4 September 1913; Act I revised as *Seven Women,* London, New Theatre, 7 April 1917;

The Will, London, Duke of York's Theatre, 4 September 1913;

Half an Hour, New York, Lyceum Theatre, 25 September 1913;

Frank Tinney's Revue, London, Savoy Theatre, 3 July 1914;

Shakespeare's Legacy, Atlantic City, N.J., 8 October 1914;

The Duke of Christmas Daisies, Dumfries, Scotland, Dumfries Academy, 12 December 1914;

Der Tag; or, The Tragic Man, London, Coliseum, 21 December 1914;

The New Word, London, Duke of York's Theatre, 22 March 1915;

Rosy Rapture, the Pride of the Beauty Chorus, by Barrie, with lyrics by F. W. Mark, music by Hermann Darewski and Jerome D. Kern, London, Duke of York's Theatre, 22 March 1915;

The Fatal Typist, London, His Majesty's Theatre, 19 November 1915;

The Real Thing at Last, 7 March 1916, Coliseum Theatre, London;

A Kiss for Cinderella, London, Wyndham's Theatre, 16 March 1916;

Irene Vanbrugh's Pantomime, London, Coliseum, 9 June 1916;

The Origin of Harlequin, with music by Herman Fincke, London, Palace Theatre, 16 February 1917;

Reconstructing the Crime, London, Palace Theatre, 16 February 1917;

The Old Lady Shows Her Medals, London, New Theatre, 7 April 1917;

Dear Brutus, London, Wyndham's Theatre, 17 October 1917;

La Politesse, London, Wyndham's Theatre, 28 June 1918;

A Well-Remembered Voice, London, Wyndham's Theatre, 28 June 1918;

The Truth About the Russian Dancers, London, Coliseum, 15 March 1920;

Mary Rose, London, Haymarket Theatre, 22 April 1920;

Shall We Join the Ladies?, London, Vanbrugh Theatre (Royal Academy of Dramatic Arts), 27 May 1921;

A Happy New Year, London, Little Theatre, 31 May 1922;

Barbara's Wedding, London, Savoy Theatre, 23 August 1927;

The Boy David, Edinburgh, King's Theatre, 21 November 1936.

J. M. Barrie's importance to children's literature can be summed up in one name: Peter Pan. The mythic boy who would not grow up has flown across countless stages throughout the Western world, starred in major motion pictures, and loaned his name to everything from peanut butter to a psychological disorder. Ironically, the creator of one of the most famous characters in children's literature was only incidentally a children's writer: Barrie built his career as a journalist, novelist, and playwright. Other than the play and book about Peter Pan and a few private theatricals, Barrie did not write for children. However, the creation of Peter Pan assures Barrie a place among the immortals.

James Matthew Barrie, the seventh of eight children was born in Kirriemuir, Scotland on 9 May 1860. His father, David Barrie, was a hand-loom weaver; his mother, known by her maiden name of Margaret Ogilvy, was the strongest influence on this third son. With eight children to clothe and feed, David and Margaret had little time for nurturing individual children, but Barrie's childhood was by no means the hand-to-mouth existence he suggested in later autobiographical writings. In fact, with careful planning the Barries were able to send their sons to private schools and to college. Barrie's earliest years were uneventful, but when he was six years old unexpected tragedy struck the family: his older brother David, seven years his senior, died in a skating accident. Margaret was inconsolable, despite her younger son's efforts to replace David in her affections and, in effect, to live David's unfinished life. In his mother's memories David would always be the thirteen-year-old golden boy. The idea of youth frozen forever in time was planted in Barrie's mind to surface years later in *Peter Pan; or, The Boy Who Wouldn't Grow Up* (1904) and other works.

Barrie's attempts to take the place of his brother resulted in a new closeness with his mother. After David's death, Margaret spent many months a semi-invalid, and her youngest son spent much time in her room, listening to her reminisce about her own childhood. Margaret's mother had died young, and Margaret, at the age of eight, had been forced to take on the care of a household and a younger brother. Barrie tucked these stories away in his own memories and in adult life would draw on them for a series of popular newspaper articles. More importantly, the young Margaret became the first model for Wendy, the little girl who took on the task of mothering Peter Pan and the Lost Boys.

Margaret also read with her son. They started with Daniel Defoe's *Robinson Crusoe* (1719) and continued through every adventure tale they could find, including the historical novels of fellow Scotsman Sir Walter Scott. Barrie developed a taste for adventure and a tendency toward hero worship that continued throughout his life. He dreamed of becoming a real-life adventurer and played at being shipwrecked on desert islands. When Barrie and his mother had exhausted the resources of the local bookshop-library, he started writing his own adventure serials to entertain them.

Margaret's influence on her son was overwhelming. All of Barrie's biographers have noted his obsessive concern for her welfare and her viselike grip on his imagination. In a 1970 biography Janet Dunbar refers to Margaret as "an emotional boa constrictor." Whether or not Barrie truly suffered from a mother fixation, the emotional tie between mother and son was certainly strong.

From the ages of thirteen to seventeen Barrie attended Dumfries Academy, boarding with his brother Alec and sister Mary. Alec was an inspector of schools, and Mary kept house for him. By his own accounts Barrie had a wonderful time at Dumfries. For perhaps the only time in his life he made friends quickly and easily — friends who shared his passion for adventure reading. He and his cronies spent many happy hours playing pirates after school. As he grew older Barrie developed an interest in the theater and attended local performances as often as he could. From the very beginning he showed an interest in stagecraft, always preferring a seat near the wings, where he could get a glimpse of backstage action.

Barrie's first public recognition as a writer came during his years at Dumfries Academy. He and a school friend started a drama society, and for one of their productions Barrie wrote a short play entitled *Bandelero, the Bandit* (1877), based on his inveterate reading of penny dreadfuls, cheap serials that specialized in sensational adventure stories for boys. This production stirred up a slight local controversy when a minister wrote to the newspaper, attacking the play for immorality. Barrie and his friends enlisted support from several London newspapers and famous men of the theater. The entire affair brought welcome publicity to the drama society and pleased Barrie immensely.

After five happy years at Dumfries Academy, Barrie returned to Kirriemuir with a determination to become a writer. His family had other plans for him: Barrie was informed that he must attend a university and become a minister, as his older brother David would have done had he lived. With Alec's wise advice, a compromise was reached whereby Barrie would attend Edinburgh University and study literature.

Barrie's first few terms at Edinburgh University were not pleasant. Always somewhat introverted, Barrie now became painfully shy. He was intensely self-conscious about his lack of height as well; he had stopped growing when he reached five feet. In his final years in Edinburgh, Barrie found a writing outlet by becoming a freelance drama critic for the Edinburgh *Evening Courant*. Despite a lack of interest in his studies, Barrie graduated with an M.A. on 21 April 1882 at the age of twenty-one.

Upon returning to Kirriemuir, the new graduate finally convinced his family to allow him to pursue his dream of becoming a writer. His older sister Jane Ann, who had always been quietly supportive of her young brother's dreams and ambitions, brought to his attention a job advertisement she saw in the *Scotsman*. An English newspaper, the *Nottingham Journal*, was looking for a writer. Barrie applied for the position and was hired in January 1883. He was given a free hand at the *Journal* to write on any topic that struck his fancy, and he began to churn out a dozen extra columns a week. This employment was short-lived, however, for the owners of the newspaper decided it would be cheaper to buy syndicated articles than to employ their own journalists. After eighteen months Barrie returned to Kirriemuir with no immediate job prospects.

While in Nottingham, Barrie had submitted unsolicited articles to several London newspapers, with occasional success. Back in Kirriemuir he began to bombard the London papers with articles. Some were accepted, many rejected. One particular article – a story based on Margaret's childhood memories of Kirriemuir – struck the fancy of the editor of the *St. James's Gazette*. At the editor's urging, Barrie wrote a series of articles set in Kirriemuir's past. Most of them concerned the Auld Lichts, a strict religious sect to which his grandfather had belonged. After the success of these articles, Barrie decided to move to London and continue his freelancing closer to his literary markets.

Although he wrote on many topics in his early years in London, Barrie's Auld Licht stories were the ones that earned him recognition as a promising new writer. These articles were gathered into one volume in 1888 and published by Hodder and Stoughton as *Auld Licht Idylls*, initiating a publishing relationship that lasted Barrie's lifetime. *Auld Licht Idylls* was the first of Barrie's "Thrums" books, named after his fictional Scottish town – a barely disguised Kirriemuir. There were three Thrums volumes in all; the two sequels were called *A Window in Thrums* (1889) and *The Little Minister* (1891). *A Window in Thrums* was another collection of previously published articles, but *The Little Minister* was an original novel – Barrie's first successful one. All three books became popular, bringing literary fame to Barrie and tourists to Kirriemuir. The success of *Auld Licht Idylls* soothed an authorial ego still stinging from the failure of Barrie's first attempt at novel writing: *Better Dead* (1888), privately printed at the author's expense.

Barrie's love for the theater had not abated one whit since his school days. Now that he was in London, he took advantage of the rich offerings of the London stage, often developing crushes on the attractive young actresses whose performances delighted him. While continuing his work as a journalist and novelist, Barrie decided to try his hand at writing plays. His first attempt, *Richard Savage* (1891), written with H. B. Marriott Watson, was hardly encouraging: the play only ran one performance. Barrie's second play, a parody of Henrik Ibsen's *Hedda Gabler* (1890), was more successful. *Ibsen's Ghost; or, Toole Up-to-Date* (1891) received good reviews and brought Barrie the critical attention he craved.

Walker, London (1892), Barrie's next play, introduced him to a young actress named Mary Ansell. Despite his private doubts about his own suitability for marriage, Barrie eventually proposed to Mary, and they were married on 9 July 1894. His wedding present to his bride was a Saint Bernard puppy, who was later to figure prominently in *The*

THE BOY
CASTAWAYS

OF BLACK LAKE ISLAND

BEING A RECORD OF THE TERRIBLE
ADVENTURES OF THE BROTHERS
DAVIES IN THE SUMMER OF 1901
FAITHFULLY SET FORTH BY

PETER LLEWELYN DAVIES

LONDON
Published by J. M. BARRIE
in the Gloucester Road
1901

Title page for Barrie's privately printed "album," a series of photographs taken on holiday and ostensibly written by one of Barrie's young friends

Little White Bird, or Adventures in Kensington Gardens (1902), the novel that introduced Peter Pan. Porthos – named after a dog in George du Maurier's *Peter Ibbetson* (1891) – was also the first model for Nana, the dog-nursemaid in *Peter Pan*. Mary herself became the model for several of her husband's heroines, and for many years Barrie gave her Christian name to characters in his books and plays.

During the early 1890s Barrie continued to write critically acclaimed plays and novels. His literary reputation was assured; in fact, some critics tossed the word *genius* into their commentaries. The recognition merely spurred Barrie to greater efforts; he produced more than a dozen books and plays during the final decade of the nineteenth century.

Barrie's prose writings were all autobiographical in nature. He had a compulsion to fictionalize the events and people in his life to a degree unprecedented in English literature. In fact, his habit of laying bare his most private thoughts and emotions under a wispy veil of fiction led to accusations that

Photograph from The Boy Castaways of Black Lake Island, *with Barrie as an early version of Captain Hook, menacing Michael Llewelyn Davies, dressed as Peter Pan*

he was overly sentimental, whimsical, and saccharine. Readers and theatergoers sometimes experienced the discomfort of the unwitting voyeur as Barrie paraded his naked emotions across the page or the stage. Late-Victorian England, however, had a strong affection for sentimentality, so the public found Barrie's works charming and touching. When he published *Margaret Ogilvy* (1896), his affectionate tribute to his mother, within a year of her death, it became an instant success, although the more reserved members of the British public found the emotionally overcharged memoir distasteful. In the United States Barrie's sentimentality was a point in his favor. In recent decades a more psychologically aware readership has seen in *Margaret Ogilvy* a very unhealthy mother-son relationship.

In 1896 Barrie's agent, Addison Bright, enticed him into taking a trip to America to meet Charles Frohman, a renowned Broadway producer. Frohman, who had an implicit belief in Barrie's genius, became the author's lifelong friend and financial backer. Although he based his operations in New York, Frohman had close theatrical contacts in London and Paris, and his sponsorship brought Barrie international fame and great financial success.

Another important figure entered Barrie's life several years later. While walking Porthos in Kensington Gardens, Barrie met five-year-old George Llewelyn Davies, who, along with his two younger brothers, Jack and Peter, was destined to provide the spark that created Peter Pan. Barrie made friends with the boys, despite the disapproval of their nursemaid, and told them stories of adventure and fantasy. The friendship became even closer after Barrie met the boys' mother, Sylvia Llewelyn Davies, the daughter of novelist du Maurier, at a dinner party. She confided to Barrie that her youngest son was named after the title character of her father's novel *Peter Ibbetson,* enabling Barrie to bring Porthos into the conversation, and Sylvia discovered that this odd little man was the storyteller about whom her sons chattered so enthusiastically. The friendship Barrie formed with Sylvia and her sons and, with more difficulty, her husband Arthur, had a tremendous impact on both his personal and professional life.

Frontispiece, drawn by H. J. Ford, for Barrie's The Little White Bird *(1902), illustrating Barrie's blending of the fantastic with everyday locales*

Peter Pan was invented to entertain George and Jack Llewelyn Davies. Because their brother Peter was only a baby, Barrie amused himself and the two older boys with the fancy that baby Peter could fly. Babies, said Barrie, were birds before they were born; parents put bars on nursery windows to keep the little ones from flying away. This grew into a tale of a baby who did fly away, not realizing that he was no longer a bird. Thus was Peter Pan born.

In 1900 Mary Barrie bought Black Lake Cottage, a vacation cottage in Surrey, and in the summer the Llewelyn Davies boys often joined the Barries from their family's nearby vacation spot. For their entertainment Barrie devised a continuing Robinson Crusoe adventure for them to act out, based loosely on the plot of R. M. Ballantyne's *The Coral Island* (1858). Barrie took many photographs of the boys at play and commemorated the holiday with a privately printed story album he entitled *The Boy Castaways of Black Lake Island* (1901). Only two copies were made: one for Barrie and one for the boys' father, who

promptly lost his copy on a train, leading some biographers and literary critics to infer that Arthur resented Barrie's influence on the family.

The Boy Castaways of Black Lake Island is short on text. It purports to be written by four-year-old Peter Llewelyn Davies, who gives a short account of being shipwrecked with his two older brothers. The photographs have appropriately adventurous captions and feature the three boys and Porthos in various poses. In his 1928 dedication to *Peter Pan; or, The Boy Who Would Not Grow Up* (the published version of the play) Barrie traces the origins of the Lost Boys, Captain Hook and his pirates, Nana the dog-nursemaid, and Tinker Bell back to *The Boy Castaways*. In addition, the fantasy island that was the setting for the earlier work would eventually become Peter Pan's Never Land.

In 1902 Barrie's most critically admired play, *The Admirable Crichton*, opened in London. The title character is an exemplary butler who is shipwrecked along with the family he serves, and whose practical survival skills elevate him to the leadership of the small group of castaways. When they are rescued and returned to civilization, social stratification is restored. The desert island setting is clearly an offshoot of *The Boy Castaways*.

During the same week that *The Admirable Crichton* opened, Hodder and Stoughton published Barrie's novel *The Little White Bird,* a lightly fictionalized account of Barrie's friendship with George Llewelyn Davies. In the novel Captain W, a lonely bachelor, plays anonymous fairy godfather to an impoverished young couple and later befriends their young son, David, with whom he goes for walks in Kensington Gardens. Barrie draws an affectionate portrait of Sylvia and Arthur in the young couple, although it would be several years before the playwright's fairy godfather fiction became reality.

As long as the narrator confines himself to recounting his supposedly reluctant assistance of a waiter's family and the newly married governess and artist, the book is amusing and enjoyable, but once the boy David enters the scene, sentimentality runs rampant. Captain W's obsessive love for David has provided much grist for biography's Freudian mills. Later accusations that Barrie was a pedophile are based largely on episodes in *The Little White Bird*. Contemporary readers tended to see a frustrated desire for fatherhood in Captain W's love for David, but later readers were intensely uncomfortable with scenes such as one in which Captain W undresses David for bed.

But also in the course of the novel, Captain W begins to tell David a story about a baby who flies out of his nursery to return to the island of the birds — a baby named Peter Pan. Believing he is still a bird, baby Peter flies back to Kensington Gardens, where he is reviled and rejected by the fairies and the other birds. Dismayed, Peter flies to the bird island to submit his case to old Solomon Caw, who sadly tells him the truth — that he is no longer a bird but a baby. Unfortunately, once he realizes he is not a bird, Peter Pan loses his ability to fly and must remain on the island.

As Captain W continues to develop the story, Peter Pan convinces the birds to make him a nest that he uses as a boat to travel to Kensington Gardens. Here he makes friends with the fairies, plays his pipes for their dances, and as a reward is given the gift of flight to return to his nursery. Once at his own window, Peter is reluctant to give up his fun with the fairies and birds and go back to being an ordinary baby, so he decides to return later, only to find that the window is barred against him, and a new baby has taken his place.

Wendy also makes her first appearance in *The Little White Bird,* in the guise of Maisie, a little girl invented by Captain W, who stays in Kensington Gardens after lockout in order to see the fairies at play. Maisie not only helps a plain little fairy find a noble husband, but she also meets Peter Pan, about whom she already knows a great deal. Despite her temptation to live with Peter on his island, Maisie decides to return to her mother instead.

The Peter Pan chapters of *The Little White Bird* reveal varied sources. There is a touch of Lewis Carroll's nonsensical logic in Peter's adventures, and, like Carroll's Alice, Maisie converses with vain flowers. Desert islands play a part in most of Barrie's works, harking back to his own childhood reading of Defoe, Robert Louis Stevenson, Frederick Marryat, and the penny dreadfuls. Barrie apparently had a fondness for the Cinderella story as well, which underlies his account of the plain fairy Brownie's attending a fairy ball and winning the heart of the Duke of Christmas Daisies. The fantasies of David's nursemaid, Irene, are explicitly linked to Cinderella by Captain W.

The interaction between Peter Pan and Maisie provides the basis for Barrie's play *Peter Pan*. Much of their dialogue would reappear in Act I and Act IV of the play. Other elements of *The Little White Bird* would resurface in the play as well. The little house that the fairies build for Maisie is the forerunner of the house the Lost Boys build for Wendy in Never Land, as well as the direct descendant of the hut in *The Boy Castaways of Black Lake Island*. A prototype of the villainous Captain Hook, Peter Pan's sworn enemy, can be found in the stern schoolmaster Pilkington, to whose school David must go.

Although *The Little White Bird* introduced Peter Pan to the world, the idea of an eternally youthful boy had been in Barrie's mind since his own childhood. In an earlier novel, *Tommy and Grizel* (1900), Barrie had applied this idea to his main character, creating a boy who *could* not grow up.

Barrie continued to ruminate over Peter Pan after the novel was finished and eventually began to write further adventures of the boy who would not grow up, this time in the form of a play. On 1 March 1904 he finished the first draft, which was to be called *Peter Pan*. Barrie combined his childhood reading, his deep love for the Llewelyn Davies family, his ambivalence about domesticity, his desire to create a modern myth of childhood, and his knowledge of stagecraft to create something new and different. Nothing like *Peter Pan* had ever been seen.

Duke of York's Theatre.

ST. MARTIN'S LANE, W.C.

Proprietors ... ... Mr. & Mrs. FRANK WYATT

Sole Lessee and Manager ... ... CHARLES FROHMAN

EVERY AFTERNOON at 2.30, and EVERY EVENING at 8.30,

CHARLES FROHMAN

PRESENTS

PETER PAN

OR

THE BOY WHO WOULDN'T GROW UP.

A Play in Three Acts, by

J. M. BARRIE.

Peter Pan	Miss NINA BOUCICAULT
Mr. Darling	Mr. GERALD du MAURIER
Mrs. Darling	Miss DOROTHEA BAIRD
Wendy Moira Angela Darling	Miss HILDA TREVELYAN
John Napoleon Darling	Master GEORGE HERSEE
Michael Nicholas Darling	Miss WINIFRED GEOGHEGAN
Nana	Mr. ARTHUR LUPINO
Tinker Bell	Miss JANE WREN
Tootles	Miss JOAN BURNETT
Nibs	Miss CHRISTINE SILVER
Slightly	Mr. A. W. BASKCOMB
Curly (Members of Peter's Band)	Miss ALICE DUBARRY
1st Twin	Miss PAULINE CHASE
2nd Twin	Miss PHYLLIS BEADON
Jas. Hook (The Pirate Captain)	Mr. GERALD du MAURIER
Smee	Mr. GEORGE SHELTON
Gentleman Starkey	Mr. SYDNEY HARCOURT
Cookson	Mr. CHARLES TREVOR
Cecco (Pirates)	Mr. FREDERICK ANNERLEY
Mullins	Mr. HUBERT WILLIS
Jukes	Mr. JAMES ENGLISH
Noodler	Mr. JOHN KELT
Great Big Little Panther (Redskins)	Mr. PHILIP DARWIN
Tiger Lily	Miss MIRIAM NESBITT
Liza (Author of the Play)	Miss ELA Q. MAY

Beautiful Mothers, Redskins, Pirates, Crocodile, Eagle, Ostrich, Pack of Wolves, by Misses Mary Mayfren, Victoria Addison, Irene Rooke, Gladys Stewart, Kitty Malone, Marie Park, Elsa Sinclair, Christine Lawrence, Mary Maddison, Gladys Carrington, Laura Barradell, Daisy Murch. Messrs. E. Kirby, S. Spencer, G. Malvern, J. Grahame. Masters S. Grata, A. Ganker, D. Ducrow, C. Lawton, W. Scott, G. Henson, R. Franks, E. Marini, P. Gicardo, A. Biserga.

ACT I.—OUR EARLY DAYS.
Inside the House. (Mr. W. Harford).
ACT II.—THE NEVER, NEVER, NEVER LAND.
Scene 1.—The House we built for Wendy. (Mr. W. Hann).
The Curtain will be lowered for a few moments.
Scene 2.—The Redskins' Camp. (Mr. W. Hann)
Scene 3.—Our Home under the Ground.

ACT III.—WE RETURN TO OUR DISTRACTED MOTHERS.
Scene 1.—The Pirate Ship. (Mr. W. Harford).
Scene 2.—A last glimpse of the Redskins.
Scene 3.—How to know your Mother.
Scene 4.—Outside the House.
Scene 5.—The Tree Tops. (Mr. W. Hann.)

The Play produced under the Direction of Mr. DION BOUCICAULT.

General Manager ... ... (For CHARLES FROHMAN) ... ... W. LESTOCQ

The Esquimaux, Pirates and Indian Costumes designed by Mr. W. NICHOLSON, and executed by Messrs. B. J. SIMMONS, 7, King Street, Covent Garden. Miss Boucicault's Dress designed by Mr. HENRY J. FORD. Miss Baird's Costumes by Madame HAYWARD 64, New Bond St. Miss Trevelyan's Dresses designed and executed by SHEBA, 17, Sloane Street. The Beautiful Mothers' Dresses designed and executed by Madame J. BLANCQUAERT & Co., 38 & 39, South Molton Street. The Dances invented and arranged by Mr. W. WARDE. The Music composed and arranged by Mr. JOHN CROOK. The Flying Machines supplied and worked by Mr. G. KIRBY. Properties supplied by Mr. LOUIS LABHART, 12, Queen's Square, W.C. Stage Mechanist, Mr. H. THOMPSON. Electrician, Mr. C. HAMBLETON. Property Master, Mr. W. BURDICK.

Stage Manager	DUNCAN McRAE	Musical Director ... JOHN CROOK
Business Manager		... JAMES W. MATHEWS

Extract from the Rules made by the Lord Chamberlain

(1.) The name of the actual and responsible Manager of the Theatre must be printed on every play bill. (2.) The Public can leave the Theatre at the end of the performance by all exit and entrance doors, which must open outwards (3.) The fire-proof screen to the proscenium opening will be lowered at least once during every performance to ensure its being in proper working order. (4.) Smoking is not permitted in the Auditorium. (5.) All gangways, passages and staircases must be kept free from chairs or any other obstructions, whether permanent or temporary.

ICES TEA AND COFFEE can be had of the Attendants.

Program for the original production of Barrie's 1904 play

The first producer Barrie approached with the script thought the author had gone mad. Charles Frohman, however, read the manuscript and fell instantly and totally in love with the story — an affection that remained with him all his life. He would, in fact, later claim that he wanted to be remembered as the man who brought *Peter Pan* to the stage. Since Frohman controlled theaters in both New York and London, he decided to produce the play in both cities. He also insisted that in New York his leading American actress, Maude Adams, should play the starring role. Barrie had not intended the lead to be played by a woman, but he could see the advantages in such casting. For one thing, British child-labor laws forbade putting children under fourteen on the stage after nine at night, a situation prohibitive to using a juvenile male lead; also, casting a woman as Peter Pan meant that the other children's roles could be scaled relative to her height rather than to a boy's height.

Peter Pan was to be an extravaganza, requiring elaborate scenery, staging, special effects. No one had ever attempted stage flight before, so Barrie had to hire a professional aerialist to invent a new kind of harness and to give lessons in its use to the actors. As usual, the author himself supervised every part of the production in London. Actors and directors had long considered Barrie the ideal playwright, always present at rehearsals in a helpful rather than an interfering way and always willing to modify the play to make it fit the actors' styles and idiosyncrasies. Even though he had poured heart and soul into *Peter Pan,* Barrie continued his practice of constant rewriting. In fact, he rewrote the play almost yearly. R. D. S. Jack, in *The Road to the Never Land* (1991), has counted more than twenty variants of the script.

The early manuscripts contain scenes later dropped. One lost scene takes place in Kensington Gardens after the children return from Never Land. The scene shows Hook as a schoolmaster surrounded by stock characters from the Italian theater's *commedia dell'arte*. Another lost scene is a Napoleonic tableau after Peter vanquishes Hook. In the early scripts the parts of Mr. Darling and Tiger Lily are much larger, but as the relationship between Peter and Wendy became more important, other roles shrank. Originally the competition among Wendy, Tinker Bell, and Tiger Lily for Peter's affection was more overtly sexual, but Barrie eventually realized that this was inappropriate for a child audience.

The initial audience, however, was not composed of children. The play had been rehearsed in complete secrecy: the actors were never given complete scripts, only the scenes they were to rehearse on a particular day. The London audience, therefore, had no idea what to expect when the curtain went up on opening night, 27 December 1904. Certainly they did not expect to see an Edwardian nursery supervised by a Newfoundland dog. Barrie's plays were known for a humorous realism and sentimentality, but such out-and-out fantasy had never been attached to his name. However, adults in the audience were enchanted by the lagoon, the pirates, the Indians, and the magic of flight, and they clapped enthusiastically when Peter Pan told them that their belief in fairies was the only thing that could save Tinker Bell's life. This appeal to the audience was another bit of risky business. Breaking the invisible fourth wall between the actors and the audience was an innovation in contemporary theatrical practice. At the last minute Barrie had panicked, fearing that nobody would clap, so he had primed the orchestra to drop their instruments and clap if the audience did not.

When *Peter Pan* opened in New York the following year, American audiences were equally charmed by the adventures of Wendy, John, and Michael Darling in Never Land. Maude Adams was such a huge success as the American Peter that she continued playing the part in various productions for two decades. Only a few phrases were changed for the American version, as when an exultant Peter compared himself to American heroes like Abraham Lincoln and George Washington.

In gratitude to his friend and producer Frohman, Barrie wrote an epilogue to the play titled "When Wendy Grew Up: An Afterthought," which was performed only once. Frohman had missed the London opening of *Peter Pan*. When Barrie learned that Frohman would be present for the last night of the 1907–1908 London season, he planned a surprise conclusion. Frohman had always wanted to know what happened when Wendy grew up, so Barrie decided to show him. The audience on 22 February 1908 was as surprised as Frohman when the curtain rose on the supposed final treetop tableau to reveal instead the Darling nursery. In this final scene a grown-up Wendy relates the well-worn story of Peter Pan to her daughter Jane, who already knows it by heart. When Peter appears to carry Wendy off for the annual spring cleaning, he is unaware that years have gone by and that Wendy has grown up. However, she convinces him to take Jane in her stead and consoles herself with the hope that someday Jane also will have a daughter who can take her place. This epilogue would later form the conclusion to Barrie's novel *Peter and Wendy* (1911), but it was never again used in the play.

Both the British and the American productions were huge financial successes. *Peter Pan* became a staple of the Christmas season in the theater world. The author, however, did not grow rich from his best-known play. Barrie gave all the royalties from the work – both the play and the later novel – to the Great Ormond Street Hospital for Sick Children in London. When the copyright expired in 1987, Parliament passed a special act to extend the royalties in perpetuity – an act in keeping with the author's own philanthropy.

Much of the action and dialogue of *Peter Pan* reflects Barrie's continuing friendship with the Llewelyn Davies family. By 1904 there were five boys – George, Jack, Peter, Michael, and Nicholas – and all had contributed inadvertently to the ideas and dialogue in the play. Their names were assigned to characters, their adventures at Black Lake Cottage were transformed into Peter Pan's adventures, and their occasional artless comments were repeated in the dialogue.

The two main characters in the play are Peter and Wendy. If Barrie had a real-life model for Wendy, no one has identified her. Barrie had always enjoyed the companionship of boys over that of girls, so he had more original boy material to draw from in his writing. Some biographers have speculated that Wendy is an idealized portrait of the young Margaret. Peter Pan may have been an amalgamation of the Llewelyn Davies boys as Barrie claimed, but he is also an aspect of his creator. When Peter looks in through the nursery window in the last scene of the play, he is the eternal outsider forever banned from hearth and home. Barrie too was an outsider, observing life from a distance. Not only was he barred from the nursery because of his childless state, but he also remained an interloper in London society – a strange little Scotsman too wealthy to be ignored but not "one of us."

Put his strange case before old Solomon Caw.

Peter Pan is the fairies' orchestra.

Two of Arthur Rackham's illustrations for Peter Pan in Kensington Gardens *(1906), Barrie's first novel-length treatment of the character*

Barrie was well aware of his outsider status; in fact, he was one of the most psychologically self-aware authors of his day. He consciously used his self-knowledge and his interest in psychology and mythology to enhance *Peter Pan*. He chose the name Pan for its connotations in Greek myth; Peter even plays the pipes like the half-human, half-goat Greek god who serves as his namesake. Barrie augments Peter's godlike status with occasional hints that Never Land exists only by Peter's whim and that all the adventures there are directed by his controlling imagination. The murky relationship between Peter and Captain Hook is full of suggestive possibilities. After Peter vanquishes Hook, the stage directions playfully indicate a dire connection: "The curtain rises to show Peter a very Napoleon on his ship. It must not rise again lest we see him on the poop in Hook's hat and cigars, and with a small iron claw." Beginning in the very first production of the play, a single actor portrayed both Mr. Darling and Captain Hook, adding another suggestive link. Because

Mrs. Darling is clearly a portrait of Sylvia Llewelyn Davies, critics often assume that Mr. Darling is based on Arthur. If so, it is not a flattering likeness of the man who possessed what Barrie longed to have. In any case, adult males come off badly in *Peter Pan*; they are childish, vain, swaggering, vindictive figures who nevertheless maintain a veneer of being true English gentlemen. Even Hook, the reader is told, is "not wholly evil: he has a Thesaurus in his cabin."

One important influence on *Peter Pan* that seldom receives mention is the traditional British Christmas pantomime, which by Barrie's day had become vulgarized performances of well-known stories. *Peter Pan* is, in effect, a high-class pantomime. Like the traditional pantomime, Barrie's play was designed to be a Christmas extravaganza for the entertainment of a youthful audience. Pantomime also typically involved much cross-dressing, with male actors taking female parts and the role of the principal boy being undertaken by a female. Actors costumed as animals were another feature of pantomime, so the sight of a Newfoundland dog cavorting on stage would not have been too surprising to the first audiences of Barrie's play. Peter's appeal to the audience to save Tinker Bell, while an innovation in terms of the legitimate stage of the time, reflects the pantomime tradition of audience interaction with the events and actors on stage. Finally, a pantomime ended with a harlequinade featuring familiar characters from Italian theater; one of the scenes dropped from *Peter Pan* was a harlequinade set in Kensington Gardens.

Barrie also drew heavily from his childhood reading. He attributed the fairy-tale elements of the play to the stories of Hans Christian Andersen. Peter Pan's island was a direct descendant of Robinson Crusoe's island by way of Ballantyne's *The Coral Island*. The Lost Boys' underground treehouse came from Johann David Wyss's *Swiss Family Robinson* (1814). The Indians were borrowed from James Fenimore Cooper's *Leather-Stocking Tales* (1823–1841). Barrie's greatest literary debt, however, was to Stevenson, with whom he corresponded until Stevenson's death in 1894. Giving directions to his home in the South Seas, Stevenson had written to Barrie, "You take the boat to San Francisco, and then my place is second to the left." This whimsy inspired the well-known directions to Never Land: "Second to the right and then straight on till morning." Captain Hook was inspired by the villainous Long John Silver in Stevenson's *Treasure Island* (1883). In the stage directions of the printed play, Barrie mentions that Peter Pan "slew Barbicue," a reference to Long John Silver's nickname (spelled "Barbeque" in *Treasure Island*). Interestingly, Stevenson had modeled Silver on his friend W. E. Henley, who had subsequently been befriended by Barrie. Henley's young daughter Margaret's lisping pronunciation of "my Friendy," her pet name for Barrie, provided the name Wendy, which soon became a popular name for little girls. In a later production of *Peter Pan* Barrie paid tribute to many of these writers by lowering a curtain designed as a sampler embroidered with his thanks to Stevenson, Andersen, Carroll, and Charles Lamb.

In 1906 Arthur Llewelyn Davies fell ill, and Barrie dropped all his other responsibilities in order to attend the sick man. During Llewelyn Davies's final illness, Barrie remained at his bedside, talking to him quietly and taking care of his physical needs. Llewelyn Davies died on 19 April 1907, and Barrie became the financial support of the widowed Sylvia. There is no record of what Barrie's wife thought of her husband's close relationship to Sylvia and the boys, but Mary usually accompanied them on trips and vacations. However, the Barries were clearly drifting apart. Mary began to spend time alone at Black Lake Cottage instead of accompanying her husband to dress rehearsals.

In the same year that Arthur fell ill, Peter Pan appeared in novel form. *Peter Pan in Kensington Gardens* (1906) was nothing more than the Peter Pan chapters of *The Little White Bird* reissued as a children's book – just in time for Christmas. The lavish illustrations by Arthur Rackham were a major selling point and received more comment from reviewers than did the text. Rackham was a well-established illustrator whose name alone could sell a book, and the play *Peter Pan* was at the height of its success. In fact, other writers were capitalizing on the popularity of Barrie's play by publishing books with titles like *The Peter Pan Keepsake, The Peter Pan Alphabet,* and *The Peter Pan Picture Book,* prompting Barrie to enter the market with his own title.

Barrie's personal life took the public stage in 1909 when he and Mary divorced after fifteen years of marriage. Mary had turned to the charms of a younger man named Gilbert Cannan – a friend and fellow writer of Barrie's. The divorce was public and unpleasant, and Barrie suffered acutely. Although he found it easy to present emotions on the stage, in his personal life he was extremely reticent. Several of his friends, knowing how painful the divorce and attendant publicity would be to Barrie, wrote to newspaper editors asking them not to cover the story – as a favor to one who was once himself a journalist. Only three papers ignored these pleas.

Not long after his divorce, Barrie suffered another blow: in August 1910 Sylvia Llewelyn Davies died after a lingering illness. In the midst of his grief Barrie discovered that he had become guardian to the five boys he adored. Several of the boys were teenagers by this time, but Barrie undertook to raise the two youngest with the help of their nurse, Mary Hodgson, who had never approved of his influence on the boys. He remained in the apartment he had rented since his divorce, while the boys lived with Mary Hodgson in the nearby Llewelyn Davies home.

The novelized version of *Peter Pan* was published the following year. *Peter and Wendy* follows the basic plot of the play but develops the characters more fully. Although the actions and dialogue remain similar, Barrie uses the narrative framework to explain personalities and motives. For example, Mr. Darling is a more sympathetic figure in the book than in the play. If his character was indeed based on Arthur Llewelyn Davies, this softening of

George Darling is no doubt in honor of the dead man. Likewise, Mrs. Darling is described in loving detail at the beginning of the book – a clear portrait of Sylvia – although by the last chapter she is "dead and forgotten." This is a rather abrupt conclusion to her life, but the pain of Sylvia's death was too recent to bear elaboration. The narrator remarks about Mrs. Darling, "Some like Peter best and some like Wendy best, but I like her best."

Peter Pan's character is presented in a more critical light in the book. Barrie elaborates on Peter's almost nonexistent memory, his vanity, his selfishness, and his heartlessness. While flying to Never Land, the Darling children are completely dependent on Peter, but he is a wayward guide, often abandoning them or nearly letting them fall to their deaths. When he leaves the children, even for short periods of time, he forgets who they are. Peter lives completely in the present moment, with no thought of yesterday or tomorrow. At the end of the book he tries to trick Wendy and her brothers into believing their mother has barred the window against them. This scene is in the play as well, but there it is limited to one paragraph of dialogue, whereas the novel expands it to several pages. In the book the connection between Peter and Hook is also made more explicit: after he conquers the pirates, Peter orders Wendy to alter one of Hook's suits to fit him.

Barrie's fond relationship with the fourth of the Llewelyn Davies boys, Michael, permeates *Peter and Wendy*. Some of the real Michael's characteristics are given to young Michael Darling in the book, but the most important addition is to Peter Pan, who has dreams "more painful than the dreams of other boys. For hours he could not be separated from these dreams, though he wailed piteously in them. They had to do, I think, with the riddle of his existence." These nightmares actually belonged to Michael Llewelyn Davies, who suffered acutely because of them; Barrie uses them in *Peter and Wendy* to add a human component to Peter's supernatural character. It is no coincidence that Peter suffers one of his bad dreams the night after he vanquishes Hook.

Peter and Wendy also elaborates on the theme of belonging. Although the Darling children can belong to Never Land because it exists in their imaginations and dreams, Peter can never belong to the real world of home, family, and school. Like his creator, he must always view domesticity from the outside, "looking through the window at the one joy from which he must be forever barred." Barrie draws his readers into a similar position as outside observers by inviting them to look in on Mrs. Dar-

"TO DIE WILL BE AN AWFULLY BIG ADVENTURE?"

F. D. Bedford's interpretation of Peter Pan for Peter *and* Wendy
(1911), Barrie's novelized version of the play

ling as she mourns for her lost children. Addressing his readers, he writes, "That is all we are, lookers-on. Nobody really wants us. So let us watch and say jaggy things, in the hope that some of them will hurt." The narrator soon begins to feel sorry for Mrs. Darling and changes his mind about making hurtful comments, but he and his readers remain mere observers to the action in the story. By his use of first- and second-person pronouns throughout the novel, the author ensures that his readers will keep him company outside the window, never fully becoming participants in the children's adventures. Whenever the action reaches a high pitch and threatens to draw the reader in, Barrie throws in an *I* or *you* to remind the reader that this is only a story – a story that Barrie controls. In effect, *Peter and Wendy* glorifies the power of imagination while at the same time limiting the reader's imaginative interaction with the story.

The last chapter of *Peter and Wendy* is based on the special epilogue Barrie had written for Frohman. Once again, Peter accepts Wendy's daughter

J. M. Barrie in his later years

many modern readers are unaware that the story originated as a drama.

Of course, Barrie could not have known that he was giving birth to a literary legend when he wrote *Peter and Wendy*. He was primarily cashing in on a financial success that would benefit the sick children at Great Ormond Street Hospital, and the Peter Pan Bequest may have been the most generous gift any hospital ever received. Barrie's British and American publishers referred to this legacy on the copyright page of every edition they published, and the editions seemed to tumble off the presses at an amazing rate.

Barrie continued to write plays that brought him further social and financial success and enabled him to indulge his boys as well as his philanthropic interests. He was also able to indulge such whims as erecting a statue of Peter Pan in Kensington Gardens, the site of Peter's literary birth. Peter's association with the park had brought it such fame that Barrie had been given an official key to its gates. In 1909 Barrie had hired sculptor George Frampton to create the statue, and it was placed in the gardens secretly on the night of 30 April 1912 so that it would seem to have appeared by magic. Not everyone was pleased by this sleight of hand. Some members of the public were upset that a private individual could do such a thing without consulting other people's wishes. Barrie, in turn, was dissatisfied with the statue because he felt it did not display the playful devilry he envisioned in Peter Pan – the spirit of Boyhood.

The next year was an eventful year for Barrie. Although he had refused a knighthood several years earlier, he now accepted a baronetcy and thus became Sir James Barrie, Bart. Also in 1913 news reached England that the renowned explorer Capt. Robert Falcon Scott had perished in Antarctica. Scott was a friend of Barrie's; in fact, Barrie was godfather to Scott's son Peter, born in 1909. Before he died, Scott had written several letters on notebook paper, which were found in his tent with his body. One of these letters was addressed to Barrie, asking him to take care of Scott's widow and son. Barrie was so proud of this scribbled letter that he carried it around with him for the rest of his life. Kathleen Scott, the widow, perceived that she and her son could easily be overwhelmed by Barrie's conception of "taking care" of them. Being a canny woman, she wisely refused to become a complete dependent, yet she managed to retain Barrie's friendship and counsel. Because of Kathleen's careful handling of her affairs, Peter Scott remained close to his godfather without ever becoming one of "Barrie's boys."

Jane as a substitute and claims her for one week every year – except when he forgets to come. When Jane grows up, her daughter Margaret takes her place, and the cycle is set to continue indefinitely.

Peter and Wendy is in many ways a book for adults. Despite Barrie's obvious intention to address young readers on their own level, he never manages to drop his cloak of adulthood. The authorial tone is often arch, whimsical, cynical, sentimental, or patronizing. Only when he allows himself to get caught up in an adventure and tell the story directly does Barrie seem to overcome his adult perspective. *Peter and Wendy* was Barrie's first and only attempt at writing a novel expressly for children, so it is not surprising that he occasionally faltered. What is surprising is that one so untried at children's fiction should have created a children's classic. *Peter and Wendy* received positive reviews both in Britain and in America and became widely popular. In fact, the book, which eventually usurped the play's title, became so well known that

Sir George Frampton's statue of Peter Pan, secretly placed in Kensington Gardens on 30 April 1912 so that it would seem to have appeared there by magic. Barrie complained that the work "doesn't show the devil in Peter."

Between the opening night of *Peter Pan* and the end of 1913, thirteen original plays by Barrie were produced on the London stage. Most of them also graced the New York stage. This prolific output kept Barrie busy, especially since he involved himself so closely with each production and continually rewrote the plays. *Peter Pan* had become a yearly Christmas treat, and he had to oversee each new production. Writing novels had once been his goal, but he no longer had time. *Peter and Wendy* was the last full-length novel he ever wrote; his only other piece of fiction was the novelette *Farewell, Miss Julie Logan* (1932), a ghost story.

On 4 August 1914 Britain declared war on Germany. Barrie was too old to fight, but George, Jack, and Peter Llewelyn Davies were young men now. Jack was already in naval service when the war broke out; George and Peter immediately sought commissions in the army. Barrie undertook a private mission to the United States to stir up support, but British officials in America persuaded him that any such attempt would offend American neutrality. To salvage the trip, Barrie gave several interviews and even wrote a fake one himself, in which he cleverly managed to insert his views on the war without directly disobeying his government's request to maintain strict neutrality.

When he returned to London, Barrie looked for ways to assist the war effort. At the request of the government he wrote a short propaganda play, *Der Tag; or, The Tragic Man* (1914) – an unusually humorless work for Barrie. Lord Lucas, a friend of Barrie's, had turned his family home into a hospital, and Barrie's financial assistance helped keep the hospital operating throughout World War I. Barrie also founded a hospital in France for displaced children which was run by his friend Elizabeth Lucas. Barrie bore the full financial burden of maintaining the institution, which was forced to close after several years because Lucas fell ill.

The war had a great impact on Barrie's life. Some of his friends were killed, including Frohman, who was on board the *Lusitania* when it was torpedoed and sunk. His last words were reputedly a paraphrase of Peter Pan's line, "To die will be an awfully big adventure." But worse was to come. On 15 March 1915 George Llewelyn Davies was shot in the head and died instantly. Barrie was devastated. George had always been special to him – the original of Peter Pan, as Barrie had told several interviewers. Barrie never fully recovered from the loss.

When the war ended in 1918 Barrie set about picking up the pieces of his life. Ever since George's death Barrie had been writing about ghosts. In *A Well-Remembered Voice* (1918), a young man killed in the war returns to visit his father. Based on Barrie's relationship with George, the play painfully recounts the father's and son's inability to express their affection for each other. In a 1920 play, *Mary Rose,* a young mother who had vanished years before returns to look for the son she left behind but does not recognize him as a grown man.

Another tragedy struck on 19 May 1921: Michael Llewelyn Davies and a fellow Oxford student drowned in the river Thames. The inquest ruled it a case of accidental death, but friends suspected it may have been a suicide pact. Michael had always been sensitive and prone to deep depressions; he had a morbid fear of water and could barely swim a stroke. In deference to Barrie the suspicion of suicide was kept quiet. Michael's death was another blow from which Barrie never recovered.

Barrie wrote few plays after Michael's death. Instead, he turned to other outlets, developing his speaking skills and giving entertaining autobiographical lectures. In the summers he rented Lady Cynthia Asquith's family home and held large house parties, surrounding himself with friends and relatives. When Barrie died on 19 June 1937, Peter and Nicholas Llewelyn Davies and Lady Cynthia Asquith, his secretary, were at his bedside.

After Barrie's death, his literary reputation, which had begun to decline after World War I, continued its downward slide. Psychoanalysis was becoming popular, and Barrie became an easy target for the new Freudian critics. Just as Rudyard Kipling was attacked for his imperial politics, Barrie was condemned for psychological crimes he would not have recognized. He was accused of being impotent, of having a mother fixation, and of being a pedophile. Except for *The Admirable Crichton* and *Peter Pan,* his works fell out of favor, and eventually he was perceived as "merely" a children's writer, undeserving of serious critical attention.

More recently, however, a few critics have taken a fresh look at Barrie's works. In 1987 Barrie was included in a series of monographs about Scottish authors published by the Scottish Academic Press. In *The Road to the Never Land* Jack responds persuasively to earlier negative criticism and concludes that Barrie is the most important playwright to come out of Scotland and that he deserves a place in his national literature.

With children's literature no longer being looked at as an unfortunate stepchild in literary studies, and psychoanalytic approaches to criticism having given way to new theories, other scholars are joining the efforts to reinstate Barrie as an important literary figure. In the introduction to his 1989 Barrie bibliography, Carl Markgraf stresses this positive criticism. Even Jacqueline Rose's highly critical *The Case of Peter Pan; or, The Impossibility of Children's Fiction* (1993) uses *Peter Pan* as the exemplar for all children's literature, thus giving Barrie an elevated status.

Whatever the critics may think of Barrie, his most successful creation has enjoyed enormous and lasting popular success. The play *Peter Pan* has become a staple of the Christmas season on the London stage. Several television productions have been made, including a well-known musical version starring Mary Martin, which first aired in 1955, and a 1976 production featuring Mia Farrow as Peter. In 1991 an all-woman troupe in London produced a lesbian version of *Peter Pan* for the Christmas season. The novelized version of *Peter Pan* has also retained its popularity. Since 1911, when it first appeared, the book has never been out of print. Disney Studios released an animated motion picture version of Barrie's story in 1952, which is considered by many to be a classic in its own right, and more recently, director Steven Spielberg released *Hook* (1992), in which an adult Peter Pan has to reclaim his forgotten heritage in order to rescue his own children from the clutches of Captain Hook. The character Peter Pan has long since attained legendary status as a cultural icon, with his name gracing a long list of products – from the Peter Pan collar to Peter Pan peanut butter. Dan Kiley's *Peter Pan Syndrome: Men Who Have Never Grown Up* (1983) goes so far as to formulate a psychological disorder in adult males by employing Barrie's character as the defining archetype.

Although Parliament extended the royalty rights for Great Ormond Street Hospital, the copyright on the work has expired, and other writers and producers will doubtless reexamine the tale of the Boy Who Would Not Grow Up and tell it anew for a modern audience. Barrie's creation has become a modern myth, which is the immortality Barrie hoped for.

Letters:

Letters of J. M. Barrie, edited by Viola Meynell (London: Davies, 1947).

Bibliographies:

Herbert Garland, *A Bibliography of the Writings of Sir James Matthew Barrie* (London: Bookman's Journal, 1928);

Bradley Dwayne Cutler, *Sir James M. Barrie: A Bibliography, with Full Collations of the American Unauthorized Editions* (New York: Greenberg, 1931);

Carl Markgraf, *J. M. Barrie: An Annotated Secondary Bibliography* (Greensboro, N.C.: ELT Press, 1989).

Biographies:

F. J. Harvey Darton, *J. M. Barrie* (London: Nisbet, 1929);

John Alexander Hammerton, *Barrie: The Story of a Genius* (New York: Dodd, Mead, 1929);

William Aubrey Darlington, *J. M. Barrie* (London: Blackie & Son, 1938);

Denis Mackail, *The Story of J. M. B.: A Biography* (London: Davies, 1941);

Lady Cynthia Asquith, *Portrait of Barrie* (London: Estate of James Barrie, 1954);

Janet Dunbar, *J. M. Barrie: The Man Behind the Image* (Boston: Houghton Mifflin, 1970);

Allen Wright, *J. M. Barrie: Glamour of Twilight* (Edinburgh: Ramsay Head Press, 1976).

References:

Lady Cynthia Asquith, *Diaries 1915–1918,* edited by Edith M. Horsley (New York: Knopf, 1969);

Andrew Birkin, *J. M. Barrie and the Lost Boys: the Love Story That Gave Birth to Peter Pan* (New York: Potter, 1979);

Roger Lancelyn Green, *Fifty Years of Peter Pan* (London: Davies, 1954);

R. D. S. Jack, *The Road to the Never Land: A Reassessment of J. M. Barrie's Dramatic Art* (Aberdeen: Aberdeen University Press, 1991);

Leonee Ormond, *J. M. Barrie* (Edinburgh: Scottish Academic Press, 1987);

Jacqueline Rose, *The Case of Peter Pan; or, The Impossibility of Children's Fiction,* revised edition (Philadelphia: University of Pennsylvania Press, 1993);

James Alexander Roy, *James Matthew Barrie: An Appreciation* (New York: Scribners, 1938);

Henry Mackinnon Walbrook, *J. M. Barrie and the Theatre* (London: F. V. White, 1922).

Papers:

The original manuscript of *Peter Pan* is in the Lilly Library of Indiana University. The largest collection of J. M. Barrie's letters, manuscripts, notebooks, and photographs is in the Beinecke Library at Yale University. Other materials are held by the Berg Collection at the New York Public Library and by the Scottish National Trust.

Hilaire Belloc

(27 July 1870 – 16 July 1953)

Gwyneth Evans
Malaspina College, British Columbia

See also the Belloc entries in *DLB 19: British Poets, 1880–1914* and *DLB 100: Modern British Essayists, Second Series.*

SELECTED BOOKS: *Verses and Sonnets* (London: Ward & Downey, 1896);

The Bad Child's Book of Beasts (Oxford: Alden / London: Simpkin, Marshall, Hamilton, Kent, 1896; New York: Dutton, 1896);

More Beasts (For Worse Children) (London & New York: Arnold, 1897; New York: Knopf, 1922);

The Modern Traveller (London: Arnold, 1898; New York: Knopf, 1923);

The Path to Rome (London: Allen, 1902; New York: Longmans, Green, 1902);

Cautionary Tales for Children, Designed for the Admonition of Children between the Ages of Eight and Fourteen Years (London: Nash, 1908; New York: Knopf, 1922);

Verses (London: Duckworth, 1910; New York: Gomme, 1916);

More Peers: Verses (London: Swift, 1911; New York: Knopf, 1914);

The Four Men: A Farrago (London & New York: Nelson, 1912; Indianapolis: Bobbs-Merrill, 1912);

The Servile State (London & Edinburgh: Foulis, 1912; Boston: Phillips, 1913);

Sonnets and Verse (London: Duckworth, 1923; New York: McBride, 1924; enlarged edition, London: Duckworth, 1938; New York: Sheed & Ward, 1939; enlarged again, London: Duckworth, 1954);

Economics for Helen (London: Arrowsmith, 1924; New York & London: Putnam, 1924); republished as *Economics for Young People: An Explanation of Capital, Labour, Wealth, Money, Production, Exchange, and Business, Domestic and International* (New York & London: Putnam, 1925);

The Cruise of the "Nona" (London: Constable, 1925; Boston & New York: Houghton Mifflin, 1925);

Hilaire Belloc in 1910 (photograph by Ian Hamilton)

New Cautionary Tales: Verses (London: Duckworth, 1930; New York: Harper, 1931);

Ladies and Gentlemen, for Adults Only and Mature at That (London: Duckworth, 1932);

Cautionary Verses: The Collected Humorous Poems (London: Duckworth, 1939); republished as *Hilaire Belloc's Cautionary Verses: Illustrated Album Edition with the Original Pictures* (New York: Knopf, 1941);

Collected Verses (Harmondsworth, U.K.: Penguin, 1958);

Complete Verse (London: Duckworth, 1970).

Hilaire Belloc was born in the middle of a thunderstorm, and it is hard for anyone writing about him now to resist observing how apt was this scene, since thunderclouds of controversy, often of his own seeking, seemed to surround him for much of his life. An impassioned controversialist and a brilliant talker, Belloc enjoyed espousing unpopular opinions and telling the British public, especially the intellectuals, about the folly and ignorance of their cherished views. However erratic his own views were – and some of them were very erratic indeed – Belloc delivered them, in person or in print, with such eloquence and fluent wit that people were usually eager to hear him out. Belloc's characteristic wit, while still recognizable in some of his polemical and descriptive prose, has survived for our time nowhere so well as in his light verse for children. *The Bad Child's Book of Beasts* (1896) and *Cautionary Tales for Children, Designed for the Admonition of Children between the Ages of Eight and Fourteen Years* (1908), along with their sequels, are masterpieces of nonsense and continue to delight children in contemporary illustrated editions.

Most of Belloc's children's verse belongs to the early part of his long career, a period marked by severe disappointments, success, and many conflicting impulses. Although he wrote more than 150 books in English and made his home in England, Belloc was born in France to a French father and British mother and was always very conscious of his paternal heritage. In addition, Belloc was raised as a Roman Catholic and remained a vigorous defender of that faith in Protestant Britain. These fundamental elements of his identity served to set Belloc apart from the mainstream of English public life, even while he participated in it most fully. The sense of ironic distance from the voice and attitudes of the Establishment, represented by the adult authority figures of his children's verse, is the key to the appreciation of that verse. Belloc implicitly sides with the child reader against the pompous, didactic person in charge, revealing the absurdity of that person's values and attitudes. This is not to say that Belloc was at heart a rebel or believed in challenging all forms of authority – in fact, he would advocate an ideal of squirearchical rule in Britain and praise the Fascist dictator of Italy, Benito Mussolini. But Belloc consciously and enthusiastically took the role of the outsider possessed of a wider knowledge and superior culture than those around him, a position from which he could join in but never be wholly part of English life.

Joseph Hilaire Pierre René Belloc was born on 27 July 1870 to Louis Belloc, a lawyer, and Bessie Parkes Belloc, a writer. His birthplace was near Paris in the village of La Celle–Saint-Cloud, in a chalet adjoining the home of his grandmother, Louise Swanton Belloc, who maintained the large house after the death in 1865 of her husband, also named Hilaire. Both of Belloc's paternal grandparents were accomplished figures in the arts: Louise had published a life of George Gordon, Lord Byron to which Stendhal contributed the preface, several children's books, and French translations of both novels and poetry, while the elder Hilaire had been a painter. Louis Belloc died when his son was barely two, leaving his wife in a state of shock and desolation from which she never entirely recovered.

Originally from England, Bessie Belloc had participated actively in the movement for woman suffrage and was a friend of George Eliot, Elizabeth Barrett Browning, and Elizabeth Gaskell, and she knew both William Makepeace Thackeray and Anthony Trollope well. On a holiday visit to France Bessie had met Louis Belloc, and they were married in London on 19 September 1867. Even after Louis's death, Bessie remained very attached to his mother, Louise, and young Hilaire might have grown up in France had it not been for the outbreak of the Franco-Prussian War two days after his birth. Within a month the family fled to England. During the siege of Paris and its aftermath, the Belloc home was occupied by German troops who vandalized the furniture and family pictures, cut down the chestnut grove, and left Belloc with a lifelong distaste for "the Prussian," which corresponded to his enthusiasm for the Latin cultures. It also perhaps encouraged his tendency toward racial hostilities and overgeneralizations.

Bessie returned to England with Hilaire and his older sister, Marie, and they lived comfortably in London on a legacy which had been left to Bessie. In 1877, however, she lost a huge sum of money in misguided stock speculation, and the family moved to Sussex. Belloc came to feel a passionate affinity for the Downs of southern England. He would spend the last five decades of his life in his rambling Sussex farm, King's Land, and the area is the subject of some of his best work.

Summers spent in La Celle–Saint-Cloud maintained Belloc's fluency in French, as well as his connection with French Catholicism. His education in England was entrusted to the Oratory School at Edgbaston, Warwickshire, presided over at a distance by the greatest of the Victorian converts, John Henry Cardinal Newman. Although he was at first dismayed by the bullying and bad food to which he was subjected at the school, Belloc received an excellent grounding there in the Greek and Latin classics, which nourished his own ear for sound and

Belloc at the Oratory School in the 1880s

meter. His academic achievement at Edgbaston was considered to be merely adequate. Among his favorite books as a schoolboy were adaptations of myth such as Sir George Webbe Dasent's *Popular Tales from the Norse* (1859) and Alfred John Church's *Stories from Homer* (1876) as well as contemporary novels of adventure and humor such as *Masterman Ready* and Mark Twain's *The Adventures of Tom Sawyer* (1876) and *The Adventures of Huckleberry Finn* (1884).

Belloc left the Oratory School in 1887 and decided to garner a larger experience of life than that afforded by the English academic world, of which he was always both jealous and suspicious. He began, and soon abruptly ended, careers in the French navy, as a land agent on the duke of Norfolk's estate, and as an architectural draftsman. The five unsettled years after he left school provided him with experience from which he drew, as much as from his more academic learning, for his writing throughout his life. During these years Belloc also cultivated the acquaintance of Cardinal Manning, another English convert to Catholicism, but of a far more militant stamp than the reserved and saintly Newman. Manning's polemical stance and vision of

a Catholic society were a great influence on the tone of Belloc's writing and the social and religious ideals behind much of his work.

Another important influence at about this time was his meeting in the summer of 1890 with an Irish-American girl, Elodie Hogan, who was visiting his mother. Intelligent but not intellectual, Elodie was attractive and a devout Roman Catholic. Although Belloc had now become interested in journalism – a more likely career for him than his previous ventures – and had founded with a friend the *Paternoster Review,* Belloc was not in a position to marry, and the twenty-two-year-old Elodie reluctantly returned to California. When Belloc appeared there some months later, having worked and gambled his way across the United States, Elodie's mother did not share her daughter's delight and awareness of his genius, and resolutely opposed their desire to marry.

Belloc, with his usual energy for changes of direction joined on 9 November 1891 the French army, in the Eighth Regiment of Artillery at Toul. The year spent in military exercises intensified what was already a fascination with military history, the subject of many of his books, and his abiding love for France. It may also have intensified less appealing attitudes. In his 1984 biography of Belloc, A. N. Wilson partially attributes the flavor of anti-Semitism which sours so much of Belloc's work to his time in the French army, where he developed many of the unpalatable attitudes that kept many of his contemporaries from taking his views seriously. Racism mars his children's writing only slightly but is evident in the illustrated verse of *The Modern Traveller* (1898) and *More Peers* (1911).

In 1892 Belloc was accepted as a student at Balliol College, Oxford, then under the mastership of the brilliant and eccentric Benjamin Jowett, who perhaps sensed the equally though differently brilliant gifts of this loud-voiced and opinionated twenty-two-year-old, who wore a dark cloak and soft hat, pronounced the letter *r* in the French way, and wrote an impressive entrance essay on poetry. Belloc chose to study history and very soon made a name for himself not only as a clever student but also as a great talker, bon vivant, and a debater of such eloquence that he became president of the Oxford Union. Belloc deeply enjoyed the stimulating intellectual male companionship of Oxford, in the prodigious walking trips and late-night drinking bouts, as well as in lectures.

Despite his impressive academic work, upon graduation Belloc was not awarded the fellowship he had expected, which would have enabled him to stay on at Oxford. What he saw as his rejection by the university rankled him all his life and fueled later vituperative verse on the academic world. His personal life, however, became stabilized by his marriage to Elodie in California on 16 June 1896. That same year he published his first collection of poetry, *Verses and Sonnets,* and also another little volume of verse which seemed ephemeral but was to prove the most durable of all his works: *The Bad Child's Book of Beasts.*

While recovering from his initial failure to win a fellowship, Belloc had traveled to Scandinavia with an aristocratic fellow student, Lord Basil Blackwood, who shared Belloc's wry sense of humor and delight in absurdity and who had a gift for comical drawing. Belloc provided amusement on the trip by making nonsense verses about animals, for which Blackwood provided humorous illustrations. The verses proved so appealing and memorable, and the drawings so perfectly apt, that when they were published as *The Bad Child's Book of Beasts,* with Blackwood signing himself as "B.T.B.," the first printing sold out in four days, and the book has been in print almost ever since. One of the charms of Belloc's verse is its air of spontaneity, with such rhymes as "platinum / flatten 'em," anticipating the work of Ogden Nash. Blackwood's pictures, too, have the air of inspired doodles. The casual and improvisational tone of the book serves to mask somewhat its polished craftsmanship and to establish a rapport with its reader, who feels invited to share in the jokes of a friendly though sardonic adult about the strangeness of the world and the folly of human behavior in it.

The beasts of this first book are mostly exotic; poet and illustrator play with the contrast of the remote and the familiar, as when the reader is exhorted to: "tell your papa where the Yak can be got, / And if he is awfully rich / He will buy you the creature." The picture interpolated between the first and second line shows parent and child at a department-store counter, with the Yak standing among assorted hats, bottles, and ads for ready-to-wear coats. In another picture the Yak is holding balls of knitting wool in the points of its enormous horns, while the text states, "It will carry and fetch, you can ride on its back, / Or lead it about with a string." In another verse a hunched man and a pleased polar bear are sitting companionably together on an ice floe, while the man notes that the bear "is unaware of cold that cuts me through: / For why? He has a coat of hair. / I wish I had one too!" The reader is cautioned not to play with the Lion,

Belloc and Basil Blackwood at Oxford. As "B.T.B.," Blackwood illustrated four of Belloc's children's books.

but the Tiger, like the Yak, is recommended as a nursery pet.

Blackwood's drawings for "The Tiger" make clear what is merely implied in the verse: the Tiger as a "pretty playfellow for any little child" is proposed to "mothers of large families (who claim to common sense)" because it will "well repay the trouble and expense" by, as the illustration shows, eating their surplus offspring. Jokes about eating and being eaten are common enough in children's literature, and usually enjoyed by children so long as they are convinced that a joke is intended. Literal-minded adults, however, may find much of Belloc's humor quite black and occasionally even offensive.

The title and introduction of this first book set the tone: the "badness" of children is tongue-in-cheek and represented with implicit sympathy as a natural rebellion against the adults who would make them "unnaturally good," while the "beasts" are not realistically presented animals but emblems in the tradition of the medieval bestiaries, which depict assorted real and legendary creatures in terms of their supposed moral qualities and significance. Blackwood's vignettes on the page facing the introduction show Man, in cravat and miniscule top hat, as one of the peculiar beasts to be considered. Both text and pictures point out the likeness between "The Big Baboon" and "Mr. So-and-so" when they are similarly clothed, and the relationship of man and ape is again sardonically noted in "The Marmozet." Scholars are pointedly mocked in the pseudopedantry of "The Whale" recommended to "every boy in Oxford town / Who wants to be a Don" and in "The Learned Fish" who "has not sufficient brains / To go into the water when it rains."

While mockery of human pretensions is an important theme in *The Bad Child's Book of Beasts,* the humans are unconcernedly shown hunting and killing the animals, an aspect of the book which may be problematic for a modern audience. Hippopotamus, Dodo, Rhinoceros, and Camelopard are all pursued with guns, while Whale is depicted as a source of blubber and oil. Tony Ross's illustrations for a 1991 edition of the book, however, make the subject more acceptable to contemporary feeling about the hunting of exotic animals by showing the hunters as particularly silly and ineffective and emphasizing the triumph of the animals (as, in fact, Blackwood had already tended to do).

While the verses of *The Bad Child's Book of Beasts* can certainly stand on their own, Blackwood's illustrations were designed to have an important role in the interpretation of the text. Although the verse gives only the hunter's insults to the Rhinoceros, the accompanying illustration shows that they are the "sour grapes" response of a would-be pursuer who has become the pursued. When inserted between lines of a poem, the drawings oblige the reader to pause and take in some pictorial information before proceeding, and the suspension of the poetic rhythm thus produced has its own comic effect, as when the sketch of an immense whale and a baffled cook interrupts the understatement of the line "Is not [picture] a table fish." The long neck of the Camelopard stretches up through the lines of verse above the rest of the picture, and the concluding couplet of this poem refers the reader to the accompanying picture for an explanation. "The Camel" is simply a captioned cartoon.

The happy collaboration between Belloc and Blackwood continued through another three children's books, as well as *The Modern Traveller* and *More Peers.* They followed the success of the first beast book with *More Beasts (For Worse Children)* (1897). The animals fare better in this second book, and indeed many of them are shown discomfiting human beings in various ways: the Infant Crocodile pops out of the missionary's breakfast egg, the Scorpion lurks in the bed of a hunter, the hunter pursuing the Chamois falls off a mountain, and both picture and text warn vividly of how unwise it is to slap the Porcupine.

The verses of this volume seem more of a piece. While none has the sublime simplicity of the "The Elephant" in the first book, the humor is generally more childlike, without the lapses into adult bitterness which occasionally crept into the earlier work. Metrical virtuosity is again apparent, playfully undercut by deliberately forced rhymes ("idea-r" with "fear" in "The Chamois") and invented words such as "Tupto-philist" – given a mock-scholarly derivation and definition ("one that loves to strike") in a footnote – and "Wanderoo." The most complex is "The Llama," with its alternating line lengths and iambic and anapestic meters. It takes some practice to read aloud well, catching the caesuras and twisting the tongue around such lines as: "The Llama of the Pampasses you never should confound / (In spite of a deceptive similarity of sound) / With the Lhama who is Lord of Turkestan."

As in bestiaries, the animals are given moral qualities: the Bison is vain, and the Vulture's "eye is dull, his head is bald, / His neck is growing thinner" because he eats between meals, leading the speaker to the moral: "Oh! what a lesson for us all / To only eat at dinner!" The "lesson" is as facetious as those of the first beast book, but the idea of the mock moral fable seemed to appeal increasingly to Belloc. While many of the poems of *The Bad Child's Book of Beasts* are either nonsensical or generally satiric, those of its sequel are unified by a meditation on the animals and what they may, or may not, have to say to humans about how they live their lives. It is always risky to write seriously about comic verse, but Belloc himself had a disconcerting habit of shifting suddenly from vituperation or nonsense to a moving and serious expression of real feeling. "The Microbe," the concluding poem of *More Beasts,* touches lightly on one of his deepest concerns – the subject of belief:

All these have never yet been seen –
But Scientists, who ought to know,

He cannot stretch out straight in bed
　　Because he is so high.
The clouds surround his lofty head,
　　His hornlets touch the sky.

How shall
　I hunt　　　　　　　　this quadruped?
　　I　　　　　　　　　cannot tell!
　　　　　　　　　　　　　　Not I!

(A picture of how people try
And fail to hit that head so high.)

Page from The Bad Child's Book of Beasts *(1896) showing the interplay between Belloc's text and B.T.B.'s illustrations*

Assure us that they must be so. . . .
Oh! let us never, never doubt
What nobody is sure about!

The "Dedication on the Gift of a Book to a Child," which was published in Belloc's *Verses* (1910) and at the front of the editions of his collected verse for children from 1939 onward, also moves between comedy and a delicate touch of the very serious. It begins: "Child! do not throw this book about! / Refrain from the unholy pleasure / Of cutting all the pictures out!" It then considers the child's "little hands," made "to take / The better things and leave the worse ones" as well as "to shake / The Massive Paws of Elder Persons," and concludes with the lovely lines:

And when your prayers complete the day,
　Darling, your little tiny hands

Were also made, I think, to pray
　For men that lose their fairylands.

These lines, like Lewis Carroll's dedicatory poems in *Alice's Adventures in Wonderland* (1865) and *Through the Looking Glass* (1872), are more likely to be meaningful to adults than to children, but they give a valuable momentary glimpse behind the mask of the ironic humorist and a sense of why the man behind it might write for children in the first place.

Belloc's first child, Louis, was born in 1897, followed by Eleanor in 1899, Elizabeth in 1900, Hilary in 1902, and Peter in 1904. For this young family Belloc and Elodie purchased in 1906 a rambling and dilapidated Tudor farmhouse, King's Land, which became very important to Belloc's sense of self and belonging. Belloc had been struggling to support his family through his earnings from his

The Porcupine

What! would you slap the Porcupine?
Unhappy child—desist!
Alas! that any friend of mine
Should turn Tupto-philist.*

* From τύπτω = I strike; φιλέω-ᾶ = I love; one that loves to strike. The
word is not found in classical Greek, nor does it occur among the writers of the
Renaissance—nor anywhere else.

Page from More Beasts (For Worse Children) *(1897), which includes a mock-scholarly
footnote by Belloc*

books and from his continuing sidelines as a lecturer, a journalist, and a literary editor of the *Morning Post*. His political interests and ambitions, however, led him to run for Parliament as Liberal member for South Salford, a manufacturing district near Manchester. Advised not to let his largely evangelical constituents know of his religion, he began his campaign by declaring to the crowd: "Gentlemen, I am a Catholic. As far as possible, I go to Mass every day. . . . If you reject me on account of my religion, I shall thank God that He has spared me the indignity of being your representative." After an astonished silence, the audience cheered him, and he was twice elected to Parliament. Because of his writing, his compulsion to travel, and his official duties, about which he quickly became disillusioned, Belloc was not often at home, but he was a loving father to his five children, as is evident from the 1956 memoir of his older daughter Eleanor Jebb.

In 1898 Blackwood illustrated a verse satire of Belloc's titled *The Modern Traveller,* which seems too adult and too dated in its subject matter to be considered a children's book today. Their next collaboration for children was *A Moral Alphabet* (1899).

Having transformed the bestiary tradition with their wit and nonsense, Belloc and Blackwood moved to the traditional form of the illustrated alphabet, which they turned into a parody of the books of moral instruction so popular in the nineteenth century. The youths whose conventional virtues are supposedly being held up for praise are cheerfully described as "justly irritating," while the moral for the letter *D,* which stands for a Dinosaur attempting to roost in branches, is "If you were born to walk the ground, / Remain there; do not fool around." Always ready to make a joke at his own expense, the poet notes, in excruciating rhyme, "No reasonable little Child expects / A Grown-up Man to make a rhyme on X," with the moral, "These verses teach a clever child to find / Excuse for doing all that he's inclined." Definitely not an alphabet book for beginning readers, the *Moral Alphabet* requires considerable sophistication of its readers, and some verses, such as those for the letter *U,* concerning the Upas Tree, make literary allusions that would elude most adults today, to say nothing of children. Nonetheless, the sardonic absurdities of the illustrations, with the jaunty humor and dashing rhythms of the verse, keep the book alive.

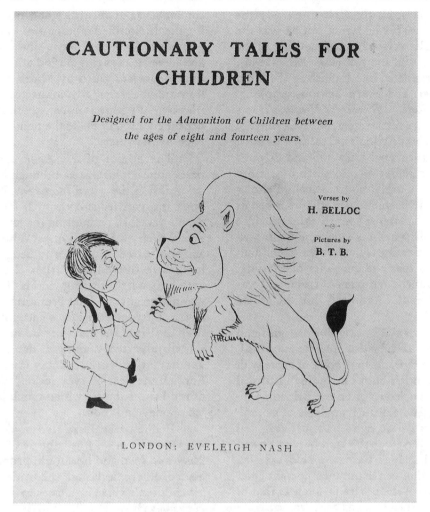

Title page for Belloc's 1907 collection of humorous verse, which parodied a genre of children's writing popular in the nineteenth century

Continuing with this rich vein of mockery, poet and illustrator produced what is perhaps their best volume, *Cautionary Tales for Children.* By this time Blackwood was living in South Africa, working for the imperial administration that Belloc despised, while Belloc labored over his journalism and his books on a variety of subjects. Belloc and Blackwood each freely criticized the other's views, but maintained their friendship and working collaboration. In the *Cautionary Tales,* such dire fates as being eaten by a lion (Jim), burned to death (Matilda), knocked flat (Rebecca), or getting a lump behind the ear (George) befall various children as the consequences of commonplace childish misdemeanors such as letting go of Nurse's hand, telling lies, slamming doors, crying, or popping a balloon. The disproportion of crime to punishment in each case points up the absurdity of the moralistic and judgmental attitudes being mocked in the verses, while the clearly obnoxious character of Charles Augustus Fortescue ("Who always Did what was Right, / and so accumulated an Immense Fortune") parodies the self-improvement books in which a commonplace, materialistic success is sure to be the reward for servility and conformity. A childlike grammatical construction results in the black humor of the subtitle of "Algernon, Who played with a Loaded Gun, and, on missing his Sister was reprimanded by his Father."

Unlike his previous books of children's verse, the *Cautionary Tales* is all in iambic meter. As in the previous collaborations, however, Blackwood's illustrations are often interposed in the middle of lines of text for humorous and sometimes dramatic effect. The pictorial explosion of George's balloon occurs in the midst of the poem's text, as does the appearance of little Lord Lundy's immensely tall and stern Grandpapa.

Belloc was far from the first to parody the moralistic verse tales for children, but he was the most successful. His verses have something of the spirit of Heinrich Hoffmann's *Struuwwelpeter* (1845), which had been translated into English in 1848, but are less gruesome and more obviously joking. Harry Graham's *Ruthless Rhymes for Heartless Homes* (1899) continues in a similar vein, but falls short of the skill and polish of Belloc's verse. Critics most often compare his work with Carroll and Edward Lear, although a number of critics see it as more pointed and less purely nonsensical. Belloc's children's verse may be more correctly described as "light" rather than "nonsense" verse, although since time has dulled the edge of his satire and the moralistic models of his parody are unknown to children now, they tend to take the accounts of Matilda, Henry King ("Who chewed bits of String, and was early cut off in Dreadful Agonies") and the others as pure nonsense.

Belloc was a man of prodigious energies and literary output. In 1911, for example, he published, in addition to *More Peers*, his final book of verse with Blackwood, seven other books including historical and political studies, an attack on the British political-party system, and a critical analysis of capitalism. In *More Peers* Belloc, who had just resigned from political life, develops the kind of joke he had made about Lord Lundy in *Cautionary Tales,* creating an upper house full of venal and incompetent characters. One or two of the portraits, such as that of Lord Finchley who "tried to mend the Electric Light / Himself," have the kind of timeless black humor which marks *Cautionary Tales,* but generally the book is shadowed by Belloc's disillusionment and by racial prejudices evident in both text and pictures.

After the death of Elodie in 1914, followed by the deaths of his oldest son and Blackwood in World War I, Belloc seems to have lost heart for his comic verse, although he kept on producing large numbers of books on a variety of subjects. He made several lecture tours of the United States, and with his friend G. K. Chesterton he founded a journal called the *New Witness* to support a Distributist social and political program. Several novels written by Belloc and illustrated by Chesterton were a popular success, and the two men influenced a number of important younger Catholics and converts such as Evelyn Waugh and J. B. Morton.

In 1930 Belloc's *New Cautionary Tales* was published with illustrations by Nicolas Bentley. Bentley's pictures for Belloc's verses have a more polished quality than Blackwood's, but impart a similar sense of absurdity and enjoyment of depicting the undignified moments of the respectable and pompous. Although they suit the verses very well and have an engaging period atmosphere (as in the flapper dresses worn by Maria and Sarah Byng), they are not essentially connected to the text as are Blackwood's illustrations, which Belloc had often depended upon to make the point of a joke only implied by the verse.

The humor of *New Cautionary Tales* is sometimes quite sophisticated although it is not as topical or cynical as the wit of *More Peers*. Nevertheless, the book is a worthy successor to Belloc's early children's verse. In recounting the experiences of characters such as Sarah Byng, "Who could not read and was tossed into a thorny hedge by a Bull," Belloc has recovered his earlier élan. Sarah escapes with only a light tossing, and is "Confirmed in her instinctive guess / That literature breeds distress." In fact, the cautionary fates encountered by the children in these later tales are no more dire than getting disinherited, making a "deplorable marriage," and having to work "All day long from 10 till 4! / For half the year or even more." The tales revolve around two subjects which much preoccupied Belloc: money and food.

Belloc's last illustrated book of verse, *Ladies and Gentlemen* (1932), is subtitled *for Adults Only and Mature at That,* and he should probably be taken at his word here, although the work is collected with his children's verse in *Cautionary Verses: The Collected Humorous Poems* (1939), and is usually (if erroneously) regarded as a children's book. The cleverness and cynicism of these poems might be enjoyed by a highly literate adolescent, but a book with drawings and funny verse is not necessarily a children's book, and Belloc did not intend *Ladies and Gentlemen* to be so.

Late in life Belloc was offered a number of the honors which had eluded him earlier, including an honorary fellowship of All Souls, Oxford, but he had lost interest in them by then. His son Peter was killed in World War II, and Mussolini proved not to be the hero-king Belloc had imagined. After the author suffered a series of minor strokes, he retired from his frantically active social and literary life and lived quietly at King's Land until his death at age eighty-three.

It is one of the ironies of literary reputation that, in the vast body of Belloc's work, the verses for children which seemed to his contemporaries such a minor and ephemeral part of his achievement, and which were never labored over and polished as his adult poetry was, seem to be the only aspect of his work which has retained its appeal. Many of his "serious" books, hurriedly written for money, are repetitive, dated, and overly polemical; few seem to have a lasting interest. In contrast, Belloc's children's verse has given pleasure and amusement to generations of readers and seems likely to continue to do so.

Although commentators on children's literature frequently observe that Belloc's verses are too verbally sophisticated for modern children, the poems continue to be anthologized, and several later twentieth-century illustrators have interpreted Belloc's Matilda, Yak, and Big Baboon for new generations of children. In 1975 Steven Kellogg illustrated a picture-book version of *Matilda* and a compilation of Belloc's animal verses entitled *The Yak, the Python and the Frog,* and 1991 saw the publication of three Belloc picture books, with illustrations by Quentin Blake, Posy Simmonds, and Tony Ross. The verbal sophistication and sardonic joking of Belloc's verses seem to be more appealing to present-day children than theorists foresaw. Belloc would be pleased to have proven the academics wrong once again.

Bibliography:

Patrick Cahill, *The English First Editions of Hilaire Belloc* (London: Privately printed, 1953).

Biographies:

J. B. Morton, *Hilaire Belloc: A Memoir* (New York: Sheed & Ward, 1955);

Eleanor and Reginald Jebb, *Testimony to Hilaire Belloc* (London: Methuen, 1956);

Marie Belloc Lowndes, *The Young Hilaire Belloc* (New York: P. J. Kenedy & Sons, 1956);

Robert Speaight, *The Life of Hilaire Belloc* (London: Hollis & Carter, 1957);

Herbert Van Thal, ed., *Belloc: A Biographical Anthology* (New York: Knopf, 1970);

Andrew N. Wilson, *Hilaire Belloc* (London: Hamilton, 1984).

References:

Ronald Knox, Preface to *Collected Verses*, by Hilaire Belloc (Harmondsworth, U.K.: Penguin, 1958);

Michael H. Markel, *Hilaire Belloc* (Boston: Twayne, 1982);

Bernard McCabe, "A Cautionary Career," *New York Review of Books* (7 November 1985): 38–41.

Papers:

A Belloc archive, containing some correspondence and literary manuscripts, is at the British Library.

L. Leslie Brooke

(24 September 1862 – 1 May 1940)

Harriet P. Williams
retired, Durham Academy

BOOKS: *Johnny Crow's Garden: A Picture Book* (London: Warne, 1903; New York: Warne, 1904);

Johnny Crow's Party: Another Picture Book (London & New York: Warne, 1907);

Johnny Crow's New Garden (London & New York: Warne, 1935).

BOOKS ILLUSTRATED: Evelyn Everett-Green, *Miriam's Ambition: A Story for Children* (London: Blackie, 1889);

Mary C. Roswell, *Thorndyke Manor: A Tale of Jacobite Times* (London: Blackie, 1890);

Everett-Green, *The Secret of the Old House; A Story for Children* (London: Blackie, 1890);

George MacDonald, *The Light Princess, and Other Fairy Stories* (London: Blackie, 1890);

Mrs. (Mary L.) Molesworth, *Nurse Heatherdale's Story* (London: Macmillan, 1891);

Annie E. Armstrong, *Marian, or, The Abbey Grange* (London: Blackie, 1892);

L. T. Meade, *A Ring of Rubies* (London: Innes, 1892);

Molesworth, *The Girls and I: A Veracious History* (London: Macmillan, 1892);

Ismay Thorn, *Bab, or The Triumph of Unselfishness* (London: Blackie, 1892);

Roma White (Blanche Oram), *Brownies and Rose-Leaves* (London: Innes, 1892);

Eva Knatchbull Hugessen, *A Hit and a Miss* (London: Innes, 1893);

Molesworth, *Mary: A Nursery Tale for Very Little Children* (London: Macmillan, 1893);

Amy Walton, *Penelope and the Others: A Story of Five Country Children* (London: Blackie, 1893);

Molesworth, *My New Home* (London: Macmillan, 1894);

White, *Moonbeams and Brownies* (London: Innes, 1894);

Molesworth, *The Carved Lions* (London: Macmillan, 1895);

Molesworth, *Sheila's Mystery* (London: Macmillan, 1895);

Molesworth, *The Oriel Window* (London: Macmillan, 1896);

E. H. Strain, *School in Fairy Land* (London: Unwin, 1896);

Andrew Lang, ed., *The Nursery Rhyme Book* (London: Warne, 1897; New York: Warne, 1898); revised as *Nursery Rhymes* (London: Warne, 1916; New York: Warne, 1917); republished in three individual booklets as *Rhymes and Lullabies; Song and Ditties;* and *Tales and Jingles* (London: Warne, 1916; New York: Warne, 1917);

Molesworth, *Miss Mouse and Her Boys* (London: Macmillan, 1897);

Robert Browning, *Pippa Passes: A Drama* (London: Duckworth, 1898);

Thomas Nashe, *A Spring Song, Now Again Published* (London: Dent, 1898);

Singing Time: A Child's Song-Book, collected by Brooke and Arthur Somervell (London: Constable, 1899);

Edward Lear, *The Pelican Chorus, and Other Verses* (London: Warne, 1899; New York: Warne, 1901);

Lear, *The Jumblies and Other Nonsense Verses* (London: Warne, 1900; New York: Warne, 1900); republished, with *The Pelican Chorus,* as *Nonsense Songs* (London: Warne, 1900; New York: Warne, n.d.);

Eleanor G. Hayden, *Travels Round Our Village* (London: Constable, 1901);

Anthony Trollope, *Barchester Towers* (London: Blackie, 1903);

The Story of the Three Little Pigs (London: Warne, 1904; New York: Warne, 1905);

Tom Thumb (London: Warne, 1904; New York: Warne, 1905); republished, with *The Story of the Three Little Pigs,* as *Leslie Brooke's Children's Books,* first series (London: Warne, 1904; New York: Warne, 1905);

The Golden Goose (London: Warne, 1905; New York: Warne, 1906);

L. Leslie Brooke in 1935

The Three Bears (London: Warne, 1905; New York: Warne, 1906); republished, with *The Golden Goose,* as *Leslie Brooke's Children's Books,* second series (London: Warne, 1905; New York: Warne, 1906); republished, with *The Story of the Three Little Pigs, Tom Thumb,* and *The Golden Goose,* as *Golden Goose Book* (London: Warne, 1905; New York: Warne, 1906);

Emily Lawless, *The Book of Gilly: Four Months Out of a Life* (London: Smith, Elder, 1906);

Jacob and Wilhelm Grimm, *The House in the Wood and Other Old Fairy Stories* (London: Warne, 1909; New York: Warne, n.d.);

George F. Hill, *The Truth About Old King Cole and Other Very Natural Histories* (London: Warne, 1910; New York: Warne, 1911);

The Tailor and the Crow: An Old Rhyme with New Drawings (London: Warne, 1911; New York: Warne, 1912);

The Man in the Moon: A Nursery Rhyme Picture Book (London & New York: Warne, 1913);

Oranges and Lemons: A Nursery Rhyme Picture Book (London & New York: Warne, 1913); republished, with *The Man in the Moon,* as *Nursery*

Rhyme Picture Books, first series (London: Warne, 1913; New York: Warne, 1914);

Little Bo-Peep: A Nursery Rhyme Picture Book (London & New York: Warne, 1922);

This Little Pig Went to Market: A Nursery Rhyme Picture Book (London & New York: Warne, 1922); republished, with *Little Bo-Peep,* as *Nursery Rhyme Picture Books,* second series (London & New York: Warne, 1922); republished, with *The Man in the Moon, Oranges and Lemons,* and *Little Bo-Peep,* as *Ring O' Roses* (London & New York: Warne, 1922);

Lawrence P. Jacks, *Mad Shepherds and Other Human Studies* (London: Williams & Norgate, 1923);

Robert H. Charles, *A Roundabout Turn* (London & New York: Warne, 1930).

L. Leslie Brooke is best known as an illustrator of children's books in the humorous story-telling tradition of Randolph Caldecott. Like many illustrators of books for children, Brooke mined the rich vein of nursery tales and rhymes. In addition, he wrote three books about that most hospitable of birds, Johnny Crow. But he began his professional career by contributing drawings to juvenile novels. As he became better known, Brooke worked increasingly for younger children, and by 1903 he had found the form in which he excelled, the picture book, comprising a slight text greatly expanded by his splendidly drawn characters in detailed surroundings. These books have delighted young children for almost a century.

Born on 24 September 1862, Leonard Leslie Brooke grew up in semirural Birkenhead, across the river from Liverpool. His parents, Leonard Brooke and Rhoda Prentice Brooke, were Irish. His father commuted by ferry to his small rope and sail manufacturing company. The family was a close one and, unlike many families of their class, sent neither their two sons nor their daughter away to boarding school. They also played a special game every Sunday evening: each child would in turn name an animal, and then Mr. Brooke would have to respond with a rhyme in which the animal did or said something in "Johnny Crow's Garden." This store of family rhymes would many years later provide the impetus for Brooke's three Johnny Crow books.

From early childhood Brooke loved to draw, but he never expected to be an artist. He attended the Birkenhead School with its classical curriculum to prepare for Oxford. In his biography, *Leslie Brooke and Johnny Crow* (1982), Brooke's son Henry describes an early example of his father's illustrative skill. In Latin class the headmaster noticed that Brooke was drawing in the margin of his copy of Julius Caesar's *Gallic Wars* and told him to come forward to show his drawing. To the amazement of the headmaster Brooke produced a "dynamic sketch of Caesar throwing his legions across the river, in the manner of an athlete throwing a discus." Brooke already had the basics of his style – vigorous line, humor, and imagination.

Holidays in the Irish countryside with relatives were part of the rhythm of Brooke's family life. But when he was seventeen, an aunt invited him to join her for a three-month tour of Italy. During the trip Brooke filled his diary with his impressions of the great Italian masters and his sketchbook with quick pencil drawings of people and scenes. Italy, unfortunately, had more than art to offer: Brooke caught typhoid fever, became seriously ill, and lost his hearing as a result. Since he would not be able to hear the lectures at Oxford, art school seemed to be an obvious alternative.

Just back from Italy with his head and notebook full of the Renaissance, Brooke set out to win a place at the Royal Academy Art School, the bastion of the High Renaissance and of painting in England. He began at the Birkenhead Art School in 1880 and after two years moved to the Saint John's Wood Art School in London. In spite of his deafness, Brooke retained his gregarious nature. He became close friends with his fellow art students and frequently visited the stimulating and lively family of his cousin and future father-in-law, Stopford Brooke, who was a preacher and an art critic. He also found time for dancing, fencing, and walking. In 1884 he qualified for the Royal Academy Art School and began his studies there. Exhibiting a watercolor landscape at the 1887 academy summer exhibition and winning the Armitage Prize in 1888, Brooke completed his training with distinction.

Now the artist literally had to seek his fortune. When his father had died a few years earlier, his brother Henry had dutifully taken over the family business; it was not very prosperous. Brooke may have wished to be a painter in the classical tradition, but he could not count on a living from such a career, as he could in the decorative art of book illustration. Although he exhibited an oil portrait of Gen. Henry Brooke at the academy in 1889 and a portrait of James Barrie in 1896, during the same period he illustrated nineteen books. In the final decades of the nineteenth century the market for children's books was expanding, serious attention was being paid to the book as an artistic whole, and the new use of photography in line-block and half-tone reproductions was producing a great flowering of black-and-white illustrations. Brooke was among a group of younger artists who took advantage of the broader range of graphic styles permitted by the new technology, and he quickly found a living illustrating novels in black and white. Though he drew with traditional pen and ink, he had to learn about new methods for reproducing his drawings. For the first books he illustrated, he used line-block process, a technique which, according to Joyce Irene Whalley and Tessa Rose Chester's *History of Children's Book Illustration* (1988), made possible "more precision and delicacy, although it had its disadvantages. The artist now had to draw for reduction, which sharpened the lines but which lost a lot of the spontaneity, and jet black ink on white board had to be used"; the method "prohibited the use of gentler tonal effects." Brooke's first professional illustrations were done for the Blackie publishing firm, starting with a frontispiece and three plates for Evelyn Everett-Green's *Miriam's Ambition: A Story for Children* (1889). He next produced a frontispiece and three plates for Mary C. Roswell's *Thorndyke Manor: A Tale of Jacobite Times* (1890), requiring historical background and costume. Another frontispiece and three plates followed for a novel by Everett-Green, *The Secret of the Old House; A Story for Children* (1890). Brooke finished that productive year with a frontispiece and two plates for an edition of George MacDonald's *The Light Princess, and Other Fairy Stories* (1890).

In 1891 Brooke was chosen by Macmillan to succeed Walter Crane as the illustrator for Mrs. (Mary L.) Molesworth's popular books for children. Beginning with *Nurse Heatherdale's Story* (1891), Brooke illustrated with line-block process eight books of Molesworth's, each of which included a picture title page, an inset frontispiece, six plates, and floral decoration on the front and spine of the binding. His next assignment for Blackie was Annie E. Armstrong's *Marian, or, The Abby Grange* (1892), for which Brooke tried a different technology, creating wash drawings to be reproduced by the monochrome halftone process, in which the drawing was photographed through a fine screen that broke it down into a pattern of dots. This technique, though it allowed for greater tonal variation, required printing separately on glossy paper unlike the matte paper of the text. Brooke returned to line-block for L. T. Meade's *A Ring of Rubies* (1892) for yet another publisher, A. D. Innes. His next work for Macmillan was Molesworth's *The Girls and I: A Veracious History* (1892). For Blackie, Brooke illustrated Ismay Thorn's *Bab, or The Triumph of Unselfishness* (1892), again employing halftone. He used line-block for Roma White's *Brownies and Rose-Leaves* (Innes, 1892) and for the first time added, in addition to the frontispiece and separate plates, pictures printed on pages with text.

In 1893 a bookplate that Brooke designed for his cousin Stopford appeared in the first volume of the *Studio,* a magazine promoting the decorative arts, in an article titled "Designing for Bookplates." The plate shows a Romantic rural background with Stopford Brooke seated by a waterfall contemplating the scene, his name in elegant lettering in white rectangles. In the same year Brooke also produced one book for each of his three publishers. He illustrated Eva Knatchbull Hugessen's *A Hit and a Miss* (1893) for Innes's "Dainty Books" imprint, so called because the books were smaller, five by five inches, rather than the more usual seven by five inches. Brooke again used line-block process for the frontispiece, four plates, and six smaller illustrations printed on the page with the text. For Macmillan, Brooke provided the illustrations for Molesworth's *Mary: A Nursery Tale for Very Little Children* (1893). For Blackie, he contributed a fron-

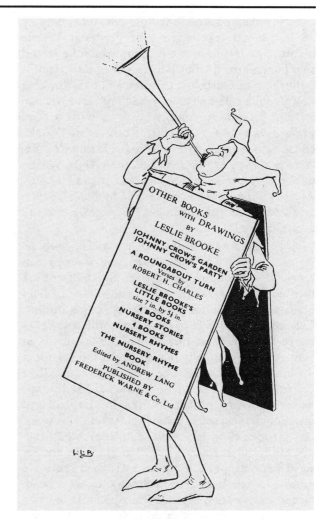

Self-caricature by Brooke used as an endpaper in his books

tispiece and three plates in the subtle halftone style to Amy Walton's *Penelope and the Others: A Story of Five Country Children* (1893). By the end of this busy year Brooke must have felt more financially secure, because in December he became engaged to his second cousin Sybil Brooke, one of his cousin Stopford's six daughters. Six months later they were married. Brooke continued to turn out work in 1894, illustrating Molesworth's *My New Home* for Macmillan and White's *Moonbeams and Brownies* for Innes, employing line-block in both instances.

The next year Brooke's first child, Leonard, was born. Both his wife and child were extremely delicate and needed much care. Brooke provided income for the family by illustrating Molesworth's *The Carved Lions* (1895), *Sheila's Mystery* (1895), and *The Oriel Window* (1896), as well as E. H. Strain's *School in Fairy Land* (1896), the latter for T. Fisher Unwin, a new publisher.

Brooke had established himself sufficiently by 1896 to begin negotiations with Frederick Warne about a nursery rhyme collection which he would select and illustrate. But Warne, one of the foremost publishers of illustrated children's books, thinking that Brooke's name alone would not carry the collection, brought in Andrew Lang to write a brief preface and add a few historical notes. Brooke chose rhymes from James Orchard Halliwell's *The Nursery Rhymes of England* (1886). In 1897 Warne published *The Nursery Rhyme Book* as edited by Lang. Although the book is only 7-3/4" by 5-3/8", it is a large collection of rhymes – 288 pages, with 107 illustrations.

For the first time Brooke had a chance to design the total book. Now the master of many current styles, Brooke here uses the capability of the line-block with great versatility and skill. The bold black-and-white lines give striking design, humor, and story to the title page. A toy soldier marches across and down the surround of the title between toy trees and gradually relaxes into a somersault at the bottom of the page. The style of illustrator Kate Greenaway inspires the first series of headpieces, which show four plump children, holding musical instruments, seated in a flower blossom and wearing upended flowers as caps. Four separated headpieces form a narrative. But these children are not so stiff and proper as Greenaway's: their socks are rumpled; their faces are too chubby. In other headpieces using stark black-and-white contrast, Brooke uses clothed animals with marvelous facial expressions to introduce various sections: Tales – two birds in tailcoats in profile showing their own tails; Proverbs – a wise old owl clothed in evening dress; Riddles – two elephants, the younger standing with trunk extended, riddling the seated elder elephant who smokes his long pipe grasped by his curled trunk. Pre-Raphaelite maidens with long flowing hair and gowns languish in the rhyme "Here Comes the Lusty Wooer," and in "I Saw Three Ships" they whistle, sing, and play the violin, lying in storm-tossed swan-prowed boats. Preindustrial, rural, jolly Caldecottian England provides the background for such rhymes as "Tom he was a Piper's son" and "Merry are the Bells." Dramatic atmospheric landscapes dominate the cold wintry scene in "The North wind doth blow" and the stormy mountain scene in "Arthur O'Bower."

But Brooke presents his own distinctive style in a full-page framed picture which encapsulates the entire story of "This little pig went to market." Brooke shows the interior of a middle-class pig family home: father seated reading his newspaper, the

Evening Sty, looks at his son at the table eating his roast beef as the son is being watched by a younger pig (who has none) in kilt. Seen through the window is a pig off to market with a basket, greeting a small pig (no doubt crying "wee wee, I can't find my way home"). This picture abounds in details for the curious child to discover. The format of each page in *The Nursery Rhyme Book* is uncrowded, with pictures or a variety of tailpieces dividing the rhymes. While many styles, sizes, and shapes of pictures make for an unharmonious whole, each element in the collection is a joy in itself.

The Nursery Rhyme Book was a great success, and from the time of its publication Brooke worked on books more congenial to his own talents. He ended his association with Macmillan after illustrating Molesworth's *Miss Mouse and Her Boys* (1897). His next books were elegantly and expensively produced. Duckworth published a limited edition of Robert Browning's *Pippa Passes: A Drama* (1898), with a frontispiece and six plates by Brooke and engraved in Paris. Dent published an edition of the Elizabethan writer Thomas Nashe's *A Spring Song, Now Again Published* (1898) in the form of sixteen folios, each including a lovely pastoral watercolor by Brooke, engraved and printed from wood by Edmund Evans. Constable published *Singing Time: A Child's Song-Book* (1899), for which Brooke hand-lettered the text and drew twelve illustrations, while his friend Arthur Somervell copied out all the music by hand.

Wishing to make use of Brooke's humorous illustrative style, Warne suggested that Brooke illustrate some of Edward Lear's nonsense songs, and so began the period of Brooke's classic work. While preparing these Lear books, Brooke realized he must move his wife and young son from the unhealthy environment of London to the countryside. They found a house in the small village of Harwell, twelve miles from Oxford and two walking or bicycling miles from the nearest railroad station. Warne initially published *The Pelican Chorus, and Other Verses* (1899) and *The Jumblies and Other Nonsense Verses* (1900) separately, later combining them into one volume, *Nonsense Songs* (1900). After the Lear titles, Warne continued to push Brooke's work by combining and dividing.

During this period Brooke developed the format which he used successfully for his most popular work, a combination of color plates using halftone color wash from watercolors and line-block drawings from black-and-white pen and ink. The challenge of illustrating Lear drew upon Brooke's talent to create humorous, fantastic figures such as pobbles, dongs, and jumblies. For each song Brooke drew a title page, a halftone color-wash full-page picture on shiny paper, and line-block drawings to appear within the text. The color is subdued, but the drawing is vigorous and, as usual, filled with humorous details.

Brooke's move to the countryside provided an added benefit – in his new village Brooke found models for strong realistic black-and-white line-block drawings of village folk and ways for Eleanor G. Hayden's *Travels Round Our Village* (1901). But Brooke often escaped the isolation of the small community by trips to Warne's office to discuss his next book. On one such visit in 1901 Warne showed him the work of an unknown artist named Beatrix Potter and asked Brooke if he thought her work should be published. The Warne brothers could not decide upon its worth, but agreed to abide by Brooke's decision. Brooke responded positively, and so began Potter's long relationship with Warne.

Warne also agreed to Brooke's idea for a book of his own, based upon the old Johnny Crow game from his childhood. Now that Brooke was playing this game with his own son, his wife had suggested that this should be the basis of his next book. In 1903 two events of great importance to Brooke occurred: his second son, Henry, was born, and his first Johnny Crow book was published. In *Johnny Crow's Garden: A Picture Book,* Brooke achieves a harmoniously as well as humorously designed picture book, with a color picture on the binding, carefully designed line-block endpapers, a color frontispiece, a decorated title page, a vignette on the half title, and a text filled with line drawings and full-page color pictures. Almost every single line of text has its own picture full of action and humor. The clothed animals, all in proper scale and with wonderfully expressive eyes, act out the nonsensical lines. Brooke has one illustrative style here but combines two printing techniques, halftone and line-block, the only interruption being the occasional presence of the shiny, blank verso pages necessary for the halftone color pictures, a problem noted more by critics than by children.

Anthony Trollope's *Barchester Towers* (1903) interrupted Brooke's steady flow of children's picture books. His work had also recently appeared in the adult world with a 1902 cartoon in the weekly humor magazine *Punch.* The editor asked Brooke to become a regular contributor, but he declined, not wishing to be on a fixed schedule for producing humor.

Brooke turned to nursery tales for the texts of his next books for Warne. He illustrated a series of

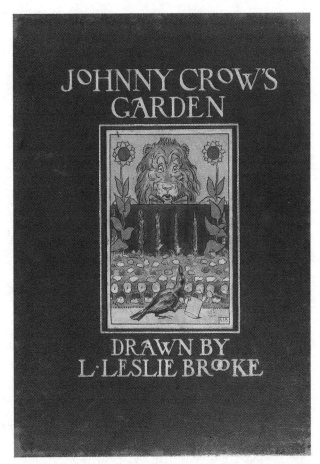

Cover for the first book that Brooke wrote as well as illustrated. The story was based on a rhyming game played by Brooke's family during his childhood (courtesy of the Osborne Collection of Early Children's Books, Toronto Public Libraries).

twenty-four-page booklets, each with a pictorial title page, eight full-page halftone color plates, and fifteen line-block drawings, beginning with *The Story of the Three Little Pigs* (1904) and *Tom Thumb* (1904). Warne then republished these two in one volume as *Leslie Brooke's Children's Books,* first series (1904) for the Christmas trade. *The Golden Goose* (1905) and *The Three Bears* (1905) followed and were republished in one volume as *Leslie Brooke's Children's Books,* second series (1905). Then all four booklets were collected in one volume titled *Golden Goose Book* (1905). Some of Brooke's most wonderful pictures appear in *The Three Little Pigs* and *The Three Bears,* where the artist's devotion to and selection of detail are particularly imaginative and abundant. The bear's mantelpiece is decorated by a bear motif, honey-bees cover the upholstery, and baby bear's quilt shows among other things the three pigs, the golden goose, and the map of Johnny Crow's garden. The highly decorated interior scenes are deriv-

Proofs for Johnny Crow's Party, *with comments by Brooke (Collection of Henry Brooke)*

ative of the Pre-Raphaelite–influenced work of illustrator Walter Crane, but without Crane's static quality; they burst with Brooke's playful humor.

In 1906 Brooke illustrated another adult book, Emily Lawless's *The Book of Gilly: Four Months Out of a Life,* using chalk reproduced in halftone. During the same year Brooke worked on the drawings for *Johnny Crow's Party,* now assisted by both his sons. Brooke's working methods were later described by his son Henry in *Leslie Brooke and Johnny Crow.* Brooke would begin with a sketch on transparent paper which he would alter until he was satisfied with the proportions, perspective, and composition of the piece. He would then turn the paper over and firmly trace the main outlines with a soft pencil, resulting in a copy of the desired illustration on the back of the transfer paper in reverse. This soft pencil image was easily transferred to a board and then delineated with pen and ink. Color always presented additional problems, and with the evolving three-color halftone process used for *Johnny Crow's Party,* Brooke sent the printer's proofs back with endless notes, trying to achieve the right tones.

Brooke was fond of the country, but, with the return of his wife's health and the need of educating his younger son, he decided to return to London, and in 1908 the family bought a house in Saint John's Wood. The move brought urban benefits such as electricity and running water and closer contact with the artistic and publishing worlds. In addition, Brooke had not lost his early love of portraiture and now found the opportunity to do commissioned chalk portraits.

Brooke adapted a selection of tales of Jacob and Wilhelm Grimm for his next book, *The House in the Wood and Other Old Fairy Stories* (1909). The volume includes his then-standard combination of full-page color, halftone, and line drawings, line-block, within the text. The pictures are not so numerous as in Brooke's collections of nursery tales, nor do they have the direct appeal or tight narrative lines of his earlier work.

Brooke joined forces with a London friend, George F. Hill, and illustrated Hill's *The Truth About Old King Cole and Other Very Natural Histories* (1910), a sophisticated takeoff in which the title character is placed in the London of 1910. The pictures are as rollicking as the text, but both now seem dated. Brooke returned to a traditional rhyme with *The Tailor and the Crow: An Old Rhyme with New Drawings*

(1911). His sure touch is evident in his illustrations of the exasperated tailor and the teasing crow in a Caldecott-like world of preindustrial rural England.

For another series Brooke went back to *The Nursery Rhyme Book* to choose a limited number of his favorites. For each booklet of twelve pages he drew twelve drawings for line-block reproduction within the text, eight plates in the three-color half-tone process, color designs for the binding, and a line drawing for endpapers. Warne published *The Man in the Moon: A Nursery Rhyme Picture Book* (1913) and *Oranges and Lemons: A Nursery Rhyme Picture Book* (1913) separately and then collected as *Nursery Rhyme Picture Books,* first series (1913). The second series, though planned for 1914, was postponed by the outbreak of World War I and did not appear until much later.

The war years were hard on the Brooke family. Publishing did not flourish, and Brooke had little heart to expend on foolishness and jollity. Warne brought out a new edition of *The Nursery Rhyme Book* titled *Nursery Rhymes* (1916), which in 1916 was published as three booklets, titled *Rhymes and Lullabies, Songs and Ditties,* and *Tales and Jingles.* Brooke's age made him unfit for military service, and his deafness made him unfit for most volunteer work, but in 1916 he found a way to help entertain soldiers on leave: he led them on walking tours of London. His elder son, Leonard, joined the army in 1915 and died on 25 September 1918 while flying a bombing mission shortly before the end of the war. During this time Brooke turned more and more to chalk portraiture, which included posthumous portraits of many young men killed in the war, including his son Leonard. Sybil Brooke was especially devastated by Leonard's death, so the family decided to return to country living.

Meanwhile, toward the end of 1920 Brooke had returned to work on his nursery rhymes, which Warne triumphantly published in 1922 in its multifaceted form. The first booklets were published separately as *Little Bo-Peep: A Nursery Rhyme Picture Book* (1922) and *This Little Pig Went to Market: A Nursery Rhyme Picture Book* (1922) and then published in one volume as *Nursery Rhyme Picture Books,* second series (1922). Finally both series were collected as *Ring O' Roses* (1922).

Before moving once again from London, Brooke was host to one of his greatest admirers, Anne Carroll Moore, director of Work with Children for the New York City Public Library. Her three idols were Brooke, Potter, and Walter de la Mare, and in all her branch libraries the librarians and children not only read Moore's favorite books

Illustration by Brooke for Robert H. Charles's A Roundabout Turn

but also celebrated her favorite authors' birthdays. All her bibliographies for core library collections contained their names. She had been one of Brooke's greatest promoters for years. Writing to her niece on 23 June 1921, Moore described "an enchanting afternoon with a family tea round the dining room table at Leslie Brooke's . . . Mr. B. is quite deaf but adorable . . . Mr. B. and I literally fell into one another's arms and he wants to give me for myself one of his originals. . . . Their eldest son was . . . finally reported lost in the War and one sees the tragedy in their eyes but in no other way." Thus began a long friendship involving an active correspondence. Moore sent Brooke copies of books by the best American illustrators for children, many of whom he met when they came to England.

When the time arrived for the Brooke family's move, finding the right house in the right village proved again to be a difficult task. After a long search they rented a house in Cumnor Village, again near Oxford, and began to build their own house. Here Brooke made his last set of drawings in black and white for an adult work, the second edition of Lawrence P. Jacks's *Mad Shepherds and Other Human Studies* (1923). He had already drawn the frontispiece for the first edition of 1910 but added a series of serious character sketches for the new edition. Brooke spent much of 1922 and 1923 planning the family's new house and garden. In 1923 the Brookes moved into their large, comfortable home, and Brooke began in earnest the creation of his new garden.

Life in the country was pleasant, and Brooke filled his time with his garden. Not until 1930 did he illustrate another book. In 1928 he had read in *Punch* a poem titled "A Roundabout Turn," by Robert H. Charles. This story of a toad setting out to go around the world struck his fancy. To draw the world from the vantage point of a toad presented an amusing challenge. The result, his next-to-last book, is full of amusing line drawings and three-color plates still using the halftone technology.

Once more Brooke moved for the comfort of his family. The harsh country wind was hard on Mrs. Brooke, so back to London they went, this time near their son Henry. Leaving his garden was difficult for Brooke, and its loss may have prompted him to write *Johnny Crow's New Garden* (1935). Again he produced his wonderful combination of pictures and text. In 1940 he died peacefully at home in London.

Brooke has been more popular in the United States, where children's librarians have always held him in high esteem, than in Britain. Upon his death Moore collected and edited an L. Leslie Brooke tribute issue of the *Horn Book* (May 1941). Maurice Sendak, writing in a 1965 *Book Week* article, "Mother Goose Garnishing," shows little respect for most illustrators of Mother Goose, but Caldecott is highly praised and Brooke is next in line: "The Brooke illustrations convey a tremendous robustness and are very funny in the real old Mother Goose way. *The Ring O' Roses* is no mere pastiche Caldecott. The pictures are pure Leslie Brooke in flavor, the warm, homely, ample flavor that can only be English." Elizabeth Nesbitt, in a 1971 article for *Horn Book,* chooses Leslie Brooke along with Howard Pyle and Beatrix Potter as the three preeminent illustrators of their time. She observes that both Caldecott and Brooke "possess the lovely quality of gentle and endearing humor, the faculty which allows the imagination to play with the content of the story or rhyme being illustrated, the mastery of the right kind and amount of detail, the ability to picture beauty in the background and setting, and yet keep background and setting unobtrusive.

These qualities are still the essential traits of a true picture-book." English scholars have also shown respect for Brooke's work. Brian Alderson in his *Sing a Song of Sixpence, The English Picture Book Tradition and Randolph Caldecott* (1986) states: "It was left to the devoted admirer of Caldecott, L. Leslie Brooke, to seek to achieve a full matching of text and picture in the nursery books that he produced under the new dispensation [technology]. More than anyone he saw the fun that could be derived from narrative illustration and brought to his work a fluent draughtsmanship." Whalley and Chester's history of the field ranks Brooke's work with that of Potter and asserts that he "perfectly interprets the rhymes with a visual humour worthy of Caldecott, but softened by a gentle benevolence. His animals are benign and companionable, drawn with his characteristically graceful and detailed line."

Brooke has remained almost continuously in print. Warne published reset editions of the Johnny Crow books in 1986. Albion (London) and Clarion (New York), using the latest technology with the original drawings and paintings, have recently produced lavish editions of Brooke's other three classics, *The Nonsense Poems of Edward Lear* (1991), *The Golden Goose Book* (1992), and *The Ring O' Roses* (1992). Children continue to delight in the works of L. Leslie Brooke.

References:

Brian Alderson, *Sing a Song of Sixpence, The English Picture Book Tradition and Randolph Caldecott* (Cambridge: Cambridge University Press, 1986), pp. 86–90;

Henry Brooke, *Leslie Brooke and Johnny Crow* (London: Warne, 1982) – includes "Leslie Brooke's Book Illustrations: A Check-list," compiled by Brian and Valerie Alderson;

Virginia Haviland, *Children and Literature: Views and Reviews* (Glenview, Ill.: Scott, Foresman, 1973);

Anne Carroll Moore, ed., *Horn Book,* special issue on Brooke, 17 (May 1941), pp. 152–162;

Elizabeth Nesbitt, "The Early Record," *Horn Book,* 47 (June 1971): 268–274;

Frances Clarke Sayers, *Anne Carroll Moore* (New York: Atheneum, 1972);

Maurice Sendak, "Mother Goose Garnishing," *Book Week* (1965);

Joyce Irene Whalley and Tessa Rose Chester, *A History of Children's Book Illustration* (London: John Murray, 1988).

Frances Hodgson Burnett

(24 November 1849 – 29 October 1924)

L. M. Rutherford
University of New England, New South Wales

See also the Burnett entry in *DLB 42: American Writers for Children Before 1900.*

BOOKS: *That Lass o' Lowrie's* (New York: Scribner, Armstrong, 1877; London: Warne, 1877); re-published with *Louisiana* (London: Macmillan, 1880);

"Theo." A Love Story (Philadelphia: Peterson, 1877; revised edition, London: Ward & Lock, 1877; New York: Scribners, 1879);

Surly Tim and Other Stories (New York: Scribner, Armstrong, 1877; London: Chatto & Windus, 1877);

Dolly: A Love Story, unauthorized edition (Philadelphia: Porter & Coates, 1877; London: Routledge, 1877); authorized edition published as *Vagabondia: A Love Story* (Boston: Osgood, 1884);

Pretty Polly Pemberton. A Love Story, unauthorized edition (Philadelphia: Peterson, 1877; London: Routledge, 1878); authorized edition (New York: Scribners, 1878; London: Chatto & Windus, 1878);

Kathleen. A Love Story, unauthorized edition (Philadelphia: Peterson, 1878; London: Routledge, 1878); authorized edition published as *Kathleen Mavourneen* (New York: Scribners, 1878; London: Chatto & Windus, 1879);

Our Neighbour Opposite (London: Routledge, 1878);

Miss Crespigny. A Love Story, unauthorized edition (Philadelphia: Peterson, 1878; London: Routledge, 1878); authorized edition (New York: Scribners, 1879);

A Quiet Life; and The Tide on the Moaning Bar (Philadelphia: Peterson, 1878); republished as *The Tide on the Moaning Bar* (London: Routledge, 1879);

Lindsay's Luck, authorized edition (New York: Scribners, 1878; London: Routledge, 1879); unauthorized edition (Philadelphia: Peterson, 1879);

Jarl's Daughter; and Other Stories (Philadelphia: Peterson, 1879); republished as *Jarl's Daughter and Other Novelettes* (Philadelphia: Peterson, 1883);

Natalie and Other Stories (London: Warne, 1879);

Haworth's (New York: Scribners, 1879; London: Macmillan, 1879);

Louisiana (New York: Scribners, 1880); republished with *That Lass o' Lowrie's* (London: Macmillan, 1880);

A Fair Barbarian (London: Warne, 1881; Boston: Osgood, 1881);

Esmeralda. A Comedy-Drama Founded on Mrs. Frances Hodgson Burnett's Story of the Same Name, by Burnett and William Gillette (New York, 1881);

Through One Administration (London: Warne, 1883; Boston: Osgood, 1883);

Little Lord Fauntleroy (New York: Scribners, 1886; London: Warne, 1886);

A Woman's Will; or, Miss Defarge (London: Warne, 1886); republished with John Haberton's *Brueton's Bayou* (Philadelphia: Lippincott, 1888);

Sara Crewe or What Happened at Miss Minchin's (New York: Scribners, 1888; London: Warne, 1888); republished with *Editha's Burglar* as *Sara Crewe; or, What Happened at Miss Minchin's: and Editha's Burglar* (London & New York: Warne, 1888); *Editha's Burglar: A Story for Children* republished separately (Boston: Jordan, Marsh, 1888);

The Fortunes of Philippa Fairfax (London: Warne, 1888);

The Pretty Sister of José (New York: Scribners, 1889; London: Blackett, 1889);

Little Saint Elizabeth and Other Stories (London: Warne, 1890; New York: Scribners, 1890);

Children I Have Known and Giovanni and the Other (London: Osgood, McIlvaine, 1892); republished as *Giovanni and the Other: Children Who Have Made Stories* (New York: Scribners, 1892);

The Drury Lane Boys' Club (Washington, D.C.: Moon, 1892);

The One I Knew the Best of All: A Memory of the Mind of a Child (New York: Scribners, 1893; London: Warne, 1893);

Piccino and Other Child Stories (New York: Scribners, 1894); republished as *The Captain's Youngest: Piccino and Other Child Stories* (London: Warne, 1894);

Two Little Pilgrims' Progress: A Story of the City Beautiful (New York: Scribners, 1895; London: Warne, 1895);

A Lady of Quality; Being a Most Curious, Hitherto Unknown History, as Related by Mr. Isaac Bickerstaff But Not Presented to the World of Fashion Through the Pages of the Tattler and Now for the First Time Written Down (New York: Scribners, 1896; London: Warne, 1896);

His Grace of Osmonde; Being the Portions of That Nobleman's Life Omitted in Relation of His Lady's Story Presented to the World of Fashion Under the Title of A Lady of Quality (New York: Scribners, 1897; London: Warne, 1897);

In Connection with The De Willoughby Claim (New York: Scribners, 1899; London: Warne, 1899);

The Making of a Marchioness (New York: Stokes, 1901; London: Smith, Elder, 1901); republished with *The Methods of Lady Walderhurst* as *Emily Fox-Seton* (New York: Stokes, 1909);

The Methods of Lady Walderhurst (New York: Stokes, 1901; London: Smith, Elder, 1902); republished with *The Making of a Marchioness* as *Emily Fox-Seton* (New York: Stokes, 1909);

In the Closed Room (New York: McClure, Phillips, 1904; London: Hodder & Stoughton, 1904);

A Little Princess: Being the Whole Story of Sara Crewe Now Told for the First Time (New York: Scribners, 1905; London: Warne, 1905);

The Dawn of a To-morrow (New York: Scribners, 1906; London: Warne, 1906);

Queen Silver-Bell (New York: Century, 1906); republished as *The Troubles of Queen Silver-Bell* (London: Warne, 1907);

Racketty-Packetty House (New York: Century, 1906; London: Warne, 1907);

The Cozy Lion, as Told by Queen Crosspatch (New York: Century, 1907);

The Shuttle (New York: Stokes, 1907; London: Heinemann, 1907);

The Good Wolf (New York: Moffat, Yard, 1908);

The Spring Cleaning, as Told by Queen Crosspatch (New York: Century, 1908);

The Land of the Blue Flower (New York: Moffat, Yard, 1909; London: Putnam, 1912);

Barty Crusoe and His Man Saturday (New York: Moffat, Yard, 1909);

The Secret Garden (New York: Stokes, 1911; London: Heinemann, 1911);

My Robin (New York: Stokes, 1912; London: Putnam, 1912);

T. Tembarom (New York: Century, 1913; London: Hodder & Stoughton, 1913);

The Lost Prince (New York: Century, 1915; London: Hodder & Stoughton, 1915);

The Little Hunchback Zia (New York: Stokes, 1916; London: Heinemann, 1916);

The Way to the House of Santa Claus: A Christmas Story for Very Small Boys in Which Every Little Reader Is the Hero of a Big Adventure (New York & London: Harper, 1916);

The White People (New York & London: Harper, 1917; London: Heinemann, 1920);

The Head of the House of Coombe (New York: Stokes, 1922; London: Heinemann, 1922);

Robin (New York: Stokes, 1922; London: Heinemann, 1922);

In the Garden (Boston & New York: Medici Society of America, 1925).

PLAY PRODUCTIONS: *That Lass o' Lowrie's,* by Burnett and Julian Magnus, New York, Booth Theater, 28 November 1878;

Esmeralda, by Burnett and William Gillette, New York, Madison Square Theater, 26 October 1881; produced again as *Young Folk's Ways,* London, Saint James' Theatre, 29 October 1883;

The Real Little Lord Fauntleroy, London, Terry's Theatre, 14 May 1888; New York, Broadway Theater, 11 December 1888;

Phyllis, adapted from *The Fortunes of Philippa Fairfax,* London, Globe Theatre, 1 July 1889;

Nixie, adapted from *Editha's Burglar,* by Burnett and Stephen Townesend, London, Terry's Theatre, 7 April 1890;

The Showman's Daughter, by Burnett and Townesend, London, Royalty Theatre, 6 January 1892;

The First Gentleman of Europe, by Burnett and Constance Fletcher, New York, Lyceum Theater, 25 January 1897;

A Lady of Quality, by Burnett and Townesend, New York, Wallack's Theater, 1 November 1897; London, Comedy Theatre, 8 March 1899;

A Little Unfairy Princess, London, Shaftesbury Theatre, 20 December 1902; produced again as *A Little Princess,* New York, Criterion Theater, 14 January 1903;

The Pretty Sister of José, New York, Empire Theater, 10 November 1903; London, Duke of York's Theatre, 16 November 1903;

That Man and I, adapted from *In Connection with The De Willoughby Claim,* London, Savoy Theatre, 25 January 1904;

Dawn of a Tomorrow, New York, Lyceum Theater, 28 January 1909; London, Garrick Theatre, 13 May 1910;

Racketty-Packetty House, New York, Children's Theater, 23 December 1912.

OTHER: "When He Decides," in *Before He Is Twenty: Five Perplexing Phases of the Boy Question Considered* (New York: Revell, 1894).

SELECTED PERIODICAL PUBLICATIONS – UNCOLLECTED: "A City of Groves and Bowers," *St. Nicholas,* 20 (June 1893): 563–571;

"How Winnie Hatched the Little Rooks," *St. Nicholas,* 34 (November 1906): 3–12;

"The First Knife in the World," *St. Nicholas,* 37 (December 1909): 99–105;

"The Christmas in the Fog," *Good Housekeeping,* 59 (December 1914): 661–671;

"The Woman in the Other Stateroom," *Good Housekeeping,* 60 (March 1915): 357–368;

Burnett's son Vivian in 1885. This photograph was sent to Reginald Birch to guide him in illustrating Little Lord Fauntleroy.

"The Attic on the House in Long Island," *Good Housekeeping,* 62 (May 1916): 549–559;

"The Passing of the Kings," *Good Housekeeping,* 68 (March 1919): 10–12, 118–128;

"The House in the Dismal Swamp," *Good Housekeeping,* 70 (April 1920): 16–18.

Frances Hodgson Burnett is chiefly remembered for her children's book *The Secret Garden* (1911). With its rich mythic resonances and detailed portrayal of its child protagonists, the novel is hailed as one of the classics of children's literature. Her biggest contemporary success, however, was *Little Lord Fauntleroy* (1886), the story of a young American boy who becomes the heir to an English title. The success of the latter book's theatrical adaptations in England and the United States and the notoriety of the small hero's distinctive costume have earned *Little Lord Fauntleroy* the status of an icon of popular culture, though the story is now considered less significant for its literary merits than for its representation of the sentimental Victorian ideal of childhood. Burnett's *A Little Princess* (1905), a revised version of an earlier story and play, is also celebrated as a work of great imaginative power. These three books are usually cited as the author's major achievements, but her adventure-romance *The Lost Prince* (1915) has also been recognized as having merit, and her autobiography, *The One I Knew the Best of All: A Memory of the Mind of a Child* (1893), is valuable for its portrait of the artist as a young child in two cultures. Although she wrote for the adult marketplace at least as much as for the juvenile, Burnett's reputation rests firmly on her achievements as a children's writer. As contemporary critic William Archer phrased it, "Mrs. Burnett shows herself a true poet though her Pegasus may be a rocking-horse."

Frances Eliza Hodgson was born on 24 November 1849 at Cheetham Hill, Manchester, the third of five children of Edwin Hodgson and Eliza Boond Hodgson. The family included two elder brothers, Herbert and John George, and two younger sisters, Edith Mary and Edwina. Her mother's relatives came from a family of some antiquity in the area and still maintained the traditions of gentility and noblesse oblige. The family's sense of its importance is dramatized in a whimsical family legend which traced the descent of the line from a mythical Welsh chieftain, Cadraad Haard, from whom, as Vivian Burnett was to remark in his biography of his mother, "it could be easily considered that many interesting and highly creditable and individual traits had descended."

Edwin Hodgson was a prosperous middle-class businessman, the head of a firm which specialized in the wholesale trade of decorative art fittings for the interior decoration of houses. The rising middle-class manufacturers in Manchester were erecting houses of some magnificence on the proceeds of the textile boom, and Hodgson's merchandise was in demand. The prosperity of the family, however, was short-lived. In 1854, following a period of illness, Edwin died of a stroke, and Frances's mother was forced to take over the business. The American Civil War proved a more decisive blow to the family fortunes. Manufacturing in Manchester was devastated by the cessation of shipments of cotton from the Southern plantations, and hardship was widespread among the mill owners as well as the factory operatives.

Although Burnett discusses these events in her 1893 memoir, the work's main focus is its portrait of the artist as a young child. It dramatizes Burnett's sense of her lifelong obsession with stories and storytelling. Her imagination is stimulated, not by the customary "improving" literature recommended for the young lady, but by stories of adventure and romance found in ballads and biblical tales, Roman histories, and works of William Shakespeare, the Romantic poets, and novelists such as Sir Walter Scott, James Fenimore Cooper, Mayne Reid, and Harrison Ainsworth and stories from bound volumes of popular magazines stored in Eliza Hodgson's *secrétaire*. Burnett dramatized and verbalized these adventure and romance stories with the aid of her doll, who played the part of the bold heroine in the child's theatrical creations. Burnett's predilection for acting out stories developed into a precocious talent for writing both stories and poetry and also into a skill at performance. She would amuse her schoolmates on sewing afternoons and other occasions with her extemporaneous performances of the story of "Edith Somerville" and later a series of other formulaic tales modeled on her reading in popular adventure and romance.

The devastating financial effect of the Civil War on the Hodgson business led Eliza Hodgson to decide on emigration. Her brother had settled in Knoxville, Tennessee, where he owned a fairly prosperous dry goods store. His offer to place her sons in his business seemed a brighter prospect than depressed Manchester could offer. Thus in 1865, when Frances was sixteen, the family sailed for the United States. They spent their first winter in a log cabin in the foothills village of New Market, about twenty-five miles from Knoxville, later settling just outside Knoxville in a hillside dwelling whimsically christened "Noah's Ark, Mt. Arafat" by the young Frances. In the chapter of her memoir entitled "Dryad Days," Burnett represents the change from industrial England to rural America in terms of a journey to the green world, which is the soul's native place – from sterility to the abundance of nature, from the stifling of potential and feeling to the freedom of the emotions and the imagination.

The scantiness of the family means led Frances to seek ways of supplementing her brothers' incomes. She set up a small school, but this proved impractical in the new home, which was too isolated from potential pupils. Thus she turned to writing to earn money. In her memoir Burnett emphasizes her own diffidence and carefully plays down any notion of ambition toward literary fame, perhaps reflecting a "feminine" reticence toward any suggestion of ambition, probably fostered by the teasing she suffered at the hands of her elder brothers on the score of her storytelling propensities. However, she was fixed on the idea of being a writer. She was determined and self-possessed enough to organize, in an isolated rural situation, the difficult process of obtaining the necessary materials and postage money in order to send her first story to a magazine without the knowledge of "the boys," whose derision she anticipated.

Burnett had noticed that popular magazines such as *Peterson's* and *Godey's Lady's Book* accepted unsolicited contributions; thus she submitted some of her stories to these markets. Her first published story, "Miss Carruthers' Engagement," appeared in *Godey's Lady's Book* in 1868. The editor, Sarah Josepha Hale, had initially doubted the story's originality, due to its striking resemblance to the popular English magazine fiction of its day. In her autobiography Burnett admitted its "evident – though unconscious – echo of like stories in *Cornhill, Temple Bar* and *London Society*": the romantic fiction which had comprised so much of her early reading. The editor was convinced after reading Burnett's second story, "Hearts and Diamonds," also published by *Godey's* in 1868. The family became increasingly dependent on Burnett's income following the death of her mother in 1872. Thus she accelerated her career as a popular writer. She sold stories to most of the American popular magazines, particularly to *Peterson's*, which later republished many of her stories in book form (though without her complete approval).

Before the publication of *Little Lord Fauntleroy*, few of Burnett's stories were intended for children. In fact, the years prior to that landmark brought her recognition as a serious writer for adults in the social-realist mode. In 1872 "Surly Tim's Trouble," a sentimental story employing the Lancashire dialect, appeared in the respected magazine *Scribner's* (later the *Century*), introducing Burnett to the literary world of New York.

Burnett received encouragement throughout her career from men associated with the magazines and publishing houses for which she wrote. Charles Peterson, the editor of *Peterson's* magazine, encouraged her financially and placed her stories with the better journals. With Richard Watson Gilder, one of the editorial staff of *Scribner's*, she established a lifelong literary relationship. As their correspondence makes clear, Gilder was influential as an editorial associate and friend who commented upon and suggested revisions to her work. In later years she became friendly with the English playwright and novelist Israel Zangwill, whose writing and critical opinion she valued highly.

The income from her stories allowed Burnett to make the first of her visits home to England in 1872. In September 1873, following her return to Tennessee, she married Swan Burnett, whom she had met in New Market during her first year in the

Burnett with her sons, Vivian and Lionel, in 1888

United States. The son of the district surgeon, he had then been preparing for a medical career. By the time of her return Dr. Burnett had begun to specialize in the treatment of the eye and ear and wished to further his specialty by studying in Europe, a desire which his wife's writing would finance. Although her husband teased Frances about her domestic shortcomings, the income from her writing always formed the largest part of the family income.

Burnett gave birth to their first child, Lionel, in Knoxville on 20 September 1874. During the first year of her marriage she had also begun work on her first major novel, *That Lass o' Lowrie's* (1877), a story set in the Lancashire pit district. The critical reception of the novel, which compared it favorably with the work of Charlotte Brontë, Elizabeth Gaskell, and Henry James, encouraged Burnett.

In 1875 the Burnett family embarked for Paris, where Swan further studied his area of specialization. Their second son, Vivian, was born in Paris on 5 April 1876. Financial pressures forced the family to return to the United States soon after. Swan moved to Washington, D.C., where he opened a specialist practice and was joined by his wife and sons in the spring of 1877. In Washington they enjoyed an expanded social life. Burnett had become known as a promising novelist in the light of the positive reviews of *That Lass o' Lowrie's*. In later years the household would become something of a literary salon, one of the hubs of Washington literary and political society, but in the first months in the new city Burnett suffered from the ill health and depression that would plague her throughout her life. She clearly felt the economic pressure on her to write as a major burden. Though her husband was to become one of Washington's most eminent medical men, the practice was initially slow to prosper, and without Burnett's income the family would not have been able to enjoy the standard of living she required for herself and her children.

She did, however, begin work on her novel *Haworth's* (1879), with which she announced her desire to be seen as a writer of serious fiction. In a letter to Gilder dated September 1877, Burnett differentiated *That Lass o' Lowrie's,* in which she was "simply writing a story," from her new work, in which she was "trying to please the critics." She also embarked on a dramatic version of *That Lass o' Lowrie's,* inspired by an unauthorized version produced in England by the novelist Charles Reade and an associate. This piracy initiated her interest in drama, which subsequently became an important facet of her literary output. Also in 1879 Burnett visited Boston, where, as the guest of the Papyrus Club under the presidency of poet and novelist John Boyle O'Reilly, she was feted by Boston's literati. There she extended her literary contacts, making the acquaintance, among others, of Louisa May Alcott, author of *Little Women* (1868), and Mary Mapes Dodge, author of *Hans Brinker, or the Silver Skates* (1865) and editor of Scribner's popular and influential juvenile magazine, *St. Nicholas.*

Burnett genuinely valued the friendship and company of children and delighted in telling stories to a child audience. One of her first children's stories, "Behind the White Brick," published in *St. Nicholas* in 1879, was invented for the amusement of an "intimate" young friend and utilizes the dream-narrative structure employed by Lewis Carroll in *Alice's Adventures in Wonderland* (1865) and *Through the Looking Glass* (1871), both of which Burnett's tale is clearly reminiscent. To her own children she related "Hair Curling Stories" – tales extemporized to amuse and pacify her sons while she curled the long hair they wore as young boys. "The Proud Little Grain of Wheat," serialized in *St. Nicholas* in 1880, may be from this series, as it mentions the boys by

name. Burnett contributed several more stories to *St. Nicholas* in the years preceding and immediately following the publication of *Little Lord Fauntleroy,* which began its serial run in the magazine in 1885.

The best known of these early stories for children is "Editha's Burglar." It appeared in *St. Nicholas* in February 1880, was published in book form in 1888, and was adapted for the stage as *Nixie* in 1890. The heroine is an exemplary character who has elements in common with the young Burnett as revealed in her autobiography. A bookish child with a well-developed imagination, she also possesses a precocious sense of moral discrimination which manifests itself in feelings of protectiveness toward the adults in her life. Editha has a real need to act as a small protectress. Like the majority of children in Burnett's fiction, she suffers from the absence of good parents. In this case the absence is due to lack of domestic responsibility – her "mamma was very young and pretty, and went out a great deal, and her papa was so busy. . . . " When a burglar pays a visit to the house, seven-year-old Editha begs him to be quiet so that he will not waken and alarm her mother, and she brings her own treasures to prevent him from taking her parents' things. The burglar eventually returns Editha's valuables. Her parents are moved by her actions. Her mother vows to become a better parent and to devote more time to her child.

As Phyllis Bixler notes in her 1984 study, Burnett's use of fairy tale and fantasy and her romantic idealization of the child are in harmony with a contemporary movement in children's fiction, seen in the work of Carroll and George MacDonald. Like the child imaged in William Wordsworth's "Ode: Intimations of Immortality" (1807), Burnett's young protagonists appear "trailing clouds of glory." They are spiritually more pure because they are less degenerate than the fallen and forgetful adult world, which they must redeem by their example and influence. In this spiritualized mode Burnett's Editha and her child successors are versions of the "Christian fool" and have Christlike redemptive power. These children are exemplars of innocent and unworldly naiveté because they have no understanding of the world of adult moral compromise. They are "Christian" and redemptive because, like all the spiritually pure, their true home is elsewhere. In her memoir Burnett writes of the child: "It is only a thing not far away from Paradise – not yet acclimatized to earth – who can so trustingly believe and be so far befooled." The naive lack of comprehension demonstrated by the child observer of adult morality rebukes the so-

Cover for the book that Burnett later rewrote as A Little Princess

phisticated but compromised adult system of values.

The following years saw a series of adult novels by Burnett, including *Louisiana* (1880), *A Fair Barbarian* (1881), and *Through One Administration* (1883). They also led to her acquaintance with certain belief systems that would influence her literary career. Burnett felt herself to be strongly affected by extremes of climate. In the early to mid 1880s she was fleeing the Washington heat, while later she was to embark on regular winter pilgrimages to escape the cold of London and New York. Her concern over her persistent illnesses led her by 1883 to an acquaintance with the "new philosophies" of Spiritualism, Theosophy, and "Mind Healing." She was also to become interested in the thought of Mary Baker Eddy, the founder of Christian Science. Though the practice of mind healing apparently made little impression on her malaise, the "new thought" concerning the power of the mind to effect personal regeneration was to take its place as a motif in some of her later writing, including *A Little Princess, The Secret Garden,* and *The Lost Prince.*

In late 1884 Burnett began work on *Little Lord Fauntleroy,* the book that so profoundly changed her life and reputation. She modeled its central character, Cedric Errol, Lord Fauntleroy, on her son Vivian. Burnett explained the genesis of the story in a magazine article titled "How Fauntleroy Occurred, and a Very Real Little Boy Became an Ideal One," later reprinted in her collection *Piccino and Other Child Stories* (1894). This essay shows Burnett's transformation of biography into fiction, and it assigns many of the novel's thematic concerns and motifs a biographical genesis. Burnett insists that her ideal of childhood innocence and maternal selflessness are practicable ones: Cedric Errol was real before he became a hero of fiction, and "Dearest" was a mother before she became a famous writer.

Both the essay and *Little Lord Fauntleroy* reveal some slippage in Burnett's construction of childhood. A gentle, ironic, and maternally indulgent tone is often employed when the author speaks of the child. The reader is intended to see through Burnett's whimsical pretense, but the gentle humor is directed from adult to adult. Burnett engages in a wink at the foibles of mothers, invoking a sense of collusive feminine conspiracy. "How Fauntleroy Occurred" is intended for an adult audience; however, its point of view has much in common with the novel and much of Burnett's early writing for children. Often she is, to borrow a phrase from Barbara Wall's *The Narrator's Voice: The Dilemma of Children's Fiction* (1991), "talking to adults in the presence of children," rather than seeking to present a focus appropriate to a child reader.

Burnett's description of her son as a quaint and picturesque child reiterates a motif central to her conception of childhood's charm, but the idyllic quality of many of her child characters often sits uncomfortably with her equal insistence of the inner life and feelings of the child as "little person." Most of Burnett's child characters are remarkable for their physical beauty. The notable exception is Mary Lennox in *The Secret Garden*, who is initially presented to the reader as an ugly and disagreeable distortion of the childlike ideal. Besides her son's appearance, his character is also depicted in "How Fauntleroy Occurred," as Burnett highlights many of the motifs to be found in the novel and in other works she wrote for children. The essence of Vivian's nature – like the fictional Cedric's – is universal consideration and generosity of spirit: "From his first hour his actions seemed regulated by the peaceful resolve never to be in the way and never to make anyone uncomfortable."

These exemplary little boys exhibit dignity, composure, and a native sense of honor, all of which indicate an innate nobility. They always comport themselves with graceful self-control and dignity, demonstrating an interested curiosity in all people and things. Because they trust in love and goodness, they perceive no separation between self and other and recognize no barriers of class or race in their friendliness. The theme of universal good fellowship is an important characteristic of Burnett's exemplary child characters. Cedric Errol is a friend to all, regardless of social standing. Ironically, this engenders a respect for and deference toward the "native" aristocrat which exceeds that shown to the de jure nobility.

Burnett's taste for the picturesque extended to clothing and had as its consequence a popular conception of the character of Cedric, Little Lord Fauntleroy, which is somewhat at variance with the character presented in the novel. Reginald Birch's illustrations for the first edition were modeled on a photograph of Vivian Burnett taken in 1884, and the velvet and lace of the infamous "Fauntleroy suit" promoted the image of an effeminate mother's boy which easily recommended itself to satire.

There is, however, more to Cedric than his pretty clothing and long, curly hair – he is, in fact, another of Burnett's versions of the Christian fool. His naive optimism and trust in goodness provide a rebuke to the adult and class-defined world of his grandfather, the misanthropic earl of Dorincourt, who lacks one fundamental Christian virtue: charity. Cedric, on the other hand, both demonstrates and symbolizes charity, and he also functions as a redemptive influence. By expecting the best of people, he produces the best in them. Motivated by emulation, shame, and love, they wish to be in truth what they seem to him.

Though descended from an aristocratic line, American-born Cedric is a little republican, the friend and confidante of grocers and bootblacks. According to the fairy-tale and romance archetype, true princes and princesses always have the common touch, engendering reverence in whatever guise they appear. As Ann Thwaite points out in her 1974 biography, this version of the American-in-Britain plot allows Burnett to exploit a double-edged appeal, indulging the reader with the exotic and romantic appeal of the aristocratic life, while at the same time endorsing egalitarian principles. Indeed, the notion of noblesse oblige is a common theme in Burnett's writing, extending beyond largesse and charity to a personal ethics and etiquette of dignity and stoicism. Like Cinderella in the fairy-tale archetype, Burnett's protagonists achieve royal status because it is theirs by natural right.

On the other hand, Cedric's grandfather Dorincourt is a lord of misrule. As lord of a great house, the earl should be obliged to perform acts of charity and to maintain justice and good order, taking his proper role as moral center of the community. Dorincourt, however, is proud and selfish, disdaining Cedric's American mother and valuing his wealth and social status as a privilege rather than as a responsibility. He functions as a potential corrupter of Cedric's innocence and goodness, offering the lure of wealth in order to separate the boy from his mother. The virtue of Cedric is thus tested in several ways. He must show himself loyal to his mother, to whom he refers as "Dearest," and to his lower-class friends. He must remain incorruptible by wealth, and he must demonstrate stoicism and dignity in the face of the prospect of reversal of fortune. When a rival claimant appears, he must show

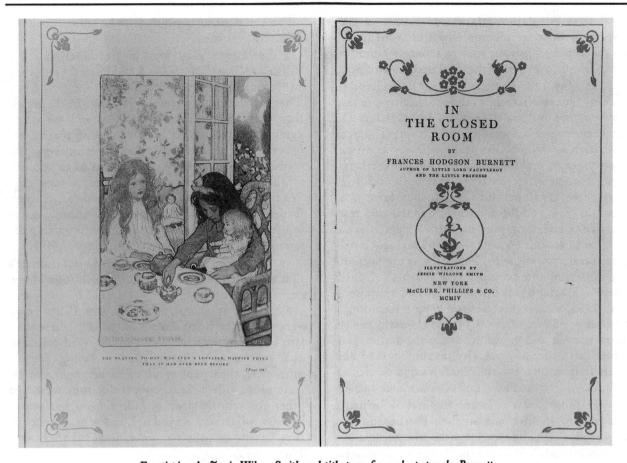

Frontispiece by Jessie Wilcox Smith and title page for a ghost story by Burnett

himself willing to surrender his position as heir to the title. By succeeding in all these challenges, Cedric demonstrates that he is indeed truly noble and worthy of his rank.

The success of *Little Lord Fauntleroy* can be partly attributed to its appeal as a classic wish-fulfilment fantasy. It embodies the dream of the profound reversal of fortune, an archetypal pattern in folktales and other modes of symbolic narrative. It also dramatizes the desire of the ego to represent itself as disguised nobility, thereby effecting a deliverance from mundane existence and heralding a new life of color, adventure, freedom, and power.

Burnett's novel, published in 1886, became a runaway best-seller in both England and the United States. It was translated into twelve languages and sold more than a million copies in English alone, earning Burnett at least one hundred thousand dollars in her lifetime. By 1893 only Lew Wallace's *Ben-Hur* (1880) appeared in more American public libraries than *Little Lord Fauntleroy*. Highly successful theatrical adaptations boosted sales of the book. Fauntleroy playing cards, toys, perfumes, and confectionery appeared, and the Fauntleroy suit be-

came a fashionable item of dress inflicted upon many little boys. Cinematic adaptations of the book also added to its popular success. In 1921, in perhaps the best known of these, Mary Pickford played both the roles of Cedric and "Dearest."

Though the novel came to be disparaged for its sentimentality, contemporary reviews were admiring, stressing the appeal of the sentimental and romantic view of the child. That of the *Manchester Guardian* is typical: "Cedric's simple, truthful, earnest and loving nature is what one would like all children to have, for it was just the same with or without wealth, in the little house in New York or in the great castle."

The success of the book also branded Burnett irrevocably as a popular and romantic writer rather than as a serious art novelist. Her acknowledgment of its biographical basis compromised the reputation of both her son and herself. Throughout her lifetime newspaper headlines patronizingly referred to the pair as "Fauntleroy" and "his Mamma." Burnett, in particular, became a celebrity, and she was subjected to frequent attacks by the press. On the positive side, however, the success of the novel and its theater adaptation guaranteed Burnett a generous independent income which allowed her to travel freely to Europe and to separate from her husband and a marriage that had become strained.

In May 1887 Burnett traveled to England to witness Queen Victoria's jubilee festivities, taking her two boys and her close friend Kitty Hall. It was the beginning of her almost yearly "shuttles" across the Atlantic, which she undertook for the next twenty years, making a total of thirty-three crossings. Burnett once remarked that both countries were necessary to her: the United States for mental stimulus, England for its picturesqueness and rest. The United States served as Burnett's place of energy, in tune with the new technological and entrepreneurial century, while England was the home of romance and the certainties of the past. Consequently, England was Burnett's base of operations until 1908. She acquired several homes, including a London residence where she could entertain her literary friends and enjoy the attention she now received as a literary celebrity. From England she made frequent trips to the Continent, in particular to Italy, which was the setting of many later stories.

Friendship was an important facet of Burnett's life. In 1887 she first met Stephen Townesend, the young physician and aspiring actor who became her second husband. She also had become acquainted with Zangwill, author and later a Zionist leader, with whom she formed a close literary and personal friendship. Interestingly, in Burnett's stories maternal, filial, and amicable relationships routinely take precedence over the depiction of the emotions of male/female romantic love. She enjoyed female friendship and usually lived and traveled with a female companion. In addition to the friendship with Hall, she engaged a secretary-companion in Lisa (or Luisa) Chiellini and in her later years spent much time with her sister Edith.

While holidaying on the Continent in 1887, Burnett discovered that E. V. Seebohm had written an unauthorized theatrical version of *Little Lord Fauntleroy*. International copyright was effectively nonexistent in the nineteenth century. British authors were routinely pirated by American publishers and vice versa, since the transatlantic pirate could reprint a book from Britain or the United States without paying royalties either to the author or to the original publisher. If it was difficult to protect the copyright of an author in a published book, the legal status of an adaptation for the stage was even more precarious. *Little Lord Fauntleroy* was a major source of income for Burnett, and though Seebohm offered a half share of the profits for her authorization, she was not to be bought

off so easily. She rushed back to London to pen her own rival version.

Seebohm's play went into production at the Prince of Wales Theatre in London on 23 February 1888. Burnett's version, which played at Terry's Theatre, did not open until 14 May. In the meantime she had been busily employed in legal action against her rival. The judicial verdict was in her favor and established a precedent effectively proscribing unauthorized dramatizations of an author's work. Burnett's victory was not only a legal one. When her *The Real Little Lord Fauntleroy* was performed, reviewers acknowledged its superiority to the "pseudo-Fauntleroy" of Seebohm, praising the artistry of Burnett's dramatic writing.

The Real Little Lord Fauntleroy was not Burnett's first attempt at dramatic success. With Julian Magnus she had dramatized *That Lass o' Lowrie's,* and she had also collaborated with William Gillette on a version of her story *Esmeralda* (1881). During the late 1880s and into the 1890s she enjoyed considerable success as a playwright, producing, for the most part, theatrical versions of her own stories. Among her other theatrical productions were two other plays for children: *A Little Princess,* performed in 1903, which had played in London as *A Little Unfairy Princess* the previous year, and *Racketty-Packetty House* (1912).

With *Little Lord Fauntleroy,* Burnett proved that popularity and success were possible with a mixed juvenile and adult audience. Her next children's book was *Sara Crewe or What Happened at Miss Minchin's* (1888), which, following a successful theatrical adaptation, she revised and expanded to create one of her greatest juvenile masterpieces, *A Little Princess.* During 1888 and 1889 *St. Nicholas* magazine published Burnett's exemplary story, "Little Saint Elizabeth," later reprinted in the collection *Little Saint Elizabeth and Other Stories* (1890). This story employs the motif of the clash of cultures, but its more serious intent is a statement concerning the morality of asceticism. Burnett's message is that too much emphasis on asceticism, so favored in nineteenth-century religious tracts for children, can stunt the natural, joyous life force in the child. Elizabeth, who has been brought up by a pious aunt, is transported to that most worldly of cities, New York, to reside with a wealthy bachelor uncle. Inspired by tales of martyrs and saints, she attempts to bring charity to the poor of the city. In her self-denying zeal she gives her coat to a poor woman and becomes ill as a result. During her recuperation Elizabeth learns to moderate her extreme self-denial and becomes more accepting of the pleasures of the world.

Cover for the most popular of Burnett's books during her lifetime.
She adapted the work for the stage in 1888.

In 1890 Burnett was struck by the greatest tragedy of her life. Her eldest son, Lionel, was diagnosed as having consumption, which at that time was almost inevitably fatal. Convinced that the high-strung, sensitive boy would be unable to face his death with anything like resignation, she decided to keep the truth from him. Maintaining the fiction that Lionel was a "Prince Imperial," traveling with entourage in search of a cure, Burnett embarked on a pilgrimage of pleasure and make-believe designed to evade the shadow of death. In the course of a tour of the sanatoriums and spas of Europe, Burnett attempted to distract her boy with expensive toys and such amusements as he was well enough to enjoy. Lionel died in Paris on 7 December 1890. To the end his mother managed to hide from him any knowledge of the terminal nature of his condition. A constant companion on this pilgrimage was Townesend. In his role as Lionel's doctor and friend, he had become a much-needed support to Burnett.

Burnett's grief and guilt over Lionel's death made itself apparent in much of her later fiction. She had frequently been separated from her children for long periods as she pursued her travels and literary interests – the image of devoted, all-contented motherhood which appears so frequently in her fiction was one which the writer, with her restless temperament and understandable human desire for a life of her own, found easier to imagine than to practice. In later stories Burnett constructed a thinly disguised version of herself as an idealized and grief-stricken mother whose whole life had been devoted to the care and love of her children. It is significant that the mother figure is inevitably a widow. Besides writing Swan Burnett out of her fiction as completely as she had written him out of her life, this casting of roles may also reflect Burnett's sense of her isolation after the death of her son. Lionel's death seems also to have influenced several stories published in two collections – *Giovanni and the Other: Children Who Have Made Stories* (1892), published in England as *Children I Have Known,* and *Piccino and Other Child Stories,* which appeared in England as *The Captain's Youngest: Piccino and Other Child Stories.* Many of these stories have an Italian setting – accompanied by Hall, Burnett had traveled in France and Italy in an attempt to recover her health and spirits following her son's death. In the title story of the 1892 collection Giovanni is a young singer befriended by an English widow who supports him so that he need not ruin his voice by overuse. As a result the boy goes on to become a famous concert tenor, and the woman appears in the audience to witness his triumph and the fruits of her good deeds. The "Other" of the story's title is a talented singer who loses his voice and dies of illness and a broken heart as a result, representing the fate Giovanni would have suffered without assistance. The Englishwoman, hearing his tragic tale, seeks out the grieving peasant mother, and an empathy based on mutual maternal feeling, which transcends class and national differences, is established.

Class relations are portrayed more satirically in "Two Days in the Life of Piccino," a story in the latter collection. An Italian peasant child of exceptional beauty is adopted from his large, poor family by Lady Aileen Chalmer, a rich young widow with no children. Bored, she decides that she "will buy [a pretty child] from a peasant some day. They will give you anything for money." Though transported from rags to riches, in a twist to the Cinderella tale Piccino is humiliated and unhappy in his rich surroundings. He is lonely for his family, scandalized by the frequent washings he must undergo, and mortified by the way in which he is treated as a pet by the heartless and whimsical woman and her monied friends. After two dreadful days of luxurious suffering, he runs back to his poor, grubby, yet loved existence with his family.

The story employs the device of the naive narrator, with frequent changes of focus to exploit the humor in the differences of perspective between simple and sophisticated observers of such processes as being bathed and clothed. The perspective of the "fool" in a sophisticated world provided by this device allows readers to examine the cultural specificity of their own assumptions and practices when seen through the distancing lenses of simple eyes. Of course, the joke is often just as much at Piccino's expense and demonstrates the ambivalence of Burnett's view of class differences in her fiction. In making her peasant and lower-class characters objects of patronizing, if affectionate, humor, or picturesque objects, Burnett compromises her social

insights into the role played by class in determining the happiness and welfare of the individual.

The theme of death is prevalent in these collections, no doubt explained by Burnett's reaction to Lionel's death. "One Who Lived Long, Long Ago" deals with the death of a child and her family in the destruction of Pompeii, while "The Daughter of the Custodian," which has travel-sketch elements in its reflections on the tour of a famous graveyard, mixes a portrait of a cheerful and picturesque little peasant girl with sentiment concerning the sensitivity and romantic angst of the artistic soul. Other stories which deal specifically with the death of children include "Little Betty's Kitten Tells Her Story" and "The Captain's Youngest." Interestingly enough, both employ first-person narrative, a rare technique in Burnett's fiction. The former is a fairly weak story concerning Kitty, the offspring of a domestic cat gone wild, who is befriended by a little girl named Betty. The girl becomes ill, however, and does not reappear to play with Kitty. Once again Burnett employs the device of the naive narrator. Kitty cannot read the signs that tell the reader that Betty has died. Nevertheless, the story maintains an elegiac tone throughout. The consolatory ending employs a paradisal image to suggest that Betty has gone to another garden, one without stain or fading.

"The Captain's Youngest," narrated in idiomatic speech by Rabbett, the Captain's former batman, is about the life and tragic death of his master's "youngest," Master Lionel. Like so many of Burnett's child characters, Lionel is born into a house of parental misrule. Formerly a fine soldier in India, the Captain made an imprudent marriage and was promptly disinherited. On "love and short commons" both parents prove selfish and imprudent. In the face of this adult misrule and mismanagement, the siblings display love and familial consideration. When his sister's would-be seducer pushes Lionel under the feet of the carriage horses, the boy remains strong in virtue to the death, a saintlike martyr. The romantic notion of the child is underlined in this death scene. Lionel is depicted as an innocent, brighter than the earth, who came from heaven and thereto, appropriately, returned.

Another story, "Eight Little Princes," provides an interesting comment on Burnett's obsession with the picturesque. Here the child subjects literally are pictures, carefully posed in a series of royal photographs. The pictures lead to speculation concerning the nature and family lives of the young royals. The story has elements of the travel sketch and history lesson as it traces the lineage of the five children of the German emperor and supplies interesting detail

Burnett's garden at Maytham Hall, which served as the inspiration for The Secret Garden

concerning domestic items, furnishings, and the dress of little boys. Burnett prefers the sentimental view of the royals as ordinary, happy parents and children. Her theme throughout is that every queen is essentially a mother and that every mother is a queen. Another interesting aspect of the story is its portrait of the young prince of Servia. With his "dark handsome face, with a rather sad and thoughtful look," he is clearly a model for Marco Loristan, the young prince of Samavia in Burnett's *The Lost Prince*.

By far the greatest proportion of the stories, however, are about lower-class children. Burnett tends to romanticize the situation of these children, portraying them as joyous beings who would resent any advancement of their social position. The matters of clothing and cleanliness required by middle-class mothers seem to be gross incursions upon their liberty. Because she views these children as

happy and close to the natural world, Burnett prefers to imagine them as really loved and secure in their own difficult but picturesque worlds. Hence the naked, unsupervised child of a Washington seamstress is "A Little Faun," Piccino is "happy as a rabbit," "A Pretty Roman Beggar" will one day grow to be an honorable man, and "The Tinker's Tom" is undisturbed by a life which includes winters spent in the workhouse and summers enduring the distrust of the local people among whom his family travels. In the last two stories, as critics have been quick to point out, Burnett shows some awareness of her own good-natured gullibility concerning the characters of her lower-class children. When the tinker child fails to return with the mushrooms for which a woman has credulously prepaid, the latter — obviously an ironic self-portrait of Burnett — prefers to invent reasons why he may have been forced to renege. The image of herself is that of the foolishly good little mother who will be taken in by any child.

Most of the stories in *Giovanni and the Other* and *Piccino and Other Child Stories* contain direct personal reference to Burnett and her children, particularly to Vivian, who appears in "What Use Is a Poet" and "The Boy Who Became a Socialist." If the stories in these two collections seem excessively sentimental and morbid today, they also contain much vitally described cultural detail, including descriptions of the architecture, artifacts, clothing, lives, customs, and ways of seeing of the Italian peasantry. These collections demonstrate Burnett's interest in customs and people whose difference she recognized and valued.

Between the appearances of these two books, Burnett published her childhood memoir, *The One I Knew the Best of All: A Memory of the Mind of a Child*. Originally intended to be a brief sketch to be included in *Giovanni and the Other*, it developed in the process of composition into a work for adults. Its comment upon Burnett's conception of childhood and her memory of her own childhood psychology is illuminating for a study of her children's fiction. The work has three major emphases: the nature of the mind of the child, the portrait of the artist as a "Small Person," and Romantic conceptions of nature and education. Burnett refers to her young self throughout as "the Small Person," and this is significant in terms of her presentation of the psychology and ethical life of the child. For Burnett, all children are persons, with well-developed emotions and moral sensibilities.

The memoir also emphasizes Burnett's lifelong obsession with gardens and the natural world. Whether or not she had been specifically influenced by Wordsworth's great evocation of childhood and nature in *The Prelude* (1805), Burnett reinforces Romantic notions of nature and childhood. Like Wordsworth she depicts nature as the great teacher of the child, nurturing spiritual and emotional health. She describes her own prelapsarian bliss in the gardens of her childhood and her feelings of entrapment in the crowded and lifeless environment of a large manufacturing city. In contrast, she recounts the flowering of her emotions and the liberation of her spirit in the wilderness of rural Tennessee.

Following the trauma of Lionel's death, Burnett turned her energies to the fortunes of surrogate sons. She threw herself into work for such charities as Invalid Children's Aid and the Drury Lane Boys Club. In the course of this work she became more acutely aware of the fate of poor children in London. Wretched street children were to figure in sev-

eral of her later stories: for example, Anne, the beggar child in *A Little Princess,* and Rat and his companion urchins in *The Lost Prince*. Burnett also attempted to play fairy godmother to Townesend, whom she saw as a "poor boy" whose theatrical aspirations had been blighted by insensitive parents. She wrote and produced *The Showman's Daughter* (1892) as a vehicle for Townesend so that he might establish himself in the professional theater.

Burnett's next work, *Two Little Pilgrims' Progress: A Story of the City Beautiful* (1895), was commissioned to commemorate the Chicago Columbian Exposition of 1893. Two twelve-year-old orphans, Meg and Robin Macleod, journey across the United States to visit the World's Fair in Chicago. The story is a secularization of John Bunyan's great Protestant allegory of salvation, *The Pilgrim's Progress* (1678), to which it makes constant reference. In Burnett's version the way to salvation for the neglected and love-starved orphans is through hard work, ingenuity, technological advance, and (finally) charity toward others. As Francis J. Molson points out in a 1975 article on Burnett, Meg and Robin represent "Young America on the March," and the story celebrates American enterprise, ambition, and "get-up-and-go."

After this work Burnett turned her efforts to adult romance, producing successful historical "costume dramas," such as *A Lady of Quality* (1896), *In Connection with The De Willoughby Claim* (1899), *The Making of a Marchioness* (1901), and *The Methods of Lady Walderhurst* (1901). The popular success of these works sealed Burnett's fate with the critics. She was now viewed as no more than a writer of third-rate potboilers who was no longer interested in attempting the serious social-realist mode which had earned praise for her early novels. Burnett, however, clearly enjoyed her successes in the marketplace.

In 1898 Frances and Swan Burnett divorced by mutual consent, based on the conveniently fictional grounds of desertion and failure to support. Vivian had completed his study at Harvard that year, and there was no longer any reason to maintain the pretense of family unity for his sake. In February 1900 she married Townesend in Genoa, Italy. Both her son's account and contemporary letters suggest that there was deep reluctance on Burnett's part. From the outset the marriage was a disaster, and the couple lived separately after 1902. Townesend died in 1914.

Burnett had always been attracted to the country and to the ideas of good rule embodied in the country-house ideal. In 1898, after the divorce, Bur-

"IT SEEMED SCARCELY BEARABLE TO LEAVE SUCH DELIGHTFULNESS"—*Page 231*

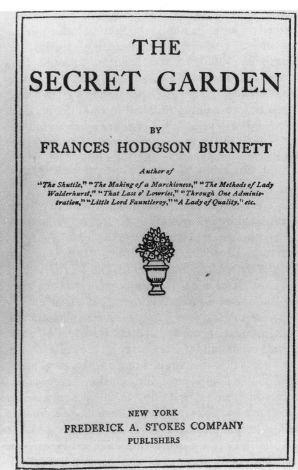

THE
SECRET GARDEN

BY
FRANCES HODGSON BURNETT

Author of

*"The Shuttle," "The Making of a Marchioness," "The Methods of Lady
Walderhurst," "That Lass o' Lowries," "Through One Administration," "Little Lord Fauntleroy," "A Lady of Quality," etc.*

NEW YORK
FREDERICK A. STOKES COMPANY
PUBLISHERS

Frontispiece and title page for Burnett's most acclaimed book

nett leased a country house, Maytham Hall at Rol-
venden in Kent, where she indulged her passions
for gardening and genteel patronage. Maytham was
her home in England for almost ten years. Burnett
had always loved gardens – her childhood memoir
describes in vivid detail the gardens of one home
which she significantly remembered as "The Back
Garden of Eden" – and Maytham boasted several
walled gardens of which one, the rose garden, became the writer's outdoor workroom and held a
special place in her imagination. Burnett wrote several of her books in this bower and began to entertain ideas that would be the genesis of *The Secret
Garden.*

The Queen Crosspatch series of stories, which
include fantasy and fairy-tale elements, appeared in
St. Nicholas between 1906 and 1909. The series is
narrated by a bad-tempered fairy, and the first
story, "The Troubles of Queen Silverbell" (1906),
relates the manner by which Queen Silverbell loses
her personified fairy "Temper" and is transformed
into an ill-tempered being. Her metamorphosis is

due to the disbelief of humans, particularly of children, which is causing consternation and loss of
powers among the fairy population. The now cross
queen decides that she will have to commission her
amanuensis, a thinly disguised version of Burnett
herself, to write thousands of books about what fairies are doing in order to restore the faith of humanity and the life of fairyland. The most entertaining
of the series is "Racketty-Packetty House" (1906),
later dramatized for the 1912 opening of the
Children's Theater in New York. Burnett loved
dolls and dollhouses, which she kept for young visitors. The doll inhabitants of the shabby and neglected Racketty-Packetty House are chiefly remarkable for their good natures and cheerfulness,
in opposition to the snobbery of those of the fashionable dollhouse, Tidy Castle.

In 1907 Burnett returned to the United States.
Her lease at Maytham was terminating, and the following year she purchased land at Plandome, Long
Island, where she set about building a fine Italianate
villa. Vivian, whose career was in publishing, was

involved with the *Children's Magazine,* and Burnett agreed to act as its nominal editor and also submitted one of her earlier "hair-curling" stories, *The Good Wolf* (1908), for serialization. A sequel, *Barty Crusoe and His Man Saturday* (1909), and *The Land of the Blue Flower* (1909) also appeared in Vivian's magazine before being published in book form. Both *The Good Wolf* and *Barty Crusoe* are episodic stories, reflecting their genesis as oral tales. The books are framed by the narrative of a little boy, Tim, whose mother relates stories to him while she does his hair, just as Burnett had originally told the stories. In the first tale Barty is taken by the Good Wolf to a Snow Feast, held by the animals in the forest. In its use of the rabbit warren as a venue and the motif of magical variations of size, the story reflects elements of Carroll's *Alice's Adventures in Wonderland.* In the second story the Good Wolf takes Barty, who has been reading Daniel Defoe's *Robinson Crusoe* (1719), on a journey to a desert island where they meet some helpful animals, including a monkey named Saturday. Barty and friends are invited to a tea party by the Perfectly Polite Pirates, who engage in a battle with a rival band, the Impolite Pirates, emerging victorious because their domestic harmony has allowed them more time to keep their weapons in order. The books are didactic and, in keeping with their oral storytelling origins, are full of direct address to the child audience. When published in book form, the stories were lavishly illustrated, with pictorial frames depicting the elements of the written narrative at the head and foot of each page.

Burnett's *The Land of the Blue Flower* is another fantasy. Young Prince Amor is sent to the mountain from the corruption of the court to learn the ancient ways of kingship. Through his mentor, a wise old man known only as "the Ancient One," the boy learns nobility and a sense of the deep meaning and purpose of existence through acquaintance with the miraculous glories of the created world. Prince Amor tends a marvelous walled garden, which once belonged to a sad young queen but grows wild after her death. Amor plants a seed from an emperor's secret garden brought to him by a swallow, and a miraculous blue flower emerges. When Amor returns to the plains of his kingdom, he finds poverty, dissension, and despair. He makes a law requiring all citizens to plant and tend a blue flower. In the process of working in the garden, they discover health, self-respect, charity, and the communal values of responsibility. Burnett's version of the dictum "tend your garden" upholds a providential view of creation and celebrates a sense of a purpose and meaning in the lives of human beings. The novel antici-

pates elements of *The Secret Garden,* and its themes include the replacement of misrule by wise and beneficent rule and the restoration of health and harmony to a society which had degenerated from its ancient wisdom and oneness with the created world.

The first decade of the twentieth century also gave rise to the second of the three children's classics for which Burnett is chiefly remembered. Burnett's play adaptation of *Sara Crewe* had been produced in London in 1902 as *A Little Unfairy Princess* but was not a remarkable success. However, the New York production in January of the following year – this time titled *A Little Princess* – won acclaim and popular success which rivaled that of *Little Lord Fauntleroy.* Scribners, Burnett's usual New York publishers, saw a chance to cash in on the success of the play and suggested that the writer rework *Sara Crewe* to incorporate the new material. The result was *A Little Princess.*

Sara's story is probably the most classic version of the Cinderella archetype in Burnett's fiction. The daughter of a young officer in India, she is placed at Miss Minchin's Select Seminary in London, where she is to receive the appropriate education for a young English lady. Although indulged in her every whim by her doting father, Sara remains unspoiled and unaffected, retaining her innate wisdom and dignity even when a shocking reversal of fortune occurs. When her father dies in India, apparently ruined, she is reduced to the status of a domestic slave by the cruel and mercenary stepmother figure, Miss Minchin. Sara rises above her humiliation to demonstrate to all that she is every inch a princess, whatever her station. Sara Crewe, like Cedric Errol before her, is a symbol of the idea that true nobility does not lie in the accidents of birth and fortune but is an inner quality of mind and heart. Eventually Sara is discovered by her father's friend and business partner – the guilt-stricken agent of his supposed "ruin" – and is restored to wealth, family life, and her true status as a little "princess."

When reduced to poverty Sara uses the power of her imagination to transform her reality. She pretends that she is a princess in order to behave like one, and she pretends that her cheerless attic is a gorgeous appartment, complete with fire and food, in order to bring comfort to herself and her fellow slave, Becky. By means of a fairy-tale pattern of events, the imagined change eventually becomes real. In this emphasis on the power of thought, which she dubs "magic," Burnett anticipates the extended development of this idea in *The Secret Gar-*

den. Moreover, Sara Crewe has elements of her creator, as revealed in Burnett's memoir and letters. She is a born storyteller, holding her classmates enthralled with her thrilling narrations; she acts out stories with the help of her doll.

Burnett's next children's book would become her most acclaimed work. Like *A Little Princess, The Secret Garden* also celebrates the power of the imagination to transform lives. Orphaned by a cholera epidemic in India, Mary Lennox is sent to live with her misanthropic uncle, Archibald Craven, at Misselthwaite Manor, on the edge of the Yorkshire moors. Abandoned to the care of servants, Mary spends her time out-of-doors in the wintry gardens. There she meets a robin, who shows her the way to the secret walled garden, which has been locked up since an accident occurred there ten years before, killing Craven's wife. In this place Mary finds her way to physical and spiritual health, through exercise, communion with other living things, and the joy of the yearly miracle of nature's rebirth.

Mary discovers another secret at Misselthwaite, the existence of her tyrannical and hypochondriac cousin, Colin. With the help of Dickon, a Yorkshire boy who lives on the moor, Mary takes Colin into the secret garden, where he too finds health and regeneration. In the process of their transformation, the children bring redemption to the fallen adult world they inhabit. By regaining health and hope, Colin inspires love and renewal in his emotionally damaged father.

Far from being the exemplary and idealized characters of Burnett's earlier fiction, the two main protagonists of *The Secret Garden* begin as thoroughly unattractive children. As the opening sentence of the novel relates, "When Mary Lennox was sent to Misselthwaite Manor to live with her uncle, everybody said she was the most disagreeable-looking child ever seen." Even more unflattering is Burnett's description of Mary as "tyrannical and selfish a little pig as ever lived." The children's malaise is attributed to lack of love and poor parental governance. Unwanted by her vain, socialite mother and her busy, sickly father, Mary has grown up physically and morally stunted. Starved of affection, she has been cared for by Indian servants, who must obey the child, rather than being able to guide and teach. Colin has been subjected to a similar neglect and misrule through both his father's rejection and the obsequious coddling of the manorial retainers.

The book reiterates the theme of illness, both physical and social, which afflicts the children because it afflicts the adult world which has formed them. Mary's uncle is another "disabled" parent.

One of Charles Robinson's illustrations for The Secret Garden

The tragic death of his pregnant wife has left him emotionally crippled. Too cowardly to accept his familial responsibilities as "Lord of the Manor," the "craven" parent seeks solace in foreign travel. When Mary arrives, he abandons her to her fate, just as he has done with his son. The redemption of Craven by his niece and son ensures the return of good rule to the ancient country house, a leadership which will be rightfully and successfully passed from father to son in accordance with tradition.

If the house is a place of masculine rule, the garden is a place of maternal fertility and rebirth. The strong symbolic structures of *The Secret Garden* account for much of its emotional power as a narrative. The pattern of fall and redemption is associated with the biblical Fall of mankind. The locked garden is a version of the Garden of Eden, representing a lost paradise of love and idyllic happiness. In the tradition of medieval romance the walled garden (often a rose garden) symbolized love, female sexuality, and fertility. The secret garden was initially a garden of love, and it symbolically remains a feminine place, the place of the maternal spirit, to which females bring the males to find healing. In the garden the spirit of Lilias (Colin's mother) watches over the regeneration of the children, employs the robin and Susan Sowerby – Dickon's mother – as her providential agents, and finally, when the time is right, calls her suffering husband back to the garden.

The Secret Garden also invokes nature myths. Burnett uses the cycle of the seasons with their traditional associations of regeneration and rebirth. Spring represents the rebirth of life after the death of winter. As Phyllis Bixler observes, Mary arrives at Misselthwaite in the winter, begins her work in the garden in the spring, and enjoys the regeneration of new life in the garden with Colin and Dickon in the summer. Colin's father returns in the autumn to witness the new life and love the children have harvested in the garden.

Dickon represents a version of the spirit of nature. He has elements of Pan, Saint Francis, and even Christ, with his ability to make lamb and fox lie down together. His mother is an archetypal earth mother. All-knowing when it comes to children, Sowerby becomes a surrogate mother for those who have been abandoned by their own guardians. The Yorkshire bluntness and plain speaking of Mrs. Medlock, the housekeeper, and her daughter Martha have a beneficial effect on the children and their guardian, who have been ruined by too much deference and too little truth about themselves and their failings. Burnett uses the Yorkshire people and their dialect to represent health: a closeness to nature and to an ancient folk wisdom which the more sophisticated world has lost.

But *The Secret Garden* is not merely an Edenic or pastoral myth. It is also a story of a child's quest for her own place. Mary is a little detective engaged in finding clues which will lead her to the garden. In the process she also finds love, companionship, and independence. Martha's rough advice to Mary and her lack of coddling foster the little girl's self-reliance. She becomes more independent. Mary is determined to find out things for herself; she explores the house, which opens all its secrets and mysteries to her. In descriptions of the ancient house Burnett gives her readers much of the luxurious detail which she considered particularly delightful to children. In this she was no doubt correct. The rich descriptions of the house of ghosts and neglect – with its many rooms, its antique pictures and toys, its mice living among the brocade cushions, its abandoned lives and artifacts from past generations – add an atmosphere of Gothic mystery.

In a house of misrule the servants have their own domain, free from any rule by master or mistress. Mary, too, is free from adult rule. In this case it is beneficial, since the authority at Misselthwaite is not trustworthy. In her search for the garden Mary seeks not only the forbidden and the exotic, but also a place of her own, free from the notice and interference of others:

> It was because it had been shut up so long that she wanted to see it. It seemed as if it must be different from other places and that something strange must have happened to it during ten years. Besides that, if she liked she could go into it every day and shut the door behind her, and she could make up some play of her own and play it quite alone, because nobody would ever know where she was but would think the door was still locked and the key buried in the earth.

The notion of a private and secret place awakens her dormant imagination as later it will do for Colin.

Burnett skillfully controls the elements of her craft, moving easily between the use of reported thought and speech, authorial direct address to a child audience, and more dramatic use of dialogue and scene. Besides its descriptive power *The Secret Garden,* in keeping with its pastoral heritage, contains many poetic passages in which the bucolic children burst forth with praise of the joys of nature and the beauties of the garden.

The providential influence of Lilias's spirit repeats an idea suggested by Sara in *A Little Princess.* Burnett believed in the existence of an afterlife and made more extensive use of the occult in two novels which deal with interaction between the living and the dead: *In the Closed Room* (1904) and *The White People* (1917). Supernatural elements also exist in *The Little Hunchback Zia* (1916), a specifically Christian fairy tale. Related to this theme is the emphasis on the power of the mind to promote positive regeneration – a feature of several books Burnett wrote in the latter part of her career. *The Secret Garden* has often been read as a tribute to the doctrines of Christian Science. The influence of the "New Thought" movement, which included the ideas of Christian Science and Theosophy, is also evident in *The Lost Prince.*

The Lost Prince is a romance dealing with the theme of return of kingship and rightful rule. The young hero, Marco Loristan, is the son of an exiled "patriot" from Samavia, a small but ancient country now torn by a desperate civil war. As her earlier story "Eight Little Princes" demonstrates, Burnett had developed an interest in the history of Serbia, its nationalist aspirations, and its royal family. Her concerns over the war which had broken out in Europe, precipitated by political instability in the smaller nations, were reflected in her portrayal of the fictional eastern European country of Samavia.

Stefan Loristan, his son Marco, and their faithful retainer, the former soldier Lazarus, are forced to move from one European country to another in order to fulfill the conspiratorial aims of Loristan's secret patriotic diplomacy. As the civil war in Samavia threatens to disrupt the economic and political stability of Europe, the other, more powerful nations begin to take an interest in its affairs. One romantic solution to its long history of misrule seems to lie in the ancient legend of "the lost Prince." Five hundred years earlier, a bad king had succeeded to the throne of Samavia, introducing vice and want into a once-idyllic land. His misrule led to a popular insurrection to supplant him with his son – a noble, generous, and godlike youth. Young Prince Ivor, however, could not be found, and his murder was suspected. Factional warfare wracked the land, the king was assassinated, and the country became a "bone fought for by dogs." In time a messianic legend arose which held that Prince Ivor had survived the plots laid for his life and would one day return to Samavia to reinstitute proper rule and so save his embattled land. Marco is fascinated by this legend and the hint given by his father that he believes he knows where the descendant of the lost prince can be found.

Another boy fascinated by the legend of the lost prince is "the Rat," Jem Ratcliffe, a crippled boy about Marco's age, the son of a gentleman who has degenerated into a life of drunkenness and ill company. Marco meets Rat in the streets of London where the cripple has gathered around him a squad of Cockney street children. He drills them with martial precision and invents adventurous games for their amusement. One of the most exciting "games" invented by Rat for the squad involves the careful strategic planning of the way in which two boys, unsuspected because of their youth and apparent lack of strategic importance, might enter Samavia to alert the members of the secret party to the imminent rising. But the "game" becomes a reality as Marco and Rat are sent alone throughout Europe to gather the secret forces loyal to the lost prince. Following the successful uprising, the novel concludes with the coronation of the lost King Ivor. Marco at last discovers what the reader has sus-

Burnett in 1888

pected all along – that his own father, the godlike Stefan Loristan, is the rightful king of Samavia.

Burnett once more makes use of the exemplary character in Stefan Loristan, who is endowed with native majesty and inspires devotion in even those who do not know his lineage. He has inherited a commander's bearing, a king's consequence, a Stoic's virtue and self-command, and a patriot's sense of selfless devotion to duty. He is unfailingly benevolent to others and courteous to those of common descent, refusing to pride himself on his lineage. When Marco feels injured that other boys might think his father to be a common artisan, Loristan reproves him gently but firmly.

Marco also shares many of these qualities. Though as shabbily dressed as any other common boy, people perceive him as a gentleman and a young soldier. While the novel seems to emphasize the romance motif of the "born king," illustrious by virtue of an ancient bloodline, this idea is in tension with Burnett's environmental and Romantic notions of education, which present virtue or vice as a consequence of good or poor education. Marco has been educated in Rousseauesque fashion as a citizen of the world, his observations guided and directed by a virtuous adult mentor (his father). He has been strictly trained in virtue, philosophical conversation, self-command, and control over his own emotions and thoughts. Since he has witnessed only models of honor and probity in his everyday life, Marco is totally free of the baser emotions of fear, mistrust, and jealousy, all of which torment Rat. The romance motifs in this novel, then, include the return of the king, the anachronistic medievalism associated with Samavia, the sense of past times and glory surrounding the adventure of the young protagonists, and the quest structure.

Even more than *The Secret Garden,* where Colin wills himself to health, *The Lost Prince* stresses the power of the mind to affect a person's future through the visualization of a better state. This power also seems to take on a stronger spiritual and spiritualist resonance in the latter work. Marco believes in a place within, some borderland of the unknown of stillness and beauty, which leads him on his quest. Messages of faith and Providence are clear as Marco points Rat to the appropriate biblical reference: "[if] a man pray believing he shall receive what he asks it shall be given him," upon which Marco comments, "It's been said so often it makes you believe it."

Burnett's story has something of the folktale in its narrative style. The exemplary characters it presents, combined with the moral impetus of the narrative, make it less dramatic than her longer works such as *The Secret Garden* that feature greater character development. Initially the narration is from Marco's viewpoint. However, as the plot develops, the perspective shifts toward that of Rat. As an outsider Rat is distanced from the naive observational stance of the main protagonist, to lead the reader to solve the mystery of "the Lost Prince."

While *The Lost Prince* celebrates Burnett's love for Europe and its history, her last years were spent in the United States, of which she had been a citizen since 1905. She planted a magnificent garden at Plandome in which she indulged her love of horticulture. She also enjoyed the society of her family, particularly that of her two granddaughters, Verity and Dorin. Despite increasing ill health she continued to write. Her last effort was, appropriately enough, an essay on gardening, published posthumously in 1925 as *In the Garden.* She died on 29 October 1924, apparently of progressive heart disease.

Critical opinions about Burnett's adult fiction have labeled her as a second-rate "relic of Victorianism," increasingly irrelevant to a generation of readers attuned to the rising tide of twentieth-century modernism. However, her reputation as a children's writer remains undiminished – *The Secret Garden,* in particular, being justly acclaimed as a classic of the golden age of British children's literature.

Biographies:
Vivian Burnett, *The Romantick Lady (Frances Hodgson Burnett): The Life Story of an Imagination* (New York: Scribners, 1927);

Constance Buel Burnett, *Happily Ever After: A Portrait of Frances Hodgson Burnett* (New York: Vanguard, 1965);

Ann Thwaite, *Waiting for the Party: The Life of Frances Hodgson Burnett 1849–1924* (New York: Scribners, 1974).

References:
William Archer, *World* (London), 23 May 1888;

Phyllis Bixler, *Frances Hodgson Burnett* (Boston: G. K. Hall, 1984);

Bixler, "*Little Lord Fauntleroy:* Continuity and Change in Popular Entertainment," in *Children's Novels and the Movies,* edited by Douglas Street (New York: Ungar, 1983), pp. 69–80;

Bixler, "The Oral-Formulaic Training of a Popular Fiction Writer: Frances Hodgson Burnett," *Journal of Popular Culture,* 15 (Spring 1982): 42–52;

Madelon S. Gohlke, "Rereading *The Secret Garden,*" *College English,* 41 (April 1980): 894–902;

Elizabeth Lennox Keyser, " 'Quite Contrary': Frances Hodgson Burnett's *The Secret Garden,*" *Children's Literature,* 11 (1983): 1–13;

Marghanita Laski, *Mrs. Ewing, Mrs. Molesworth and Mrs. Hodgson Burnett* (New York: Oxford University Press, 1951);

Francis J. Molson, "Frances Hodgson Burnett (1848–1924)," *American Literary Realism,* 8 (Winter 1975): 35–41;

Molson, "*Two Little Pilgrims' Progress:* The 1893 Chicago Columbian Exposition as Celestial City," *Markham Review,* 7 (Spring 1978): 55–59.

Papers:
The Scribner Archives at the Princeton University Library has a large collection of Burnett's professional correspondence.

Lucy Clifford

(1853? – 21 April 1929)

Lois Rauch Gibson
Coker College

See also the Clifford entry in *DLB 135: British Short-Fiction Writers, 1880–1914: The Realist Tradition.*

BOOKS: *Children Busy, Children Glad, Children Naughty, Children Sad,* as L. C. (London: Wells, Gardner, 1881; New York: Nelson, 1881);

The Dingy House at Kensington, anonymous (New York: Munro, 1882);

Anyhow Stories, Moral and Otherwise (London: Macmillan, 1882); republished as *Anyhow Stories for Children* (London: Macmillan, 1885); revised and enlarged as *Anyhow Stories for Children* (London: Duckworth, 1899);

Marie May; or, Changed Aims, anonymous (London: Warne, 1884); as Clifford (London & New York: Warne, 1893);

Under Mother's Wing, as L. C. (London: Wells, Gardner, Darton, 1885; New York: Young, 1885);

Mrs. Keith's Crime: A Record, anonymous (London: Bentley, 1885); republished as *Mrs. Keith's Crime: A Novel* (New York: Harper, 1885); revised edition (London: Eveleigh Nash & Grayson, 1925);

Very Short Stories and Verses for Children, anonymous (London: Scott, 1886);

Love-Letters of a Worldly Woman (London: Arnold, 1891; New York: Harper, 1892; enlarged edition, London: Constable, 1913);

The Last Touches and Other Stories (London: Black, 1892; New York & London: Macmillan, 1892);

Aunt Anne (London: Bentley, 1892; New York: Harper, 1892);

A Wild Proxy (London: Hutchinson, 1893); republished as *A Wild Proxy: A Tragic Comedy of To-day* (New York: Cassell, 1893);

A Grey Romance (London: Allen, 1894);

A Flash of Summer; The Story of a Simple Woman's Life (London: Methuen, 1894); republished as *A Flash of Summer: A Novel* (New York: Appleton, 1894);

"Dear Mr. Ghost": A Christmas Story (London: Dean, 1895);

Mere Stories (London: Black, 1896); republished as *The Dominant Note, and Other Stories* (New York: Dodd, Mead, 1897);

A Woman Alone (New York & London: Macmillan, 1898); enlarged as *A Woman Alone, Three Stories* (London: Methuen, 1901);

The Likeness of the Night. A Modern Play in Four Acts (London: Black, 1900; New York: Macmillan, 1900);

A Long Duel: A Serious Comedy in Four Acts (London & New York: Lane, 1901);

Woodside Farm (London: Duckworth, 1902); republished as *Margaret Vincent: A Novel* (New York & London: Harper, 1902);

The Getting Well of Dorothy (London: Methuen, 1904; New York: Dutton, 1917);

The Way Out (London: Daily Mail, 1904);

A Honeymoon Tragedy. A Comedy in One Act (London & New York: French, 1904);

The Modern Way (Eight Examples) (London: Chapman & Hall, 1906);

The Shepherd's Purse [A Play] (Cambridge: Macmillan & Bowes, 1906);

Proposals to Kathleen (New York: Barnes, 1908);

Plays: Hamilton's Second Marriage; Thomas and the Princess; The Modern Way (London: Duckworth, 1909; New York: Kennerley, 1910);

Sir George's Objection (London & New York: Nelson, 1910; New York: Duffield, 1910);

A Woman Alone, in Three Acts (London: Duckworth, 1915; New York: Scribners, 1915);

The House in Marylebone: A Chronicle (London: Duckworth, 1917);

Mr. Webster, and Others (London: Collins, 1918);

Miss Fingal (Edinburgh & London: Blackwood, 1919; New York: Scribners, 1919);

Eve's Lover, and Other Stories (New York: Scribners, 1924);

The Searchlight. A Play in One Act (London & New York: French, 1925).

SELECTED PERIODICAL PUBLICATION –
UNCOLLECTED: "A Supreme Moment. A Play in One Act," *Nineteenth Century,* 46, no. 7 (July 1899): 153–172.

In her own day, Lucy Clifford was a respected novelist and playwright whose works were translated into foreign languages and published in both legitimate and pirated editions outside England. Her first book was a collection of poems and stories for children titled *Children Busy, Children Glad, Children Naughty, Children Sad* (1881) and inscribed, "stories by L. C." It sold thirty-one thousand copies and was attributed by some to Lewis Carroll. Although

her most commercially successful works were her adult novels *Mrs. Keith's Crime: A Record* (1885), *Love-Letters of a Worldly Woman* (1891), and *Aunt Anne* (1892), Clifford is primarily remembered for her friendships with such influential literary figures as Henry James, Rudyard Kipling, George Eliot, James Russell Lowell, Oliver Wendell Holmes, Leslie Stephen, and Violet Hunt, and her children's book *Anyhow Stories, Moral and Otherwise* (1882). This book, particularly the story "The New Mother," firmly established Clifford's reputation as a children's author.

Clifford was born Sophia Lucy Lane in Barbados, British West Indies, around 1853. Her father, John Lane, was a prosperous planter, and her grandfather Brandford Lane was Speaker of the House of Assembly. She spent her girlhood in the English countryside near Eltham Palace with her maternal grandmother. In a 1920 interview for *Windsor* magazine Clifford implied that her girlhood was not particularly interesting and claimed that she was not what might be called a "literary child," but she did read "everything that came in her way, especially the old novelists and poets." She also showed some early talent as a writer: as a young girl she had several of her stories published in Cassell's magazines.

She later studied art in London, where she met the brilliant Cambridge mathematics professor and philosopher William Kingdon Clifford, whose close friends included Charles Darwin, Herbert Spencer, John Tyndall, and Thomas Huxley. On 7 April 1875 Lane and Clifford were married. The Cliffords shared a love of literature, travel, and children, and their home became a meeting place for scientific, literary, and other friends of almost every taste and opinion imaginable. They were also regular visitors at Eliot's gatherings, where Clifford was one of the few women.

The Cliffords traveled widely, especially after the spring of 1876, when William showed signs of serious pulmonary disease. When he died at age thirty-four on 3 March 1879, Clifford was left with two young daughters to support. With the help of Eliot and others, she received a small Civil List pension of eighty pounds. She had published occasional writings earlier – at least one story appeared in the *Quiver* in 1877 – and she now began to write for a living, beginning with reviews in the *Standard*.

Her first published book, *Children Busy, Children Glad, Children Naughty, Children Sad,* included some stories apparently written for her own children. It was a critical and commercial success, so far exceeding the publishers' expectations that they sent her a generous addition to the twenty guineas they had originally paid. Still, it is not really her best work and was undoubtedly attributed to Carroll because of the shared initials. Conventional in subject and style, these short poems and stories bear little resemblance to Carroll's unique blend of sophisticated wit, imaginative fantasy, and nonsense. Clifford's frequently personified flowers and animals are sweet rather than intriguing. In "The Violets" a small boy gathers flowers to sell so he can buy breakfast for his poor, sick mother, and the violets sigh in sympathy. In "The Children and the Garlands" the pale, sickly protagonist worries that the "poor roses" whose leaves are drooping may be "lonely away from the garden" and kindly has them sleep near him; they reciprocate by sighing and stealing softly into his cheeks as he sleeps. The setting of the poem "Round the Tea Table" mildly echoes a scene from Carroll's *Alice's Adventures in Wonderland* (1865), but no Mad Hatter appears in Clifford's treatment. Instead, "the dollies all seem very glad" to have a "nice little party," and party and poem end with the children promising to sing the dolls a song which "shall not be sad . . . and shall not be long." The "Song," taken up by the following poem in the collection, does have a surprisingly violent chorus ("Time to cut off the dickie birds' noses"), but the verses in this book are generally pleasant and rhythmic. Two poems ("Come Home, Father" and "A Coming Down the Street") deal with a father's absence and the children's eagerness for his return, a theme common in Clifford's books. In these poems the father is expected; in many other stories and poems he has died – as the father of Clifford's children had. Frequently Clifford's families are headed by strong, loving, independent women.

Of the stories in this volume, two deserve special comment. "The Duck Pond" fictionalizes an incident that occurred while the Cliffords were vacationing in Wales in 1877. On this particular holiday William Clifford constructed a duck pond for a family of ducks his little daughter enjoyed feeding at a roadside ditch. Unfortunately a local authority thought the pond was too close to the highway and filled it with dirt. Clifford's version of the event is clearly designed to please children, especially her two daughters, Ethel (who later became a poet) and Amelia; she emphasizes the fictional little girl's reactions: joy in feeding ducks and chickens, fear of an old turkey who "was so fond of her it would run after her until she screamed," and fascination with two black pigs that came and stared at her. She also describes the father's "blue eyes, and [his] voice that you seemed to hear with your heart" and alludes to the fact that the beloved father has now died. Clifford alludes also to the origins of her daughters' nicknames, Blue Eyes (after the trait she shared with her father) and the Turkey. The two girls in her best-known story, "The New Mother," have these names.

The other noteworthy story in her first book is "The Light on the Hills," about a boy struggling to paint the beauty of the natural world before him. It employs themes that recur in many of Clifford's works: the beauty of the world and the role of art in conveying it; the importance of doing one's best; the power of love to inspire; and the closeness of sorrow to joy. All of these themes are interwoven as the boy brings joy to others with his work, which is inspired by love of his sister who has died.

The following year Clifford published the children's book for which she is best remembered, *Anyhow Stories, Moral and Otherwise.* Neither pure fan-

ANYHOW STORIES

MORAL AND OTHERWISE

BY

MRS. W. K. CLIFFORD

WITH ILLUSTRATIONS BY DOROTHY TENNANT

London

MACMILLAN AND CO.

1882

Frontispiece and title page for Clifford's collection of stories for children

tasy nor realistic fiction, *Anyhow Stories* combines philosophy and magic in its best tales and is merely moralistic in others; it is the only book published before 1891 to which Clifford willingly signed her name. Usually insisting on anonymity to avoid capitalizing on her late husband's reputation, she wrote in *Athenaeum* on 25 February 1893 that she allowed her name (Mrs. W. K. Clifford) to appear on the book because some of the stories "were an attempt to carry out an idea of my husband's." Clifford is referring primarily to a series of tales about a cobbler's son and the philosophy he learned from his dying father.

In "The Cobbler's Children," the first of the *Anyhow Stories*, a cobbler's son works at building the best little table he can, all the time thinking of his father's teachings about the beauty of the world and each person's responsibility to work well and to do good, to make the world better for everyone. With

his dying breath the cobbler advises his son that one must "do a thing as well as it can be done — that is all the great men do." These characters and ideas recur in several stories of the collection. For example, "In the Porch" reveals that the cobbler's daughter, seven-year-old Sarah Short, has also heeded her father's words: her sampler, on which she has stitched "Good works go on forever," inspires a discouraged artist to paint great pictures and so bring joy to many.

Other stories are less blatantly philosophical and more magical. In "The Story of Willie and Fancy," a particularly delightful allegory, Clifford exhibits a sense of humor probably directed toward parents. In Willie's boyhood, golden-haired Fancy leads him to the land of his dreams — beyond the seas and stars at the end of the world. But when school and work enter Willie's life, Fancy grows "small and thin and sad." Then the boy decides to be a lawyer, and "when Fancy heard that word, she fled away from him swiftly and for ever." But Fancy finds a permanent home with the blacksmith's daughter who is often "dreaming over her poetry books." Eventually the girl becomes a teacher, and the young lawyer, Willie, decides to marry her. The reason for his choice, Clifford's narrator adds whimsically, is "that the blacksmith's daughter had taken his Fancy."

Several stories have a less playful, more haunting quality, akin to the bittersweet tones of Hans Christian Andersen. In "The Imitation Fish" a child loves his toy fish, made of tin, but the fish worries that the boy will discover it is not real and reject it. Ironically, the boy worries that the fish *is* real and lonely; so he tearfully kisses it goodbye and throws it out to sea, where it is ignored by the real fish. They, unlike the child, know the difference between imitation and real. After a long, lonely stay underwater, the fish is washed ashore and retrieved by the child's mother. Relieved to think its loneliness is over, the fish learns that the child has died, but the fish remains to console the now-lonely mother. This sentimental and simple story is made significant by its many ironies and by its examination of the relationship between the real (nature) and an imitation (art).

Without question, most outstanding in *Anyhow Stories* is the unique and troubling "The New Mother." Reminiscent at times of fairy tales, and at times of the popular Victorian moral and cautionary tales, it also contains dark, Edenic undertones and veiled sexual imagery. Some readers have suggested that it recalls the primitive world of voodoo, about which Clifford may have heard in Barbados. But most striking is the mingling of the bizarre and the commonplace, the matter-of-fact presentation of strange, and even terrifying, events – characteristics later associated with Franz Kafka and, more recently, with the magic realists. Though "The New Mother" introduces the traditional conflict between good and evil, the conflict is never satisfactorily resolved: good is not victorious, and the sources of evil are left unexplained and mysterious. Furthermore, there is punishment for sin with no hope of redemption, and a loss of innocence without any gain in knowledge. The reader is left with no end to the terror the story arouses. Critic F. J. Harvey Darton recounts in his *Children's Books in England* (1932; third edition, 1982) how he found the book so full of pity and terror that he was haunted by it – and by the image of "The New Mother" – fifty years later.

The story begins like many Clifford tales, with a loving mother living alone in a cozy cottage with her two little girls and a baby, while their father is away at sea. The children are called Blue Eyes and the Turkey, the nicknames of Clifford's own daughters, and they are proud to help their mother by going off to the post office to see if there is a letter from Father. In the fairy-tale tradition of "Little Red Riding Hood," the mother warns them, "Don't be long. Go the nearest way and don't look at any strangers you meet, and be sure you do not talk with them." On the way to town the girls discover that they have missed a fair held the day before; they see a man with two dancing dogs, but they do not stop. In town there is no letter, and the girls slowly turn toward home. Just outside the village they come across a girl who is shabbily dressed and seems to have been weeping. The sisters forget their mother's warning and approach the strange-looking girl. Despite her unhappy appearance, she claims to be happy, rich, and a resident of the village, though the two children have never seen her there. She has hidden under her shawl something which at first they think is a baby but later discover is a peardrum with a mysterious little square box attached to one side. The girl claims that a little man and woman are in the box, and she talks into this box, describes the little people's clothes to the children, and says they dance "most beautifully" on the lid of the box. The good little girls long to see the little man and woman, and especially to learn a "secret" from the woman; but the strange girl claims only naughty children may do so. The temptation is enormous; the sisters try to be naughty, but they do not know how. Furthermore, their mother has warned them that if they misbehave, she will be forced to go away and be replaced by a "new mother" with a glass eye and a wooden tail.

But the children seem bewitched; they beg the strange girl to let them see the little people, but she calmly and cheerily refuses, scoffing both at the idea of "a new mother" (there is no such thing; they would be too expensive to make, she claims) and at the children's potential for misbehaving. Inevitably, despite their love for their mother and their cozy home, the children follow the strange girl's directive and misbehave, breaking crockery and clock and looking glass, dancing on the butter, dousing the fire; but no matter what they do, the girl insists they are not truly naughty. The children are pained by their mother's unhappiness and fearful of her leaving, yet they seem unable to wrench free of their guilty desire to learn the forbidden secret. Finally, their mother does leave, but when the strange girl passes their cottage at the appointed hour and the children ask once more to see the little man and

Engraved by C.H. Jeens from a Photograph by Barraud & Jerrard

Clifford's husband, William Kingdon Clifford

woman, she refuses, showing them only the empty box and chanting, "The little man and woman are far away. See, their box is empty." Of the children's mother, she sings, "No, she'll never come back, she'll never come back." As the girl dances farther and farther on her way out of town, the children hear her dreadful words, "Your new mother is coming. She is already on her way; but she only walks slowly for her tail is rather long. . . . she is coming – coming – coming."

The children rush home and desperately clean and tidy the home they have wrecked, but it is too late to recapture the lost innocence of the cozy cottage; remorse and repentance are to no avail. They hear "a sound of something heavy being dragged along the ground outside, and then there was a loud and terrible knocking on the door." Peeking out the window, they see the fearful figure clad in black, with what they assume are her glass eyes flashing beneath her black satin bonnet. She breaks the door, apparently with her wooden tail, and the children flee to the forest beyond the house, cast out forever from their home. They live on berries and nuts, occasionally stealing back to their lost home in which the dreadful new mother dwells.

The difference between this sophisticated and terrifying story and Clifford's usual tales for chil-

dren is striking. Not only is it more complex, but it also leaves the reader astounded and awed at the total disaster that befalls the children. The children's "sin" is misbehavior, along with an implied desire for sexual knowledge (the "secret"); but throughout they seem spellbound, trapped like the heroes in the Greek tragedies by their fate, over which they have little or no control. This is far more than a cautionary tale. Its rich texture and thematic complexities invite Christian, Jungian, Freudian, and other interpretations and continue to intrigue readers. In a 1990 article concerning "The New Mother," Heather Schell explores the sociological significance of the threat posed to a cozy middle-class home by the clearly lower-class girl with the peardrum. The influence of William Clifford's philosophy is also evident in the tale – he had written, "There is one thing in the world more wicked than the desire to command, and that is the will to obey." In this context the children's sin is primarily that of obeying the external authority of the strange girl rather than following their own instinctive desire to be good. But the conclusion still remains terrifying, and "The New Mother" remains the best known of all Clifford's many publications. *Anyhow Stories* was republished in 1885 and revised and enlarged in 1899. In 1976 Garland published a reprint edition of the work, which also included Clifford's story "The Wooden Tony: An Anyhow Story" (1892).

Not quite as impressive as "The New Mother" but a complex and interesting story nonetheless, "The Wooden Tony" presents a boy who seems not quite normal. The people in his Swiss village call him "Wooden-head" because they believe his "wits [have] gone a-wandering." Certainly, he perceives the world differently from most. At one point he tells his mother he wants to be both far away and still at home with her; that is, he wishes to be "little and far off," like people one sees in the distance, for that is the only way he can imagine being small enough again to lie in his mother's arms as he did when a baby – small enough so no one will ask him to do any tasks. Eventually Tony's wish is granted, but in a bizarre way. Two acts of artistic creation are involved: his father's carving out of wood a little woman; and Tony's learning of a strange, sweet song. A dealer comes from Geneva to buy carved figures from Tony's father and asks to take Tony and his song back with him. On the way down the mountain Tony moves more and more mechanically, like a puppet, singing and walking and getting stiffer all the time. When his parents come to look for him, they discover Tony as a little wooden figure inside a clock, playing his song when the door opens and standing beside the little woman his father had carved. This reversal of the Pinocchio story offers either a happy ending, about the immortality one gains through art, or an unhappy, symbolic withdrawal of a person who does not "fit," – or perhaps it suggests something else. Like "The New Mother," its complexities invite various interpretations, and the two little figures suggest simultaneously the innocence of dolls and the magic of voodoo. Like many other Clifford works, the story also introduces the contrast between art and nature.

In the spring of 1884 Clifford was in Italy working on *Mrs. Keith's Crime,* another psychologically interesting work, which she completed and published in England during the winter of 1885. Though not a children's book, it is largely about a mother's relationship with her children; it is Clifford's most controversial novel and firmly established her as a serious writer. Mrs. Keith, a young widow dying of consumption, poisons her consumptive daughter to spare her the further agony of a lonely and motherless end. Defending her choice of so painful a subject, Clifford wrote in the preface to the book's sixth edition, "Human life is often an agony borne in silence; and because of the silence it sometimes does not occur to us to give the sympathy and the help that might leaven it. Besides, it is surely the business of fiction to make us familiar with the joys and sorrows of life."

Her children's book *Under Mother's Wing* (1885), dedicated to her daughters, offers conventional stories and verse on conventional subjects: personified toys, cats, and birds; the evils of pride and boasting; and good and bad children. The poems are perhaps a bit livelier than the stories, but none is particularly noteworthy. In 1886 Clifford published a similar collection, *Very Short Stories and Verses for Children.* In 1893 Clifford was distressed when Warne republished, under her name, *Marie May; or, Changed Aims,* a semireligious girls' story previously published anonymously, first in a magazine in 1877 and then as a book in 1884; she felt that it was not up to her more recent standards, and that Warne was capitalizing on her reputation.

Perhaps because her own children were getting older, Clifford spent most of the rest of her career writing books for adults. Besides the unauthorized republication of *Marie May,* her only children's books published during the 1890s were *"Dear Mr. Ghost": A Christmas Story* (1895) and a revised and enlarged version of *Anyhow Stories for Children* (1899). During this decade, however, Clifford trav-

eled to the United States, incidentally discovering pirated editions of her *Love-Letters of a Worldly Woman* and other books. She also wrote several of her most successful novels, including *Aunt Anne; A Wild Proxy* (1893), Clifford's own favorite among her work; *A Flash of Summer; The Story of a Simple Woman's Life* (1894); and *A Woman Alone* (1898).

By this time Lucy Clifford had become widely known as a warm, charming woman of lively intelligence who made her home and her literary connections available to aspiring young writers. Her insistent recommendations to skeptical publishers led to the printing of Kipling's early writings. "Ruddy," as she called him, was a frequent visitor to her home, playing with her children and their cat, and perhaps learning some social graces from her, as Lord Birkenhead suggests in his 1978 Kipling biography. In a 1985 biography of Henry James, Leon Edel quotes James late in life, speaking of "that admirable Lucy Clifford – as a character, a nature, a soul of generosity and devotion."

By 1900 Clifford had begun writing and publishing plays, including *The Likeness of the Night* (1900); *A Woman Alone* (1915), adapted from her novel; and *The Searchlight* (1925). Meanwhile, Clifford continued to write novels and short stories, many with her trademark main character: a strong, resilient woman. Whether widowed, single, married, or with husband at sea, Clifford's woman would almost always struggle and prevail. Some reviews of Clifford's books complain about the absence of equally positive male characters; in fact, her children's books focus almost entirely on mothers and children. Yet Clifford often makes clearly antifeminist statements. More often than not she argues against social change and for following social and moral rules, even as she portrays sympathetically those who break the rules. In life as in her novels, Clifford tried to be both kind and socially correct.

In 1904 Clifford's last children's book, *The Getting Well of Dorothy,* was published. A 9 December 1917 *New York Times* review recommends it as a "Christmas book for young readers," calling it a "nice natural little story." To the reviewer's "nice" and "little," one might add "dear," invoking the three most frequently used words in the book. Though the book reveals Clifford at her most conventional, certain aspects of it arouse interest. Because Dorothy has been ill, her mother takes her traveling for her health, allowing Clifford to demonstrate her knowledge of sea travel and of foreign lands, such as Gibraltar, Genoa, and Switzerland. Events are filtered through Dorothy's eyes and those of her younger sister Betty. As in Clifford's other books, the family is without a father (he is far away and writes letters), devoted to one another, appreciative of beauty, and kind to others. Despite their conventional morality, Clifford's works are not religious in the manner of many other Victorian children's books – for example, even when Dorothy's family celebrates Christmas in Montreux, no one mentions God or church. However, her children's books are relentlessly wholesome, with the notable exception of that formidable story "The New Mother."

From 1904 until shortly before her death on 21 April 1929, Clifford continued to publish plays, novels, and short stories; contribute to the literary periodicals; hold her Sunday gatherings; and encourage young writers. Upon her death Clifford's obituary in the London *Times* emphasized her literary friendships and her many adult works; from a strictly critical standpoint these works are superior to most of those for children. But her masterpiece, "The New Mother," has attained near-classic status – praised by Darton, reprinted by Garland in 1976, and included in *The Oxford Book of Modern Fairy Tales* (1993). This story alone secures her reputation as a significant figure in the history of children's literature.

References:

Lord Birkenhead, *Rudyard Kipling* (New York: Random House, 1978), pp. 117–118;

Virginia Blain, Patricia Clements, and Isobel Grundy, eds., *The Feminist Companion to Literature in English* (New Haven: Yale University Press, 1990);

William Kingdon Clifford, Introduction, *Lectures and Essays,* volume 1, edited by Leslie Stephen and Sir Frederick Pollock (London: Macmillan, 1901);

F. J. Harvey Darton, *Children's Books in England: Five Centuries of Social Life* (Cambridge: Cambridge University Press, 1932); third edition, revised by Brian Alderson (Cambridge: Cambridge University Press, 1982);

Mary Angela Dickens, "A Chat with Mrs. W. K. Clifford," *Windsor,* 40 (March 1920): 483–485;

Leon Edel, *Henry James: A Life* (New York: Harper & Row, 1985);

Mrs. Belloc Lowndes, *The Merry Wives of Westminster* (London: Macmillan, 1946), pp. 62–66;

Alison Lurie, *Don't Tell the Grown-ups: Subversive Children's Literature* (Boston: Little, Brown, 1990), pp. 67–73;

Anita Moss, "Mothers, Monsters, and Morals in Victorian Fairy Tales," *Lion and the Unicorn,* 12 (December 1988): 44–60;

Wilfred L. Randell, "Mrs. W. K. Clifford," *Bookman,* 57 (January 1920): 136–138;

Heather Schell, "Clifford's 'The New Mother' and the Menace of the Lower Classes," *Turn-of-the-Century Women,* 5 (Summer/Winter 1990): 43–47.

Kenneth Grahame

(8 March 1859 – 6 July 1932)

R. J. Dingley
University of New England, New South Wales

BOOKS: *Pagan Papers* (London: Mathews & Lane, 1894; Chicago: Stone & Kimball, 1894);

The Golden Age (London: John Lane, 1895; Chicago: Stone & Kimball, 1895);

The Headswoman (New York & London: John Lane, 1898);

Dream Days (New York & London: John Lane, 1898);

The Wind in the Willows (London: Methuen, 1908; New York: Scribners, 1908);

Fun O' the Fair (London & Toronto: Dent, 1929);

The Kenneth Grahame Book (London: Methuen, 1932);

The Reluctant Dragon (New York: Holiday House, 1938);

First Whisper of 'The Wind in the Willows,' edited by Elspeth Grahame (London: Methuen, 1944; Philadelphia & New York: Lippincott, 1945);

Bertie's Escapade (Philadelphia: Lippincott, 1949);

Paths to the River Bank: The Origins of 'The Wind in the Willows' from the Writings of Kenneth Grahame, edited by Peter Haining (London: Souvenir, 1983).

OTHER: Eugene Field, *Lullaby-Land. Songs of Childhood,* selected, with a preface, by Grahame (New York: Scribners, 1897; London: John Lane, 1898);

A Hundred Fables of Aesop from the English Version of Sir Roger L'Estrange, introduction by Grahame (London & New York: John Lane, 1899);

The Cambridge Book of Poetry for Children, edited by Grahame, 2 volumes (Cambridge: Cambridge University Press, 1916; New York: Putnam, 1916; revised edition, Cambridge: Cambridge University Press, 1932; New York: Putnam, 1933);

"Lord" George Sanger, *Seventy Years a Showman,* preface by Grahame (London & Toronto: Dent, 1926).

Kenneth Grahame

For more than eighty years, Kenneth Grahame's works have been among the most widely read of English children's writers. In his 1959 biography of Grahame, Peter Green reports that *The Wind in the Willows* (1908) had gone into more than one hundred editions and had enjoyed an annual sale of about eighty thousand copies. The book has been dramatized for both the stage and motion pictures, including two separate animated versions in 1983. Its enduring popularity confirms A. A. Milne's claim, in his introduction to a 1940 edition, that *The Wind in the Willows* is "a Household Book; a book which everybody in the household loves, and quotes continually, a book which is read aloud to every new guest and is regarded as the touchstone of his worth." Milne's rather complacent assertion, however, passes off as universal what is probably a rather more limited appeal. The "household" of which he speaks is unquestionably middle-class, moderately well-off, and most likely English. Its enthusiasm for Grahame's writing derives from his ability to articulate its most deeply cherished images of itself, to communicate deeply felt needs of his own that are also culturally representative. The circumstances of Grahame's life are thus crucial to an assessment both of his achievements and of his limitations.

Kenneth Grahame was born in Castle Street, Edinburgh, on 8 March 1859. He was the third child and second son of Bessie and James Cunningham Grahame, a well-liked advocate and gastronome who paid more attention to his table than to his legal practice. The Grahame family was a thoroughly prosperous and respectable one, and the only creative writer it had produced prior to Kenneth was his great-granduncle, James Grahame, whose lengthy and somber poem *The Sabbath* (1804) had briefly attracted George Gordon, Lord Byron's ironic attention in *English Bards, and Scotch Reviewers* (1809). Apart from this one outbreak of imaginative energy, the Grahames had mostly devoted their labors to the law and to finance, a tradition which was to have an unfortunate impact on Kenneth's future.

In 1860 Cunningham Grahame made the surprising decision to leave his moderate practice and flourishing social life in Edinburgh and accepted an appointment as sheriff-substitute of Argyll, which necessitated a move to Inveraray in the western Highlands. For all of the Grahame children this seems to have been a happy time, but it ended abruptly after only four years. In March 1864 Bessie Grahame gave birth to a fourth child, Roland, and then, within a few weeks, she died from scarlet fever. On the day of her death Kenneth, too, became infected, and for some time his life was in danger. He recovered very slowly, and the disease left him with a tendency to suffer from bronchial illness. But of more immediate concern was the effect on Cunningham Grahame of his wife's death. They

had been a devoted couple, and the loss proved devastating. Grahame's father lapsed into a lethargic depression, and what had earlier passed for heavy social drinking rapidly became unmistakable alcoholism. The children were sent away to their maternal grandmother at Cookham Dene in Berkshire, and the father remained alone at Inveraray.

The removal to England marked a significant change in Grahame's life. His grandmother Mrs. Ingles was a strict Presbyterian in her sixties, with a limited income, and she conducted her duties as a surrogate parent with correctness rather than enthusiasm. But her large, sprawling house, the Mount, and its smaller successor, Fernhill Cottage at nearby Cranbourne, became for the Grahame children, and for Kenneth in particular, places of adventure and delight whose memory was later to inspire *The Golden Age* (1895) and *Dream Days* (1898). The absence of both mother and father seems to have created a gulf between the children and adults, so that even the amiable uncle David, a clergyman who lived with Mrs. Ingles and the children until his marriage in 1866, was no more than an occasional intruder into the jealously guarded world that the children formed for themselves. From an early date, too, literature began to play a significant part in that world. According to Grahame's sister Helen, while they were at Cranbourne, Kenneth first began to show an interest in poetry, reciting lines from William Shakespeare, then Thomas Babington Macaulay's *Lays of Ancient Rome* (1842), then Alfred Tennyson.

In 1866 Cunningham Grahame recalled his children to Inveraray, but the attempt to reconstitute his family turned out to be a dismal failure and lasted for less than a year. In 1867 he resigned from the judicial post, whose duties he could no longer competently fulfill, and went to France, where he lived for the next two decades as an English-language teacher. It appears that none of his children ever corresponded with him or saw him again. Kenneth certainly never spoke of his father, and his diary record of a brief visit to Le Havre in 1887 to attend Cunningham Grahame's funeral and to wind up his scanty estate is chillingly detached and businesslike. Yet in some ways the career of Cunningham Grahame conformed to a recurrent image in his son's writing – that of the outwardly respectable professional man who suddenly opts for bohemian liberation. It is as though, by re-creating Cunningham Grahame's flight from reality as a release into the pastoral, Grahame was exorcising a part of his past which was too painful for direct confrontation. The memory of childhood as a golden age had to be preserved intact.

But by 1868 childhood was already drawing to a close, for Grahame was sent off to Saint Edward's School in Oxford (an event which is probably commemorated in the story "Lusisti Satis"). Rather surprisingly, perhaps, for a reclusive and sensitive Victorian child, his school career seems to have been anything but traumatic. Despite bronchial troubles he became a good all-around sportsman, and his academic ability was recognized with a succession of prizes; in 1874 he became senior prefect, and he always afterward referred to his school days with pious affection. He seems to have developed a capacity to blend in with his surroundings and conform to expectations while preserving a vulnerable, private self – a talent that would continue into his adult life.

The other abiding legacy of Grahame's school years was a deep love of Oxford and of the values it appeared to embody. He saw the university as a repository of age-old traditions and the guardian of a particular and privileged kind of classical culture. Grahame left Saint Edward's School a competent classicist, but his conception of the value of Greek and Latin, as well as of the university which devoted itself to them, had more to do with being a gentleman than with being a scholar, and his knowledge was employed in making telling allusions and apt quotations rather than as a means of access to the ancient world.

As his school days ended, Grahame no doubt saw entry to the university, to be followed preferably by a not-too-demanding academic career, as the natural next step. But family tradition, in which universities had played little part, intervened, and his uncle John Grahame, who held the purse strings, insisted that Grahame seek employment as a gentleman-clerk at the Bank of England. This frustration of Grahame's hopes meant that for the rest of his working career he would have to exist simultaneously in two worlds – the public world of professional obligations on the one hand and the private world of cultivated bookmanship on the other. The two worlds would have been perfectly adjusted in an academic milieu, but they were separate in that of a banker.

Yet the instinctive conformism which had ensured Grahame's smooth passage through Saint Edward's also went far to reconcile him to the Bank of England, which he joined on New Year's Day 1879. In addition, residence in London put him into stimulating contact with a metropolitan culture from which he would have been exiled by permanent incarceration in an Oxford college. A chance meeting in a Soho restaurant, for example, led to a

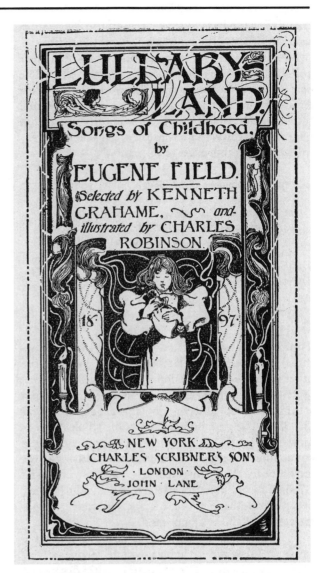

Title page for Grahame's edition of children's verses by Eugene Field

lasting friendship with Frederick James Furnivall, one of the most flamboyant and energetic figures of the Victorian literary scene. Through him Grahame made his first contacts with writers, and with Furnivall's guidance and encouragement he made a practice of jotting down poems and short prose pieces.

The next ten years were uneventful. Grahame's work at the bank required little exertion, and he was able to spend a good deal of his time exploring London and the Thames, discovering Italy, and generally pursuing the self-indulgent career of a well-heeled bachelor. In 1888 his first piece was published in the *St. James's Gazette,* and in 1891 he found a regular outlet in the *National Observer,* whose bellicose editor, W. E. Henley, became a personal friend. For the next four years, until the *National Observer* folded, Grahame was a frequent contributor, producing nearly forty items, many of which were collected in his first book, *Pagan Papers* (1894). The essays in *Pagan Papers* struggle to emulate Robert Louis Stevenson, but they lack his intellectual toughness. Grahame's stylistic preciosity, instead of generating irony and paradox, often seems merely inflated, as in this passage in "Orion":

> Truly, we Children of the Plough, but for yon tremendous Monitor in the sky, were in right case to forget that the Hunter is still a quality to reckon withal. Where, then, does he hide, the Shaker of the Spear? Why, here, my brother, and here; deep in the breasts of each and all of us! And for this drop of primal quicksilver in the blood what poppy or mandragora shall purge it hence away?

The first sentence seems little more than a cumbersome imitation of seventeenth-century prose (Sir Thomas Browne was among Grahame's favorite authors), but the mannered archaisms serve no purpose other than to draw attention to themselves. The final sentence, similarly, exists chiefly in order to provide a setting for an allusion to Shakespeare's *Othello* (3.3.335). The gratuitous artifice of the whole passage, moreover, fatally undercuts the message it is trying to communicate: seldom can humanity's predatory urge have been less threateningly articulated, and Grahame's attempt to get stern and manly ("Why, here, my brother, and here") appears merely incongruous amid all the daintiness.

Still, *Pagan Papers* retains some interest because it introduces themes which recur in Grahame's later work. The collection's title declares a faith that both underwrites *The Wind in the Willows* and is also characteristic of its period. For a generation in which orthodox Christian belief had been rendered problematic by science but which still hankered after some form of epistemological certainty, nostalgia for a slightly bowdlerized classical nature worship had obvious appeal. The years around the turn of the century saw an extraordinary resurgence of literary and artistic interest in the goat god Pan, a figure whose savage animal lusts could encapsulate a post-Darwinian version of the natural world but whose divine status could simultaneously invest nature with a spiritual presence. Pan, consequently, became the subject of a whole spectrum of creative treatments, ranging from the malign supernatural power of Arthur Machen's "The Great God Pan" (1894) to the gentle, elegiac figure encountered in James Stephens's *The Crock of Gold* (1912). Grahame's contribution, "The Rural Pan," which first appeared in the *National Observer* in 1891, is perhaps the most anodyne representation of the goat god to be found in the literature of the period. His Pan is the tutelary spirit of a timeless rustic England, shyly retreating before the advance of urban civilization and contemporary technology. The countryside over which this "kindly god" presides is an endangered haven where the world's cares can be forgotten and where the human inhabitants – shepherds and ditchdiggers – appear picturesque rather than functional.

Grahame's version of the Pan myth expresses little more than a nostalgic yearning for pastoral ease and innocence, a longing which would find more extended embodiment in *The Wind in the Willows* and which is unashamedly escapist. In *Pagan Papers* and in the other writings of this time, Grahame repeatedly introduces anecdotes of conscientious bourgeois executives who suddenly become possessed by a desire for flight and who abandon their desks and their responsibilities (though never their families; Grahame's fugitives are all bachelors). In "The Wayfarer" a secretary "to some venerable Company or Corporation that dated from Henry VII" impulsively sends in his resignation and spends his declining years wandering around Venice. "An old cashier in some ancient City establishment" passes his annual holiday "relieving some turn-pike man at his post" in order to observe "the flowing, hurrying, traveling, marketing Life of the Highway" ("The Eternal Whither"). The most notable feature of these stories, perhaps, is that in each case Grahame presents headlong retreat from everyday reality as a truly courageous option. Any contradiction between flight and adventure is eliminated and an impulse to escape into contemplative indolence is held in delicate balance with an urgent desire for novelty and exploration.

In addition to its inferior Stevensonian essays, the first edition of *Pagan Papers* contains six short stories about children. Over the next year or so Grahame wrote a further dozen episodes (some of which appeared in the influential literary magazine the *Yellow Book*), and early in 1895 he published all eighteen stories under the title *The Golden Age*. The unassuming little book met with an overwhelmingly favorable reception: A. S. Swinburne rhapsodized for two columns in the *Daily Chronicle*, and other admirers included Theodore Roosevelt (who repeatedly invited the reclusive Grahame to stay at the White House) and Kaiser Wilhelm II of Germany.

Of the several related reasons for the extraordinary success of *The Golden Age*, the first, unquestionably, is its originality. The book's five orphaned

Now don't you hit me

One of Ernest Shepard's illustrations for Grahame's The Reluctant Dragon

children in their rather remote country home have little or nothing in common with children in the works of Grahame's predecessors. The smugly virtuous children of Charlotte M. Yonge or of Louisa Molesworth are patterns of conduct to which the young reader is invited to conform (and even their infrequent lapses from grace inculcate useful moral lessons). Grahame's children, conversely, inhabit a world with largely autonomous values and regard the precepts of their elders (the "Olympians") with puzzled disdain. They learn not through adult instruction but from experience and observation, and the books they read are turned to uses different from those intended by the authors. In "A Holiday," for example, Edward, Harold, and Charlotte discuss the incident in John Bunyan's *The Pilgrim's Progress* (1678) where Christian walks between two chained lions on either side of his route to the Heavenly City – an incident designed to test his faith in a benignly protective God. For the children, however, the incident has been divorced from its original allegorical purpose and has become instead an enticingly hazardous prospect; indeed, the whole attraction of the passage resides for them in the possibility that the lions will slip their chains and devour the wayfarer.

The impact of this episode from "A Holiday" depends on the reader's recognition of the distance that separates the children's apprehension of Bunyan's work from its traditional interpretation. Such a reader is likely to be an adult, and this is the source of another clear distinction between Grahame and his most obvious predecessors: *The Golden Age* is written not for a juvenile but for a mature audience – an audience which can simultaneously delight in the freshness of the children's vision and perceive the limitations of knowledge and experience which make that freshness possible – as is clear in "The Argonauts," one of Grahame's subtlest and most tightly controlled narratives.

In the story Harold, Edward, and the narrator steal Farmer Larkin's boat, rechristen it the *Argo,* and proceed to explore the tiny local stream in search of Medea and the Golden Fleece. When the boys finally land, Edward characteristically strides off to inspect the local village, but the two younger children linger in a garden that "from the brooding quiet lapping it round, appeared to portend magical possibilities." As the young Argonauts puzzle over the inscription "TIME:TRYETH:TROTHE:" on a sundial, a woman whom they take to be Medea herself suddenly appears to them, "dark-haired, supple, of a figure lightly poised and swayed, but pale and listless." Greeting the children with delight, Medea enters into their games with "gusto and abandonment." Returning to the sundial, Harold asks Medea the meaning of its inscription, and her mood instantly changes: "They shut me up here – they think I'll forget – but I never will – never, never!" Another woman then approaches; she leads Medea away and dismisses the children. The two boys are then rejoined by Edward, and the expedition returns homeward, ingeniously evading the vengeful Farmer Larkin.

While the boys' encounter with Medea is clearly, for an adult reader, the story's central incident, the narrative structure works to reduce that centrality. For the children the discovery of the garden and its strange occupant is only one event in an intrinsically unconnected series, and, indeed, by the end of the story it seems to have been forgotten in the excitement of outwitting the irate farmer. Moreover, the identification of the young woman (whose name turns out to be Lucy) with Medea seems inappropriate: there is no real parallel between the homicidal witch of classical legend and the rather pathetic inhabitant of the neglected garden. For the children, of course, this discrepancy is unimportant, since for them the status of Medea is not a fixed quantity but can be adapted at will to suit the shifting needs of the adventure they are constructing. For adult readers, however, the curious mismatching of myth and reality is likely to constitute another of the story's disturbing features, another of the non sequiturs which Harold and the narrator find it so natural and so easy to accept. Adult readers, in fact, will almost certainly find other, closer analogues for Lucy/Medea of which the children are unaware. The boys do not understand the hints that suggest she is convalescing from a nervous breakdown after being jilted by a lover nor that this aligns her with a long Romantic literary tradition of imprisoned maidens. Harold and the narrator cannot recognize these things because, unlike the story's presumed reader, they are unable to deduce from Medea's broken sentences the adult sexual tragedy of which she has been the victim, and for them she simply takes her place among a select band of grown-ups capable of entering the child's world.

"The Argonauts," then, works on two levels. Re-creating the innocent perspective of the children, it nevertheless lays sufficient clues to enable experienced readers to construct an alternative story. This dual perspective is largely instrumented through an ambivalent narrative voice: the unnamed speaker in *The Golden Age* is both observer and participant, able both to express the naive vision of the child and to establish an ironic perspective on that vision. At the end of the book's prologue, the speaker asks plaintively of himself: "Can it be that I too have become an Olympian?" But anyone who can remember Arcady so vividly is clearly in no danger of joining his joyless aunts and uncles; rather, he is in the position of the book's "good" adults, capable of inhabiting both worlds and thus of conducting his readers into a similarly dual focus.

In a story such as "The Argonauts" this precarious balance is brilliantly sustained, but elsewhere it can result in embarrassing archness. As Roger Sale argues in *Fairy Tales and After* (1978), "Sawdust and Sin," where Charlotte's male doll Jerry sprawls across the female doll Rosa until she falls "flat on her back in the deadest of faints," is recounted in such a prurient tone that it exposes, rather than bridges, the rift between childish and adult viewpoints. The collection's successes, however, far outnumber its failures, and Grahame's double focus (to which some early reviewers took exception) enables him to embrace positions which might otherwise be mutually antagonistic: to present childhood as both heartlessly selfish and idyllically innocent; to assert that children are at the same time profoundly wise and amusingly ignorant; to portray prepubescence as a golden age while insisting that it needs to be outgrown. Grahame ultimately preserves the Romantic idealization of the child within a basically realistic narrative mode that seems to guarantee its truth and this reassuring formula proved instantly successful at the turn of the century, a time of intellectual uncertainty in which conventional wisdom was everywhere being subjected to skeptical reassessment.

Despite its episodic nature *The Golden Age* charts a sporadic progression through time and ends with the departure of Edward for his boarding school, signaling the breakup of the tightly knit group and prefiguring a far-from-golden future. The narrator describes Edward "as he would appear a short three months hence, ragged of attire and lawless of tongue, a scorner of tradition and an adept in strange new physical tortures, one who would in the same half-hour dismember a doll and shatter a hallowed belief" and concludes, "But which of us is of mental fibre to stand the test of a glimpse into futurity?"

But this did not mark the end of Grahame's dealings with Charlotte, Harold, Selina, and the narrator. Over the next few years he produced eight further episodes (three of them first appeared in *Scribner's* magazine, attesting to the author's popularity in the United States), collected as *Dream Days.*

The stories in this book are a good deal more disparate than are those of its predecessor, and some of them exhibit a decline in quality. Even so, *Dream Days* contains two of Grahame's finest achievements. The opening story, "The Twenty-First of October," begins with an observant account of the way in which children cultivate specialized private areas of knowledge. Selina, the elder girl, has turned herself into an expert on naval history, and on the anniversary of Adm. Horatio Nelson's great victory in 1805 at Trafalgar, otherwise universally ignored, she decides to mark the occasion in fitting style. Enlisting the uncomprehending support of Harold, she builds a great bonfire (the Olympians are temporarily absent) and piles it higher and higher in a kind of ecstatic frenzy:

> Selina, a Maenad now, hatless and tossing disordered locks, all the dross of the young lady purged out of her, stalked around the pyre of her own purloining, or prodded it with a pea-stick. And as she prodded she murmured at intervals, "I *knew* there was something we could do! It isn't much – but still it's *something!*"

The repeated "something" hints that Selina is less than fully conscious of the meaning of her actions, and the narrator seems equally unable to account for her uncharacteristically lawless fervor. But the glancing reference to Selina as a Maenad suggests a possible sexual origin for her excitement, so that the fire can be read as an expression of energies not yet understood but seeking forms of release. The bonfire thus becomes both a last climactic eruption of childhood play and a first step toward the emotional turmoils of adolescence. But progress toward maturity for Selina will also involve a subjection of her own desires to the socially acceptable but constricting norms of "ladylike" conduct (she is already, in fact, beginning to enjoy tea parties), and so the bonfire, with its originating cause in the world of masculine heroic action from which she is about to be excluded, can also be interpreted as a half-conscious gesture of protest against the passive role to which her sex will condemn her. The story's poignancy derives from Grahame's suggestion of a variety of motivations for Selina's action, ranging from her conscious intent, through her half-conscious defiance of adult restrictions, to an unrecognized expression of developing sexual energies. The implication of these different levels of consciousness evokes for the reader a liminal experience – the protagonist's rite of passage from the secure and known past to the uncertain future.

"The Reluctant Dragon," the penultimate story in *Dream Days,* is quite unlike anything else in the two collections – Grahame even had to devise an elaborate framing device to justify its inclusion. The title character is actually less reluctant than downright lazy, and it is, in fact, his indolence that has preserved him (a little like the fugitive clerks of *Pagan Papers*) when more "active and *earnest*" dragons have perished. After centuries of contented entombment underground, he decides to tunnel his way to the surface to do nothing more disruptive than contemplate the scenery and write poetry. Unfortunately the local villagers, though prepared to accept that the dragon is harmless, feel that convention demands his elimination; therefore they summon Saint George. Everyone, even the Boy who has befriended the dragon, feels momentarily elated at the prospect of a fight, but anxiety that some real injury might follow induces the Boy to bring dragon and saint together to arrange a peaceful compromise. The two stage a convincing battle which ends with the dragon's ritual submission, and the villagers, feeling that the proprieties have now been observed, accept him as a neighbor and throw a banquet.

On first inspection "The Reluctant Dragon" seems a rather slight achievement, a made-over fairy tale in which marvels and wonders are parodied as prosaic commonplaces, but it is thematically related to other significant preoccupations of the collection as a whole. The villagers, for example, occupy the role elsewhere allocated to the Olympians, but here their damaging lack of imagination is extended beyond the limited sphere of adult/child relations. The villagers are cruel (they bait "dogs, bulls, dragons," and even "a poor innocent badger," the Boy tells Saint George); they lie habitually (inventing examples of the dragon's harmful behavior); above all, they are enslaved by mindless and inflexible conventions: dragons *have* to be exterminated because that is the rule. These conventions, moreover, cannot be defied; they can only be circumvented by guile and on the condition that appearances be maintained. Saint George, the boy, and the dragon have to arrange a sham that will conform to the prejudices of the unthinking adult, human majority. Implicitly only saints, children, and animals are able to transcend ideological constraints, and since Saint George, though decent, is a rather stolid figure, and the boy, though wise, is a little disappointed when he thinks he is going to be cheated of the spectacle of bloodshed, the kindly dragon, the animal, alone fully emerges as an embodiment of positive value.

The decade between Grahame's first article in the *St. James's Gazette* and the publication of *Dream*

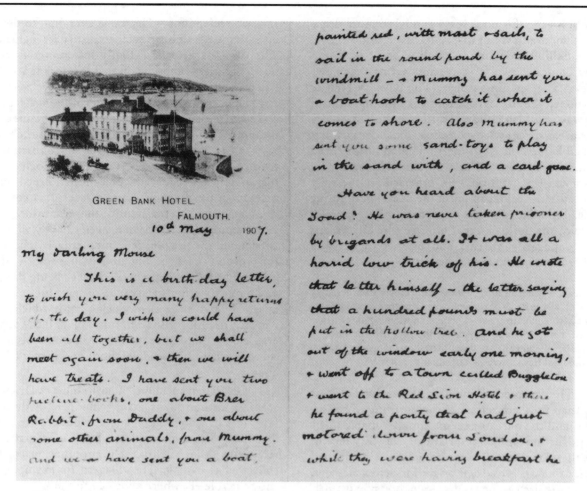

GREEN BANK HOTEL.
FALMOUTH.
10th May 1907.

My darling Mouse

This is a birthday letter, to wish you very many happy returns of the day. I wish we could have been all together, but we shall meet again soon, & then we will have treats. I have sent you two picture-books, one about Brer Rabbit, from Daddy, & one about some other animals, from Mummy. And we have sent you a boat, painted red, with mast & sails, to sail in the round pond by the windmill — & mummy has sent you a boat-hook to catch it when it comes to shore. Also mummy has sent you some sand-toys to play in the sand with, and a card-game.

Have you heard about the Toad? He was never taken prisoner by brigands at all. It was all a horrid low trick of his. He wrote that letter himself — the letter saying that a hundred pounds must be put in the hollow tree. And he got out of the window early one morning, & went off to a town called Buggleton & went to the Red Lion Hotel & there he found a party that had just motored down from London, & while they were having breakfast he

A letter from Grahame to his son, Alastair. It includes the beginning of the earliest written version of Grahame's The Wind in the Willows *(Ms. Misc d. 281, fol. 1ᵛ-2ʳ; Bodleian Library, Oxford).*

Days had been a productive and eventful one. He not only had written all of the essays in *Pagan Papers* and all of the short stories of childhood, but also had published a handful of poems, reviews, and introductions and, more importantly, his one foray into adult fiction, a short novella called *The Headswoman,* which had appeared in the *Yellow Book* in 1894 and was published separately by Lane in 1898. Also during this period, probably in 1897, Grahame met Elspeth Thomson, the thirty-six-year-old stepdaughter of a moderately distinguished barrister and politician named Fletcher Moulton. Denied a demanding formal education and unable to step into a responsible profession, Elspeth had no disciplined outlet for her energy; so she became a kind of fringe dweller in London's literary and artistic circles, where she met Grahame, by then a well-known author who was also a solid and successful professional man (in 1898 he became secretary of the Bank of England, one of its three highest executive officers).

Early in 1899 Grahame succumbed to one of his regular bronchial illnesses, and Elspeth bombarded him with fruit and often visited him without a chaperone. They began to correspond in a mawkish baby talk, and Grahame gradually discovered that he had become committed to an engagement. Asked by his sister Helen whether he intended to marry Elspeth, he replied despondently, " I suppose so; I suppose so." Their wedding took place at Fowey in Cornwall on 22 July 1899.

The marriage was a failure almost from the start, and their lives and interests, though generally pursued under the same roof, became increasingly separate as the years passed. They were united only by a doting love for their one child, Alastair, who was born prematurely in May 1900. The boy was blind in one eye and had severe defects in the other, and he became the object of his mother's exclusive and overprotective devotion. Elspeth seems to have lavished on the hapless Alastair all of the passion which had been thwarted in her marriage, and Grahame came to be partially excluded from the claustrophobic bonding of mother and son.

It seems likely that the most intimate moments shared by father and child, in the intervals between their frequent separations, came in the evenings when Grahame would invent tales for Alastair's delight. As early as 1904 he reports in a letter to Mrs. Stanley Ward telling Alastair (whom he called Mouse) "stories about moles, giraffes & water-rats (he selected these as subjects) till after 12." But not until 1907 were any of these tales written down. Grahame spent the summer of that year in London, while Elspeth and Alastair remained at home in Cookham Dene. Over the course of the season, he wrote a series of letters to Alastair that forms the basis, the "first whisper" as Elspeth later put it, of *The Wind in the Willows*. The purpose of the letters, it seems clear enough, was to continue a narrative which had already been begun in the evening storytellings, and the first letter begins in *medias res:* "Have you heard about the Toad? He was never taken prisoner by brigands at all. It was all a horrid trick of his. He wrote that letter himself — the letter saying that a hundred pounds must be put in the hollow tree."

After this unfamiliar opening, however, Toad immediately arrives at the Red Lion Hotel, steals a car belonging to "a party that had just motored down from London," and begins the series of adventures which, with a good deal of later embellishment, became chapters 6, 8, and 10 through 12 of the finished book. Chapters 1 through 5, which deal primarily with the story's other major characters, Rat, Mole, and Badger, and are not formed into a sequential narrative, made no appearance in the original letters and may well have been written later. Chapters 7 and 9, which are as much essays as episodes, were probably written last and inserted in an almost completed draft. After being rejected by the Bodley Head, the book was published by Methuen in October 1908.

Although *The Wind in the Willows* was put together in a rather haphazard way, the story's development is far from careless. The first five chapters cumatively establish the principal characters — the Mole, the Water Rat, the Toad, and the Badger — and their various dwellings (the leisurely Riverbank, opulent Toad Hall, and the ominous Wild Wood, home of stoats and weasels). The story gathers momentum when the reckless Toad, rebelling against the well-meant pressure of his friends, begins his series of adventures by stealing a car. Arrested and imprisoned, he escapes by disguising

Alastair Grahame

himself as a washerwoman and, after several further episodes, arrives back at the Riverbank, only to find that his home has been occupied by the lawless inhabitants of the Wild Wood. Under Badger's leadership, however, he, the Rat and the Mole recapture Toad Hall in a climatic battle which provides an epic conclusion to the book's events.

The gradual, even sporadic, development of *The Wind in the Willows* from bedtime story to printed book may partly explain its curiously eclectic quality. Toad's adventures, with which the project began, form a relatively self-contained narrative within the book, a narrative which owes a great deal to the picaresque tradition of the eighteenth-century novelists Henry Fielding and Tobias Smollett. An improvident hero leaves, or is expelled from, his sheltered parental home and embarks on a series of loosely related experiences, culminating in a crisis in which his essential qualities are tested. Once that test has been passed, the hero is permitted to return home: his innate virtue not only has been established but has been disciplined and refined by experience, and he is now fit to take his place as a responsible member of his society's ruling elite.

Toad's return to Toad Hall in The Wind in the Willows,
illustrated by Ernest H. Shepard

As in all mock epic, the effect of such allusions is ambivalent, both subverting Toad's heroic pretensions by lining him up against a genuine epic protagonist and yet enhancing his status as a hero: there is, after all, something really Homeric about the way he goes for the Chief Weasel and sends him "flying across the table with one blow of his stick."

But the story of Toad is not the only part of the book which draws on the conventions of other genres and the achievements of other writers. The first chapter is strongly reminiscent of Jerome K. Jerome's *Three Men in a Boat* (1889) in its depiction of holiday leisure on the Thames and its evocation of a pastoral release from workaday responsibilities. Again, when the Rat, in chapter 3 ("The Wild Wood"), deduces from the cleanness of the cut on Mole's shin the presence of a door scraper, and from that their proximity to the safety of Badger's mansion, Grahame is obviously imitating the conventions of the detective story ("I've read about that sort of thing in books," Mole comments).

Besides these occasionally intrusive episodes of parody and pastiche, whole sections of the book seem stylistically inconsistent. The five opening chapters, in their lovingly detailed descriptions of natural life through the changing seasons and in their central concern with the precise definition of mood (for example, Mole's poignantly evoked homesickness in chapter 5, "Dulce Domum"), seem to belong to a category of writing different from that of the chapters that follow, with their accelerated momentum and their predominantly comic (and largely externalized) narration of Toad's vicissitudes. Chapter 7 ("The Piper at the Gates of Dawn") and chapter 9 ("Wayfarers All"), however, halt that momentum and temporarily suspend the comedy, providing intermissions of speculative calm in the picaresque progress.

But this dazzling assortment of modes and genres is not as unsettling as it sounds, for an overall thematic consistency welds together the book's heterogeneous voices. The whole of *The Wind in the Willows* is concerned with a central binary opposition whose poles might broadly be described as love of adventure and nostalgia for home. Thus the first chapter opens with the Mole, like one of the romantic fugitives of *Pagan Papers,* impulsively abandoning his respectable domestic labors and tunneling his way up to the surface world, a world whose infinite possibilities contrast with the starkly limited scope of his subterranean home. "Bewitched, entranced, fascinated" by the sheer novelty of all that he sees, he meets the Water Rat and becomes captivated by the river. For him, "messing about in boats" is an

As in much picaresque fiction, the episodic narrative progression of the Toad story accommodates a fair amount of literary parody. The ending of chapter 6 ("Mr. Toad"), in which Toad is incarcerated in "the remotest dungeon of the best-guarded keep of the stoutest castle in all the length and breadth of Merry England," is, as has often been pointed out, a comic reduction of the historical novels produced by Harrison Ainsworth and his host of imitators. The scene in chapter 10 ("The Further Adventures of Toad") in which Toad sells the bargewoman's horse to a canny gypsy is clearly and intentionally reminiscent of George Borrow, a writer whose work was enjoying a popular revival at the turn of the century. Of rather more structural significance than these isolated parodies, however, is the undercurrent of Homeric reference which pervades the book. The final chapter, for example, is actually called "The Return of Ulysses," and that title makes explicit a subdued but consistent parallelism between Toad's adventures and the *Odyssey.*

adventure. For Rat, however, it is the norm, and in the following chapter, "The Open Road," Rat's instinctive response to the lure of Toad's caravan is one of dismissive rejection (" 'I *am* going to stick to my old river, *and* live in a hole, *and* boat, as I've always done' "). While Mole seeks to embrace what Grahame calls the "Life Adventurous," Rat inclines to deny it. But Grahame emphasizes that these are not fixed choices – that the relationship between homebound security and outward-bound quest is always a dialectical one. In "Dulce Domum" the adventurous Mole is dragged back to his abandoned home by an almost magnetic attraction, while in "Wayfarers All" the mesmerized Rat has to be physically restrained from following the Sea Rat to new and unknown worlds.

This central preoccupation extends, of course, to the various experiences of Toad. Secure in the possession of Toad Hall (" 'really one of the nicest houses in these parts,' " the Rat concedes), Toad's only desire seems to be to leave it for distant horizons. Once separated from his ancestral home, however, Toad spends most of his time trying first to return to it and then to recapture it from the stoats and weasels.

If the disparate generic conventions in Grahame's book are to some extent reconciled by the common theme to which they are all subordinate, their juxtapositions nevertheless create a certain ambivalence. The abrupt shifts from picaresque comedy to pastoral idyll to spiritual meditation leave the reader uncertain about the level of seriousness on which a given passage is operating. In chapter 11 ("Like Summer Tempests Came His Tears"), for example, when Toad tries to row back to his occupied home and a couple of stoats sink his boat by dropping a "great stone" on it from a bridge, it is difficult to gauge whether the reader is meant to find the episode of Toad's discomfiture comic or pathetic. These two possibilities are not, of course, mutually exclusive, but Grahame's prose seems designed to exploit them in succession, to offer them as alternatives, rather than to effect any kind of synthesis: the boat sinks, and Toad finds himself "struggling in deep water"; he rises to the surface and sees the two stoats falling about with merriment ("they nearly had two fits – that is, one fit each, of course"). Finally he retraces "his weary way on foot."

This calculated uncertainty of tone is analogous to other uncertainties in the book. Grahame's apparently inconsistent presentation of his characters makes it unclear whether they are more human than animal or vice versa. In chapter 1 ("The River Bank"), for example, the narrator insists on the otherness of animal mores ("animal-etiquette forbade any sort of comment on the sudden disappearance of one's friends at any moment") while at the same time equipping Mole and Rat with a picnic hamper and having Rat talk about his new friend's fur as though it were detachable (" 'I'm going to get a black velvet smoking-suit myself one day' "). Badger "had never been a very smart man," but he refers to Toad's father as "a worthy animal." The bargewoman speaks of her passenger as "a horrid nasty, crawly Toad" yet recognizes Toad Hall as an important local landmark.

Examples of this kind of contradiction abound: the Great God Pan (in chapter 7, "The Piper at the Gates of Dawn"), with his half-divine, half-animal status, seems an appropriate tutelary spirit for the book in more ways than Grahame perhaps intended. But this doubleness of perspective, where contrary positions miraculously became equally true, is apparent elsewhere: in *Pagan Papers* the fugitives' neurotic retreats from reality are presented as manly initiative; in the construction of childhood that informs *The Golden Age* and *Dream Days,* prepubescent innocence is both allowed its own voice and is subjected to ironic commentary, and realistic and romantic versions of the same phenomenon are held in fine balance. So, too, in *The Wind in the Willows* the generic juxtapositions and the deliberately indeterminate characterization permit Grahame once again to get the best of many alternatives while committing himself to none.

The function of this strategy is also closely bound up with the social and political allegiances that underpin the book. Surprisingly, *The Wind in the Willows,* the most overtly fantastic of Grahame's fictions, is also the one in which both the relationship and the potential friction between classes become for the first time explicit. The children of *The Golden Age,* though clearly well heeled, are innocent of any adult consciousness of social difference, so that in "The Roman Road" the narrator can announce that the maidservant Martha is "my idea of a real lady." The narrator of "Dies Irae" from *Dream Days* concludes that the gardener's boy is "a red proletariat, who hated me just because I was a gentleman," but the facetious tone (reinforced by the childish misuse of "proletariat") reduces class conflict to a playful war, of no more significance than a game of cowboys and Indians.

When it comes to animals, however, Grahame delineates social boundaries with scrupulous care. The principal characters are all quite clearly members of the middle and upper classes, but there are

SHE ARRANGED THE SHAWL WITH A PROFESSIONAL FOLD,
AND TIED THE STRINGS
OF THE RUSTY BONNET UNDER HIS CHIN

*Arthur Rackham's illustration of Toad's escape from prison, in a 1940
edition of Grahame's* The Wind in the Willows

clear distinctions within that area of broad equality. Mole appears to be the least exalted member of the group: his little house with its "plaster statuary," its "meagre dimensions," and its "shabby contents" suggests that he belongs to the lower middle class, which clings precariously to its bourgeois status on a limited income. The Water Rat, on the other hand, is comfortably well-off; unlike Mole, who is first discovered busily spring-cleaning, Rat's commodious riverside villa is equipped with invisible servants (" 'Surely I heard the chink of dishes on a tray,' " says Toad when he and Rat are apparently alone together), and he is required to do nothing except "mess about in boats" and write poetry. Toad, of course, occupies a splendid house, but it is not at all clear that the house is a truly ancestral one. His behavior certainly conforms to popular Edwardian stereotypes of the nouveau riche, with his tendency to conspicuous displays of affluence (the endless succes-

sion of expensive motorcars) and his slightly suspect insistence on his genteel status (the synopsis of his undelivered speech at the final banquet ends with a section titled "A Typical English Squire"). Badger, by contrast, is the book's only real aristocrat. His lineage stretches back to the dawn of history, his residence is vast and antique, and his authority is absolute. His carelessness toward conventional good manners and grammatical correctness (" 'What's the matter with his English?' " he demands when the pedantic Rat reproves Toad for using "learn" instead of "teach": "'It's the same what I use myself '") implies an assured superiority to the rules that bind lesser beings.

Despite the fine distinctions within their circle, however, the inhabitants of the River Bank stick together, supporting one another and endorsing the same code of belief. Mole, for example, despite his humbler origins, is instantly recognized as a member of the little clique, as one of nature's gentlemen. Toad, conversely, though his social and economic status is not in doubt, needs to be taken firmly in hand so that he will not compromise his peer group by indecorous behavior. What he lacks, and what the book insists on as of crucial importance, are conservative values such as stability (" 'no stability — especially in a boat,' " is how Otter describes Toad in chapter 1), soundness (" 'How *sound* you always are,' " says Toad to Rat), and solidity (Badger has "solid qualities").

These qualities connote an obligation to maintain the status quo, and they assume the prominence they do because the class that espouses them is, in fact, under threat from below and so needs to preserve a defensive solidarity. When Mole decides to explore the Wild Wood in chapter 3, he finds it a deeply intimidating experience. Under the "hard steely sky" of winter, the denuded copses and dells display a "shabby poverty," but the Wood shows evidence of being densely populated ("he passed another hole, and another, and another"), and the creatures Mole glimpses ("a little evil wedge-shaped face") are not welcoming. He soon finds himself chased by unseen enemies and finally conceals himself in the hollow of a tree, where he listens, terrified, to the whistles with which his pursuers signal to one another.

With fairly minor alterations this whole episode could come from some late-nineteenth-century novel of slum life, and the stoats, weasels, and ferrets could be considered Grahame's version of an urban proletariat (thus constituting a double threat to the rural bourgeoisie). Although the Wild Wooders appear to be dominated by Badger in a kind of feudal polity, the appearance of order is deceptive, and Rat prophetically warns Mole in chapter 1 that " 'they break out sometimes, there's no denying it.' "

But the eventual occupation of Toad Hall by the lower orders, whose filthy habits, Rat reports, reduce the place " 'to such a mess . . . it's not fit to be seen,' " is a temporary reversal of the social hierarchy. The mass of stoats and weasels is easily routed by four representatives of the established order, and the former insurgents are set to appropriately menial tasks such as sweeping bedrooms and delivering letters. Everything thus ends happily and, Grahame reports, "after this climax, the four animals continued to lead their lives, so rudely broken in upon by civil war, in great joy and contentment, undisturbed by further risings or invasions."

Grahame's conservative exorcism of the specter of revolution anchors his book firmly within the cultural life of its period. It is one response to the complex array of social and political upheavals that characterized Edwardian England, the most prominent of which was perhaps the dramatic increase in the incidence and the intensity of working-class agitation. But it is difficult to read *The Wind in the Willows* simply, or even primarily, as a political parable because the ambiguous status of Grahame's animal protagonists makes it impossible to identify them fully with the human situations they seem to reflect. Toad has most of the characteristics of the Edwardian "masher," but he is also the "nasty, crawly Toad" which the bargewoman disgustedly ejects from her boat. Mole and Water Rat may talk like a pair of former public-school boys, but they are also inhabitants of the animal world who pass somnolent winters and follow scents.

This equivocal characterization is not of service only in redeeming the book from an appearance of bald political didacticism or mechanical allegory. By insisting that his characters lead their own distinctively animal lives — lives which are determined by natural rhythms and an instinctive responsiveness to seasonal change — Grahame also, by implication, naturalizes the human values and material conditions they represent. Since what is natural is, by implication, what is right, the ideology of the Edwardian middle class, with its comfortable world of velvet smoking suits and lobster salad, is exalted into a myth whose timeless validity is guaranteed by nature. This universalization of the historically specific is consolidated by the welter of literary allusion with which the book is suffused: references to ancient epic confer the gloss of primal heroism on Edwardian interiors (the Badger's kitchen is a place "where heroes could fitly feast after victory"), and even the parody of Ainsworth at the end of chapter 6 converts imprisonment for theft and for dangerous driving into an episode of romantic escapade. Everything, in short, conspires to translate the temporary present (or a favored version of it) into mythic permanence, the local into the universal, the contingent into the natural.

Grahame's deeply conservative version of pastoral, where private incomes are the norm, where the "red proletariat" can be kept in its place with a few sweeps of the cudgel, where the innocence of male camaraderie can be kept, as he put it in a blurb, "clean of the clash of sex," has established itself as a classic of children's, and indeed of adult, literature. The strongest source of its enduring appeal, perhaps, is its unashamed celebration of leisure. Like Charles Dickens's *Pickwick Papers* (1837), an earlier mythologization of bourgeois life, its princi-

Grahame, circa 1920 (photograph by J. Russell & Sons)

pal characters inhabit a recognizable contemporary world, but, supported by a wealth whose sources are invisible and unspecified, they are able to transform that world from workplace to playground, to spend, if they please, their whole lives simply "messing about."

Indeed, after the book's publication in 1908, Grahame clearly decided to follow his characters' example. He had already resigned, earlier in the same year, from the Bank of England, and in 1910 he moved with his family to a Tudor farmhouse at Blewbury, near Didcot. He occasionally toyed with suggestions from publishers, but the only substantial project that he brought to completion was *The Cambridge Book of Poetry for Children* (1916), a rather bland anthology from which, as Grahame boasted in his preface, he had tried as far as possible to exclude the subject of death and which grouped its generally predictable selections under thematic headings like "Toys and Play" and "Fairyland." Apart from this volume, a few essays, and a preface to the 1926 memoirs of the flamboyant showman "Lord" George Sanger, Grahame produced nothing after the publication of *The Wind in the Willows*.

Almost the only incident that ruffled the indolent serenity of his last years was the tragic death of his son. Alastair had grown up to be a melancholy, withdrawn young man plagued by spiritual doubts, and in May 1920, while he was at Oxford, he wandered onto a railway line and was killed by a train (the verdict of accidental death was probably more charitable than accurate). Grief brought Grahame and Elspeth closer than they had been for years. They traveled a good deal in Italy, where Grahame became a connoisseur of Rome's architecture and restaurants. They moved their English headquarters from Blewbury back to the riverbank at Pangbourne, and they became increasingly reclusive, even a little eccentric, in a world with which, not altogether reluctantly, they were losing touch. In the early morning of 6 July 1932 Grahame suffered a cerebral hemorrhage, went into a deep coma, and died without regaining consciousness.

Grahame is an especially appropriate subject for critical biography because the circumstances of his life have such a formative and direct relationship to the small body of work he produced. The fugitive clerks and secretaries of *Pagan Papers* clearly

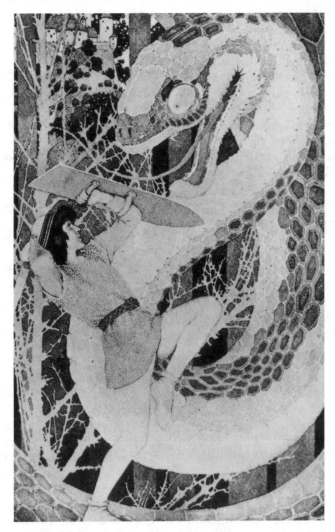

One of Maxfield Parrish's illustrations from Grahame's The Golden Age

encapsulate his own frustration with an uncongenial, deskbound career at the Bank of England. The childhood world of *The Golden Age* and *Dream Days* is unquestionably based on his memories of growing up with his siblings under the stern eye of his Olympian grandmother. Indeed, the particular emphasis in those books on the autonomy of the children's world and on the failure of communication between the children and their adult guardians is implicitly dependent on the absence of parents. Grahame is presenting as a general truth about children what may in fact be a quality specific to orphans. Like Grahame's earlier work, *The Wind in the Willows* is a reflection of its author's experience — not only of his experience as a conservative member of a middle class which felt itself to be under attack, but also of his private experience as an individual. The River, on which

Rat enjoys "messing about in boats," is also the Thames, which Grahame loved to explore as a boy, on which he rowed with Furnivall as a young man, and to which he returned in maturity when he bought two of his three family homes. The sunny Mediterranean world that the Sea Rat conjures up in "Wayfarers All" is also the world to which Grahame himself retreated constantly from the pressure of family and professional cares.

All of these widely different exploitations of the self and its experiences — essays, stories about children, fables about animals — are united in their longing for escape. Each sets up an ideal world as a refuge from tension and anxiety, whether it is the itinerant gypsy life of *Pagan Papers,* the innocent childhood of *The Golden Age* and *Dream Days,* or the secure middle-class leisure of the River Bank in *The Wind in the Willows.* In each case retreat is not presented as timid surrender or headlong flight but as a challenging prospect, a demanding option. The city clerks of the early essays who buy carts and become peddlers are striking manly blows against deadening conformism; the adults who can participate in the children's vision of *The Golden Age* are rare and privileged people, gifted with special insight. As for the inhabitants of the River Bank, they are heroic defenders of eternal values, and their right to pastoral ease is established by their epic victory over the anarchic forces of the Wild Wood.

It is, then, Grahame's special achievement — and also the source of his enormous influence and appeal — not merely to have created evocative escapist fantasies but to have presented those fantasies as credible, even morally preferable, alternatives to the prosaic realities in which most of his readers must live. To make retreat sound convincingly like advance is an uncommon gift, and Grahame possessed it in full measure; it should ensure that *The Golden Age* and *Dream Days* will be occasionally reprinted and that *The Wind in the Willows* will enjoy lasting popularity with future generations.

Biographies:

Patrick R. Chalmers, *Kenneth Grahame: Life, Letters and Unpublished Work* (London: Methuen, 1933);

Peter Green, *Kenneth Grahame 1859–1932: A Study of His Life, Work and Times* (London: John Murray, 1959); abridged as *Beyond the Wild Wood: The World of Kenneth Grahame* (Exeter, Devon: Webb & Bower, 1982);

Eleanor Graham, *Kenneth Grahame* (London: Bodley Head, 1963).

References:

John Anderson, "Kenneth Grahame," in *Art and Reality: John Anderson on Literature and Aesthetics,* edited by Janet Anderson, Graham Cullum, and Kimon Lycos (Sydney: Hale & Iremonger, 1982), pp. 157–161;

Humphrey Carpenter, *Secret Gardens: A Study of the Golden Age of Children's Literature* (London: Allen & Unwin, 1985), pp. 115–125, 151–169;

Mary DeForest, "*The Wind in the Willows:* A Tale for Two Readers," *Classical and Modern Literature,* 10 (Fall 1989): 81–87;

Peter Green, Introduction to *The Wind in the Willows* (Oxford & New York: Oxford University Press, 1983), pp. vii–xx;

Lois R. Kuznets, *Kenneth Grahame* (Boston: Twayne, 1987);

Naomi Lewis, Foreword to *The Golden Age* (London: Bodley Head, 1979), pp. 7–12;

Geraldine D. Poss, "An Epic in Arcadia: The Pastoral World of *The Wind in the Willows,*" *Children's Literature,* 4 (1975): 80–90;

Laura Krugman Ray, "Kenneth Grahame and the Literature of Childhood," *English Literature in Transition (1880–1920),* 20 (1977): 3–12;

W. W. Robson, "On *The Wind in the Willows,*" in his *The Definition of Literature and Other Essays* (Cambridge: Cambridge University Press, 1982), pp. 119–144;

Roger Sale, *Fairy Tales and After: From Snow White to E. B. White* (Cambridge, Mass.: Harvard University Press, 1978), pp. 165–193.

Kate Greenaway
(17 March 1846 – 6 November 1901)

Anne H. Lundin
University of Wisconsin – Madison

BOOKS: *Under the Window, with Coloured Pictures and Rhymes for Children* (London: Routledge, 1879);
Almanack for 1883 (London: Routledge, 1882);
Almanack for 1884 (London: Routledge, 1883);
A Painting Book (London: Routledge, 1884);
Almanack for 1885 (London: Routledge, 1884);
Marigold Garden (London: Routledge, 1885);
Kate Greenaway's Alphabet (London: Routledge, 1885);
Almanack for 1886 (London: Routledge, 1885);
Almanack for 1887 (London: Routledge, 1886);
Almanack for 1888 (London: Routledge, 1887);
Kate Greenaway's Painting Book (London & New York: Warne, [1888]);
Almanack for 1889 (London: Routledge, 1888);
Kate Greenaway's Book of Games (London: Routledge, 1889);
Almanack for 1890 (London: Routledge, 1889);
Kate Greenaway's Almanack 1891 (London: Routledge, 1890);
Kate Greenaway's Almanack 1892 (London: Routledge, 1891);
Kate Greenaway's Almanack 1893 (London: Routledge, 1892);
Kate Greenaway's Almanack 1894 (London: Routledge, 1893);
Kate Greenaway's Almanack 1895 (London: Routledge, 1894);
Kate Greenaway's Almanack and Diary for 1897 (London: J. M. Dent, 1896);
Mother Goose or Old Nursery Rhymes: the Complete Facsimile Sketchbooks from the Arents Collection, the New York Public Library (New York: Abrams, 1988).

BOOKS ILLUSTRATED: William Henry Giles Kingston, *Infant Amusements, or How to Make a Nursery Happy* (London: Griffith & Farran, 1867);
Aunt Louisa's Nursery Favourite: Diamonds and Toads (London: Warne, 1870);

Kate Greenaway in 1880

Margaret S. Jeune, *My School Days in Paris* (London: Griffith & Farran, 1870);
Madame D'Aulnoy's Fairy Tales, 9 volumes (Edinburgh: Gall & Inglis, 1870) – comprises *The Fair One with Golden Locks; The Babes in the Wood; Tom Thumb; Bluebeard; Puss in Boots; The Blue Bird; The White Cat; Hop O' My Thumb; Red Riding Hood;*
Lisa Lockyer, *A Child's Influence, or Kathleen and Her Great Uncle* (London: Griffith & Farran, [1872]);

Aunt Cae (H. C. Selous), *The Children of the Parsonage* (London: Griffith & Farran, 1873);

Kathleen Knox, *Fairy Gifts, or a Wallet of Wonders* (London: Griffith & Farran, 1874; New York: Dutton, 1875); revised edition with extra illustrations by Greenaway (London: Ward, 1875);

Miranda Hill, *The Fairy Spinner* (London: Ward, 1875);

Alice Jerrold, *A Cruise in the Acorn* (London: Ward, [1875]);

Mary Senior Clark, *Turnaside Cottage* (London: Ward, 1875);

Children's Songs With Pictures and Music (London: Ward, [1875]);

Frederick Scarlett Potter, *Melcomb Manor: A Family Chronicle* (London: Ward, [1875]);

Rosa Mulholland, *Puck and Blossoms, A Fairy Tale* (London: Ward, [1875]);

Knox, *Seven Birthdays or The Children of Fortune, A Fairy Chronicle* (London: Griffith & Farran, 1875);

W. J. Loftie, ed., *The Quiver of Love: A Collection of Valentines Ancient and Modern* (London: Ward, 1876);

Alice Hepburn, *Two Little Cousins* (London: Ward, 1876);

What Santa Claus Gave Me (London: Griffith, Farran, Okeden & Welsh, [1876]);

H. Rutherford Russell, *Tom Seven Years Old* (London: Ward, 1876);

Fanny Lablache, *Starlight Stories Told to Bright Eyes and Listening Ears* (London: Griffith & Farran, 1876);

Pretty Stories for Tiny Folk (New York, London & Paris: Cassell, 1877);

C. L. Mateaux, *Woodland Romances; or Fables and Fancies* (London: Cassell, Petter, Galpin, [1877]);

Bonavia Hunt, *Poor Nelly* (London: Cassell, Petter, Galpin, 1878);

G. E. Brunefille (Lady Colin Campbell), *Topo: A Tale about English Children in Italy* (London: Ward, 1878);

Geraldine Butt, *Esther: A Story for Children* (London: Ward, 1878);

Charlotte M. Yonge, *Heartsease, or The Brother's Wife* (London: Macmillan, 1879);

Yonge, *The Heir of Redclyffe* (London: Macmillan, 1879);

Walter Herries Pollock, *Amateur Theatricals* (London: Macmillan, 1879);

Trot's Journey, with Pictures, Rhymes and Stories (New York: Worthington, 1879);

Toyland, Trot's Journey, and Other Poems and Stories (New York: Worthington, 1879);

George Weatherly, *The Little Folks Painting Book* (London: Cassell, Petter, Galpin, 1879);

Weatherly, *The Little Folks Nature Painting Book* (London: Cassell, Petter, Galpin, 1879);

A Favourite Album of Fun and Fancy (London: Cassell, Petter, Galpin, 1879);

Christmas Snowflakes (Boston: Lothrop, 1879);

Ellen Haile, *Three Brown Boys and Other Happy Children* (London: Cassell, Petter, Galpin, 1879);

Art in the Nursery (Boston: Lothrop, [1879]);

A Book for Every Little Jack and Gill (New York: Dodd, Mead, [1879]);

Emma E. Brown, *Once Upon a Time: Play-Stories for Children* (Boston: Lothrop, [1879]);

Haile, *The Two Gray Girls and Their Opposite Neighbors* (New York, London & Paris: Cassell, Petter, Galpin, [1880]);

Mrs. Sale Barker, *Kate Greenaway's Birthday Book for Children* (London: Routledge, 1880);

Chatty Cheerful (William Martin), *The Little Folk's Out and About Book* (London: Cassell, [1880]);

F. E. Weatherly, ed., *The Illustrated Children's Birthday Book* (London: Mack, [1880]);

Freddie's Letter: Stories for Little People (London: Routledge, 1880);

Cousin Daisy, *The Youngster* (Philadelphia: Lippincott, 1880);

Stevie's Visit (New York: Dodd, Mead, 1880);

The Purse of Gold (New York: Dodd, Mead, [1880]);

The Lost Knife (New York: Dodd, Mead, 1880);

Little Sunbeam Stories (New York, London & Paris: Cassell, Petter, Galpin, [1880]);

Pleasant Hours and Golden Days (New York: Lupton, [circa 1880]);

Baby Dido; and Other Stories (Boston: Lothrop, [circa 1880]);

Archie Fell, *Dumpy* (Boston: Lothrop, [1880]);

The Easy Book for Children (London: Pictorial Literature Society, [circa 1880]);

Laura E. Richards, *Five Mice in a Mousetrap* (Boston: Lauriat, [1880]);

Grandmamma's Surprise Baby (New York: Dodd, Mead, [1880]);

Austin Dobson, "English Illustrated Books," in Andrew Lang, *The Library* (London: Macmillan, 1881);

Frederick Locker, *London Lyrics* (London: Chiswick, 1881; New York: White, Stokes & Allen, 1881);

Myles B. Foster, *A Day in a Child's Life* (London: Routledge, 1881);

You see, merry Phillis, that dear little maid,
    Has invited Belinda to tea;
Her nice little garden is shaded by trees,—
    What pleasanter place could there be?

There's a cake full of plums, there are strawberries too,
    And the table is set on the green;
I'm fond of a carpet all daisies and grass,—
    Could a prettier picture be seen?

A blackbird (yes, blackbirds delight in warm weather)
    Is flitting from yonder high spray;
He sees the two little ones talking together,—
    No wonder the blackbird is gay!

Page from Under the Willow, *the first book to be written as well as illustrated by Greenaway*

Mother Goose, or The Old Nursery Rhymes (London: Routledge, 1881);

Elise (New York: Dodd, Mead, [1881]);

Hide and Seek Illustrated (New York: Dodd, Mead, [1881]);

King Christmas (New York: Dodd, Mead, [1881]);

Whose Fault Was It? (New York: Dodd, Mead, 1881);

George Kringle, *Some Little People* (New York: Dodd, Mead, [1881]);

Olive Patch, *Happy Little People* (New York: Cassell, 1882);

Helen Zimmern, *Tales from the Edda* (London: Sonnenschein, 1882);

Mary D. Brine, *Papa's Little Daughters* (New York, London & Paris: Cassell, Petter, Galpin, 1882);

Margaret Eleanora Tupper, *Little Loving-Hearts Poem-Book* (New York: Dutton / London: Griffith & Farran, 1882);

Little Gatherers (New York, London & Paris: Cassell, Petter, Galpin, [1882]);

Greenaway Pictures to Paint (New York: McLoughlin, [1882]);

Jane and Ann Taylor, *Little Ann and Other Poems* (London: Routledge, 1882);

Aunt Ella, *The Wonderful Fan* (New York: Dutton, 1882);

B. M. Montgomerie Ranking and Thomas K. Tully, *Flowers and Fancies, Valentines Ancient and Modern* (London: Ward, 1882);

Brine, *Jingles and Joys for Wee Girls and Boys* (New York: Cassell, 1883);

Aunt Hattie, *Baby Chatterbox: Stories and Poems for Our Little Ones* (New York: Worthington, 1883);

John Ruskin, *Fors Clavigera: Letters to the Workmen and Labourers of Great Britain* (London: Allen, 1883);

Juliana Horatia Ewing, *Brothers of Pity and Other Tales of Beasts and Men* (London: Society for Promoting Christian Knowledge / New York: Young, 1884);

The Language of Flowers (London: Routledge, 1884);

A Summer at Aunt Helen's (New York: Dodd, Mead, 1884);

Baby's Birthday Book (London: Ward, 1884);

William Mavor, *The English Spelling Book* (London: Routledge, 1884);

Chatterbox Hall (New York: Worthington, [1884]);

The Children's Birthday Book (London, Belfast & New York: Ward, [1884]);

Kringle, *Little Castles with Big Wings* (New York: Dodd, Mead, [1884]);

Robert Ellice, ed., *Songs for the Nursery* (London: Mack, [1884]);

"A Lady of Ninety," *Dame Wiggins of Lee and Her Seven Wonderful Cats* (London: Orpington, 1885);

Tick, Tick, Tick and Other Rhymes (New York: Mayer, Merkel & Ottmann, [1885]);

Mrs. E. P. Miller, *Mother Truth's Melodies: Common Sense for Children, A Kindergarten* (Springfield, Mass.: Bay State, 1885);

Barker, ed., *Little Patience Picture Book* (London & New York: Routledge, [1885]);

A Apple Pie (London: Routledge, 1886);

Bret Harte, *The Queen of the Pirate Isle* (London: Chatto & Windus, 1886; Boston & New York: Houghton Mifflin, 1887);

William and Helen Allingham, *Rhymes for the Young Folk,* illustrated by Greenaway, Helen Allingham, Caroline Paterson, and Harry Furniss (London: Cassell, 1886);

Bib and Tucker: With Pictures and Stories for Little People in the Nursery (Boston: Lothrop, [1886]);

Brine, *Christmas Dreams* (New York: Cassell, [1886]);

Queen Victoria's Jubilee Garland (London: Routledge, 1887);

Laurie Loring, *Lucy's Troubles and Other Stories* (Boston: Lothrop, 1887);

Loftie, *Orient Line Guide: Chapters for Travellers by Sea and Land* (London: Sampson, Low, Marston, Searle & Rivington, 1888);

Around the House: Stories and Poems (New York: Worthington, 1888);

Robert Browning, *The Pied Piper of Hamelin* (London: Routledge, 1888);

The Old Farm Gate: Stories in Prose and Verse for Little People (London, Glasgow & New York: Routledge, [1888]);

Miss Rosebud and Other Stories (Boston: Lothrop, [1888]);

Beatrice F. Cresswell, *The Royal Progress of King Pepito* (London & Brighton: Society for Promoting Christian Knowledge, 1889; New York: Young, 1889);

Our Girls, Stories and Poems for Little Girls (Chicago, New York & San Francisco: Belford, Clarke, 1890);

Lucie E. Villeplait, *Songs of the Month* (New York: Worthington, 1891);

Fanny Barry, *Soap Bubble Stories for Children* (London: Skeffington, 1892);

Doll's Tea Party, Merry Play Time (Boston: Lothrop, [1895]);

Grace Aguilar, Geraldine Butt, and Jane Butt, *Every Girl's Stories* (London: Routledge, 1896);

Stories Witty and Pictures Pretty (New York & Chicago: Conkey, [1896]);

To Pass the Time (New York: McLoughlin, [circa 1897]);

Little Folks' Speaker (Boston: Lothrop, 1898);

Mary Annette Beauchamp Russell, Countess von Arnim, *The April Baby's Book of Tunes, with the Story of How They Came to be Written* (New York & London: Macmillan, 1900);

Loftie, *London Afternoons* (London: Cassell, 1901);

Mrs. M. H. Spielmann, *Littledom Castle and Other Tales* (London: Routledge, 1903);

Anne Greaves, *The Birthday Bouquet* (London & New York: Warne, 1903);

Dobson, *De Libris: Prose and Verse* (London: Macmillan, 1908).

Kate Greenaway's vision of arcadian childhood dramatically changed the art of the picture book. Her work was innovative in its imaginative renderings of a romanticized childhood, a departure in subject matter from traditional folklore for children. Greenaway's books represent the apotheosis of artistic picture books, with attention to the artistry of the book from cover to cover, especially in the key element of color. Her stature was recognized at the time and continues to be acknowledged in the modern age — virtually every historical survey of children's literature mentions her work in the development of the picture book. Greenaway titles continue to be published through the Warne/Viking imprint, and her stylized images are commercially

One of Greenaway's twelve illustrations for "Christmas in Little Peopleton Manor," published in the Illustrated London News *in 1879*

produced on posters, stationery, coloring books, paper dolls, and needlework patterns. In some ways the Greenaway style is still as much an article of folk culture as it was in her time.

Kate Greenaway was born in London on 17 March 1846, the second child of John and Elizabeth Greenaway. While her parents intended to call her Kate, her name was registered as Catherine Greenaway. Her father was a draftsman and engraver apprenticed to Ebenezer Landells, one of the giants of the new profession of wood engraving. John Greenaway worked on his own, taking freelance commissions for illustrated children's books and for periodicals, such as the *Illustrated London News*. Her mother was a seamstress and milliner, who opened a shop in Islington when her husband's business waned.

The family often stayed with relatives in the village of Rolleston, in Nottinghamshire countryside, an old-fashioned country setting which inspired much of her subsequent art. Here Greenaway was touched by the commonplace sights of oldfashioned England: villagers in their antiquated eighteenth-century dress; men working in the fields in embroidered smocks dyed blue; women wearing their Sunday best of frilly lace and large poke bonnets; and roads edged with primroses or fields filled with poppies. Greenaway's unfinished autobiography reveals her delight in the sights, sounds, and smells of the country.

Behind her mother's shop in the city was a large back garden, which soon became "Kate's domain," although shared with two other families. While this small patch of earth was little more than abandoned flower beds beside makeshift sheds, the garden led into a pocket of pastureland where sheep grazed. This rural retreat behind the busy Islington streets became her secret garden, a vision recounted in a letter to a friend years later and recorded in Rodney Engen's 1981 biography of Greenaway: "I often think just for the pleasure of thinking, that a little door leads out of the garden wall into a real old flowering garden, full of deep shades and deep colours. Did you always plan out delightful places just close and unexpected, when you were young? My bedroom used to look out over red roofs and chimney pots, and I made steps up into a lovely garden up there with nasturtiums growing and brilliant flowers so near to the sky."

A shy, solitary child, Greenaway let her artwork express these fantasies. Her formal art training lasted at least twelve years. Her early watercolors, exhibited at the Dudley Gallery in 1868, caught the eye of an editor and led to a commission for illustrations for *People's* magazine and later for Christmas cards and valentines for Marcus Ward. In 1870 she received a commission to illustrate an edition of *Madame D'Aulnoy's Fairy Tales*. She also began contributing to *Little Folks*, the *Illustrated Lon-*

don News, and *Cassell's* magazine, and she exhibited for the first time at the Royal Academy in 1877.

Greenaway's ambition was to publish a book of her own verses and drawings based on her memories of Rolleston, street rhymes, and favorite childhood stories. She dressed her characters in the old-fashioned clothing so common in Rolleston: high-waisted gowns, smocks, and mobcaps. She accompanied these drawings with her own verse, based on nursery-rhyme morals and make-believe. John Greenaway showed the manuscript to a colleague in the engraving business, Edmund Evans, a pioneer color printer who had already created successful productions of Walter Crane's toy books and had recently engaged Randolph Caldecott for a similar series. Evans in his *Reminiscences* (1967) describes the notebook as "miscellaneous odd drawings with nonsense verses written to them," and he decided that the sixty-four-page manuscript had all the markings of commercial promise. Routledge, the leading publisher of children's books at the time, agreed to act as the distributor but insisted on some changes in the verses. Evans arranged for Frederick Locker to edit the volume – though few changes were made. Greenaway and Evans agreed on the volume's title, *Under the Window,* taken from the first line of the first verse.

Then Evans set about the delicate process of transposing the images onto paper: "I photographed these original drawings on to wood and engraved them as nearly 'facsimile' as possible, then transferred wet impressions to plain blocks of wood – 'Transfers' to engrave the several colours on, red, flesh tint, blue, yellow. This was a costly matter but it reproduced the character very well indeed of the original drawings." Evans printed the books on his own and then issued them through Routledge's organization and imprint, with their British and American branches. *Under the Window* appeared in the July 1879 Routledge catalogue, which contained the Christmas book list sent to booksellers.

Aestheticism was an art movement of the last quarter of the nineteenth century that revolutionized classical Victorian art and led the way for art nouveau. Partial aesthetic motifs resound in *Under the Window.* The children in the illustrations exhibit a subdued and melancholy air even when accompanied by cheerful verse. Merry Phillis and her friend sit on William Morris rush-seated chairs to take tea on blue and white china. The predominant colors are the soft yellows and greens in vogue at the time and are displayed on the cover with a border of children waving lilies. White plays an integral part in Greenaway's designs, as it does in Japanese prints, creating a light effect.

Under the Window received much attention in the United States, where aestheticism was particularly influential after the 1876 Centennial Exhibition Exposition, an international trade fair that championed decorative arts. While the first few American reviews were more notices than criticism, the reviewer for *Scribner's* (December 1879) described the dual appeal of the book: children would enjoy "the prettiest pictures available"; adults would appreciate "the grace of an unconscious childhood." The children's magazine *St. Nicholas* (December 1879) stressed the work's lighthearted manner and artistry: "every grown person of taste" would want to explore it first and then share it with a child who "deserves to be happy."

The most extensive review – for this or for any of Greenaway's books – appeared in the *Spectator* (20 December 1879), which called *Under the Window* "an artistic story-book" which should be an important part of artistic nursery education. The reviewer took the novel approach of quoting the responses of children, who reacted adversely to other picture books after viewing Greenaway's book. Pages were described in detail, with strengths or weaknesses noted. The page with Phillis and Belinda at tea was singled out, with its images symbolizing an idealized world, "a better land, where strawberries are larger, cakes plummier and sweeter, and children prettier and more engaging than in this work-a-day world."

With such a warm reception, *Under the Window* exceeded even Evans's expectations. The first edition of twenty thousand, which Routledge had considered to be excessive, quickly sold out; the second edition and foreign editions totaled nearly seventy thousand copies. Receipts from Evans's accounts listed the book on every quarterly report of royalties, with the exception of the summer and fall of 1888. Greenaway first arranged with Evans to secure one-third of the profits for herself, after the initial sale of twenty-five thousand copies, which paid his printing costs; the figure was raised to one-half profits by 1881. Throughout the 1890s *Under the Window* was listed as a perennial seller, along with Greenaway's three other most popular works: *Kate Greenaway's Birthday Book for Children* (1880), *Mother Goose, or The Old Nursery Rhymes* (1881), and *A Painting Book* (1884). Sales were enhanced in 1892 by the catalogue promotion of inexpensive editions of *Under the Window, Marigold Garden* (1885), and *The Pied Piper of Hamelin* (1888).

Greenaway's drawings for *Under the Window,* exhibited at the Fine Art Society, attracted the attention of art critic John Ruskin. Encouraged by Stacy Marks, one of Greenaway's mentors, Ruskin wrote

Georgie Peorgie, pudding and pie,
Kissed the girls and made them cry;
When the girls begin to play,
Georgie Peorgie runs away.

Here am I, little jumping Joan,
When nobody's with me,
I'm always alone.

Two pages from Greenaway's Mother Goose, or The Old Nursery Rhymes

to the artist in 1880, initiating a twenty-year friendship, in which Ruskin advised her on her work and inspired her affection. Engen's biography reveals the intense, unrequited love of Greenaway for Ruskin and speculates on the influence of Ruskin on Greenaway's work, which led her to indulge his proclivities for images of innocent girlhood and for naturalistic detail, even as she resisted much of his dictatorial direction.

Under the Window also spawned the "Greenaway Vogue," as it was known. Numerous imitations, piracies, and spinoffs were produced without her permission, an onslaught that popularized her name but adversely affected her livelihood and stature. She was certainly one of the most copied artists of all time. Several anecdotes in M. H. Spielmann and G. S. Layard's 1905 biography relate Greenaway's dismay with this phenomenon. She apparently witnessed a bookseller touting his books by Kate Greenaway, none of which was hers. H. H. Emmerson, Constance Hazelwood, George

Lambert, and T. Pym are a few who copied her style during the 1880s. The most celebrated imitation was *Afternoon Tea* (1881) by J. G. Sowerby and Emmerson, produced by Routledge's rival Frederick Warne. The McLoughlin Brothers, New York's largest publisher of children's picture books, pirated many of Greenaway's books or adapted them and billed them as "after Kate Greenaway."

Under the Window launched Greenaway's successful commercial and critical reception: a fashion with the public as well as the academic fine-art world. Curiously, Greenaway departed from the format of *Under the Window* in her next publication. *Kate Greenaway's Birthday Book for Children* was an example of a popular genre of the day, a journal that provided spaces for signatures by designated birthdays. Greenaway's entry in the genre was accompanied by 382 drawings and the verse of Mrs. Sale Barker – its title attests to the illustrator's newly found fame. The book was enthusiastically received in England and the United States, although the critical notice was slighter and more subdued than the initial response to *Under the Window*. Nevertheless, the book sold readily in England and the United States, with editions also published in French and German. The book persisted as one of Greenaway's best-selling titles throughout the 1880s and 1890s. Moreover, the *Birthday Book* inspired Robert Louis Stevenson's *A Child's Garden of Verses* (1885).

Greenaway's illustrated edition of *Mother Goose* appeared in the following year, and while the commercial response was less than that of the *Birthday Book*, the critical reception was better. The work was proposed by Evans, and Greenaway chose the verses, most likely from *Popular Nursery Rhymes*, edited by James Orchard Halliwell, a collection common at the time. However, peculiar printing problems associated with the book displeased the author. Greenaway insisted on the printing of the book on rough-textured paper for an antique effect. Evans improvised by pressing the rough paper smooth between copper plates, printing the pages, and then dipping them into water. The method produced the desired effect but created problems in color register. The timing of the publication was such that Greenaway had no opportunity to proof copies before it was published.

Reviewers, however, praised the book's illustrations although they were somewhat critical of its text. Greenaway's original verses had been scrutinized in *Under the Window*, with the suggestion that she employ more traditional nursery poetry. Now that she had done so, reviewers questioned the version of the traditional fare that she had selected. American reviews of *Mother Goose* appeared later than in British publications, suggesting a delay in the book's stateside release. The reviews were positive, and, for the first time, the *New York Times* (24 November 1881) covered one of Greenaway's books and placed her ahead of all other illustrators of children's books.

With the publication of *Mother Goose*, Greenaway moved into a higher echelon of critical notice. She was covered in the December 1881 issues of the *Art Journal* and the *Magazine of Art*, both of which only sporadically reviewed books and rarely children's titles. The former referred to the dual appeal of her books for young and old in its quaintness and originality, while the latter called Greenaway "an artistic Fairy Godmother" who created a kind of "nursery Arcadia," which in itself made for her a place in nursery literature.

Mother Goose marked the pinnacle of Greenaway's reputation, becoming one of her most pop-
ular titles and consistently one of the top four Greenaway best-sellers throughout the 1880s and 1890s. From then on, her work would be less favorably reviewed. *A Day in a Child's Life* (1881), with lyrics by Miles Foster and illustrations by Greenaway, appeared simultaneously with *Mother Goose* and was only marginally successful, either commercially or critically. The book was advertised in the January 1882 Routledge catalogue as "Uniform with 'Under the Window.'" Sales of English editions reached twenty-five thousand, a respectable number but insufficient to bring royalties for Greenaway under the already-explained arrangement by which she shared profits after a certain total of copies was sold.

In 1882 Greenaway published the first of her series of almanacs, for which the author is well known. The almanacs were booklets with variant bindings that contained monthly calendars and in which the surprise from year to year was in Greenaway's choice of decorations for the seasons. From 1882 to 1894 annual volumes appeared, printed by Evans and published by Routledge. No edition appeared for 1896, and the 1897 edition was published by Dent. The most successful of these was the *Almanack for 1883*, which received favorable reviews and sold some ninety thousand copies in England, the United States, France, and Germany. The subsequent thirteen almanacs (1884–1895, 1897) received minimal coverage every year. There was some interest in how Greenaway would symbolize the months, the seasons, or the zodiac. The 1883, 1886, and 1888 almanacs received the most comment, with favorable response from such frequent Greenaway commentators as the *Graphic, Saturday Review, Publishers' Weekly*, and *Punch*. In the 1890s the Greenaway almanacs were virtually neglected by the press. From 1891 on, the almanac's title was altered to include Greenaway's name. The almanacs remained in print throughout the decade, as indicated by the Routledge catalogues. As collectible items the almanacs held commercial appeal in subsequent years, and the publisher's catalogue mentioned the availability of all previous almanacs when it announced the new year's offering. Some of these advertisements might have been prompted by the existence of a backlog of unsold almanacs. Evans's receipts indicated that only about half of the ninety thousand copies of the 1884 almanac sold that year, prompting a run of fifty thousand for the next year's edition. Later almanacs incorporated images from other Greenaway works, such as the 1895 almanac, which was entirely composed of images from William Mavor's *The English Spelling Book*

(1884). The almanacs had a stronger following in the United States, with sales often twice that of the British market. In a final appraisal of Greenaway's work, biographers Spielmann and Layard regret that so much of her creative attention was diverted to the almanacs, although the books demonstrate her "endless resource and inexhaustible faculty of design."

For many years the almanacs competed for critical attention with major Greenaway publications. The 1884 almanac was issued at the same time as one of her most important works, *Little Ann and Other Poems,* which was printed in, and thus dated, 1882, but published in 1883. Sixty-four illustrations by Greenaway illustrated the text, a collection of the poetry by Jane and Ann Taylor, whose verses were some of Greenaway's earliest and fondest childhood reading. The Taylors' first collection of poetry, *Original Poems, for Infant Minds* (1804–1805), was published in two volumes, followed by *Rhymes for the Nursery* (1806). Their poems (such as "Twinkle, Twinkle, Little Star") were some of the most celebrated and commonly known poetry of the early nineteenth century.

Little Ann and Other Poems was well advertised in periodicals and given top billing as Routledge's leading Christmas juvenile book. Routledge cited it in a select list inside the front cover of the January 1883 catalogue, included a full-color plate from the book on the title page of the August 1883 catalogue, and even inserted a frontispiece from the book in the 1885 catalogue.

The book appeared in early fall of 1883, shortly after Ruskin's tribute to Greenaway in his Slade Lecture at Oxford University. In "Fairy Land: Mrs. Allingham and Kate Greenaway," later published in his collection of essays *The Art of England* (1884), Ruskin touted Greenaway for her fancy, for images of "the radiance and innocence of re-instated infant divinity showered among the flowers of English meadows." What he particularly admired was the idealized setting, a preindustrial England of rural integrity, where, as he observed, "There are no railroads in it to carry the child away . . . no tunnel or pit mouths . . . no league-long viaducts . . . no blinkered iron bridges." References to Ruskin's speech appeared in subsequent reviews and commentary on Greenaway.

Little Ann received wide coverage in reviews of holiday books in England and the United States. Its most striking feature was the congruence of the Greenaway style with the subject matter: the poetry of the Georgian period. Greenaway's old-fashioned costumes seemed aptly suited to the poetry of the

Frontispiece for Greenaway's 1885 book, a collection of verse about childhood games and make-believe

Taylors. Evans's name, or a reference to his printing process, was also mentioned in virtually every review. Yet, despite the sympathetic match of style and subject matter, not all critics were delighted with the choice of text. The reviewer for the *Outlook* (13 December 1883), for example, appreciated the nostalgic appeal of the poetry and the improved aesthetics of Greenaway's art but questioned whether the poetry was too didactic for current tastes. While the moral, improving tone was commendable, the overall spirit of the poetry seemed out of harmony with the more progressive educational approach of the age.

At the end of 1884 several new Greenaway gift books appeared for the Christmas book market. Evans and Routledge selected engravings from previous Greenaway volumes to comprise *A Painting Book* and issued forty thousand copies. In addition to another almanac, there was *The Language of Flowers,* in which Greenaway illustrated floral lyrics from classic poets, and Mavor's *The English Spelling Book,* a reprint of a well-known spelling text. The Mavor book was a famous primer first published in 1801, which included, besides the alphabet, lessons in natural history; a selection of fables, poems, and moral tales; and a catechism. The drawings of the alphabet letters were also published separately as

Kate Greenaway's Alphabet (1885), which was more in the style and size of her almanacs and other gift books. Of the three 1884 titles, only *The Language of Flowers* attracted much critical attention. In fact, Greenaway received some of her most fulsome praise for this book. Choosing it as the leading juvenile book of the season, the *Saturday Review* (29 November 1884) raved about it, comparing the experience of examining it to looking at medieval manuscripts, adorned with decorative borders and illuminated initials.

The year 1885 brought the publication of *Marigold Garden,* the second book written as well as illustrated by Greenaway. *Under the Window* had been her first effort at picture-book making, and its text was questioned as poetry. Her more experienced effort to create a unified picture book of art and poetry produced a collection of verses on favorite childhood activities, such as playing games or make-believe, with pronounced flower imagery. Unlike its predecessor, the work suggests none of the darker, more fearsome elements of childhood. A color plate from the book graced the title page and frontispiece of Routledge's summer 1885 catalogue, and the Christmas supplement carried a full-page advertisement for *Marigold Garden.* Critical response was mixed. Considering that a famous author and illustrator was creating her own book of art and verse, and that it was printed by the virtuoso engraver in the field, the attention was slight. Though the *Illustrated London News,* the *Athenaeum,* and *Publishers' Weekly* all praised the book, the reviewer for the London *Times* (21 December 1885) criticized the contrivances of Greenaway's most recent production, asserting that Greenaway's "childish grace," so "irresistibly seductive" in the past, had been lost. Noting that Caldecott was away on holiday in the United States, where he would surely return with fresh ideas, the reviewer suggested that a trip there would be appropriate for Greenaway, who needed new inspiration. The commercial reception of the book was satisfactory for a limited run. Of the 20,000 copies of *Marigold Garden* printed in the fall of 1885, 16,810 were sold by 31 December, representing a dramatic departure from the sales of *Under the Window,* which had reached nearly 100,000 in its various editions.

In 1886 two new Greenaway titles were published, but only one of them by Routledge. *A Apple Pie* was Greenaway's illustrated version of a traditional nursery alphabet jingle, which had often been published as a separate book, as in John Harris's *History of the Apple Pie, Written by Z* (1808). Presumably, Greenaway was familiar with the rhyme from her own childhood reading or from her research in illustrating the Mavor reprint. Sales of the book reached a total of 13,500 copies, making the book a marginal success but also indicating a shrinking market for Greenaway's work. The book was only sketchily covered by the press. Two American reviews, in *Publishers' Weekly* and *Literary World,* were enthusiastic about its educational utility. The British reviews were less interested in the book's instructional value than its artistic quality. The *Saturday Review* (27 November 1886) singled out *More Graphic Pictures by Randolph Caldecott* as the best book of the season and mentioned *A Apple Pie* only in passing, as "sure of a favourable reception," with one of the young female figures described as "a charming conception." The most enthusiastic British response came from the *Athenaeum* (11 December 1886), which applauded the book's color and its depiction of childish whims and fancies; the reviewer claimed that it demonstrated the qualities that justified Greenaway's reputation: "grace, vivacity, homeliness, and Englishness."

The Queen of the Pirate Isle also appeared in 1886. This children's story by Bret Harte was published by Chatto and Windus, marking the first time Greenaway and Evans had worked with a publisher other than Routledge. Beyond the fact that Evans engraved the volume's thirty illustrations, very little publishing information exists about this book.

The story of *The Queen of the Pirate Isle* opens with nine-year-old Polly, her cousin Hickory, and a Chinese boy, Wan Lee, engaging in imaginative play, including being pirates. Joined by Patsey, a gold miner's son, they explore the California countryside and come upon a mine tunnel. Inside they find the Red Rovers, actually miners in disguise, who discover, through the children's fall, the famous lost lode of Red Mountain.

The popularity of author and illustrator attracted attention to the book in the press. The seeming incompatibility of Bret Harte's robust writing and Kate Greenaway's delicate artistry piqued the curiosity of critics, who frequently commented on the odd match. The estimate of the *Saturday Review* (11 December 1886) expressed the views of many: while the reviewer found Greenaway's drawings charming, there seemed little connection between them and the story. The American press was equally skeptical about the collaboration of Harte and Greenaway. The reviewer for the *Nation* (16 December 1886) felt that Greenaway's conventional style kept Harte's realism at a distance — the children could play at a mine and even tumble down a hill without soiling their clothes. The

Two of the letters designed by Greenaway for William Mavor's The English Spelling Book *(1884), later published separately as* Kate Greenaway's Alphabet *(1885)*

function of Greenaway's illustrations, in short, was "almost purely decorative."

One of Greenaway's most important works appeared in 1888: an edition of Robert Browning's *The Pied Piper of Hamelin* with thirty-five illustrations. The poem was first published in 1842 in Browning's *Bells and Pomegranates*. Browning knew the story from a version his father had written, and examples of the tale appear in other books, the oldest dating from 1450. Browning's rendition of the story was quickly recognized as a children's classic and was included in Coventry Patmore's pioneer anthology, *The Children's Garland from the Best Poets* (1862). Greenaway met Browning in 1882 when the author was seventy and several years later secured his permission to use the text. She worked closely with Ruskin in planning the book.

The critical reception of *The Pied Piper of Hamelin* was mixed. Generally, the American press found the book to represent Greenaway in her prime, and the collaboration between Browning's text and Greenaway's art was viewed sympathetically, with Greenaway's contributions bringing new life to old verse. However, there was some American resistance, including the *Nation* (20 December 1888), which found that Greenaway's illustrations displayed "the old qualities and the old defects." The attractiveness of the color and the decorative arrangement were unchanged, but deficiencies in draftsmanship were worse, according to the review.

Kate Greenaway's Book of Games, the last of her books to be both printed by Evans and published by Routledge, and *The Royal Progress of King Pepito* appeared in the fall of 1889. Evans printed ten thousand copies of each, and both were considered to be commercial failures. The *Book of Games* is a pictorial anthology of fifty-three games, with each described as to its structure and rules. About half of them are illustrated with Greenaway-style children at play in quaint villages and picturesque countryside. Its twenty-four full-sized plates were praised for their designs and coloring. The *Saturday Review* (7 December 1889) chose the book as the season's best — "the most pleasurable book of diversions that children could possess." The reviewer applauded Greenaway's choice of subject as the most sympathetic to her style and talents and the expertise of Evans.

The Royal Progress of King Pepito was published by the Society for Promoting Christian Knowledge (SPCK), a leading producer of award books and tracts. The story concerns a young boy who imagines himself as "King Pepito" and wanders away into the countryside, with animals and toys as his royal accompaniment, only to be rescued later by his family. Few reviewers noted the book at all, commenting mainly on the boy's lace-trimmed clothes, which suggested the Fauntleroy craze inspired by Frances Hodgson Burnett's popular book, *Little Lord Fauntleroy* (1886).

During the 1890s only Greenaway's almanacs kept her name visible. Evans retired in 1892, with his business continued by his two sons. Routledge brought out almanacs until 1894; the final edition was published by Dent in 1896. In 1900 Routledge sold its Greenaway copyrights to the rival firm of Frederick Warne, which began to reprint her major titles.

One of the last books Greenaway illustrated was published by Macmillan: *The April Baby's Book of Tunes* (1900) was ascribed to the mysterious "Author of Elizabeth and Her German Garden," who was, in fact, Mary Annette Beauchamp Russell, the Countess von Arnim, one of Greenaway's favorite authors. The earlier book had created a stir when it was published anonymously in 1898 by Macmillan; the story recounted the author's life in Germany with her first husband and her children who were named after the spring months in which they were born: "the April baby, the May baby, and the June baby." The sequel, *The April Baby's Book of Tunes,* is a loosely framed story of the mother instructing her three daughters in nursery rhymes, with music and lyrics woven into the text. The illustrations by Greenaway were reproduced by chromolithography, a departure from Evans's process of wood engravings.

The book was widely reviewed. The mystery of the author and Kate Greenaway's name on the title page after a decade of absence (apart from the predictable almanacs) stimulated interest. The fact that the illustrations were not engraved by Evans, who had become aligned with Greenaway's work, was not specifically noted, but the *Athenaeum* (15 December 1900) referred to the absence of Greenaway's customary delicacy and finish. The *Critic* (December 1900) agreed that the illustrations could not be compared in quality to her earlier efforts.

It was the end of an era. Greenaway deeply mourned Ruskin's death on 20 January 1900. Then, after suffering from a long bout with breast cancer, Greenaway died on 6 November 1901, at the age of fifty-five. Her ashes were buried in the family plot at Hampstead cemetery. Evans, her masterful engraver and commercial impresario, died in 1905.

When the newspapers announced Greenaway's death, they often followed with lengthy commentary on her style, influence, and major works, and these listings of significant titles helped to establish "the Greenaway canon." Since Greenaway's death occurred almost a decade after her prime in publishing, enough distance allowed some objective examination of her life and works. The *New York Times* was the first major paper to an-nounce her death, in an article which appeared on 8 November 1901. The paper listed her major works as *The Pied Piper of Hamelin, Marigold Garden, The Language of Flowers, Under the Window, A Day in a Child's Life, Little Ann, Mother Goose, Birthday Book, A Painting Book, The English Spelling Book, Kate Greenaway's Alphabet,* and *A Apple Pie.* Of her many books, only those printed by Evans and published by Routledge were mentioned. The London *Times* (9 November 1901) examined her career and influence in terms of the age: the advancement of the engraving and color printing process; the fanciful drawings which caught and held the public taste; the fascination of the age for "retrospection and curiosity-hunting"; and Ruskin's enthusiasm for her work.

The *Academy* (16 November 1901) published a lengthy memorial by E. V. Lucas, which was excerpted by various periodicals. He viewed her genius to be "repose" rather than "action" and expressed a perception that was later to be echoed by F. J. Harvey Darton's definitive history, *Children's Books in England* (1932): "To illustrate was not her *metier;* but to create – that she did to perfection."

Several celebrated tributes came from Spielmann, editor of the *Magazine of Art.* Spielmann's words carried much influence due to his standing as an art critic and from his personal knowledge of and friendship with the artist. Spielmann wrote about Greenaway in articles in the *Bookman,* the *Magazine of Art,* and, later, in a full-length biography, *The Life and Work of Kate Greenaway* (1905), coauthored with Layard. In the *Bookman* (December 1901), Spielmann acknowledged that Greenaway's stature could not be measured by ordinary standards of literary and artistic achievement. Instead, her work must be viewed by its effects: "simple, exquisite, and dainty, it came home to all; it was within the comprehension of all; and child and parent and child-lover alike delighted in her pictures." Despite her limitations as a writer for children, she aspired to be a poet and preferred to illustrate her own writing, which was more in harmony with her art than with the texts of others. In the *Magazine of Art* (January 1902) Spielmann addressed the nature of her appeal, which went to "the universal heart." She was the head of a school, the creator of a new style of depicting childhood. While Crane and Caldecott had interested and amused the reader, Greenaway interested the reader in the children themselves: "their graces, their little foibles, their thousand little prettinesses, the sweet little characteristics and psychology of their tender age." What she created was, in essence, "a fairy world" that

A page from Greenaway's illustrated edition of Robert Browning's The Pied Piper
of Hamelin

readers recognized as their own, more fantastic world.

Another influential tribute came in a two-part essay in the *Art Journal* (February and April 1902) by Austin Dobson, a distinguished poet and man of letters who had been her close friend and mentor. In this lengthy commentary Dobson placed Greenaway's work within a particular tradition of illustration. After comparing the more formal world of Stothard's art and the animated rural scenery of Caldecott, Dobson portrayed Greenaway's art as "a third country," a child-land peopled by diminutive characters in picturesque dress, playing in a decorous manner, and surrounded by Queen Anne architecture and landscapes.

Dobson attributed Greenaway's strength to the fidelity of her distinctive vision. Her personal perception was best represented in her almanacs, her *Birthday Book, Mother Goose, A Day in a Child's Life, Little Ann,* and *Marigold Garden.* At her best, her works were "little masterpieces of refined line and fairy tinting." Dobson reiterated Ruskin's advice to Greenaway: "Holbein lives for all time with his grim and ugly 'Dance of Death'; a not dissimilar

and more beautiful immortality may be in store for you if you worthily apply yourself to produce a 'Dance of Life.'"

Greenaway's status as an eminent children's book author and illustrator has fluctuated, with her reputation at its lowest at the time of her death. Numerous obituaries made reference to her fading glory, to her powerful influence rather than presence in children's books. The many imitations of her work over two decades had so saturated the market that the public had tired of her style. The artistic mood at the turn of the century privileged all things new, such as the work of Aubrey Beardsley and the Impressionists, making Greenaway's work seem merely old-fashioned – a label bearing pejorative rather than positive associations, as it had in the prime of the aesthetic movement.

Greenaway's waning reputation was revived by book collectors, who had continued to buy her works even when they had fallen from public favor. Warne reprinted many of her major titles in 1900. Spielmann and Layard's biography helped to elevate her status in the public eye. An auction of the Meacham Collection in 1921 was well publicized by a

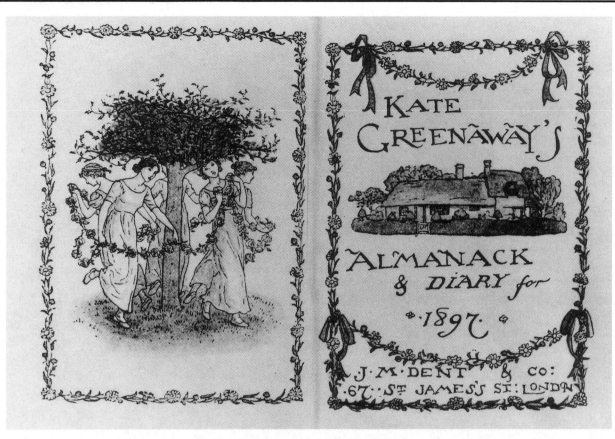

Frontispiece and title page for the last of Greenaway's series of almanacs, which began in 1882

catalogue with important bibliographic detail. Warne published an elaborate edition of *Kate Greenaway Pictures* (1921), introduced by H. M. Cundall, who predicted that Greenaway would survive long after the current craze for the Cubists had faded.

The centenary of Greenaway's birth in 1946 inspired many exhibits, articles, and reprintings. The British journal *Junior Bookshelf* and the American journal *Horn Book* published special commemorative issues in honor of Greenaway and Caldecott, who share the same birth year and month. Covelle Newcomb wrote a biography for children, *The Secret Door: The Story of Kate Greenaway* (1946), and Anne Carroll Moore, distinguished New York City Public Library's children's librarian and critic, offered her memorial book, *A Century of Kate Greenaway* (1946). She compared Greenaway's work to that of William Blake, reviewed Greenaway's publishing history, and relayed anecdotes about modern readership and circulation of Greenaway's books.

The last several decades have witnessed a wealth of publications about Greenaway's life and works. Anthologies of Greenaway illustrations and writings appeared by Edward Ernest in 1967 and by Bryan Holme in 1976. Publication of collections of

Greenaway material from the Rare Book Room, Detroit Public Library (1977), and from the Hunt Institute, Carnegie-Mellon University (1980), provided new bibliographic information. Engen authored a 1981 biography of Greenaway and co-authored with Thomas E. Schuster *Printed Kate Greenaway: A Catalogue Raisonné* (1986), which lists approximately 150 books that Greenaway illustrated or wrote in part or in whole, and at least ninety periodicals that include her work, greatly enlarging knowledge of the body of Greenaway's work.

Greenaway remains a major figure in the history of children's picture books. Her best known works today are *A Apple Pie,* which appears frequently on recommended lists for alphabet books, and *Mother Goose.* Despite her ambition to be a poet, Greenaway is much better known as an illustrator. Along with Evans, she helped to raise the stature of the picture book to a work of art, with studied appeal for adults as well as children. Her distinctive contribution was the fantastic landscape she created for English childhood, a juvenile Arcadia with contours shaped by childish play and parody of adult rituals. Greenaway's artistic images readily appealed to a popular audience, which led to the phenomenal "Greenaway

Vogue" of ephemera, commercial products, and imitations of her highly original designs. Her work remains a part of folk culture as well as a landmark in the history of children's bookmaking.

Bibliography:
Thomas E. Schuster and Rodney Engen, *Printed Kate Greenaway: A Catalogue Raisonné* (London: Schuster, 1986).

Biographies:
Marion H. Spielmann and George S. Layard, *The Life and Work of Kate Greenaway* (London: A&C Black, 1905);
Covelle Newcomb, *The Secret Door: The Story of Kate Greenaway* (New York: Dodd, Mead, 1946);
Rodney Engen, *Kate Greenaway: A Biography* (New York: Schocken, 1981).

References:
Brian Alderson, "Heavy Boots in the Marigold Garden: An Extended Comment on Current Kate Greenaway Literature," *Phaedrus,* 9 (1982): 7–10;
Alderson, *Sing a Song for Sixpence: The English Picture-Book Tradition and Randolph Caldecott* (Cambridge: Cambridge University Press, 1986), pp. 75–78;
Jonathan Cott, ed., "A Dialogue with Maurice Sendak," *Victorian Color Print Books, Masterworks of Children's Literature,* volume 7 (New York: Stonehill/Chelsea House, 1983), pp. ix–xxi;
M. H. Cundall, "Kate Greenaway," *Junior Bookshelf,* 10 (March 1946): 3–8;
F. J. Harvey Darton, *Children's Books in England: Five Centuries of Social Life* (Cambridge: Cambridge University Press, 1932); third edition, revised by Alderson (Cambridge: Cambridge University Press, 1982);
Patricia Dooley, "Kate Greenaway's *A Apple Pie*: An Atmosphere of Sober Joy," in *Touchstones: Reflections on the Best in Children's Literature,* volume 3, edited by Perry Nodelman (West Lafayette, Ind.: Children's Literature Association, 1989), pp. 63–69;
Rodney Engen, "Charting the Course of the Greenaway Legend," *Antiquarian Book Monthly Review,* 7 (March 1980): 115–123;
Edmund Evans, *The Reminiscences of Edmund Evans,* edited by Ruari McLean (Oxford: Clarendon Press, 1967);
Michael Patrick Hearn, "Mr. Ruskin & Miss Greenaway," *Children's Literature,* 8 (1980): 22–34;

Bryan Holme, *The Kate Greenaway Book* (New York: Viking, 1976);
Robert Kiger, ed., *Kate Greenaway: Catalogue of an Exhibition of Original Artworks and Related Materials Selected from the Frances Hooper Collection* (Pittsburgh: Hunt Institute for Botanical Documentation, Carnegie-Mellon University, 1980);
Selma G. Lanes, "Greenaway Went Thataway," in her *Down the Rabbit Hole: Adventures and Misadventures in the Realm of Children's Literature* (New York: Atheneum, 1971), pp. 31–43;
Anne Carroll Moore, *A Century of Kate Greenaway* (London: Warne, 1946);
Frank Arthur Mumby, *House of Routledge* (London: Routledge, 1934);
Jacqueline Overton, "Tuppence Colored: Walter Crane, Randolph Caldecott, and Kate Greenaway," in *Contemporary Illustrators of Children's Books,* edited by Bertha Mahoney and Elinor Whitney (Boston: Bookshop for Boys and Girls, 1930), pp. 110–125;
Anne Parrish, "Flowers for a Birthday: Kate Greenaway, March 17, 1846," *Horn Book,* 22 (March 1946): 97–108;
John Ruskin, "Fairy Land: Mrs. Allingham and Kate Greenaway," in his *The Art of England* (Kent: Allen, 1884), pp. 115–157;
Ina Taylor, *The Art of Greenaway: A Nostalgic Portrait of Childhood* (Gretna, La.: Pelican, 1991);
Susan Ruth Thomson, *Kate Greenaway: A Catalogue of the Kate Greenaway Collection, Rare Book Room, Detroit Public Library* (Detroit: Wayne State University Press, 1977);
Gleeson White, "Children's Books and Their Illustrators," *Studio* (Winter 1897–1898): 31–32, 36–40.

Papers:
Approximately three hundred of Kate Greenaway's original illustrations, books, correspondence, ephemera, and woodblocks are in the de Grummond Children's Literature Research Collection at the University of Southern Mississippi. The Hunt Institute for Botanical Documentation at the Carnegie-Mellon University has an extensive collection of Greenaway illustrations, books, and original materials, such as Greenaway's holograph journal. Among other important collections are those at the Rare Book Room, Detroit Public Library; the Keats House (Hampstead, England), holding books and materials donated by John Greenaway, Kate's brother, to the local public library; and the Library at University College, London, holding the Routledge archives.

G. A. Henty

(1832? – 16 November 1902)

Nicholas Ranson
University of Akron

See also the Henty entry in *DLB 18: Victorian Novelists After 1885.*

BOOKS: *A Search for a Secret,* 3 volumes (London: Tinsley, 1867);

The March to Magdala (London: Tinsley, 1868);

All but Lost, 3 volumes (London: Tinsley, 1869);

Out on the Pampas; or, The Young Settlers (London: Griffith & Farran, 1871; New York: Burt, n.d.);

The Young Franc-Tireurs, and their Adventures in the Franco-Prussian War (London: Griffith & Farran, 1872; New York: Dutton, 1892);

The March to Coomassie (London: Tinsley, 1874);

Seaside Maidens (London: Tinsley, 1880);

The Young Buglers: A Tale of the Peninsular War (London: Griffith & Farran, 1880; New York: Dutton, 1880);

In Times of Peril: A Tale of India (London: Griffith & Farran, 1881; New York: Dutton, 1881);

The Cornet of Horse: A Tale of Marlborough's Wars (London: Low, Marston, Searle & Rivington, 1881; Philadelphia: Lippincott, 1881);

Winning His Spurs: A Tale of the Crusades (London: Low, Marston, Searle & Rivington, 1882); republished as *The Boy Knight, Who Won His Spurs Fighting with King Richard of England: A Tale of the Crusaders* (Boston: Roberts, 1883);

Facing Death; or, The Hero of the Vaughan Pit: A Tale of the Coal Mines (London: Blackie, 1882; New York: Scribner & Welford, 1882);

Under Drake's Flag: A Tale of the Spanish Main (London: Blackie, 1883; New York: Blackie-Scribner, 1883);

Friends, though Divided: A Tale of the Civil Wars (London: Griffith & Farran, 1883);

Jack Archer: A Tale of the Crimea (London: Low, Marston, Searle & Rivington, 1883); republished as *The Fall of Sebastopol; or, Jack Archer in the Crimea* (Boston: Roberts, 1884);

G. A. Henty in 1856

By Sheer Pluck: A Tale of the Ashanti War (London: Blackie, 1884; New York: Scribner & Welford, 1884);

With Clive in India; or, The Beginnings of an Empire (London: Blackie, 1884; New York: Scribner & Welford, 1884);

True to the Old Flag: A Tale of the American War of Independence (London: Blackie, 1885; New York: Scribner & Welford, 1885);

St. George for England: A Tale of Cressy and Poitiers (London: Blackie, 1885; New York: Scribner & Welford, 1885);

The Young Colonists: A Story of the Zulu and Boer Wars (London: Routledge, 1885);

In Freedom's Cause: A Story of Wallace and Bruce (London: Blackie, 1885; New York: Scribner & Welford, 1885);

Through the Fray: A Tale of the Luddite Riots (London: Blackie, 1886; New York: Scribner & Welford, 1886);

For Name and Fame; or, Through Afghan Passes (London: Blackie, 1886; New York: Scribner & Welford, 1886);

The Dragon and the Raven; or, The Days of King Alfred (London: Blackie, 1886; New York: Scribner & Welford, 1886);

The Lion of the North: A Tale of Gustavus Adolphus (London: Blackie, 1886; New York: Scribner & Welford, 1886);

With Wolfe in Canada: or, The Winning of a Continent (London: Blackie, 1887; New York: Scribner & Welford, 1887);

The Young Carthaginian: A Story of the Times of Hannibal (London: Blackie, 1887; New York: Scribner & Welford, 1887);

A Final Reckoning: A Tale of Bush Life in Australia (London: Blackie, 1887; New York: Scribner & Welford, 1887);

The Bravest of the Brave; or, With Peterborough in Spain (London: Blackie, 1887; New York: Scribner & Welford, 1887);

In the Reign of Terror: The Adventures of a Westminster Boy (New York: Scribner & Welford, 1887; London: Blackie, 1888);

For the Temple: A Tale of the Fall of Jerusalem (New York: Scribner & Welford, 1887; London: Blackie, 1888);

Bonnie Prince Charlie: A Tale of Fontenoy and Culloden (New York: Scribner & Welford, 1887; London: Blackie, 1888);

Sturdy and Strong; or, How George Andrews Made His Way (New York: Scribner & Welford, 1887; London: Blackie, 1888);

Orange and Green: A Tale of the Boyne and Limerick (New York: Scribner & Welford, 1887; London: Blackie, 1888);

Gabriel Allen, M.P. (London: Blackett, 1888);

The Curse of Carne's Hold: A Tale of Adventure, 2 volumes (London: Spencer, Blackett & Hallam, 1889);

The Plague Ship (London: Society for the Propagation of Christian Knowledge, 1889; New York: Young, 1889);

The Cat of Bubastes: A Tale of Ancient Egypt (London: Blackie, 1889; New York: Scribner & Welford, 1889);

The Lion of St. Mark: A Tale of Venice (London: Blackie, 1889; New York: Scribner & Welford, 1889);

Captain Bayley's Heir: A Tale of the Gold Fields of California (London: Blackie, 1889; New York: Scribner & Welford, 1889);

One of the 28th: A Tale of Waterloo (New York: Scribner & Welford, 1889; London: Blackie, 1890);

Tales of Daring and Danger (London: Blackie, 1890; New York: Scribner & Welford, n.d.);

With Lee in Virginia: A Story of the American Civil War (London: Blackie, 1890; New York: Scribner & Welford, 1890);

By Pike and Dyke: A Tale of the Rise of the Dutch Republic (London: Blackie, 1890; New York: Scribner & Welford, 1890);

By Right of Conquest; or, With Cortez in Mexico (New York: Scribner & Welford, 1890; London: Blackie, 1891);

By England's Aid; or, The Freeing of the Netherlands (1585–1604) (New York: Scribner & Welford, 1890; London: Blackie, 1891);

A Chapter of Adventures; or, Through the Bombardment of Alexandria (New York: Scribner & Welford, 1890; London: Blackie, 1891);

Those Other Animals (London: Henry, 1891);

Maori and Settler: A Story of the New Zealand War (London: Blackie, 1891; New York: Scribner & Welford, 1891);

A Hidden Foe (2 volumes, London: Low, Marston, 1891; 1 volume, New York: National Book Company, n.d.);

Held Fast for England: A Tale of the Siege of Gibraltar (New York: Scribners, 1891; London: Blackie, 1892);

The Dash for Khartoum: A Tale of the Nile Expedition (New York: Scribners, 1891; London: Blackie, 1892);

Redskin and Cow-Boy: A Tale of the Western Plains (New York: Scribners, 1891; London: Blackie, 1892);

Beric the Briton: A Story of the Roman Invasion (New York: Scribners, 1892; London: Blackie, 1893);

The Ranche in the Valley (London: Society for the Propagation of Christian Knowledge, 1892; New York: Young, 1892);

Condemned as a Nihilist: A Story of Escape from Siberia (New York: Scribners, 1892; London: Blackie, 1893);

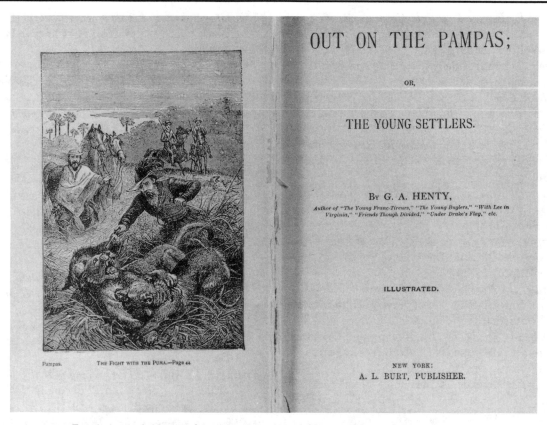

Frontispiece and title page for an American edition of Henty's first novel for young readers

In Greek Waters: A Story of the Greek War of Independence (1821–1827) (New York: Scribners, 1892; London: Blackie, 1893);

Rujub, the Juggler, 3 volumes (London: Chatto & Windus, 1893); republished as In the Days of the Mutiny: A Military Novel (New York: Ogilvie, 1893);

Through the Sikh War: A Tale of the Conquest of the Punjaub (New York: Scribners, 1893; London: Blackie, 1894);

Saint Bartholomew's Eve: A Tale of the Huguenot Wars (New York: Scribners, 1893; London: Blackie, 1894);

A Jacobite Exile: Being the Adventures of a Young Englishman in the Service of Charles XII of Sweden (New York: Scribners, 1893; London: Blackie, 1894);

Wulf the Saxon: A Story of the Norman Conquest (New York: Scribners, 1894; London: Blackie, 1895);

In the Heart of the Rockies: A Story of Adventure in Colorado (New York: Scribners, 1894; London: Blackie, 1895);

When London Burned: A Story of Restoration Times and the Great Fire (New York: Scribners, 1894; London: Blackie, 1895);

Dorothy's Double (3 volumes, London: Chatto & Windus, 1894; 1 volume, Chicago: Rand McNally, 1895);

A Knight of the White Cross: A Table of the Siege of Rhodes (New York: Scribners, 1895; London: Blackie, 1896);

The Tiger of Mysore: A Story of the War with Tippoo Saib (New York: Scribners, 1895; London: Blackie, 1896);

A Woman of the Commune: A Tale of Two Sieges of Paris (London: White, 1895); republished as Two Sieges of Paris; or, A Girl of the Commune (New York: Fenno, 1895);

Through Russian Snows: A Story of Napoleon's Retreat from Moscow (New York: Scribners, 1895; London: Blackie, 1896);

Surly Joe: The Story of a True Hero (London: Blackie, 1896);

White-Faced Dick: A Story of Pine-Tree Gulch (London: Blackie, 1896);

On the Irrawaddy: A Story of the First Burmese War (New York: Scribners, 1896; London: Blackie, 1897);

At Agincourt: A Tale of the White Hoods of Paris (New York: Scribners, 1896; London: Blackie, 1897);

Cover for an American edition of Henty's 1880 adventure novel, set during the Peninsula War (1808–1814), in which the British fought along with Portuguese troops and Spanish guerrillas to drive Napoleon's troops from the Iberian Peninsula

With Cochrane the Dauntless: A Tale of the Exploits of Lord Cochrane in South American Waters (New York: Scribners, 1896; London: Blackie, 1897);

The Queen's Cup: A Novel (3 volumes, London: Chatto & Windus, 1897; 1 volume, New York: Appleton, 1898);

Among Malay Pirates: A Tale of Adventure and Peril (New York: Hurst, 1897);

With Moore at Carunna: A Tale of the Peninsula War (New York: Scribners, 1897; London: Blackie, 1898);

A March on London: Being a Story of Wat Tyler's Insurrection (New York: Scribners, 1897; London: Blackie, 1898);

With Frederick the Great: A Story of the Seven Years' War (New York: Scribners, 1897; London: Blackie, 1898);

Both Sides the Border: A Tale of Hotspur and Glendower (New York: Scribners, 1898; London: Blackie, 1899);

Colonel Thorndyke's Secret (London: Chatto & Windus, 1898; New York: Hurst, 1901); abridged as *The Brahmins' Treasure: Or, Colonel Thorndyke's Secret* (Philadelphia: Lippincott, 1900);

Under Wellington's Command: A Tale of the Peninsular War (New York: Scribners, 1898; London: Blackie, 1899);

At Aboukir and Acre: A Story of Napoleon's Invasion of Egypt (New York: Scribners, 1898; London: Blackie, 1899);

On the Spanish Main (London: Chambers, 1899);

The Golden Canon (New York: Mershon, 1899);

A Roving Commission; or, Through the Black Insurrection of Hayti (New York: Scribners, 1899; London: Blackie, 1900);

No Surrender!: A Tale of the Rising in La Vendée (New York: Scribners, 1899; London: Blackie, 1900);

Won by the Sword: A Tale of the Thirty Years' War (New York: Scribners, 1899; London: Blackie, 1900);

The Lost Heir (London: Bowden, 1899);

Do Your Duty (London: Blackie, 1900);

Out with Garibaldi: A Story of the Liberation of Italy (New York: Scribners, 1900; London: Blackie, 1901);

In the Irish Brigade: A Tale of the War in Flanders and Spain (New York: Scribners, 1900; London: Blackie, 1901);

With Buller in Natal; or, A Born Leader (New York: Scribners, 1900; London: Blackie, 1901);

In the Hands of the Cave-Dwellers (New York: Harper, 1900; London: Blackie, 1903);

At the Point of the Bayonet: A Tale of the Mahratta War (New York: Scribners, 1901; London: Blackie, 1902);

To Herat and Cabul: A Story of the First Afghan War (New York: Scribners, 1901; London: Blackie, 1902);

John Hawke's Fortune: A Story of Monmouth's Rebellion (London: Chapman & Hall, 1901);

Queen Victoria: Scenes from Her Life and Reign (London: Blackie, 1901);

With Roberts to Pretoria: A Tale of the South African War (New York: Scribners, 1901; London: Blackie, 1902);

The Sole Survivors (London & Edinburgh: Chambers, 1901); republished as *Redskins and Colonists* (New York: Stitt, 1905);

With the British Legion: A Story of the Carlist Wars (New York: Scribners, 1902; London: Blackie, 1903);

The Treasure of the Incas: A Tale of Adventure in Peru (New York: Scribners, 1902; London: Blackie, 1903);

With Kitchener in the Soudan: A Story of Atbara and Omdurman (New York: Scribners, 1902; London: Blackie, 1903);

Through Three Campaigns: A Story of Chitral, Tirah, and Ashantee (New York: Scribners, 1903; London: Blackie, 1904);

With the Allies to Pekin: A Tale of the Relief of the Legations (New York: Scribners, 1903; London: Blackie, 1904);

By Conduct and Courage: A Story of the Days of Nelson (New York: Scribners, 1904; London: Blackie, 1905);

Gallant Deeds (London & Edinburgh: Chambers, 1905);

In the Hands of the Malays and Other Stories (London: Blackie, 1905);

Redskins and Colonists (New York: Stitt, 1905);

Among the Bushrangers (London: Blackie, 1906);

Cast Ashore (London: Blackie, 1906);

Cornet Walter (London: Blackie, 1906);

The Highland Chief (London: Blackie, 1906);

An Indian Raid (London: Blackie, 1906);

A Soldier's Daughter and Other Stories (London: Blackie, 1906);

The Two Prisoners (London: Blackie, 1906);

The Young Captain (London: Blackie, 1906);

The Young Patriot (Dublin: Blackie, 1906).

SELECTED PERIODICAL PUBLICATIONS:
"Coming Together," *Tinsleys'* (March 1869);
"The King of Clubs," *Tinsleys'* (September 1869);
"A Simple Story," *Tinsleys'* (November 1869);
"Sir Salar Jung and the Berars," *Tinsleys'* (1876);
"Bears and Dacoits," *Union Jack* (June 1881);
"Do Your Duty," *Union Jack* (1882);
"The Spy of Belfort," *Grip* (15 November 1883);
"A Coaching Adventure," *Our Annual* (1883);
"The Golden Cañon," *Boys Illustrated Annual,* 1 (1892/1893);
"Jack Dillon of Dunnamore," *Chums Annual,* 1 (1892/1893);
"A Prevision of Evil," *Western Weekly News* (Christmas 1893);
"A Close Shave," *Ludgate* (1894);
"An Anxious Time," *Western Weekly News* (Summer 1894);
"A Simple Story," *Tinsleys'* (November 1896);
"Life as a Special Correspondent," *Boy's Own Annual,* 18 (1896);
"The Fetish Role," *Boy's Own Annual,* 19 (1896–1897);
"Among Malay Pirates," *Boy's Own Annual,* 20 (1897–1898);
"The Sole Survivors," *St. Nicholas* (1898–1899);
"Torpedo Boat 240," *Chambers's Journal* (1899);
"The Old Pit Shaft," *Captain* (1901);
"Down a Crevasse," *Boy's Own Paper* (Summer 1901);
"In the Hands of the Cave Dwellers," *Boy's Own Annual,* 22 (1901);
"A Frontier Girl," *Girl's Realm Annual* (1901);
"In Troubled Times," *Nister's Holiday Annual* (1902);
"A Soldier's Daughter," *Girl's Realm Annual* (1903);
"How a Drummer Boy Saved the Regiment," *Nister's Holiday Annual* (1909).

When Victoria ascended the British throne on 20 June 1837, G. A. Henty was not yet five years old. Yet in thousands of young boys' lives Henty was destined to be as important as the queen. In a 1980 review of the most recent biography of Henty, Eric Stokes commented that "No other writer for the young exercised a tithe of his influence." Henty

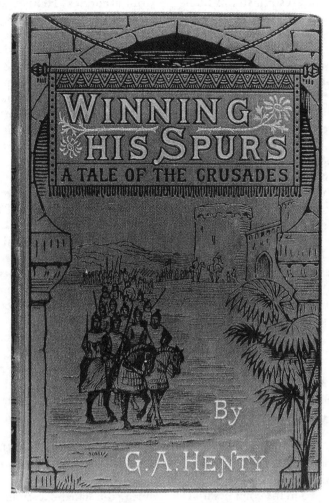

*Cover for an 1895 edition of one of Henty's popular historical
adventure novels*

was one of the most influential of all Victorian children's writers and remained in print for three generations of young British and American readers. The circumstances of his birth are a mystery: he told *Captain* magazine in 1899 that he was born in the small village of Trumpington, two miles south of Cambridge, England, on 8 December 1832 (the year of the Great Reform Act). This date is usually repeated in subsequent biographies, but parish records show no documentation of a Henty family for the period 1797 to 1890. The admissions register of Gonville and Caius College, Cambridge, indicates that Henty was born in Godmanchester (a town some twelve miles northwest of Cambridge) and baptized on 27 April 1833, a fact confirmed in the parish register of the church of Saint Mary. He died on 16 November 1902, nearly two years after Queen Victoria's death, placing Henty's life and ca-

reer squarely within that period of British history (1837–1901) called the Victorian age. Perhaps more than any other writer of his time, Henty was instrumental in the creation, promotion, and upholding of the age's values and beliefs. Indeed, his whole life may be seen as a living out of the Victorian values of manliness and tenacity and the relentless capacity for exploration and acquisition that characterized the period of British imperial history between 1830 and 1900.

George Alfred Henty was born into a "respectable" household, his father, James, being a stockbroker and his mother, Mary Bovill, being the daughter of a Dr. Edwards, a physician practicing in Wandsworth, London. As a boy, Henty suffered from bouts of profuse bleeding and a nearly fatal attack of rheumatic fever. His grandfather taught him natural history. On 24 September 1847 Henty was sent, along with his younger brother Frederick, to the well-known public school Westminster in London. Henty was nearly fifteen, a comparatively late age to enter Westminster, a situation later explained by the author as the result of his sickly childhood. Picked on due to his puny appearance, Henty took boxing and wrestling lessons outside school hours. In addition, as he later recalled, students at Westminster either had to row or play cricket – Henty chose rowing. He received a "Good drilling in Latin" at the school, which he claimed was of use to him later when he became a war correspondent, since Latin served as a "key to modern Italian," and that meant, "wherever I could come across a priest I had a friend and an interpreter."

Sometime in 1850 Henty's father began coal- and iron-mining operations at Banwen, at the top of the Neath Valley in southern Wales. Henty's exposure to the family business fostered a lifelong interest in mining, which would lead him to visit the gold and silver mines of the Sierra Nevada in California in 1874 and later still to become a director, and then chairman, of the Lake Superior Copper Company, formed in 1885 and dissolved in 1889. Henty was admitted to Gonville and Caius College, Cambridge, on 14 April 1851 and matriculated in the Michaelmas term of 1851. By his own account he was below the necessary academic standard, crammed too hard, and suffered a breakdown, which led to his taking a year's leave. Within a short period he returned to Cambridge for another year, and then he left sometime in 1853 without taking a degree because he enlisted in the commissariat department of the British army.

In the spring of 1855 Henty was sent to the Crimea as a member of the purveyor's department. He was present at the siege of Sebastopol and wrote letters home concerning what he saw. Some of these were shown to the editor of the newspaper *Morning Advertiser,* and he engaged Henty to send reports about any aspects of the campaign which would interest the newspaper's readers. Henty's position gave him an inside view of military affairs. Although these eleven letters were published without a byline, Nicholas Ranson identifies Henty as their author in a 1990 article for the *Henty Society Bulletin.* The letters deal with everything from the excellence of the Turkish army's riflemen to the appearance of the Sardinian contingent, from Florence Nightingale to the superior provisioning arrangements of the French army.

Sometime in June 1855 Henty's brother Frederick arrived from England to join the purveyor's department but contracted cholera at Scutari and died within a fortnight. Having caught the fever from Frederick, Henty was returned to England as an invalid shortly after 18 June 1855, the date of his last letter for the *Morning Advertiser.* Following a brief convalescence, he was posted by the War Office on 30 November 1855 to Turin to join the Anglo Italian Legion as purveyor. But his time in Italy was short: in February 1856 he was recalled by the War Office and sent as purveyor in charge of the Belfast Purveying District; on 19 March 1857 Henty was appointed to take charge of the Portsmouth Purveying District. He soon returned to Ireland, where he married Elizabeth Finucane on 1 July 1857. The couple would have four children: Charles Gerald, born 1858; Hubert, born 1860; Maud, born 1861; and Ethel, born 1862.

Henty suddenly resigned his commission on 29 January 1858. G. Manville Fenn, in his 1907 biography, asserts that Henty resigned over a general lack of encouragement from his superiors. The War Office letter book tells another story, however, with the War Office claiming upward of five hundred pounds for unpaid bills for which Henty had withdrawn money and more than one thousand pounds unaccounted for. Henty appears to have left the army under a cloud, and he was now faced with making a career somewhere else.

Henty seems to have left the country for several years, returning to England to take care of his children after his wife, Elizabeth, had died on 20 August 1865. He was hired by the London *Standard* as a special correspondent to Italy in May 1866, during the Italian-Austrian war. He immediately left England, and, in a series of letters beginning at Basle on 13 June 1866, he reported his following of Giuseppe Garibaldi's Tyrolese campaign against the Austrians.

Returning to England overland, he busied himself with his yacht – a lifetime recreation – until the *Standard* sent him in December 1867 with Sir Robert Napier's expedition to Abyssinia to punish King Theodore for imprisoning the British consul. Henty equipped himself in Bombay and set out with the expedition to Magdala, Theodore's capital. Napier's troops stormed Magdala, released the European captives, and killed King Theodore. Henty returned to England; collected his dispatches as a book, *The March to Magdala* (1868); and wrote *All but Lost* (1869), a three-volume novel. These books received little notice, and sales seem to have been poor.

After several other assignments for the *Standard,* in March 1871 Henty suddenly found himself in the center of the Paris Commune uprising. Henty

Sir Cuthbert's introduction to Lady Margaret, an illustration by H. Petherick for Henty's Winning His Spurs:
A Tale of the Crusades *(1882)*

saw much of the massacres that followed the suppression of the Commune, which he reported for the *Standard.*

Returning to England, he wrote the first two of his boys' novels – *Out on the Pampas* (1871) and *The Young Franc-Tireurs* (1872) – in return for a substantial payment. The two works proved very successful, much to Henty's surprise.

For the next several years Henty continued to report on military campaigns as an international correspondent for the *Standard.* But by 1876 his health had given out from all the travel, and he returned to England. Henty never did any more reporting from the field, though almost to the end of his life he was retained to edit the reports and telegrams that *Standard* correspondents sent back to London. Apart from a mysterious visit to the United States to see copper mines around Lake Superior in 1874 and then on to Nebraska and California, he never left England again.

With the publication of *Out on the Pampas,* Henty had experimentally begun his career as an author of children's fiction, and after his retirement as a field reporter he turned his energies to the continuation of this career. In 1880 Henty succeeded another popular boys' writer, W. H. G. Kingston, as editor of the *Union Jack;* it ceased publication in 1883. He tried again in 1888 as editor of Beeton's *Boy's Own Magazine,* but it closed in 1890. Another editing venture, *Camps and Quarters,* produced only a single annual in 1889. As a writer of juvenile novels, he experienced greater success, however – from 1882 to 1902 Henty produced three or four books each year for Blackie, writing roughly a chapter (6,500 words) a day . The length of a Henty boys' novel was typically 130,000–150,000 words – about the length of the old three-volume Victorian novel, the form Henty had tried first.

Henty's gifts as a narrator are derived from his ability to tell a story full of incident. He used a characteristic formula in his fiction – choosing as the protagonist a young boy who is of middle-class origin, often orphaned, and with no great expectations of estate or fame. This character is typically fourteen to sixteen years of age, physically brave, naturally courteous, intuitively honorable, far-sighted, and quick acting. He is the embodiment of the ideals of the Victorian public-school boy. Henty places this protagonist in a historical situation (usually of military significance), where he then becomes closely associated with the principal British authority and rises to the position of trusted assistant and adviser. His progress involves adventures by sea, capture by brigands, several amazing escapes, unexpected assistance from the local population (including a friendship with a young native boy his own age), a share in the inevitable material spoils of conquest, and finally a return to London to receive the grateful thanks of the government. Henty disposes of his character's future in a brief, final chapter that sees the young hero married to a childhood sweetheart, with the clear implication that he will settle down, have a family, and take up a position in society to which his exploits and newly acquired wealth entitle him.

With Clive in India (1884) serves as a typical example of this formula. In its preface, a feature which became standard in all Henty's juvenile stories, the author identifies the historical focus of the novel – "the wonderful events of the ten years, which at their commencement saw Madras in the hands of the French – Calcutta at the mercy of the Nabob of Bengal – and the English influence apparently at the point of extinction in India – and which ended in the final triumph of the English both in Bengal and Madras." Henty also asserts that the "historical details are, throughout the story, strictly accurate."

The hero, Charlie Marryat, is a "lad of sixteen" who, though "slight in build," has "firm and hard" muscles as well as a "reputation for being a leader in every mischievous prank; but he was honorable and manly, would scorn to shelter himself under the semblance of a lie, and was a prime favorite with his masters as well as his schoolfellows." Charlie has lost his father, a former naval officer, and he must help support his mother and his two younger sisters. Fortunately, his mother has an uncle who has an interest in the East India Company, and this benign, gruff man secures Charlie a writership in the company. He sails to India in a ship attacked successively by privateers and then pirates, and he saves the life of a nineteen-year-old Irish soldier by diving into the ocean and rescuing him. Having arrived in Madras, Charlie Marryat is commended to Baron Robert Clive and joins his forces, exchanging the pen for the sword, as Clive himself had done. They set off on the morning of 26 August 1751 to attack the French at Arcot. Charlie

returns to England following the successful English siege of Pondicherry in 1761 and France's consequent loss of India. In the final chapter Charlie is promoted to lieutenant colonel, and he announces airily to his uncle and mother on his return to England: "I have earned in my way close upon one hundred thousand pounds." He marries his childhood sweetheart, Ada, and his friend Peters, who has shared in Charlie's adventures, marries Charlie's youngest sister, Katie.

It is convenient to group Henty's eighty-one historical adolescent novels into categories for analysis and examine the structure, the themes, and the outcomes. Twenty-five of these novels take British history as their theme and reveal Henty's views on British imperialism. Serious attention has been paid to him as a propagator of British imperialism since a seminal article by Godfrey Davis was published in 1955. Henty's role as a purveyor of British history has been the focus of this critical attention, and critical debate has coalesced around this aspect of his work. In his 1955 article Davis finds Henty's use of sources largely uncritical, repeating both the political prejudices and inaccuracies embodied in them. For instance, in the four novels dealing with Britain's peninsular war campaign (1808–1814) – *The Young Buglers* (1880), *Under Wellington's Command* (1898), *With Moore at Corunna* (1897), and *One of the 28th* (1889) – Henty took his historical material from Sir William Napier's *History of the War in the Peninsula* (1828–1840). Napier was a Whig and admirer of Napoleon, and in uncritical acceptance of his source Henty belittles the contribution of the Spaniards to the war and berates the British Tory government. Henty also grossly simplifies the difficulties of a military struggle against Napoleon. Worse, he even includes such incidents as those in *The Young Buglers* where the young hero leads the French to attack a Spanish guerrilla stronghold and in *Under Wellington's Command* where British prisoners join the French against the guerrillas. No such events are known, and they are improbable since the Spanish were the allies of Britain, but they give a dismissive cast to the contributions of the Spanish and suggest Henty's ignorance of the actual conditions of peninsular warfare.

Other careless mistakes are glaring. In *With Moore at Corunna* Henty gives two different figures on the same page for the number of men commanded by General Moore; and the account of the battle of Busaco has several mistakes based on Henty's misunderstanding of the terrain. Davis concludes that "Small mistakes matter little in novels written for boys, but the distortion of the whole

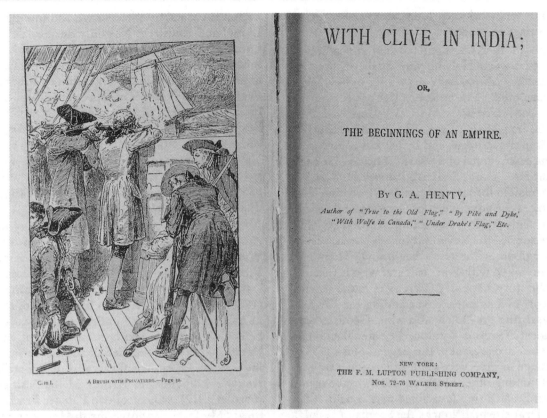

C. in I.   A BRUSH WITH PRIVATEERS.—Page 32.

Frontispiece and title page for an American edition of one of Henty's imperialist historical novels

course of the war is serious." The cumulative effect of these errors is that no young reader who relied on Henty's books on the peninsular war would be able to give a good answer to the question which demands an answer: why did Napoleon with his superiority in numbers fail to defeat Arthur Wellesley, first Duke of Wellington, and hold down the Spanish?

Mark Naidis's 1964 study of nine Henty novels set in India presents a more complex view of Henty's imperialism as found in *With Clive in India, For Name and Fame* (1886), *In Times of Peril* (1881), *Through the Sikh War* (1893), *The Tiger of Mysore* (1895), *Rujub, the Juggler* (1893), *To Herat and Cabul* (1901), *At the Point of the Bayonet* (1901), and *On the Irrawaddy* (1896). Henty had visited India in 1875 and 1876, when he reported on the tour of the Prince of Wales, later Edward VII, and he saw the British Raj at one of its heights of pomp and circumstance. But he was not all admiration. The British under Clive pursued a policy that was not driven by ethical considerations. Naidis points out that Charlie Marryat is lectured by an experienced young man of twenty-six: "You will see after a time that right has nothing at all to do with the dealings of the Company in their relations to the native princes."

This implicit acknowledgment of the amoral, pragmatic British interest in India contrasts with Henty's presentation in *At the Point of the Bayonet* of the British freeing of India from many warring factions as something of a moral crusade. While it is clear that Henty had little firsthand knowledge of Indian life outside the official bounds of the military and civil service, he notes, accurately enough, a significant difference between Clive's rule and that of Victoria, where the swashbuckling and acquisitive Briton seeking his fortune abroad has been replaced by the bureaucrat. *In Times of Peril* describes the peaceful domesticity of the compounds where the colonial elite lived, presumably drawing on Henty's own observations.

Naidis therefore concludes that Henty believed the British Raj benefited the Indians, but he portrays most Indians as cowards. The best that may be hoped for is that the British may also come to those parts of the country as yet unconquered. In *Through the Sikh War* a character remarks of the future of Kashmir: "A generation or two at the outside and the English will be rulers in Seringur I think, sahib. What a blessing it would be for the country! In the first place, there would be neither over-taxation nor oppression. All would live and till their lands and work their loom, secure of enjoying their earnings in peace."

Still another war depicted in a Henty novel was that between Holland and Spain in the sixteenth century. *By England's Aid* (1891) shows Henty in a typical mode. The book has Henty's customary preface, addressed as usual to "My Dear Lads," in which he explains: "England ... threw herself openly into the struggle, and by her aid contributed to the successful issue of the war." Thus, as far back as Elizabeth's time, England is presented as being responsible for another nation's freedom. The novel traces the adventures of Geoffrey and Lionel Vickars, "boys of fourteen and thirteen years old" who are sons of the Reverend John Vickars, rector of Hedingham at the tale's beginning. Their fortunes are linked with Francis Vere, who is twenty-five at the story's opening. Vere rises in the service of the earl of Leicester, commanding the English forces assisting the Dutch, and when Geoffrey and Lionel meet Francis in London, they are taken on as pages. They are present at the siege of Sluys (1587) and manage to save Vere's life and reveal a traitorous plot, among other heroic acts. They manage to get on an English ship (captained by a cousin of Sir Francis Drake) which attacks the Spanish Armada. Geoffrey is captured by the Spanish when his ship's mast – with him on it – breaks and falls onto the Spanish ship's deck. Taken to Spain, Geoffrey learns the language in six weeks; befriends Gerald Burke, an Irishman who has an ample estate in Ireland; and rescues two merchants from robbers, for which he is handsomely rewarded. He unites his Irish friend with his Spanish ladylove, Donna Inez. All three run away by sea, but Geoffrey is captured by Moorish corsairs and befriended by an English prisoner, Stephen Boldero. Their captor commends their work ethic: "I have watched you while you have been at work, and truly you have not spared yourselves in my service, but have labored for me with all your strength, well and willingly. I see now that it is true that the people of your nation differ much from the Spaniards, who are dogs." Later Juan Mendez (who turns out to be a rich merchant) and his daughter arrive as captives, and Geoffrey and Stephen rescue them, steal a boat, and sail back to Cartagena. They travel to Cadiz, the merchant's home city, and Geoffrey marries Dolores Mendez.

Henty's version of history, derived from his reading of Clement Markham and other historians, is again central to his plot. The novel creates the impression that the victory of the Dutch is possible only because of the British, and the victory of the

nation is caused by the courage and intelligence of Lionel and Geoffrey. Not only do they defeat and outmaneuver the opposition, they also win the hearts and minds, the daughters and the treasure, of their enemies. Mendez offers Geoffrey a share in his business, and Dolores accepts the faith of her husband. The pattern of the romance, where youth and beauty triumph, is clearly present in *By England's Aid,* as it is in more than eighty of Henty's novels. Three generations of English children followed such adventures, with their vision of life as adventurous service rewarded with a grateful kingdom's thanks and an estate in the country.

Henty also influenced the way many notable Americans viewed historical events, as Kenneth Wiggins Porter documents in "Some American Views of G. A. Henty" (1980). The respected American social historian Arthur M. Schlesinger, Sr. (1888–1965), recounted that by the age of fourteen he had read nearly six hundred books whose titles he could recall. He was particularly captivated by Henty's works and credited them as a "formative influence" on his choice of career. Equally striking is Henty's influence on Arthur M. Schlesinger, Jr. (born in 1917), winner of two Pulitzer Prizes in history: "My father exposed me to Henty at an early point, and I read book after book with enjoyment and fascination. Such knowledge as I have of ancient Egypt, the republic of Venice, India, southern Africa, the rise of the Dutch republic, the struggle for Chilean independence, the Franco-Prussian War, the Boxer rebellion, and many other historical episodes, had its roots in Henty." Many other influential Americans, such as U.S. Navy admiral Elmo Zumwalt, have expressed their admiration for Henty's works and the powerful impact that their reading of these books had on their adult careers. Porter also produces convincing evidence to show that several American writers were influenced by Henty.

Thus Americans had their historical perspectives molded by Henty, who had very definite ideas about American history, particularly in regard to the revolutionary war. In *True to the Old Flag: A Tale of the American War of Independence* (1885) the hero, Harold Wilson, a Boston lad of fifteen, is sent in 1774 to a family friend's farm by Lake Huron so that he can learn what life is like on the frontier. There he helps fight off an attack by Iroquois Indians, returns to Boston, and when war breaks out, stays loyal to Britain. He helps John Burgoyne capture Ticonderoga, rescues his cousin Nelly from Indians, fights later with the British in the defense of Savannah, is captured by revolutionary forces and

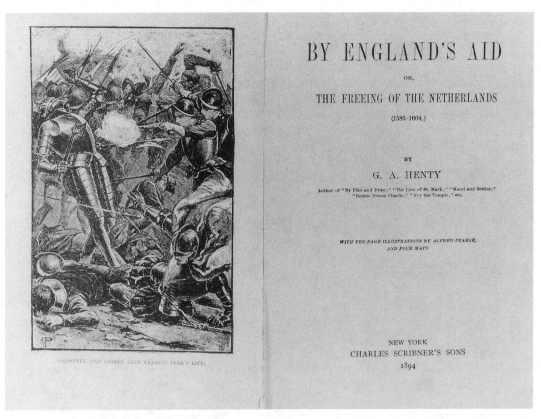

GEOFFREY AND LIONEL SAVE FRANCIS VERE'S LIFE.

BY ENGLAND'S AID

OR,

THE FREEING OF THE NETHERLANDS

(1585–1604.)

BY

G. A. HENTY

Author of "By Pike and Dyke;" "The Lion of St. Mark;" "Maori and Settler,"
"Bonnie Prince Charlie;" "For the Temple," etc.

WITH TEN PAGE ILLUSTRATIONS BY ALFRED PEARSE,
AND FOUR MAPS

NEW YORK
CHARLES SCRIBNER'S SONS
1894

Frontispiece and title page for an American edition of the novel Henty set during the war between Holland and Spain in the sixteenth century

then rescued by his black friend Jake, and finishes the war as a scout. When Cornwallis surrenders at Yorktown, Harold migrates to Canada, buys a farm on the Saint Lawrence, marries Nelly, and lives out his life as an Empire Loyalist. In a 1980 article Dennis Butts comments on the discontinuity in this novel "between Harold's *personal* adventures, which are mainly accounts of success and triumph over the Indians – though he is present at some Canadian victories – and the major *historical* events of the War, which are mainly accounts of British failures and disasters, but which Harold for some reason or another misses." The unusual failure to integrate the hero's adventures with the historical setting lies in Henty's purposes. His preface announces that he will adopt a British point of view for his story because American historians have largely dominated such narratives. Henty believes the colonists were wrong to rebel, although he admits the British government made foolish errors in their prosecution of the war and, in a series of coercive acts, united the population against them.

In *With Lee in Virginia: A Story of the American Civil War* (1890) the young hero, Vincent Wing-

field, the son of a Virginian plantation owner, joins the Confederate army and works for Gen. Robert E. Lee as a spy. When Wingfield realizes that the war will finish with a Southern defeat, he persuades his mother to release their slaves. In the typical Henty formula the hero then marries his sweetheart, Lucy Kingston, and inherits his family's estate. In "Henty's Representative Significance: A Reading of *With Lee in Virginia*" (1983), Butts finds much ambiguity beneath its surface, commenting that "Henty's position is essentially that of a liberal-minded supporter of the South." Henty, however, in his preface to the Scribner and Welford edition, expresses his belief that the system of slavery was such that "taken all in all the Negroes on the well-ordered estate, under kind masters, were probably a happier class of people than the labourers upon any estate in Europe." Even a sympathetic analysis by Butts can hardly diminish the force of that statement.

In "Writing to a Formula: G. A. Henty, Historical Novelist or Reporter?" (1980), Butts analyzes the strengths and weaknesses Henty possessed as a children's writer. Beginning with the author's

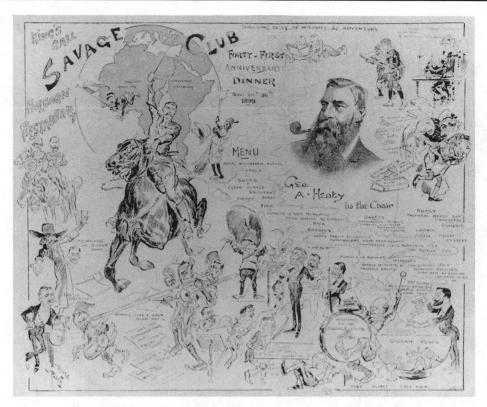

Bill of fare for an 1898 dinner meeting of the Savage Club, chaired by Henty

acknowledged method of composition (dictating while smoking, with three or four texts spread out before him), Butts identifies the recurring formulaic quality that such a procedure imposes. The same elements of adventure recur: the capture, the escape, the fight; the same moral purpose and scheme of values; the undifferentiated character of the hero; and the lack of understanding of the special historical conditions of the age in which the story is set. Butts concludes that "Henty's historical stories, then, whether of Empire or otherwise, seem to be of greatest value now for what they tell us, not of Roman times or eighteenth-century India, but of the late nineteenth century when Henty wrote them. They reveal what late Victorians made of the Napoleonic Wars, and how they wished to interpret their imperial history." Butts asserts that the real interest in Henty lies in his stories that deal with contemporary events – such as *Jack Archer* (1883), *Facing Death* (1882), and *The Young Franc-Tireurs.* Indeed, if, as Butts concludes, Henty's "gifts as an imaginative writer were slender," and his works have a sociological rather than a literary interest today, then modern critics must still account for the spell he cast on contemporary readers.

Another kind of analysis thus may be brought into play. As Fred Inglis discusses in *The Promise of*

Happiness: Value and Meaning in Children's Fiction (1981), Henty's work falls into the category of romance, a genre with a long history but now in critical disrepute. A representative work such as *Winning His Spurs* (1882), written at the beginning of Henty's "formula" fiction period, reveals several elements which place him within a long tradition of Western European romance. Set in England and the Holy Land during the Third Crusade, the novel has as its hero Cuthbert, son of Sir William de Lance, a follower of Sir Walter, Earl of Evesham. Cuthbert grows up fatherless; accompanies Sir Walter to the Holy Land; saves the life of Richard the Lionhearted three times; accompanies Blondel, Richard's minstrel, on his successful search for the imprisoned Richard; and finally gains the hand of his childhood sweetheart, Lady Margaret (Sir Walter's daughter), and the estate and station of the deceased earl of Evesham. As in all serious romances, the hero receives his rewards of rank, station, wealth, and true love.

It may be objected that below the novel's sentimental, highly Victorian conclusion lurk murky depths. There are clearly moral evasions: "Fortunately, he [Cuthbert] had, at the storming of Acre, become possessed of a valuable jewel, and this he now sold, and purchased a charger for himself " –

implying the nonheroic action of looting. Of King Richard, one baron ambivalently remarks: "Although he may be fierce and proud, he is the worthiest knight in Christendom, and resembles the heroes of romance rather than a Christian king." Despite such suggestions of moral imperfections, there is really no pain evident in this world of Henty's. Characters are said to be "overwhelmed with grief" but are active within the next few sentences; dying men "go to the next world" by pressing their lips to their sovereign's hand and breathing their last. One episode presenting the breadth between Henty's rhetoric and simple probability occurs when Cuthbert is journeying south through France to catch up with the main English host and is attacked by assassins:

> The man next to him sprang upon him, and endeavored to drag him from the saddle. Cuthbert drew the little dagger called a *misericorde* from his belt, and plunged it into his throat. Then seizing the short mace which hung at the saddlebow, he hurled it with all his force full in the face of his enemy, the page of Sir Philip, who was rushing upon him sword in hand. The heavy weapon struck him fairly between the eyes, and with a cry he fell back, his face completely smashed in by the blow, the sword which he held uplifted to strike flying far through the air.
>
> Cuthbert struck his spurs into his horse, and the animal dashed forward with a bound, Cuthbert striking with his long sword at one or two men who made a snatch at the reins. In another minute he was cantering out of the village, convinced that he had killed the leader of his foes, and that he was safe now to pursue the rest of his journey on to Marseilles.
>
> So it turned out.
>
> Without further incident he traveled through the south of France.

This scene represents the essential Henty moral vision: in the heat of physical danger, evil is met, recognized, and responded to on its own terms, and no tears are wasted on the demise of one's enemy. Cuthbert's superior strength and agility repeatedly save him; where that is not sufficient, his quick wits get him out of trouble. He is always devoted to his friend and servants, to whom he becomes a paternal figure despite his youth. He never urges impetuous action; at all times he is the wise counselor.

Henty wrote within a rich tradition; he was a historian of the English race's slow but inevitable rise, from the Anglo-Saxon conquest of Britain in the fifth century through fifteen hundred years to its destined role as the great civilizer of the modern world. Henty believed in this destiny, and his novels struck a deep chord in the hearts of Victorian parents as well as in their children. His novels did not so much propagandize for this destiny as simply celebrate it. Victorian parents agreed and for twenty years regularly bought the newest Henty books for their children.

Henty is the essential Victorian because he shares that predilection for hard work, that preference for action, that admiration for success, that belief in the mission of nineteenth-century England to enlighten the world, characteristic of the social elite of which he was a member. Henty's view of life was uncomplicated: any proper chap could see what the moral code called for, and then it was simply a matter of acting swiftly and in accordance with that instinct for rightness, which was the special English gift nurtured over the centuries. Even the spilling of blood was no great matter — Henty's young heroes did it routinely, though only when forced, and in any case it was expected of those who must make their way through an uncertain world.

Inglis puts the matter succinctly: "Historical romances by the best children's novelists are the political myths of the powerlessly genteel in modern industrial states." Henty's right to present magnificent simplifications of the historical romance was earned through his own extraordinary exertions as a young man, his own frequently commented on physical endurance, and his own experiences in dangerous situations in battle and reporting from the front line. One feels slightly more inclined to indulge a romantic when his creations are scarcely more than the echoes of his own early life.

But the ghost of Henty's imperialism currently gets short shrift, as Edward W. Said's *Culture and Imperialism* (1993) still names him in a preeminent group of adventure-imperialism writers which includes H. Rider Haggard, Sir Arthur Conan Doyle, Charles Reade, and Vernon Fielding. This is perhaps the right company for the author whom Edmund Downey, in his book *Twenty Years Ago: A Book of Anecdote* (1905), calls "the most Imperialist of all Imperialists I ever encountered." Downey goes on to describe Henty's reaction to the news of Majuba Hill, a Boer defeat of a small British force in Africa in 1881:

> "Have you heard this awful news?" he asked me as he arrived in the office. And then the big man burst into tears.
>
> "The disgrace can never be wiped out," he blubbered. "Never! Never!"

The conflict with the Boers indeed signaled to the rest of the world the twilight of the British Empire that Henty had done so much to promote. The

G. A. Henty

foundations of Henty's British Tory world were to suffer more Majuba Hills before World War I descended finally on Europe, destroying forever the Pax Britannica along with so many of Henty's "Dear Lads."

Bibliographies:

R. S. Kennedy and B. J. Farmer, *Bibliography of G. A. Henty and Hentyana* (London: Farmer, 1955);

Robert L. Dartt, *G. A. Henty, A Bibliography* (Altrincham: Sherratt & Son / Cedar Grove, N.J.: Dar-Web, 1971);

Dartt, *A Companion to G. A. Henty, A Bibliography* (Cedar Grove, N.J.: Privately published, 1972);

David Sandler, comp., *G. A. Henty: A Collector's Ready Reference* (N.p.: Henty Society, 1992).

Biographies:

G. Manville Fenn, *George Alfred Henty: The Story of an Active Life* (London: Blackie, 1907);

Guy Arnold, *Held Fast for England: G. A. Henty: Imperialist Boys' Writer* (London: Hamish Hamilton, 1980).

References:

William Allan, "G. A. Henty," *Cornhill Magazine,* no. 1082 (Winter 1974/1975): 71–100;

Raymond Blathwayt, "How Boys' Books Are Written: A Talk with Mr. G. A. Henty," *Great Thoughts from Master Minds,* fifth series 2 (October 1902);

Dennis Butts, "Henty's Representative Significance: A Reading of *With Lee in Virginia,*" *Henty Society Bulletin,* 3 (June 1983): 6–10;

Butts, "Writing to a Formula: G. A. Henty, Historical Novelist or Reporter?," *Henty Society Bulletin,* 2 (March 1980): 3–8;

Godfrey Davis, "G. A. Henty and History," *Huntington Library Quarterly,* 17 (May 1955): 159–167;

Edmund Downey, *Twenty Years Ago: A Book of Anecdote* (London: Hurst & Blackett, 1905);

Fred Inglis, *The Promise of Happiness: Value and Meaning in Children's Fiction* (Cambridge, U.K.: Cambridge University Press, 1981);

Mark Naidis, "G. A. Henty's Idea of India," *Victorian Studies,* 8 (September 1964): 49–58;

Kenneth Wiggins Porter, "Some American Views of G. A. Henty," *Henty Society Bulletin,* 2 (March 1980): 9–12;

Eric Quayle, "Rise and Fall of Henty's Empire," *Times Literary Supplement,* 7 November 1968, p. 1251;

Nicholas Ranson, "Henty and the Accounts: New Discoveries on George Alfred Henty," *Henty Society Bulletin,* 8 (Autumn 1992): 3–10;

Ranson, "Henty in the Crimea," *Henty Society Bulletin,* 8 (Spring 1990): 3–19;

Edward W. Said, *Culture and Imperialism* (New York: Knopf, 1993);

Gail L. Savage, "G. A. Henty: Recent Scholarship in the United States," *Henty Society Bulletin,* 3 (December 1982): 4–5;

Eric Stokes, "From Mexico to Mysore," *Times Literary Supplement,* 11 April 1980, p. 406;

James Cargill Thompson, *The Boy's Dumas: G. A. Henty: Aspects of Victorian Publishing* (Cheadle Hulme: Carcanet, 1975);

W. T. Thurbon, "George Alfred Henty: The Trumpington Mystery," *Henty Society Bulletin,* 2 (December 1977): 6–7;

C. F. Willey, "G. A. Henty and Mining: The Henty Family Welsh Mines Located," *Henty Society Bulletin,* 4 (June 1978): 6–10.

Papers:

Collections of Henty materials are located in the Osborne Collection, Toronto, Canada, which includes a recent private collection of Henty and Hentyana comprising over 3,000 items; Cornell University Libraries, New York; the Lilly Library, Indiana University; the British Library, London; the Bodleian Library, Oxford; and Battersea Public Library, London, which has 247 items, many donated by Elizabeth Henty.

Joseph Jacobs

(29 August 1854 – 30 January 1916)

Mary E. Shaner
University of Massachusetts – Boston

BOOKS: *Bibliotheca Anglo-Judaica, a Bibliographic Guide to Anglo-Jewish History,* by Jacobs and Lucien Wolf (London: Office of the "Jewish Chronicle," 1888);

The Jewish Race: A Study in National Character (London: Privately printed, 1889);

English Fairy Tales (London: Nutt, 1890; New York: Putnam, 1891; revised edition, London: Nutt, 1892; revised again, 1898);

Studies in Jewish Statistics, Social, Vital and Anthropometric (London: Nutt, 1891);

George Eliot, Matthew Arnold, Browning, Newman: Essays and Reviews from the 'Athenaeum' (London: Nutt, 1891); enlarged as *Literary Studies* (London: Nutt, 1895);

Celtic Fairy Tales (London: Nutt / New York: Putnam, 1892);

Indian Fairy Tales (London: Nutt / New York: Putnam, 1892);

Science of Folk Tales & the Problem of Diffusion (London: Nutt, 1892);

Tennyson and "In Memoriam": An Appreciation and a Study (London: Nutt, 1892);

The Jews of Angevin England (London: Nutt / New York & London: Putnam, 1893);

Yiddish-English Manual, by Jacobs and Herman Landau (London: Rabbinowicz, 1893);

More Celtic Fairy Tales (New York: Putnam, 1893; London: Nutt, 1894);

The Fables of Aesop. Selected, Told Anew, and Their History Traced (London: Macmillan, 1894);

Little St. Hugh of Lincoln, Boy and Martyr: Researches in History, Archaeology and Legend (London: Office of the "Jewish Chronicle," 1894);

More English Fairy Tales (London: Nutt / New York: Putnam, 1894);

Studies in Biblical Archaeology (London: Nutt / New York: Macmillan, 1894);

An Inquiry into the Sources of the History of the Jews in Spain (London: Nutt / New York: Macmillan, 1894);

Joseph Jacobs

As Others Saw Him: A Retrospect, A.D. 54, anonymous (London: Heinemann, 1895; Boston & New York: Houghton, Mifflin, 1895); republished as *Jesus as Others Saw Him* (New York: Richards, 1925);

Glossary of Jewish Terms (New York & London: Macmillan, 1896);

Jewish Ideals, and Other Essays (London: Nutt / New York: Macmillan, 1896);

The Story of Geographical Discovery: How the World Became Known (London: Newnes / New York: Appleton, 1899);

The Dying of Death (New York: Tucke, 1900);

The Mean Englishman (New York: Tucke, 1900);

The Jewish Encyclopedia: A Guide to Its Contents and Aid to Its Use (New York & London: Funk & Wagnalls, 1906);

European Ideals: A Study in Origins (New York: Privately printed, 1911);

Europa's Fairy Book (New York & London: Putnam, 1916); republished as *European Folk and Fairy Tales* (New York: Putnam, 1967);

Jewish Contributions to Civilization: An Estimate (Philadelphia: Jewish Publication Society of America, 1919);

Jews of Distinction (1815–1915) (New York: Privately printed, 1919);

Molly Whuppie, An Old English Fairy Tale (London & New York: Oxford University Press, 1939).

OTHER: Sir T. North, *The Earliest English Version of the Fables of Bidpai, "The Morall Philosophie of Doni,"* edited by Jacobs (London: Nutt, 1888);

The Fables of Aesop as First Printed by William Caxton in 1484 with Those of Avian, Alfonso, and Poggio, 2 volumes, edited, with an introduction, by Jacobs (London: Nutt, 1889);

William Painter, *The Palace of Pleasure,* edited by Jacobs (London: Nutt, 1890);

Epistolae Ho-Elianae: The Familiar Letters of James Howell, Historiographer Royal to Charles II, edited by Jacobs (London: Nutt, 1890);

Balthasar Gracián y Morales, *The Art of Worldly Wisdom,* translated by Jacobs (London & New York: Macmillan, 1892);

"The Science of Folk-Tales and the Problem of Diffusion," in *International Folk-Lore Congress, 1891: Papers and Translations,* edited by Jacobs and A. Nutt (London: Nutt, 1892);

The Most Delectable History of Reynard the Fox, edited, with an introduction, by Jacobs (London & New York: Macmillan, 1895);

Barlaam and Josaphat. English Lives of Buddha, edited, with an introduction, by Jacobs (London: Nutt, 1896);

The Book of Wonder Voyages edited by Jacobs (London: Nutt / New York: Macmillan, 1896) — includes Jacobs's adaptations of "Hasan of Bassorah" and "The Journeyings of Thorkill and of Eric the Far Travelled";

The Jewish Year Book: An Annual Record of Matters Jewish, edited by Jacobs (London: Greenberg, 1896).

SELECTED PERIODICAL PUBLICATIONS – UNCOLLECTED: "Mordecai," *Macmillan's* (June 1877);

"The Folk," *Folk-Lore,* 4 (June 1893): 233–238;

"Andrew Lang as Man of Letters and Folklorist," *Journal of American Folklore,* 26 (October–December 1913): 367–372.

Joseph Jacobs is remarkable for his learning, especially in folklore, history, ethnology, and anthropology. Also impressive is his productiveness: he wrote, edited, and translated at least twenty-nine books and composed innumerable articles, reviews, and encyclopedia entries. Some of his early work was published anonymously and cannot be identified now. According to his daughter, May Bradshaw Hays, Jacobs once told her that his first published book, titled *Dental Bridges and Crowns,* was ghostwritten for a dentist. Perhaps he was joking, but he had been supporting himself (and later his young wife and family) by his pen since the late 1870s, and no task was too tedious. Jacobs's varied canon might suggest hackwork, but that is certainly untrue in his case. Although many of his works are now out of print, his books on the history of the Jewish people in Spain remain valuable sources for the researcher, and his writing maintained a high quality. But the best evidence of Jacobs's fine talents as a writer and his best-known works are his fairy-tale collections for children. These collections, from their introductions through their notes, constitute Jacobs's lasting achievement.

Born in Sydney, Australia, on 29 August 1854, Joseph Jacobs attended a Sydney grammar school before going to England in 1872 to study at Cambridge University. Hays says that her father originally planned to qualify in law and return to practice in Australia, but while he was at Cambridge, his interests changed. Literature, history, anthropology, mathematics, and moral philosophy all attracted him, and he began to lay the foundations for the diversified intellectual exploration that characterized his life's work. In 1876 he received his B.A. from Saint John's College, Cambridge, as senior moralist, having scored highest in the examination in moral philosophy. He left Cambridge for London, intending to become a writer.

Jacobs began his career with short pieces, articles, and reviews for newspapers and literary journals. In 1877 he wrote "Mordecai" (later collected in *Jewish Ideals, and Other Essays,* 1896), a critical essay about George Eliot's *Daniel Deronda* (1876), whose sympathetic treatment of Jews had drawn hostility and bad reviews. The youthful Jacobs saw

An illustration by John D. Batten for Jacobs's Celtic Fairy Tales

the anti-Semitism underneath the pretended objectivity of these reviews and saw also that such hateful feelings were widely prevalent in English culture. He may have felt for the first time the reality of such bias. At any rate, "Mordecai" attempts to accord *Daniel Deronda* its proper value. Although Eliot later told Jacobs that she never read her books' reviews, someone must have brought "Mordecai" to her attention, for she invited Jacobs to an afternoon reception at her and her companion George Lewes's home. According to Jacobs's daughter, May, Eliot's hospitality to Jacobs resulted in his meeting several artists, writers, and intellectuals of the time. Some of these valuable contacts, such as William Morris, remained dear friends for life. His career as a writer, so promisingly launched, was suspended. As Mayer Sulzberger says, "Under the spur of the feeling which produced 'Mordecai,' he went in the same year to Berlin and there studied Jewish litera-

ture and bibliography under [Moritz] Steinschneider and Jewish philosophy and ethnology under [Moritz] Lazarus."

Upon his return to England in 1878, Jacobs again studied anthropology, this time with Sir Francis Galton as his mentor. The anthropological folklorists organized the Folk-Lore Society in London in 1878, and Jacobs was an early member. Through the society Jacobs met Alfred Nutt of the publishing family, who would publish several of Jacobs's works. With his involvement in the Folk-Lore Society, Jacobs began the work that would produce his most lasting writings, the fairy-tale books.

Jacobs continued not only his studies of the history of the Jewish people but also his observation of and protest against the ways nations and governments treated them. He never, in the busy and active life that lay ahead of him, set aside his commitment to his people. In his 1916 bibliography of

Jacobs's works, Sulzberger notes, "From 1878 to 1884, he was Secretary of the Society of Hebrew Literature. When Russia, in 1881, began her present cruel persecution of the Jews, it was Jacobs who, in *The Times* (London) of January 11 and 13, 1882, drew the attention of Europe to this new development of barbarism. The result was the Mansion House meeting of February 1, 1882, and the formation of the Mansion House Fund and Committee, whose secretary he was from 1882 to 1900." From 1881 Jacobs was also an editorial writer for the *Jewish Chronicle* in London. In 1887 he helped organize the Anglo-Jewish Historical Exhibition, and he and Lucien Wolf edited its monumental catalogue and bibliography. In 1888 they also edited *Bibliotheca Anglo-Judaica, a Bibliographic Guide to Anglo-Jewish History,* a basic reference in the field.

In 1888 Jacobs edited *The Earliest English Version of the Fables of Bidpai, "The Morall Philosophie of Doni,"* his first major folkloric publication. Jacobs believed these fables originally derived from Buddhist sources and estimated that nearly one-tenth of European folktales derived from the Bidpai literature. This material constitutes an important part of Jacobs's "diffusionist" argument concerning the origins and dispersion of folktales. His opponents, the "casualists," among whom Jacobs inaccurately included Andrew Lang, theorized that many similar folktales simply arose independently of each other in different cultures. This argument lasted among folklorists for some time, ultimately resolving itself mostly in favor of the diffusionists.

Continuing his interest in the fable, Jacobs edited *The Fables of Aesop as First Printed by William Caxton in 1484 with Those of Avian, Alfonso, and Poggio* (1889). The first volume of this two-volume work contains a history of the Aesopic fable. *The Fables of Aesop. Selected, Told Anew, and Their History Traced* (1894), an edition for children, contains no scholarly apparatus but has "A Short History of the Aesopic Fable" appended. This book reflects Jacobs's frequent practice of incorporating his scholarly findings into his writings for children, although never in a pedantic or intimidating way. He simply assumed that what he found interesting, a child might find interesting; what he wanted to know, a child might want to know. But he included such material only in prefaces, notes, or appendices, which the child reader could easily ignore. The actual contents of *The Fables of Aesop* are among the most popular of the versions of Aesop available to children, even today.

The introductions to *The Fables of Aesop* and to other editions of folktales by Jacobs constitute important elements in the folklorists' argument about

diffusion. In his 1987 article on Jacobs, Gary Alan Fine characterizes Jacobs's introduction to the 1894 edition, along with those to *The Most Delectable History of Reynard the Fox* (1895) and *Barlaam and Josaphat* (1896), as the "most notable of Jacobs' essays on the diffusion of printed matter." Fine stresses that Jacobs's interest in printed collections of tales and fables was less literary in nature than sociological – he analyzed these texts primarily as "artifacts which provide evidence about the structure of the Medieval world-system and the trade routes within it." Hence, Fine classifies Jacobs as a "sociological folklorist" and claims that he was more modern than many of his contemporaries in his approach to folklore, which in fact led to controversy with his fellow folklorists during the late 1880s and early 1890s. As was common in British controversy of the time, the exchanges between combatants were often sarcastic and sometimes vitriolic. Jacobs could wield words with the best of them, as in a paper read at the 1891 International Folklore Congress:

> The Casual Theory of our worthy opponents assumes the chance medley of clashing incidents coming together, and forming everywhere the same slot.... Mr. Lang, as an Oxford man, cannot be expected to know anything about the doctrine of probabilities, and that the chances against such an order of incidents occurring twice casually are greater than my bowling out Dr. Grace first ball ... Mr. [Edwin Sidney] Hartland one can forgive, for he is a lawyer; but that Mr. Lang, of all persons, should fail to feel that many folktales are masterpieces of constructive literary art, surprises me, I must confess.

Such exchanges, surprising though modern readers may find them, do not seem to have generated lasting ill-will or permanent ruptures among opponents. Jacobs's 1913 obituary of Andrew Lang is admiring and even affectionate; Israel Zangwill, whose last contact with Jacobs was in what he calls "a duel" over "the real Jewish problem of the Bible's breakdown as a verbally inspired document," called Jacobs "a prince of good fellows" in a 1916 memorial address. That Jacobs was esteemed by the very folklorists with whom he quarreled is shown by his selection as editor of *Folk-Lore* in 1890, a position he held until 1893, a period which Fine calls the publication's era "of greatest vitality and importance for decades." From 1893 to 1900 Jacobs remained on the editorial board, having given up the editorship because of the demands of his writing.

By 1890 Jacobs and his wife, Georgina Horne, had three children: Philip, Sydney, and May. In

"Memories of My Father, Joseph Jacobs" (1952), Hays recalls thinking as a small child "that all fathers wrote fairy tales to earn a living for their families." His children, the first audience of his fairy tales and a kind of field test of quality, inspired the creation of Jacobs's most lasting and most controversial works, the fairy-tale books.

The controversy, one of the fiercest in which Jacobs ever engaged, arose immediately upon publication of *English Fairy Tales* in 1890. Unlike Lang's "rainbow" fairy-tale collections, Jacobs's anthologies have apparatuses – prefaces explaining his goals and methods, and notes and references to the individual tales. Jacobs's melding of the scholarly habit of annotation and attribution with the storyteller's instinct to adapt and modify stories for particular effects upon particular audiences produced excellent books and a firestorm of criticism from folklorists because he had altered the texts of his sources. The accusation is true; Jacobs never pretended otherwise, and indeed, the purpose of the notes in each book was partially to point out such alterations and to explain their purpose. His specific folkloric "sins" were the occasional use of literary rather than oral sources; the cutting, expanding, or adding of details to the plot; and the "prosing" of ballads or otherwise altering original folklore materials. Jacobs was also attacked by critics for his use of "vulgar" dialects, and by parents who feared that their children's language would be corrupted by exposure to the colloquial usages in some of the tales.

Jacobs defended himself strongly on all counts, especially in the preface to *More English Fairy Tales* (1894). Since he considered printed collections of tales and fables to hold an important place in the diffusion of folk materials, he saw nothing wrong with the use of so-called literary sources of folktales. The alteration of materials that had been inevitably changed in centuries of oral transmission seemed to him to be an appropriate part of the storyteller's role, and for these books he saw himself as just another storyteller. Furthermore, he asserted that the Norwegian folklorist Peter Christen Asbjørnsen and the Brothers Grimm had done exactly the same as he. Jacobs's retelling of ballads in story or mixed form is the result of his theory that all folktales originated as *cantes-fable,* a genre composed partially in poetry or song and partially in prose. Jacobs thought that at some point the *cantes-fable* split, some becoming altogether prose and hence folktales, others becoming entirely poetry and ballads. In retelling the ballads in his fairy-tale books as *cantes-fable* (he always retained part of the verses), he merely attempted to restore them to what he believed to be

their original form. As to the possible corruption of children's language, Jacobs found dialect usages amusing and assumed children would too, but he saw no reason why a child would begin to say "darter" instead of "daughter" in speech just because the child had read it in a funny tale.

The contents of the fairy-tale volumes fulfill the author's intent to fill "our children's imaginations with bright trains of images," as stated in his Preface to *More English Fairy Tales*. They also illustrate his maxim from the Preface to *Celtic Fairy Tales*: "The success of a fairy book, I am convinced, depends on the due admixture of the comic and the romantic." Accordingly, he uses "fairy tale" loosely and includes in his volumes legends, beast tales, cumulative stories, and nonsense stories. Jacobs's judgment and taste in the selecting of fairy tales produced collections uniquely attractive for their varied and occasionally rare contents.

In *English Fairy Tales* Jacobs included some of the standard selections of the genre, such as "Jack and the Beanstalk," "Jack the Giant-Killer," "Henny-Penny," and "The History of Tom Thumb." Less well known are the tales with strong and assertive heroines: "Cap O'Rushes," "Molly Whuppie," and "Kate Crackernuts." These women shape their own fates, rescue themselves and others, and add a subtle feminist slant to the collection. The humor that Jacobs so loved is especially well illustrated by the absurd "Mr. Vinegar," who trades all his money for a cow, the cow for bagpipes, the bagpipes for gloves, and so on, until he has nothing. Beast fables like "The Magpie's Nest" are balanced against high romance like "Childe Rowland." The old ballads "Binnorie" and "Earl Mar's Daughter" are "prosed," and the ballad "Kempe Owein" makes an appearance as the beautifully written "The Laidly Worm of Spindleston Heugh." Although Jacobs always showed considerable awareness that his audience was composed of children, he sometimes selected stories that, to modern taste, are too frightening for the very young, such as "Mr. Fox" (a variant of the Bluebeard legend), "The Golden Arm," in which a woman's ghost reclaims her golden arm, and "Mr. Miacca," who eats bad little boys. Still, they contribute to the surprising variety characteristic of Jacobs's collections and contrast with the more predictable collections of other contemporary editors.

In *Celtic Fairy Tales* (1892) Jacobs assembled a broad cross section of Celtic folk materials: Irish, Scots, Welsh, and even one Cornish tale. Some of these tales are tragic, like "The Story of Dierdre"; others, such as the cumulative tale "Munachar and Manachar," show Jacobs's sense of fun:

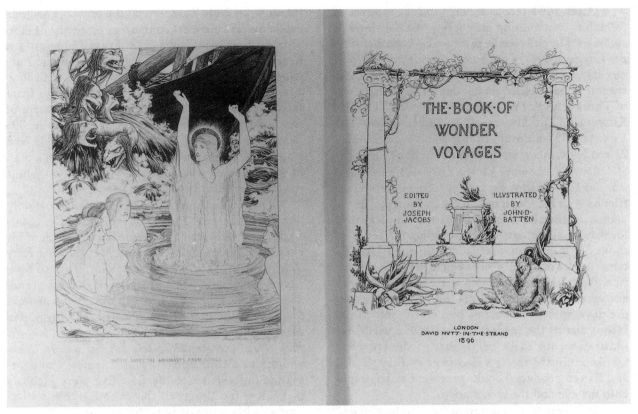

Frontispiece and title page for Jacobs's collection of four mythic journey sagas adapted for children

He came to the miller. "What news today?" said the miller. "It's my own news I'm seeking. Going looking for the makings of a cake which I will give to the threshers, the threshers to give me a whisp of straw, the whisp of straw I will give to the cow, the cow to give me milk, milk I will give to the cat, cat to scrape butter, butter to go in claw of hound, hound to hunt deer, deer to swim water, water to wet flag, flag to edge axe, axe to cut a rod, a rod to make a gad, a gad to hang Manachar, who ate my raspberries every one."

Jacobs's *Indian Fairy Tales* contains a fine selection of comic and serious tales from India, several of them previously little known in the West. But because Jacobs altered few of his sources, and those mostly by cutting, most of these stories are not in his characteristic style. Two exceptions are "The Lion and the Crane," which Jacobs rewrote almost entirely, and "The Soothsayer's Son," which he abridged and adapted.

More English Fairy Tales (1894) continues where *English Fairy Tales* leaves off, numbering the first tale 44. Jacobs uses more chapbook material here than in the previous volume; for instance, he prints the chapbook ballad "The Children in the Wood" without any revision. Also included are nonsense selections, like "Sir Gammer Vans" and "The Wise Men

of Gotham," a *cante-fable* version of the ballad "Tamlane." Some tales of the strange and supernatural might frighten children: "The Hobyahs" is one of Jacobs's scariest stories, in which the mysterious title characters threaten every night to "kill the old woman, kill the old man, and carry off the little girl," but are driven away by the faithful dog. But the old man, annoyed at being wakened by the dog, cuts a leg a day off the dog and finally kills it. The Hobyahs then kill the old couple and carry off the little girl. A version of "The Three Bears," called "Scrapefoot," may be much closer to the primal original of this folktale than the version with a mischievous human female told by Robert Southey in *The Doctor* (1812). In Jacobs's selection a nosy fox prowls through the bears' castle, breaks furniture, drinks up the milk, is at last found in the softest bed, and is thrown out the window.

Jacobs's version of *The Fables of Aesop* for children appeared in 1894, and the same year saw his *More Celtic Fairy Tales,* which contains a fine abridgment of "The Fate of the Children of Lir," one of the "Three Sorrowful Tales" of Ireland, a work well suited to Jacobs's *cante-fable* theories. He also sprinkled several comic stories among the tales of high romance and heroism.

After 1894 Jacobs seemed to lose interest in folktales, contributing only a few book reviews to *Folk-Lore*. For children he produced *The Book of Wonder Voyages* (1896), a collection of four mythic journey sagas. Jacobs himself adapted only two of these stories: "Hasan of Bassorah" and "The Journeyings of Thorkill and of Eric the Far-Travelled." Charles Kingsley's "The Argonauts" and a version of "The Voyage of Maelduin," adapted and annotated by Alfred Nutt, make up the rest of the book.

During his work on the fairy-tale books and *The Book of Wonder Voyages*, Jacobs became close friends with his illustrator, John D. Batten. The romantic, neomedieval style of Batten's illustrations for romances and sagas and the rollicking action of those for humorous tales complemented Jacobs's tales. Jacobs obviously worked closely with the artist and often mentions Batten as the source of a variant version, or as having made suggestions about the development or origins of a motif. Sometimes Jacobs directs the reader's attention to a particular illustration, for instance, to that of the fat, commalike Hobyahs in *More English Fairy Tales*. Jacobs and Batten produced books that were satisfying to both the eye and the imagination.

If Jacobs's commitment to folklore faded somewhat in the late 1890s, his interest in Jewish history and ethnology did not. His *Studies in Jewish Statistics, Social, Vital and Anthropometric* appeared in 1891, and during the early 1890s he wrote a series of articles on biblical archaeology, culminating in the book *Studies in Biblical Archaeology* (1894). In 1893 his important history, *The Jews of Angevin England*, was published. Jacobs's edition of *The Jewish Year Book* (1896), became an institution in the Anglo-Jewish community. Also in 1896 Jacobs first visited the United States, lecturing on "The Philosophy of Jewish History" before the Council of Jewish Women in New York, Philadelphia, and Chicago and delivering a series of lectures on "English Style and Composition" at Johns Hopkins University. His daughter recalls his saying upon his return, "I've found the country I want you children to grow up in." Four years later, when offered the revising editorship of the *Jewish Encyclopedia*, Jacobs moved with his family to the United States.

From 1900 on, Jacobs was as prolific as ever, but what he produced was primarily articles: about 450 for the *Jewish Encyclopedia*, others for *Publications of the American Jewish Historical Society*, still others for the 1911 edition of the *Encyclopaedia Britannica*, and one, "Fable," for the *Encyclopaedia of Religion and Ethics*. The *Jewish Encyclopedia* was finished in 1906, by which time Jacobs was teaching literature in New York City at the Jewish Theological Seminary. He worked there as professor of literature and registrar until 1913. From 1906 until his death, he was editor of *The American Hebrew*. Published posthumously, *Jewish Contributions to Civilization: An Estimate* (1919) was pieced together from Jacobs's articles and his unfinished manuscript of what many hoped would be his magnum opus, *The Jewish Race: A Study in National Character*. He had planned such a work as early as 1889, when a plan of the projected work was privately printed, but it never came to fruition.

During his American years, Jacobs wrote only one book, *Europa's Fairy Book* (1916). In the 1890s Jacobs had dedicated a fairy-tale book to each of his children: *English Fairy Tales* to May; *Indian Fairy Tales* to Philip; and *More English Fairy Tales* to Sydney. According to May, he declared that his granddaughter must have her own fairy-tale book as well. So *Europa's Fairy Book* is dedicated "*To Peggy, and Madge, and Pearl, and Daisy, and Pegg, and Margaret Hays (How many granddaughters does that make?).*" This whimsical dedication (the six names make *one* granddaughter, since the first five were Jacobs's nicknames for Margaret) shows both Jacobs's affection and his sense of fun, characteristics to which those who knew him repeatedly referred in their assessments of his character. Jacobs intended the book as a collection of "the Common Folk-Tales of Europe," stories which occur, with variations, in many European cultures. Jacobs attempts to get back to the common original form of such tales as "Snow White" ("Snowwhite"), "Cinderella" ("Cinder-Maid"), "Puss-in-Boots" ("The Earl of Cattenborough"), and "Hansel and Gretel" ("Johnnie and Grizzle"). Although the humorous tales are, as in previous volumes, presented in the fast-paced, comic style that typifies Jacobs's storytelling at its best, something has gone awry in the classic fairy tales. In the preface to *Europa's Fairy Book*, Jacobs acknowledges that, in the interests of his "young audience," he has "bowdlerized" the tales, and in "Johnnie and Grizzle" the portrayal of the parents and their motivations has been softened considerably, leaving the reader puzzled by their abandonment of the children. In "Beauty and the Beast" Beauty does not visit home and overstay her time; in fact, her father comes to visit her and leaves feeling better because she is so happy! There is thus no motivation for the beast's death, but he dies, nevertheless. Beauty cries that she loves him; he comes back to life as a handsome prince and explains the spell that held him and how it was broken — all in one sentence. The unsatisfying rush of this summarized happy ending is not typical of Jacobs. Also, the original form of these tales may have caused Jacobs to focus more on their formulas and to neglect those original touches of detail and style that had originally characterized his fairy tales.

Jacobs planned to collect the folktales of New England, and, according to Zangwill, he and Batten had agreed to create another fairy-tale book, illustrating the continuing fertility of his intellect and his devotion to children's literature. In the spring of 1914 Jacobs journeyed to Nauheim, Germany, seeking treatment for "heart-weakness." Zangwill recounts that Jacobs "had booked his passage home via Naples. But he was caught in Germany by the mobilization [of the German army] half-an-hour before the train reached the Italian frontier, and he was turned out at a wayside station to shift for himself. He managed to struggle back and up to Holland, where he crossed to England again, arriving more dead than alive, not expected to live through the night. But under the kindly care of the Battens he rallied, and my last glimpse of him before he sailed back to New York was in their spacious suburban garden, alarmingly ashen-faced indeed, yet mercurial as ever. . . ." Jacobs lived only about a year and a half longer.

In a lifetime of great industry Jacobs made solid contributions both to the history of the Jewish people and to the study of folklore. But his reputation rests more in the area of children's literature with the lasting heritage of his fairy-tale books.

Bibliographies:

Israel Abrahams, "Dr. Joseph Jacobs' Contributions to Anglo-Jewish History, Literature, and Statistics," *Transactions of the Jewish Historical Society of England,* 8 (1915–1918): 150–152;

Mayer Sulzberger, "Necrology," *Publications of the American Jewish Historical Society,* 25 (1916): 156–173.

References:

Richard Dorson, *The British Folklorists* (Chicago: University of Chicago Press, 1968);

Gary Alan Fine, "Joseph Jacobs: A Sociological Folklorist," *Folklore,* 98 (1987): 183–193;

May Bradshaw Hays, "Memories of My Father, Joseph Jacobs," *Horn Book,* 28 (1952): 385–392;

Brian C. Maidment, "Joseph Jacobs and English Folklore in the 1890s," in *Studies in the Cultural Life of the Jews in England,* edited by Dov Noy and Issachar Ben-Ami (Jerusalem: Magnes Press, 1975), pp. 190–191;

Israel Zangwill, "Memorial Address," *Transactions of the Jewish Historical Society of England,* 8 (1915–1917): 131–146.

Richard Jefferies

(6 November 1848 – 14 August 1887)

Kathy Piehl
Mankato State University

See also the Jefferies entry in *DLB 98: Modern British Essayists, First Series.*

BOOKS: *Reporting, Editing, and Authorship, Practical Hints for Beginners in Literature* (London: Snow, 1873);

Jack Brass, Emperor of England (London: Pettitt, 1873);

A Memoir of the Goddards of North Wilts, Compiled from Ancient Records, Registers, and Family Papers (Swindon, U.K.: N.p., 1873);

The Scarlet Shawl: A Novel (London: Tinsley, 1874);

Restless Human Hearts: A Novel, 3 volumes (London: Tinsley, 1875);

Suez-cide!! Or, How Miss Britannia Bought a Dirty Puddle and Lost Her Sugar-plums (London: Snow, 1876);

World's End: A Story in Three Books, 3 volumes (London: Tinsley, 1877);

The Gamekeeper at Home: Sketches of Natural History and Rural Life (London: Smith, Elder, 1878; Boston: Roberts, 1879);

Wild Life in a Southern County (London: Smith, Elder, 1879; Boston: Roberts, 1879); republished as *An English Village* (Boston: Little, Brown, 1903);

The Amateur Poacher (London: Smith, Elder, 1879; Boston: Roberts, 1879);

Greene Ferne Farm (London: Smith, Elder, 1880);

Hodge and His Masters, 2 volumes (London: Smith, Elder, 1880);

Round About a Great Estate (London: Smith, Elder, 1880; Boston: Roberts, 1880);

Wood Magic: A Fable, 2 volumes (London, Paris & New York: Cassell, Petter, Galpin, 1881); adapted as *Sir Bevis: A Tale of the Fields,* edited by Eliza Josephine Kelley (Boston: Ginn, 1899);

Bevis: The Story of a Boy, 3 volumes (London: Low, Marston, Searle & Rivington, 1882; New York: Dutton, 1905); abridged as *Bevis and*

Richard Jefferies

Mark, edited by Guy N. Pocock (London: Dent, 1937); abridged again as *Bevis at Home* (London: Dent, 1940);

Nature Near London (London: Chatto & Windus, 1883; New York: Crowell, 1907);

The Story of My Heart: My Autobiography (London: Longmans, Green, 1883; Boston: Roberts, 1883);

Red Deer (London: Longmans, Green, 1884; New York: Longmans, Green, 1892);

142

The Life of the Fields (London: Chatto & Windus, 1884; New York: Crowell, 1907);

The Dewy Morn: A Novel, 2 volumes (London: Bentley, 1884; London & New York: Macmillan, 1900);

After London; or, Wild England (London & New York: Cassell, 1885);

The Open Air (London: Chatto & Windus, 1885; New York: Harper, 1886);

Amaryllis at the Fair: A Novel (London: Low, Marston, Searle & Rivington, 1887; New York: Harper, 1887);

Field and Hedgerow: Being the Last Essays of Richard Jefferies, Collected by His Widow (London & New York: Longmans, Green, 1889);

The Toilers of the Field (London & New York: Longmans, Green, 1892);

Thoughts from the Writings of Richard Jefferies, edited by S. H. Waylen (London: Longmans, Green, 1895);

The Early Fiction of Richard Jefferies, edited by Grace Toplis (London: Simpkin, Marshall, Hamilton, Kent, 1896);

Jefferies' Land: A History of Swindon and Its Environs, edited by Toplis (London: Simpkin, Marshall, Hamilton, Kent, 1896);

The Pageant of Summer (Portland, Maine: Mosher, 1896);

T.T.T. (Wells, U.K.: Young, 1896);

Hours of Spring and Wild Flowers (Portland, Maine: Mosher, 1899);

Bits of Oak Bark and Meadow Thoughts (Portland, Maine: Mosher, 1900);

Saint Guido, by Richard Jefferies; Queen Mary's Child-Garden, by Dr. John Brown (Portland, Maine: Mosher, 1901);

Nature and Eternity: With Other Uncollected Papers (Portland, Maine: Mosher, 1902);

A Little Book of Nature Thoughts, edited by Thomas Coke Watkins (Portland, Maine: Mosher, 1903);

Amaryllis at the Fair (London: Duckworth, 1904; New York: Dutton, 1906);

The Pocket Richard Jefferies, edited by Alfred H. Hyatt (London: Chatto & Windus, 1906);

The Hills and the Vale (London: Duckworth, 1909);

The Makers of Summer, An Essay (Birmingham, U.K.: Birmingham School of Printing, 1933);

Out-of-Doors with Richard Jefferies (London & Toronto: Dent, 1935);

Jefferies' England: Nature Essays by Richard Jefferies, edited by Samuel Looker (London: Constable, 1937; New York & London: Harper, 1938);

The Nature Diaries and Note-Books of Richard Jefferies, with an Essay, "A Tangle of Autumn," Now Printed for the First Time, edited by Looker (Billericay, Essex: Grey Walls, 1941);

Jefferies' Countryside: Nature Essays by Richard Jefferies, edited by Looker (London: Constable, 1944);

Richard Jefferies' London, edited by Looker (London: Lutterworth, 1944);

The Wood from the Trees (London: Pilot, 1945);

The Spring of the Year, and Other Nature Essays, edited by Looker (London: Lutterworth, 1946);

Beauty is Immortal ("Felise of The Dewy Morn") with Some Hitherto Uncollected Essays and Manuscripts, edited by Looker (Worthing, Sussex: Aldridge, 1948);

The Essential Richard Jefferies, edited by Malcolm Elwin (London: Cape, 1948);

The Jefferies Companion, edited by Looker (London: Phoenix, 1948);

The Old House at Coate, and Other Hitherto Unpublished Essays, edited by Looker (London: Lutterworth, 1948; Cambridge, Mass.: Harvard University Press, 1948);

Chronicles of the Hedges, and Other Essays, edited by Looker (London: Phoenix, 1948);

Readings from Richard Jefferies: An Anthology of the Countryside, edited by Ronald Hook (London: Macmillan, 1948);

Field and Farm: Essays Now First Collected, with Some from MSS, edited by Looker (London: Phoenix, 1957);

Landscape & Labour. Essays and Letters Now First Collected with an Introduction, Notes and Bibliography by John Pearson (Bradford-on-Avon: Moonraker Press, 1979).

OTHER: *Society Novelettes*, by various authors, 2 volumes (London: Vizetelly, 1883) – includes Jefferies's "Kiss and Try" (volume 1) and "Out of Season" (volume 2);

Gilbert White, *The Natural History of Selbourne*, introduction by Jefferies (London: Scott, 1887).

SELECTED PERIODICAL PUBLICATIONS –
UNCOLLECTED: "A Sin and a Shame," *New Monthly Magazine*, 59 (November 1875): 584–593;

"The Monkbourne Mystery," *New Monthly Magazine*, 60 (January 1876): 1–14;

"The Rise of Maximin, Emperor of the Occident," *New Monthly Magazine* (October 1876–July 1877).

Richard Jefferies defies easy literary categorization. Labels such as essayist, journalist, novelist,

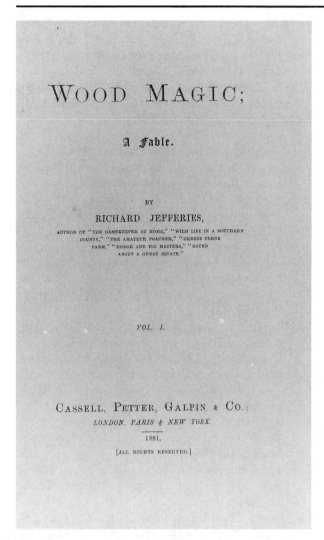

WOOD MAGIC;

A Fable.

BY

RICHARD JEFFERIES,

AUTHOR OF "THE GAMEKEEPER AT HOME," "WILD LIFE IN A SOUTHERN
COUNTY," "THE AMATEUR POACHER," "GREENE FERNE
FARM," "HODGE AND HIS MASTERS," "ROUND
ABOUT A GREAT ESTATE."

VOL. I.

CASSELL, PETTER, GALPIN & CO.:
LONDON, PARIS & NEW YORK.
1881.
[ALL RIGHTS RESERVED.]

*Title page for the book that introduced Bevis, Jefferies'
best-known character*

rural observer, naturalist, and mystic have all been applied to this British writer who chronicled nineteenth-century rural life, including the adventures of his own boyhood. His two novels of childhood, *Wood Magic: A Fable* (1881) and *Bevis: The Story of a Boy* (1882), effectively portray the interactions of a boy and his natural surroundings. Although the books retained their popularity for more than half a century, they are likely to be read today primarily by scholars interested in Jefferies' influence on such later writers for children as Kenneth Grahame and Arthur Ransome.

John Richard Jefferies was born at Coate Farm in Wiltshire on 6 November 1848. Coate Farm was part of an agricultural society in the throes of vast social changes. The town of Swindon, two miles distant, which developed into a major rail center, exemplified the mechanization that would alter agriculture before the end of Jefferies' short lifetime.

But as a boy Jefferies was more aware of his proximity to the rolling hills of The Downs and to Coate Reservoir.

Jefferies' father, James Luckett Jefferies, had received Coate Farm freehold upon his marriage to Elizabeth Gyde of Islington. In his youth James had traveled through Canada, and the accounts of his adventures may have inspired his son to attempt some youthful foreign travel himself. At sixteen, Jefferies, with his cousin James, planned to travel to Moscow but made it only as far as France, where their ignorance of French forced their return to England. A similar quest, this time to reach America, was aborted in Liverpool when they discovered that the tickets they had purchased with all their available cash did not include food for the voyage.

Jefferies' formal education seems to have been sporadic. Much of his early schooling took place in Sydenham, a London suburb, where he lived for extended periods with his aunt and uncle until he was about nine. When he resumed regular residence at Coate Farm, he attended various schools in Swindon. His walks through the countryside afforded him opportunities for observation, which supplemented his formal education. His immersion in rural life prepared him for his later career as a writer, and he drew extensively on his own explorations of nature and such youthful activities as swimming and hunting for the foundation of his books for children, *Wood Magic: A Fable* and *Bevis: The Story of a Boy*.

As his own writings reveal, Jefferies was an eclectic reader as a boy. Homer's *Odyssey*, Miguel de Cervantes's *Don Quixote*, Johann Wolfgang von Goethe's *Faust*, and the works of William Shakespeare are noted as favorites. Although his father enjoyed tending the orchards on the small farm, they never produced much income. His mother seems to have held little enthusiasm for rural life, and household tensions may have spurred Jefferies' fondness for solitary rambles. After he left school at fifteen, he spent his days walking outdoors – a way of life that struck observers as profitless. Apparently he provided little help with farm work and instead spent time wandering with his gun to engage in observation and hunting.

Jefferies' first writing was as a reporter for the *North Wilts Herald*, a position he undertook at seventeen. During 1867 he experienced the first bouts of prolonged illness that were to mark much of his later life, but by 1868 he had been hired as the Swindon correspondent for the *Wilts and Gloucestershire Standard*. His short stories, historical sketches, poems, and descriptions paid little but provided a chance for Jefferies to get his writing into print. His attempts to write for London newspapers on a regular basis or to convince publishers to accept a novel were unsuccessful.

Then in 1872 a letter Jefferies wrote to the London *Times* about the Wiltshire laborers brought him the attention he had been seeking. Jefferies' descriptions of the life of agricultural laborers reveal a journalistic detachment that exhibits little sympathy. Although the letter's conservative tone may have been adopted in part to appeal to the readership of the *Times,* its views reveal Jefferies' sympathy with the farmer, who depends on the laborer but struggles with his own economic problems. The newspaper picked up the theme in a lead article, which in turn generated other letters, including two more by Jefferies. After 1872 Jefferies found increased success in getting his writing published in national magazines such as *Fortnightly Review,* the *New Quarterly Magazine,* and *Fraser's Magazine.* Many of these essays were later collected in *The Toilers of the Field* (1892).

However, for Jefferies, publication was proceeding too slowly. His desire to publish a novel was apparent as early as 1871, when his book "Fortune" made the rounds of publishers before acceptance by Smith, Elder. The work was never published. In 1873 Jefferies paid John Snow of London to issue a pamphlet called *Reporting, Editing, and Authorship, Practical Hints for Beginners in Literature,* though the work's authority on the subject is questionable, given Jefferies' lack of success to that date. That same year the Goddard family paid part of the publication costs for Jefferies's *A Memoir of the Goddards of North Wilts,* and Jefferies paid for the printing of his political pamphlet, *Jack Brass, Emperor of England.* This work and a later satire, *Suez-cide!! Or, How Miss Britannia Bought a Dirty Puddle and Lost Her Sugar-plums* (1876), are equally forgettable. Clearly, Jefferies' future as an author did not lie in the realm of political satire.

Nor did his first published novels achieve acclaim or financial success for Jefferies or his publisher, William Tinsley. *The Scarlet Shawl* (1874), *Restless Human Hearts: A Novel* (1875), and *World's End: A Story in Three Books* (1877) are seldom read. The publication of his first novel coincided with Jefferies' marriage to Jessie Bade. The young couple soon moved to Swindon, where their first child was born. But Jefferies' drive for publication led him to spend increasing amounts of time in London, often with his aunt and uncle in Sydenham. His growing success in placing articles in London journals convinced him that relocation would enhance his literary possibilities. His search for a home on the outskirts of the city ended in 1877, when he and his family moved to Surbiton, a suburb of southwest London. He was never to live in the Coate Farm area again.

Weekly contributions to the *Livestock Journal,* beginning in January 1877, provided Jefferies with a regular outlet for his writings. Essays on rural topics in other publications resulted in the first book-length work that met with critical success. Smith, Elder published *The Gamekeeper at Home* (1878), which had appeared as a series in the *Pall Mall Gazette.* Three other series from the *Pall Mall Gazette* collected and issued as books were *Wild Life in a Southern County* (1879), *The Amateur Poacher* (1879), and *Round About a Great Estate* (1880). Together with *Hodge and His Masters* (1880), these volumes reveal Jefferies' power to evoke the country life with which he was familiar. The popularity of the country books seemed to carry the promise of future success.

The Amateur Poacher introduces readers to Jefferies' use of incidents from his childhood, anticipating his creation of the Bevis character. The early chapters, written in first person, contain accounts of the activities of the narrator, his companion Orion, and Orion's spaniel. Some of the boys' pursuits described in *The Amateur Poacher,* such as sailing to an island and hunting, would receive extended treatment in *Bevis,* as would the recurring image of Ulysses. The narrator confides that "Ulysses was ever my pattern and model: that man of infinite patience and resource."

Bevis first appears in the anthropomorphic romance, *Wood Magic: A Fable.* Little "Sir" Bevis is a child about seven years old who spends most of his time outdoors and possesses the ability to converse with creatures on his father's farm. Not only do the birds and animals speak with Bevis, but he also receives advice from plants, such as the reeds, as well as the wind and the brook. However, Jefferies does not simply present a sentimentalized world of childhood as remembered by a nostalgic adult. When he introduces Bevis in the first paragraph, the boy pulls petals off daisies from the farmhouse garden and squeezes the juice from a dandelion stem. In the next few pages Bevis recalls how an old toad had outwitted a spider to prevent him from eating all the flies. After convincing the spider to move his web to a shed window, the toad watched as the spider gorged himself until he became easy prey for a robin. "The old toad shut his eye and opened it again, and went on thinking for that is just what he knew would happen."

Bevis is fooled by a weasel, who first persuades the boy to free him from a trap, despite the

Illustration by Ernest H. Shepard for a 1932 edition of Bevis: The Story of a Boy

protests of a mouse. As the story progresses, Bevis learns to share the animals' hatred of the weasel because of his cunning. The weasel manages to have Bevis fire his "cannon stick" at a thrush instead of him, and as the weasel feasts on the egg which had been knocked from the shattered nest, "he thought how cleverly he had deceived them all." The weasel, though, is only one player in the political intrigue which comprises most of the plot. Various animals give Bevis information about one-eyed Kapchack, the magpie, their cruel and greedy king. He holds his position because of his wealth, advanced age, and a farmer's protection. However, his authority is being challenged by the rebel Choo Hoo, the wood pigeon.

The old magpie also faces insurrection at home because of his desire for the lovely La Schach, the youngest jay in the wood. The owl tells the animal assembly that custom dictates marriages between animals of the same species. Kapchack's courtiers spend much time in devising plots against each other. As Choo Hoo approaches, several of

Kapchack's commanders offer to throw their support to the rebels' cause. However, Kapchack has offered to divide the kingdom. His compromise is foiled, and a monumental battle for territorial control ensues.

The political overtones of the story offer Jefferies opportunities to comment on various issues under the guise of reporting woodland intrigue. For example, when commander Ah Kurroo Khan receives authority from Kapchack to attack the enemy, he rejoices that "he should thus enter the field of battle unhampered with any restrictions, and without the useless and unpleasant companionship of a political officer, appointed by the council of his nation." Such observations do not overwhelm the narrative, however, which is complex enough with its shifting allegiances.

Although Bevis is the only person who overhears the animals' conversations, the human element is an integral part of the Kapchack plot. The farmer who protects the magpie does so because he thinks Kapchack is the original bird that inhabited the tree where he and his sweetheart used to meet. The story reveals that the original Kapchack had died long ago, but not before pecking out the eye of his successor. The kingdom, in fact, has been ruled by a succession of Kapchacks, until the victor of the battle with Choo Hoo is shot by the farmer, who has discovered that the original magpie had hidden his sweetheart's pledge of faithfulness and caused a misunderstanding that separated the lovers forever.

This element of chance is one that interests Jefferies, and several times in *Wood Magic* he digresses to consider how a seemingly insignificant event such as the loss of a piece of flint from a wagon can affect several lives in unexpected ways. When a fox chases a hare, Jefferies notes, "Even yet the fox did not know what was going to happen, or why he was doing this, for such is commonly the progress of great events."

Throughout the book Bevis enjoys a virtually unlimited amount of freedom. Although he is warned to stay out of Little Field, he frequently wanders away, necessitating several searches early in the book. But once Kapchack's tale begins, he is totally absorbed in the animal realm. Bevis's similarities to animals are apparent in passages such as one in which he eats cake while he considers how greedy a young rook is to demand sweets from his parents. "Bevis, who had another large slice in his pocket, having stolen both of them from the cupboard just after breakfast, felt angry to see such greediness." Bevis's closest contact with the domesticated world is his association with Pan, his spaniel. Bevis treats the dog cruelly on several occasions, teasing him by placing his food out of reach, or whipping him for a minor offense.

The final chapter of *Wood Magic*, "Sir Bevis and the Wind," in some ways seems oddly disconnected from the rest. Battles over, Bevis accompanies his father and the bailiff to The Downs to load straw, but he quickly tires of the work. Climbing a hill, he realizes the world is strangely silent, until a butterfly leads him to the top of the ridge, where he encounters the wind. In the book's best-known conversation, the wind reveals that people never listen because they are too busy and encourages Bevis to drink deeply, to ingest the wind's stories rather than relying on devices such as telescopes to explore nature. "How can they know anything about the stars who never stopped on the hills, or on the sea all night?," the wind asks. Furthermore, the wind tells Bevis, there is no yesterday and no tomorrow. The man buried in the hillside has been there but a minute. Bevis "felt with his soul out to the far-distant sun just as easily as he could feel with his hand to the bunch of grass beside him." Such passages relate directly to Jefferies' later adult writings, most notably *The Story of My Heart: My Autobiography* (1883). Little Sir Bevis is drawn from the world of the copse to contemplation of the universe.

Jefferies's second autobiographical novel, *Bevis: The Story of a Boy,* features the protagonist of *Wood Magic* when he is approximately eleven years old. No longer does he converse directly with plants and animals, although he still spends most of his life outdoors. Bevis is joined in his pretend adventures by a companion, Mark, modeled on Jefferies' younger brother. Pan the spaniel also participates in the boys' games.

The novel's structure is loosely organized around two major events: a battle and a shipwreck. Most of the action occurs around and on the New Sea, which contains two islands, New Formosa and Serendib. Bevis devotes much of his time and energy to making sailing vessels of one kind or another, a pursuit introduced in the first pages, when he attempts to turn a wooden case into a raft.

Bevis's preoccupation with sailing and adventures receives a strong impetus from his familiarity with the *Odyssey*. In fact, he often relates the experiences he and Mark have to those of Ulysses; for example, as the boys plan their shipwreck, they imagine themselves washed up against a cliff on the island and bring to mind how Ulysses clung to similar rocks. After they are on the island, Bevis consults his copy of the *Odyssey* to see "how Ulysses constructed his ship or raft." Before the boys' play battle he checks the well-worn book to see how his "favourite hero" had defeated his adversaries. "With his own bow in his right hand, and the book in his left, Bevis read, marching up and down the room, stamping and shouting aloud as he came to the passages he liked best."

Nor is the *Odyssey* the only book that influences Bevis. He makes numerous references to "The Ballad of King Estmere" and has obviously absorbed the knightly lore. In fact, the name Bevis itself is associated with a legend recounted in *Bevis of Southampton,* which first appeared in England in the sixteenth century. Variations in the legend of Bevis, a knight errant who battles pagans, evil Christians, and wild animals, appeared as children's books in the seventeenth and eighteenth centuries before becoming a chapbook standard.

Although Jefferies' Bevis expresses knowledge of knights, his imagination ranges to all types of heroic adventures. The book's first central event consists of a battle. Bevis and Mark debate about which battle they should use as the model for their war.

Rejecting Waterloo, Agincourt, Troy, and others, they settle on the clash between Julius Caesar and Pompey. Bevis assumes the role of Caesar, Mark acts as Mark Antony, and another friend, Ted, leads his band of boys as Pompey. Preparations for "war" and the "combat" extend over several chapters and end with Bevis's fall off a cliff, his ride across the New Sea on a punt, and his shipwreck. Mark eventually comes to his rescue but envies his companion "because Bevis had been really shipwrecked and he had not." The boys stage a "jolly shipwreck" after provisioning New Formosa, making a gun, creating a story to cover their absence from home, and completing other preparations. Their adventures on the islands after the shipwreck comprise most of the rest of the book's action.

Although Jefferies' writing is sometimes tedious, as in his extended descriptions of the battle or the construction of a matchlock gun, for the most part the characters' lively imaginations endow their activities with interest. Jefferies does a masterful job of describing the natural environment and the boys' absorption in their surroundings. Particularly during their adventures on the island and their exploration of the New Sea, the longing their friends feel to accompany Bevis and Mark is powerfully evoked. For them the landscape is magic. The Mississippi River and the Nile are both within sailing distance. Savages lurk constantly just beyond sight.

The theme of magic often creeps into the boys' conversations. They encounter it in an encyclopedia and in the light of summer falling on the water near Serendib. "There was magic in everything, blades of grass and stars, the sun and the stones upon the ground."

As in *Wood Magic,* lyrical and mystic descriptions of the natural world are interjected among more mundane events. Bevis and Mark exhibit cruelty toward animals as easily as they contemplate natural wonders. They steal eggs from birds' nests; they beat a donkey unmercifully. They devote many hours to building a gun and increasing their proficiency as hunters. The animal with which Bevis and Mark have the most contact is Pan, and the spaniel's personality is so well developed that he seems a genuine companion, particularly during the time on the island. Pan sails with the boys on expeditions, retrieves game they shoot, and warns them of intruders. He even fools them by swimming back to the mainland each night to take advantage of the "fleshpots," bones thrown out by his house. Yet his cleverness does not save him from periodic thrashings.

Bevis has more contact with other people in this volume than in *Wood Magic.* Not only is Mark his frequent companion, but the two also involve other boys. Though adults provide some supervision, Bevis and Mark have a great deal of freedom. For example, Bevis's father gives the boys swimming lessons after he recognizes their insatiable desire to explore the New Sea and makes mastery of the skill a prerequisite for their receiving a sailboat. When he is satisfied with the boys' progress, he allows them to sail. However, he restrains himself from rigging the sails and teaching them proper techniques because "he considered it best that they should teach themselves, and find out little by little where they were wrong." Bevis's mother has much less direct involvement, and Mark's parents have an insignificant role. However, his sister Frances participates in some adventures from a distance, by sewing sails, for instance. Bevis and Mark mention her often when they discover the tedium of cooking and decide she might be useful for such a chore.

The girl who eventually does join them on the island is Loo, the daughter of a laborer. The harshness of her life presents Bevis with an alternative to his usually romantic views. Because her father buys ale instead of food for his family, Loo has been coming from the mainland to steal food for her younger brother to stop his cries of hunger. Loo briefly becomes the boys' "slave" and gladly joins the adventure, which is cut short when they find out Bevis's mother is planning a trip to the home of the person with whom they had told their families they would be staying.

Bevis's encounter with Loo's poverty is only part of the maturation process he undergoes. At the beginning of the novel he is impatient and bossy, constantly relegating Mark to the secondary role in their play. However, on the island Mark's hunting ability earns Bevis's admiration, and they develop a more equal comradeship.

No matter how interesting Bevis and Mark's exploits, the book as a whole suffers from excessive length. Authorial intrusions and comments range from practical advice for ladies on learning to swim at the sea, to musings on setting "the clock of your senses," to descriptions of the soul's encounter with the natural world that anticipate the mystical tone of *The Story of My Heart.*

The publication of *Wood Magic* and *Bevis* roughly coincided with the onset of the illness that would result in their author's death. After Jefferies was diagnosed with a tubercular fistula, he underwent a series of operations to alleviate the condition. In the hope that sea air might bring relief, the Jefferies family moved to the Sussex coast. This was the first of a series of moves to various locations in southern

Coate Water in Wiltshire, the "New Sea" of Jefferies' Bevis: The Story of a Boy

England before the writer's final relocation in 1886 to Goring, where he died of tuberculosis the following year. Because these moves to restore Jefferies' health caused severe financial hardship, he reluctantly accepted a grant from the Royal Literary Fund as well as private donations to help support the family.

The final years of his life included much publication activity, although none of the works were aimed at children or drew on his own childhood in the direct manner of *Wood Magic* and *Bevis*. In many ways, these books may be viewed as the first two parts of an autobiographical sequence that concludes with *The Story of My Heart*. Here the moments of mystic communication with nature that appear in the earlier books become central. Jefferies' first-person account of his development of "soul-thought" over a seventeen-year period details his search for a fourth idea beyond the soul, immortality, and the Deity. His absorption in nature, his love of the sea and sun, his perception that the present is all of time that exists, even his admiration of Caesar are all foreshadowed in his books of boyhood. Yet, *The*

Story of My Heart has a level of abstraction that separates it from the practical descriptions and daily routines of the Bevis books.

In 1884 Jefferies published *Red Deer,* which is based on a trip to Exmoor he had made in 1883. Three other volumes of essays collected from journals also appeared during his lifetime. Chatto and Windus published *Nature Near London* (1883), *The Life of the Fields* (1884), and *The Open Air* (1885). This last volume contains an essay, "Saint Guido," which had originally appeared in the December 1884 edition of *English Illustrated Magazine.* The essay is notable because it recounts the activity of its title character, a little boy who converses with the wheat in much the same way Bevis carries on conversations with animals in *Wood Magic.*

In 1884 the novel *The Dewy Morn: A Novel* was published, followed in 1885 by *After London; or, Wild England.* The latter describes a future time when London has been flooded and England has lapsed into barbarism. Scholars have suggested that the romance continues Bevis's story with men instead of boys. Bevis has been renamed Felix Aquila and

Mark is called Oliver. The inland sea over which they sail might be a greatly enlarged Coate Reservoir. Their construction of a canoe resembles similar boat-building in *Bevis,* and a sailing adventure that leads to the stagnant swamp covering London recalls Bevis's preoccupation with the *Odyssey.* However, this futuristic romance seems unlikely to have held much appeal for children.

Jefferies continued to suffer in his personal life. In 1884 his younger son Oliver died of meningitis, leaving behind a brother and sister. In 1885 Jefferies' spine deteriorated, and he dictated to his wife his last novel, *Amaryllis at the Fair* (1887) as well as many of his last essays. Edited by his widow, the collection *Field and Hedgerow* (1889) concludes with what is thought to be Jefferies' final essay, "My Old Village," in which he returns in thought to Coate and muses on the changes in the familiar landscape.

Jefferies' death on 14 August 1887 did not end the publication of his writings. The collection edited by his widow was followed in 1892 by *The Toilers of the Field,* issued by Longmans, Green, and in 1909 by *The Hills and Vale,* introduced by Edward Thomas. Since then, Jefferies' writings have appeared in various combinations, including editions compiled by Samuel J. Looker from the late 1930s to the 1950s. Such anthologizing continued into the 1970s.

In the history of children's literature, Jefferies is probably more notable for his influence on other writers than for his own books of boyhood, although *Bevis* retained its popularity well into the twentieth century. In his introduction to the 1948 edition, C. Henry Warren notes the book's enduring appeal for both adults and children. Few contemporary children, however, are likely to read *Wood Magic* or *Bevis.* Yet Jefferies influenced other authors whose names are still familiar. In his introduction to a 1974 edition of *Wood Magic,* Richard Adams claims that the book is a precursor of other fantasies such as Grahame's *The Wind in the Willows* (1908), Rudyard Kipling's *The Jungle Book* (1894) and *The Second Jungle Book* (1895) and T. H. White's *The Sword in the Stone* (1939). Other critics have noted the influence of Jefferies' autobiographical novels and some of his nature essays on the writing of Grahame in particular. Ransome's *Swallows and Amazons* (1931) might also draw on Jefferies' writings, particularly the adventure sequences in *Bevis.*

Although the observations of time and place expressed in Jefferies' essays now receive more attention than his children's writing, his accounts of a rural boyhood continue to reveal a vanished way of life to modern readers. Few writers have captured so skillfully the sensations and rhythms of a boy's involvement in the natural world.

Bibliographies:

Harold Jolliffe, *A Catalogue of the Books in the Richard Jefferies Collection of the Swindon Public Libraries* (Swindon: Libraries, Museum, Arts & Music Committee, 1948);

John G. Pearson, "Newly-Discovered Works Written by Richard Jefferies," *Victorian Periodicals Review,* 12 (Spring 1979): 33.

References:

W. Richard Adams, Introduction to *Wood Magic* (New York: Third Press, 1974), pp. i–viii;

Reginald Arkell, *Richard Jefferies and His Countryside* (London: Jenkins, 1946);

Walter Besant, *The Eulogy of Richard Jefferies* (London: Chatto & Windus, 1888);

Peter Hunt, Introduction to *Bevis* (Oxford: Oxford University Press, 1989), pp. vii–xx;

W. J. Keith, *Richard Jefferies: A Critical Study* (London: Oxford University Press, 1965);

Keith, *The Rural Tradition: A Study of the Non-Fiction Prose Writers of the English Countryside* (Toronto: University of Toronto Press, 1974), pp. 127–147;

Q. D. Leavis, "Lives and Works of Richard Jefferies," *Scrutiny,* 6 (March 1938): 435–446;

Samuel J. Looker, ed., *Concerning Richard Jefferies, by Various Writers* (Worthing: Aldridge, 1944);

Looker, ed., *Richard Jefferies: A Tribute by Various Writers* (Worthing: Aldridge, 1946);

Looker and Crichton Porteous, *Richard Jefferies: Man of the Fields* (London: John Baker, 1965);

Edna Manning, *Richard Jefferies: A Modern Appraisal,* (Windsor: Goldscheider, 1984);

H. S. Salt, *Richard Jefferies: A Study* (London: Sonnenschein, 1894);

Brian Taylor, *Richard Jefferies* (Boston: Twayne, 1982);

G. R. Stirling Taylor, "Richard Jefferies: I – His Study of Nature," *Nineteenth Century and After,* 95 (April 1924): 530–540;

Taylor, "Richard Jefferies: II – His Philosophy of Life," *Nineteenth Century and After,* 95 (May 1924): 686–696;

Edward Thomas, *Richard Jefferies: His Life and Work* (London: Hutchinson, 1909);

C. Henry Warren, Introduction to *Bevis* (London: Eyre & Spottiswoode, 1948).

Rudyard Kipling

(30 December 1865 – 18 January 1936)

Corinne McCutchan
Lander University

See also the Kipling entries in *DLB 19: British Poets, 1880–1914* and *DLB 34: British Novelists, 1890–1929*.

SELECTED BOOKS: *Schoolboy Lyrics* (Lahore: Privately printed, 1881);

Echoes, by Kipling and Alice Kipling (Lahore: Privately printed, 1884);

Departmental Ditties and Other Verses (Lahore: Privately printed, 1886; enlarged edition, Calcutta: Thacker, Spink / London & Bombay: Thacker, 1890); republished as *Departmental Ditties, Barrack-Room Ballads, and Other Verses* (New York: United States Book Company, 1890); republished as *Departmental Ditties and Ballads and Barrack-Room Ballads* (New York: Doubleday & McClure, 1899);

Plain Tales from the Hills (Calcutta: Thacker, Spink / London: Thacker, 1888; New York: Lovell, 1890; London & New York: Macmillan, 1890);

Soldiers Three: A Collection of Stories Setting Forth Certain Passages in the Lives and Adventures of Privates Terence Mulvaney, Stanley Ortheris, and John Learoyd (Allahabad: Wheeler, 1888; London: Low, Marston, Searle & Rivington, 1890);

The Story of the Gadsbys: A Tale Without a Plot (Allahabad: Wheeler, 1888; Allahabad: Wheeler / London: Low, Marston, Searle & Rivington, 1890; New York: Lovell, 1890);

In Black and White (Allahabad: Wheeler, 1888; Allahabad: Wheeler / London: Low, Marston, Searle & Rivington, 1890);

Under the Deodars (Allahabad: Wheeler, 1888; Allahabad: Wheeler / London: Low, Marston, Searle & Rivington, 1890; New York: Lovell, 1890);

The Phantom 'Rickshaw and Other Tales (Allahabad: Wheeler, 1888; Allahabad: Wheeler / London: Low, Marston, Searle & Rivington, 1890);

Wee Willie Winkie and Other Child Stories (Allahabad: Wheeler, 1888; Allahabad: Wheeler / Lon-

Rudyard Kipling in the 1880s

don: Low, Marston, Searle & Rivington, 1890);

Soldiers Three [and *In Black & White*] (New York: Lovell, 1890);

Indian Tales (New York: Lovell, 1890) – includes *The Phantom 'Rickshaw and Other Tales* and *Wee Willie Winkie and Other Child Stories*;

The Courting of Dinah Shadd and Other Stories (New York: Harper, 1890);

The Light That Failed (London: Ward, Lock, Bowden, 1891; Philadelphia: Lippincott, 1891; revised edition, London & New York: Macmillan, 1891);

The City of Dreadful Night and Other Places (Allahabad: Wheeler, 1891; Allahabad: Wheeler / London: Low, Marston, 1891; New York: Ogilvie, 1899);

The Smith Administration (Allahabad: Wheeler, 1891);

Letters of Marque (Allahabad: Wheeler, 1891; republished in part, London: Low, Marston, 1891);

American Notes (New York: Ivers, 1891);

Mine Own People (New York: United States Book Company, 1891);

Life's Handicap: Being Stories of Mine Own People (New York: Macmillan, 1891; London: Macmillan, 1891);

The Naulahka: A Story of West and East, by Kipling and Wolcott Balestier (London: Heinemann, 1892; New York & London: Macmillan, 1892);

Barrack-Room Ballads and Other Verses (London: Methuen, 1892); republished as *Ballads and Barrack-Room Ballads* (New York & London: Macmillan, 1892);

Many Inventions (London & New York: Macmillan, 1893; New York: Appleton, 1893);

The Jungle Book (London & New York: Macmillan, 1894; New York: Century, 1894);

The Second Jungle Book (London & New York: Macmillan, 1895; New York: Century, 1895);

Out of India: Things I Saw, and Failed to See, in Certain Days and Nights at Jeypore and Elsewhere (New York: Dillingham, 1895) – includes *The City of Dreadful Night and Other Places* and *Letters of Marque;*

The Seven Seas (New York: Appleton, 1896; London: Methuen, 1896);

"Captains Courageous": A Story of the Grand Banks (London & New York: Macmillan, 1897; New York: Century, 1897);

An Almanac of Twelve Sports, text by Kipling and illustrations by William Nicholson (London: Heinemann, 1898; New York: Russell, 1898);

The Day's Work (New York: Doubleday & McClure, 1898; London: Macmillan, 1898);

A Fleet in Being (London & New York: Macmillan, 1898);

Kipling's Poems, edited by Wallace Rice (Chicago: Star Publishing, 1899);

Stalky & Co. (London: Macmillan, 1899; New York: Doubleday & McClure, 1899);

From Sea to Sea and Other Sketches, 2 volumes (New York: Doubleday & McClure, 1899; London: Macmillan, 1900);

The Kipling Reader (London: Macmillan, 1900; revised, 1901);

Kim (New York: Doubleday, Page, 1901; London: Macmillan, 1901);

Just So Stories: For Little Children (London: Macmillan, 1902; New York: Doubleday, Page, 1902);

The Five Nations (London: Methuen, 1903; New York: Doubleday, Page, 1903);

Traffics and Discoveries (London: Macmillan, 1904; New York: Doubleday, Page, 1904);

Puck of Pook's Hill (London: Macmillan, 1906; New York: Doubleday, Page, 1906);

Collected Verse (New York: Doubleday, Page, 1907; London: Hodder & Stoughton, 1912);

Letters to the Family (Toronto: Macmillan, 1908);

Actions and Reactions (London: Macmillan, 1909; New York: Doubleday, Page, 1909);

Rewards and Fairies (London: Macmillan, 1910; Garden City, N.Y.: Doubleday, Page, 1910);

A History of England, by Kipling and C. R. L. Fletcher (Oxford: Clarendon Press / London: Frowde / Hodder & Stoughton, 1911; Garden City, N.Y.: Doubleday, Page, 1911);

Songs from Books (Garden City, N.Y.: Doubleday, Page, 1912; London: Macmillan, 1913);

The New Army, 6 pamphlets (Garden City, N.Y.: Doubleday, Page, 1914); republished as *The New Army in Training,* 1 volume (London: Macmillan, 1915);

France at War on the Frontier of Civilization (London: Macmillan, 1915; Garden City, N.Y.: Doubleday, Page, 1915);

The Fringes of the Fleet (London: Macmillan, 1915; Garden City, N.Y.: Doubleday, Page, 1915);

Sea Warfare (London: Macmillan, 1916; Garden City, N.Y.: Doubleday, Page, 1917);

A Diversity of Creatures (London: Macmillan, 1917; Garden City, N.Y.: Doubleday, Page, 1917);

The Eyes of Asia (Garden City, N.Y.: Doubleday, Page, 1918);

Twenty Poems (London: Methuen, 1918);

The Graves of the Fallen (London: Imperial War Graves Commission, 1919);

The Years Between (London: Methuen, 1919; Garden City, N.Y.: Doubleday, Page, 1919);

Rudyard Kipling's Verse, Inclusive Edition, 1885–1918 (3 volumes, London: Hodder & Stoughton, 1919; 1 volume, Garden City, N.Y.: Doubleday, Page, 1919);

Letters of Travel (1892–1913) (London: Macmillan, 1920; Garden City, N.Y.: Doubleday, Page, 1920);

Selected Stories From Kipling, edited by William Lyon Phelps (Garden City, N.Y. & Toronto: Doubleday, Page, 1921);

A Kipling Anthology: Verse (London: Methuen, 1922; Garden City, N.Y.: Doubleday, Page, 1922);

A Kipling Anthology: Prose (London: Macmillan, 1922; Garden City, N.Y.: Doubleday, Page, 1922);

Kipling Calendar (London: Hodder & Stoughton, 1923; Garden City, N.Y.: Doubleday, Page, 1923);

Land and Sea Tales for Scouts and Guides (London: Macmillan, 1923); republished as *Land and Sea Tales for Boys and Girls* (Garden City, N.Y.: Doubleday, Page, 1923);

Songs for Youth (London: Hodder & Stoughton, 1924; Garden City, N.Y.: Doubleday, Page, 1925);

A Choice of Songs (London: Methuen, 1925);

Debits and Credits (London: Macmillan, 1926; Garden City, N.Y.: Doubleday, Page, 1926);

Sea and Sussex (London: Macmillan, 1926; Garden City, N.Y.: Doubleday, Page, 1926);

Songs of the Sea (London: Macmillan, 1927; Garden City, N.Y.: Doubleday, Page, 1927);

Rudyard Kipling's Verse, Inclusive Edition, 1885–1926 (London: Hodder & Stoughton, 1927; Garden City, N.Y.: Doubleday, Page, 1927);

A Book of Words: Selections from Speeches and Addresses Delivered Between 1906 and 1927 (London: Macmillan, 1928; Garden City, N.Y.: Doubleday, Doran, 1928);

The Complete Stalky & Co. (London: Macmillan, 1929; Garden City, N.Y.: Doubleday, Doran, 1930);

Poems 1886–1929, 3 volumes (London: Macmillan, 1929; Garden City, N.Y.: Doubleday, Doran, 1930);

Thy Servant a Dog, Told by Boots (London: Macmillan, 1930; Garden City, N.Y., 1930);

Limits and Renewals (London: Macmillan, 1932; Garden City, N.Y.: Doubleday, Doran, 1932);

Souvenirs of France (London: Macmillan, 1933);

Rudyard Kipling's Verse, Inclusive Edition, 1885–1932 (London: Hodder & Stoughton, 1933; Garden City, N.Y.: Doubleday, Doran, 1934);

Something of Myself for My Friends Known and Unknown (London: Macmillan, 1937; Garden City, N.Y.: Doubleday, Doran, 1937);

Rudyard Kipling's Verse, Definitive Edition (London: Hodder & Stoughton, 1940; New York: Doubleday, Doran, 1940).

Collections: *The Sussex Edition of the Complete Works of Rudyard Kipling,* 35 volumes (London: Macmillan, 1937–1939); republished as *The Collected Works of Rudyard Kipling, The Burwash Edition,* 28 volumes (Garden City, N.Y.: Doubleday, Doran, 1941);

Kipling at about the time he was placed in foster care in England

Kipling's India: Uncollected Sketches, 1884–1888, edited by Thomas Pinney (London: Macmillan, 1985);

Early Verse by Rudyard Kipling 1879–1889: Unpublished, Uncollected, and Rarely Collected Poems, edited by Andrew Rutherford (Oxford & New York: Oxford University Press, 1986);

Something of Myself and Other Autobiographical Writings, edited by Pinney (Cambridge: Cambridge University Press, 1990).

From the 1890s to the 1920s the most popular writer in the English-speaking world was Rudyard Kipling. He won at the outset of his career the favorable attention of writers and critics, and in 1907 he received the first Nobel Prize in literature given to an author writing in the English language. He published hundreds of short stories and poems, four novels, and volumes of pamphlets, speeches, and journalism. Yet, of his vast body of work, his novel *Kim* (1901) and his other writing for children have kept Kipling popular. His children's books have remained in print while his tales for adults of ethics, aesthetics, and empire have gone out of fashion — though they are receiving renewed attention in the wake of recent critical interest in imperialism. The author loved children and enjoyed their company, and he probably would have been content to go down in history as the creator of Kim and Mowgli and the Elephant's Child. The roots of Kipling's alliance with children go back, predictably, to his own childhood.

Joseph Rudyard Kipling was born 30 December 1865 in Bombay, India, the first child of John Lockwood Kipling and Alice Macdonald Kipling. Although his parents were a relatively obscure young couple in India, connected neither with the all-important army or the Indian Civil Service, they had ties to celebrated figures back in England. Kipling's mother was the sister-in-law of the Pre-Raphaelite painter Edward Burne-Jones and Academy painter Edward Poynter, so she had grown up in an atmosphere of lively culture. John Lockwood Kipling was an educated, cultivated man, who had come to India to teach art in Bombay, where Kipling spent his early childhood. Kipling remained devoted to a family circle in which art and work were synonymous. Work, or to use Kipling's term, *craft*, was inseparable from everyday life and directly related to the Pre-Raphaelite concern with realism in presentation and idealism of content, as well as commitment to both the life of the mind and the life of the populace. Lockwood Kipling's particular tasks were to preserve and revive native Indian crafts and art forms as well as to help Indians adapt to an industrial age – concerns that influenced Rudyard Kipling's entire career.

His first six years were idyllic, stimulating, and indulgent. He had two Indian servants of his own, and with them he spoke the vernacular Hindustani and had to be reminded to speak English to his parents. Being brought up by Indians may also have laid the foundation of Kipling's rather polymorphous religious beliefs: his bearer Meeta took him to Hindu shrines, and his Goan ayah took him to Roman Catholic services. In sum, he had no reason to doubt the goodness and benevolence of life and the world.

Then everything changed. When Rudyard was three, Alice Kipling gave birth to a daughter, named after her mother but called Trix, and in 1870 she gave birth to a second son who died almost immediately. This event set the Kipling parents on a course of action quite common among colonial families though disastrous for their son and daughter. To remove Rudyard and Trix from the Indian heat and diseases, they took them back to England and placed them in the care of hired foster parents whom they had found through a newspaper adver-

tisement. Why they did not place the children with any of Alice's three married sisters remains a mystery. For whatever reason, they found it best to deposit a six-year-old son and a three-year-old daughter in the care of strangers with painfully hasty goodbyes and not a word of explanation. They did not see them again for over five years.

The woman in charge of the fostering establishment in Southsea was a Mrs. Holloway. Her husband, an old sailor, lived with her for part of the Kipling children's stay, but died, leaving Mrs. Holloway and her son in complete control. In his autobiography *Something of Myself for My Friends Known and Unknown* (1937), Kipling refused to write their names and referred to mother and son as "The Woman" and "The Devil Boy," and to Downe Lodge, the house in which he had lived, as "The House of Desolation." Another record of Kipling's reaction to being in Mrs. Holloway's care is his short story "Baa, Baa, Black Sheep," published in *Wee Willie Winkie and Other Child Stories* (1888). The boy in the story suffers verbal abuse, beatings, public humiliations, solitary confinement, fire-and-brimstone religious threats, and consequent fury, violence, despair, hallucinations, and attempted suicide. How much of the short story is factual and how much invention can never be known, but according to a witness who saw Kipling while he was writing the story, Kipling went about in a state of fury at the recollection. In the story three things save the boy: reading, telling stories, and the furtive affection of his sister and a succession of housemaids. The story leaves out the fourth thing that saved Kipling: his Christmas vacations with the genial Burne-Jones family. There he also came to know William Morris (Uncle Topsy to Kipling) and Dante Gabriel Rossetti and played with their children. Kipling wrote in *Something of Myself* that later in life he asked for the bellpull from the Burne-Jones house that had let him "into all felicity" and put it on his own house "in the hope that other children might also feel happy when they rang it." Despite such exceptional furloughs, Downe Lodge was the rule until his mother returned suddenly from India and whisked her children away, but the Downe Lodge regime had affected him profoundly. In the final words of "Black Sheep": "when young lips have drunk deep of the bitter waters of Hate, Suspicion, and Despair, all the Love in the world will not wholly take away that knowledge; though it may turn darkened eyes for a while to the light, and teach Faith where no Faith was." Though embittered by the experience, Kipling saved his aggression for the printed page, and he never forgot the vulnerability of children. On the other hand, his own resilience may have led him to overestimate the robustness of others based on his own recovery. He became enormously successful and was happily married for forty-four years, but he had had two breakdowns by the time he was twenty-five and suffered from insomnia from his teens to the end of his life. His resilience evidently had its limits.

In 1878 Kipling enrolled at the United Services College, run by a close family friend, Cromell ("Crom") Price. The school's sole aim was to get its students through the army entrance examination or into the Indian Civil Service and do it cheaply. In such a relentlessly practical setting, Kipling was odd boy out – too nearsighted for the army, too irrepressible for the civil service. Instead, "Uncle Crom" fostered Kipling's literary interests, printing his juvenilia in school papers and giving Kipling unlimited access to his personal library, which Kipling devoured. Back home, Kipling's parents collected these poems and, without consulting their son, published a selection of them in 1881 as *Schoolboy Lyrics*.

The school proved crucial to Kipling's development as a children's writer, providing the setting and characters of the stories collected as *Stalky & Co.* (1899), in which the author appears as Beetle and his friends George Beresford and L. C. Dunsterville as M'Turk and Stalky respectively. The extravagant exploits of the characters have no originals except in the fantasies of children who long for the power of adult authority and, conversely, in the nostalgia of adults who long for the freedom of children. The Stalky stories, published over a span of twenty-two years, cannot be taken as faithful reconstructions of unadulterated truth, but they reflect what Kipling felt and thought about his experiences in retrospect. Kipling began to memorialize his school in his thirties, publishing ten stories between 1897 and 1899, an eleventh in 1917, and the last three between 1924 and 1929, when *The Complete Stalky & Co.* appeared. The first ten, however, were collected in 1899, and it was to this *Stalky & Co.* that critics first reacted. It was immediately recognized as a collection for and about educating boys for the duties of empire – which is exactly what the United Services College was all about – the pragmatic values of which varied from those of the standard public-school story.

The violence in the stories is undoubted, but it is not violence alone which appeals to the reader. The majority of the stories concern a species of poetic justice in the form of practical jokes: jokes in which effect is less important than creativity and "stalkiness" – to be stalky is to be "clever, well-

Kipling as a student at the United Services College

considered and wily, as applied to plans of action." Stalkiness allows the boys of Number Five Study to humiliate officious gamekeepers, paranoid or insulting masters, and overgrown bullies, and to play on intellectual prejudices of examiners and rescue less stalky pranksters from irate farmers. Kipling also considers more complex matters, advocating classical studies for army candidates in "Regulus," suggesting compromise in "The Satisfaction of a Gentleman," teaching patriotism in "The Flag of Their Country," or defining heroism in "A Little Prep." If the stories are partly a school for building character, this last tale is perhaps the best example. In it the boys are all dazzled by the heroic appearance of alumni on leave from the army who have come for a reunion; they are thrilled by Crandall's account of the rescue of a fallen comrade during a skirmish on the Northwest Frontier. Meanwhile, the Head has been mysteriously absent from the school and has risked his own life to save a boy dying from diphtheria by using a tube to suck the infected mucus from the child's lungs. Moreover, he has kept his action a secret. When Stalky learns what has happened, he immediately recognizes the Head's action as more heroic than Crandall's exploit, and Crandall agrees: "It's about the bravest thing a man can do." So at the end of the story it is the self-effacing Head who is cheered by the school, rather than the flashy officers and gentlemen.

In 1882 Kipling started the working life for which Price and other masters at the college had tried to prepare him. He arrived in Bombay on 18 October 1882 and joined his family in Lahore, where his father was now principal of the Mayo School of Art and curator of the Lahore Museum. Rudyard Kipling's work had less refined accommodations at the *Civil and Military Gazette,* the local paper for the Punjab province. He owed his position of assistant editor to Price's and his father's connections to one of the paper's owners, who also owned a substantial part of the all-India *Pioneer,* based in Allahabad. The home of the provincial paper was the more interesting city, its ancient, predominately Islamic district coming close to the Occidental's fantasy conception of an Asian city in a golden age. Unfortunately, the difficulties of everyday life included the absence of refrigeration and electric fans and throughout his tenure in India, Kipling suffered from malaria and dysentery.

Kipling nevertheless worked long hours writing articles, acting as editor, and seeing the paper through the press, quite often without the help of his editor, who was frequently incapacitated by fever and the heat. Kipling fared better, perhaps because his father encouraged him, and by 1884 his mother and sister had joined them, reconstituting "the Family Square," a pleasant and emotionally self-sufficient group that fostered Kipling's creative work. In 1884 Rudyard and Trix Kipling published *Echoes,* a book of imitations and parodies in verse. With his family Kipling spent some of the hotter months of the year in the hill towns of Dalhousie or Simla, which was the viceroy's summer seat. And when a new viceroy, Lord Dufferin, arrived, the Kiplings unexpectedly found themselves included in the upper echelon of the caste-ridden Anglo-Indian society.

Kipling thus found himself with access to India at virtually every level. Work for the paper sent him to public events — receptions for maharajas, reviews of troops — and to different parts of India — the Himalayas, the Khyber Pass, Benares, Calcutta, and the ruins of Chitor, which he explored by moonlight. His insomniac night wanderings took him to opium dens, to the marginalized world of Eurasians, to bat-infested minarets, and to conversations with punkah wallahs who worked his cooling system. At the same time, his family connections kept him in contact with Indian arts, ancient

and modern, and gave him entrée into Simla society, complete with dances, polo, picnics, and recreational flirting. This cross-caste way of living made the casteless ideal of Freemasonry naturally attractive to Kipling; it systematized and ritualized his ideas about what was possible when all races and religions met on an even footing. As he wrote of the society in his autobiography: "Here I met Muslims, Hindus, Sikhs, members of the Araya and Brahmo Samaj, and a Jew tyler who was priest and butcher to his little community in the city. So yet another world opened to me which I needed." In return for this living model of what he hoped the imperial unification might accomplish, he gave the Freemasons his undying loyalty, and Masonic references appear throughout his works, including those for children.

Kipling's literary career began in earnest in 1886 with the publication of *Departmental Ditties and Other Verses,* a collection of light and satiric poems about Anglo-Indian careers and courtships. Then in 1886 Kay Robinson arrived to edit the *Civil and Military Gazette* and set Kipling to producing "turnovers," short stories limited to one and a half columns — about two thousand to twenty-five hundred words. Kipling wrote thirty-two of these before the end of 1887 and collected them with eight more stories as *Plain Tales from the Hills* (1888). Late in 1887 Kipling moved to the *Pioneer* in Allahabad, where he supplied the paper's weekly magazine with readable fiction. Released from the constraints of the turnover, he wrote longer stories that were, along with a short novel, collected in six volumes by the Indian Railway Library. These editions sold quickly and attracted international attention.

In Allahabad, Kipling met Prof. S. A. Hill and his wife, Edmonia ("Ted"), an American woman who was about thirty, and who was plump and cheerful. Kipling seems to have been infatuated with her — he wrote to her every day when they were separated. He lived with the Hills as their guest during his last year in India, and he sailed with them when he felt ready to return to England to pursue his career. The trio sailed from India on 9 March 1889, visiting China, Japan, and many locations in the United States, including Elmira, New York, where Kipling interviewed Mark Twain for the *Pioneer.* All of his impressions of America are collected in *From Sea to Sea and Other Sketches* (1899). In Pennsylvania Kipling met and began courting Ted's sister, Caroline Taylor. Both sisters and their father went to England with Kipling, but once he was settled in London in October 1889, they returned to India. Kipling's religious beliefs became a barrier to a match with Caroline: her father was a

WEE WILLIE WINKIE and other Stories by Rudyard Kipling.

A. H. Wheeler & Co's Indian Railway Library No. 6 One Rupee

LONDON:
SAMPSON LOW, MARSTON & COMPANY,
Limited,
St. Dunstan's House, Fetter Lane, Fleet Street, E.C.

*Title page of an 1890 edition of Kipling's first collection of stories
for children*

strict Methodist and wanted assurance that Kipling was a thoroughgoing Christian. The young man made an idiosyncratic declaration of faith in a letter to Caroline, with the result that the engagement (such as it was) was broken off.

Kipling had more success with the literary establishment of London. Especially helpful were the critic Andrew Lang, who wrote favorable reviews of Kipling's Indian works, and magazine editors W. E. Henley and Mowbray Morris, who published his stories and poems in the *National Observer* and *Macmillan's* magazine.

Indeed, Kipling had plenty of stories and poems to publish. Disappointed in love, depressed, lonely, sick with malaria and influenza, and broke because he was too proud to borrow money from a relative or ask a publisher for an advance, Kipling nevertheless entered one of his most productive and successful periods. By August 1890, when he suffered a breakdown from overwork and left for a cruise to Italy, Kipling's new publications included short stories and also the verses that would be collected in 1892 as *Barrack-Room Ballads and Other Verses.* His critical reception was overwhelmingly positive, his reputation made, his success assured — though Kipling never counted on any assurances. "Up like a rocket, down like the stick" was his motto.

When he returned to London from Italy, he held a different view of his professional world. His copyright was not protected in the United States, and Harper's effectively pirated a collection of his short stories under the slack laws. In London the literary establishment provided no help to Kipling, and three of the most eminent authors of the day — Walter Bezant, Thomas Hardy, and William Black —

printed a letter in the *Times* (London) supporting the pirates. Thereafter Kipling sought comradeship and criticism elsewhere, first from his family and then from Wolcott Balestier, an American publisher's agent, who became Kipling's closest friend. When Balestier made his way in London, his family joined him. His elder sister, Caroline (Carrie), kept house for him and one day, visiting his office to go over the housekeeping books, met Kipling.

As the two friends collaborated on a novel, *The Naulahka: A Story of West and East* (1892), Kipling fell in love with Carrie and quietly began courting her. Before they could announce an engagement or marry, Kipling's health relapsed again in 1891, and he set off on another recuperative cruise, this time to South Africa, Australia, New Zealand, and India. Back in Lahore for Christmas with his parents, Kipling received a telegram from Carrie telling him that Wolcott had died suddenly of typhus. Kipling left immediately, stopping only to visit his old ayah in Bombay, and was back in London in fourteen days. He never saw India again.

Eight days after arriving in London, on 18 January 1892, Kipling married Carrie Balestier in a small, rather dreary service (all their relatives had influenza). Three years older than her husband and less beautiful than her sister Josephine, Carrie had characteristics that Kipling loved even though his friends and family did not. Kipling, with good reason, is not considered a great feminist. It does, however, speak something for him that when he married, he chose an independent, intelligent woman with a strength of character to match his own. She was considered unladylike by Henry James, and Lockwood Kipling called her "a good man spoiled." Even some of Kipling's biographers have been baffled by the attraction and have evolved extraordinary theories to account for the match, usually trying to see the marriage as a mere extension of the friendship with Wolcott. That Kipling might have loved Carrie because of, rather than in spite of, her strength is at least as likely.

On their round-the-world honeymoon tour, the couple learned that their bank had failed, taking with it Kipling's entire savings, except for one hundred dollars in a New York bank. Forced to give up their trip, they returned to the United States and set up housekeeping at Bliss Cottage near Brattleboro, Vermont. There, on 29 December 1892, Josephine Kipling was born. Her sister Elsie was born on 2 February 1896 in a house the Kiplings had built and christened Naulahka. Content with a home of his own, a wife, and children, Kipling enjoyed a richly productive literary period that saw the beginning of his ca-

reer as a children's author, producing *The Jungle Book* (1894), *The Second Jungle Book* (1895), *"Captains Courageous": A Story of the Grand Banks* (1897), *Kim* (1901), and *Just So Stories: For Little Children* (1902).

The best-known character in *The Jungle Book* is Mowgli, the boy raised by wolves, but both *Jungle Book* volumes include other stories about animal/human relationships: four in the first *Jungle Book* and three in the second. Besides their surface similarity in their interest in animals, the non-Mowgli stories are thematically akin to the Mowgli stories, especially in the case of the second volume in which both kinds of stories are more obviously and carefully arranged in an alternating pattern. Nevertheless, Kipling himself authorized a collection entitled "All the Mowgli Stories," singling out the character for special attention.

The Jungle Book begins with "Mowgli's Brothers," in which Mowgli is adopted by the mother wolf and her mate. In doing so they deprive the man-eating tiger Shere Khan of his prey, leading to the tiger's hatred of Mowgli, his many attempts to kill the boy, and the war between them. Mowgli is accepted into the pack – his patrons being his parents, the chief wolf Akela, Baloo the Bear, and Bagheera the black panther. But when Akela grows old, a new generation comes to power, and, bribed by Shere Khan and afraid of Mowgli's power to stare them down, they vote to eject the boy from the pack. Hurt and furious, Mowgli reluctantly goes to live with men.

"Kaa's Hunting," set before Mowgli's ostracism, concerns Mowgli's kidnapping by the *Bandarlog,* the Monkey People; his imprisonment in the Cold Lairs, an ancient ruined city; and his rescue by Baloo, Bagheera, and a new ally, Kaa the python. "'Tiger! Tiger!'" picks up from the end of "Mowgli's Brothers," telling how a village woman takes in Mowgli as her lost son. His foster wolf brothers and Akela warn him that Shere Khan is coming to kill him, and they help Mowgli kill the tiger instead. After a jealous rival starts rumors of Mowgli's magic powers, the villagers call him a devil and stone him. Outcast once again, he returns to the jungle but turns down the pack's offer to make him their leader, withdrawing instead to live with his brothers and old patrons.

In *The Second Jungle Book,* "How Fear Came" presents a version of the Fall of Man, an appropriate preface to "Letting In the Jungle" in which fear comes upon the villagers, who cast out Mowgli and then send a hunter to kill him. Meanwhile, out of superstition and greed, they decide to burn the "devil's" human foster parents as witches and di-

The Kipling children: Elsie, John, and Josephine

vide their property among themselves. Mowgli and his friends rescue the couple; then Mowgli orchestrates a slow but inevitable destruction of the village, forcing the inhabitants to flee. "The King's Ankus" varies and amplifies the themes of violence, cruelty, and greed as six men kill each other in a single night, fighting for possession of a ceremonial elephant goad made of gold and precious stones. Mowgli follows its trail of death through the forest, finally retrieving the deadly stick and returning it to oblivion in the Cold Lairs. Although he was treated badly by men, he still feels some pity for them and tries to protect them. In "Red Dog" he protects the jungle and the pack from an invasion of imperialistic dholes, who ravage the jungle. The dholes' motto is "All Jungles are our Jungle," but Mowgli, Kaa, and the pack prove them wrong. At the end of a celebrated battle scene between the wolves and the dholes, Akela lies dying in Mowgli's arms. Mowgli affirms that he is a wolf: "I am of one skin with the Free People," Mowgli cries. "It is no will of mine that I am a man." But Akela tells him that he will return to men in the end. This return is the subject of the last story, "The Spring Running," in

which Mowgli's sexual awakening draws him out of the jungle to follow "new trails."

In *Rudyard Kipling and His World* (1975), Kingsley Amis points out that when the stories appeared in *St. Nicholas* magazine, "the normally vocal readership was silent"; he suspects that the perpetually high sales of the books have more to do with adult gift-giving than juvenile preference. But Amis also quotes a six-year-old reader who praises the stories' action and humor, concluding that Kipling "writes things that sound a bit truish really." For the young reader, being "a bit truish" may be a comment on the lyrical realism with which Kipling describes his jungle, but from an adult point of view, it applies equally to such ideas, values, and themes in the tales as liminality, dual identity, rejection, and acceptance; the human need for variety and the dangers of living in a monoculture; the fragility of societies; the deadliness of greed and the sterility of acquisition; and, the favorite of critics and interpreters, the Law.

The first of these is the most obvious: man by birth, wolf by choice, Mowgli is accepted and rejected at different times by both men and wolves.

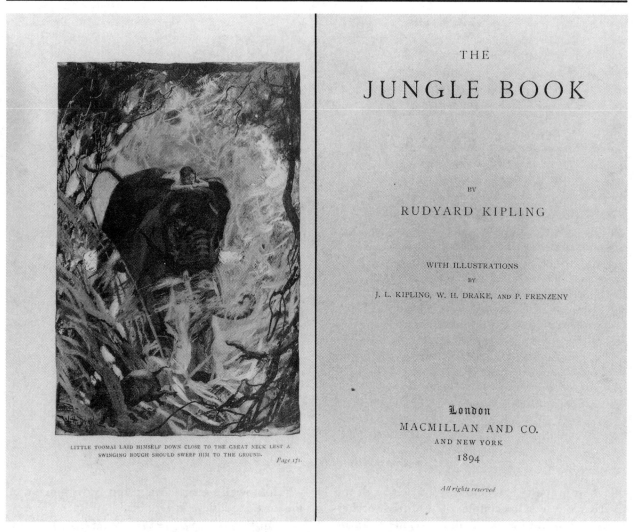

LITTLE TOOMAI LAID HIMSELF DOWN CLOSE TO THE GREAT NECK LEST A
SWINGING BOUGH SHOULD SWEEP HIM TO THE GROUND.
Page 171.

THE

JUNGLE BOOK

BY

RUDYARD KIPLING

WITH ILLUSTRATIONS

BY

J. L. KIPLING, W. H. DRAKE, AND P. FRENZENY

London
MACMILLAN AND CO.
AND NEW YORK
1894

Frontispiece and title page for the collection of stories that introduced Kipling's popular character Mowgli

They drive him out because he has displayed superior characteristics, which may mark Mowgli as a figure for imperialist-racist (human) domination of inferior (animal) peoples. Yet it is difficult to see the imperialist mentality in Mowgli's saying to his supposed inferiors that he would have been a wolf with them to the end of his life or claiming them as his parents or vowing that he and they are the same species. Mowgli is not only master of the jungle because he is a man, but he also is master of men because he is of the jungle, and he would have been master of neither if he had not been carefully and exhaustively educated by his jungle patrons. His greatness lies in the combination of human capacities for thought and compassion with the jungle's law of "Wisdom, Strength, and Courtesy" which frees him from human greed and fear.

What goes for Mowgli goes for societies as well: variety marks healthy group interaction in the jungle. In "Red Dog" Mowgli repels a violent invasion, but the wild bees he uses to dispose of the dholes allows no intrusion whatsoever. The hives of the Little People are given a half-mile berth by other animals, and their vast hives line a marble canyon, the "stale" honey "staining" the marble where the "clotted millions" live. Then their hives collapse under their own weight "like decayed tree trunks" above "huge masses of spongy rotten trash" compounded of "wasted honey" and "rubbish" – the perfect picture of a closed society. The difference between the Little People and the Free People of the jungle is that the bees have the paranoia of a monoculture, indiscriminately killing all strangers, while the pack entertain as observers and sometimes as decisive counselors and members Shere Khan, Bagheera, Kaa, and, of course, Mowgli.

Still, throughout the *Jungle Book* stories, mere multiplicity is not enough to hold a society

Illustration by W. H. Drake from The Jungle Book *depicting Bagheera the panther, Mowgli, and Baloo the bear*

together or guarantee its future. The prime necessity is the Law, the lack of which renders any society fragile and vulnerable to attack from without and decay from within. The chief figure for this fragility is the Cold Lairs, the ruined kingly city deep in the jungle. The two stories involving the Cold Lairs point to social decadence and its causes. In "Kaa's Hunting," the Cold Lairs are the retreat of the *Bandar-log,* who are "very many, evil, dirty, shameless, and they desire, if they have any fixed desire, to be noticed by the Jungle-People." Kipling attacks their lack of memory, of purpose, of follow-through, of any interest in anything for its own sake:

> Whenever they found a sick wolf, or a wounded tiger, or bear, the monkeys would torment him and would throw sticks and nuts at any beast for fun and in the hope of being noticed. Then they would howl and

shriek senseless songs, and invite the Jungle-People to climb up their trees and fight them, or would start furious battles over nothing among themselves, and leave the dead monkeys where the Jungle-People could see them. They were always just going to have a leader, and laws and customs of their own, but they never did, because their memories would not hold over from day to day, and so they compromised things by making up a saying: "What the *Bandar-log* think now the jungle will think later," and that comforted them a great deal.

When searching for an insult bad enough for the covetous, murderous humans in "Letting in the Jungle," Mowgli chooses "Men are blood-brothers of the *Bandar-log.*"

The brotherhood is most marked by the human/monkey association with the Cold Lairs, where the mental bankruptcy of the monkeys lives atop the moral bankruptcy of men. Beneath the ruined city lives an ancient, savage, possessive, and

Illustration by P. Frenzeny for Kipling's "Servants of the Queen," in The Jungle Book

sickly cobra, placed there to guard an immense treasury: "No mere money would begin to pay the value of this treasure, the sifted pickings of centuries of war, plunder, trade, and taxation." Although the treasure and the white cobra have endured together, the society that valued the one and set the other to kill for its sake has vanished. But as the cobra remarks, "Little do men change in the years." The moment a piece of the treasure gets above ground, six men kill each other for its possession, reenacting the strife that implicitly destroyed the ancient civilization.

If contempt for money, possessions, and empty talk protects the jungle-people from the behaviors that destroy human societies, obedience to the Law gives them a society to protect. This Law is a complex set of commands and prohibitions – part tradition, part practicality – that keeps relations among the jungle-people optimal, considering that most of them are either prey or predators. The Law is difficult to sum up partly because the elements are usually brought out situationally and partly because the Law is also something like destiny or necessity that is beyond maxims and prescriptions. When Mowgli exceeds the requirements of the Law, he fulfills the Law nevertheless, as when he defends and provides for Akela when the Law

would allow his successor to kill him and his age would drive him to starvation. The Law is finally difficult to define because specific definitions tend to reduce it to conventional wisdom and rob it of its poetry, though some of the laws versified in "The Law of the Jungle" sound remarkably contemporary: negotiate to avoid fighting, do not drag other people into private quarrels, be considerate of others' needs, kill only for food and never for pleasure, do not allow the poor and weak to starve, children must be fed before adults, mothers must be subsidized, and fathers must have paternity leave.

With such maxims as these drumming in their ears, why are the wolves (and other jungle-people) called "The Free People?" Their freedom lies in their ability to accept or reject the Law. Shere Khan rejects it, as do the *Bandar-log* and even some wolves, bribed and goaded by Shere Khan (to their ruin). The dholes have no Law but aggression; the white cobra has none but possessiveness; human beings past and present are generally Lawless as well, often with disastrous results.

For Mowgli, the Law is not only the guarantor of social harmony, but also the guardian of identity and sanity. In "The Spring Running" both are put to the test when he must leave the jungle and live among the blood brothers of the *Bandar-log*. The

Tailpiece for The Second Jungle Book, *drawn by Kipling's son, John Lockwood Kipling*

Law has saved his life, and now it saves his conscience and dignity. In earlier stories Mowgli has been cast out of one group or another, but this time he chooses to leave the jungle. The animals who raised him understand completely; there is no embarrassment, no jealous clinging, nor any attempt to deny the pain of separation. The Law allows Mowgli to go freely, assured that his animal family loves him, that he can come home again, that his wolf brothers will come with him, and that in leaving he is acting not selfishly but lawfully. Kipling's theme of the Law is thus used to allay the fears children have about growing up and leaving home.

The primary themes in the Mowgli stories tend to recur in the non-Mowgli stories as well. Duality, Law, and compassion infuse the best of them, "The Miracle of Purun Bhagat," in which an Indian prime minister gives up everything to seek spiritual enlightenment as an anonymous beggar. Interspecies integration appears in the well-known "Rikki Tikki Tavi," about a heroic mongoose living in an Anglo-Indian garden. "The White Seal" is perhaps the most modern in its interests, being a story about the slaughter of baby seals and the need for a human-free sanctuary. "Toomai of the Elephants" is sheer fantasy, in which Kipling sends an elephant catcher's son off to witness the nocturnal, mystical dance of the wild elephants. The most adult-oriented story is "The Undertakers," a rich satire on the fragility of the empire and the epidemic cruelty and death of the 1857 mutiny. The weakest stories are "Quiquern," an Eskimo story, and "Her Majesty's Servants," a talking-animal fable about livestock in the British army. But even these lesser efforts cannot detract from the overall excellence of the two collections, with their luminous prose, imaginative power, emotional intensity, and consistent decency.

"Quiquern" and "The White Seal" also display Kipling's interest in stories with a North American setting, and *Captains Courageous,* written in 1896, explores a specialized American setting in great detail. As was often the case with Kipling, the details came before the story. Kipling and the family doctor James Conland made a visit to Boston Harbor, attending the annual memorial service for drowned fishermen. To gather background, the two men explored the old T-wharf of Boston Harbor, clambered aboard ships, and collected quaint paraphernalia. So much does this passion for accuracy and atmosphere saturate the book, that one hesitates to classify *Captains Courageous* as strictly for

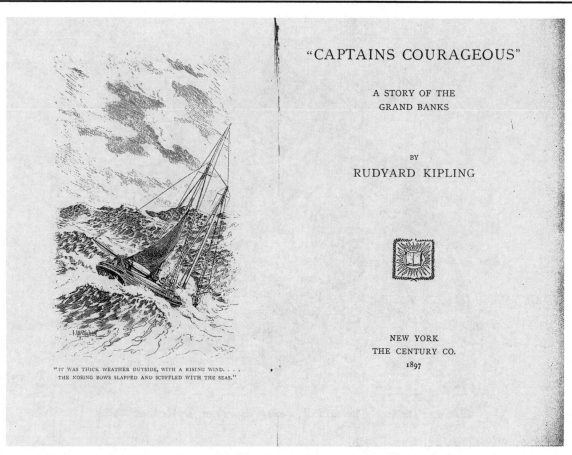

"CAPTAINS COURAGEOUS"

A STORY OF THE
GRAND BANKS

BY

RUDYARD KIPLING

NEW YORK
THE CENTURY CO.
1897

"IT WAS THICK WEATHER OUTSIDE, WITH A RISING WIND. . . .
THE NOSING BOWS SLAPPED AND SCUFFLED WITH THE SEAS."

Frontispiece and title page for Kipling's juvenile adventure novel, set primarily at sea

children, even though the main character is a boy. It is less a children's book than a meticulous and loving elegy for a dying way of life. The men of the ship *We're Here* fish from dories with hooks and lines, and it is remarked more than once that her captain Disko Troop "ain't no ways progressive." Instead of reveling in the latest maritime technology, Kipling devotes himself to the traditional character of the New England fleet.

Harvey Cheyne, fifteen-year-old son of a railway king, is spoiled, arrogant, and overprotected. While crossing to Europe on an ocean liner, he falls overboard and is picked up by the *We're Here*. He tries to buy a passage back to New York, but the tales he tells of his extravagant wealth are unbelievable to the captain and crew. Concluding that Harvey has hit his head too hard in falling from the liner, Captain Troop instead offers him $10.50 a month to work out the rest of the fishing season. Harvey rejects the offer and calls Troop a thief. Troop punches him in the nose and tells him to get to work. After a day of manual labor Harvey is meekly apologizing and looking forward to earning

his pay. Although his old personality collapses rather easily, the point seems to be that when he boards the *We're Here,* he has no personality to speak of, only a Kipling-like impressionability: "Harvey was a very adaptable person, with a keen eye and ear for every face and tone about him." Gradually he becomes like the good men around him, genuinely humble yet justly proud of his accomplishments. In keeping with Harvey's less grandiose place in life, the bulk of the book subordinates his adventures to the larger fortunes of the ship and its motley crew – the Gloucester captain and his son; an Irishman from Galway; a Portuguese; a Gaelic-speaking, clairvoyant black cook from Cape Breton; and an amnesiac Moravian farmer hired on as an act of charity because he lost his family in the disastrous Johnstown flood of 1889. The last two chapters concern Harvey's grieving parents, their race by rail to meet Harvey when they learn he is alive, and the improvement wrought by Harvey's reformation.

Whatever kind of American literature Kipling might have gone on to produce was lost before *Cap-*

tains Courageous saw print in 1897. Tensions between the Kiplings and Carrie's improvident brother Beatty Balestier over his mishandling of money grew until, in a moment of anger, the latter threatened to kill Kipling, who foolishly decided to prosecute his brother-in-law. The resulting publicity drove the intensely private Kiplings to return to England, setting up house first in Torquay and then in Rottingdean, Sussex, in 1897. There, instead of a hostile Beatty for a neighbor, Kipling had his beloved Uncle Ned Burne-Jones, his Aunt Georgina, and cousins the age of his own daughters. His son John was born in August.

The return to England and the birth of a son may well have revived Kipling's literary interest in his own boyhood, sparking the beginning of the Stalky stories. In addition, Kipling produced two more works for adults: *The Day's Work* (1898) and *From Sea to Sea and Other Sketches* (1899). Two of Kipling's best-known and somewhat contradictory political poems were also written in 1898: "Recessional," addressed to the English as they celebrated Queen Victoria's Diamond Jubilee; and "The White Man's Burden," addressed to the Americans as they prepared to annex the Philippines. After the Boer War broke out in 1899, Kipling returned to journalism, working briefly on the *Friend,* a British army newspaper based in South Africa. His connection with South Africa had developed through friendships with Sir Arthur Milner and Cecil Rhodes. Rhodes went so far as to build for the Kiplings a house dubbed "The Woolsack" adjoining his estate near Cape Town so that they could escape the English winter in comfort, a practice they continued from 1898 to 1908.

Despite the difficulties with Beatty Balestier and the family ties to Rottingdean, the Kiplings decided in 1899 to make a voyage to the United States, arriving in New York at the beginning of February. Carrie wanted to visit her relatives, Kipling had some copyright litigation to pursue, and perhaps they also hoped that they could return to what had once been a happy home. The trip was an unqualified disaster: on the voyage all the children suffered a series of illnesses, including whooping cough and bronchitis; on arrival, Carrie too fell ill. Three weeks into the visit both Kipling and six-year-old Josephine came down with pneumonia. Kipling's condition deteriorated, and he was delirious with fever for days. Doctors virtually despaired of his life, and concerned crowds of people blocked traffic outside his New York hotel, some of them kneeling on the sidewalk to pray for his recovery. The lobby was packed with reporters who sent the news in headlines around the world, provoking a landslide of letters and telegrams. By 27 February 1899 Kipling had rallied, and on 4 March he was pronounced out of danger, though he was still very weak. However, two days later Josephine died. Josephine had been a precocious and beautiful child with her father's arrestingly intelligent blue eyes. She had been Kipling's favorite and his constant companion. Her loss seemed irreparable and Kipling was never able to speak of her or hear her name again, alluding to her life or his grief only indirectly here and there in his poetry and fiction.

Typically, Kipling kept working in the aftermath of disaster, continuing to publish and to travel. In 1901 he published *Kim,* the novel about India that he had projected since his journalist days in Lahore and Allahabad. The novel was immediately recognized as something uniquely fine in Kipling's career and in English letters in general. In *Kim,* perhaps naively, Kipling presents the imperial British regime as the best possible agency for the fullest appreciation of India. As Judith A. Plotz explains in "The Empire of Youth" (1992): "With a freedom impossible for any actual Indian, necessarily bound by rules of caste and community, Kim slides in and out of the multiple inhibiting rules of Indian life just as in and out of the rules of different games. What is the realm of necessity and law for Indians is the realm of choice and freedom for Kim. He inhabits an idyll, but it is an idyll of imperialism." Readers have often been troubled by what they perceive to be an insoluble conflict in *Kim* between East and West.

Imperialism aside, *Kim* has been admired for its fluency and beauty of language, for its clarity of detail, for its vivid depiction of place and character, and for the affection it attaches to the places and people of India. Kipling called the book "a naked picaresque," yet it has a distinct, if subtle, plot: a double quest. Kim searches for his destined work so that he can begin his adult life by turning his gifts for language, observation, and imitation to a responsible purpose. Meanwhile, a Buddhist lama searches for a sacred river so that he can end his long life — one that has had worldly and militant passages — with freedom from sin. They take up this double search together and move in and out of each other's quests for the beginning and ending of a life's work, both searches requiring constant ethical self-examinations.

A readable and energetic adventure story, *Kim* has been classified as a children's book, although most critics agree that it appeals to adults as well. Kim O'Hara is the orphan child of an Irish sergeant

" ' There was a bit of scrimmage.' "   *(See page 205.)*

Frontispiece and title page for Kipling's collection of school stories

retired from the Mavericks, a British regiment serving in India. Kim's Irish mother predeceased his father, so the boy has been left in the care of an Indian woman who has virtually let him run wild in the streets of Lahore. His friendliness leads him to help the unworldly lama when he appears in front of the Lahore Museum and earns Kim a place at the holy man's side. In the midst of their search Kim is discovered by the Mavericks, who, when they establish his parentage, decide to send him to an Anglo-Indian school. The lama, eager that Kim's education should be the best, pays his tuition and retires to a Jain monastery. On holidays from the school Kim readily returns to his un-Anglicized habits and the company of the lama, but their wanderings take on a special purpose for Kim under the guidance of members of the secret service, who have been quick to recognize in Kim a virtually ready-made spy. Toward the end of the novel Kim induces the lama to turn his steps into the Himalayas so that Kim, with spymaster Huree Babu leading the way at a discreet

distance, can help to foil an invasion-reconnaissance mission by a pair of Russian spies. The demands of the return journey to get the lama safely to the plains again and to deliver the Russians' papers to his superiors exhaust Kim, who recovers at the house of the Sahiba, an elderly, outspoken, and commanding widow of a minor king. On her maternal estate Kim grasps his identity, and the lama finds his river, achieving enlightenment and, like Buddha before him, returning for a time to the earth for the sake of his follower, smiling "as a man may who has won Salvation for himself and his beloved."

Generally, critics have seen the need to choose between the lama's "Eastern" passivity and spiritualism and the British Empire's "Western" activity and materialism as the watershed decision that Kim must make if he is to enter adulthood. But Kim's decision is never made explicit. Some have argued that Kipling was reluctant or unable to end Kim's childhood. On the other hand, Kipling may well

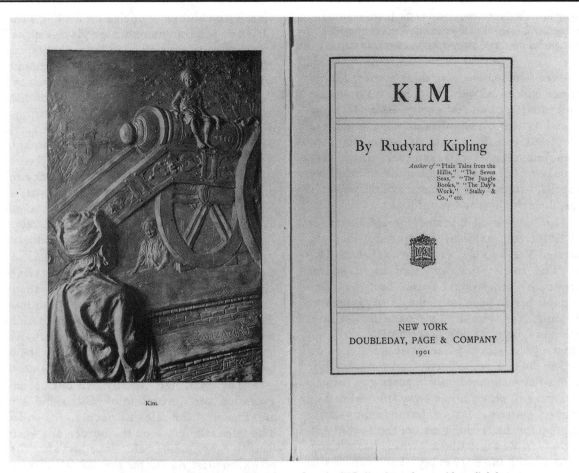

KIM

By Rudyard Kipling

Author of "Plain Tales from the Hills," "The Seven Seas," "The Jungle Books," "The Day's Work," "Stalky & Co.," etc.

NEW YORK
DOUBLEDAY, PAGE & COMPANY
1901

Kim.

Frontispiece and title page for Kipling's popular story of an Anglo-Indian boy who provides a link between the two cultures

have recognized that the cultural-ethical-political synthesis that is Kim must be permanently in process, that the price paid for being Kim is never to be presented with a single definitive decision between the great game of the government or the buddhist way of enlightenment.

In Kipling's works variety is richness, and Kim ultimately asserts a working identity based on the world around him, variegated yet solid. The blending of cultures in *Kim* develops familiar Kipling concerns – liminal identity, surrogate parentage, education, the quest for belonging, the primacy of friendship, and the discovery of worthwhile work.

Kim proved that Kipling could master both the short story and the more prestigious novel. Following its success, Kipling returned to shorter forms. Perhaps the most interesting of these is the collection *Just So Stories: For Little Children*. The stories are literary versions of orally composed tales made up for Kipling's own children; its title, Angela Thirkell explains in her autobiography *Three Houses* (1931),

refers to "a ritual about them, each phrase having its special intonation which had to be exactly the same each time" – in other words, *just so*. Although Kipling's other children's books were literary from the beginning, *Just So Stories* originated as performances, and their range of verbal virtuosity and play reaches a new baroque height, perhaps because the ritual intonations made him responsible first to sound and only second to sense. An example is the opening of "How the Rhinoceros Got His Skin":

Once upon a time, on an uninhabited island on the shores of the Red Sea, there lived a Parsee from whose hat the rays of the sun were reflected in more-than-oriental splendour. And the Parsee lived by the Red Sea with nothing but his hat and his knife and a cooking-stove of the kind that you must particularly never touch. And one day he took flour and water and currants and plums and sugar and things, and made himself one cake which was two feet across and three feet thick. It was indeed a Superior Comestible (*that's* Magic), and he put it on the stove because *he* was allowed to cook on that stove, and he baked it and he baked it till it was all done brown and smelt most sentimental. But just as he was going to eat it there came down to the beach from the Altogether Uninhabited Interior one Rhinoceros with a horn on his nose, two piggy eyes, and few manners.

Even while composing these stories, Kipling remained concerned with creation, transformation, and incantation of art and poetry. Animals, alphabets, and written communication are created, varied, mutated, transformed. Gods, butterflies, cavewomen, jinn, dingoes, cats, and every sort of creature make or fall under incantations, invocations, and spells, witnesses to or masters of the power of words, their rhythms and repetitions.

The book itself mutated for the better, as Brian Alderson explains in "Just-So Pictures: Illustrated Versions of *Just So Stories for Little Children*." The stories first appeared in magazines illustrated by professional artists, but when they were published in book form, the illustrations were by Kipling. Nor were they ordinary illustrations: the pictures have varying degrees of relevance to the text of the story. Some illustrate scenes described in the text, while others depict events never mentioned or mentioned only in passing in the narrative, and still others break away from what they "illustrate" entirely, a fact confessed in the whimsical caption for the "inciting map of the Turbid Amazon done in Red and Black," which "hasn't anything to do with the story except that there are two Armadilloes in it – up by the top." Since Kipling worked in more than one graphic style, the kinds of jokes and comments possible increase with each new pictorial technique. The captions which presumably would clarify the relationship between the drawing and the story do so, but they also ask questions of the reader, answer the reader's implied questions, provide irrelevant information and noninformation, and apologize for the achievements and limitations of the artist. The verbal playfulness of the stories is kept up in the captions and transposed to visual playfulness in the illustrations. This shared richness of invention and facetiousness of tone, rather than any functional or rational link, unify the stories, pictures, and captions in a unique authorial game.

In 1902 Kipling settled permanently at Bateman's near Burwash in Sussex. The most meticulously imagined and fervently realized product of the ensuing period is a pair of books for children, *Puck of Pook's Hill* (1906) and *Rewards and Fairies* (1910), both collections of stories and poems that had previously appeared in magazines. Unlike the *Jungle Book* collections and *Just So Stories,* however, the Puck books are unified by a frame-narrative de-

vice. Two children, modeled on Kipling's children Elsie and John, summon up the playful sprite Puck by acting out a portion of William Shakespeare's *A Midsummer Night's Dream* (1595) on Midsummer eve while standing in a fairy ring on their Sussex farm. Puck, modeled on Kipling in his role of mediator for otherwise inarticulate people of action, introduces them to a series of ghosts from England's past: a British-Roman soldier, a Norman knight, a Renaissance artist, a thirteenth-century Jewish physician, Elizabeth I (incognito), a Regency miss, a prehistoric hunter, a Franco-English gypsy of the Napoleonic era, a seventh-century bishop, a Civil War physician, and an Elizabethan boatwright. Each ghost in turn tells a story to the children.

Their stories form a history of England from the perspective of unsung heroes. They remember kings and cabbages with impartiality – the operations of time have rendered all equal. Although didactic, the stories are not dull: the heroes and heroines of the Puck books are vividly alive, passionate about lives and times still immediate to them, and endowed with distinct and complex personalities.

The characters usually live during times of evolution and devolution of "Cities and Thrones and Powers," the title of a poem in the collection. The tales take place on the border of a shrinking Roman Empire, just before and just after the Norman Conquest, during the rise and fall of Napoleon, in the infancy of the United States, and so on. The fall of one order overlaps the ascent of the new, the adversaries in one story becoming the heroes of the next or their ancestors. For instance, the heroes of the Roman stories fend off Vikings whose descendant is the Saxon hero of another tale. Thus Kipling's fascination with conflicting and complementary elements of identity ranges from personal to national, and his old faith in inclusiveness and "melting pot" unification is upheld. Whereas in Mowgli's jungle the unification depends on filial love between a child and his foster parents, in the Puck books unification is a function of varied friendships: Roman with Viking, Norman with Saxon, Gypsy and Moravian with Seneca, saint with pagan, Roundhead with Cavalier. Kipling hoped this spirit of friendship and love would unite and (no doubt) extend the British Empire.

But mere justification was not enough for Kipling; he could justify his past by becoming its historian, but he could only describe and define it by becoming its poet. Although there had been poetry in his other children's books, the verses in the Puck books are some of Kipling's best, the work of a mature poet at the top of his form: "Harp Song of the

Kipling's illustrations for "The Elephant's Child" and "The Cat that Walked by Himself," in Just So Stories

Dane Women," "Cities and Thrones and Powers," "A Smuggler's Song," "Cold Iron," "If – ," "Eddi's Service," and "The Way through the Woods." Amis calls this last poem "a pastoral lyric so well done and so far outside its author's usual range, whatever that is, as to make it difficult to think of a literary parallel."

The blend of story and verse creates a piece of didactic romancing about the provenance and continuity of the English and English virtues (and vices) combined with a lyrical hymnody about the beauty and richness of the English countryside and character. Interestingly, however, these British characters fall neatly into the Indian caste system: physicians and priests, soldiers, merchants, artisans (who cast considerable light on Kipling's concept of himself), and farmers. Kings appear but are, with one exception, seen from the perspective of the less exalted. "A Charm" in *Rewards and Fairies* tells us that the author's concern is not with the overtly powerful, but with the obscurely good: "Not the great or well-bespoke, / But the mere uncounted folk / Of whose

life and death is none / Report or lamentation." It is fitting, therefore, that one of the recurring symbols in the Puck books is iron – a common metal capable of endurance, brightness, and magic – whether as a singing sword, compass needle, cannon, or horse-shoe.

With their idyllic frame narrative and absorption in good characters, the Puck books are fundamentally hopeful in tenor. But this does not prevent Kipling from dealing with old age, loneliness, grief, incurable diseases, blindness, maiming, alienation, vendetta, violence, racism, religious persecution, madness, melancholia, and death in these stories. His children's England belongs to children whose names, Dan and Una, evoke the biblical hero and the heroine from book 1 of Edmund Spenser's *Faerie Queene* (1590), and it is no place of facile safety any more than the empire of Nebuchadnezzar in the Bible or the haunts of Duessa and Archimago in Spenser's work. No victory is assured, no defeat impossible. The last story, "The Tree of Justice," deals with the respect and gentleness owing to the defeated and the guilt-ridden melancholy that falls upon the conquerors.

Though modern children may relish the Puck books less than adults do, Kipling declares in *Something of Myself* that the tales were designed for both groups: "Yet, since the tales had to be read by children, before people realized that they were meant for grown-ups; and since they had to be a balance to, as well as a seal upon, some aspects of my 'Imperialistic' output in the past, I worked the material in three or four overlaid tints and textures, which might or might not reveal themselves according to the shifting light of sex, youth, and experience." But if reviewer Brander Matthews, writing in 1926, is correct, then the appeal is weighted toward the adults: "Only the mature, who have come to an understanding of life . . . have experience enough to relish the rich savor of *Puck of Pook's Hill* and *Rewards and Fairies,* that incomparable pair of volumes." Though less regarded by contemporary critics, the Puck books are arguably the last long masterpiece of Kipling's career.

The life led by Kipling after moving to Bateman's until his death can be thought of as a period of losses — of parents, another child, friends, health, and public standing. Kipling's mother died in November 1910, and his father outlived her by less than three months, dying in January 1911. Kipling consoled himself through his wife and two children, and when his son John began school, Kipling frequently visited him, evidently determined not to re-enact his own parents' willingness to dispense with his company for years at a time. John Kipling was popular and pleasant and, though no great scholar, was accepted by the army readily in 1914 when World War I began. He was commissioned in the Irish Guards and left with them for France on his eighteenth birthday, 17 August 1915. He served creditably for six weeks and was then reported wounded and missing in action. His body was never found. It seems characteristically stoic of Kipling that after the war he served on the Imperial War Graves Commission, writing epitaphs and inscriptions and inspecting cemeteries, attending to the graves of other people's children when there was none for his own. He wrote a history of his son's regiment, in which John's name appears only on a list of casualties, but otherwise the author was as reticent about this grief as he had been about his loss of Josephine and his parents.

The Imperial War Graves Commission was not the only official or public connection that Kipling made after settling in Sussex. He was as indefatigable as ever, strengthening ties with increasingly extreme right-wing politicians, indulging his Francophilia by traveling to France and studying its literature, watching his friend Sir Robert Baden-Powell institutionalize Mowgli-like ideas of education by founding the Boy Scouts, becoming in the 1920s a friend of King George V, and using his popularity with the armed services to study at close hand the Royal Navy and the infantine Royal Aircraft Establishment. He declined knighthood twice; he declined membership in the British Academy, which would have required him to criticize other writers; and he declined the Order of Merit in 1921 and again in 1924. He received honorary doctorates from McGill University in Canada; the Universities of Durham, Cambridge, Oxford, Edinburgh; and the Universities of Paris and Strasbourg. He won the Nobel Prize in literature in 1907, and in 1923 he became lord rector of Saint Andrew's University. At home he carried on more like an undergraduate: always hungry for information, Kipling studied ancient manuscripts, botany, Jacobean poets, John Donne, and the history of medicine, and he pursued his love of Horace by reading his works and by writing English imitations of his poems.

Perhaps more distressing than the state of his health was the loneliness he and Carrie felt after Elsie married George Bambridge in 1924 and followed her husband abroad for his diplomatic career. Kipling wrote to friends the familiar complaint about the excessive size and quietness of his house with his children gone, but the Kiplings were scarcely living in enforced isolation. There was a steady procession of friends, admirers, and, best of all for Kipling, their friends' children who were, as always, Kipling's favorite company. Carrington records that when writing to invite friends and their children, Kipling "always insisted that they should come in their oldest clothes, fully prepared to fall into the pond."

Despite such amusements, his losses, his painfully failing health, his hobbies, and more formal commitments, Kipling continued to write, though no longer for children, barring some verses to accompany chapters in C. R. L. Fletcher's *A History of England* (1911). In 1923 he made up a collection intended for Baden-Powell's Scouts, *Land and Sea Tales.* This awkward assortment had only two or three short stories that might actually interest a young reader: "Stalky," collected for the first time since its publication in 1898; "His Gift," a harmless tale about a misfit Boy Scout who discovers a talent for cooking; and "The Son of His Father," the precocious escapades of the small son of Strickland, the policeman hero of several of Kipling's earliest tales.

But with the exception of "'Stalky'" these stories for children are lackluster. More successful at the end of his career were his fictions intended for adults, which include some of his finest mature work.

After 1919 Kipling's interest in medicine was more than omnivorous amateurism. He was beginning to suffer from gastric disorders which went undiagnosed for fourteen years and were ineffectively treated for the rest of his life. He feared cancer but was in fact afflicted with ulcers; thus, he lived the rest of his life in acute and unremitting pain which ended only when the ulcers ruptured, and he died on 18 January 1936 of the consequent stroke.

At the nadir of its popularity at his death, Kipling's work never entirely lost its readership. The fairly negligible *Thy Servant a Dog, Told by Boots* (1930) sold one hundred thousand copies in six months. When Kipling died his British publishers had sold seven million copies of his works and his American publishers eight million, excluding articles in magazines and newspapers, numerous translations, and the uncountable number of pirated editions which broadened his audience, even if they did not enrich his bank account.

Kipling was cremated at Golders Green and interred in Poets' Corner at Westminister Abbey. Conspicuous by their absence at his funeral were the members of his own profession and professional critics who had turned out in force, Kipling included, to bury Thomas Hardy only a few years before. But Westminster Abbey was nevertheless filled with friends and admirers, and the crowd overflowed into the streets.

Hardly a decade has passed since without one critic or another attempting to restore Kipling's reputation, damaged by its inevitable association with imperialism. The recent lapse of copyright and the consequent availability of paperback editions from Oxford and Penguin may do more than any critical revision to restore Kipling to the public. With the exception of a small boom in imperialist readings, critical attention has continued at a steadily modest rate. Kipling was the most popular British author since Charles Dickens and the most read and recited poet since Alfred Tennyson, yet he has not accumulated a fraction of their scholarly apparatus, possibly because he was such a controversial figure. Whether or not his critical reputation ever changes, one thing is assured: his work for children (or writing disguised as work for children) called out the best in him at every level.

Rudyard Kipling

Letters:

'O Beloved Kids': Rudyard Kipling's Letters to His Children, edited by Elliot L. Gilbert (London: Weidenfeld & Nicolson, 1983);

The Letters of Rudyard Kipling, edited by Thomas Pinney, volume 1, 1872–1889; volume 2, 1890–1899 (London: Macmillan, 1990).

Interviews:

Kipling: Inverviews and Recollections, edited by Harold Orel (Totowa, N.J.: Barnes & Noble, 1983).

Bibliographies:

Flora V. Livingston, *Bibliography of the Works of Rudyard Kipling* (New York: Wells, 1927);

Catalogue of the Works of Rudyard Kipling Exhibited at the Grolier Club from February 21 to March 30, 1929 (New York: Grolier Club, 1930);

Ellis Ames Ballard, *Catalogue Intimate and Descriptive of My Kipling Collection* (Philadelphia: Privately printed, 1935);

Livingston, *Supplement to Bibliography of the Works of Rudyard Kipling* (Cambridge, Mass.: Harvard University Press, 1938);

James McG. Stewart, *Rudyard Kipling: A Bibliographical Catalogue,* edited by A. W. Yeats (Toronto: Dalhousie University Press/University of Toronto Press, 1959).

Biographies:

C. E. Carrington, *The Life of Rudyard Kipling* (Garden City, N.Y.: Doubleday, 1955);

Kingsley Amis, *Rudyard Kipling and His World* (London: Thames & Hudson, 1975);

Angus Wilson, *The Strange Ride of Rudyard Kipling* (New York: Viking, 1978);

Lord Birkenhead, *Rudyard Kipling* (London: Weidenfeld & Nicolson, 1978);

Marghanita Laski, *From Palm to Pine: Rudyard Kipling Abroad and at Home* (New York: Facts on File, 1987).

References:

Brian Alderson, "Just-So Pictures: Illustrated Versions of *Just So Stories for Little Children,*" *Children's Literature,* special issue on Kipling, 20 (1992)147–174;

Harold Bloom, *Rudyard Kipling* (New York: Chelsea House, 1987);

T. S. Eliot, Preface to *A Choice of Kipling's Verse* (London: Faber & Faber, 1941) pp. 5–36;

Elliot L. Gilbert, *The Good Kipling: Studies in the Short Story* (Manchester: Manchester University Press, 1972);

Gilbert, *Kipling and the Critics* (New York: New York University Press, 1965);

Roger Lancelyn Green, *Kipling and the Children* (London: Elek, 1965);

Green, ed., *Kipling: The Critical Heritage* (New York: Barnes & Noble, 1971);

Phillip Mallett, ed., *Kipling Considered* (New York: St. Martin's Press, 1989);

Brander Matthews, Review of *Debits and Credits, Literary Digest International Book Review,* 9 (November 1926): 745–746;

Judith A. Plotz, "The Empire of Youth: Crossing and Double-Crossing Cultural Barriers in Kipling's *Kim,*" *Children's Literature,* special issue on Kipling, 20 (1992): 111–131;

Andrew Rutherford, ed., *Kipling's Mind and Art: Selected Critical Essays* (Stanford, Cal.: Stanford University Press, 1964);

Angela Thirkell, *Three Houses* (Oxford: Oxford University Press, 1931);

J. M. S. Tompkins, *The Art of Rudyard Kipling* (London: Methuen, 1959).

Papers:

The Kipling Papers are the property of the National Trust, London. The manuscripts for his children's works are at Princeton University Library (*Kim*), the Pierpont Morgan Library (*Captains Courageous*), the Bodleian Library (*Puck of Pook's Hill*), Cambridge University Library (*Rewards and Fairies*), Haileybury (*Stalky & Co.,* no access), and the British Library (*The Jungle Book, The Second Jungle Book, Just So Stories*). Other major collections are held at the Library of Congress and the University of Sussex.

Andrew Lang

(31 March 1844 – 20 July 1912)

Jan Susina
Illinois State University

See also the Lang entry in *DLB 98: Modern British Essayists, First Series.*

BOOKS: *Ballads and Lyrics of Old France* (London: Longmans, Green, 1872; Portland, Maine: Mosher, 1896);

Oxford: Brief Historical and Descriptive Notes (London: Seely, Jackson & Halliday, 1879; London: Seeley / New York: Macmillan, 1890);

XXII Ballades in Blue China (London: Kegan Paul, 1880);

The Library (London: Macmillan, 1881);

XXII and X: XXXII Ballades in Blue China (London: Kegan Paul, 1881);

Helen of Troy (London: Bell, 1882; New York: Scribners, 1882);

Custom and Myth (London: Longmans, Green, 1884; New York: Harper, 1885);

Much Darker Days, as A. Hugh Longway (London: Longmans, Green, 1884);

Ballades and Verses Vain (New York: Scribners, 1884);

The Princess Nobody: A Tale of Fairy Land after the Drawings by Richard Doyle (London: Longmans, Green, 1884);

Rhymes à la Mode (London: Kegan Paul, Trench, Trübner, 1885; London & New York: Longmans, Green, 1907);

That Very Mab, by Lang and May Kendall (London: Longmans, Green, 1885);

Books and Bookmen (London: Longmans, Green, 1886; New York: Coombes, 1886);

In the Wrong Paradise and Other Stories (London: Kegan Paul, Trench, 1886; New York: Harper, 1886);

Letters to Dead Authors (London: Longmans, Green, 1886; New York: Scribners, 1886);

The Mark of Cain (Bristol: Arrowsmith, 1886; New York: Scribners, 1886);

The Politics of Aristotle, Introductory Essays (London: Longmans, Green, 1886);

He, by Lang and Walter Herries Pollock as the "Author of 'It' . . ." (London: Longmans, Green, 1887; New York: Munro, 1887);

King Solomon's Wives; or, The Phantom Mines, as Hyder Ragged (London: Vizetelly, 1887; New York: Munro, 1887);

Myth, Ritual, and Religion, 2 volumes (London: Longmans, Green, 1887; London & New York: Longmans, Green, 1889);

The Gold of Fairnilee (Bristol: Arrowsmith, 1888; New York: Longmans, Green, 1888);

Grass of Parnassus: Rhymes Old and New (London & New York: Longmans, Green, 1888);

Pictures at Play; or, Dialogues of the Galleries by Two Art Critics, by Lang and William Ernest Henley (London: Longmans, Green, 1888);

Letters on Literature (London & New York: Longmans, Green, 1889);

Lost Leaders (London: Kegan Paul, Trench, 1889; New York: Longmans, Green, 1889);

Prince Prigio (Bristol: Arrowsmith / London: Simpkin, Marshall, 1889; New York: Crowell, 1901);

How to Fail in Literature: A Lecture (London: Field & Tuer, 1890);

Life, Letters, and Diaries of Sir Stafford Northcote, First Earl of Iddesleigh, 2 volumes (Edinburgh & London: Blackwood, 1890);

Old Friends: Essays in Epistolary Parody (London & New York: Longmans, Green, 1890);

The World's Desire, by Lang and H. Rider Haggard (London: Longmans, Green, 1890; New York: Harper, 1890);

Angling Sketches (London & New York: Longmans, Green, 1891);

Essays in Little (London: Henry, 1891; New York: Scribners, 1891);

Homer and the Epic (London & New York: Longmans, Green, 1893);

Prince Ricardo of Pantouflia (Bristol: Arrowsmith, 1893; Bristol: Arrowsmith / New York: Longmans, Green, 1893);

St. Andrews (London & New York: Longmans, Green, 1893);

Ban and Arrière Ban: A Rally of Fugitive Rhymes (London & New York: Longmans, Green, 1894);

Cock Lane and Common-Sense (London & New York: Longmans, Green, 1894);

A Monk of Fife: A Romance of the Days of Jeanne d'Arc (London & New York: Longmans, Green, 1895);

My Own Fairy Book (Bristol: Arrowsmith, 1895; New York: Longmans, Green, 1895);

The Book of Dreams and Ghosts (London, New York & Bombay: Longmans, Green, 1897);

The Life and Letters of John Gibson Lockhart, 2 volumes (London: Nimmo, 1897; London: Nimmo / New York: Scribners, 1897);

Modern Mythology (London, New York & Bombay: Longmans, Green, 1897);

Pickle the Spy; or, The Incognito of Prince Charles (London, New York & Bombay: Longmans, Green, 1897);

The Companions of Pickle (London & New York: Longmans, Green, 1898);

The Making of Religion (London & New York: Longmans, Green, 1898);

Parson Kelly, by Lang and Alfred Edward Woodley Mason (London & New York: Longmans, Green, 1899);

A History of Scotland from the Roman Occupation to the Suppressing of the Last Jacobite Rising, 4 volumes (Edinburgh & London: Blackwood, 1900–1907; New York: Dodd, Mead / Edinburgh & London: Blackwood, 1901–1907);

Prince Charles Edward (Paris & New York: Goupil/Manzi, Joyant, 1900; London: Goupil, 1900);

Alfred Tennyson (Edinburgh & London: Blackwood, 1901; New York: Dodd, Mead, 1901);

The Disentanglers (London & New York: Longmans, Green, 1901);

Magic and Religion (London, New York & Bombay: Longmans, Green, 1901);

The Mystery of Mary Stuart (London, New York & Bombay: Longmans, Green, 1901);

James VI and the Gowrie Mystery (London & New York: Longmans, Green, 1902);

Social Origins (London, New York & Bombay: Longmans, Green, 1903);

The Story of the Golden Fleece (London: Kelly, 1903; Philadelphia: Altemus, 1903);

The Valet's Tragedy and Other Studies (London & New York: Longmans, Green, 1903);

Historical Mysteries (London: Smith, Elder, 1904);

Adventures Among Books (London, New York & Bombay: Longmans, Green, 1905);

The Clyde Mystery: A Study in Forgery and Folklore (Glasgow: MacLehose, 1905);

John Knox and the Reformation (London, New York & Bombay: Longmans, Green, 1905);

New Collected Rhymes (London & New York: Longmans, Green, 1905);

The Puzzle of Dickens's Last Plot (London: Chapman & Hall, 1905);

The Secret of the Totem (London, New York & Bombay: Longmans, Green, 1905);

Tales of a Fairy Court (London: Collins, 1906);

Homer and His Age (London & New York: Longmans, Green, 1906);

Portraits and Jewels of Mary Stuart (Glasgow: MacLehose, 1906);

Sir Walter Scott (London: Hodder & Stoughton, 1906; New York: Scribners, 1906);

A merry chase.

Two of Richard Doyle's illustrations for his In Fairyland: A Series of Pictures from the Elf-World *(1869). Lang rearranged the pictures and wrote an accompanying text to create* The Princess Nobody.

The Story of Joan of Arc (London: T. C. & E. C. Jack, 1906; London: T. C. & E. C. Jack / New York: Dutton, 1906);

The King Over the Water, by Lang and Alice Shield (London, New York, Bombay & Calcutta: Longmans, Green, 1907);

Tales of Troy and Greece (London & New York: Longmans, Green, 1907);

The Maid of France: Being the Story of the Life and Death of Jeanne d'Arc (London & New York: Longmans, Green, 1908);

La Jeanne d'Arc de M. Anatole France (Paris: Perrin, 1909);

Sir George Mackenzie, King's Advocate of Rosehaugh: His Life and Times 1636(?)–1691 (London & New York: Longmans, Green, 1909);

Sir Walter Scott and the Border Minstrelsy (London & New York: Longmans, Green, 1910);

The World of Homer (London & New York: Longmans, Green, 1910);

Method in the Study of Totemism (Glasgow: Mac-Lehose, 1911);

A Short History of Scotland (Edinburgh & London: Blackwood, 1911; New York: Dodd, Mead, 1911);

History of English Literature from "Beowulf" to Swinburne (London: Longmans, Green, 1912; New York: Longmans, Green, 1912);

Shakespeare, Bacon, and the Great Unknown (London & New York: Longmans, Green, 1912);

Highways and Byways in the Border, by Lang and John Lang (London: Macmillan, 1913).

OTHER: Wilhelm and Jacob Grimm, *Grimm's Fairy Tales,* translated by Margaret Hunt, with an introduction by Lang (London: Bell, 1884);

Charles Lamb, *Beauty and the Beast,* introduction by Lang (London: Field & Tuer, 1887; New York: Scribners, 1887);

Apuleius Madaurensis, *The Most Pleasant and Delectable Tale of the Marriage of Cupid and Psyche,* translated by William Adlington, with an introduction by Lang (London: Nutt, 1887);

Charles Perrault, *Perrault's Popular Tales,* edited, with an introductory essay, by Lang (Oxford: Clarendon Press, 1888);

The Blue Fairy Book, edited, with a preface, by Lang (London & New York: Longmans, Green, 1889); republished in part as *Prince Darling and Other Stories Based on the Tales in the Blue Fairy Book* (London: Longmans, Green, 1893; New York: Longmans, Green, 1908); republished in part again as *Princess on the Glass Hill and Other Stories* (New York: Longmans, Green, 1899; London: Longmans, Green, 1901); republished in part again as *The History of Jack the Giant-Killer and Other Stories Based on the Blue Fairy Book* (London: Longmans, Green, 1902; New York: Longmans, Green, 1908); republished in part again as *Cinderella, or the Little Glass Slipper, and Other Stories from the Blue Fairy Book* (London & New York: Longmans, Green, 1902); republished in part again as *Dick Whittington and Other Stories Based on Tales in the Blue Fairy Book* (New York: Longmans, Green, 1905);

The Red Fairy Book, edited, with a preface, by Lang (London & New York: Longmans, Green, 1890);

The Blue Poetry Book, edited, with an introductory essay, by Lang (London & New York: Longmans, Green, 1891);

The Green Fairy Book, edited, with a preface, by Lang (London & New York: Longmans, Green, 1892);

Marian Roalfe Cox, *Cinderella: Three Hundred and Forty-Five Variants,* introduction by Lang (London: Publications of the Folk-Lore Society, 1892);

The True Story Book, edited, with a preface, by Lang (London: Longmans, Green, 1893; New York: Longmans, Green, 1894); revised as *The Blue True Story Book* (New York: Longmans, Green, 1896: London: Longmans, Green, 1909);

The Yellow Fairy Book, edited, with a preface, by Lang (London & New York: Longmans, Green, 1894);

The Red True Story Book, edited, with an introductory essay, by Lang (London & New York: Longmans, Green, 1895);

Frederick van Eeden, *Little Johannes,* translated by Clara Bell (London: Heinemann, 1895) — includes "Literary Fairy Tales" by Lang;

The Animal Story Book, edited, with a preface, by Lang (London & New York: Longmans, Green, 1896; revised, 1901);

The Pink Fairy Book, edited, with a preface, by Lang (London & New York: Longmans, Green, 1897);

The Nursery Rhyme Book, edited, with a preface, by Lang (London & New York: Warne, 1897);

Arabian Nights Entertainments, edited, with a preface, by Lang (London & New York: Longmans, Green, 1898);

The Red Book of Animal Stories, edited, with a preface, by Lang (London & New York: Longmans, Green, 1899);

The Grey Fairy Book, edited, with a preface, by Lang (London & New York: Longmans, Green, 1900);

The Violet Fairy Book, edited, with a preface, by Lang (London & New York: Longmans, Green, 1901);

The Book of Romance, edited, with a preface, by Lang (London & New York: Longmans, Green, 1902); revised as *Tales of Romance* (London & New York: Longmans, Green, 1907); revised again as *Tales of King Arthur and the Round Table* (London & New York: Longmans, Green, 1909);

The Crimson Fairy Book, edited, with a preface, by Lang (London & New York: Longmans, Green, 1903); republished in part as *Little Wildrose and Other Stories From the Crimson Fairy Book* (London & New York: Longmans, Green, 1906);

The Brown Fairy Book, edited, with a preface, by Lang (London & New York: Longmans, Green, 1904);

The Red Romance Book, edited, with a preface, by Lang (London & New York: Longmans, Green, 1905);

Irene Mauder, *The Plain Princess and Other Stories,* preface by Lang (London: Longmans, Green, 1905);

The Orange Fairy Book, edited, with a preface, by Lang (London & New York: Longmans, Green, 1906);

The Olive Fairy Book, edited, with a preface, by Lang (London & New York: Longmans, Green, 1907);

The Book of Princes and Princesses, edited, with a preface, by Lang (London & New York: Longmans, Green, 1908);

The Red Book of Heroes, edited, with a preface, by Lang (London & New York: Longmans, Green, 1909);

The Lilac Fairy Book, edited, with a preface, by Lang (London & New York: Longmans, Green, 1910);

All Sorts of Stories Book, edited, with a preface, by Lang (London & New York: Longmans, Green, 1911);

The Book of Saints and Heroes, edited, with a preface, by Lang (London & New York: Longmans, Green, 1912);

The Strange Story Book, edited by Lang, with a preface by Leonora Blanche (London & New York: Longmans, Green, 1913).

TRANSLATIONS: Homer, *The Odyssey,* translated by Lang and Samuel Henry Butcher (London: Macmillan, 1879; New York: Macmillan, 1883);

Theocritus, Bion, and Moschus (London: Macmillan, 1880; New York: Macmillan, 1889);

Homer, *The Iliad,* translated by Lang, Walter Leaf, and Ernest Myers (London: Macmillan, 1883; New York: Alden, 1883);

Aucassin and Nicolete (London: Nutt, 1887; New Rochelle, N.Y.: Clarke Conwell, 1902);

Charles Deulin, *Johnny Nut and the Golden Goose* (London: Longmans, Green, 1887);

The Dead Leman and Other Tales from the French, translated by Lang and Paul Sylvester (London: Swan, Sonnenschein, 1889; New York: Scribner & Welford, 1889);

The Miracles of Madame Saint Katherine of Fierbois (Chicago: Way & Williams, 1897);

Homer, *The Homeric Hymns* (New York: Longmans, Green, 1899; London: Allen, 1899);

Victor Hugo, *Notre-Dame of Paris* (London: Heinemann, 1902).

More than any other British writer of the second half of the nineteenth century, Andrew Lang successfully championed the fairy tale as appropriate reading material for children. This astonishingly productive man of letters influenced children's literature in two ways: as the editor of the immensely popular twelve-volume color fairy book series begun with the publication of the *Blue Fairy Book* (1889), and as the author of five literary fairy tales for children.

Despite Lang's repeated assertions in prefaces to the color fairy books that he was merely the editor and did not invent the stories, his readers frequently incorrectly credited him as their author. While Lang selected the tales, assigned the translations, and wrote the prefaces to the color fairy books, his wife, Leonora Blanche Lang, did much of the other work of the series. In the preface to *The Lilac Fairy Book* (1910), the final volume in the series, Lang acknowledges that "the fairy books have been almost wholly the work of Mrs. Lang" and suggests that his part in their creation was that of "Adam, according to Mark Twain, in the Garden of Eden. Eve worked, Adam superintended." So to think of Lang as the sole or even the primary editor of the color fairy books is a mistake. This does not, however, diminish Lang's important role in the series. He was clearly a well-established author and editor whose name lent the volumes credence and respectability.

A prolific writer, Lang produced 120 books and pamphlets, edited or appeared as a contributor in another 150 volumes, and penned more than 5,000 essays, articles, and reviews. He was a folklorist, classical scholar, poet, novelist, journalist, and editor who lived by his pen, capable of producing something worth saying on nearly any topic that caught his fancy, which earned him the reputation, coined by William Ernest Henley, of "the divine amateur of letters."

Born in Selkirk, Scotland, on 31 March 1844, Andrew Lang recalls in his *Adventures Among Books* (1905) that "When I was a little boy, it is to be sup-posed that I was a little muff: for I read every fairy tale that I could lay my hands on." A bookish child, Lang seemed more at home in fairyland than in his own period. His deep love of the Scottish border country, with its folktales and legends, was to become a consistent theme in his writing.

Lang attended Edinburgh Academy in 1854 and entered the University of Saint Andrews in 1861, where he lived at Saint Leonard's Hall. There he and friends began *St. Leonard's Magazine,* with Lang as the editor and chief contributor. He transferred to the University of Glasgow in 1864 to qualify for the Snell exhibition, a major scholarship that would enable him to attend Balliol College, Oxford. Entering Balliol in 1868 with the distinguished classical scholar Benjamin Jowett as his tutor, Lang was later elected to the Open Fellowship to Merton College that he held for seven years. Ill health caused him to end his academic career, and Lang left Oxford in 1872 for the French riviera to recover from his bout with consumption.

On 17 April 1875 Lang married Leonora Blanche Alleyne, the youngest daughter of Charles Thomas Alleyne of Clifton, whose family had been planters in Barbados for generations. Leonora Lang, particularly proficient at languages, worked closely with the production of the twenty-five children's collections Lang edited for Longmans, providing many of the French, German, and Italian translations for the color fairy books. Especially concerned with the readability of the texts, Leonora attempted to limit the vocabulary and sentence structure so that the collections were accessible to children with average reading abilities. Her influence in this regard is apparent in the many adaptations of the original color fairy books produced by Longmans as school editions or versions for younger readers.

After Lang resigned his Merton fellowship, he and his wife moved to Kensington, where he began his career as a London journalist, contributing articles and reviews to a large variety of journals and newspapers. Of Lang's prodigious journalistic output, Richard Le Gallienne has said, "His 'leaders' in the *Daily News* read like fairy tales written by an erudite Puck." His work quickly attracted the attention of publisher Charles Longman of Longmans, Green, and Company, and Lang soon became the chief literary adviser to the well-established firm that was to publish many of his books. From 1882 to 1905 Lang's column, "At the Sign of the Ship," appeared in *Longmans Magazine;* Lang dealt with a wide range of subjects, including fairy tales, mythology, folklore, cultural anthropology, psychic phe-

PRINCE RICARDO OF PANTOUFLIA

BEING THE ADVENTURES OF PRINCE
PRIGIO'S SON, BY ANDREW LANG
AUTHOR OF PRINCE PRIGIO

ILLUSTRATED BY
GORDON BROWNE

PUBLISHED AT BRISTOL BY J. W. ARROWSMITH,
QUAY STREET, AND AT LONDON BY SIMPKIN,
MARSHALL, HAMILTON, KENT & COMPANY LIMITED

Title page for Lang's 1893 literary fairy tale (courtesy of the Lilly Library)

nomena, and superstition. Longman gave Lang a sixty-volume *Cabinet des Fées* (1786), the massive collection of French literary fairy tales produced during the period of Louis XIV. In a 1913 article Joseph Jacobs notes that, with the editing of the color fairy books, Lang was creating a Victorian version of *Cabinet des Fées* for British children.

While at Oxford Lang had earned a first-class rank in the Greek and Latin classics and was influenced by Edward B. Tylor's pioneering work in anthropology. Using Tylor's concepts of cultural evolution and folklore as "survivals," Lang became the best-known and most-vigorous spokesperson for the anthropological school of folklore. Using his knowledge in mythology and folktales from around the world, Lang expanded Tylor's limited concept of folklore as an European peasant tradition and incorporated a more comparative methodology. Lang established himself as a leading Victorian folklorist with the publication in the *Fortnightly Review* (May

1873) of his article "Mythology and Fairy Tales," which successfully refuted the claims of Max Müller, who had argued that philologically all myths could be reduced to one great myth of a common Aryan ancestry and that the variations were the result of the "disease of language." Lang countered that instead of being derived from the same source, fairy tales evolved in various cultures as the result of societies undergoing the same cultural evolution. Throughout his career, including comic asides found in his literary fairy tales *Prince Prigio* (1889) and *Prince Ricardo of Pantouflia* (1893), Lang continued to ridicule Müller's theory that all myths are linked to solar mythology and that all myths trace their origins to India. Lang elaborated these points in *Custom and Myth* (1884) and in *Myth, Ritual, and Religion* (1887). By the time Lang contributed his entry on tales to the eleventh edition of the *Encyclopaedia Britannica* (1910) he had modified his position to take into account the cultural diffusion of fairy tales.

Lang's first literary fairy tale for children was completed at the request of Longman, his friend and publisher, who asked if he would write a story around some illustrations of fairies by Richard Doyle that had originally appeared in a book titled *In Fairyland: A Series of Pictures from the Elf-World* (1869). The forty fanciful paintings of elves and fairies are Doyle's masterwork, surpassing his long-running cover for *Punch* and his illustrations of John Ruskin's *The King of the Golden River* (1851); they are certainly the most famous and elaborate example of Victorian fairy painting. Lang reorganized the illustrations, omitted five, cut up several, and reproduced some without color. Drawing on his knowledge of fairy lore, he created *The Princess Nobody* (1884), an amusing tale in the French fairy-court tradition of the romantic misadventures of the Princess Niente and Prince Comical.

In Lang's fairy tale a king has unwittingly promised his daughter in marriage to a dwarf. Princess Niente, known to her to subjects as Princess Nobody, is saved from this unpleasant marriage by the Queen of the Water Fairies, who makes the girl invisible and spirits her away to Fairy Land. Her father promises Niente to the prince who can locate and return his invisible daughter. The kindhearted Prince Comic locates Niente and is eventually transformed into a handsome Prince Charming. Lang's tale is an ingenuous attempt to sequence Doyle's random illustrations into a cohesive plot, but since Doyle rarely repeated characters, Lang was forced to have his protagonists undergo multiple magical transformations. While Lang's story is vastly superior to the poem by William Allingham that originally accompanied the pictures, the chief attraction of *Princess Nobody* remains Doyle's illustrations.

Lang's second fairy tale, *The Gold of Fairnilee* (1888), is a haunting story told in the Scottish-border-ballad tradition using the folk beliefs in fairies and set in the locale of his childhood. This dramatic switch from the charming winged fairies of *Princess Nobody* is considered by critics to be the most successful of his five children's books. Drawing inspiration from the folk ballads "Tam Lin" and "Thomas Rymer," Lang's moody tale deals with the disappearance of the young Randal Ker of Fairnilee. Inspired by his nurse's tales of fairy treasure, Randal sets out with his companion Jean to discover the fairy gold. On Midsummer Eve Randal is lured away by the Fairy Queen at the Wishing Well into the Fairy Land. Seven years later, Jean uses magic water to bring Randal back from the fairies, whereupon he uncovers the gold of Fairnilee, a cache of long-buried Roman coins.

Lang returns to the fairy-court tradition in *Prince Prigio*, which owes a debt to William Makepeace Thackeray's *The Rose and the Ring* (1855), the literary fairy tale that Lang recommends in his preface to *The Yellow Fairy Book* (1894) as "quite indispensable in every child's library"; it also reflects the Christmas pantomime tradition. In the preface to *The Lilac Fairy Book,* Lang complains that authors think writing a new fairy tale is easy, but he notes: "They are mistaken: the thing is impossible. Nobody can write a *new* fairy tale; you can only mix up and dress up the old, old stories, and put the characters in new dresses." This is clearly the case in *Prince Prigio,* which borrows freely from both the folktale and literary fairy-tale conventions.

Fairies are not invited to the christening of Prigio, since the skeptical Queen of Pantouflia does not believe in the supernatural. Nevertheless, the fairies arrive and present Prigio with the traditional magic gifts, which include a sword of sharpness, seven-league boots, the purse of Fortunatus, a flying carpet, and a cap of darkness. As punishment the young prince is cursed with the burden of being "*too* clever." The Queen discards the gifts in the attic, and Prigio develops into such a clever and rational fellow that he is generally despised by everyone in the kingdom except his mother. When the Firedrake causes destruction in Pantouflia, King Grognio encourages his son to battle the beast. Prigio, who has been educated to reject the supernatural, refuses to believe in the existence of such a fabulous beast and observes that according to fairy-tale logic, it would be useless to send him, the first son, to fight the Firedrake, as it is always the youngest sibling who succeeds in such tasks. When Prigio's less intelligent but far more popular younger brothers, Alphonso and Enrico, fail to return from their attempts to defeat the Firedrake, the entire court abandons Prigio in disgust. Alone in the castle, Prigio uncovers his magical christening gifts, and he sets out to kill the Firedrake for his love, Lady Rosalind. The clever Prigio manages to have the Firedrake battle Remora, the Ice-Beast, and the two monsters are destroyed. Prigio brings his brothers back to life, marries Rosalind, and becomes beloved by his subjects when he wishes to "*SEEM* NO CLEVERER THAN OTHER PEOPLE."

Lang continues his gentle burlesquing of the fairy-court tradition in a sequel, *Prince Ricardo of Pantouflia;* the two texts were subsequently published collectively under the name "The Chronicles of Pantouflia" in *My Own Fairy Book* (1895). While Lang's literary fairy tales were popular, they never achieved the popularity of the color fairy books. J. R. R. Tolkien, in "On Fairy-stories" (1964), finds "The Chronicles of Pantouflia" to be flawed in that, like Prigio, Lang delights in being too clever, having "an eye on the faces of other clever people over the heads of his child-audience."

In 1889, along with the publication of *Prince Prigio,* Lang edited *The Blue Fairy Book,* which his biographer Roger Lancelyn Green claims renewed the public's interest in fairy tales. Louise Frances Field's *The Child and His Book* (1891), a pioneering study of children's literature, announces, "At the present moment the fairy-tale seems to have given way entirely in popularity to the child's story of real life." With the enormous impact of *The Blue Fairy Book,* Field obligingly added, "Since the above was written eighteen months ago, the tide of popularity seems to have set strongly in the direction of old fairy tales."

Initially published in an edition of six thousand, *The Blue Fairy Book* and the second volume in the series, *The Red Fairy Book* (1890), were published simultaneously in trade and limited editions for book collectors, with the latter intended to help defray the cost of the general edition. Lang did not plan to create a fairy-tale series, and in the preface to *The Red Fairy Book* he suggests that he had already selected the best tales. Despite Lang's well-known status, *The Blue Fairy Book* was a publishing risk for Longmans in that the appeal for fairy tales for children seemed to have peaked. Instead, it was the first of a popular twelve-volume series of color fairy books and the first of twenty-five annual children's collections Lang produced for the publisher from 1889 to 1913.

The Blue Fairy Book, a wide-ranging assortment of thirty-seven tales, includes both traditional folktales and literary fairy tales compiled from various printed sources. Lang announced in his introduction to the limited edition of *The Blue Fairy Book* that the volume was intended "for the pleasure of children without scientific purpose." Illustrated by H. J. Ford and G. P. Jacob Hood, the first color fairy book contains seven tales from Charles Perrault, seven from the Brothers Grimm, three from the *Arabian Nights,* as well as literary fairy tales from the French tradition by Jeanne-Marie de Beaumont and Marie-Catherine d'Aulnoy and those from the Norwegian folk tradition collected by Peter Asjørnsen and Jørgen Moe. Lang's initial selection favors well-known European folktales including "Little Red Riding Hood," "Sleeping Beauty," "Cinderella," "Hansel and Gretel," "Blue Beard," and "Beauty and the Beast." Lang was well served by Ford's richly detailed black-and-white illustrations; Ford would be the illustrator for all the color fairy books and many of Lang's other children's collections. *The Blue Fairy Book* also contains selections that are clearly not fairy tales, including an abridgment of the voyage to Lilliput from Jonathan Swift's *Gulliver's Travels* (1726) and Lang's adaption of the Greek myth of Perseus and the Medusa entitled "The Terrible Head," in which he omits the local and personal names so it will better resemble a folktale.

The Red Fairy Book, quickly published to follow on the success of *The Blue Fairy Book,* was issued by Longmans with an initial edition of fifteen thousand copies and reissued in an edition of five thousand the following year. Longmans quickly began to repackage and simplify material from the existing color fairy books into volumes to be marketed as school readers and versions for younger readers. *The Red Fairy Book,* like its predecessor, contained thirty-seven selections but had fewer French fairy tales. Lang expanded the range to include Russian, Norwegian, Finnish, and Romanian tales as well as a version of the story of Sigurd and Brynhild adapted from William Morris's translation *Sigurd the Volsung* (1876).

The Blue Poetry Book (1891) is a collection of poems selected by Lang and intended for children. The volume had an initial printing of three thousand copies and was not as popular as the fairy-tale series. In making his choices Lang recalled those poems that had pleased him in his childhood and had developed his love of poetry. The selections show a marked preference for narrative verse, and while not written specifically for children, they are poems which Lang felt could be accessible to chil-

dren. He warns in his preface that it is a mistake when authors "write down" to children or when adults tell children that they should not read a poem because they will not understand it, arguing instead that children understand far more than adults assume. He adds that nothing crushes the love of poetry more swiftly than the use of poems in schoolbooks, but that warning did not prevent Longmans from quickly producing a school edition of the volume.

In the preface to *The Green Fairy Book* (1892) Lang suggests it would be "probably the last, of the Fairy Books of many colours." Fairy tales from the French tradition dominate this collection, although the most familiar stories in this collection are those from the English tradition: "Three Little Pigs" and Robert Southey's "The Story of the Three Bears." While Lang made minor editorial changes to the folktales in his collections, the literary fairy tales, particularly those from the French fairy-court tradition by d'Aulnoy and de Beaumont, were substantially reduced in length, and in the case of Perrault, the rhymed morals were dropped. In his preface Lang discusses the function of fairy tales, arguing that they are the oldest stories in the world and were created "not only to amuse, but to teach goodness." He defends the reading of fairy tales by children, suggesting that young readers are capable of distinguishing between real and make-believe.

The preface concludes, "If we have a book for you next year, it shall not be a fairy book," and the following year Longmans published *The True Story Book* (1893), which included various retellings of lives of historical figures composed by writers including H. Rider Haggard, Florence Sellar, and Lang's own version of the life of Joan of Arc. Later collections including *The Red True Story Book* (1895), *The Book of Princes and Princesses* (1908), *The Red Book of Heroes* (1909), and *The Book of Saints and Heroes* (1912) would expand the true-story series, Lang reminds his readers that although such stories might be considered less thrilling than fairy tales, facts can sometimes be "curious and interesting."

The publication of *The True Story Book* was overshadowed by the publication in the same year of *Prince Ricardo of Pantouflia,* the continuation of Lang's fairy court cycle. Unlike Prigio, who had been skeptical in his belief in fairies, Ricardo was raised on a steady diet of fairy tales and, according to his bewildered father, "is always after a giant, or a dragon or a magician." In order to teach his son independence, Prigio replaces Ricardo's magic weapons with fakes, and, consequently, Ricardo fails in his attempt to restore Bonnie Prince Charlie

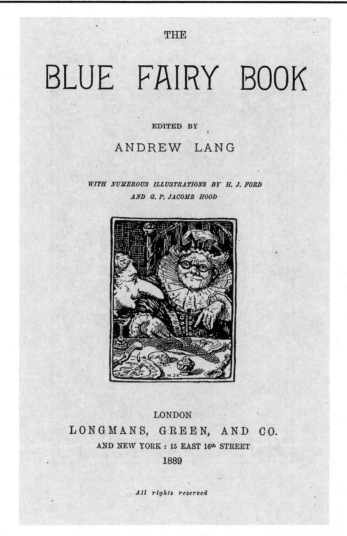

THE

BLUE FAIRY BOOK

EDITED BY

ANDREW LANG

WITH NUMEROUS ILLUSTRATIONS BY H. J. FORD
AND G. P. JACOMB HOOD

LONDON
LONGMANS, GREEN, AND CO.
AND NEW YORK: 15 EAST 16th STREET
1889

All rights reserved

Title page for the first volume of the popular series edited by Lang. The illustration by H. J. Ford includes what might be a caricature of Lang at left (courtesy of the Lilly Library).

to the English throne. Ricardo is rescued by the resourceful Princess Jacqueline, who is in love with him. Ricardo continues his adventures by slaying the horrible Yellow Dwarf, the famous and triumphant villain of d'Aulnoy's fairy tale, in a fair fight and ultimately defeating the Giant-who-does-not-Know-when-he-has-had-Enough by dropping on him the heaviest material in existence: stupidity. Much of *Prince Ricardo* is a sly commentary of the Lang-Müller debate over solar mythology. More episodic in form than *Prince Prigio,* the sequel is less satisfying, and its humor is a bit more forced. Regrettably, Lang often took good ideas and expanded them into a series of books with the later volumes suffering from his flagging enthusiasm; such was the case with "The Chronicles of Pantouflia."

The following year *The Yellow Fairy Book,* the fourth volume of the series, was published; Lang

used his preface to respond to the attacks directed at previous volumes by George Laurence Gomme, president of the Folk-Lore Society. As a folklorist, Gomme objected to Lang's non-scholarly approach to his fairy-tale collections and in particular to Lang's practice of adapting and editing traditional tales and of mixing literary tales with folktales in the volumes. As the president of the Folk-Lore Society before Gomme, Lang had published scholarly work on folklore in addition to the color fairy books for children. Lang's preface responds to Gomme with the assertion, "If children are pleased, and they are so kind to say that they *are* pleased, the Editor does not care very much for what other people have to say." His criteria for selection of the tales for the series were based on whether the tales were pleasant to read and not that they conformed to any academic definition of a fairy tale. *The Yellow Fairy Book*

PRINCE DARLING TRANSFORMED INTO THE MONSTER.   *See p. 284.*

Frontispiece by H. J. Ford for The Blue Fairy Book *(courtesy of the Lilly Library)*

continues the mix of traditional folktales from Russia, Germany, and Iceland, with literary fairy tales by d'Aulnoy and Hans Christian Andersen.

In the preface to *The Red True Story Book,* Lang had promised his readers that the next collection would be "something quite as true as History, and quite as entertaining as Fairies!" That volume was *The Animal Story Book* (1896), a compilation of stories dealing with "the friends of children and of fairies – the beasts." Lang continued the animal series with *The Red Book of Animal Stories* (1899), a collection which deals with ordinary and fabulous creatures such as griffins, unicorns, and dragons.

In *The Pink Fairy Book* (1897) Lang observes that "all people in the world tell nursery tales to their children," and with this collection he further expands his international scope of fairy tales to include Japanese and Catalonian tales as well as examples from Sweden, Sicily, and Africa. Despite their different geographic origins, Lang suggests the tales have a universal moral in that "Courage, youth, beauty, kindness have many trials, but they always win the battle."

Lang returns to his love of poetry in *The Nursery Rhyme Book* (1897), a collection aimed at younger children. He groups the rhymes into such categories as proverbs, songs, riddles, charms, and lullabies. In his preface Lang admits that while nursery rhymes do not provide useful information, they will be remembered long after children have forgotten history and geography. L. Leslie Brooke brilliantly illustrated the collection with more than one hundred lively drawings; the volume was his first major success as a children's book illustrator.

Lang's *Arabian Nights Entertainments* (1898), an adaptation for children of twenty-six tales from Antoine Galland's *Arabian Nights* (1704–1717), includes "Aladdin and the Wonderful Lamp," which Lang recycles from *The Blue Fairy Book,* but with new illustrations by Ford. In his preface Lang recalls reading *The Arabian Nights* as a child but observes that these "fairy tales of the East" were not originally intended for children and reassures any concerned parent that his edition omits "pieces only suitable for Arabs and old gentlemen."

In *The Grey Fairy Book* (1900), *The Violet Fairy Book* (1901), *The Crimson Fairy Book* (1903), *The Brown Fairy Book* (1904), and *The Orange Fairy Book* (1906) Lang dutifully continues to widen his international scope of fairy tales. Sensitive to the problem that readers of the expanding series were faced with variations on the same theme in many of the tales, he notes that, like the bits of colored glass that go into the making of a kaleidoscope, the possible combinations of fairy-tale incidents are limited. Observing that he had frequently been asked how he has managed to invent so many more stories than William Shakespeare, Alexandre Dumas, and Charles Dickens combined, Lang felt compelled by a "sense of literary honesty" to insist repeatedly in the prefaces to these various volumes that he was simply the editor and not the author of the collected fairy tales. He acknowledges that his versions are not literal translations and that he has altered them in various ways to make them "suitable for children," adding that fairy tales that include cruel incidents had been "softened down" as much as possible. His progressively more crotchety prefaces to the fairy color books suggest that Lang had become trapped by his own success and had grown weary of the project.

Lang's *Tales of Troy and Greece* (1907) splendidly retells Homer's *Odyssey* and *Iliad,* with the addition of the stories of Theseus and Perseus from Greek mythology. Lang was a considerable Homeric scholar, having published *Homer and the Epic* (1893), *Homer and His Age* (1906), and *The World of Homer* (1910) as well as translating with Samuel Henry Butcher *The Odyssey* (1879), which became a standard nineteenth-century edition of the poem, and, with Walter Leaf and Ernest Myers, *The Iliad* (1883). Lang relied on his knowledge and recently discovered artifacts excavated by Heinrich Schliemann at Troy and Arthur Evans at Myceane to add authenticity to his narrative. His retelling of the Greek tales as a boy's adventure story was well received by reviewers and is considered by critics to be one of his best children's books: it ranks alongside Charles Kingsley's *The Heroes* (1856) as an outstanding children's adaptation of the Greek myths.

The final installment of Lang's chronicle of Pantouflia appeared in *Tales of a Fairy Court* (1906), a series of short tales that explore events after Prince Prigio has matured but before his marriage to Lady Rosalind. Prigio discovers among his magical gifts a fairy timepiece that allows him to travel in time, and he visits first the twentieth century, where he is troubled by the vast number of automobiles, and then the court of James VI of Scotland, where he plays a match of golf with the prince and is accused of practicing witchcraft. The most amusing story involves Prigio arranging a marriage between his brother and a giant's daughter.

In the preface to *The Green Fairy Book* Lang muses that few people can write good fairy tales because they do not believe enough in their stories and because the authors try to be wittier than they actually are. Yet Lang was frequently insecure about his abilities and once complained to Edith Nesbit that his fairy tales were "like everything of mine, utterly unpopular." While *Tales of a Fairy Court,* illustrated by Arthur Dixon, provides some history of Pantouflia and the major characters of *Prince Prigio* and *Prince Ricardo,* by the third volume of the Pantouflia series Lang seems culpable of the same errors that he observed in other literary fairy tales.

Alternating with the publication of the color fairy books were *The Book of Romance* (1902) and *The Red Romance Book* (1905), collections of tales that Lang called "fairy tales grown up." Lang's most imaginative romance was written for adults rather than children: *The World's Desire* (1890), cowritten with his friend Haggard, continues the *Odyssey,* with Odysseus's seeking out Helen in Egypt.

The Lilac Fairy Book is the final volume in the series, and Lang's exasperation is apparent in his preface. It is his last attempt to reiterate that he is not the author of the color fairy books: an undeserved reputation whose weight "is killing me." He takes the opportunity to recommend to the reader *Prince Prigio, Prince Ricardo,* and *Tales of a Fairy Court* — tales that, he admits, may be "poor things, but my own." As he had previously noted in his introduction to Fredrich Van Eeden's *Little Johannes* (1895) and his preface to Irene Mauder's *The Plain Princess and Other Stories* (1905), Lang points out the difficulties, if not sheer impossibility, in composing a completely new and satisfying fairy tale. As the literary adviser for Longmans, he laments the "dreadful kind of sham fairy tale," done in imitation of Lewis Carroll's *Alice's Adventures in Wonderland* (1865), constantly submitted for publication.

The All Sorts of Stories Book (1911) and *The Strange Story Book* (1913) come the closest in content

Lang, circa 1902

to Lang's "The Grey True Ghost-Story Book" — a proposed volume of "the deadliest, creepiest ghost-stories he could find or invent" that was shelved in deference to the concern of anxious mothers and aunts.

Lang died of angina pectoris on 20 July 1912 and, following his request that no official biography or collection of letters should appear, Leonora dutifully destroyed his personal papers. It is reported that she complained that her wrists ached for weeks after tearing up the massive collection. *The Strange Story Book* was published after Lang's death and includes a brief reminiscence of Lang by Leonora, who describes her husband as "the man who loved fairies." Despite their never having children, Leonora recalls that Lang quickly adapted himself to the company of children, no matter where he was.

Fellow folklorist Jacobs wrote the most fitting tribute to Lang for the *Journal of American Folk-Lore* (1913). After recounting Lang's many accomplishments that had helped to establish the emerging discipline of folklore, Jacobs singles out the publication

of *The Blue Fairy Book* and its subsequent multicolored offspring for having "revived the vogue of the folk-tale among English-speaking children." Jacobs predicts that "Lang's name will be added to those of Perrault, Grimm, and Andersen, as one of the chief delights of the nursery library."

Green's *Andrew Lang: A Critical Biography* (1946), the standard study of the man and his work, firmly established Lang's reputation as the English historian of fairy tales for children. It is unfortunate that the success of the color fairy books has overshadowed Lang's own literary fairy tales. While not quite so memorable as Carroll's Alice books or the mystical fairy tales written by George MacDonald, they certainly are as clever and as crafted as Thackeray's *The Rose and the Ring* or those written by Oscar Wilde or Nesbit.

One measure of Lang's continued popularity and importance is that the color-fairy-tale collections have remained constantly in print and have even inspired several imitations, including Jacobs's five-volume collection of the fairy tales of many nations (1890–1916); Edwin Sidney Hartland's *English Fairy and Other Folk Tales* (1890); and the anonymous *The Golden Fairy Book* (1895). Besides the reprinting of the original color fairy books, two revised editions were published under the general editorships of Mary Gould Davis, beginning with *The Blue Fairy Book* (1948), and Brian Alderson, beginning with *The Blue Fairy Book* (1975). While both of these series add background material, Alderson's notes are far more extensive in identifying Lang's literary sources and editorial changes. Unfortunately, both series introduce new illustrations and rearrange and, in some cases, omit tales. Several one-volume compilations of the color fairy books have been produced, including Green's *The Rainbow Fairy Book* (1977), Cary Willkins's *The Andrew Lang Fairy Tale Treasury* (1979), and Michael Patrick Hearn's *The Andrew Lang Fairy Tale Book* (1986).

Despite his wide-ranging interests and his astonishing productivity, Lang was a modest and self-effacing writer. Perhaps his brief evaluation of his career most accurately sums up his literary accomplishments: "I confess that I still have a child-like love of a fairy-story for its own sake; and I have done my best to circulate Fairy Books among children."

Biography:

Roger Lancelyn Green, *Andrew Lang: A Critical Biography* (Leicester: Ward, 1946).

References:

Glenn S. Burne, "Andrew Lang's *The Blue Fairy Book:* Changing the Course of History," in *Touchstones: Reflections on the Best in Children's Literature,* edited by Perry Nodelman, volume 2: Fairy Tales, Fables, Myths, Legends and Poetry (West Lafayette, Ind.: Children's Literature Association, 1986), pp. 140–150;

Richard M. Dorson, *The British Folklorists: A History* (Chicago: University of Chicago Press, 1968);

Louise Frances Field, *The Child and His Book* (London: Wells, Gardner, 1891);

Roger Lancelyn Green, "Andrew Lang and the Fairy Tale," *Review of English Studies,* 20 (July 1944): 227–231;

Joseph Jacobs, "Andrew Lang as Man of Letters and Folk-Lorist," *Journal of American Folklore,* 26 (1913): 367–372;

Eleanor De Selms Langstaff, *Andrew Lang* (Boston: Twayne, 1978);

Eric L. Montenyohl, "Andrew Lang and the Fairy Tale," Ph.D. dissertation, Indiana University, 1986;

J. R. R. Tolkien, "On Fairy-stories," in *Tree and Leaf* (London: Allen & Unwin, 1964), pp. 11–70:

A. B. Webster, ed., *Concerning Andrew Lang: Being the Andrew Lang Lectures Delivered Before the University of St. Andrews. 1927–1937* (London: Oxford University Press, 1949).

Papers:

Major collections of Andrew Lang material are located at the Lilly Library, Indiana University, and the Houghton Library, Harvard University.

L. T. Meade
(5 June 1844 – 26 October 1914)

Mavis Reimer
University of Winnipeg

BOOKS: *Ashton Morton* (London: Newby, [1866]);
Lettie's Last Home (London: Shaw, [1875]);
Great St. Benedict's: A Tale (London: Shaw, 1876); republished as *Dorothy's Story; or, Great St. Benedict's* (London: Shaw, [1879?]);
David's Little Lad (London: Shaw, [1877]; New York: Harper, 1878; New York: Munro, 1878);
A Knight of To-day (London: Shaw, [1877]);
Scamp and I: A Story of City By-Ways (London: Shaw, [1877]; New York: Carter, [1878]);
Bel Marjory: A Story of Conquest (London: Shaw, 1878);
The Children's Kingdom: The Story of a Great Endeavour (London: Shaw, [1878]; Boston, 1893);
Miss Toosey's Mission (London, 1878);
Outcast Robin; or, Your Brother and Mine: A Cry from the Great City (London: Shaw, [1878]);
Water Lilies and Other Tales (London: Shaw, 1878);
Dot and Her Treasures (London: Shaw, 1879);
Laddie (London, 1879);
The Water Gipsies; or, The Adventures of Tag-Rag and Bob-Tail (London: Shaw, 1879); republished as *The Water Gipsies: A Story of Canal Life in England* (New York: Carter, 1879; New York: Munro, 1879);
Andrew Harvey's Wife (London: Isbister, 1880);
A Dweller in Tents (London: Isbister, 1880);
The Floating Light of Ringfinnan, and Guardian Angels (Edinburgh: Macniven & Wallace, 1880);
Mou-Setsé, A Negro Hero, with *The Orphan's Pilgrimage,* by T. von Gumpert (London: Isbister, 1880);
Mother Herring's Chicken (London: Isbister, 1881; New York: Carter, 1881);
A Band of Three (New York: Seaside Library, [1882]; London: Isbister, 1884);
A London Baby: The Story of King Roy (London: Nisbet, 1882);
The Children's Pilgrimage (London: Nisbet, 1883);
Hermie's Rosebuds and Other Stories (London: Hodder & Stoughton, 1883);

L. T. Meade

How It All Came Round (London: Hodder & Stoughton, 1883; New York: Lovell, [1883]);
The Autocrat of the Nursery (London: Hodder & Stoughton, 1884; New York: Armstrong, 1886);
Scarlet Anemones (London: Hodder & Stoughton, 1884);
Tip Cat (London, 1884);
The Two Sisters (London: Hodder & Stoughton, 1884);
The Angel of Love (London: Hodder & Stoughton, 1885; Boston: Earle, 1887);
A Little Silver Trumpet (London: Hodder & Stoughton, 1885);
Our Little Ann: A Tale (London, 1885);

A World of Girls: The Story of a School (London: Cassell, 1886; New York: Burt, n.d.; New York: Mershon, n.d.; Chicago: Donohue, n.d.);

Beforehand (London, 1887);

Letters to Our Working-Party (London, 1887);

The O'Donnells of Inchfawn (London: Hatchards, 1887; New York: Harper, 1887);

The Palace Beautiful: A Story for Girls (London: Cassell, 1887; New York: Grosset & Dunlap, n.d.; New York: Hurst, n.d.; New York: Burt, n.d.);

"Sweet Nancy" (London: Partridge, [1887]);

Daddy's Boy (London: Hatchards, 1888; New York: White & Allen, 1889);

Pen (London, 1888);

Deb and the Duchess: A Story for Boys and Girls (London: Hatchards, [1888]; New York: White & Allen, 1889);

Nobody's Neighbours (London: Isbister, [1888]; New York: Seaside Library, n.d.);

A Farthingful (London & Edinburgh: Chambers, 1889);

The Golden Lady (London & Edinburgh: Chambers, 1889; New York: Whitaker, n.d.);

The Lady of the Forest: A Story for Girls (London: Partridge, [1889]; New York: Warne, 1889);

The Little Princess of Tower Hill (London: Partridge, [1889]);

Polly: A New-Fashioned Girl (London: Cassell, 1889; New York: Burt, [1897]);

Poor Miss Carolina (London & Edinburgh: Chambers, 1889);

The Beresford Prize (London: Longman, 1890);

Dickory Dock (London & Edinburgh: Chambers, 1890);

Engaged to be Married: A Tale of To-day (London: Simpkin Marshall, 1890); republished as *Daughters of Today* (London: Hodder & Stoughton, 1917);

Frances Kane's Fortune (London: Warne, 1890; New York: Lovell, 1890);

A Girl of the People: A Novel (London: Methuen, 1890; New York: Lovell, 1890);

Heart of Gold (London & New York: Warne, 1890; New York: United States Book Company, 1890);

The Honourable Miss: A Story of an Old-Fashioned Town (New York: United States Book Company, 1890); 2 volumes (London: Methuen, 1891);

Just a Love Story (London: Blackett, 1890); republished as *The Beauforts* (London: Griffith & Farran, 1900);

Marigold (London: Partridge, [1890]);

The Children of Wilton Chase (London & Edinburgh: Chambers, 1891; New York: Cassell, 1891);

Hepsy Gipsy (London: Methuen, 1891);

A Life for a Love: A Story of To-Day (New York: United States Book Company, 1891; London: Digby, Long, [1894]);

Little Mary and Other Stories (London & Edinburgh: Chambers, 1891);

A Sweet Girl-Graduate (London: Cassell, 1891; New York: Allison, n.d.; New York: Grosset & Dunlap, n.d.);

Bashful Fifteen (London & New York: Cassell, 1892);

Four on an Island: A Story of Adventure (London & Edinburgh: Chambers, [1892]); also published as *Four on an Island: A Book for the Little Folks* (New York: Cassell, 1892);

Jill, a Flower Girl (London: Isbister, 1892; New York: United States Book Company, 1892);

The Medicine Lady, 3 volumes (London: Cassell, 1892; New York: Cassell, [1892]);

Out of the Fashion (London: Methuen, 1892; New York: Cassell, [1892]);

A Ring of Rubies (London: Innes, 1892; New York: Cassell, 1892; New York: Chatterton-Peck, 1892; New York: Grosset & Dunlap, 1892; New York: Mershon, 1892);

Beyond the Blue Mountains (London: Cassell, 1893);

This Troublesome World, by Meade and Clifford Halifax (3 volumes, London: Chatto & Windus, 1893; 1 volume, New York: Macmillan, 1893);

A Young Mutineer (London: Gardner, [1893]; New York: Hurst, 1893);

Betty, a School Girl (London & Edinburgh: Chambers, 1895 [1894]; New York: Cassell, [1894]);

In an Iron Grip, 2 volumes (London: Chatto & Windus, 1894);

Red Rose and Tiger Lily; or, In a Wider World (London & New York: Cassell, 1894);

A Soldier of Fortune (3 volumes, London: Chatto & Windus, 1894; New York: Grosset, 1894; Chicago: Hill, 1894; 1 volume, New York: Fenno, 1894);

Stories from the Diary of a Doctor (First Series), by Meade and Halifax (London: Newnes, 1894; Philadelphia: Lippincott, 1895);

Girls, New And Old (London & Edinburgh: Chambers, 1896 [1895]; New York: Cassell, 1895);

The Least of These and Other Stories (New York: Hunt & Eaton, 1895; Cincinnati: Cranston & Curtis, 1895);

A Princess of the Gutter (London: Gardner, 1895; New York: Putnam, [1896]);

The Voice of the Charmer, 3 volumes (London: Chatto & Windus, 1895);

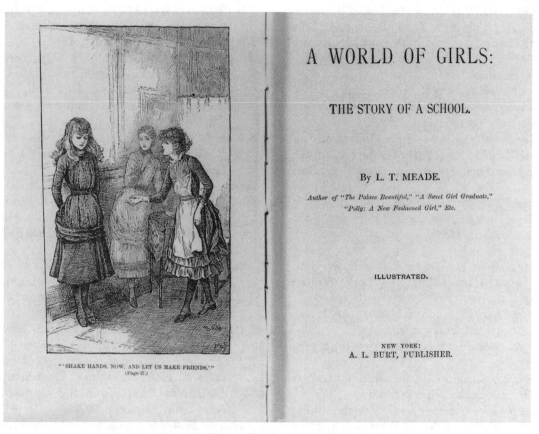

A WORLD OF GIRLS:

THE STORY OF A SCHOOL.

By L. T. MEADE.

Author of "The Palace Beautiful," "A Sweet Girl Graduate,"
"Polly: A New Fashioned Girl," Etc.

ILLUSTRATED.

NEW YORK:
A. L. BURT, PUBLISHER.

"'SHAKE HANDS, NOW, AND LET US MAKE FRIENDS.'"
(Page 27.)

Frontispiece and title page for Meade's first girls' school novel

Catalina: Art Student (London & Edinburgh: Chambers, 1896; Philadelphia: Lippincott, 1897);

Dr. Rumsey's Patient: A Very Strange Story, by Meade and Halifax (London: Chatto & Windus, 1896; London & New York: International News, [1896]);

A Girl in Ten Thousand (Edinburgh: Oliphant, [1896]; New York: Whittaker, 1897);

Good Luck (London: Nisbet, 1896; Boston, 1897);

The House of Surprises (London: Longman, 1896);

A Little Mother to the Others (London: White, 1896);

Merry Girls of England (London: Cassell, 1896; Boston: Bradley, [1897]);

Playmates: A Story for Boys and Girls (London & Edinburgh: Chambers, 1896);

A Son of Ishmael: A Novel (London: White, 1896; New York: New Amsterdam Book Company, 1896);

Stories from the Diary of a Doctor (Second Series), by Meade and Halifax (London: Bliss, Sands, 1896);

The White Tzar (London: Marshall, Russell, [1896]);

Bad Little Hannah (London: White, 1897; New York: Mershon, n.d.);

A Handful of Silver (Edinburgh: Oliphant, 1897; New York: Dutton, 1898);

Under the Dragon Throne, by Meade and Robert Kennaway Douglas (London: Gardner, [1897]);

The Way of a Woman (London: White, 1897);

Wild Kitty: A School Story (London & Edinburgh: Chambers, 1897); also published as Wild Kitty: A Story of Middleton School (New York: Burt, n.d.);

A Bunch of Cherries: A Story of Cherry Court School (London: Nister, [1898]; New York: Dutton, 1898);

Cave Perilous (London: Religious Tract Society, [1898]);

The Cleverest Woman in England (London: Nisbet, 1898; Boston: Bradley, 1899);

The Girls of St. Wode's (London & Edinburgh: Chambers, 1898; Chicago: Donohue, n.d.);

Mary Gifford, M.B. (London: Gardner, 1898);

A Master of Mysteries, by Meade and Robert Eustace (London: Ward, Lock, [1898]);

Me and My Dolls: Miss Bo-Peep and Her Doll-Family, to which is added The Strange Adventures of Mopsy and Hans (Boston: Lothrop, [1898]);

On the Brink of a Chasm: A Record of Plot and Passion (London: Chatto & Windus, 1898; New York: Buckles, 1899);

The Rebellion of Lil Carrington (London: Cassell, 1898; London & New York: Neely, 1898);

The Siren: A Novel (London: White, 1898);

Adventuress (London: Chatto & Windus, 1899);

All Sorts (London: Nisbet, 1899);

A Brave Poor Thing (London: Isbister, 1900 [1899]);

The Brotherhood of the Seven Kings, by Meade and Eustace (London: Ward, Lock, 1899; New York: New Amsterdam Book Company, n.d.);

The Desire of Men: An Impossibility (London: Digby, Long, 1899);

The Gold Star Line, by Meade and Eustace (London: Ward, Lock, 1899; New York: New Amsterdam Book Company, n.d.);

Light o'the Morning: The Story of an Irish Girl (London & Edinburgh: Chambers, 1899; New York: Dutton, [1900?]);

The Odds and the Evens (London & Edinburgh: Chambers, 1899; New York: Burt, n.d.);

A Public School Boy: A Memoir of H. S. Wristbridge (London: Nisbet, 1899);

The Temptation of Olive Latimer (New York: Mershon, 1899; London: Hutchinson, 1900);

Daddy's Girl (London: Newnes, 1900; Philadelphia: Lippincott, 1901); republished as *Daddy's Girl, and Consuelo's Quest of Happiness* (New York: New York Book Company, 1911);

Miss Nonentity: A Story for Girls (London & Edinburgh: Chambers, 1900; New York: Grosset & Dunlap, n.d.; New York: Platt & Peck, n.d.; Chicago: Donohue, n.d.);

A Plucky Girl (Philadelphia: Jacobs, [1900]);

The Sanctuary Club, by Meade and Eustace (London: Ward, Lock, 1900);

Seven Maids (London & Edinburgh: Chambers, 1900);

The Time of Roses: A Story for Girls (London: Nister, [1900]; New York: Hurst, n.d.; New York: Burt, n.d.);

Wages: A Novel (London: Nisbet, 1900; Boston, [1900]);

Where the Shoe Pinches, by Meade and Halifax (London & Edinburgh: Chambers, [1900]);

The Blue Diamond (London: Chatto & Windus, 1901);

Cosey Corner; or, How They Kept a Farm (London & Edinburgh: Chambers, 1901);

Girls of the True Blue: A School Story (London & Edinburgh: Chambers, 1901; New York: Dutton, 1901);

The New Mrs. Lascelles (London: Clarke, 1901); republished as *Mother Mary: A Story for Girls* (London: Chambers, 1916);

A Race with the Sun, by Meade and Halifax (London: Ward, Lock, 1901);

The Secret of the Dead (London: White, 1901);

A Sister of the Red Cross: A Tale of the South African War (London: Nelson, 1901);

A Stumble by the Way (London: Chatto & Windus, 1901);

A Very Naughty Girl (London & Edinburgh: Chambers, 1901; New York: Grosset & Dunlap, n.d.; New York: Hurst, n.d.);

Wheels of Iron (London: Nisbet, 1901);

Confessions of a Court Milliner (London: Long, [1902]);

A Double Revenge (London: Digby, Long, 1902);

Drift (London: Methuen, 1902);

Girls of the Forest (London & Edinburgh: Chambers, 1902; New York: Dutton, [1912?]);

The Lost Square, by Meade and Eustace (London: Ward, Lock, 1902);

Margaret (London: White, 1902);

The Princess Who Gave Away All, and The Naughty One of the Family (London: Nister, 1902);

The Pursuit of Penelope (London: Digby, Long, 1902);

Queen Rose (London & Edinburgh: Chambers, 1902; New York: Dutton, 1902);

The Rebel of the School (London & Edinburgh: Chambers, 1902; New York: Burt, n.d.);

The Squire's Little Girl (London & Edinburgh: Chambers, 1902);

Through Peril for a Wife (London: Digby, Long, 1902);

The Burden of Her Youth (London: Long, 1903);

By Mutual Consent (London: Digby, Long, 1903);

A Gay Charmer: A Story for Girls (London & Edinburgh: Chambers, 1903);

The Manor School (London & Edinburgh: Chambers, 1903; New York: Mershon, 1903);

Peter the Pilgrim (London & Edinburgh: Chambers, 1903);

Resurgam (London: Methuen, 1903);

Rosebury (London: Chatto & Windus, 1903);

The Sorceress of the Strand (London: Ward, Long, 1903);

Stories from the Old, Old Bible (London: Newnes, 1903);

That Brilliant Peggy (London: Hodder & Stoughton, 1903);

The Witch Maid (London: Nisbet, 1903);

The Adventures of Miranda (London: Long, 1904);

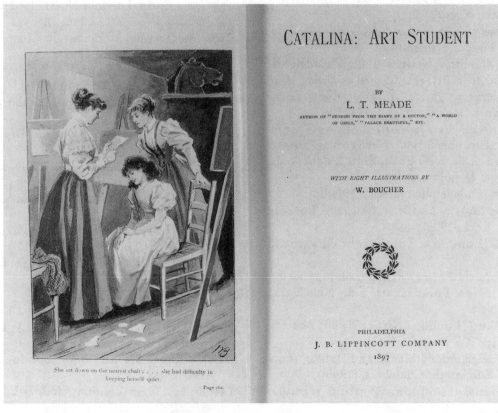

Frontispieces and title pages for American editions of two of Meade's girls' stories

At the Back of the World (London: Hurst & Blackett, 1904);

Bride of To-morrow (London: Daily Mail, [1904]);

Castle Poverty (London: Nisbet, 1904);

The Girls of Mrs. Pritchard's School (London & Edinburgh: Chambers, 1904; New York: Grosset & Dunlap, [1904]; New York: Hurst, 1904; New York: Mershon, [1904]);

The Lady Cake-Maker (London: Hodder & Stoughton, 1904);

A Maid of Mystery (London: White, 1904);

Love Triumphant (London: Unwin, 1904);

A Madcap (London: Cassell, 1904; New York: Mershon, 1904);

A Modern Tomboy (London & Edinburgh: Chambers, 1904; New York: Dutton, n.d.; Chicago: Donohue, n.d.);

Nurse Charlotte (London: Long, 1904);

The Oracle of Maddox Street (London: Ward, Lock, 1904);

Petronella; and The Coming of Polly (London & Edinburgh: Chambers, 1904);

Silenced (London: Ward, Lock, 1904);

Bess of Delaney's (London: Digby, Long, 1905);

A Bevy of Girls (London & Edinburgh: Chambers, 1905; New York: Still, 1905);

Dumps: A Plain Girl (London & Edinburgh: Chambers, 1905; New York: Dutton, 1905);

His Mascot (London: Long, 1905);

Little Wife Hester (London: Long, 1905);

Loveday: The Story of an Heiress (London: Hodder & Stoughton, 1905);

Old Readymoney's Daughter (London: Partridge, 1905);

The Other Woman (London: Scott, 1905);

Virginia (London: Digby, Long, 1905);

Wilful Cousin Kate: A Girl's Story (London & Edinburgh: Chambers, 1905);

The Colonel and the Boy (London: Hodder & Stoughton, 1906);

The Face of Juliet (London: Long, 1906);

From the Hand of the Hunter (London: Long, 1906);

The Girl and Her Fortune (London: Hodder & Stoughton, 1906);

The Golden Shadow (London: Ward, Lock, 1906);

The Heart of Helen (London: Long, 1906);

The Hill-Top Girl (London & Edinburgh: Chambers, 1906; New York: Burt, n.d.);

The Home of Sweet Content (London: White, 1906);

In the Flower of Her Youth (London: Nisbet, 1906);

The Maid with the Goggles (London: Digby, Long, 1906);

Sue: The Story of a Little Heroine and Her Friend (London & Edinburgh: Chambers, 1906);

Turquoise and Ruby (London & Edinburgh: Chambers, 1906; New York: Chatterton-Peck, 1906);

Victory (London: Methuen, 1906);

The Chateau of Mystery (London: Everett, 1907);

The Colonel's Conquest (Philadelphia: Jacobs, 1907);

The Curse of the Feverals (London: Long, 1907);

A Girl from America (London & Edinburgh: Chambers, 1907);

The Home of Silence (London: Sisley's, 1907);

Kindred Spirits (London: Long, 1907);

The Lady of Delight (London: Hodder & Stoughton, 1907);

The Lady of Jerry Boy's Dreams: A Story for Girls (London & Edinburgh: Chambers, n.d.; Philadelphia: Jacobs, 1907);

Little Josephine (London: Long, 1907);

The Little School-Mothers: A Story for Girls (London: Cassell, 1907; Philadelphia: McKay, 1907);

The Love of Susan Cardigan (London: Digby, Long, 1907);

The Red Cap of Liberty (London: Nisbet, 1907);

The Red Ruth (London: Laurie, 1907);

The Scamp Family: A Story for Girls (London & Edinburgh: Chambers, 1907; New York: Burt, n.d.);

Three Girls from School (London & Edinburgh: Chambers, 1907; New York: Burt, n.d.);

The Aim of Her Life (London: Long, 1908);

Betty of the Rectory (London: Cassell, 1908; New York: Grosset & Dunlap, [1908]);

The Court-Harman Girls (London & Edinburgh: Chambers, 1908);

The Courtship of Sybil (London: Long, 1908);

Hetty Beresford (London: Hodder & Stoughton, 1908);

A Lovely Fiend and Other Stories (London: Digby, Long, 1908);

Sarah's Mother (London: Hodder & Stoughton, 1908); republished as *Colonel Tracy's Wife* (London: Aldine, 1914);

The School Favourite (London & Edinburgh: Chambers, 1908; Chicago: Donohue, [1913]);

The School Queens (London & Edinburgh: Chambers, 1908; New York: New York Book Company, 1910);

Alwyn's Friends (London & Edinburgh: Chambers, 1909);

Betty Vivian: A Story of Haddo Court School (London & Edinburgh: Chambers, 1909);

Blue of the Sea (London: Nisbet, 1909);

Brother or Husband (London: White, 1909);

The Fountain of Beauty (London: Long, 1909);

THE YOUNG
MUTINEERS

L·T·MEADE

Cover, illustrated by Gordon Browne, for the first American edition of one of Meade's novels with an independent female protagonist

I Will Sing a New Song (London: Hodder & Stoughton, 1909);

The Necklace of Parmona (London: Ward, Lock, 1909);

Oceana's Girlhood (New York: Hurst, 1909);

The Princess of the Revels (London & Edinburgh: Chambers, 1909; New York: New York Book Company, 1910);

The Pursuit of Penelope (London: Digby, Long, 1909);

The Stormy Petrel (London: Hurst & Blackett, 1909);

Wild Heather (London & New York: Cassell, 1909);

The A.B.C. Girl (London: White, 1910);

Belinda Treherne (London: Long, 1910);

A Girl of To-day (London: Long, 1910);

Lady Anne (London: Nisbet, 1910);

Micah Faraday, Adventurer (London: Ward, Lock, 1910);

Miss Gwendoline (London: Long, 1910);

Nance Kennedy (London: Partridge, 1910);

Pretty-Girl and the Others (Edinburgh: Chambers, 1910);

Rosa Regina: A Story for Girls (London & Edinburgh: Chambers, 1910);

A Wild Irish Girl (London & Edinburgh: Chambers, 1910; New York: Hurst, 1910);

A Bunch of Cousins, and The Barn "Boys" (London & Edinburgh: Chambers, 1911; New York: Hurst, 1910);

Desborough's Wife (London: Digby, Long, 1911);

The Doctor's Children (London & Edinburgh: Chambers, 1911; Philadelphia: Lippincott, 1911);

For Dear Dad (London & Edinburgh: Chambers, 1911);

The Girl from Spain (London: Digby, Long, 1911);

The Girls of Merton College (New York: Hurst, 1911);

Mother and Son (London: Ward, Lock, 1911);

Ruffles (London: Paul, [1911]);

The Soul of Margaret Rand (London: Ward, Lock, 1911);

Twenty-four Hours: A Novel of To-day (London: White, 1911);

Corporal Violet (London: Hodder & Stoughton, 1912);

The House of Black Magic (London: White, 1912);

Kitty O'Donovan: A School Story (London & Edinburgh: Chambers, 1912; New York: Hurst, 1912);

Lord and Lady Kitty (London: White, 1912);

Love's Cross Roads (London: Paul, 1912);

Peggy from Kerry (London & Edinburgh: Chambers, 1912; New York: Hurst, 1912);

The Chesterton Girl Graduates: A Story for Girls (New York: Hurst, 1913);

The Girls of Abinger Close (London & Edinburgh: Chambers, 1913);

The Girls of King's Royal: A Story for Girls (New York: Hurst, 1913);

The Passion of Kathleen Duveen (London: Paul, 1913);

A Band of Mirth (London & Edinburgh: Chambers, 1914);

Elizabeth's Prisoner (London: Paul, 1914);

A Girl of High Adventure (London & Edinburgh: Chambers, 1914; New York: Hurst, [1914]);

Her Happy Face (London: Ward, Lock, 1914);

The Queen of Joy (London & Edinburgh: Chambers, 1914; New York: Hurst, 1914);

The Wooing of Monica (London: Long, 1914);

The Darling of the School (London & Edinburgh: Chambers, 1915);

The Daughter of a Soldier: A Colleen of South Ireland (London & Edinburgh: Chambers, 1915; New York: Hurst, 1915);

Greater than Gold (London: Ward, Lock, 1915);

Jill the Irresistible (London & Edinburgh: Chambers, 1915; New York: Hurst, 1915);

Hollyhock: A Spirit of Mischief (London & Edinburgh: Chambers, 1916);

Madge Mostyn's Nieces (London & Edinburgh: Chambers, 1916);

The Maid Indomitable (London: Ward, Lock, 1916);

Better Than Riches (London & Edinburgh: Chambers, 1917);

The Fairy Godmother (London & Edinburgh: Chambers, 1917);

Miss Patricia (London: Long, 1925);

Roses and Thorns (London: Long, 1928).

PLAY PRODUCTION: *The Brotherhood of the Seven Kings,* South Shields, County Durham, 1900.

SELECTED PERIODICAL PUBLICATIONS – UNCOLLECTED: "From the Editor's Standpoint," *Atalanta,* 6 (1892/1893): 839–842;

"Girton College," *Atalanta,* 7 (1893/1894): 325–331;

"Newnham College," *Atalanta,* 7 (1893/1894): 525–529;

"Girls' Schools of To-Day: Cheltenham College," *Strand,* 9 (January–June 1895): 283–288;

"Girls' Schools of To-Day: St. Leonards and Great Harrowden Hall," *Strand,* 9 (January–June 1895): 457–463;

"How I Began," *Girls' Realm,* 3 (1900/1901): 57–60.

L. T. Meade was the most prolific writer of girls' books in the nineteenth century. She established the girls' school story with *A World of Girls* (1886), but only 30 of the approximately 280 books she authored during her forty-year writing career are school stories. Meade wrote in a wide variety of other genres for both juvenile and adult audiences, including "street arab" tales, historical adventure stories, fantasies, domestic stories, robinsonnades (island survival tales, a genre established by Daniel Defoe's *Robinson Crusoe,* 1719), nursing stories, detective tales, medical mystery novels, and crime stories. Between 1887 and 1893 she also edited the girls' magazine *Atalanta.*

Elizabeth Thomasina Meade was born in Bandon, County Cork, Ireland, on 5 June 1844, the daughter of the Reverend Richard Thomas Meade. Her recollections of childhood are of summer afternoons spent with her six siblings in the large garden of their country home at Nohoval. Educated at home by a governess, Meade enjoyed making up and telling stories to her brothers and sisters. At the age of twelve she began to write stories featuring fair heroines and dark villainesses. Her first book, written when she was fifteen, was published several years later by the London publisher Newby. Meade submitted the manuscript on the advice of a Mr. Morrow, who operated a circulating library in Dublin. Newby's offer to publish the book was conditional on Meade's guarantee of the sale of forty copies. Meade sold seventy books. *Ashton Morton* (1866) is the story of a woman's life from the age of seventeen through her married life and to old age. The heroine was not modeled on any particular person, but the heroine's daughter, with whose death the book ends, was based on a girlfriend who died of fever at fifteen. Meade's description of her friend as "gay and bright," with "a winning way, a lively tongue, and a fascinating manner," and "wild of the wild, but deeply affectionate," could double as a description of many of the heroines of her girls' books. She later described this early writing as "very crude," but also maintained that it was "alive, honest, and unaffected."

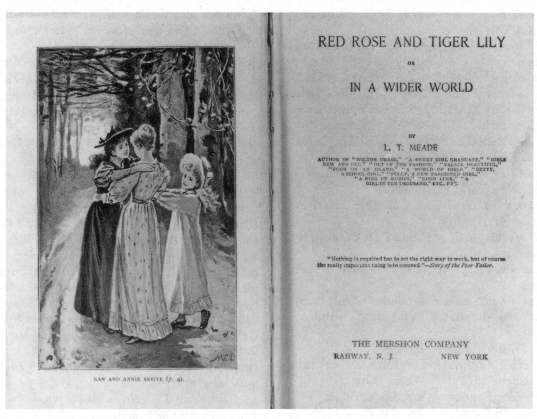

RED ROSE AND TIGER LILY

OR

IN A WIDER WORLD

BY

L. T. MEADE

AUTHOR OF "WILTON CHASE," "A SWEET GIRL GRADUATE," "GIRLS
NEW AND OLD," "OUT OF THE FASHION," "PALACE BEAUTIFUL,"
"FOUR ON AN ISLAND," "A WORLD OF GIRLS," "BETTY,
A SCHOOL GIRL," "POLLY, A NEW-FASHIONED GIRL,"
"A RING OF RUBIES," "GOOD LUCK," "A
GIRL IN TEN THOUSAND," ETC., ETC.

"Nothing is required but to set the right way to work, but of course
the really important thing is to succeed."—*Story of the Poor Tailor*.

THE MERSHON COMPANY

RAHWAY, N. J.   NEW YORK

NAN AND ANNIE ARRIVE (*p.* 4).

Frontispiece and title page for an American edition of Meade's 1894 family story, a sequel to her A World of Girls

Meade received little encouragement at home for her storytelling and writing. Her father was displeased by her announcement that she would like to earn money, raising the conventional objection that the family would be disgraced if its women worked for themselves rather than being kept by its men. She earned angry reprimands from her governess for scribbling stories in the margins of newspapers when she was supposed to be working on lessons. Her mother found her ambition amusing; but it was her mother's tears at hearing Meade's reading of the final scene of *Ashton Morton* that "clinched" her conviction that she had the gift "of seeing pictures in their true proportions."

Her mother died when Meade was a young woman, and her father soon remarried. Feeling that she no longer had a home, Meade went to live in London. She had submitted a manuscript to the publishing house of John F. Shaw shortly before she left home. When the Shaws informed her that they would publish the book and pay her four guineas if she could expand the story by four thousand words, she enthusiastically accepted the offer and set to work at the British Museum. She had been deprived of paper at home to curtail her "scribbling"; in the reading room she was taken seriously as a writer and provided with the desk, books, blotting paper, pens, and ink she required for her work. The novel that resulted, *Lettie's Last Home* (1875), portrays a little East End girl whose drunken mother sells unwanted babies to rich clients. After Lettie is convinced by a sermon that a wonderful life awaits her after death, she returns a little boy to his real mother and is beaten to death by her parent. Meade came to regard the story as immature, and subsequent commentators have verified her judgment.

Having a second book accepted for publication, however, made Meade determined to win fame and fortune through her writing. Her father settled a small yearly allowance on her, insufficient for her living expenses, so that from the outset of her career she supported herself. A doctor and his wife, friends with whom she lived in London, encouraged her to write an exposé of the abuses of the outpatient system of the London hospitals and supplied the facts for the work. The outpatient department of the major London hospital depicted in Meade's *Great St. Benedict's* (1876) is supposed to meet the medical needs of patients who cannot afford the clinical rates of private doctors, but it is chronically understaffed and typically used to train medical students. The consequent rate of misdiagnosis, the resistance to admitting seriously ill but poor patients to the hospital, and the illicit use of the services by middle-class people with the ability to pay complicate the attempts of Arthur Shirley to establish a medical practice among the indigent people of East End London. The story is told in the first person by Arthur's stepsister, seventeen-year-old Dorothy, who has left home after the death of her father to earn money to assist her widowed mother; much of her story details her involvement with the "street arab" (a runaway or abandoned child who lived on the streets of major cities) Captain Jack and a runaway gypsy girl he befriends. Meade saw this novel as the pivotal book of her career.

Encouraged by her sale of the manuscript of *Great St. Benedict's* to the Shaws for forty pounds, Meade produced another book within a fortnight, for which she earned another thirty pounds. *Scamp and I* (1877) concerns another East End waif, little Flo, who ekes out a living for herself by mending old boots and who takes comfort in the companionship of the mongrel Scamp, a survivor like herself. Both books sold well, and *Scamp and I* went into several editions and was translated into many languages. With these early successes Meade established herself as a popular professional writer.

During the 1870s Meade produced many stories about the life of poor London children, based on her observations of East End life. Patterned on the genre popularized by Hesba Stretton's *Jessica's First Prayer* (1867), these early stories emphasize the transforming possibilities of an emotional and personal commitment to the teachings of Christ, not only allowing Meade's pathetic street children to transcend the horrors of their material circumstances by a contemplation of the heavenly comforts awaiting them, but also motivating her middle-class reformers, who forsake comfortable lives to give themselves to the work of ameliorating the circumstances of "outcast London."

On 20 September 1879 Meade married solicitor Alfred Toulmin Smith, but she continued to be known professionally as "L. T. Meade" or "Mrs. L. T. Meade." During the 1880s she and Smith had three children — Alfred Kendal, Hope, and Lucy Lilian Joy — and Meade produced thirty books. For most of their married life, the Toulmin Smiths lived in Dulwich, a suburb of London that Meade had used as the setting for Dorothy's family home in *Great St. Benedict's,* where she describes it as "a small, old-fashioned place . . . [where] no man with

much money would have chosen to live." But it recommends itself to Dorothy — and, it seems, to Meade — for just those reasons: it is a place where children can grow up "unsophisticated and childlike, on the borders of the great world, and yet not of it," with "true English woods and lanes" and "a glorious old garden" for rambles.

The connection of children to the natural world is a prominent theme in Meade's family stories. In *The Children's Kingdom* (1878) six siblings have built a private place for themselves away from adult eyes within the natural world. Their kingdom is a fort, complete with paling and bridge, situated at the top of a hill and "shut away from all observation" by a belt of trees. When their father loses the family estate in Ireland, the children determine to re-create their kingdom in the attic of the London house to which they move. It is clear, however, that the move from country to city constitutes a fall from grace and into adulthood for Guy and Molly, the oldest children. In *The Scamp Family* (1907) the city setting reinforces the theme of the neglected childhood of Nora and Snowball.

Nature is less kind, but the children equally resourceful, in *Four on an Island* (1892). A day that begins as an idyllic picnic for two sets of cousins ends with their being shipwrecked on a deserted island. In a story that recalls *Robinson Crusoe* or Johann Wyss's *The Swiss Family Robinson* (1812–1813), the children tangle with the native creatures of the Brazilian island, are battered by a hurricane, and become separated from each other in the pathless forest. But the children prove equal to the tests, and, after pillaging a variety of useful objects from a ship wrecked on the beach, they succeed in building themselves a snug house before the rainy season. When Ferdinand and Isabella's father arrives to rescue them, he decides that they will all be safer remaining on the island to weather the worst of the seasonal storms.

In *Cave Perilous* (1898), a family story set during the Chartist revolts of the 1840s, nature provides a refuge from the conflicts of civilization. The three children of a village miller discover a secret cave, which proves fortuitous when bread riots break out in their neighborhood. Meg, Jack, and Dick hide both themselves and the flour from their father's mill in the cave, although the children survive in their underground home only because they have planned carefully for most contingencies and have carried with them as many implements of domestic life as possible.

In *Cosey Corner* (1901) the four Ross children propose to keep a small farm to help their parents

L. T. Meade, circa 1898

pay off a large debt they owe to a hard-hearted businessman. The children's delight at keeping house for themselves is infectious, and their adventures with the thieving gypsies who prey upon them are chilling, but, as in many of Meade's family stories, the realism of the domestic story undercuts the romance of the adventure story. Farmer Burgin and his wife ensure the success of the children's experiment by supplying crockery, pies, and even livestock when the children's fortunes or spirits flag. The invincible child of most adventure stories is replaced in Meade's books by plucky but vulnerable children.

Meade's books were published by a variety of publishing houses. Beginning with *Cosey Corner,* Meade published most of her juvenile fiction with Chambers. Her contract with them from 1904 to 1906 specified that she was to be paid £150 for a book of ninety thousand words and an additional £50 when sales reached ten thousand copies. Chambers usually limited to three the number of books she published for the juvenile market in any one year; but, at the height of her career, she often produced three titles for other audiences in addition to her work for children.

Meade wrote family stories throughout her career, but after 1886 the majority of her juvenile pub-

lications were girls' books. *A World of Girls*, Meade's first school story, was extremely popular. By 1902, when Cassell issued a new edition of the novel, it had sold thirty-seven thousand copies. Several American firms reprinted it. This novel established the basic formula for her school stories. Hester Thornton is sent to school when her home is disrupted by her mother's death. Her arrival causes a disturbance of established routines and loyalties within the school body. She soon finds herself in an untenable situation, her better self prompting her to declare allegiance to a girl who upholds the values of disciplined work, moral openness, and the good of the group, while she is simultaneously drawn to a dangerous girl who inveigles her way to personal advantage and influence. Finally, when Hester recognizes that her secrecy and her scheming have endangered the life and health of other girls, including her own sister, she embraces the school community.

In 1887 Meade took over the editorship of Routledge's *Every Girl's Annual,* retitled *Atalanta.* The magazine, largely a literary publication, featured fiction by Robert Louis Stevenson, Mrs. (Mary) Molesworth, and George MacDonald; poetry by Christina Rossetti, Jean Ingelow, and Edith Nesbit; and essays by Charlotte Yonge, Thomas Hughes, and Mary Ward. The annual's new name, borrowed from the Greek legend of the young woman who refused to marry unless a suitor could defeat her in a race, suggests the magazine's celebratory tone toward girls' aspirations. The education of girls and women, in particular, was a frequent topic of both editorials and readers' letters to the magazine, and many issues featured reports on or from women's colleges. In 1892 Meade became an active participant in the feminist Pioneer Club. As well as providing its women members with a comfortable environment for meeting like-minded women, the club sponsored lectures and debates on cultural, social, and literary issues.

Some of Meade's girls' books are domestic stories that, like the family stories, emphasize girls' resourcefulness. A novel such as *Red Rose and Tiger Lily* (1894), which continues the story of the characters first introduced in *A World of Girls,* turns into a family story when the main characters become involved with neighbors threatened with losing their ancestral home. But most of the girls' books focus on problems specific to girls. The story of *Polly* (1889), clearly based on Charlotte Yonge's *The Daisy Chain* (1856), details young Polly Maybright's attempts to manage the household after her mother's death. In *Merry Girls of England* (1896) the Underhill sisters run a farm to support themselves after the death of their guardian, much as the children in *Cosey Corner* do, but a second plot in the novel follows the career of one of the sisters who tries to define an independent, intellectual life for herself as a writer in London.

Meade's interest in the particular problems faced by the girls of her day is perhaps most obvious in her social-realist fiction. Meade continued to tell stories about the slums and the lower-working-class neighborhoods of English cities she had used as settings in her street arab tales, but without her earlier religious ardor. Although Meade occasionally gestures toward conventional pieties, the problems of the central female characters in the later books have to do with their survival in brutal living conditions and with their negotiation of the cultural codes regulating women's behavior. In *A Girl of the People* (1890) the evangelical fervor of Bet's mother is inadequate to meet the desperate situation of her family, headed as it is by a drunken and violent father. She dies in the first chapter, with all of her visions of heaven intact. Bet is left to protect herself and her brothers from her father's attempts to sell the boys into apprenticeships and her into marriage. She succeeds only after two women who have befriended her galvanize the community into action against the sadistic sailor to whom her father has

promised her. In *A Princess of the Gutter* (1895) Girton graduate Joan Prinsep works with the factory girls of the East End. While she is welcomed by the local priest, her work is seen as a secular rather than spiritual mission. The novel's conflicts include her middle-class family's disapproval of her decision to live alone in the East End and Joan's difficulties in understanding the mores of the factory girls. In *The Palace Beautiful* (1887) three orphaned middle-class girls are shamefully exploited and physically abused by the other inhabitants of their derelict tenement while they try to earn their own living. This was among Meade's most popular novels, selling over twenty-four thousand copies for Cassell by 1902.

Meade also wrote more school stories. In the novels set in boarding schools, including *A World of Girls, A Bunch of Cherries* (1898), *The Manor School* (1903), and *The School Favourite* (1908), the central moral dilemma often involves a writing contest and the opportunity to plagiarize another girl's work. In Meade's stories set in women's colleges, such as *A Sweet Girl-Graduate* (1891), *The Girls of St. Wode's* (1898), and *The Girls of Merton College* (1911), the plot turns on a debate or dramatic production. A third group of school stories, set in large day schools, deals with an individual who does not wish to fit the school's mold. *Wild Kitty* (1897) and *The Rebel of the School* (1902) portray their rebellious heroines as Irish girls whose high spirits and need for affection are misunderstood by the more conventional English girls and headmistresses. The Irish heroines and the society of malcontents they head eventually capitulate to the headmistresses' appeals for cooperation, but the reader's sympathy is directed largely to the free-spirited girls.

Much of the interest of the school stories lies in the girls' explorations of their own needs and desires, their development of social and emotional relationships with one another unmediated by adults, and the passionate pleasure they take in learning. In these novels both narrator and characters delight in the rooms of their own that the girls find in the academies devoted to them. Many of the fictional schools are thinly disguised versions of actual schools and colleges, and the fictional headmistresses resemble well-known participants in the campaigns for reform of women's education. In fact, Dorothea Beale, the famous headmistress of Cheltenham Ladies' College, appears in *The Girls of Merton College* as the teacher who has inspired the college head when she was a girl. The school stories function not only as entertaining tales but also as introductions to opportunities available to middle-class girls at the end of the nineteenth century.

Meade died on 26 October 1914 at her home in Oxford, where the Toulmin Smiths had lived for eighteen months, but new books continued to appear under her name until 1928. Contemporary reviewers commonly described her fiction as "absorbing," with "plenty of action." They praised her "winning" or "charming" writing style and applauded her as a "wholesome" storyteller for children. At the end of her career, notices of new books by Meade often alluded to her considerable accomplishments and her established reputation. Her name on the title page, reviewers suggested, was sufficient to guarantee a story of quality. The voices that dissented from this general opinion typically censured Meade's fiction for its overwrought emotional tone or suggested that her stories were "old-fashioned."

The terms of the critical assessment of Meade have not changed much since her death. While she continues to be acknowledged by some commentators as an accomplished teller of exciting tales and dismissed by others for the highly charged emotional atmosphere of her books, she is most often simply passed over as a conventional writer of popular fiction. Studies on the school story mention her as the first practitioner of the genre, but they usually credit another writer, Angela Brazil, with developing its characteristic tone and themes. None of Meade's books is currently in print, nor is there a biography, comprehensive bibliography, or major critical study of Meade's work. Her writing, nevertheless, continues to have historical importance. Not only did she pioneer the new style of girls' school story, but also, in telling the stories from the girls' points of view, she helped to create a separate, popular culture for girls.

References:

Jacquelline S. Bratton, *The Impact of Victorian Children's Fiction* (London: Croom Helm, 1981; Totowa, N.J.: Barnes & Noble, 1981), pp. 191–217;

Gill Frith, " 'The Time of Your Life': The Meaning of the School Story," in *Language, Gender and Childhood,* edited by Carolyn Steedman, Cathy Urwin, and Valerie Walkerdine (London: Routledge & Kegan Paul, 1985), pp. 113–136;

Sally Mitchell, "Children's Reading and the Culture of Girlhood: The Case of L. T. Meade," *Browning Institute Studies,* 17 (1989): 53–63;

Maureen Nimon, "A Chart of Change: The Work of L. T. Meade," *Children's Literature in Education,* 18 (1987): 163–175;

Kimberley Reynolds, *Girls Only?: Gender and Popular Children's Fiction in Britain, 1880–1910* (Philadelphia: Temple University Press, 1990), pp. 111–156;

Judith Rowbotham, *Good Girls Make Good Wives: Guidance for Girls in Victorian Fiction* (Oxford: Blackwell, 1989).

E. Nesbit

(15 August 1858 – 4 May 1924)

Claudia Nelson
Southwest Texas State University

BOOKS: *Fading Light: Verses by E. Nesbit* (London & New York: Hagelberg, n.d.);

Apple Pie (N.p., n.d.);

Miss Mischief (London: Nister / New York: Dutton, n.d.);

Fairies (London: Tuck, n.d.);

The Prophet's Mantle, by Nesbit and Hubert Bland, as Fabian Bland (London: Drane, 1885; Chicago: Clarke, 1889);

Lays and Legends (London: Longmans, Green, 1886);

The Lily and the Cross (London: Griffith, Farran, 1887; New York: Dutton, 1887);

The Star of Bethlehem (London: Nister, 1887; New York: Dutton, 1887);

All Round the Year, by Nesbit and Caris Brooke (London: Von Portheim, 1888);

The Better Part, and Other Poems (London: Drane, 1888);

Easter-tide: Poems by E. Nesbit and Caris Brooke (London: Drane, 1888; New York: Dutton, 1888);

Landscape and Song (London: Drane, 1888; New York: Dutton, 1888);

The Message of the Dove (London: Drane, 1888; New York: Dutton, n.d.);

Leaves of Life (London: Longmans, Green, 1888);

Corals and Sea Songs (London: Nister, 1889; New York: Dutton, 1889);

Songs of Two Seasons (London: Tuck, 1890);

The Voyage of Columbus: Discovery of America (London: Tuck, 1891);

Sweet Lavender (London: Nister, 1892; New York: Dutton, 1892);

Lays and Legends: Second Series (London & New York: Longmans, Green, 1892);

Grim Tales (London: Innes, 1893);

Something Wrong (London: Innes, 1893);

The Butler in Bohemia, by Nesbit and Oswald Barron (London: Drane, 1894);

The Marden Mystery (Chicago: Clarke, 1894);

Pussy Tales (London: Ward, 1895);

Doggy Tales (London: Ward, 1895);

E. Nesbit, circa 1887

Rose Leaves (London: Nister, 1895);

A Pomander of Verse (London: Lane, 1895; Chicago: McLurg, 1895);

Holly and Mistletoe: A Book of Christmas Verse by E. Nesbit, Norman Gale and Richard Le Gallienne (London: Ward, 1895);

As Happy as a King (London: Ward, 1896);

In Homespun (London: Lane, 1896; Boston: Roberts, 1896);

The Children's Shakespeare, edited by Edric Vredenburg (London: Tuck, 1897; Philadelphia: Altemus, 1900);

Romeo and Juliet, and Other Stories (London: Tuck, 1897);

Royal Children of English History (London: Tuck, 1897);

Dog Tales, and Other Tales, by Nesbit, A. Guest, and Emily R. Watson, edited by Vredenburg (London: Tuck, 1898);

A Book of Dogs: Being a Discourse on Dogs, with Many Tales and Wonders Gathered by E. Nesbit (London: Dent, 1898; New York: Dutton, 1898);

Songs of Love and Empire (Westminster: Constable, 1898);

Pussy and Doggy Tales, (London: Dent, 1899; New York: Dutton, 1900);

The Story of the Treasure Seekers: Being the Adventures of the Bastable Children in Search of a Fortune (London: Unwin, 1899; New York: Stokes, 1899);

The Secret of Kyriels (London: Hurst & Blackett, 1899; Philadelphia: Lippincott, 1899);

The Book of Dragons (London & New York: Harper, 1900);

Nine Unlikely Tales for Children (London: Unwin, 1901; New York: Dutton, 1901);

The Wouldbegoods: Being the Further Adventures of the Treasure Seekers (London: Unwin, 1901; New York & London: Harper, 1901);

To Wish You Every Joy (London: Tuck, 1901);

Thirteen Ways Home (London: Treherne, 1901);

The Revolt of the Toys, and What Comes of Quarrelling (London: Nister, 1902; New York: Dutton, 1902);

Five Children and It (London: Unwin, 1902; New York: Dodd, Mead, 1905);

The Red House: A Novel (London: Methuen, 1902; New York & London: Harper, 1902);

The Rainbow Queen, and Other Stories (London: Tuck, 1903);

Playtime Stories (London: Tuck, 1903);

The Literary Sense (London: Methuen, 1903; New York: Macmillan, 1903);

Cat Tales, by Nesbit and Rosamund Bland (London: Nister, 1904; New York: Dutton, 1904);

The Phoenix and the Carpet (London: Newnes, 1904; New York: Macmillan, 1904);

The New Treasure Seekers (London: Unwin, 1904; New York: Stokes, 1904);

The Story of the Five Rebellious Dolls (London: Nister, 1904; New York: Dutton, 1904);

Pug Peter (Leeds & London: Cooke, 1905);

Oswald Bastable and Others (London: Wells, Gardner, 1905);

The Rainbow and the Rose (London: Longmans, Green, 1905);

The Railway Children (London: Wells, Gardner, 1906; New York & London: Macmillan, 1906);

The Story of the Amulet (London: Unwin, 1906; New York: Dutton, 1907);

The Incomplete Amorist (London: Constable, 1906; New York: Doubleday, Page, 1906);

Man and Maid (London: Unwin, 1906);

The Enchanted Castle (London: Unwin, 1907; New York & London: Harper, 1908);

Twenty Beautiful Stories from Shakespeare: A Home Study Course, Being a Choice Collection from the World's Greatest Classic Writer, William Shakespeare, Retold by E. Nesbit, edited by E. T. Roe (Chicago: Jenkins, 1907);

The Old Nursery Stories (London: Frowde/Hodder & Stoughton, 1908);

The House of Arden: A Story for Children (London: Unwin, 1908; New York: Dutton, 1909);

Jesus in London (London: Fifield, 1908);

Ballads and Lyrics of Socialism, 1883–1908 (London: Fifield, 1908);

Harding's Luck (London: Hodder & Stoughton, 1909; New York: Stokes, 1910);

These Little Ones (London: Allen, 1909);

Daphne in Fitzroy Street (London: Allen, 1909; New York: Doubleday, Page, 1909);

Salome and the Head: A Modern Melodrama (London: Rivers, 1909); republished as *The House with No Address* (New York: Doubleday, Page, 1909; London: Newnes, 1914);

Cinderella: A Play with Twelve Songs to Popular Airs (London: Sidgwick & Jackson, 1909);

Garden Poems (London & Glasgow: Collins, 1909);

The Magic City (London: Macmillan, 1910);

Children's Stories from English History, by Nesbit and Doris Ashley (London: Tuck, 1910);

Children's Stories from Shakespeare (London: Tuck, 1910; Philadelphia: McKay, n.d.);

Fear (London: Paul, 1910);

The Wonderful Garden, or the Three C's (London: Macmillan, 1911; New York: McCann, 1935);

Ballads and Verses of the Spiritual Life (London: Matthews, 1911);

Dormant (London: Methuen, 1911); republished as *Rose Royal* (New York: Dodd, Mead, 1912);

The Magic World (London & New York: Macmillan, 1912);

Wet Magic (London: Laurie, 1913; New York: McCann, 1937);

Wings and the Child: Or, the Building of Magic Cities (London & New York: Hodder & Stoughton, 1913);

The Incredible Honeymoon (New York & London: Harper, 1916);

The New World Literary Series, Book Two, edited by Henry Cecil Wyld (London & Glasgow: Collins Clear Type Press, 1921);

The Lark (London: Hutchinson, 1922);

Many Voices: Poems (London: Hutchinson, 1922);

To the Adventurous (London: Hutchinson, 1923);

Five of Us—and Madeline (London: Unwin, 1925; New York: Adelphi, 1926);

The Complete History of the Bastable Family (London: Benn, 1928);

Long Ago When I Was Young (London: Whiting & Wheaton, 1966; New York: Watts, 1966).

PLAY PRODUCTIONS: *Cinderella,* Deptford Board School, December 1892;

A Family Novelette, by Nesbit and Oswald Barron, New Cross, February 1894;

Sleeping Beauty, Deptford Board School, December 1895;

Aladdin, Deptford Board School, December 1896;

The King's Highway, by Nesbit and Dorothea Deakin, Woolwich, Freemasons' Hall, 13 May 1905;

The Philandrist, or the Lady Fortune-Teller, by Nesbit and Deakin, Woolwich, Freemasons' Hall, 13 May 1905;

The Magician's Heart, London, St. George's Hall, 14 January 1907;

Unexceptionable References, London, Royalty Theatre, Autumn 1912.

OTHER: *Spring Songs and Sketches; Summer Songs and Sketches; Autumn Songs and Sketches; Winter Songs and Sketches; Morning Songs and Sketches; Noon Songs and Sketches; Eventide Songs and Sketches; Night Songs and Sketches,* 8 volumes, selected and arranged by Nesbit and Robert Ellice Mack (London: Griffith, Farran, 1886–1887; New York: Dutton, 1886–1887);

River Sketches (London: Von Portheim, 1887; New York: Dutton, 1887);

The Time of Roses (London: Drane, 1888) – includes poem by Nesbit;

By Land and Sea, selected by Nesbit (London: Drane, 1888);

Autumn Leaves, selected and arranged by Nesbit (London: Drane, 1888; New York: Dutton, 1888);

Winter Snow, selected and arranged by Nesbit (London: Drane, 1888; New York: Dutton, 1888);

Lilies and Heartsease: Songs and Sketches; Falling Leaves: Songs and Sketches, 2 volumes, arranged by Nesbit and Mack (London: Griffith, Farran, Okeden & Welsh, 1888; New York: Dutton, 1888);

Daisy Days (London: Griffith, Farran, Okeden & Welsh, 1888) – includes poems by Nesbit;

Evergreen from the Poet's Corner, selected by Mack (London: Nister, 1889; New York: Dutton, 1889) – includes two poems by Nesbit;

The Lilies Round the Cross, by Nesbit and Helen J. Wood (London: Nister, 1889; New York: Dutton, 1889);

Life's Sunny Side (London: Nister, 1890; New York: Dutton, 1890) – includes poems by Nesbit;

"The Excursion," in *Told by the Fireside* (London: Griffith, Farran, Okeden & Welsh, 1890);

Songs of Scotland, selected by Nesbit (London: Nister, 1890; New York: Dutton, 1890);

"Finding a Sister," in *Twice Four* (London: Griffith, Farran, Browne, 1891);

The Poets and the Poetry of the Century. Vol. 8, Robert Bridges and Contemporary Poets, edited by Alfred H. Miles (London: Hutchinson, 1891) – includes eleven poems by Nesbit;

"Allie's House-Keeping," in *Story upon Story, and Every Word True* (London: Tuck, 1892; New York: Publishers' Union, 1896);

Flowers I Bring and Songs I Sing (London: Tuck, 1893) – includes seven poems by Nesbit, as E. Bland;

Our Friends and All About Them (London: Tuck, 1893) – includes poems and three stories by Nesbit: "The Self Respecting Pussies"; "Down at Grannie's"; "Mabel's Pussy";

Listen Long and Listen Well (London: Tuck, 1893) – includes two stories by Nesbit, "Midsummer Day" and "The Oak Panel";

"Ella's Adventure," in *Sunny Tales for Snowy Days,* edited by Vredenburg (London: Tuck, 1893);

Told by the Sunbeams and Me, edited by Vredenburg (London: Tuck, 1893) – includes two stories by Nesbit, "Dorothy's Birthday" and "Being Bandits";

"The Babe in the Wood, or What Happened at Kitty's Party," in *What Really Happened* (London: Tuck, 1893);

We've Tales to Tell (London: Tuck, 1893) – includes two stories by Nesbit, "How Jack Came to Tea" and "A Crooked Tail";

Hours in Many Lands, edited by Vredenburg (London: Tuck, 1894) – includes two stories by Nesbit, "The Little Heroine" and "Effie's Birthday";

"Lonely Mabel," in *Tales That Are True for Brown Eyes and Blue,* edited by Vredenburg (London: Tuck, 1894);

"Mother's Present," in *Tales to Delight from Morning till Night,* edited by Vredenburg (London: Tuck, 1894);

Cover for the 1899 novel that introduced the Bastable children, among the most popular of Nesbit's characters

"More Haste, Less Speed," in *Fur and Feathers, Tales for All Weathers* (London: Tuck, 1894), pp. 15–19;

"Hot Pies," in *All But One, Told by the Flowers,* edited by Vredenburg (London: Tuck, 1894);

The Girls' Own Birthday Book, selected and arranged by Nesbit (London: Drane, 1894);

"The Glordy John," in *Tick Tock: Tales of the Clock* (London: Tuck, 1895);

"The Rainbow Queen," in *Stories in a Shell* (London: Tuck, 1895);

"Linda and the Prince," in *Treasures from Storyland,* edited by Vredenburg (London: Tuck, 1895);

"A House of Her Own," in *Friends in Fable: A Book of Animal Stories,* edited by Vredenburg (London: Tuck, 1895);

"Finding a Sister," in *Dulcie's Lantern, and Other Stories* (London: Tuck, 1895);

Poets' Whispers: A Birthday Book, selected and arranged, with an introductory poem, by Nesbit (London: Drane, 1895);

Dinna Forget (London: Nister, 1897; New York: Dutton, 1897) – includes two poems by Nesbit and G. Clifton Bingham;

Tales Told in the Twilight (London: Nister, 1897; New York: Dutton, 1897) – includes twenty stories by Nesbit;

The Children's Bookcase, volumes 1–5, 7 edited by Nesbit (London: Frowde/Hodder & Stoughton, 1908–1911);

"The Fairy Godmother," in *Days of Delight,* edited by Vredenburg (London: Tuck, 1910);

Our New Story Book (London: Nister, 1913; New York: Dutton, 1913) – includes two stories by Nesbit, "Our Black Cat" and "The Likeness";

Battle Songs, selected by Nesbit (London: Goschen, 1914);

Hubert Bland, *Essays,* edited by E. Nesbit-Bland (London: Goschen, 1914).

SELECTED PERIODICAL PUBLICATIONS – UNCOLLECTED:

FICTION

"The Social Cobweb," by Nesbit and Hubert Bland, as B., *Weekly Dispatch* (6 January–23 March 1884);

"Something Wrong," by Nesbit and Bland, as Fabian Bland, *Weekly Dispatch* (28 March–4 July 1886);

"The Hour Before Day," by Nesbit and Hubert Bland, as Fabian Bland, *Weekly Dispatch* (20 September–4 October 1885);

Nister's Holiday Annual (1894) – includes Nesbit's "The Play Times, Vol. 1 No. 1" and "The Tiger's Story" (1894);

Nister's Holiday Annual (1895) – includes Nesbit's "The Play Times, Vol. 1 No. 2" and "Dolly's Voyage";

"The Play Times, Vol. 1 No. 3," *Nister's Holiday Annual* (1896);

"The Revolt of the Toys," *Nister's Holiday Annual* (1897);

Nister's Holiday Annual (London: Ernest Nister, 1898) – includes verses and four stories by Nesbit: "The Pen Fairy"; "The Rat Princess"; "Prince Feather-Head and the Mer-Princess"; and "No Good";

"The Criminal," *Neolith,* no. 1 (November 1907): 17–22;

"In the Queen's Garden," *Neolith,* no. 4 (August 1908): 1–11;

"The Doll's House," *Children's Annual 1920* (1920).

NONFICTION

"When I Was a Girl," *John O'London's Weekly* (15 November 1919).

Reviewing Edith Nesbit's verse collection *Leaves of Life* (1888) in the Socialist periodical *To-Day* (January 1889), popular novelist Adeline Sergeant singled out for praise Nesbit's "passionate sympathy," her "fine enthusiasm for splendid deeds," and her "strong and tender feeling," concluding, "She has the gift of inward vision." Nesbit was struggling at the time to support her family through hack writing and to establish herself as an important Victorian woman poet, the equal of Elizabeth Barrett Browning and Christina Rossetti. Yet while she gained a measure of evanescent fame for her verse — accolades from Algernon Charles Swinburne and Oscar Wilde, as well as admission to *Who's Who* as "poet and novelist" in 1897 — the stories and novels she wrote in middle life, from *The Story of the Treasure Seekers* (1899) to *Wet Magic* (1913), won her lasting renown as one of the greatest Edwardian fantasists for children. Nesbit's children's writings rather than her poetry best display the qualities pointed out by Sergeant.

Nesbit liked to describe herself as a child who had never grown up, further explaining in *Wings and the Child* (1913) that children "cannot be understood by imagination, by observation, nor even by love. They can only be understood by memory." This ability to reenter childhood at will, ironically enough, did not always help her deal tactfully with her own offspring; yet it is crucial to the success of her writings for children. From the Bastable stories through the posthumously published *Five of Us — and Madeline* (1925), Nesbit drew on her own youthful experiences and recollections to produce lively and heartfelt works, both gently mocking childhood's manners and mores and wholly sympathetic to children themselves.

Born on 15 August 1858 to Sarah Alderton Nesbit and her second husband, John Collis Nesbit, Edith was the youngest of six children. The siblings closest to her in age were her two brothers, Alfred and Harry, so she spent her early childhood as the participant and occasional victim in their rough-and-tumble escapades. Childhood was for her a golden time of imaginative play and freedom from responsibility, as she recounts in a series of articles titled "My School-Days" (published in the *Girl's Own Paper* between October 1896 and September 1897 and collected as *Long Ago When I Was Young* [1966]) and subsequently in her various fictional reworkings of this material. While she never lost her love for charades, "devil-in-the-dark" (a form of hide-and-seek), and the building of "magic" model cities, irresponsibility was to become an impossible luxury in her adult life. Hence, much of her juvenile fiction focuses on the child's attempt to carry out adult duties such as looking after children, earning money, or upholding family honor — all concerns of the grown-up Nesbit.

Nesbit's father (a pioneering agricultural chemist who had studied under John Dalton and had made his own galvanic battery at fifteen) died unexpectedly at the age of forty-three when Edith was four years old. This blow shifted family responsibilities onto his wife; it may also help explain the prevalence of absent parents in Nesbit's fiction. For four years, Sarah Nesbit followed in her husband's footsteps by administering the agricultural college, founded by her father-in-law and located adjacent to the house at Kennington (South London) where Edith was born. In 1866, however, Edith's sister Mary was diagnosed as consumptive, and the family gave up life at Kennington to seek a climate that might restore Mary's health.

The loss of the Kennington house may rank above even the loss of her father in terms of the effect it had on Nesbit. She now had to attend school, or rather a variety of schools, ranging from private academies to Continental convents, almost all of which she hated. The separation from her mother and siblings and familiar surroundings and the imposition of boarding-school regulations and pecking orders upon one accustomed to fun proved traumatic. Her memoirs trace a pattern alternating unpleasant schools with delightful homes or surrogate homes, both in England and in France, where Mary was eventually ordered for her health. In general, schools work in this pattern to squelch the imagination, homes to stimulate it; and although she conceded that allowing free rein to fancy may prove dangerous, she nonetheless believed it to be essential to happiness. Thus, while her fictions acknowledge the inconveniences to which imagination (often symbolized by magic) can give rise, it is not imagination but boredom and repression, two elements that sometimes loomed large in Nesbit's childhood after she left Kennington, that touch off real evil in her works.

After Mary's death in 1871 at age nineteen, Sarah Nesbit rented a house in Halstead, Kent, and Edith's boarding-school days ended. It was at Halstead that she produced her first published works (verses in the magazines *Good Words* and the *Argosy*). In 1875, however, her mother experienced the kind of financial reversals that so often plague Nesbit's characters, and the family settled instead in London. Two years later, Nesbit met her future husband, Hubert Bland. The youngest son of a Cockney clerk, Bland displayed two characteristics that

One of Gordon Browne's illustrations for Nesbit's The Story of the Treasure Seekers

would strongly influence in his married life with Nesbit: ambivalence toward class hierarchies and irresponsibility toward women. Although he and Nesbit became founding members of the Socialist Fabian Society, he simultaneously desired conservative doctrine and a gentlemanly pedigree. When on 22 April 1880 he married Nesbit (their first child, Paul, was born two months later), he apparently had not confided in her that he was simultaneously engaged to his mother's companion, Maggie Doran, with whom he had also had a son; nor did he subsequently abandon his connection with Doran.

Marriage to Bland provided Nesbit with stimulating company; the freedom to behave unconventionally; and the dramatic situations, quarrels, and reconciliations that appealed to her tendency to view herself as the heroine of any episode. Among their friends were fellow Socialists Bernard Shaw, H. G. Wells, Olive Schreiner, and Annie Besant. Through her work Nesbit would also meet Rudyard Kipling, Laurence Housman, and Richard Le Gallienne, and Noël Coward.

Though Bland was a poor provider financially, he seemed ideally suited to give Nesbit the kind of social environment she most wanted. As a young writer, Nesbit thrived on collaborative efforts, her partners in various projects including Bland and her sister, Saretta Green Deakin (as "Caris Brooke"). The professional sympathy and companionship Bland could both furnish and help attract to her were invaluable. In return, she steered him toward journalism, a field in which he attained some prominence, although he continued to devote much of his time to the Fabian Society.

Despite its overall success, their marriage was never without strain, most of it stemming from Bland's infidelities. The most important of his affairs was a long-standing relationship with Nesbit's close friend Alice Hoatson, whom he seduced at about the time she came to nurse Nesbit through the birth of her fourth child (a stillborn daughter). When the unmarried Hoatson's pregnancy became known, Nesbit suggested that the mother-to-be move in with her family, who would pass off the child as their own while Hoatson managed the household. Apparently, Nesbit discovered only after this arrangement had been effected that her adopted child's father was Bland. As had been the case with Maggie Doran, Bland saw no reason to break off the romance after his wife became aware of it; the Bland-Nesbit-Hoatson household continued until Bland's death. Nesbit's children, then, included not only her biological progeny – Paul, Iris (born 1881), and Fabian (born 1885) – but also Hoatson's offspring, Rosamund (born 1886) and John (born 1899).

The tense situation affected the children, who, unaware of the truth until adolescence, could not understand the emotions swirling around them: Hoatson, who had to settle for being "Auntie" instead of mother; Bland, who had to keep this delicate constellation in balance; and Nesbit, always prone to resent any arrangement in which she did not come indisputably first. Nesbit embarked upon infidelities of her own, perhaps attempting not only to gain revenge or to prove her attractiveness but also to create for herself a more satisfactory "family" circle. As Julia Briggs notes in her 1987 biography, the relationships between Nesbit and her lovers resembled the less romantic camaraderie that characterizes the relationships of her fictional children. In fact, she named the three oldest Bastable boys in her novel *The Story of the Treasure Seekers* (1899) for some of her suitors.

Her marital situation served as the catalyst to prod Nesbit into producing children's fiction. First, it provided the financial incentive: Bland's attack of smallpox and the subsequent loss of his business early in the marriage forced his wife to turn her taste for writing to good account by selling as much work as possible. It also gave her the professional contacts she needed to find a market. Perhaps most importantly, the complicated emotions of the Bland household seem to have moved her to approach juvenile literature with respect and sympathy. Sexuality, which she had learned to distrust, could be omitted from her children's books, allowing her to focus instead on safer issues: dealing with adversity, behaving honorably while avoiding priggishness, and learning that actions have consequences.

Some critics present Nesbit as an antididactic children's writer, but it is more precise to say that she offers morals obliquely rather than forcefully; the Fabian Society, one might note, advocated indirect influence rather than revolutionary action in its attempts to change society. Her earliest publications for children follow the fashion set by the authors of her own childhood in underscoring the lesson to be learned – a technique at which Nesbit was not always expert. *The Children's Shakespeare* (1897), for instance, a prose retelling of twelve plays along fairy-tale lines, asks the reader of "Hamlet" to interpret the story as a homily on courage and the propriety of revenge: "if [Hamlet] had found the heart to [kill his uncle] long before, all these lives had been spared, and none suffered but the wicked King, who well deserved to die."

This condescending tendency to oversimplify complex moral issues is much less overt in Nesbit's later work, where it typically appears only in the form of didactic asides on pet themes such as rural beautification. Indeed, she was to explain to her friend Berta Ruck, "I make it a point of honour never to *write down* to a child." Ultimately, one of her greatest strengths as a children's author is precisely this recognition of the complexity of the child's moral universe.

Nesbit moved from her slight early work in children's literature to her first mature contribution to the field in December 1897, when she published the first installment of *The Story of the Treasure Seekers* in a Christmas supplement to the *Illustrated London News*. (Subsequent chapters appeared in the *Pall Mall* and *Windsor* magazines; whenever possible, Nesbit published her prose and poetry both seriatim and in book form, the *Strand* being her preferred forum for stories involving magic.) The installment introduced the Bastable family, a group of six motherless children living in reduced circumstances in Blackheath who determine "to restore the fallen fortunes of [their] House."

The Treasure Seekers contains sixteen episodes, most of them focusing on the children's ill-fated attempts to earn money. Their liveliness and generosity eventually come to the attention of a childless great-uncle, who takes the whole family under his financial wing and returns them to middle-class comfort. The events were frequently suggested by Nesbit's remembered experiences or the exploits of her children; some, such as the burial of Albert-next-door or the establishment of the home newspaper, rework material she had recently published in "My School-Days" and in volumes of *Nister's Holiday Annual*. The comedy, usually more evident to adults than to children, arises from the gap between grown-up expectations and the Bastable children's perceptions of the world. This gap, of course, becomes particularly pronounced when they attempt adult activities, from Oswald's and Noël's literary endeavors – Oswald narrates the stories, periodically adopting a grand style; Noël is perennially busy writing poetry, after the fashion of the young Nesbit – to Dicky's expedition to a moneylender.

The child reader may be no more sophisticated than the child characters, thus missing many of the jokes. What appeals across the generations

Nesbit's husband, Hubert Bland

are the Bastables' vivid personalities, the clarity of the relationships, and the children's fertile imaginations. While the Bastables lack the funds to attend school or to get the silver out of pawn, they have the freedom to explore the city by themselves. As a result, they combine the flexibility of mind that Nesbit saw as a product of middle-class reading with the physical freedom associated with working-class youth, embodying in a new form Bland's straddling of social strata.

A similar balance exists between the narrative's effort to delight and its effort to instruct. As the narrator, Oswald propounds "manly" values: courage, calmness, justice, and honesty. At the same time, narrative events expose a competing code of feminine virtues to which Oswald is less sensitive: kindness, peacekeeping, and responsibility. Neither set of qualities is adequate by itself. Oswald's belief that he embodies true manliness is as mistaken as it is arrogant, and Dora's attempt as the eldest to mother her siblings verges on priggishness. Both boys and girls, Nesbit suggests, should strive for virtues appropriate alike to manliness and to womanliness, while never losing the ability to enjoy life, which Nesbit saw as childhood's most attractive characteristic.

This pattern continually resurfaces in her works for children. For instance, it recurs in her next effort for young readers, *The Book of Dragons* (1900), a collection of seven unrelated stories, all featuring dragons and all including line drawings by H. R. Millar, who became the best-known illustrator of her works of fantasy. A common thread in several of these tales is the neuter quality of true worth. This theme occurs in many of her other short stories in the genre, notably "The Prince, Two Mice, and Some Kitchen-Maids" (*Nine Unlikely Tales,* 1901), "The Twopenny Spell" (*Oswald Bastable and Others,* 1905), and "The Princess and the Hedge-Pig" (*The Magic World,* 1912). Bravery and kindness are equally important to boys and to girls, and Nesbit's princesses are as likely as her princes to fight off dragons or foil evil fairies. This implicit feminism owed nothing to Nesbit's professed politics; at Bland's urging, she opposed woman suffrage, a goal he found repellent.

Another characteristic pattern that carries over from the dragon stories into Nesbit's later works of fantasy is her modernizing of the fairy-tale world, which occurs even in her retellings of classic stories, such as "Beauty and the Beast" in *The Old Nursery Stories* (1908). Whereas most Victorian creators of "art" fairy tales (Hans Christian Andersen, George MacDonald, and Wilde, for instance) evoke a traditional, preindustrial setting, Nesbit mixes the timeless impossible and the modern-day prosaic – her dragons drink petrol and prey on the South Lambeth Infirmary; her kings build modern villas; and her princes study arithmetic – thus reinforcing the stories' humor and ratifying the reader's perception that magic may exist in any setting.

A second collection of stories incorporating magic, titled *Nine Unlikely Tales,* and a new installment of the Bastable saga, *The Wouldbegoods,* appeared in 1901. The latter recounts the adventures of the Bastables and their friends Denny and Daisy after forming a "society for being good in," an organization the girls have started because they "wish not to be such a nuisance to grown-up people and to perform prodigies of real goodness." Structurally very similar to *The Treasure Seekers, The Wouldbegoods* likewise draws on Nesbit's childhood memories – the character Daisy, in fact, bears Nesbit's youthful nickname. The novel plays on the question of how to define "good" behavior. As Mervyn Nicholson observes in a 1991 article, a major Nesbit theme is "the conflict of desire and frustration," often presented in terms of the adult effort to control self-expression by establishing codes of conduct. Children in Nesbit's fiction show much ingenuity in balancing these competing drives by adhering to the letter of the law while still pursuing their own wants.

The Wouldbegoods places several systems of conduct in competition. Denny and especially Daisy, the "white mice," represent the overly obedient children of adult preference, those conforming to the prim and unimaginative pattern that Dora Bastable sometimes approaches. This form of goodness, so convenient to adult authority, is codified in the books that the girls have read and the Bastable boys reject: Maria Louisa Charlesworth's *Ministering Children* (1854) and tracts such as "a horrid little blue book about the something or other of Little Sins." That the earnest works of the girls' preference – which also include Susan Coolidge's (Sarah Chauncy Woolsey) *What Katy Did* (1872) and other works "all about being good" – date from Nesbit's own childhood or earlier helps to condemn this Victorian model of deportment as old-fashioned.

In contrast, the other children invoke classic works such as John Bunyan's *Pilgrim's Progress* (1678) and Geoffrey Chaucer's *The Canterbury Tales* (1387–1400) and contemporary titles such as Kipling's *The Jungle Book* (1894) and *The Second Jungle Book* (1895). While literal reenactments of Kipling's works prove inconvenient in a domestic setting, the

values they stress – honor, courage, loyalty – are indeed essential to "being good." Daisy and Denny have as much to learn about the best kind of goodness as Oswald does, and their gradual acquisition of childlike mischief is no less important than the other children's attempts to channel these qualities into activities that will not annoy the authorities.

In October 1900 Nesbit's son Fabian died under anesthesia while undergoing a routine tonsillectomy. Her horror and grief pervade much of her post-1900 writing. Whereas the Bastable stories tend to rework her own youth and to memorialize the companionship she enjoyed with friends of her young adulthood, later works often rewrite the family situation of her children, allowing the reincarnation of Fabian (for example, as Robert in the "Five Children" books) or suggesting the removal of Hoatson's offspring by depicting three children rather than five.

Nesbit's productions for adults paradoxically tend to be more "childish" than her children's books in their reflection of the pain of Fabian's loss. The *Neolith,* for instance (a short-lived literary magazine Nesbit edited from 1907 to 1908), featured in its first number her story "The Criminal," a somewhat sentimental exercise in parental guilt that recalls Fabian's punishment for stealing sweets intended for poor children and notes that "it is your Mother who has [it] to remember." Likewise, the final number of the *Neolith* included Nesbit's "In the Queen's Garden," a blank-verse drama about Maacah's feelings after the death of her son Absalom. Here Maacah blames her cowives for Absalom's loss, suggesting Nesbit's resentment of Hoatson and her other rivals.

Among Nesbit's juvenile stories *Harding's Luck* (1909) seems especially to recall Fabian, presenting a situation in which the best of three children dies to the modern world and survives only in the now-unreachable past. Nesbit's favorite among her children's books, the work achieves a level of maturity absent from the *Neolith* contributions.

Ironically, Fabian's death preceded the most profitable year of Nesbit's career. The volumes of stories she published in 1901 – two for children and one for adults, besides an illustrated gift booklet put out by Raphael Tuck – brought in serial fees, royalties, and bids for American publication rights; she was also still receiving royalties from reprints of *The Treasure Seekers* and *The Book of Dragons. The Wouldbegoods* alone netted her eleven hundred pounds (not counting serial fees) in one year, which would prove to be her record.

Illustration by Arthur H. Buckland for Nesbit's The Wouldbegoods, *the sequel to* The Story of the Treasure Seekers

In the January 1903 issue of *Harper's Bazaar,* just after *The Red House* had concluded its serialization there, reviewer Marshall Steele praises Nesbit as a writer for adults but notes that her true preeminence is in juvenile fiction: "With the single exception of *The Jungle Book,* no child's book of recent years has had success to compare with that of *The Wouldbegoods.*" Thus, when "The Psammead" began in the *Strand* in April 1902, Nesbit was established as a major children's writer; her *Who's Who* entry for 1903 for the first time added the phrase "and author of children's books" to her identification as "poet and novelist."

"The Psammead," published in book form as *Five Children and It* (1902), is Nesbit's first extended fantasy. Like her shorter magic tales, it owes something to other fantasists of the day; Kenneth Grahame's "The Reluctant Dragon" (1898) obviously influenced her *Book of Dragons,* as Grahame's *The Golden Age* (1895) had helped shape the Bastable tales. In the case of *Five Children and It,* the workings of the magic, so inconvenient to everyday life, suggest F. Anstey's *The Brass Bottle* (1900).

The chief delight of *Five Children and It,* however, is the family life of the five children themselves and their relationship to "It," the snappish Psammead (or sand fairy). Cyril, Anthea, Robert, Jane, and the baby, known as the Lamb, portray, respectively, Paul, Iris, Fabian, Rosamund, and John Bland. The story begins with the onset of their summer holiday in a house in the country and, as the narrator notes, could well continue as "a most interesting story about all the ordinary things that the children did," à la the Bastable tales. Instead, the first chapter introduces the Psammead and its power to grant wishes, so that the "things that the children did" need not be ordinary at all. What the central characters fail to take into account, however, is that they must still contend with rules; instead of freeing them from the requirements of the everyday world, the magic adds more. This conflict between the wish to gratify the imagination and the need for obedience moves the narrative.

Their wishes — whose expression is not always intentional — are of several kinds. Some represent long-held dreams, such as being as "beautiful as the day" or having a sandpit full of gold coins. Some hold out freedom from responsibility, such as Robert's and Cyril's inadvertent wishes to be free of having to baby-sit the Lamb, or Anthea's desire for wings, which the children imagine will excuse them from observing certain human codes. Robert's wish to be "bigger than the baker's boy" reflects the child's anger at powerlessness; the wishes to be in a besieged castle or to be under attack by Red Indians directly express the importance of imaginative play in a child's life.

However, none of these wishes entirely succeeds; indeed, the children speculate that the Psammead secretly hopes that none of their wishes will turn out well. The rules of the magic seem to be stacked against them – the only convenient aspect (although even this can lead to problems) being that the wish ceases to work at sunset. In her biography of Nesbit, *A Woman of Passion* (1987), Briggs suggests that the novel's psychological appeal depends on children's ambivalent feelings about wish fulfillment: "The child's realization that wishes have no power in the real world is at once deeply disappointing and yet also reassuring, since it protects the ill-controlled self from the appalling consequences such power would confer." Significantly, the children's final wishes provide for the (temporary) relinquishment of the Psammead and the clearing up of the problems created by their wish that their mother should find a cache of stolen jewels; ultimately, what they desire most is a return to the status quo, where all they need to worry about are the rules of daily life.

Minor works of this period include short-story anthologies and booklets and a collection of four whimsical *Cat Tales* written with Rosamund in 1904; Nesbit also published an adult novel, *The Red House* (1902), one episode of which features a visit from the Bastables. Nesbit's next important work for children was the sequel to *Five Children and It, The Phoenix and the Carpet* (1904), which combines two magical entities, the Phoenix and the wishing carpet. The latter provides more opportunities for disaster than did the Psammead, in part because it permits the children to travel farther afield. Still, although they encounter real danger, their use of the magic is somewhat more successful than in the preceding work, due to the Phoenix's supervision. While he is as prone as his charges to make mistakes about the everyday world, the Phoenix is naturally more expert in dealing with magic. Another key difference between this novel and its predecessor resides in the children's hopes for the carpet: this time they seek only adventure, and any material benefits go to others. While their earlier dealings with the Psammead were aimed chiefly at selfish pleasures, the carpet is used to bestow benefits on others.

This change reflects the beginning of a shift in Nesbit's work as a whole; increasingly, her writings tend to display a moral as well as a narrative complexity absent from her early stories. The Phoenix's concern for the children's good behavior is noticeably greater than that of the Psammead, who merely grumbles about their manners; even the mute carpet is capable of pointing out to them that "good and kind actions" might best be performed at home. Similarly, the Bastables' adventures in *The New Treasure Seekers* (1904) and *Oswald Bastable and Others* (1905) introduce more frequently themes such as class conflict or the amelioration of poverty.

The Wouldbegoods takes note of these issues occasionally, as in the episodes "Bill's Tombstone" and "The Benevolent Bar," each describing ill-considered attempts at doing good. In *The New Treasure Seekers,* however, the children's encounters with the poor are more extended and more serious. "The Turk in Chains," for instance, examines Dicky's run-in with a railroad guard, in which all the children but Dora play a trick, immediately exposed as morally shabby, upon a working-class family; they must then expiate their deed. Similarly, "The Poor and Needy" looks at social prejudice among the poor themselves, while two of the Bastable stories in *Oswald Bastable and Others* suggest the consequences to the less fortunate that may result from the children's failure to think things through. In *The Wouldbegoods* the solution offered by the Bastables' father is simply that of "minding your own business," but in *The New Treasure Seekers,* active involvement with the lives of others is advocated.

In addition to providing a forum for social issues that reach beyond individual goodness, *The New Treasure Seekers* affords Nesbit an opportunity for narrative experiments. The time sequence of the collection is looser than that of the earlier books: "The Conscience-Pudding" takes place much earlier than the rest of the stories, while "Archibald the Unpleasant" refers to an episode that was not to appear between covers until the 1905 volume. Another new feature is a narrative game represented by an episode about "The Young Antiquaries" that reprises the visit by the Bastables in *The Red House.* The same events occur, this time told from Oswald's point of view rather than that of the hero of the adult novel, Len. This playing with overlapping events and perceptions recurs in more extended form in *Harding's Luck* (1909).

Just as the Bastable stories become progressively more earnest, the last of the three "Five Children" novels, *The Story of the Amulet* (1906), is also the most serious. The machinery of this novel owed much to the keeper of Egyptian and Assyrian antiquities at the British Museum, Ernest Wallis Budge, to whom the story is dedicated (he appears in its pages as the "nicest gentleman" among the crowd of museum officials whose anger the Babylonian Queen has aroused). Budge suggested the Amulet, the Words of Power, and many of the settings and historical data that are essential to the plot. Nesbit's *Wings and the Child: Or, the Building of Magic Cities*

"Now, then, what's the trouble?"

An illustration by C. E. Brock for Nesbit's The Railway Children

(1913), however, suggests that the dioramas of savages and the Egyptian court she had encountered on visiting the Crystal Palace as a child may have furnished the original impetus for her excursion into the past.

The Story of the Amulet focuses on the children's journey to Atlantis, Babylon, and a future London to find the lost half of the Amulet that when whole can give them their heart's desire. Their understanding of the magic derives from the Psammead, whom they have rescued from a pet store. This adventure provides wider social commentary than any Nesbit had hitherto offered.

Thus, the present consistently appears as inferior to the noble past or the utopian future. Although the past is violent, its greater sense of social responsibility is evident in the beauty of its cities and the comparative happiness of its workers. Best of all is the future, modeled on the proposals of Wells. Nesbit's theories about ideal child rearing,

based on those of Johann Pestalozzi, Friedrich Froebel, and Maria Montessori and detailed more fully in *Wings and the Child,* hold sway in her utopia, and good citizenship is the primary lesson every inhabitant must learn.

In contrast, the present is criticized for its widespread indifference to human life, especially with regard to children and the working classes. It is no accident that at the end of the novel, the Psammead's heart's desire turns out to be escape into the distant past, while that of the children's friend and adviser "the learned gentleman" is possession of the Amulet and unification with his counterpart, the Ancient Egyptian priest Rekh-Mará. In different ways, each has turned his back on Edwardian England. The children also wish for union in the restoration of their family circle, disrupted by their father's being in Manchuria as a war correspondent and their mother's being in Madeira, where she and the Lamb have gone during her convalescence from an illness. Once the family is again whole, magic is no longer needed.

This longing for family completion, which recalls Nesbit's loss of her father, her siblings (all dead by 1899 save a brother who had moved to Australia), her son, and her mother (in 1902), also drives her other juvenile novel of 1906, *The Railway Children*. Here the father of Roberta (Bobbie), Peter, and Phyllis has been wrongfully imprisoned for selling state secrets, and their mother – whose comic verses and writing career recall Nesbit – has moved the family to a spartan existence in the country. The children's main entertainment is provided by the nearby railroad and its station personnel, while their moral task has to do with learning responsibility. Such duty has many forms, both domestic (giving up treats they cannot afford; controlling their bickering) and social (preventing an accident on the line; saving a boy with a broken leg; helping their railway-porter friend, Perks).

Money, which except in *The Treasure Seekers* has little part in Nesbit's earlier work for children, becomes a central theme of *The Railway Children,* as does social class. The narrative suggests that children may have a more sensible attitude toward these adult preoccupations than do adults. The children's stance on generosity, for instance, is that it should be directed toward any deserving person. Thus, they define its possible objects not only as those less fortunate than themselves but also as their own family. Peter steals coal from the railway to be helpful at home; all three request a loan from an "Old Gentleman" to buy food for their sick mother; Bobbie asks the doctor to reduce his bill. Since their mother defines generosity (or charity) as tied to class, she is willing to extend it to others but not to accept it herself; to do so would offend against the code of the class to which she belongs by education if not by current economic standing.

But while the narrative recognizes the class pride of adults as significant, it suggests that the children's disregard for hierarchies when dealing with others is preferable to adult self-consciousness. Consequently, Bobbie, presented as the best of the three, is both the quickest to give help and the quickest to ask for it. Her trustful openness is finally rewarded when the Old Gentleman succeeds in clearing her father and thus reunites the family.

Like most of Nesbit's children's books, *The Railway Children* first appeared in an adult forum, the *London Magazine;* as Anthea Bell notes in her 1960 Nesbit biography, these works appealed to adults as well as to children. And some critics have complained that Nesbit's next magic book, *The En-*

chanted Castle, which ran in the *Strand* during most of 1907, is not altogether suitable for young readers. They single out the episode of the Ugly-Wuglies (dummies who come alive in response to an absent-minded wish) as unnecessarily horrific. Nevertheless, *The Enchanted Castle* has more to do with Nesbit's own childhood than do any other of her fantasy tales.

The story concerns three siblings, Gerald, Jimmy, and Kathleen, and their friend Mabel, the castle housekeeper's niece. Mabel discovers a magic ring while she is playing a trick on the others. The form and duration of the ring's magic change according to several variables: it is sometimes a ring of invisibility, sometimes a wishing ring, sometimes a ring that alters the wearer's form, and so on, depending on how its user has described it. To complicate the situation still further, the ring is but a key to a place of greater magic, the Hall of Granted Wishes, where one's heart's desire may be found. Not until comparatively late in the novel do the children master the rules of this magic, and as is usual in Nesbit's fiction, they continue to make mistakes in practice even after they understand the theory. Hence, Kathleen accidentally turns herself into a statue, and Mabel grows to be four yards high. Worse, those who do not happen to be wearing the ring when confronting the magic are prey to panic.

The narrative presents this fear as supernatural in origin. Nevertheless, it would appear to have several more earthly sources: the children's involvement with forces so much stronger than themselves, for instance. Significantly, *The Enchanted Castle* is unique among Nesbit's full-length tales in providing the central characters with no kind of instruction in the magic's use, and the loss of control over the self through fear reflects the lack of control exemplified by the lack of guidelines or mentors. The adults in this novel are not surrogate parents but surrogate siblings; not until the end is there a sense that anyone's life is well ordered.

Moreover, just as various episodes incorporate some of the delights of Nesbit's own childhood, such as the Crystal Palace's life-size model of a dinosaur and the Great Exhibition's classical statues – all relocated to the castle grounds, where they come alive after dark – others incorporate some of her terrors. The Ugly-Wuglies mirror the figures Nesbit made, well into her adulthood, in an attempt to control the fear she felt on visiting the mummies of Bordeaux, which she had described in "My School-Days" as "the crowning horror of my childish life." If Nesbit usually gloried in her role as grown-up child, *The Enchanted Castle* may be read as an explo-

One of H. R. Millar's illustrations for Nesbit's The Story of the Amulet, *the third and last of Nesbit's "Five Children" novels, which began with* Five Children and It

ration of some of the negative aspects of that feeling, in which repressed horrors may burst their bonds and overpower even adults (the Ugly-Wuglies knock down Lord Yalding) and bring children to the breaking point. The denouement not only unites the story's lovers but also restores order by providing an explanation of the magic and undoing all its works, even those apparently beneficial.

In contrast, Nesbit's next works, *The House of Arden* (1908) and *Harding's Luck,* employ a magic with lasting if bittersweet effects. Of the two, *Arden* more closely approximates the typical Nesbit narrative, its episodes culminating in the restoration of the family circle. The first chapter introduces Edith Arden and her niece and nephew, Elfrida and Edred. The children's father and Edith's fiancé have both been reported dead in South America, so the Ardens are in reduced circumstances until old Lord Arden dies and Edred succeeds to the title. The legacy includes land and a castle but no money, as the family fortune was hidden from the Parliamentarians during the civil war and never recovered. As Edred and Elfrida discover, however, the

advantages of nobility also include magic, as the family crest of a white mole takes form in the living Mouldiwarp. Under the guidance of the latter, they can travel back in time to discover the treasure. Each time trip moves the children another century away from their own day, where they invariably find that they have stepped into the lives of the Edred and Elfrida of that era. This apparatus permits Nesbit to describe the daily lives and attitudes toward childhood of bygone centuries and to introduce appropriate local color: smugglers, wise women, "gentlemen of the road," and so forth.

The rules of magic presented in the novel also allow the author to forge her plainest link yet between magical success and virtue. The crusty Mouldiwarp, for instance, requires the children to summon it in verse they have composed themselves; furthermore, the magic will not work unless they have not quarreled for three days. At its most basic level, then, the magic demands both creativity and self-control. Nor is mere access to its workings enough. Perseverance, courage, and generosity are also essential not only to the success of the quest but to the Ardens' adult future, when they will have to "remember the poor and needy," as an Edwardian caretaker instructs Edred.

At once more talented in versifying, more adventurous, and more ready to engage with the people they meet in the past than is Edred, Elfrida has less difficulty living up to the demands the magic places on them. Appropriately, the final episode asks more of Edred than of Elfrida: he must prove himself a true Arden by behaving with unwonted bravery and relinquishing the title that marks him as superior to Elfrida in the eyes of the world. His willingness to perform these tasks permits the rescue of the missing father and uncle from South America to make the family circle whole.

But *Arden* leaves a deliberate loose end in the shape of Cousin Richard, whom Edred and Elfrida first encounter in 1607 and who turns out to be another visitor from the present, via his own brand of Arden magic. He is thus obviously a member of the Arden family, but where he fits into it is unclear. The answer has to do with another theme that *Arden* introduces and *Harding's Luck* develops, that of what Elfrida and Edred's father terms "the wicked cruelties of modern civilization."

The least episodic of all Nesbit's tales, *Harding's Luck* is also unusual among her works for children in employing a slum child as the central character instead of as a foil for a middle-class protagonist. Indeed, this novel reworks an idea expressed more simplistically in one of her *Neolith* stories for adults, "The Ashpits" (collected in *These Little Ones*, 1909). The hero/victim of the latter story, Bert, closely resembles Nesbit's ideal child, having "courage as well as imagination, enterprise, eyes clear enough to see beauty, and a heart big enough to hold love"; society and his family, however, allow him no scope to use these talents, leaving Bert no future but a providential death. This, in miniature, is also the story of *Harding's Luck*.

The novel, however, introduces time magic to transform Dickie Harding, a lame slum child, into Richard Arden, the rightful heir of the Arden estates. Because of an episode of family history recounted in *Arden,* Dickie's branch of the family has been lost. Dickie is thus emblematic both of the hidden Arden treasure (restored to the family through his efforts) and, in a larger sense, of the relationship between the well-to-do and the urban poor: he is good material who has been neglected, crippled, and abused. Only his excursions into the Jacobean past give Dickie the ethical and practical training that his own society should have afforded him.

Nesbit portrays seventeenth-century England as a utopia. Not only is Richard physically and emotionally whole, provided with a family and a fortune, but society is healthier as well. The unpolluted countryside is beautiful; the rich live in harmony with the poor. The modern Dickie, to be sure, has more options than his counterpart in "The Ashpits," as he is offered an assortment of acceptable surrogate parents ranging from the genial tramp Beale to Lady Talbot and finally to Edred and Elfrida's father. But his knowledge of Jacobean society makes it easier for Dickie to turn his back on Edwardian times even after he is restored to his proper station and to membership in the Arden family. Unwilling to deprive Edred and Elfrida's father of the title and fortune, which the latter will use responsibly to improve the lot of the village poor, Dickie employs the magic a final time to vanish into the family's past.

The Arden saga thus repeatedly stresses the need for self-sacrifice as well as for the enterprise always demanded of Nesbit's fictional children. While the two novels introduce no new themes, they go further than Nesbit's earlier work in developing such tropes as the androgyny of virtue and the failings of modern society.

Her next book for the young, *The Magic City* (1910), retains the emphasis on individual moral growth (exemplified by the passing of various tests of character) but turns away from the straightforward representation of social issues by employing not a real world but a toy world as its setting. The problem animating the novel is the construction of a blended family: Philip's sister and foster mother, Helen, has married Lucy Graham's father, much to Philip's resentment. Staying with Lucy and her domineering nurse while the newlyweds are on their honeymoon, Philip is sullen and angry. His chief recreation is in building a model city, a project that Lucy wants to assist and the nurse wants to clear away. Magic is introduced, and the pretend world becomes real. Philip finds that he must perform seven tasks to save the city, aided by Lucy and threatened by a veiled woman known as the Pretenderette – who turns out to be the nurse.

The Pretenderette is usually interpreted as a sardonic portrayal of suffragists. The novel, however, in no way dismisses the feminine. While each of Philip's tasks centers on a particular virtue – including atonement, neatness, courage, resourcefulness, generosity, industry, and book learning – his overarching lesson deals with accepting Lucy as a friend and sister. Lucy shares fully in the accomplishment of the tasks, although she takes no credit;

E. Nesbit, circa 1903

nor does she need to make any moral advances akin to Philip's.

The Pretenderette mistakenly assumes that "You can let your evil passions go in a dream and it don't hurt any one." The narrative suggests the contrary: the dreamworld of magic and imagination is the best place to reorder oneself and even, perhaps, society. Along the way, Philip and Lucy are instructed about the dangers of moneygrubbing and technology, among other Nesbit pitfalls. Thus, when they leave the magic world after solving the assorted problems of its inhabitants, they find that the drawbacks of their everyday situation have disappeared. This lesson in the uses of fantasy is implicit in other Nesbit works as well, but *The Magic City* represents its clearest statement. Most critics hold that this novel initiates the decline of Nesbit's powers as a writer for children; certainly the period after 1910 was filled with worries likely to distract her attention from her work, such as Bland's increasing blindness and heart trouble and her own financial difficulties.

The Wonderful Garden, or the Three C's (1911) invokes the halcyon days of the Bastables through minor characters who also appear in *The New Treasure Seekers* and through similar plot situations. Caroline, Charlotte, and Charles, whose parents are in India, go to live with their great-uncle, the author of

a scholarly work-in-progress on magic. They find two mislaid books on herbal magic and medicine which, together with a book on the language of flowers, serve as the initiating factors in a series of adventures with disputably supernatural elements, shared with their friend Rupert, who has run away from school.

In her 1960 study of Nesbit, Bell describes *The Wonderful Garden* as "the gentlest" of the author's books, a quality she attributes to the girls' predominance in the story. Indeed, while Caroline, Charlotte, and Charles engage in the same sorts of activities as the Bastables, their exploits seem somehow less spirited. But the concern for courage, truth, kindness, and responsibility that animates so many Nesbit tales is still at work; the need for ingenuity and the difficulty of submitting to authority are also again stressed.

By this time the reunification of the family had become the predictable resolution of Nesbit's tales. *The Wonderful Garden* provides such an ending on several levels. Rupert is reconciled to his schoolmaster, denoting the restoration of one kind of order, while the "three C's" relinquish the books to their uncle and thus take the final step in accepting him as one of themselves. They are rewarded with the sight of a figure who may be a ghost or merely an actress; she tells them that because of their belief in "the old and beautiful things" and their attempts to help those in need they shall have their hearts' desire. This turns out, of course, to be the conveyance of all four children to their parents in India, under the escort of Great-Uncle Charles.

The *Strand* contained no Nesbit serial in 1912, a year that saw only the publication in book form of twelve previously published stories. Her next *Strand* serial, *Wet Magic* (1913), was her last novel for children. Most of its action takes place undersea. This milieu may have been suggested by "Our Cat's Tale," included in the stories Nesbit had written with her daughter Rosamund in 1904, which recounts the adventures of the Bland cat among the mermaids. Likewise, much of the novel's plot depends upon the coming to life of characters out of books, which Nesbit, always fond of incorporating references to the works of other authors and her own earlier publications, had last used in *The Magic City*. The theme of militarism, on the other hand, clearly reflects the coming war.

The story begins with the departure of four children, Francis, Mavis, Bernard, and Kathleen, for the seaside; while on the train, they see a newspaper article describing the discovery of a mermaid at their destination. After they rescue the mermaid from captivity in a circus sideshow, acquiring another companion in the circus boy Reuben, they accompany her to the undersea world. A breach of rules by Kathleen lays open the merpeople's realm to attack by the Under Folk and then by wicked or boring book characters. While the children ward off the latter by raising an army of heroes and heroines, they find themselves the prisoners of the Under Folk and must restore proper order and true amity throughout the undersea world before they may return home. In the novel's final scene Reuben is reunited with his upper-class parents, who have been the amnesiac rulers of the Under Folk country.

The central value of *Wet Magic* is bravery, which consists of both moral courage and pluck in battle. The narrative invokes some of war's attractions: gorgeous parades, opportunities for courage, the sense of community arising from facing a common enemy. Thus, the lasting result of the "battle of the books" is that literature takes on for the children "an interest far above any [that it] had ever held before." At the same time, however, the novel ultimately establishes peace as a higher good. As Francis points out to the merprincess, "Why, don't you see, all these people you're at war with are *nice.*" Just as the best courage occurs in peaceful contexts, the highest patriotism works for amity rather than strife.

But as events were soon to prove, Nesbit's preachments would have little immediate effect; and she herself was to succumb to the war fever to some extent, editing a 1914 anthology entitled *Battle Songs* and helping with war work at Well Hall despite her disapproval of jingoism. Before the war broke out in August 1914, however, came Hubert Bland's death on 14 April. A devastating, unexpected blow, his death precipitated a series of troubles, including family strife over Bland's will and further financial difficulties and ill health for Nesbit.

On 20 February 1917 Nesbit married Thomas Terry Tucker, a marine engineer known to his friends as "the Skipper." With the exception of Rosamund, most of the Bland offspring disapproved of the union on class grounds. Indeed, Nesbit's *Who's Who* entry for 1919, an updated one describing her occupations as "literary work, poultry farming, fruit and vegetable growing, [and] keeping a shop for the sale of garden and farm produce," omits all mention of her second marriage. Nonetheless, the step provided Nesbit with new contentment and emotional security. She no longer had to share her husband with Hoatson, who soon left Well Hall, and Tucker's fund of anecdotes furnished the basis for some of Nesbit's late stories.

But the final years brought other difficulties. In 1922 financial considerations forced the sale of Nesbit's longtime home Well Hall, the setting for a number of her books. Her health deteriorated rapidly, perhaps from lung cancer, and she died on 4 May 1924. Nesbit had produced little work for children since 1913, except for a few short stories; some of these, linked together by Rosamund Bland Sharp, were published posthumously as *Five of Us— and Madeline* (1925), a Bastable-like family sequence using material provided by Tucker and reminiscences of Nesbit's life from "My School-Days."

Despite the lighthearted tone of her best works for children, the issues Nesbit explores in them are by no means trivial. Yet she feared that her juvenile tales, certainly her most lucrative productions, might detract from her "real" work as a poet; as she wrote in 1905 to her agent, J. B. Pinker: "I don't think it is good for my style to write *nothing* but children's stuff." Nesbit's first biographer, Doris Langley Moore, explains, "She knew that her books for children were good books . . . but she never imagined that they were the highest manifestation of her literary capacities."

Nevertheless, in writing for children Nesbit proved her ability to combine humor and sympathy, the personal and the universal. Not only does her popularity in this genre continue today, she also served as a major influence upon other writers for the young, including Edward Eager and C. S. Lewis. Her work, in turn, owes much to Victorian authors, so that in reading Nesbit's productions one gets a glimpse of a much wider range of literature beloved by young and old alike. She thus stands as an important transitional figure, both participating in the final years of an era often referred to as the Golden Age of children's books and anticipating the children's literature of the later twentieth century.

Biographies:

Doris Langley Moore, *E. Nesbit: A Biography* (London: Benn, 1933);

Anthea Bell, *E. Nesbit* (London: Bodley Head, 1960);

Julia Briggs, *A Woman of Passion: The Life of E. Nesbit 1858–1924* (London: Century Hutchinson / New York: New Amsterdam Books, 1987).

References:

Joan Evans de Alonso, "E. Nesbit's Well Hall, 1915–1921: A Memoir," *Children's Literature,* 3 (1974): 147–152;

Gloria G. Fromm, "E. Nesbit and the Happy Moralist," *Journal of Modern Literature,* 11 (March 1984): 45–65;

U. C. Knoepflmacher, "Of Babylands and Babylons: E. Nesbit and the Reclamation of the Fairy Tale," *Tulsa Studies in Women's Literature,* 6 (Fall 1987): 299–325;

Colin N. Manlove, "Fantasy as Witty Conceit: E. Nesbit," *Mosaic,* 10 (Winter 1977): 109–130;

Mervyn Nicholson, "What C. S. Lewis Took from E. Nesbit," *Children's Literature Association Quarterly,* 16 (Spring 1991): 16–22;

Stephen Prickett, "Worlds within Worlds: Kipling and Nesbit," in his *Victorian Fantasy* (Brighton, U.K.: Harvester / Bloomington: Indiana University Press, 1978), pp. 198–239;

Suzanne Rahn, "News from E. Nesbit: *The Story of the Amulet* and the Socialist Utopia," *English Literature in Transition,* 28, no. 1 (1985): 124–144;

Elmar Schenkel, "Domesticating the Supernatural: Magic in E. Nesbit's Children's Books," in *The Victorian Fantasists: Essays on Culture, Society and Belief in the Mythopoeic Fiction of the Victorian Age,* edited by Kath Filmer (New York: St. Martin's Press, 1991), pp. 205–216;

Adeline Sergeant, "Books of To-Day," *To-Day,* 11 (January 1889): 24–27;

Barbara Smith, "The Expression of Social Values in the Writing of E. Nesbit," *Children's Literature,* 3 (1974): 153–164;

Marshall Steele, "E. Nesbit: An Appreciation," *Harper's Bazaar,* 37 (January 1903): 78–79;

Noel Streatfeild, *Magic and the Magician: E. Nesbit and Her Children's Books* (London: Benn / New York: Schuman, 1958).

William Nicholson

(5 February 1872 – 16 May 1949)

Michael Scott Joseph
Rutgers University Libraries

BOOKS: *An Alphabet* (London: Heinemann, 1898 [1897]; New York: Russell, 1898 [1897]);

An Almanac of Twelve Sports, by Nicholson and Rudyard Kipling (London: Heinemann, 1898 [1897]; New York: Russell, 1898 [1897]);

London Types, by Nicholson and William Ernest Henley (London: Heinemann, 1898; New York: Russell, 1898);

Twelve Portraits (London: Heinemann, 1899; New York: Russell, 1899);

The Square Book of Animals, by Nicholson and Arthur Waugh (London: Heinemann, 1900 [1899]; New York: Russell, 1900);

Characters of Romance (London: Heinemann, 1900; New York: Russell, 1900);

Twelve Portraits, second series (London: Heinemann, 1902; New York: Russell, 1903);

Oxford (Oxford: Stafford Gallery, 1905);

Clever Bill (London: Heinemann, 1926; Garden City, N.Y.: Doubleday, Page, 1926);

The Pirate Twins (London: Faber & Faber, 1929; New York: Coward-McCann, 1929);

The Book of Blokes (London: Faber & Faber, 1929).

BOOKS ILLUSTRATED: Edwin Pugh, *Tony Drum, a Cockney Boy* (London: Heinemann, 1898; New York: Holt, 1898);

Margery Williams Bianco, *The Velveteen Rabbit: or, How Toys Become Real* (London: Heinemann, 1922; New York: Doran, [1922]);

William Henry Davies, *The Hour of Magic and Other Poems* (London: Cape, 1922; New York & London: Harper, 1922);

John Gay, *Polly* (London: Heinemann, 1923; New York: Doubleday, 1923);

Davies, *True Travellers: A Tramps Opera in Three Acts* (London: Cape, 1923);

Davies, *Moss and Feather* (London: Faber & Gwyner, 1928);

Siegfried Sassoon, *Memoirs of a Fox-hunting Man* (London: Faber & Faber, 1929; New York: Coward-McCann, 1929).

When England knighted William Nicholson in 1936, it was in recognition of his international prominence as a painter of still lifes, lucid and sedate landscapes, and portraits, including such English luminaries as Max Beerbohm, Ellen Terry, and J. M. Barrie. While Nicholson's stature as a painter has not diminished since his death in 1949, his original accomplishments in the fields of graphic art, stage design, and book illustration have enjoyed greater critical attention, as has his work in children's literature. The artist's first books for children, appearing from 1897 to 1899, were boldly conceived graphic works for which Nicholson employed the technique of wood engraving as a medium of direct artistic expression rather than a means of transferring line drawings onto a page. Nicholson's *An Alphabet* (1898) and *The Square Book of Animals* (1900), sold both to collectors of art and to children, anticipated the modern elevation of children's book illustration to the level of fine art. Nicholson's other children's books include *Clever Bill* (1926) and *The Pirate Twins* (1929), which he both wrote and illustrated. In a 1977 article in *Horn Book* Selma G. Lanes notes Nicholson's "mesmerizing synchronization between spare text and uncluttered drawings" in *Clever Bill.* The literary historian Marcus Couch places both works in "the front rank among picture-books of the century." In the field of children's literature Nicholson is most often remembered as the illustrator of Margery Williams Bianco's *The Velveteen Rabbit: or, How Toys Become Real* (1922), a mainstay of the nursery library.

Born in Newark-on-Trent in 1872 – the same year as Beerbohm, Aubrey Beardsley, and Edward Gordon Craig – William Newzam Prior Nicholson was the youngest of the three children of William Newzam Nicholson, an engineer, and his second wife, Ann Elizabeth Prior. As a boy, Nicholson found learning to read difficult and did so only by puzzling over captions to illustrations. His early favorites were works of Alexandre Dumas père and Sir Walter Scott and the picture books of Randolph Caldecott, whose

William Nicholson, circa 1898. His son Ben and his partner,
James Pryde, are looking through the window.

illustrations he continued to admire throughout his life.

Like his father Nicholson attended the Magnus Grammar School. Before he was twelve, Nicholson discovered a penchant for caricature and sharpened his skill upon the Magnus staff, moving his father to comment that his son had an "overdeveloped" sense of humor. Turning twelve, Nicholson was permitted to take weekly drawing lessons from the school's drawing master, William H. Cubley, who, believing that drawing was a preliminary to painting, also instructed him in traditional methods of oil painting. Nicholson continued with Cubley for about four years and then entered a school of art founded at Bushey by Herbert Von Herkomer, a successful exponent of High Victorian art, including sentimental narrative paintings and scenic landscapes. He proved a harsh pedant with a jealous disdain for modern art – a disdain Nicholson could not help but provoke. In 1889 Nicholson and Von Herkomer parted ways after

the teacher raged at his young student over what he imagined "a piece of Whistlerian impertinence." In his abbreviated sojourn at Bushey, Nicholson acquired the nickname "The Kid," which, to his occasional displeasure, would stick to him for the rest of his life. He also met Mabel Pryde, who won Nicholson's admiration by driving a flock of geese into life class one day. Her strong sense of the ridiculous excited Nicholson's sense of humor, and they became friends. Mabel's brother, Jimmy Pryde, had already earned a reputation as a painter working in the pastel style of James McNeill Whistler. He also possessed an irresistible self-confidence and an ability to convince anybody of anything. His occasional visits to Bushey certainly hastened Nicholson's decision to reject Von Herkomer's complacent provincialism, and it was also due to Jimmy Pryde's influence that Nicholson enrolled in the Académie Julian in Paris.

The academy was a suite of studios crowded with boisterous pupils, the walls caked with palette

Cover for Nicholson's first children's book

scrapings gilded with crude caricatures; it was hot, airless, and unrelentingly noisy. As happy as Nicholson was with the greater artistic freedoms of his new school, his strong sense of decorum caused him to be appalled by its unruliness and the absence of instruction. Whenever he could, he fled into the boulevards of Paris where he came into contact with modern paintings being exhibited at the Exposition Universelle by artists such as Henri de Toulouse-Lautrec and Edouard Manet.

After a scant half year in Paris, Nicholson left Julian's and returned to his parents' house in Newark, where a small studio was constructed for him in the garden. His feelings for Mabel Pryde had deepened during their separation. After a brief engagement they married in April 1893. Upon returning from their honeymoon, the couple moved to Denham, Buckinghamshire, and occupied a former public house, reputedly haunted, called Eight Bells. In 1894 their first child, Ben, was born.

That same year Craig, an actor, son of actress Dame Ellen Terry, and a friend of Jimmy Pryde, requested a decorative poster for a production of *Hamlet* in which he was appearing. Pryde and Nicholson designed a bold black silhouette on brown paper, which met with such a favorable reception from the cast that an edition was printed for collectors. The artists con-

jectured that making posters might buy them time to paint, and, taking on the name "J. & W. Beggarstaff," Pryde and Nicholson embarked upon the career of poster artists.

In their use of clear outline and unbroken areas of flat color, Pryde and Nicholson revealed a knowledge of Toulouse-Lautrec and French poster art gained during their days at Julian's. The Beggarstaffs produced a series of theatrical posters (including a design for a production of *Cinderella*) and speculative advertisements for such wares as candles, pianos, and washing blue. The Beggarstaff posters charmed cultured English society and brought Nicholson some professional success. Unfortunately the advertising managers — the audience the young artists had set out to impress — found their work beyond the grasp of the average person and therefore unsuccessful as advertising.

Alongside his work as W. Beggarstaff in his early twenties, Nicholson developed an interest in wood engraving. A burst of enthusiasm for the old book arts had inspired English artists such as Charles Ricketts, Sturge Moore, and Walter Crane to explore line engravings in the Gothic style of sixteenth-century Venice. The elder Joseph Crawhall, a Northumbrian artist, had discovered another source of inspiration nearer to

Two of Nicholson's illustrations for An Alphabet. *The Beggar is a caricature of James Pryde, and the beggar's staff is a visual pun on their joint pseudonym, Beggarstaff.*

hand in the English chapbook cuts of the late eighteenth and early nineteenth centuries. Crawhall opposed the sinuous black-line drawings of the Vale group — artists and craftsmen associated with the Vale Press, one of the foremost presses of the Arts and Crafts movement — with simple, boldly contrasting masses of black and white. Crawhall's work, and perhaps the deceptively simple woodcuts of the Swiss artist Felix Valloton, inspired Nicholson to begin engraving on wood himself. Sometime after 1895 he began a series of engravings of farmyard and domesticated animals, probably to amuse Ben, and these eventually were gathered into Nicholson's second children's book, *The Square Book of Animals.*

The first, *An Alphabet,* appeared in 1897 (with a copyright date of 1898), under the imprint of William Heinemann. Heinemann had been encouraged to speak to Nicholson by Whistler after the latter had seen a wood engraving of his exhibited at the Fine Art Society. Nicholson's relationship with Heinemann was to prove fruitful for both men and endured for over a quarter of a century. *An Alphabet* was commissioned as a pictorial book, with no letterpress, the only text being that which the artist carved upon the block. It alludes

not only to a long tradition of children's alphabet books but also to the woodcut and wood-engraved illustrations used in primers and chapbooks of the past. In order to give himself time to prepare for the Christmas market, Heinemann allowed Nicholson only four months to complete his work. Two editions were planned: for collectors, a limited edition pulled from Nicholson's engravings, which the artist would color at sixpence per impression; and, for children, a lithographically produced edition. Nicholson received five pounds for each woodblock and 10 percent of the first edition of five thousand copies at five shillings each, in addition to the pay he received for his coloring.

Like Crawhall's *Old Aunt Elspa's ABC* (1884), Nicholson's *Alphabet* slightly distorted the form by conflating archaic prototypes, such as "O for Ostler," "R for Robber," and "P for Publican," with more contemporary models, such as "W for Waitress" and "J for Jockey." *An Alphabet* also stepped outside the tradition by introducing contemporary figures into the work, placing them within the various emblematical guises as though they were actors modeling their roles for an illustrated theater program. Identifying the faces was certainly not intended for children. The "Dandy," for example, caricatures Herbert Beerbohm-Tree, half brother of Nicholson's friend Max, and the "Keeper" was one of Nicholson's patrons, George Carpenter. A cut created for the "Executioner," satirizing a contemporary art critic, was excluded by Heinemann from the lithographic edition as being too gory for children.

The "Beggar" caricatures Pryde, who, at this time, had come to visit, squeezing himself into the Nicholsons' small basement flat in Avonmore Gardens, West Kensington, and Nicholson modestly portrayed himself in "A was an Artist" as a mere street artist. His "H for Huntsman" is an unabashed homage to Caldecott, whose own inspiration had been drawn from early English cultural modes, and "T for Trumpeter" acknowledges Nicholson's fascination with Diego Rodríguez de Silva Velázquez, the seventeenth-century Spanish artist.

Nicholson's *Alphabet* engravings surpass chapbook cuts as well as Crawhall's revivals in their delicate coloring and shading – leading some critics to compare his work to Japanese woodcuts. Nicholson applied broad washes of subdued colors, which served to mellow the contrast between white paper and his black shapes. On certain designs he employed a brush stroke of primary color for spirit. Nicholson's use of shadow both strengthens the composition of these designs and insinuates information about the character portrayed. In "U for Urchin" the boy's passive, indifferent posture is betrayed by his menacing, crouching shadow. The shadows pressing upon "V is for Villain" threaten to erase the character's physical features, his lack of moral distinction made manifest. Shadows become amusing puzzles as well. In "O for Ostler" (innkeeper) they challenge the eye to guess what are objects draped in shadow and what are empty shapes merely conjured by shadows. His Villain shadows, when looked at sideways, become a ferretlike mask. Subtle visual games recur throughout Nicholson's children's books, constantly surprising the eye, tempting the reader beneath the pleasant surface of his creations. He once wrote that "the incongruity of life is far more abundant than the circumstantial evidence of it." In his multilayered designs, in *Alphabet* as well as in later works, Nicholson hints at the incongruities buried in circumstance.

Despite his wife's illness, which caused the upkeep of the flat and the care of baby Ben to fall squarely on Nicholson, the work was completed well before the deadline. The reviews were good. *Athenaeum* found the work to be spirited and original. The *Magazine of Art* observed: "there is vastly more than the charm of the old chap-books in *An Alphabet*." While *Athenaeum* deemed the images of Robber,

Ostler, and Idiot unacceptable for children, the *Magazine of Art* proposed that many of the designs would better appeal to the understanding of children than other contemporary picture books aimed at adult sensibilities. The *Art Journal* compared Nicholson's work with that of Velázquez and Caldecott.

Another son, Anthony, was born to the Nicholsons in 1897. Also that year Heinemann commissioned the artist to do another series of engravings, this time on the subject of athletics, published in December under the title *An Almanac of Twelve Sports*. Each of twelve illustrations depicts a different seasonal sport. Critics proved cordial to *An Almanac*, although some questioned the relevance of the verse supplied by Rudyard Kipling – solicited by Heinemann in hopes of boosting sales. Although copies of the popular edition served as Christmas gifts for children, there is nothing about *An Almanac* to challenge the prevailing judgment that it is primarily aimed at an adult audience.

Heinemann followed *An Alphabet* and *An Almanac* with a third proposal, a book to exploit a wave of national affection for the everyday characters of London. The terms of payment for *London Types* (1898) were more advantageous to Nicholson due to a surge in his popularity following a series of portraits he had published in the *New Review*. Among these the most sensational was an engraving of Queen Victoria based upon a photograph in the *Illustrated London News*. Nicholson's controversial illustration portrayed a humble old lady out on a walk with her pet dog. Although this image did not chime with the emblematic regent whom artists had used for so long to glorify the crown, it struck a responsive chord with the public, remaining for many years the most widely known of Nicholson's portraits. That he depicted it twenty-eight years later within an illustration in *Clever Bill* (1926) suggests the artist's humorous awareness of its persistence in the public mind.

In 1899, the same year Mabel gave birth to their third child, Nancy, Nicholson published *The Square Book of Animals*. He had been at work on the illustrations for about five years, and, surrounded by the bucolic beauties of Chaucer's House, Woodstock, the home once inhabited by the artist's maternal grandparents, and companioned by a growing family, the artist brought the second of his children's books to completion.

The Square Book contains twelve block prints, with appropriate verses by Arthur Waugh. As in *An Alphabet*, the artist uses low, flat tones with an occasional dash of bright pigment. More than twenty years later, in *Clever Bill* and, to a lesser extent, *The Velveteen Rabbit*, Nicholson would play upon the as-

Nicholson's woodblock illustrations for three months in An Almanac of
Twelve Sports, *with text by Rudyard Kipling:* Golf *(October);*
Boxing *(November); and* Cricket *(June)*

sociations of primary color and childhood to portray the persona of the book's artist as a child. Decorative patterned backgrounds, such as his ripple effect in "Lucky Duck," the black and gold grid structure in the "Cock O' The North," and the dreamy reflections of "The Beautiful Swan," once again prompted talk of Nicholson's debt to Japanese art, a topic of continuing debate.

In 1900 Nicholson set aside engraving as his principal medium of expression, partly in reaction to his need for a more promising source of income, and began to devote more of his time to painting. *Characters of Romance* (1900) marks the artist's first exploration of a medium other than wood engraving for his book illustration – in this case, colored drawings. Nicholson received twenty-one pounds for each design and 10 percent on the published price of all copies sold. The selection of characters was completely Nicholson's, but, as well as pleasing himself, he made choices with the intention of pleasing W. E. Henley, the widely admired editor of the *New Review*. Henley had dared to publish Nicholson's controversial Queen Victoria – after the more timid Heinemann had refused – and secured celebrity for the artist. *Characters of Romance* failed to engage as wide an audience as Nicholson's engravings had done. But Walter de la Mare wrote the artist in 1936 to tell him that during a recent stretch of illness he had set up *Characters* in a place where he could view it from his bed and it had brought him a great deal of pleasure. He apologized to Nicholson for coming to it so late after publication. Nicholson, an admirer of de la Mare's poetry, was touched.

In 1904, the year another son, Christopher, was born, the illustrator's affinity for children's literature stimulated Barrie to invite him to design the costumes for the premiere of *Peter Pan* at the Duke of York Theatre. Nicholson was pleased to design both the costumes and the stage sets, but he disappointed Barrie, who hoped that he would design a poster showing "Esquimaux boys looking thro' legs at wolves." (A Peter Pan poster was eventually designed by Nicholson's son Ben, then eleven years old.) Before the play opened, Nicholson painted Barrie's portrait in oils, and about a year later he published a colored drawing he had based upon it in the *Outlook* (27 May 1905).

By 1910 Nicholson had become a national celebrity with a flair for entertaining society. He and Mabel were habitués of the theater, and stories circulated of his raining tears over the edge of his box and upon the kettle drum during a performance that much moved him and his stretching out on the floor to sleep during performances that did not. He ap-

peared in the *Tatler*. He was known to dabble at mysticism. He decorated his home in extraordinary taste, with blue ceilings, black mirrors, and maps on the walls, which the painter Paul Nash thought ahead of his time. His exhibitionistic clothing became the source of popular amusement. His suspenders, which he described as "ostler's braces," were bright orange and, according to a contemporary, caused men to "wince" when he removed his coat. He frequently sported luxurious silk dressing gowns. When he painted, he routinely donned immaculate white ducks, a spotted shirt, black socks, and shiny patent-leather shoes – indeed, the black socks were a permanent article of apparel, whether he was painting or dancing or playing tennis.

Unfortunately Nicholson's earnings were unable to keep pace with his extravagant expenses despite an increase in portrait requests. The playwright Edward Knoblock came to the artist's rescue with a commission to decorate his suite in the Palais Royal. With Knoblock's timely invitation came the opportunity to attend one of the quintessentially Parisian spectacles, the great masked balls at the opera. A well-regarded artist at the height of his powers, possessed of a whimsical, boyish charm and a love for Paris he had gained during his days at Julian's, Nicholson could not help but make an unforgettable impression upon the French.

Nicholson's charm extended to children and generally tended toward playfulness. During World War I a commission was obtained for him by the architect Edward Luytens to paint a full-length, life-size portrait of the Indian viceroy, Baron Charles Hardinge – an assignment Nicholson afterward remembered as the most difficult he ever faced. Visited daily by the viceroy's daughters, Nicholson entertained them by giving them paintbrushes to doodle about at the foot of the canvas, which, purportedly, the viceroy considered an act of lèse-majesté. Nicholson was unconcerned, and the children were happy.

Nicholson was forty-two when Britain declared war on Germany. Still young enough to be admitted into the armed forces, he chose not to enlist. He drilled for a time with the Artist's Rifles but deserted when he learned that he would have to support the cost of a uniform himself. Instead Nicholson placed his art at the service of wartime fund-raising efforts by designing posters and theater programs in aid of charitable organizations such as the Red Cross.

With two mature sons Nicholson could reasonably expect that the war would intrude further into his life. Yet its first incursion came from an unexpected direction. In January 1917 Nancy married a soldier she had met through her brother Ben. De-

Nicholson's woodblock illustration for the cover of his 1898 book with text by W. E. Henley

spite his youth Capt. Robert Graves impressed Nicholson with his intellectual vigor and sense of humor, and the artist felt they had much in common. Years later, writing about father and husband, Nancy wryly concurred: "I never know two men who cried so much." Several successful collaborations materialized between Nicholson and his son-in-law, and over the next six years each seems to have derived influence from the other. Beginning in 1918, they coedited an art and literary journal, the *Owl,* with Graves soliciting the poems and stories from among his literary acquaintances and Nicholson taking charge of the art. In advance of publication Graves had announced that the *Owl* was to show contemporary work exclusively, but the first issue, oddly enough, included drawings by Crawhall and Caldecott. While works by notable contemporaries Thomas Hardy, John Masefield, Beerbohm, and Siegfried Sassoon, as well as Graves and Nicholson, appeared in the *Owl,* the editors evidently thought highly enough of Caldecott's art to make an exception of him again in the third and final issue, published in 1923. This, with its title adjusted to the *Winter Owl,* issued two previously un-

published drawings the great Victorian illustrator had omitted from his picture book, *The Queen of Hearts* (1881).

For one of his several unfinished children's stories, "Fowler in Love," Nicholson used a prose version of Graves's poem "Love Without Hope" for an illustration captioned "The Birdcatcher and the Lady." Another of Nicholson's unfinished children's books, "The Tale of Paul and Mary Bright," figures as an interesting antecedent to Graves's *Two Wise Children,* the story of Avis Deeds and Bill Brain. In the latter Avis and Bill each possess magical abilities complementary to the other's: Avis can perform wondrous physical feats, such as riding on the back of an enraged bull or flying into the air, merely by willing it; Bill can look into the future. In the Nicholson poem Paul and Mary Bright are exact opposites in style and ability: "His cat called Scratch her dog called Bite / He used his charm She used her might / Paul slept by day his wife by night." As with the differing abilities of Avis and Bill, the differences between the Brights tend to play upon gender stereotypes. Another unconventional similarity is that in both accounts, the girl or woman possesses superior physical coordination or force. Nicholson also illustrated covers for a handful of Graves's books, including *Mock Beggar Hall* (1924), *Feather Bed* (1923), and *Whipperginny* (1923). A caricature he drew of his son-in-law and William H. Davies, the tramp-poet, appeared in *Form* (November–December 1921).

Nicholson remarked that in 1918 fate started throwing bricks at him. On 13 July Mabel died of Spanish influenza, and on 5 October Anthony died of wounds received in France. As it had for so many bereaved Londoners, the long-awaited Armistice, with its spontaneous celebrations and sweeping outpourings of hope, quickened the healing process for Nicholson. In 1919 he married Edith Stuart-Wortley, a wealthy friend of the family who had been widowed by the war.

The marriage brought financial independence, freeing Nicholson from the treadmill of bread-and-butter portrait painting. During the twenties, in addition to the work he undertook with Graves, he produced landscape paintings rich in their reflection of the English Downs around Rottingdean and Sutton-Veny, where he and Edith lived, and more children's books. In 1922 he agreed to illustrate Bianco's *The Velveteen Rabbit,* a story the author based upon imaginary interactions among toys she remembered from her childhood.

The Velveteen Rabbit connects two loosely parallel stories: the first is a psychologically perceptive tale of how a toy rabbit is made real by the love of the boy who owns him; the second shows the velveteen toy transformed into a natural rabbit through the magical intervention of a fairy. Nicholson's seven watercolor illustrations emphasize the themes of growth and maturation, occasionally blurring the story's narrative elements. His captions, including "Christmas Morning," "Spring Time," and "Summer Days," suggest a seasonal progression analogous to the rabbit's metamorphosis from the artificial to the organic. Similarly, depictions of sources of light advance from night-lights to candles to sunlight, tracing a path from the manmade to the natural, and this is accompanied by a progressive lessening of shadow, which is offered, and then shed, as an ambivalent symbol of cocoonlike containment. In the earlier illustrations, connotative of an infantile stage of being, shadows flatten perspective, lending intimacy and looming immediacy to the animate objects which are thrust outward by the near two-dimensionality of the shallowed depth, in the manner of caricatures. In the latter illustrations

shadows cast in natural light weight the representational credibility of the drawing and deepen perspective. Just as the rabbit matures through successive developmental stages of self-refinement, point of view becomes increasingly refined, maturing from the murky and unreal still lifes of "Christmas Morning" and (slightly less so) "The Skin Horse Tells His Story" to the simple portrait "Spring Time," in which childlike brushstrokes further encourage an identification between illustrator and reader, to the playful and subdued eroticism of "The Fairy Flower." The progression finally completes itself in the sophisticated and complex landscape "At Last! At Last!"

Nicholson's highly choreographed variations overcome the problematical passivity of the author's rabbit by evoking a dynamic reciprocity between the developing self and the world, asserting an active engagement. The composition of "At Last! At Last!" excites lively attention. The eye must jump clockwise around the page and burrow into conflations of tone to discern the multitude of natural rabbits darting about their newly "naturalized" peer. At the center the transformed rabbit vertically leaps into the air, parodying his former immobility, just as the shadow beneath him punctuates his voyage from the nursery (and the cloistered realm of seeming) to the airy and more inspiriting realm of being.

Two years prior to the publication of *The Velveteen Rabbit,* Edith had given birth to a daughter, Liza, and several grandchildren were also born during this period, setting a stage of domestic felicity for Nicholson. Liza would toddle into his bed in the morning or into his studio, and he would scribble caricatures for her. His "blokes," as he called them, were eventually published by Faber and Faber as *The Book of Blokes* (1929). In 1927 he designed a poster entitled "Food and Fruits of Empire" (measuring 44 by 230 inches) for the Empire Marketing Board, whose seven puttylike children, eating breakfast surrounded by an Edenic plenitude of Empire produce, were modeled upon his grandchildren.

Heinemann published the fourth of Nicholson's children's books in 1926. *Clever Bill* consists of twenty-two full-page color drawings and a text, written by Nicholson, of 150 words. Like *The Velveteen Rabbit,* the hero of *Clever Bill* is a toy belonging to a child. When Mary accepts an invitation to visit her aunt, she confronts the new task of packing an overnight bag. Although rearranging her suitcase several times in an effort to include everything, she manages to neglect her toy soldier, Bill Davis. Bill,

One of Nicholson's woodcuts for The Square Book of Animals

after a good, long cry, races down the stairs and out into the world after her, cleverly finding his way to Dover in time to meet Mary's train. The brief, colloquial text is a model of concision. Each illustration is boxed, like those in *The Velveteen Rabbit,* or enclosed within a boxed oval frame. Serried black horizontal lines shade in the empty corners, endowing the latter illustrations with a look comparable to enlarged eighteenth-century chapbook cuts.

Clever Bill succeeds for precisely the same reasons Sir Kenneth Clark found Nicholson's paintings successful. They express a "humorous sympathy" for his subjects and a "half ironical reticence." Of Nicholson's first thirteen drawings, eight are still lifes of Mary's clothes and toys. One includes a toy horse whose square torso and tinting recall the Skin Horse of *The Velveteen Rabbit.* Nicholson substitutes a bobbin for one of the wheels on the horse's platform, a lovely flourish reminiscent of Cruikshank's peg-leg table in *Billy Culmer & The Grave* (1826). Unhampered by a text of any density, Nicholson's assembled combinations achieve an elliptical coherence of their own, attempting to locate a logical frame of reference within the reader's imagination.

The reader looks over Mary's shoulder as Clever Bill is crammed and then folded into Mary's case and, finally, unpacked and allowed to fall out of sight. That Mary does not wish to neglect Bill and removes him because she is displeased that she is mauling him must be construed from the pictures, just as it may be construed that the task of packing a suitcase is new and difficult for her.

Nicholson employs three landscape drawings to depict the toy soldier's racing down the road, over the hills, and toward the sea in an effort to catch up with Mary's train. Throughout *Clever Bill,* Nicholson tended to limit himself to the colors of a child's crayon set, suggesting that the story occurs within the medium of a book and that it has been made by a child. The text, printed in an imitative childlike cursive hand, lends the illusion of additional verisimilitude, as does the occasional distortion of perspective. He demonstrates the artifactuality of the book dramatically in an early drawing where his caption points the reader to the legible contents of a trompe l'oeil, upside-down letter, thereby expanding the child's awareness of the book that must, for a moment, be turned upside

A poster advertising Nicholson's fourth book for children

down in order to follow the story. Graves makes use of a similar trope in his *The Big Green Book* (1962), whose polysemous title refers to a book in the story as well as the book in hand. In each case the author expands the child's awareness of the possibilities for interacting with the book.

Nicholson's second landscape is a subtler demonstration in which he uses systematic linear perspective to entice the reader into the landscape's "depths." Clever Bill, however, practically bursting into the illustration from the left margin (the gutter of the book), ignores the delectably artificed landscape. By positioning Bill directly in the foreground of the illustration, facing straight ahead, Nicholson makes him seem to be darting across the page, as if his real goal were the next page and the story's subsequent happy conclusion. Even though he has appeared to fly off in the wrong direction and, as delineated unambiguously in the final landscape, fallen far behind the disappearing train, Clever Bill

somehow shows up at the station, in the penultimate drawing, saluting just as the train arrives. The reader can hardly ask how he had done it, although it is a virtue of the book's engaging irony that creates this curiosity. Traveling the margins of the endpapers is the train, whose caboose scoots along just ahead of its engine, a schematic metonym for the plot: lighting out from the center of the page, Clever Bill seems to be running toward the departing tail of the caboose, betraying his simplicity and childlike inexperience of the physical world. However, the back of the caboose also happens to be at a point just far enough ahead of the front of the oncoming train to encourage the belief that Clever Bill has chosen exactly the right path withal.

The final illustration concludes the book with an ingenious puzzle. Mary seems to be playing the role of courtly lady as she accepts a bouquet from Bill, who gallantly bows his head to her. The caption "Clever Bill" appears to render Mary's exclamation of delight. Yet, another reading is possible: Clever Bill may be accepting a bouquet from Mary for his steadfastness and yeomanlike exertions, and his bow may be intended to express deference or to conceal embarrassment. "Clever Bill" might be intended as Mary's exclamation of admiration or affection. By spreading the plenitude of Mary's playthings before her, Nicholson seems to be gently suggesting that the nature of Mary's relation to Clever Bill intended by the illustration can be determined, along with the exact value of *Clever Bill*, the book, within the reaches of one's own imagination. Just as in his earlier illustration he had subverted the conventional norm by licensing young readers to turn their picture book upside down, the artist's concluding illustration flouts convention by its cheerful inconclusiveness.

Although certainly the artist and his relationships with both of the book's dedicatees – his daughter Liza (then called Penny) and granddaughter, Jenny – provided material for elements of *Clever Bill*, the illustration of the abandoned toy crying into a pool of his tears may have been intended as gentle self-mockery. But Clever Bill may have been named after Nicholson's friend William Henry Davies, for whose books, including *The Hour of Magic and Other Poems* (1922) and *True Travellers: A Tramps Opera in Three Acts* (1923), Nicholson had supplied illustrations. The poet was generally referred to as Bill, and, in writing, Nicholson addressed him as Davis rather than Davies. Several characteristics of Clever Bill can be traced to Davies, such as the latter's train-chasing aptitude, sharpened during his twenty years of tramping around England and America. The bobbin replacement for one of the horse's wheels may have been privately intended to charm the poet, who suffered embarrassment over his wooden leg, the result of a train accident. Indeed, Clever Bill's fleetness, despite the handicap of his two stiff wooden legs, may have conveyed a similarly private homage as well.

As a result of the popularity of *Clever Bill*, Nicholson and Faber discussed a successor, "Lucky Susan," which would have been about Clever Bill and Mary's doll. Unfortunately, Faber surmised that the public would accept only one new children's book from Nicholson and preferred the chances of another of Nicholson's ideas. In *The Pirate Twins* (1929), the titular pair are discovered by Mary inside a seashell. Mary promptly adopts them, but despite her affectionate care one day the twins run away. They leave a note that says they have gone forever, adding, "don't worry, back soon." And, true to their word, after various ad-

ventures they return. Like *Clever Bill*, the drawings fuel the story, and the text comprises a mere hundred or so words. Landscapes predominate over still lifes, and once again the endpapers, in their whimsical mimicry of Sandro Botticelli's *Birth of Venus*, image the book's maritime associations.

An American publisher for *The Pirate Twins* proved difficult to obtain, but Nicholson, whose income was ever falling behind his expenses, eventually secured Coward-McCann. Relief turned to disgust, however, when he beheld the low quality of the firm's color printing. In his own copy of *The Pirate Twins*, he scribbled a note describing the plates as "poisonous," with the added reminder "don't give out."

In addition to "Lucky Susan," "Fowler in Love," and "The Tale of Paul and Mary Bright," the latter half of the 1920s saw Nicholson begin other projects for children. Devised in collaboration with the composer Elizabeth Luytens, "Water Music" was to be made of a waterproof material that could be immersed in a bath. For another proposed work, "Twelve Days of Christmas" — whose choice of a traditional theme reverts to his works of the preceding century – he seems to have completed the full complement of twelve colored drawings, albeit two have yet to be recovered. In 1927 Nicholson collaborated with his daughter Nancy on a story called "Poor Gladys," but he could find no publisher who would accept the work.

That Nicholson initiated no new children's projects in the 1930s reflects no diminished fondness for children's literature or for children. Rather, Nicholson's separation from children's literature echoed his marital separation from Edith and the intimate contact with children that he regarded as an indispensable ingredient of his work in this genre. Explaining his inability to finish his last children's book, "The Tale of Paul and Mary Bright," Nicholson said to biographer Marguerite Steen that to write children's books "you must have children about you." Even though he had photographs taken of himself and Steen to use for drawings of the Brights, he could produce nothing from them.

Steen met Nicholson in 1935 in Málaga, Spain, at the home of Sir Peter Chalmers Mitchell. They became companions soon afterward and remained together until Nicholson's death in 1949, living in London and traveling extensively through Spain, Italy, and France. Steen made a lively and inspiring companion for Nicholson. Like him she was a hard worker and possessed a gifted imagination. Their home, Apple Tree Yard, became a place for painters and friends to congregate, enjoy luncheons that lasted into the evening, and talk about painting. Nicholson's old friend Beerbohm became such a frequent guest that eventually Nicholson made his silk top hat into a paintbrush holder. In this hectic social atmosphere Steen sometimes complained she found it hard to concentrate, but Nicholson, at the eye of the storm and far surer of himself than during his student days at Julian's, continued to paint and draw with unperturbable calm. As always, Nicholson created because it was the primary imperative of his nature to do so and because he needed funds. His knighthood in 1936 and retrospective exhibitions of his work at the Nottingham Museum and Art Gallery (1933), the Beaux-Arts Gallery in London (1933), and the National Gallery (1942) added to his considerable reputation, but new adventures abroad and lavish entertainments at home dissuaded him from resting on his laurels. Geoffrey Taylor, to whom he once expressed the opinion that a man ought to be able to choose his own epitaph, immortalized Nicholson's hapless economics:

Here lies the painter Nicholson, Alas!
  But to posterity his genius sends,
A monument "more durable than brass,"
  Of which he kept but little – having friends.

With much work unfinished, Nicholson died at Blewbury, Berkshire, on 16 May 1949.

His children's books have made an ineradicable contribution to the development of children's book illustration in the twentieth century. His earliest works, utilizing wood engraving, synthesize the raw energy of English chapbook cuts and the delicacy of Japanese woodcuts, providing children and adults alike with original works of graphic art within a traditionally informed context. As much as they look backward upon a century of engraved children's book illustrations, they look ahead to the emergence of the modern children's book artist. In his illustrations for *The Velveteen Rabbit, Clever Bill,* and *The Pirate Twins,* Nicholson creates opportunities for the reader to look beneath the text and become a collaborator in the creation of the story. Not the least aspect of their charm lies in the fact that they are among the century's most beautiful picture books.

Biography:

Marguerite Steen, *William Nicholson* (London: Collins, 1943).

References:

Colin Campbell, *William Nicholson: The Graphic Work* (London: Barrie & Jenkins, 1992);

Edward Craig, *William Nicholson's 'An Alphabet': An Introduction to the Reprint from the Original Woodblocks* (Andoversford, U.K.: Whittington, 1978);

Duncan Robinson, *William Nicholson: Paintings, Drawings and Prints* (London: Art Council of Great Britain, 1980);

William Nicholson (London: Benn, 1923).

Papers:

Many of the original illustrations for William Nicholson's children's books are in private collections. Woodblocks for *An Alphabet* and *An Almanac of Twelve Sports* are owned by William Heinemann, a sketchbook belongs to Stanford University, and six preparatory drawings for *The Square Book of Animals* are in the Australian National Gallery, Canberra.

Beatrix Potter

(28 July 1866 – 22 December 1943)

Ruth K. MacDonald

BOOKS: *The Tale of Peter Rabbit* (London: Strangeways, 1901; London & New York: Warne, 1902);

The Tailor of Gloucester (London: Strangeways, 1902; London & New York: Warne, 1903);

The Tale of Squirrel Nutkin (London & New York: Warne, 1903);

The Tale of Benjamin Bunny (London & New York: Warne, 1904);

The Tale of Two Bad Mice (London & New York: Warne, 1904);

The Tale of Mrs. Tiggy-Winkle (London & New York: Warne, 1905);

The Pie and the Patty-Pan (London & New York: Warne, 1905);

The Story of a Fierce Bad Rabbit (London & New York: Warne, 1906);

The Story of Miss Moppet (London & New York: Warne, 1906);

The Tale of Mr. Jeremy Fisher (London & New York: Warne, 1906);

The Tale of Tom Kitten (London & New York: Warne, 1907);

The Tale of Jemima Puddle-Duck (London & New York: Warne, 1908);

The Roly-Poly Pudding (London & New York: Warne, 1908); republished as *The Tale of Samuel Whiskers* (London & New York: Warne, 1926);

The Tale of the Flopsy Bunnies (London & New York: Warne, 1909);

Ginger and Pickles (London & New York: Warne, 1909);

The Tale of Mrs. Tittlemouse (London & New York: Warne, 1910);

The Tale of Timmy Tiptoes (London & New York: Warne, 1911);

Peter Rabbit's Painting Book (London & New York: Warne, 1911);

The Tale of Mr. Tod (London & New York: Warne, 1912);

The Tale of Pigling Bland (London & New York: Warne, 1913);

Appley Dapply's Nursery Rhymes (London & New York: Warne, 1917);

Beatrix Potter with her husband, William Heelis, on their wedding day

Tom Kitten's Painting Book (London & New York: Warne, 1917);

The Tale of Johnny Town-Mouse (London & New York: Warne, 1918);

Cecily Parsley's Nursery Rhymes (London & New York: Warne, 1922);

Jemima Puddle-Duck's Painting Book (London & New York: Warne, 1925);

Peter Rabbit's Almanac for 1929 (London & New York: Warne, 1928);

The Fairy Caravan (Philadelphia: McKay, 1929; Ambleside, U.K.: Middleton, 1929);

The Tale of Little Pig Robinson (London & New York: Warne, 1930);

Sister Anne (Philadelphia: McKay, 1932);

Wag-by-Wall (Boston: Horn Book, 1944);

The Tale of the Faithful Dove (London & New York: Warne, 1955);

The Journal of Beatrix Potter from 1881 to 1897, edited by Leslie Linder (London & New York: Warne, 1966);

The Tailor of Gloucester: From the Original Manuscript (London & New York: Warne, 1969);

The Sly Old Cat (London & New York: Warne, 1971);

The Art of Beatrix Potter, edited by Leslie and Enid Linder (London & New York: Warne, 1955; revised edition, 1972);

The Tale of Tuppenny (London & New York: Warne, 1973).

Beatrix Potter is best known for her extraordinary accomplishment in children's literature: the twenty-three illustrated storybooks comprising the Peter Rabbit series. Beginning with *The Tale of Peter Rabbit* (1901) and continuing for three decades, she managed regular output of small storybooks, illustrated with her own subtly detailed watercolors, featuring small animals found in the woodlands, open fields, and sometimes in close proximity to human beings. The care with which she portrayed animals, capturing the nuances of their coloring and their habitats, and the precision with which she told their stories, with vocabularies of more complexity than current easy-to-read picture books, yet clearly defined by context, attest to the focused attention of her pen and paintbrush. Potter's love of things small, as well as her willingness to portray the brutal, sometimes violent, events in the lives of animals, makes her books perennial favorites. Because of their charming miniaturization and her portrayal of rural English life, they have become heirlooms of the nursery, antique yet still vibrant for young readers.

Potter was born into an upper-middle-class family in London on 28 July 1866. Her parents were both members of the nouveau riche, having inherited a fortune earned by their immediate forebears. Thus, though they were not aristocrats with a tradition of leisure and service, they had the means to live as they chose, without a heritage of past family deportment. Neither Rupert nor Helen Potter worked for a living, and they had full-time child care and ample household help to deal with their large home. As a young girl Potter spent most of her time on the third floor of their Kensington home, cared for by nannies and governesses, with her parents rarely troubling themselves about her. She took her meals separately and seldom saw her parents except for a short visit in the evening. Her pets, small animals that were sometimes hardly tame (frogs, mice, rats – never larger than cats and thus appropriate for urban, third-floor life) were sometimes her only companions, though she was seldom alone – a nanny was always posted to keep watch. Her parents led lives of stultifying regularity, where the exuberance and outbursts of childhood could hardly be tolerated. Given her parents' disinterest, it is surprising that Potter was not allowed to attend school outside the house; but, with no family tradition of school attendance for her to follow, her parents simply hired teachers. A younger brother, Walter Bertram, born when Potter was five, was, however, sent off to boarding school at the appropriate age.

In her own way young Potter sought to deal with the boredom and isolation that might have threatened the mental state of a less resilient child. She took to writing and sketching as a means of occupying herself, as a form of mental purpose and discipline, though her parents hardly encouraged her. Her extensive journal, begun in 1881 and continued for over a decade, was written in code and in a hand so small as to be virtually impenetrable. Perhaps the code not only served to prevent prying eyes from understanding but also served Potter as a mental exercise. Her parents were parsimonious about art materials and lessons, using them as a way of punishing and rewarding a daughter who, by today's standards, would hardly be considered wayward. Their requirement of utter subordination of her will sometimes meant denial of her most favored activities.

Potter's sole excursions during her childhood were to the newly built museums in Kensington, and during the lengthy Easter and summer vacations her family spent four months of the year in the Lake District in England. There Potter closely observed the animals that she so lovingly and faithfully drew and about which she told stories in her adulthood. Apparently allowed to roam unsupervised, Potter and her brother skinned and boiled dead animals until only the skeletons remained to be examined. They also had a brief adventure with an abandoned printing press found in an outbuilding on one of the properties the family rented. One

The Tale of
PETER RABBIT.

By BEATRIX POTTER.

COPYRIGHT.

Title page for Potter's first children's book, which introduced her most beloved character (Osborne Collection of Early Children's Books, Toronto Public Libraries; by permission of Frederick Warne)

Her family took particular interest in contemporary artists of their time and established a personal acquaintance with James Whistler. Original Caldecott works hung in the nursery, and the family visited art shows, where the teenage Potter could overhear others' criticisms of the artists' works. This isolation from normal social interaction led her to concentrate her attention on sketching pets while in London and sketching anything and everything when she was on holiday. Potter showed the professionalism with which she took her art studies by her use of signatures: some works were preliminary, others more professional and finished, and she designated the latter as such with a discreet signature. But her parents sometimes curtailed even her interest in art. She suffered in silence, though not without some ill effects: in her twenties Potter was frequently totally confined and enervated by unexplained, vaporlike illnesses, from which she would recover without much medical intervention.

Potter remained something of a recluse, both by her parents' design and sometimes her own inclination, until she was thirty, when the burden of such dependence became too great. Because they were of a new social set, the family had a limited circle of social acquaintances through which to introduce their daughter to eligible young men who might have been potential husbands; neither parents nor daughter seemed to have taken any initiative on this score. Perhaps by the time she was old enough to marry, either Potter was too intimidated by crowds to want to go to parties, or her parents wanted her to remain at home and dependent. While they succeeded until Potter was in her late forties, her desire to be productive with her life eventually prevailed.

Certainly in her young adulthood Potter was not a prisoner of the third floor; some of her minor excursions had clear results in books produced later in her life. Most notable among these trips were visits to her last governess, Annie Moore, a woman only slightly older than Potter who left her position to marry and start a family. During these visits Potter formed an acquaintance with some of the only children she met in those years, to whom the story of *Peter Rabbit* was originally addressed in a letter. When Noel, the oldest Moore boy, contracted scarlet fever in 1893, Potter wrote him an illustrated letter which became the original outline of the Peter Rabbit story. Clearly the letter was significant to Noel and his brothers and sisters, for he kept the letter until Potter asked for it in 1900, when she made the little story into a book. Apparently she wrote other such story

of Potter's other vacation interests focused on mushrooms, and in her young adulthood she would document different species in their various stages of maturity as objects of scientific study.

In the museums Potter found special pleasure in studying and sketching animal skeletons. Her later understanding of the way animal bodies functioned made her illustrated animals particularly vital – no false movement, no oddly shaped limbs – so that they always remain true to their various species. Because the Kensington museums also preserved such decorative, domestic artifacts as furnishings and clothing, Potter accumulated various subjects in her sketchbooks, using them to study perspective to much advantage in her later books, where the low-to-the-ground vantage points of her animals show familiar objects from new angles.

letters, including the draft of *The Tale of Squirrel Nutkin* (1903), although none survived.

The other trip of note was a visit to Gloucester with a cousin in 1894, during which Potter first heard a local tale of a tailor named Prichard who was assisted in his stitching by mice. The story would later serve as the inspiration for *The Tailor of Gloucester* (1902), which was originally drafted in an exercise book and illustrated as a Christmas gift from Potter for Freda, Noel Moore's sister.

The impetus for Potter's venture into publishing is not clear, though she had been casting about for a career to give meaning to the extended idleness imposed by her parents. She had tried her hand at illustrating greeting cards and the stories of other authors. In 1897 she even published a scientific article on the reproductive cycles of certain kinds of mushrooms, "On the Germination of the Spores of the *Agaricineae*," which was publicly presented to the Linnaean Society of London, though not by Potter. Because women were not permitted to appear before scientific groups at the time, her work was presented by a male friend of the family, a circumstance hardly likely to be satisfying to her. Her original findings have been verified. None of these efforts at finding a life's work brought the kind of notice or purpose that Potter desired.

Intrigued by a family friend's question about the possibility of publishing a children's book, Potter found the first publisher she approached uninterested. Consequently, in 1901 she published an early version of *The Tale of Peter Rabbit* with funds from her greeting-card venture. When the book came to the attention of Warne, a publishing house with a list of famous children's illustrators and authors, Warne agreed to reprint it, with revisions and full-color illustrations. Thus began a long and usually happy association. Author and publishing house worked closely together at first, while Potter developed her style and method of revision. The first book underwent extensive editing, but Potter edited, critiqued, and redrew her own illustrations for her later books.

The story of *Peter Rabbit* is simple: a naughty but interesting little boy rabbit disobeys his mother's injunctions to stay out of a farmer's garden where the father rabbit has already met an untimely end. The son ventures in, eats his fill of greens, loses his new jacket and shoes, and barely escapes the farmer's wrath. He returns to the warmth of his mother's burrow, where she punishes him, though lovingly, with a distasteful home remedy and an early bedtime.

Potter, circa 1876

Peter's journey and his escape back home provide most of the story's interest. The full indulgence in the pleasures of the garden is amply realized, at least from Peter's limited perspective; the simpleminded naughtiness and the real peril in which he finds himself as a result develop the tension in the story. Children readily identify with his loss of his clothing, the only items that identify him as humanlike. Though Potter originally was concerned that the simple, natural tones of rabbit brown and lettuce green might not provide enough variety of color in the illustrations, she keeps the reader's eye busy and provides variation in the hues with a red-breasted robin; sister rabbits dressed in pink; Peter's jacket in an unusually regal, elegant blue; and mother rabbit in a red cloak. The minuteness of detail, right down to the ragged edges on a particular species of lettuce – she later identified it as "Sutton's Perfection" – is so consistently and conscientiously attended to that the story of a rabbit family living in a parallel, but otherwise unnoticed existence so close to humankind, is entirely convincing and endearing. The vulnerability of these

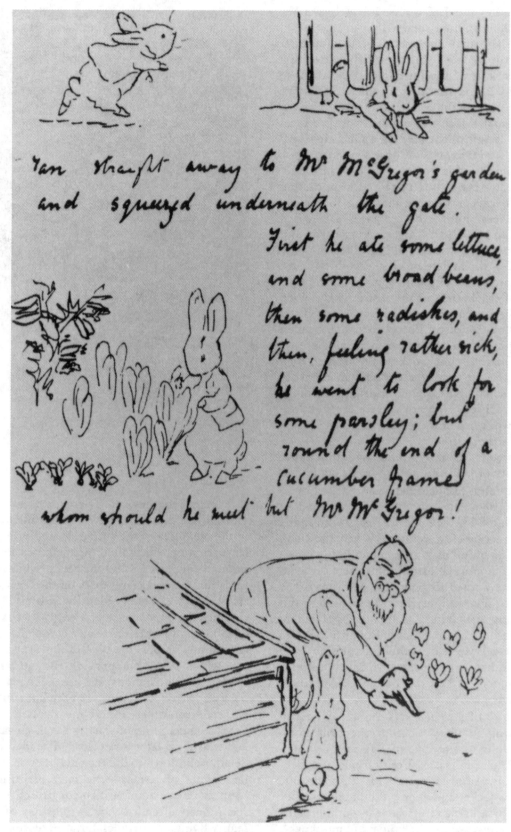

Page from Potter's letter to Noel Moore with the first version of The Tale of Peter Rabbit *(Bodleian Library, Oxford; by permission of Frederick Warne)*

animals makes their survival all the more remarkable. Small children can sympathize with their animal status as frightened prey, and their furriness gives a tactile appeal to their already alluring characteristics in illustration and text.

The changes imposed as the study evolved from original letter to first self-published book to final commercial publication are substantial, especially in the text. Yet the items that remain unchanged are even more striking: the arrangement on the page of the words introducing Flopsy, Mopsy, Cottontail, and Peter; the almost cryptic line drawing of Mr. McGregor in the background, chasing Peter with a rake; and the ending at home in the rabbit burrow. Potter worked over her illustrations relentlessly, adding color to the original line drawings; adding characters, such as robin, sparrow, and cat; reworking onomatopoeia to be more accurately reflective of the noises they represent; and, finally, managing punctuation to make lines more readable, especially for young, less experienced readers. The points at which the pages must be turned, indicating the passage of time, were of special concern to her, as were the divisions of lines on the page. The result is a simple adventure elegantly told, with illustrations surprising for both their miniaturization and their expansiveness.

Warne requested that another book be published as quickly as possible to take advantage of the success and popularity of *Peter Rabbit*. Potter rummaged through her files and found "The Tailor of Gloucester," which, in its original form as a homemade gift, was more of a fairy tale, heavily burdened with long interpolations of nursery rhymes and not nearly as concise as the published form. In this story Potter found a use for her frequent visits to the Victoria and Albert Museum in Kensington, which still holds in its collection the elegantly embroidered waistcoat Potter so faithfully copied for *The Tailor of Gloucester*.

The story of the tailor near starvation with an impending deadline for an important client and the willingness of the mice in his shop to finish the job for him recalls the Grimms' "The Shoemaker and the Elves." Since the tailor is ill and unable to work, the mice finish the Lord Mayor's waistcoat in time for his wedding on Christmas Day. They manage all but the final buttonhole, which they do not have the special thread to work, and so leave a note to the tailor to finish the waistcoat. Their intervention on the tailor's behalf is made more magical by the story's time frame of Christmas Eve, when, traditionally, animals have been able to talk in honor of their presence at the birth in Bethlehem. The published version still has some nursery-rhyme songs, though the ones that Potter chose to keep in revision from the earlier version are clearly related to mice and to Christmas. The smallness of the mice lets them live in close observation of the tailor and empathize with his pressured situation while escaping his gaze. They must deal with his boon companion, the cat Simpkin, who worries them for fun and food, though at the end he can see their helpfulness to his master and therefore declares a truce. The size of the mice also makes them especially apt choices as embroiderers, expert handlers of the needles, and crafters of fine stitchery. Their work on buttonholes, some of the most careful stitching required of a tailor, is a mark of their expertise. A tailor's whole work could be judged by his buttonholes, and the townspeople consider the tailor a master, as judged by the prominence of his work on the chest of the mayor.

While *The Tailor of Gloucester* has attained the status of a nursery classic partly because of its success in the Christmas trade, after its publication Potter's editors at Warne wanted to wean the author away from her dependence on fairy tale and nursery rhyme. They recognized, quite rightly, that her real strength was her own creations, anthropomorphized yet essentially animal, even when they wore human clothes and stood upright. In order to provide some diversity among her other books about mice and rabbits, Potter returned to the animal kingdom in *The Tale of Squirrel Nutkin*. She had originally told the story to the children of Annie Moore in a letter. She remarked on the odd behavior of some squirrels she had observed while on holiday in Derwentwater. The author had found several inhabiting an island and wondered how they could have journeyed from shore to shore; in the letter she invented the possibility of their sailing on leaves, using their tails to catch the wind. The existence of one squirrel without a full tail further captured her imagination and inspired the character of Nutkin.

Nutkin is a naughty squirrel, though more of a tempter of fate than Peter Rabbit. While Peter simply reacts without thinking, Nutkin deliberately taunts Old Brown, an owl, by chattering riddles and jokes. The squirrels beg the owl's kind permission to scavenge for nuts in his territory over the course of a week, offering him tasty gifts in return for his favors; in contrast, Nutkin offers only jests and even offense. Nutkin eventually receives his comeuppance, and though he could have lost his life, he manages to escape with only the loss of part of his tail. Although the English topicality of Nutkin's rid-

Hunca Munca arriving to clean the dollhouse, in The Tale of Two Bad Mice *(by permission of Frederick Warne)*

dles renders them obscure for American readers, the first readers of the book would have found them familiar and easily answered, beginning with the schoolchild for whom attaining such verbal cleverness was a mark of distinction. Overall, the tale cautions children who are too clever and do not mind their manners enough to ask permission; it is serious enough to warn children, but not so serious as to deny them pleasure in the high-stepping fun of the riddles and the antics of the squirrels.

Potter next returned to Peter Rabbit's world, with the approval of both publisher and public. *The Tale of Benjamin Bunny* (1904) continues Peter's story after he recovers from his adventures in Mr. McGregor's garden. Peter's cousin Benjamin lures him back into the garden in order to retrieve his clothes. They succeed, although Peter is nervous the whole time, having already visited the forbidden garden once with bad results. They gorge themselves and tangle with a cat. They bring home a bunch of onions as a peace offering to Peter's mother, but they receive a thrashing from Benjamin's father after he rescues them from the paws of McGregor's cat.

In this sequel Potter shows a more cunning, less reactive, more human kind of rabbit than Peter has been. Benjamin is calculating in luring Peter into the garden and more clever in going not under the fence but up a tree, a safer though more unlikely route into the garden for a rabbit. He is less prone to anxiety than is Peter. The two join other complementary pairs of boys – such as Huck and Tom in the works of Mark Twain – as friends with disparate interests and abilities which lead them through adventures.

The rabbit world receives more detailed treatment in *The Tale of Benjamin Bunny,* including a discussion of Mrs. Rabbit's economic situation, an adult male presence in Mr. Bunny, and a more fully described home for the bunnies. Some of the details in the story, recycled from earlier versions of *The Tale of Peter Rabbit,* find a more appropriate home in the sequel, which expands rather than establishes the fullness of the fictional world. Overall, the book shows Potter growing in her sense of confident authorship. Her connection with Warne included a continuing relationship with Norman Warne, her

Potter's illustration of Lucie and Mrs. Tiggy-Winkle, from The Tale of Mrs. Tiggy-Winkle
(by permission of Frederick Warne)

editor and the youngest brother of the firm. While he gently guided her prose and illustration, Potter found much satisfaction in their growing professional and personal relationship. They visited each other, Potter usually being the one who traveled, though her ability to visit was severely restricted by her parents, who disapproved of her acquaintance with a family of businesspeople. Nevertheless, the relationship flourished into romance, and over the strenuous objection of her parents, Potter and Warne became engaged in 1905. Her parents did not acknowledge the presence of the simple engagement ring she wore, nor did they discuss what it meant. However, Warne's family welcomed Potter into their large, loving family as their own "Aunt Beattie."

A dollhouse in the Warnes' home and Potter's fascination with mice led to her next book, *The Tale of Two Bad Mice* (1904). Potter's love of small things extended to dolls, which she collected even in late adulthood. The mice of the title find a dollhouse and attempt to eat the doll food they find in it. Though tempting, the food is inedible. Infuriated, they make a mess of the dollhouse, committing vandalism and theft, taking whatever they can move. No particular harm comes to the mice, though a

doll policeman is called in to investigate. The mice make amends by cleaning the dollhouse early every morning, explaining why dollhouses are so neat.

The lithe, busy activity of mice and their incessant investigation of their environment had always made them attractive to Potter. In this book Potter draws on her interest in animals and small things and also comments on the sterility of Victorian decorative arts and lifestyles. While the dollhouse and the dolls are lovely, the mice, who invade the house and steal anything they can, are more interesting and charming. While the doll residents, Jane and Emma, are expressionless about the mess created in their home, the mice make good use of what they have stolen, including clothing, which is charming on the lady mouse and makes for one of the best portraits of animals in any of Potter's books. The mice find a real use for items such as the cradle, which they fill with offspring, in contrast to the sterility of the dolls. Essentially, the dollhouse is all display, but no home; the real coziness is in the mouse hole and in mouse family life, which exists in close proximity to both the dolls and even the unseen humans in the book.

Potter seems to be criticizing her parents' lifestyle and home, contrasting it perhaps with the busy, warm household of the Warnes or, even more likely, with the kind of ideal house she envisioned. It is no wonder that, as soon as she was able, she bought Hill Top, a small country cottage on a farm, and set to work establishing the domestic felicities she had imagined for the mice. Unfortunately, Norman Warne was unable to join her in her new arrangements. With very little warning, he fell ill and died of leukemia. The notice came to Potter while she was on another long summer vacation away from London with her parents. Unaware of his illness, she received a telegram announcing his sudden death. Apparently the Potters did not speak of the death, and she could express her sorrow only to Warne's sister.

The Tale of Two Bad Mice was Potter's last book about an exclusively urban scene and the last book that Norman Warne supervised from start to finish. During that summer away, Potter found a new focus for her work. Having dealt with favorite rodents for two books in a row, Potter turned to the countryside for two truly wild animals in *The Tale of Mrs. Tiggy-Winkle* (1905) and *The Tale of Mr. Jeremy Fisher* (1906). At Warne's death, one or another of his brothers took over editorship of Potter's works, though her relationship with the brothers was never as cordial. In fact, at this point, when Potter's career truly flowered, the editors were more a source of contention than guidance, as the author found new stories and illustrational possibilities that took her beyond the realm of mice, rabbits, dollhouses, and walled gardens. Even after Warne's death, Potter found it possible to be productive, possibly as a way of dealing with her grief. She had other motives as well. While the profits from the earlier books were substantial enough for Potter to purchase property, with the commitment to the house, Potter felt the need to step up her production of books to two a year in order to improve her property. Potter's enjoyment of and absorption in her home probably provided her with further compensation for the death of her fiancé. In this new setting, she found all the inspiration she needed to continue a pace of two books a year for nearly a decade.

The Tale of Mrs. Tiggy-Winkle features Mrs. Tiggy, a hedgehog and a washerwoman known for her skill at getting out spots and ironing and starching delicate white fabrics. When Lucie, a girl from the village, comes looking for her lost handkerchiefs and pinafore, she finds Mrs. Tiggy doing the laundry of animal friends, including Peter Rabbit, Benjamin Bunny, Henny Penny, and Tom Titmouse. Finally, Lucie and Mrs. Tiggy locate Lucie's lost clothes and launder them to perfection, but as Lucie leaves she finds not a washerwoman but a hedgehog scampering away on all fours, leading her to question the reality of the experience.

Potter asserts the reality of Mrs. Tiggy and her humanlike world in a coda where she intrudes in her own voice. That she felt this need to intrude into the narrative is evidence of the difficulty in plotting; after all, not much goes on in this fictional world, and there is not much tension or motivation in Mrs. Tiggy's existence or Lucie's wanderings. Mrs. Tiggy receives the reader's whole attention and interest. Instead of the stolid shape and prickly exterior of the hedgehog limiting plot and character, Potter has transformed Mrs. Tiggy into a busy, accomplished entrepreneur with useful skills in demand. She gets around on her two hind legs; has a jolly expression on her face to enliven the illustrations; and lives in a cozy, if humid and somewhat strange, subterranean world. Drawing Lucie, a little girl of Potter's acquaintance, was troublesome for Potter, as was illustrating most human forms. While the child's blond hair and chubby features make her charming, Potter had so much trouble with deciding on the color of her clothing and with posing her that the pictures were redrawn several times. The result is that Lucie is wooden, like a doll, and her features, through numerous redrawings, are fuzzy, drawn with none of the sureness of Mrs. Tiggy's less probable but much more lively form. The model for the hedgehog was a pet of Potter's; obviously, she was much more familiar with and adept at drawing the form of the somewhat strange animal than she was at drawing the much more common form of a human child. Throughout her life this dichotomy characterized Potter: she knew and drew animals well, but though she wrote for children, she did not know them or draw them with skill.

Potter had much less trouble drawing *The Tale of Mr. Jeremy Fisher* and found the nonmammalian cast of frog, fish, tortoise, and newt much more to her liking and her ability. Jeremy Fisher is an eighteenth-century frog gentleman dressed in waistcoat and pumps, who enjoys the sport of fishing and has as his friends some other eighteenth-century animals of leisure. The fishing adventures include catching a stickleback, hooking a game fish that gets away, and nearly being eaten by a trout, a near-catastrophe that leads Jeremy to resolve never to go fishing again. Though the animals have limited facial expressions and glassy, unfocused eyes, Potter manages through their clothing to accentuate their animalness while giving them both human and antique qualities with their eighteenth-century full-dress regalia. In the case of the frog Potter uses a

Potter's illustration of the title character in The Tale of Mr. Jeremy Fisher *(by permission of Frederick Warne)*

waistcoat, long stockings, and pumps to accent the motion of Jeremy's skinny legs and makes use of his lack of a neck to express much of the frog's emotion through his shoulders. The newt's waistcoat takes advantage of the naturally colorful pigmenting of his underbelly, and the cravats of the frog, newt, and tortoise make their heads seem more human than animal.

Like gentlemen on permanent vacation, these three are dining partners and tellers of tall tales about the fish that got away. Their world is well realized through Potter's vision of their dated quality as dandies. Fishing was a hobby Potter's father avidly pursued with his friends, and the author probably saw many other such vacationing fishermen around her farm village, which was also a popular summer holiday location. While Jeremy and his friends are precious, they are somewhat ridiculous in their clothing, which is unsuitable for rough, wet

sporting, and their highly proper manners are a comment on Potter's father and his cohort of gentlemen on permanent vacation from care and from the realities of early-twentieth-century life.

The Pie and the Patty-Pan (1905) and *The Tale of Tom Kitten* (1907) celebrate Potter's establishment of a home of her own at Hill Top Farm. Both stories concern pet animals: cats who lived in her own household and a Pomeranian dog who lived in the neighborhood. On a farm cats are useful, working animals; in contrast, a Pomeranian is a house pet kept solely for the pleasure of its master or mistress. Potter invests an approving homespun quality in the cats, who may try to dress up by putting on a clean apron, though much greater decoration is beyond them; on the other hand, the dog is clearly a show dog and a decoration, somewhat silly, especially when compared to the good-willed, if stodgy cats. In these first two "Sawrey" books (named after the town where Hill Top Farm was located), Potter found a new impetus to experiment with characterization and more complex plots. The reassurance she drew from her home and the distancing from her parents benefited her work as an author and illustrator.

The Pie and the Patty-Pan features Ribby, an appropriately named striped cat, who invites the Pomeranian dog Duchess to tea. The dog finds out that the menu will be mouse pie, not at all to her liking, and so decides to substitute a veal and ham pie in her neighbor's oven while the cat is out making last-minute purchases. Unfortunately, the old brick oven has two sections, and the veal and ham pie goes into the part not in use. When served the mouse pie from the other section, the dog assumes it is her own and gorges herself. At this point, the patty-pan, a metal liner to give pies baked in crockery dishes their shape, becomes an issue, since the mouse pie did not have one and the veal and ham pie did. The dog, having finished the pie, assumes she has eaten the metal patty-pan – the idea that the pies have been switched is beyond her. The hostess cat is confounded by the dog's distress, there having been no patty-pan as far as she knows. A rushed visit from the doctor and the revelation of the veal pie's existence in the remaining oven does not reassure the dog, since she now feels ill at the thought of having eaten mouse. A commotion ensues, with the hostess cat never really understanding that there has been a substitution.

The trickery is fairly complex, based on the similarity of crockery pie plates that both animal housekeepers have. Potter was fond of country crockery: she collected it, displayed it, and left instructions in her will that these displays were to remain undisturbed when she bequeathed her home to the National Trust for public viewing. The dog's feigning distaste for mouse pie, all the while eating it with relish, betrays her tastes as not being so discerning or particular after all; it is more the thought than the actuality of eating mouse that offends her. Perhaps Potter is poking fun at the narrow experiences of country folk that lead them to such false conclusions about dishes they have never eaten. The dog's attractive portrait – in fancy neck ribbon, walking on her back legs, and carrying a gift bouquet as she arrives at her neighbor's house – defines her as a pet and contrasts sharply with the more homey appearance of the matronly cat, with shawl and apron, who is just trying to provide a nice party for her friend. The story mirrors the prim manners of village ladies with particular palates. The small-town manners and the rumors swirling among the observing neighbors, especially after the emergency visit of the doctor, give Potter the opportunity to comment critically, although with a light-handed humor, about the behavior of those she observed in her new neighborhood. The fuss and the doctor's visit are both over nothing; the dog is fine, but the flurry of activity provides much of the interest in a small town where everyone knows everyone else's business.

The Tale of Tom Kitten carries on the theme of the manners of small-town ladies and their excessively correct etiquette. Tabitha Twitchit, one of the gossiping cats in *The Pie and the Patty-Pan,* is the subject of the story. She has her own family of typically playful kittens, whom she tries to keep in order by washing them and dressing them in party clothes. After some rough-and-tumble play, the boy cat, Tom Kitten, finds himself without his clothing. While Potter first shows him in his Little Lord Fauntleroy outfit, stiff and upright with a surprised and perhaps pained look on his face, she later pictures him dirty, kitten-like, and without clothes. To the reader, he is not naked, but rather simply a cat in his normal, natural state, and his mother's exclamation, "I am affronted," thus seems incongruous. But fine ladies must insist on manners, and because Tabitha is about to play hostess to neighbors who are coming in for tea, she sends the kittens to their rooms – they are no longer fit for exhibition as proper kittens. There they play rambunctiously and with no penitence – that is, after all, what kittens naturally do. That Tabitha sent them outside to play, which is their ruin in her eyes, does not seem to enter her mind. Her own responsibility, first in making them unnatural by forcing them into clothing and then creating the circumstances that led to their undoing, does not occur to her. Of course, it does to the reader, whose sympathy lies entirely with the playful kittens and not with the twitchy, nervous, overbearing mother. In *The Tale of Tom Kitten* Potter comments on the pleasing, natural fun of children as well as on the pretentiousness and unnatural expectations of some mothers.

Potter was also experimenting with a new form for a new, younger audience. Designed more as toys than as books, *The Story of a Fierce Bad Rabbit* (1906) and *The Story of Miss Moppet* (1906) show the author's willingness to see her characters in other forms than strictly literary and her willingness to attempt to address a preliterate audience. Originally designed as panoramas – or pages arranged on long strips of paper, folding out, accordion-fashion, to tell a story – these two books are now formatted as regular books in the Peter Rabbit series. Originally

Potter's frontispiece for The Pie and the Patty-Pan, *including a view of*
Hill Top Farm in the background (by permission of Frederick Warne)

Potter was experimenting with a new literary form as well as a new bookbinding technique: a story of slight action and little characterization, more involved with naming objects and people than with plot, as opposed to a more complicated narrative with several characters and extensive use of language. In the panorama books there is almost no style, so thoroughly has Potter stripped down the stories to their essential elements. Each book has a good creature and a bad creature: a good rabbit and a fierce one in the first book, and a mouse and a cat in the other. There is some confrontation between the two, a climax, and a denouement. The fierce rabbit bothers the good one, but a hunter shoots the offender, leaving the good rabbit with his carrot, content at the end. The mouse bothers the cat, the cat worries the mouse, but the mouse gets away to live another day. With little character motivation, the resolutions of the stories offer slight satisfaction.

But Potter's close observation of animals is again evident in her illustrations, where she portrays the characters with much human emotion in various playful and antagonistic poses.

A third panorama was planned, to be titled "The Sly Cat," but the relative failure of the first two scuttled plans for a third in Potter's lifetime. *The Sly Old Cat* (1971) was published posthumously, and Potter's failure to pursue other toy books and their simple stories was part of an apt recognition that her forte lay in more developed tales, where language and plot could have freer play.

Increasingly, Potter spent most of her time at the farm, dividing her time between her parents and their London home and her new life. She would return to her farm at the slightest pretense and became increasingly socially independent, as she had already become financially. She prospered as a breeder of animals, especially sheep, and began to acquire other small farms in the area around Hill Top. Yet the business activities of the farm did not detract from her writing and illustrating; Potter had only to look in her own yard to find inspiration for further books. The ridiculous behavior of one particular duck in her thoughtless placement of her eggs inspired *The Tale of Jemima Puddle-Duck* (1908). The duck on Potter's farm was so elusive in her quest to establish her clutch that her nests were dangerously distant from the safety of the walled farmyard. One of Potter's tenant farmers was in the habit of transplanting ducks' eggs into hens' nests to assure that they hatched but had trouble finding the eggs of Jemima's model.

Jemima is equally muddleheaded about her brooding, never having successfully hatched her eggs. She wanders about looking for an appropriate nesting spot away from the farmer's gaze but finds herself in the territory of the "sandy-whiskered gentleman," who attempts to capture her for his own feast. Though he is never called by his rightful name, he is clearly depicted as a fox, of the crafty sort found in fable and folktale. When he invites Jemima to join him for an omelette, she accepts, never making the connection between her own eggs and the ingredients of the main course. Even when he asks her to bring the herbs usually associated with omelettes and roast duck, she is oblivious to his intentions. She even tries out a possible nest in his home among a room full of feathers, the leavings of his other "guests." Though he becomes increasingly rude and orders her about as he prepares to butcher her, she still does not understand what is happening. Finally, a neighboring farm dog meets her and recognizes what is happening; he summons the hounds from other nearby farms to destroy the fox's home. The fox escapes, to find a tale of his own in a later Potter book. Jemima finally has a chance to lay and brood her eggs, though only half of them hatch. Yet even at story's end, she is none the wiser as to the close circumstances of her life.

This work has been called Potter's "poem about the farm" by biographer Margaret Lane. The environs have changed little in the years since the book's writing, nor had they changed much in the century before. Jemima's antique poke bonnet and shawl were still in style when Potter wrote and illustrated the book, and the ability of a suave gentlemen to be "foxy," to snare naive country ladies is legendary. The world that Potter portrays is as old as Aesop's fables, yet still in existence continuing as it has for centuries. While most of the world has passed by this out-of-the-way place, it is preserved for posterity in this slender volume.

Interspersed among these stories of Hill Top Farm is *The Tale of the Flopsy Bunnies* (1909), Potter's return to the world of Peter and his family. When Flopsy Rabbit, Peter's sister, marries Benjamin Bunny, the new family becomes the Flopsy Bunnies. Like good bunnies, they reproduce, though Flopsy and Benjamin are unconcerned about the support of their brood. In contrast, Peter and his mother have gone into business for themselves as garden-destruction experts; they give handouts when Flopsy and Benjamin need them. But the new parents leave the little bunnies sleeping on a pile of grass clippings (the implied source of the clippings being a human presence), and the babies are captured in a burlap sack by Mr. McGregor, who lives on in his animosity to rabbits. When the parents notice that the little ones are missing, they call on Peter, who rescues them, foiling Mr. McGregor's plans for the baby-rabbit skins. The rabbits live happily ever after, while Mr. and Mrs. McGregor bicker over a sack of rotten vegetables that he has given her, thinking it full of bunnies – a switch arranged by clever Peter.

The animosity between bunnies and gardeners, especially professional gardeners who grow their produce for commercial purposes, has existed ever since there have been gardens. Potter's rabbit world has matured in *The Tale of the Flopsy Bunnies,* with babies to be cared for and Peter Rabbit having become an independent gardener. Benjamin's youthful daring has turned into adult carelessness, while Flopsy has turned into a more responsible, though anxiety-ridden mother. The most memorable picture in the whole book shows her in rear view, alone in front of a vast landscape, her apron tied behind, her ears and tail perked up in nervous attention, trying to find her children; the pinkness of the apron suggests her human emotions of concern, the tension in her body her rabbit origins, the depth of the landscape her smallness and vulnerability and therefore that of her children. In such a small picture there is much emotional depth, showing Potter at her most mature. While drafting the story, Potter had such difficulty with the figures of Mr. and Mrs. McGregor that any use of them in the illustrations were finally abandoned; this is, in fact, the last appearance of Mr. McGregor.

Potter returned to village life for the inspiration for her next book. *Ginger and Pickles* (1909) picks up the story of daily village activity in the more public domain of a general store run by two inept entrepreneurs, a cat named Ginger and a terrier named Pickles. They do not understand the profit motive in running their shop and extend un-

The two larcenous rats preparing to cook Tom Kitten, from The Roly Poly Pudding *(by permission of Frederick Warne)*

limited credit to their animal customers, many of whom are characters from Potter's other books. When it becomes clear that they have no income because they do not collect on their credit accounts, they send out collection notices and turn to eating their own stock in order to survive. Their cheerful disregard for their impending doom and their incomprehension of finances create a safe environment with no real negative consequences. All the characters live happily ever after, Ginger and Pickles in other occupations after they are forced to close up shop and the neighboring store in secure prosperity, since without competition the proprietor can raise prices and still refuse to extend credit. The gossipy townspeople, the pleasures of new things, and the array of items and customers in the general store are particularly appealing in this story. Even the technical aspects of commerce, which Potter explains to young readers, do not weigh down the narrative flow. The parade of characters and events brings the pleasures of constant activity if little real action. Ginger and Pickles are so ineffectual that it is difficult to take their hand-wringing

over their business failures seriously. The small-town gossip, the naiveté of the main characters, and the happy ending make for a story that gently chides small-town life while glorifying in the simple pleasures of neighborliness and material comforts as provided by a country general store.

Potter returns one last time to her farm's cats in *The Roly-Poly Pudding* (1908). Tabitha Twitchit still lives in the same big old farmhouse. Hill Top Farm is used as a background for the story, illustrated from a cat's perspective, about a foot from floor level. Her son Tom decides to climb up the kitchen chimney, where he and his precious jacket are soiled with soot. He finds two larcenous rats, part of the hoard that lives in the thick walls, and they tie up Tom and roll him in some stolen dough in order to cook him. When they are discovered and Tom is rescued by his kitten siblings, the rats leave in a hurry. They carry a wheelbarrow full of stolen items out to the barn, where Tom's siblings establish their reputation as mousers. Tom, however, has been permanently frightened and stigmatized by the rats and so fails to live up to his name as a grown-up Tom Cat.

Once again the pleasures of the farm, the details of furnishings and crockery, and the mysteries of rats and mice and their runs dominate the story. The antics of the amoral rats, stealing everything they can, eating to the point of gluttony, and arguing rather rudely with each other, can be seen as commentaries on human life; but Potter's affection for such daring effrontery to human property makes the rats admirable and laughable, even though their real-life counterparts harried her on the farm and in her kitchen. At this point in her career, Potter had royalties sufficient to support herself and a freer hand in defying her editors. Her previous successes gave her enough confidence and persuasive power to convince her editors that amoral, rude rats would not offend her audiences.

Potter wrote *The Tale of Timmy Tiptoes* (1911) while preoccupied with expanding her farm. Timmy and his wife Goody are gray squirrels. The book displays less focus and commitment than her other books of the same period. Her choice of animals she had observed only in museums, rather than the living animals in places she knew more intimately, did not bode well for the book. In the story Timmy accidentally falls into a hollow tree where he stores gathered nuts. After gorging himself at the insistence of a chipmunk who inhabits the tree, he finds himself unable to get through the hole to the outside. Goody does not know what has happened; she assumes, after a lady chipmunk tells of her own husband's disappearance, that Timmy has deserted her. But news of Timmy's temporary imprisonment finally reaches Goody, and she rescues him and waits a fortnight for him to slim down. The missing chipmunk spouse is also discovered in the hollow tree. Though less eager to rejoin his garrulous mate, he finally emerges.

The point of this story is not entirely clear. The lady chipmunk, with her public, rhyming complaints about her husband's inconstancy, is humorous, and her complaints are chattery in rhythm like a chipmunk, but none of the characters has enough charm or characterization to carry the story. The tale is also vaguely anachronistic, with the colonial period name Goody and the sometimes archaic phrasing that the squirrels use to address each other, but the point of this antiquity is vague: there is nothing particularly old about the forest, nor is the mythology surrounding squirrels so strong as to give the story some kind of resonance. Even the motions of the squirrels are not as interesting as those of the earlier squirrel Nutkin.

Potter was more successful with *The Tale of Mrs. Tittlemouse* (1910), perhaps because she stays closer to home in her choice of characters and setting. The book is Potter's celebration of the satisfactions of housekeeping and cleanliness. Mrs. Tittlemouse makes her first appearance in *The Tale of the Flopsy Bunnies,* where she gnaws at the string ties on the burlap bag that holds the little bunnies captive. She is rewarded with rabbit wool to make herself some clothing. Hers is the closing picture of the story, and she appears as charming in her clothing as did the animals in *The Tale of Two Bad Mice* and as ready for development in her own story, where she is spring-cleaning her underground home.

Mrs. Tittlemouse's nemeses are a bullfrog, who keeps trying to invade her snug domain, and a variety of insects, who make themselves at home uninvited. When she finally gets rid of the unwanted guests and makes her home as tidy as she wants, she has a party for other mice. The bullfrog attempts to reenter the home, but is prevented by the smaller entrance she has made; however, to keep up appearances, she sends out a beverage, and he returns thanks with a toast to her good health.

The extreme orderliness of the little mouse, her tidiness, and her wish not to offend are marks of true womanhood among the country women Potter had come to admire and whose hard work at housecleaning she had experienced firsthand. The intensity and frequency of pink tones and other pastels mark the book's setting as an interior, female world, to be ordered to the pleasure of the lady mouse herself. Potter found intense pleasure in ordering her own domain when she first bought her farm, and the pleasure of knowing that one's own efforts could be efficacious in establishing one's own space was sacred to her even after several years of housekeeping and farming. Her affection for housekeeping in snug quarters is thus embodied in the small mouse world. While Potter makes subtle fun of the lady mouse who wishes her uninvited guests to go but cannot quite bring herself to ask them to leave, she clearly respects the kindness that such consideration for others' feelings represents. Again, in the mouse world she creates a perfect image of the tidy, cozy home she had come to know – not imagined as in *The Tale of Two Bad Mice,* but actualized.

Potter's relationship with her editors became increasingly difficult over the years. She spent less time in London and less time on writing and illustration, but in turn she became more sure of herself and her craft. Her audience's continued interest in her books was underscored by continuing royalties. At the same time, she was growing older, with eyesight no longer up to the fine brushwork of her earlier books. Certainly, she was reluctant to take on large projects, choosing rather to invest herself only in stories that were more adventurous and daring than the tidier worlds of the earlier books.

In her next book, the sandy-whiskered gentleman from *The Tale of Jemima Puddle-Duck* reappears with a full name and pedigree in *The Tale of Mr. Tod* (1912), with all his wild, foxy predilections for bunnies clearly in evidence. This story is the last of the Peter Rabbit saga, taking up the story in Peter Rabbit's and Benjamin Bunny's adulthood, transplanted this time to the woodlands surrounding Potter's farm. Flopsy and Benjamin Bunny have had another litter of babies who are stolen this time by the badger Tommy Brock. The rabbit parents may have learned to be concerned about their offspring but have not learned enough caution to protect them adequately. The badger bags the litter and takes them to the home of Mr. Tod, the fox, who has temporarily abandoned his dwelling. Benjamin and Peter attempt a rescue by tunneling under the house, only to be cornered by the returning Mr. Tod. The fox and the badger battle it out for possession of the fox's home to the end of mutual routing, while Peter and Benjamin rescue the little bunnies and return them home to a joyous family reunion.

The motivations in this story are sometimes hard to follow for the reader who is not well versed in the habits of wild predators. Badgers are smelly omnivors much less fastidious than foxes, who are more attentive to their grooming rituals and to cleanliness in their habitats. Badgers will sometimes invade the nests and burrows of other animals and will eat anything. They are not particularly active, hence Tommy Brock displays a propensity to sleep through most of this story. His ominous presence is made the more obnoxious because of his smell, which is particularly menacing to the rabbits, whose noses are part of their defense against predators. In this story, Peter appears to be the clever rabbit, more human because of his deviousness in attempting the baby rabbits' rescue, but finally, it is just luck and not planning that enables him to get the babies back. The entire atmosphere of this story is much more threatening and dark than any of the earlier Peter Rabbit stories, not only because of the characterization of Tommy Brock, but also because of the presence of animal bones in the home of Mr. Tod. The remains of previous meals are displayed in the gathering gloom of an afternoon and are not as easily ignored as is the simple story of Mr. Rabbit being made into a pie, a cautionary example told to Peter in his first adventure.

Potter's frontispiece for The Tale of Mr. Tod *(by permission of Frederick Warne)*

The story contains no human characters and marks a shift from Potter's less bloodthirsty animals to clearly disagreeable ones who are part of the world that Potter and her rabbits inhabited in rural farm life. Potter's intention to write about a truly unpleasant animal was a source of contention with her editors, though she finally won out, producing one of the most interesting and realistic stories in the whole Peter Rabbit series. While the book includes fewer full-color illustrations (Potter complained that her eyes could not bear the work), there are more thick-line drawings that resemble woodcuts, giving the book an antique quality found in none of Potter's other books. The work shows Potter still willing to invest herself in a compelling, dangerous story; in fact, the pages are much more text-dense than earlier books, perhaps because the author became so involved in the dastardly deeds of her protagonists.

Potter was progressing in her personal life as well as her writing. At age forty-seven she was engaged to William Heelis, a country lawyer slightly younger than herself, whom she had met in the process of buying the small farms she acquired after Hill Top. Potter's parents still felt free to object to her choice of partners, even though she had been living an independent life as both author and farmer for over a decade. Disregarding their objections, Potter married Heelis on 14 October 1913. *The Tale of Pigling Bland* (1913), Potter's only love story, was inspired by her impending marriage and also by three nursery rhymes about pigs: "Tom, Tom, the Piper's Son," "To Market, To Market," and "This Little Piggie." The three rhymes surface from time to time in the story, in which Pigling is sent to market. As a young naïf, he is lured away from the path by Thomas Peter Piperson, whose name conflates two nursery-rhyme characters ("Tom, Tom, the Piper's Son," and "Peter Piper"). Old Mr. Piperson shuts Pigling up in a house with a little girl pig, a black Berkshire named Pigwig. She and Pigling manage to elude their captor and run away to the next county, hand in hand, "over the hills and far away." The last picture shows them dancing together in a traditional country social dance, high-spirited and clearly in love.

While the love interest here is coupled with an escape motif and is sometimes subordinate to it, the story takes on greater poignancy given the biographical details: Potter was engaged to marry; her parents were opposed to her choice of a country lawyer; the couple planned to escape to her country farm and life. These two pigs are nothing like the mature couple that Potter and Heelis made, but their glee, Pigling Bland's solicitous attention to his beloved's sweet tooth, and her high spirits suggest the childlike pleasure that Potter found in marriage even later in life. That she knew her husband was not spectacularly exciting or a prime candidate for marriage may be evident from Potter's choice of a last name for the male pig – Bland. Still, no evidence suggests that she had the slightest reservation about the marriage. The two even tried, unsuccessfully, to start a family, so thoroughly did they relish the prospect of home and traditional family life.

Potter's pleasure in her married life is the clear underpinning of one of few books she wrote after her marriage, *The Tale of Johnny Town-Mouse* (1918). A version of Aesop's fable of the city mouse and the country mouse, the story is set not in a city, but in Hawkshead, a neighboring village near Potter's farm. The mice in the city are the kind of vermin Potter so lovingly portrays in *The Tale of Two Bad Mice,* though the country cousin is a field mouse. While the city mouse and his life are given their due, including more elegant and reliable food, the country mouse receives preferential treatment in Potter's portrayal of his sunny, colorful summer home in the country; there is no real menace to his existence, only noise from a lawn mower, to which his city cousin objects. The conclusion that Potter explicitly states at the end, that she certainly prefers the country to the city, is not necessarily Aesop's. Her clear preference becomes the reader's, since there is almost no compensation for the noise and danger of the city in Potter's depiction of it. The pictures of the mice in the city are not as colorful or as detailed; even the pleasant, charming expression of the country mouse reveals the author's preference.

After her marriage Potter complained that her eyes were too tired to do the fine work required in her earlier drawings and that her time was consumed with domestic responsibilities. Both these excuses for her reduced literary output are credible, but the prodigious effort of her earlier career and her unwillingness to submit to such a level of toil in her later, more successful period, are also likely explanations for some of the weaker volumes of her later output.

Certainly *Appley Dapply's Nursery Rhymes* (1917) and *Cecily Parsley's Nursery Rhymes* (1922) met the demands of Potter's readers for more books in the Peter Rabbit series – the pictures and rhymes were from earlier, unfinished drafts and projects. Both books feature the animals Potter enjoyed illustrating best: mice, rabbits, pigs, cats, dogs, and other farm animals. But there is no continuous story line in either book to link the rhymes together, and there are so few rhymes in each that two volumes hardly seem justified. Potter had not lost her ability to create a nursery-rhyme story that sounded enough like another rhyme to reveal its heritage, while different enough that it was original, yet the scant text and the uneven and carelessly framed illustrations betray her lack of interest in these two books.

Potter dabbled in adaptations of her books for large-format painting books, such as *Peter Rabbit's Painting Book* (1911) and *Tom Kitten's Painting Book* (1917). She took pictures from earlier Peter Rabbit books, enlarged them, and simplified the text as captions for the pictures. Sometimes Potter simply lent her name and book title, permitting another artist to redraw the pictures for a larger format. On a larger page the pictures look wispy and shaky, with only a black line where formerly watercolors had defined depth and edges. Potter's books worked well in miniature, where simple pen sketches with backgrounds edited for suggestiveness rather than full detail were more effective. On a full page the eye expects detail and definiteness of line, which were not Potter's expertise. There were no particular instructions for painting the books' pictures; today they are more accurately classed as coloring books. Once again, they show Potter's willingness to try other forms and to commercialize her works, and, like the panorama books, they are subordinate to her greatest success in her original genre, the tale illustrated on the small page.

The Fairy Caravan (1929), written at the request of David McKay, an American publisher, is another project done to order, out of the reach of the customary editorial scrutiny Potter's works had received at Warne. Potter may have felt more comfortable and certainly freer to ramble and to illustrate with simple line drawings for McKay than is evidenced in any of her books published by Warne; perhaps she thought that an ocean's space between herself and her publisher gave sufficient leeway for a less energetic work to be published. The closest work to a novel that Potter wrote, this story of a gypsy caravan of guinea pigs wanders through improbable, pointless episodes in picaresque fashion, supported by some hasty line drawings that are more sketches than formally prepared illustrations. Though lengthy, the volume has none of the satisfactions of plot, illustration, or language of the earlier tales. *Sister Anne* (1932), a retelling of the Bluebeard story, constitutes Potter's return to the less strenuous literary standards of the fairy tale, where she felt free to ramble rather than revise carefully for tight plotting. Done for profit rather than to satisfy a commitment to literary and illustrational excellence, these books suggest Potter's preoccupation with other matters besides her books. Nowhere do these works approach the high standards for text and illustration shown earlier in the Peter Rabbit series.

Potter also resorted to her files of unpublished materials to satisfy the continuing demands of her publishers and readers for more books. *The Tale of Little Pig Robinson* (1930) is a long, winding, ill-formed story dependent on nursery rhyme and Daniel Defoe's *Robinson Crusoe* (1719) and more suited to Potter's personal pleasure than the audience's desires. Little Pig Robinson, like Pigling Bland, is sent to market but does not end up there. He is pressed into naval service, not so much to perform nautical duties as to provide an eventual meal for the sailors. When his fate becomes clear to him, he escapes on a lifeboat to the Land where the Bong Tree Grows, a place invented by Edward Lear as the destination of the Owl and the Pussy-Cat. While the story contains much credible, human detail about life in a seaport and aboard ship, the final, abrupt landing, and Pig Robinson's taking up a leisure chair on the beach under a Bong Tree, contrast jarring fantasy with the unfulfilled promise of a more realistic ending. As one of the longest of Potter's books, the scope of the story is at once ambi-

Potter in later years

tious and disappointing. Invoking the tradition of the robinsonnade, the title promises more adventure on the island, but once escape from the ship is effected, the story is over; even the Owl and the Pussy-cat fail to appear. Pig Robinson becomes more tourist than adventurer. As the last of Potter's small picture books, *The Tale of Little Pig Robinson* shows the author's increasing lack of interest in her literary and artistic creations.

The decline in the quality and quantity of her literary output after her marriage did not reflect a general lack of energy or ambition on Potter's part. Having submerged her former identity, Mrs. Heelis became a champion sheep breeder and active supporter of the National Trust, an organization devoted to preserving the English countryside for future generations. Potter successfully raised funds for the purchase of properties, located the properties, negotiated their purchases, and saw to their repairs and upkeep. In this effort she became acquainted with Bertha Mahony, an editor of *Horn Book,* a magazine about children's books. Trying to raise funds, Potter offered for sale some of the sketches from the original Peter Rabbit book for Mahony to sell to Americans. The two became friends, based on their mutual interest in high literary values in literature for children. The sale of the sketches allowed the National Trust to purchase more farms.

At her death on 22 December 1943, Potter's holdings reverted to the National Trust, where they remain in perpetuity as undeveloped spaces for public enjoyment. Potter also left a legacy of books, especially the Peter Rabbit series, that continue to be loved and purchased, at least partly because of the growing gift trade during the Easter season and Potter's tie-in with rabbits and other springtime animals. China, toys, wallpaper, and other spin-offs from her characters, including book adaptations by other writers, often bear little resemblance and sometimes no attribution to their originator, though they have made Potter's works a veritable industry.

Potter's books, especially the earlier ones, remain popular and accessible, although the taste for such dense language in children's picture books has declined. Young readers now expect much more expansive illustrations than the exquisite pastels and natural colors in Potter's miniature books and may lose patience with such convoluted stories as Potter produced later in her career. Nevertheless, while some of these later works will undoubtedly fade into obscurity, her triumphs such as *The Tale of Peter Rabbit* and *The Tailor of Gloucester* remain popular standards in nursery libraries, and their powerful legacies continue to be felt in the field of children's literature. Peter also survives through the many framed prints and stuffed imitations of himself, lovable through generations and changes, yet still basically Peter Rabbit.

Letters:

Letters to Children (New York: Walker, 1966);

Beatrix Potter's Americans: Selected Letters, edited by Jane Crowell Morse (Boston: Horn Book, 1982);

Letters to Children from Beatrix Potter, edited by Judy Taylor (London & New York: Warne, 1992).

Bibliography:

Leslie Linder, ed., *A History of the Writings of Beatrix Potter: Including Unpublished Works* (London & New York: Warne, 1971).

Biographies:

Margaret Lane, *The Tale of Beatrix Potter* (London & New York: Warne, 1946; revised edition, London: Fontana/Collins Books, 1970);

Lane, *The Magic Years of Beatrix Potter* (London & New York: Warne, 1978).

References:

Delmar Banner, "Memories of Beatrix Potter," *Nineteenth Century and After,* 140 (October 1946): 230–232;

Marcus Crouch, *Beatrix Potter: A Walck Monograph* (New York: Walck, 1961);

Rumer Godden, "Beatrix Potter," *Horn Book,* 42 (1966): 390–392;

Grahame Greene, "Beatrix Potter," in *Collected Essays* (New York: Viking, 1969), pp. 232–240;

Roger Sale, "Beatrix Potter," in *Fairy Tales and After: From Snow White to E. B. White* (Cambridge, Mass.: Harvard University Press, 1978), pp. 127–163;

Maurice Sendak, "Aliveness of Peter Rabbit," *Wilson Library Bulletin,* 40 (1965): 345–348.

Papers:

Most of the correspondence between Beatrix Potter and her publishers is held by Warne in their London archives; other papers are held by the National Trust in Near Sawrey.

Arthur Rackham
(19 September 1867 – 6 September 1939)

Lucy Rollin
Clemson University

BOOKS: *The Peter Pan Portfolio* (London: Hodder & Stoughton 1912; New York: Brentano's, 1914);

Mother Goose (London & New York: Heinemann, 1913);

Arthur Rackham's Book of Pictures (London: Heinemann, 1913; New York: Century, 1914);

The Arthur Rackham Fairy Book (London: Harrap, 1933; Philadelphia: Lippincott, 1933).

SELECTED BOOKS ILLUSTRATED: Thomas Rhodes, *To the Other Side* (London: Philip, 1893);

Annie Berlyn, *Sunrise-Land Rambles in Eastern England* (London: Jarrold, 1894);

Anthony Hope, *The Dolly Dialogues* (London: Westminster Gazette, 1894);

Washington Irving, *Tales of a Traveller,* 2 volumes (London & New York: Putnam, 1895);

S. J. Adair Fitzgerald, *The Zankiwank and the Bletherwitch* (London: Dent, 1896; New York: Dutton, 1896);

Margaret Wise Browne (Margaret Hamer), *Two Old Ladies, Two Foolish Fairies and a Tom Cat* (London: Cassell, 1897);

Thomas Ingoldsby (Richard Harris Barham), *The Ingoldsby Legends: Or, Mirth & Marvels* (London: Dent, 1898);

Charles and Mary Lamb, *Tales from Shakespeare* (London: Dent, 1899);

Jacob and Wilhelm Grimm, *Fairy Tales of the Brothers Grimm,* translated by Mrs. Edgar Lewis (London: Freemantle, 1900);

Jonathan Swift, *Gulliver's Travels into Several Remote Nations of the World* (London: Dent, 1900; New York: Dutton, 1909);

May Bowley, *Queen Mab's Fairy Realm* (London: Newnes, 1901);

Miranda Hill, *Cinderella,* Little Folks Plays series (London: Cassell, 1903);

Browne, *The Surprising Adventures of Tuppy and Sue* (London: Cassell, 1904);

Arthur Rackham in the 1890s

Irving, *Rip Van Winkle* (London: Heinemann, 1905; New York: Doubleday, Page, 1905);

Sam Hield Hamer, *The Little Folks Fairy Book* (London: Cassell, 1905);

Arthur Lincoln Haydon, *Fairy Tales Old and New* (London: Cassell, 1905);

J. M. Barrie, *Peter Pan in Kensington Gardens* (London: Hodder & Stoughton, 1906; New York: Scribners, 1906);

Rudyard Kipling, *Puck of Pook's Hill* (New York: Doubleday, Page, 1906);

One of Rackham's illustrations for his Mother Goose: The Old Nursery
Rhymes. *He included a self-portrait in the lower left corner.*

Lewis Carroll (Charles Lutwidge Dodgson), *Alice's Adventures in Wonderland* (London: Heinemann, 1907; New York: Doubleday, Page, 1907);

The Land of Enchantment (London & New York: Cassell, 1907);

William Shakespeare, *A Midsummer Night's Dream* (London: Heinemann, 1908; New York: Doubleday, Page, 1908);

Friedrich de la Motte Fouqué, *Undine,* adapted by W. L. Courtney (London: Heinemann, 1909; New York: Doubleday, Page, 1909);

Richard Wagner, *Siegfried & the Twilight of the Gods,* translated by Margaret Armour (London: Heinemann, 1911; New York: Doubleday, Page, 1911);

Aesop's Fables, translated by V. S. Vernon Jones (London: Heinemann, 1912; New York: Doubleday, Page, 1912);

Charles Dickens, *A Christmas Carol* (London: Heinemann, 1915; Philadelphia: Lippincott, 1915);

The Allies' Fairy Book (London: Heinemann, 1916; Philadelphia: Lippincott, 1916);

Jacob and Wilhelm Grimm, *Little Brother & Little Sister* (London: Constable, 1917; New York: Dodd, Mead, 1917);

Sir Thomas Malory, *The Romance of King Arthur and His Knights of the Round Table,* abridged by Alfred Pollard (London & New York: Macmillan, 1917);

Flora Annie Steel, *English Fairy Tales* (London & New York: Macmillan, 1918);

A. C. Swinburne, *The Springtide of Life, Poems of Childhood* (London: Heinemann, 1918; Philadelphia: Lippincott, 1918);

Julia Ellsworth Ford, *Snickety Nick* (New York: Moffat, Yard, 1919);

Charles S. Evans, *Cinderella* (London: Heinemann, 1919; Philadelphia: Lippincott, 1919);

Evans, *The Sleeping Beauty* (London: Heinemann, 1920; Philadelphia: Lippincott, 1920);

Jacob and Wilhelm Grimm, *Snowdrop and Other Tales* (London: Constable, 1920; New York: Dutton, 1920);

Jacob and Wilhelm Grimm, *Hansel & Gretel & Other Tales* (London: Constable, 1920; New York: Dutton, 1920);

James Stephens, *Irish Fairy Tales* (London & New York: Macmillan, 1920);

Nathaniel Hawthorne, *A Wonder Book* (London: Hodder & Stoughton, 1922; New York: Doran, 1922);

Christopher Morley, *Where the Blue Begins* (London: Heinemann, 1925; New York: Doubleday, Page, 1925);

Margery Williams Bianco, *Poor Cecco* (London: Chatto & Windus, 1925; New York: Doran, 1925);

Shakespeare, *The Tempest* (London: Heinemann, 1926; New York: Doubleday, Page, 1926);

Abbie Farwell Brown, *The Lonesomest Doll* (Boston & New York: Houghton Mifflin, 1928);

Irving, *The Legend of Sleepy Hollow* (London: Harrap, 1928; Philadelphia: McKay, 1928);

May Clarissa Byron, *J. M. Barrie's Peter Pan in Kensington Gardens, Retold for Little People* (London: Hodder & Stoughton, 1929; New York: Scribners, 1930);

Clement Clarke Moore, *The Night Before Christmas* (London: Harrap, 1931; Philadelphia: Lippincott, 1931);

Izaak Walton, *The Compleat Angler,* edited by Richard Le Gallienne (London: Harrap, 1931; Philadelphia: McKay, 1931);

Hans Christian Andersen, *Fairy Tales* (London: Harrap, 1932; Philadelphia: McKay, 1932);

John Ruskin, *King of the Golden River* (London: Harrap, 1932; Philadelphia: Lippincott, 1932);

Christina Rossetti, *Goblin Market* (London: Harrap, 1933; Philadelphia: Lippincott, 1933);

Robert Browning, *The Pied Piper of Hamelin* (London: Harrap, 1934; Philadelphia: Lippincott, 1934);

Edgar Allan Poe, *Tales of Mystery and Imagination* (London: Harrap, 1935; Philadelphia: Lippincott, 1935);

Henrik Ibsen, *Peer Gynt* (London: Harrap, 1936; Philadelphia: Lippincott, 1936);

Shakespeare, *A Midsummer Night's Dream* (New York: Limited Editions Club, 1939);

Kenneth Grahame, *The Wind in the Willows* (New York: Limited Editions Club/Heritage, 1940; London: Methuen, 1950).

Although Rackham wrote no children's books, he created them: through his illustrations the great classics of children's literature gained lives and identities beyond those which their authors and other illustrators could give. Through Rackham's pictures readers enter a world of goblins and elves, of delicate androgynous children with wings, of twisted grotesque trees with faces – in short, the world of faerie, where everyday surroundings are touched by magic.

Long after his death Rackham's works continue to fascinate, not least for the remarkable craftsmanship that made his books treasures in his day and collector's items today. But the chief fascination seems to lie in how this proper, Edwardian gentleman, so businesslike and meticulous in his life, could have dwelt daily with witches and fairies and could have created them so believably for generations of children and adults alike. Part of the answer is that he was reflecting his times. In *Fantastic Illustration and Design in Britain, 1850–1930* (1979) Diana L. Johnson notes that the fantastic permeated the literature, illustration, and design of this period to a degree not equaled before or since, but that this trend found its strongest expression in book illustration. Other illustrators in this vein, however, such as Rackham's contemporaries Richard Doyle and George Cruikshank, have not had Rackham's lasting power. In his memoir *Another Part of the Wood* (1974) art critic Kenneth Clark remembers the fear as a child of opening Rackham's illustrated collection of the Grimms' fairy tales, not because of the violence of the narratives but because of the pictures.

Arthur Rackham, the third surviving child of Alfred and Annie Rackham, was born in London on 19 September 1867. His father was a public servant, rising from junior clerk at Doctors' Commons (the location of the Ecclesiastical and Admiralty Courts) to the high post of admiralty marshal; Rackham once sketched his father in full regalia, carrying out ceremonial duties. His mother was a quiet and deeply religious woman who bore twelve children but buried several in infancy. Both parents were liberal in their child raising and were much influenced by Frederick Denison Maurice, a theologian who preached freedom of thought. Yet Alfred Rackham's journals reveal his pride in his civil service as well as in his family; biographer James Hamilton comments that Alfred was, in spite of his freethinking, a company man. This combination of conservatism and liberality may partly explain that balance of qualities in his son Arthur.

Rackham at his drawing board in 1909

Though not especially academic, Rackham won prizes in mathematics and early revealed a drawing ability that made him popular both with other boys and with his school's drawing master, who encouraged his talent. However, Rackham's health was poor, and a sea voyage was recommended as a cure. Accordingly, he left school in 1884, at age sixteen, for a six-month journey to Australia. On the trip he kept a detailed journal, listing not only the passengers (along with their notable characteristics) but also each day's distance and the latitude and longitude reached. He painted twenty-four watercolors of the sea, the harbors, and the trees and rocky outcroppings near Sydney. Hamilton proposes that Rackham began this voyage as a schoolboy and returned as a dedicated artist.

Family finances prevented Rackham's studying art full-time upon his return to London, so he compromised by attending art school at night while job hunting during the day, eventually finding work as junior clerk at the Fire Office in 1885. Though he was frequently bored with clerking, he seems to have accepted it as a means to something more fulfilling. When he resigned from the position in 1892 and moved from his parents' house soon thereafter,

he carefully chose a neighborhood inhabited by both barristers and artists, as if he had an eye to future contacts.

During the late 1880s and early 1890s, Rackham submitted illustrations to various magazines, honing his skills for that lucrative market. After a year of publishing illustrations in the *Pall Mall Budget,* a liberal magazine with varied appeal, he accepted a position on its staff and was at last assured of an income from his drawing. He was sent out on a variety of assignments each day, from illustrating bank robberies to stray dogs. In 1893 he moved to the *Westminister Budget,* which gave him more "literary" kinds of work and a freer artistic hand. One of his illustrations from this period is for a poem by Richard Le Gallienne, "To Spring" (1893). Rackham has surrounded this rather overrefined verse with trees, a female figure with swirling hair and garments, and scattered daffodils. Though markedly different from Rackham's later work, the illustration does have a lyricism which anticipates his mature style.

Rackham seems to have been at pains to discourage critics and interested collectors from viewing these early journalistic efforts, and with good reason, for they show little of the technique that made him famous. On the other hand, they reveal variety, interesting detail, and a facility for line – especially the curvilinear line which later so distinguished his work. In his 1976 book on Rackham's art Fred Gettings argues persuasively that Rackham's experience in graphic journalism, though it seemed at the time to delay his individual achievements, was in fact responsible for his development. The chief advantage of this tradition, according to Gettings, is that it gives the artist time to develop until he really has something original to express. From this work of observing and reproducing Rackham slowly developed his individual style: that peculiar blending of the fantastic with carefully observed nature that makes his work entirely believable.

For Rackham, though, hindsight produced only painful memories of this time in his life. The *Bookman* (October 1925) asked several artists to describe "The Worst Time In My Life." Rackham identified this early period in his career, when he worked as a freelance graphic artist for journals and magazines: "Work was hard to get and not well paid, and such efforts as I made along the lines I have since followed received little encouragement." The Boer War caused a demand for work unsuited to his interests or aptitude, and he realized that the camera would soon supplant illustrated journalism. But his special bent began to be recognized by other artists. Indeed, within ten years of this "very thin time," Rackham would reach a pinnacle of success unlike that of any of his contemporaries.

Though he had already contributed realistic drawings for several books, his first venture into fantasy came when he illustrated a children's tale by S. J. Adair Fitzgerald titled *The Zankiwank and the Bletherwitch* (1896). Rackham drew the Zankiwank as a strange, ostrichlike creature running through the town on attenuated feet in down-at-the-heels carpet slippers, two calm-looking children under its arms. Hamilton suggests that these illustrations represent the real Rackham breaking out at last. Moreover, the title page of this book announces that the book contains "pictures by Arthur Rackham"; his illustrations were beginning to sell books.

In 1897 Rackham made his first trip to Bayreuth, Germany, where he saw a performance of Richard Wagner's music-drama cycle *Der Ring des Nibelungen* (1874). Rackham returned to Bayreuth and nourished himself on Wagnerian themes throughout his career, these interests emerging most noticeably in his illustrations for adaptations of Wagner's *Siegfried & the Twilight of the Gods*

(1911). The quality of these illustrations fascinated C. S. Lewis, whose childhood discovery of them was, he said, a turning point in his life; he was enraptured with the "Northern" vision they invoked "of huge, clear spaces" with their "remoteness, severity." While this quality may seem different from the grotesque dwarfs and delicate fairies that identify Rackham for many, critics have suggested that it springs from the same source. Rackham acknowledged "Teutonic influences" on his work, and in a 1977 article tracing Rackham's debt to the romantic tradition, Christa Kamenetsky points out that Norse mythology may have supplied the inspiration for the "thievish, gray, and grotesque dwarfs" of his fairy-tale illustrations.

Dent continued to offer commissions to Rackham; in 1898 the artist received £150 for one hundred black-and-white illustrations for *The Ingoldsby Legends* (1837), by Richard Harris Barham. Like *The Zankiwank and the Bletherwitch,* these quaint tales and poems allowed Rackham, as Hamilton says, to exercise his penchant for macabre humor. By this time he had mastered a variety of styles: the journalistic tradition of action, costume, and adventure; the tradition of caricature, of exaggerating and stylizing for humorous or whimsical effect; and what he called "the fantastic and the imaginative," in which Rackham combined the first two to create something new and entirely individual.

Given this interesting combination of techniques, it is probably not surprising that he would be drawn to the tales of Jacob and Wilhelm Grimm. His first commission for them came in 1900, but he returned to them many times during his career, adding illustrations, coloring ones that had originally been black-and-white, constantly reworking the themes and images. He did not shrink from their more violent motifs in his earlier interpretations, though later, during wartime, he would soften his images somewhat. Evidently after some urging from his family he exhibited these illustrations at the Royal Watercolor Society, beginning in 1902. A critic for the *Outlook* (24 October 1903) responded to Rackham's painting for "Rumpelstiltskin" exhibited at the Society of Oil Painters: "[Rackham] is a man with a special kink in his mind, a faculty for exaggerating certain odd developments of humanity to the pitch of monstrosity, yet with an affectionate liking for the monster."

In 1903 Rackham married Edyth Starkie, whom he had met in 1901. Edyth amused friends and family throughout her life with stories of her robust childhood in Ireland. An accomplished portrait painter, she won a medal at the Barcelona Interna-

Rackham's frontispiece for a 1915 edition of Charles Dickens's A Christmas Carol

tional Exhibition in 1911, the same year her husband won. The marriage was evidently a happy one, with deep emotional involvement on both sides. Edyth, however, always suffered from delicate health and had a serious heart attack in 1916, after which her health continued to decline.

An important year for Rackham was 1905. He received a commission from Brown and Phillips for fifty color illustrations for a 1905 edition of Washington Irving's *Rip Van Winkle* (1820), but the paintings were to be exhibited at Brown and Phillips's Leicester Galleries, along with thirty-nine other Rackham works, before the book's publication. This shrewd business move by Rackham and his publishers ensured that the paintings themselves would bring a good profit and that the book would get excellent advance publicity. Rackham made similar arrangements for many of his major books, though he retained all the rights to the originals, allowing himself the option of later enhancing and reselling them.

Rip Van Winkle was an unqualified success; critics compared Rackham's work to that of the sixteenth-century German artist Albrecht Dürer and remarked on the accomplished draftsmanship. The

illustrations were all gathered at the back of the book, thus allowing the story to be told first in words, then in Rackham's pictures. And while Rackham's pictures do not exactly tell a different story – Rackham was scrupulously true to the text in all his illustrations – they reveal Rackham's ability to enhance, to re-create, to open the world of the text in ways the author might have envisioned but did not put into words.

Gettings has commented on a particular example of this technique, which he calls Rackham's "irrelevancy." In Irving's tale Rip is harangued by his wife while they are in bed: "A curtain-lecture is worth all the sermons in the world for teaching the virtues of patience and long-suffering," writes Irving. Rackham took this small statement and created a remarkable fantasy: in the upper left of the painting, Rip and his wife are in a bed with flowered curtains and richly patterned bedding, but clinging to the bed curtains is an assortment of playful goblins, obviously much amused by the suffering Rip. In the foreground one lone goblin has tried on Rip's slippers, which he evidently finds hilariously funny, as do two small mice nearby who are supporting each other in laughter. Gettings believes that such irrelevancy tends to comment on rather than merely illustrate the text, a tendency he traces back to medieval manuscript illumination. Certainly one of the most characteristic of Rackham's techniques is to choose moments in the text that suggest no action or image and to create both in pictures which Gettings calls "contiguous to the text"; this is "Rackham's way to extend the narrative into another, more rarified dimension of imagination," and it came into its own with *Rip Van Winkle*.

Following immediately on this success came another, perhaps the one with which Rackham is most associated. Brown and Phillips arranged for Rackham to illustrate J. M. Barrie's *Peter Pan in Kensington Gardens* (1906), giving him almost twice the time to complete it as he had had for *Rip Van Winkle*. By December 1906 he had completed the fifty illustrations contracted, and once again the publication of the book followed an exhibition of the paintings. This time the critics were not so enthusiastic, though their complaint seemed to be directed at the publisher rather than the artist. The *Times* (London) criticized the book for being aimed more at catching the eye of adult Christmas shoppers than at pleasing young readers – identifying a peculiar marketing situation that still exists for expensively produced illustrated books and that Rackham may have partly created. Rackham's own problems with

Peter Pan were more literary, as Barrie had created a very young Peter for *Peter Pan in Kensington Gardens* and an older Peter in the version he wrote for the theater, where the action was set not in a specific London locale but in Never Land. Rackham chose to illustrate the Kensington Gardens Peter, believing that "Never Never lands are poor prosy substitutes" for real places which might be peopled with fairies. Certainly his illustrations of Kensington Gardens achieved for his public what Barrie's more popular incarnations of Peter Pan did not: the transformation of a real place into fairyland. The continuing popularity of Rackham's pictures and their frequent republication suggest the truth of his later comment to Eleanor Farjeon: "What power localizing a myth has."

With the success of *Peter Pan* came a certain financial and professional freedom. At age thirty-nine he bought 16 Chalcot Gardens, Hampstead; he also was able to refuse any assignments he found uncongenial and to spend as much as eighteen months planning his work – a luxury for an illustrator. At the same time he was developing the persona that identified him so closely with his pictures. He often drew his balding head, spectacles, lanky figure, and carpet slippers on elves, gnomes, and trees, creating little caricatures of himself and making him a resident of his own fairy world. In a 1904 illustration for *Punch* called "Common Objects at the Seaside by our Goblinesque Artists," he drew a crowded scene of goblins, maidens, and sundry creatures taking photographs of each other, catching lobsters, hiding in bathing tents, boating, and generally making confused seaside merriment. At least four of these goblins appear to be self-portraits. For *Peter Pan* he portrayed himself as an elf hiding behind a tulip, with a postage stamp placed in the foreground to show his relative size. As Rackham's fame grew and his public saw photographs of him, the recognition of his face in goblin guise established him as "the Goblin master," or "Court Painter to King Oberon and Queen Titania," an identity he seems not to have discouraged.

Yet a 1934 formal self-portrait depicts Rackham against a background of London chimney pots and cloudy skies, titling the picture *A Transpontine Cockney*. His daughter Barbara said that he was "neat, tidy, punctual, conscientious, hardworking," a conformist in a navy blue suit and navy and white bow tie, an outfit he seldom varied. He kept meticulous records of his materials and his models; he took regular exercise in the form of golf and swinging on a trapeze which he kept in his studio chiefly for use in modeling.

In 1907 the copyright on Carroll's *Alice's Adventures in Wonderland* (1865) lapsed, and Heinemann commissioned Rackham to produce new illustrations. Rackham once again depended on reality for Wonderland, just as he had Kensington Gardens for Never Land. He chose a real little girl for his Alice and his own cook for Alice's, used Edyth's best china and his own big chair for the tea-party scene – he even threw a few plates to get broken ones right. But his delicately colored, dreamlike paintings, with their heightened reality, evoked outrage from many fans of Sir John Tenniel, the original illustrator, who felt that Rackham had encroached on sacred territory. Yet Rackham's was one of five new editions of *Alice's Adventures in Wonderland* published that same year and the only one to survive. Sales, in fact, far surpassed those of *Peter Pan*, reaching a career high for the artist.

During the next several years Rackham was at the peak of his popularity. The birth of his daughter Barbara in 1908 was heralded in the press. He won many awards, his works went into multiple printings, publishers battled for his services, his opinions were sought not only on illustration and caricature but also on dolls and children's education, and his work was parodied by other artists – a sure sign of fame. In 1914 *St. Nicholas*, the popular American children's magazine, published Farjeon's profile of Rackham, firmly establishing his romantic persona for his child audience. Farjeon calls him a "wizard" who "only pretended to call himself Arthur Rackham, and hobgoblins really hailed him by some more mystic name on stormy nights on Hampstead Heath, which is an easy broomstick ride from a certain little house in Chalcot Gardens." Farjeon whimsically claims that "a magic carpet is kept in the house for personal use."

All this attention made Rackham busier than ever. One self-caricature that may date from this period shows Rackham working on five books at once, pens in both hands and both feet, and one in his mouth. Yet in a 1911 letter to Lewis Melville he described himself as a "slow and painful worker" and spent long hours on relatively minor projects. He worried constantly about the reproduction of his paintings, often expressing frustration with the three-color process then in use: the method tended to blur detail, such as his rendering of delicately printed fabric. In a 1911 book on painting technique, A. L. Baldry describes Rackham's painstaking technique for figure work: he began with "a careful drawing in pencil" to fix the essentials and the details, then added pen-and-ink work. The pencil marks were erased, and color washes were then added. At times

Pandora's box, one of Rackham's illustrations for an edition of
Nathaniel Hawthorne's A Wonder Book

he had to go over a colored illustration again in pen and ink to ensure that the most important lines would be visible. Despite Rackham's frustration with the three-color process, perhaps its drawbacks were in some measure responsible for his distinctive style, for it forced his use of the pale washes that give his paintings their quality of old vellum and encouraged his facility with the curvilinear line. Rackham also reversed the usual process of composition in his figure drawing; he sketched the surroundings and settings before drawing the figures. Baldry conjectures that this technique accounts for the particular unity of Rackham's work: his figures are firmly anchored in their surroundings, no matter how fantastic or imaginative either might be.

At this time, too, Rackham's affection for the Germanic became more noticeable. His illustrations for Friedrich de la Motte Fouqué's *Undine* (1909) and Wagner's *Siegfried & the Twilight of the Gods* evoke the "Northern" qualities that so entranced a young C. S. Lewis. Unfortunately, his larger book-buying audience did not respond especially well to his forays into adult picture books, though the de-

cline in sales may have been partly due to the beginning of the war. At any rate, in 1913 Heinemann commissioned a Rackham *Mother Goose* and published a collection of Rackham illustrations in *Arthur Rackham's Book of Pictures;* these, says Hamilton, reunited him with children's literature, where his publishers could be assured of sales.

The patriotism of wartime England inspired two Rackham contributions to the war effort: *The Allies' Fairy Book* (1916), a collection of tales in honor of the cooperation among the Allies, and *The Romance of King Arthur and His Knights of the Round Table* (1917), an abridgment of Thomas Malory's *Morte Darthur* (1485). Soon the stresses of air raids caused Rackham to move his family to safer quarters while he continued his work and his social life in London. Following the war, Rackham published two books with silhouette illustrations, Charles S. Evans's *Cinderella* in 1919 and *The Sleeping Beauty* in 1920, which revealed mastery of this unusual form. Also in 1920 the Rackhams moved to Houghton House, a farm with vistas, outbuildings, gardens, and a medieval thatched barn which Rackham used

Rackham's illustration of "The Elder-Tree Mother," for a 1932 collection of Hans Christian Andersen's Fairy Tales

as his country studio. He would test his brushes on the wall, and he once commented to Barbara that they should one day sell the area of paint-daubed plaster, adding, "It'll be worth a lot of money!"

Money was not yet a problem. Rackham was a rich man, thanks to sucessful exhibitions and to sales of his work in America. His image in America differed somewhat from that in England, due to his only venture into commercial art. The Colgate Company wanted to create an image of English aristocracy for the American buyers of its Cashmere Bouquet soap, so between 1922 and 1925 Rackham created a series of thirty illustrations of delicate young women in ruffled, crinoline skirts, surrounded by flowers. In a 1931 essay for *Artist and Advertiser* William P. Gibbons of the Colgate advertising department claims that many American art galleries, as well as the Metropolitan Museum of Art, asked to display Rackham's Cashmere Bouquet paintings during the campaign, and years later the

company continued to receive requests from the American public for reproductions. But this rise in his American popular reputation corresponded with a fall in Rackham's English status. Younger artists were emerging, and postwar printing emphasized cheaper methods less congenial to Rackham's work; this combination of circumstances prompted Rackham to comment that the "freely illustrated 'Rackham' book is no longer possible" and would probably never come back.

To foster his American reputation and to shop for more commissions, Rackham traveled to America, for the first and only time, in November 1927. Despite bouts of depression and initial bewilderment at New York City, Rackham obtained a commission for an edition of *A Midsummer Night's Dream* (performed circa 1595–1596): a hand-lettered version of the highest quality, finished in 1930 but never published, for the New York Public Library, which had a large bequest for such projects. He had

Rackham's 1934 self-portrait, A Transpontine Cockney

previously illustrated the work for a 1908 edition and would do so again in 1939. Rackham also met Anne Carroll Moore of the library's children's room, unexpectedly spending the evening with her and a young companion named Nicholas riding in a taxi, watching the city light up, and having supper at the Brevoort Grill.

His return to England began a period of ill health for both Rackham and his wife. But it also began what Hamilton calls his second great period of creativity (the first being 1905–1916). Harrap commissioned him to illustrate a 1932 edition of Hans Christian Andersen's *Fairy Tales* and sent him and Barbara to Denmark to absorb the atmosphere. He also entered the world of the stage, designing Basil Dean's production of *Hansel and Gretel* in 1933. The same year saw the publication of *The Arthur Rackham Fairy Book,* a selection of twenty-three tales chosen by Rackham and accompanied by new illustrations. Rackham's brief preface to this collec-

tion, probably the only thing he ever wrote deliberately for children, expresses his belief in the value of fairy tales: "There's no doubt that we should be behaving ourselves very differently if Beauty had never been united to her Beast, or Sir Richard Whittington listened to the bells." More important, as Gillian Adams notes in her 1989 analysis of *The Fairy Book,* the multiplicity of styles in its illustrations offers a retrospective of Rackham's work. The full range of Rackham styles is represented: finished painting, silhouette, sketch, and decorative head- and tailpieces that constitute his ephemeral yet distinctive doodling. Rackham's compositional devices are also in evidence: his pleasure in the vignette, his use of the close-up, his gathering of action into an inverted triangle, his placing the mass of the picture in the upper half or lower half of the frame, and his use of strong verticals at the center or at the sides of a picture. A recurrent argument among Rackham critics centers on whether Rackham was primarily an artist of line or color; the illustrations in *The Fairy Book* demonstrate his facility with both.

Rackham produced illustrations for a 1934 edition of Robert Browning's *The Pied Piper of Hamelin* (1842) and, in an interesting change of pace, a 1935 collection of Edgar Allan Poe's short stories. Of the latter he commented once that the illustrations he was creating "were so horrible I was beginning to frighten myself." The finished pictures, however, are as much parodic as horrific.

By this time Rackham had been diagnosed as having cancer and was often hospitalized or under enforced rest at home. But one of his most famous works was yet to come. In 1936 George Macy of the Limited Editions Club of New York visited Rackham at his studio. The two talked about various possible commissions, one of which was Rackham's third time at illustrating *A Midsummer Night's Dream.* Macy also casually mentioned Kenneth Grahame's *The Wind in the Willows* (1908). As Macy recalled in a 1940 article for *Horn Book:* "Immediately a wave of emotion crossed his face; he gulped, started to say something, turned his back on me and went to the door for a few minutes. Then he came back and said that he had for many years been trying to persuade an English publisher to let him illustrate *The Wind in the Willows.* He had been asked by Kenneth Grahame, nearly thirty years ago, to illustrate that book; and had for all those years deeply regretted his refusal."

Permission was obtained from Scribners, holder of the copyright in America, to issue for subscribers a limited edition printed on the finest paper and to the most exacting specifications. Despite his exhaustion and illness, Rackham embarked on the project enthusiastically, keeping Macy informed of his progress. In his last letter to Macy, written two weeks before his death, Rackham revealed that he was almost entirely bedridden and had done many of the pictures in bed, though he added, "I think some of them are as good as I have ever done." As he finished the last picture, of Rat and Mole about to set off in the boat, he realized that he had forgotten to draw oars in the boat. He drew them, then lay back, saying "Thank goodness, that is the last one." Rackham died shortly afterward, on 6 September 1939, three days after Britain declared war on Germany. He was cremated at Croydon, and his ashes were scattered in the rose garden at Golders Green crematorium. Edyth died two years later, and her ashes joined his. *The Wind in the Willows* was published in America in 1940 to general acclaim but was not published in England until 1950.

Curiously, despite his considerable fame and popularity, Rackham was never awarded any state honors in England, nor was he ever admitted to the Royal Academy. Moreover, his work is better represented by collections in American libraries than in those of his native country. Yet he was quintessentially British. Comparing Rackham to Maurice Sendak, Selma G. Lanes suggests that his Britishness took the form of diffidence, a reluctance to reveal his emotions. As she puts it, whereas Sendak is involved in the emotional pain of childhood, Rackham kept his distance from such feelings. The result is a certain detachment in the viewer. Kamenetsky sees this detachment as evidence of Rackham's sense of humor and of his ability to move freely between reality and imagination. American writer and illustrator Robert Lawson proposes in a 1940 *Horn Book* essay that Rackham always respected the central task of an illustrator, which is not to reveal himself but to render visible the ideas and moods of the author. Certainly this is the goal at which Rackham aimed. Yet he did not believe this made the illustrator a slave to the text. He once commented to a group of authors that the illustrator must first be a partner and that one of the illustrator's chief duties is to bring to the work an individual sense of delight. Rackham far surpassed his contemporaries in the achievement of this goal, for although he never essentially departed from the text, his pictures recreate it on a new plane, one that expresses Rackham's own delight in the work.

Rackham's particular gifts for line, color, and composition make his works a rich new celebration of the imagination. For him illustration had its own rewards; he never confused the purpose of a picture meant to be hung on a wall with one meant to accompany a text, believing that the former had to be individual and complete in itself as an object of contemplation, while the latter, often done to order, was usually examined only briefly as an accompaniment to words and to other pictures. Yet Rackham's pictures often transcend this division: done to order, yet highly individual; accompanying a text, yet compositionally as satisfying as any classic painting; suggesting a tale, yet offering possibilities for contemplation in themselves. When he achieved this balance, Rackham set a standard by which the success of all other illustrators of children's books may be judged.

Interview:
Arthur Rackham, "The Worst Time in My Life," *Bookman* (October 1925): 7.

Biographies:
Derek Hudson, *Arthur Rackham: His Life and Work* (New York: Charles Scribner's Sons, 1960);

James Hamilton, *Arthur Rackham* (New York: Arcade, 1990).

References:

Gillian Adams, "Arthur Rackham's *Fairy Book:* A Confrontation with the Marvelous," in *Touchstones: Reflections on the Best in Children's Literature,* volume 3, edited by Perry Nodelman (West Lafayette, Ind.: Children's Literature Association, 1989), pp. 107–121;

Alfred. L. Baldry, "Arthur Rackham: A Painter of Fantasies," *International Studio,* 25 (May 1905): 189–201;

Baldry, *The Practice of Water-Colour Painting* (London: Macmillan, 1911), pp. 109–113;

Kenneth Clark, *Another Part of the Wood* (New York: Harper & Row, 1974);

Eleanor Farjeon, "Arthur Rackham: The Wizard at Home," *St. Nicholas,* 41 (March 1914): 385–391;

Fred Gettings, *Arthur Rackham* (New York: Macmillan, 1976);

William P. Gibbons, "Sir Arthur Rackham's Adventure in Advertising Art," *Artist and Advertiser* (January 1931): 6–8;

Diana L. Johnson, *Fantastic Illustration and Design in Britain, 1850–1930* (Providence: Rhode Island School of Design, 1979), pp. 82–85;

Christa Kamenetsky, "Arthur Rackham and the Romantic Tradition," *Children's Literature,* 6 (1977): 115–129;

Selma G. Lanes, "Rackham and Sendak," in her *Down the Rabbit Hole: Adventures and Misadventures in the Realm of Children's Literature* (New York: Atheneum, 1971), pp. 67–78;

Robert Lawson, "The Genius of Arthur Rackham," *Horn Book,* 16 (May–June 1940): 147–151;

C. S. Lewis, *Surprised by Joy* (New York: Harcourt, Brace & World, 1955), pp. 72–78;

George Macy, "Arthur Rackham and *The Wind in the Willows,*" *Horn Book,* 16 (May–June 1940): 153–158;

Susan E. Meyer, "Arthur Rackham," in *A Treasury of the Great Children's Book Illustrators,* edited by Meyer (New York: Abradale/Abrams, 1987), pp. 157–175;

Anne Carroll Moore, "The Three Owls' Notebook: A Christmas Ride with Arthur Rackham," *Horn Book,* 15 (November–December 1939): 369–372;

Walter Starkie, *Scholars and Gypsies: An Autobiography* (Berkeley & Los Angeles: University of California Press, 1963).

Papers:
The largest collection of Rackham's work is housed in the Butler Library at Columbia University, New York City. The University of Texas at Austin has almost every issue of every periodical to which Rackham contributed. Smaller holdings are at the University of Louisville Library, the Free Library of Philadelphia, and the Cambridge (U.K.) City Libraries.

Talbot Baines Reed

(3 April 1852 – 28 November 1893)

Patrick Scott
University of South Carolina

BOOKS: *The Adventures of a Three Guinea Watch* (London: Religious Tract Society, [1883]);

"Follow My Leader": or, The Boys of Templeton (London & New York: Cassell, 1885);

A History of the Old English Letter Foundries, with Notes, Historical and Bibliographical, on the Rise and Progress of English Typography (London: Stock, 1887); revised and enlarged by A. F. Johnson (London: Faber & Faber, 1952);

The Fifth Form at St. Dominic's: A School Story (London: Religious Tract Society, [1887]);

The Willoughby Captains: A School Story (London: Hodder & Stoughton, 1887);

My Friend Smith: A Story of School and City Life (London: Religious Tract Society, [1889]);

Sir Ludar: A Story of the Days of the Great Queen Bess (London: Low, 1889);

Old and New Fashions in Typography (London: Caslon, 1890);

Roger Ingleton, Minor (London: Low, 1891);

John Baskerville, Printer: A Paper Read before the Archaeological Section of the Birmingham and Midland Institute on 23 November 1892 (N.p., [1892]);

The Cock-House at Fellsgarth (London: Religious Tract Society, [1893]);

Tom, Dick and Harry (London: Religious Tract Society, [1894]);

Reginald Cruden: A Tale of City Life (London: Religious Tract Society, [1894]);

A Dog with a Bad Name (London: Religious Tract Society, [1894]);

The Master of the Shell (London: Religious Tract Society, [1894]);

Kilgorman: A Story of Ireland in 1798, by Reed and John Sime (London & New York: Nelson, 1895 [i.e., 1894]);

A List of Books and Papers on Printers and Printing, under the Countries and Towns to Which They Refer, by Reed and A. W. Pollard (London: Blades, East & Blades, [1895]);

A Book of Short Stories, edited by G. Andrew Hutchison (London: Religious Tract Society, [1897]);

Parkhurst Sketches and Other Stories, edited by Hutchison (London: Religious Tract Society, [1899]);

Parkhurst Boys: And Other Stories of School Life, edited by Hutchison (London: Religious Tract Society, [1905]);

The School Ghost, and Boycotted; With Other Stories (London: Boy's Own Paper, [1930]).

OTHER: "The Rise and Progress of Typography and Type-Founding in England," in *Caxton Celebration, 1877: Catalogue of the Loan Exhibition of Antiquities, Curiosities, and Appliances Connected with the Art of Printing* (London, 1887), pp. 422–425;

"Memoir of the late William Blades," in William Blades, *The Pentateuch of Printing* (London: Stock, 1891; Chicago: McClurg, 1891), pp. ix–xviii.

SELECTED PERIODICAL PUBLICATIONS – UNCOLLECTED: "Camping Out," anonymous, *Morning of Life,* 1 (1875): 95–97, 101–104;

"My First Football Match," as "An Old Boy," *Boy's Own Paper* (18 January 1879): 1;

"Rough Preliminary List of Books Printed in the Irish Character and Language," *Celtic Magazine,* 10 (October 1885): 584–586;

"On the Use and Classification of a Typographical Library," *Library,* 4 (February 1892): 33–44.

Remembered chiefly for his realistic novels of boarding-school life, Talbot Baines Reed was among the most influential boys' writers of his generation. Reed was never a full-time author, and his writing career lasted barely more than a decade, but he produced thirteen novels, in addition to sketches, articles, and scholarly publications on the history of printing.

Reed's works played a crucial role in the late-nineteenth-century movement of boys' books away from religious didacticism toward a morally sensitive realism. In his serials for the *Boy's Own Paper,*

No. 1.—Vol. I.

SATURDAY, JANUARY 18, 1879.

Price One Penny.
[ALL RIGHTS RESERVED.

MY FIRST FOOTBALL MATCH.

BY AN OLD BOY.

IT was a proud moment in my existence when Wright, captain of our football club, came up to me in school one Friday and said, "Adams, your name is down to play in the match against Craven to-morrow."

I could have knighted him on the spot. To be one of the picked "fifteen," whose glory it was to fight the battles of their school in the Great Close, had been the leading ambition of my life—I suppose I ought to be ashamed to confess it—ever since, as a little chap of ten, I entered Parkhurst six years ago. Not a winter Saturday but had seen me either looking on at some big match, or oftener still scrimmaging about with a score or so of other juniors in a scratch game. But for a long time, do what I would, I always

seemed as far as ever from the coveted goal, and was half despairing of ever rising to win my "first fifteen cap." Latterly, however, I had noticed Wright and a few others of our best players more than once lounging about in the Little Close where we juniors used to play, evidently taking observations with an eye to business. Under the awful gaze of these heroes, need I say I exerted myself as I had never done before? What cared I for hacks or bruises, so only that I could distinguish myself in their eyes? And never was music sweeter

"Down!"

Short story by Reed on the front page of the first issue of a paper published by the Religious Tract Society

Reed perfected the school novel as a genre – boarding-school life, athletic achievement, school-boy conflict and adventure – creating a formula followed for the next fifty years or more. In a 1914 essay on the genre, Ian Hay comments that Reed's school novels "have never been bettered . . . anybody who has ever attempted to write a tale which shall be probable yet interesting, and racy yet moral, will realize how admirably Mr. Reed has achieved this feat." Yet Reed is oversimplified if he is identified solely with this formula. His school novels are only part of his writing for boys, and increasing recognition is now being given to his other achievements, such as the psychological acuteness of his characterization and the broader social implications of his often-neglected stories of young adult life.

Talbot Baines Reed was born in London on 3 April 1852 and lived in the London area all his life. Over several generations his family had been influential in religious dissent and liberal politics; his father was a Liberal member of Parliament, and so was his maternal grandfather, the radical newspaper editor Edward Baines. The family's religious beliefs were expressed through a variety of philanthropic endeavors. Reeds were involved with hospitals, orphanages, asylums, nonconformist religious schools, the Bible Society, and, important for his writing career, the Religious Tract Society. He came from a family tradition of charitable activism.

Reed was educated first in a small suburban school and then, from the age of twelve, at the City of London School, a downtown day foundation strongly focused on preparation of young men for commercial life but struggling also in the 1860s to give more of a classics-based, "public-school" education for university-bound boys. The notion of building up a school's status and credit would be central in Reed's later fiction. Reed, commuting daily from the suburbs, organized football and cricket teams, and when these later lapsed, he protested fiercely, in a letter to the school magazine, that "the fair fame of the Old School" rested on its traditions "not only of scholarships won and degrees taken but of goals kicked and runs scored." As a schoolboy Reed, known to his friends as "Tibi" ("O Thou," a Latinate pun on his initials "T. B."), was popular, vivacious, and athletic. His contemporaries remembered his feats, not only at football and cricket, but also in rowing, mountaineering, rifle shooting, and swimming. He twice walked overnight from London to Cambridge to visit a cousin, and in 1869 the Humane Society gave him a medal for rescuing another cousin from drowning. Though Reed did not go to a traditional elite boarding school, he certainly experienced firsthand the values that such schools increasingly embodied.

Reed was only sixteen when he left school and entered his father's typefounding business. In due time he became managing director of the foundry, steering the firm effectively through a period of enormously expanded printing demand and of dramatic changes in typesetting technology. London commercial life, printing, and newspaper production feature in several of his novels, notably *My Friend Smith: A Story of School and City Life* (1889), *Reginald Cruden: A Tale of City Life* (1894), and *Sir Ludar: A Story of the Days of the Great Queen Bess* (1889).

From the foundry, also, Reed developed an absorbing intellectual interest in the new field of printing history. Reed's achievements as a historical bibliographer, not as a boys' writer, elicited Stanley Morison's 1960 biography. Reed's Caxton Exhibition essay (1877), his still-standard *History of the Old English Letter Foundries* (1887), his published lectures on type design and the fine-printing movement, and his completion of William Blades's *The Pentateuch of Printing* (1891) all attest to his knowledge in this field. In 1892 he applied his organizational ability as founding secretary of a new scholarly group, the Bibliographical Society. In addition, throughout the 1880s he contributed a weekly essay or book review to his cousin's newspaper, the *Leeds Mercury*. By most standards his was an already full life, completed by his marriage to Elizabeth Greer on 15 June 1876 and the subsequent birth of three children.

It seems extraordinary, therefore, that shortly after his marriage Reed committed himself to what was, effectively, a third career, as a writer for boys. The key lies in the Reed family's long involvement with the influential Religious Tract Society. His grandfather had attended the society's inaugural meeting in 1799; several of his family wrote for its publications; and his eldest brother, Charles, served on the RTS governing committee. The landmark Education Act of 1870, making primary education compulsory, sharpened the society's concern about the quality of reading material available to newly literate youngsters, especially boys. Consequently, the society resolved to combat the myriad cheap, illustrated crime-and-adventure magazines – the "penny dreadfuls" – with a new boys' magazine, intended to be morally healthy while still being entertaining. It would be formally titled the *Boy's Own Paper,* though usually called the *B.O.P.* In the words of the prospectus, "Its editors understand boyhood

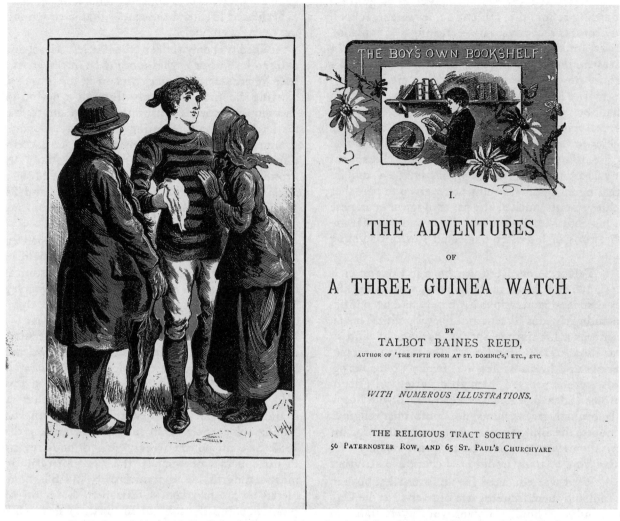

Frontispiece and title page for Reed's first book, narrated from the point of view of a timepiece (Collection of Patrick Scott)

well, enter heartily into its pursuits and pleasures. True religion, in their view, is a spirit pervading all life, in work, in play; and in this conviction, rather than any purpose of direct doctrinal teaching, this tone is given to the Paper."

As Patrick Dunae has shown in *"Boy's Own Paper:* Origins and Editorial Policies" (1976), it was difficult in practice to maintain this balancing act and to satisfy the society's evangelical supporters as well as the targeted readership. Most modern accounts rely on Reed's memoirist, George A. Hutchison (subeditor and then editor of the *B.O.P.*), and so downplay the tense evolutionary period during which the periodical renegotiated its pious origins and established its editorial image. Reed's early contributions are by no means free of direct religious reference, and much about his writing can be understood only in terms of the society's moral agenda. The *B.O.P.* never really competed directly with the

penny dreadfuls; it was relatively upmarket both in physical format and in social assumptions. But it did win middle-class parental and schoolmasterly endorsement, and the contents increasingly attracted a substantial readership, especially among boy-readers in the ten-to-sixteen-year age range. Within a few months circulation was over two hundred thousand per week, and by the late 1880s the society was printing well over half a million copies weekly. Dunae plausibly asserts that the *B.O.P.,* which survived until 1967, was "the most important and influential juvenile periodical ever published."

Reed wrote the opening item for the first issue of the *B.O.P.* in January 1879. He had already had some experience writing for boys (as, for example, in his 1875 articles on "Camping Out" for the magazine *Morning of Life*). The opener was his short story "My First Football Match," topping a half-page illustration, and using Thomas Hughes's pen name, "An Old Boy." Reed's match differs significantly from its superficial source, the football chapter in Hughes's *Tom Brown's Schooldays* (1857), for its hero, Adams, is a sixteen-year-old, and the match is his first for the Parkhurst school team against another school. Moreover, the focus is on Adams's earning his place in the team, not the newness of the football experience. Reed followed this initial effort with a series of short historical articles on "Boys from English History" (nearly all kings or princes), further short stories about Adams of Parkhurst (nearly all athletic), and a series of character sketches of "Boys We Have Known," deftly mixing humor with moral commentary. These early series show the strong initial moral and informational bent of the *B.O.P.*

Reed's first serial book, *The Adventures of a Three Guinea Watch* (1883), written at Hutchison's suggestion and serialized in the *B.O.P.* from October 1880 to April 1881, is told entirely from the point of view of the timepiece. The novel begins as a school story, following the *Tom Brown* theme as the proud young watch owner, Charlie Newcome, adapts to boarding-school life. The watch soon passes from the moral Charlie to his wastrel friend Tom Drift, who goes to the bad as a medical student in London. From the inevitable pawnshop, it passes on to a pious but unathletic Cambridge undergraduate (who dies from overwork), to his clergyman friend (a prison chaplain), to Tom Drift's equally inevitable prison cell, and then back to Charlie, just in time to save his life by stopping a bullet in the Indian Mutiny (where his wounds are tended by the now-reformed and medically qualified Tom). The sprawling plot, moral stereotyping, and occasional preachiness are utterly different from Reed's later work. As Claudia Nelson has argued in *Boys Will Be Girls: The Feminine Ethic and British Children's Fiction, 1857–1917* (1991), the role given to Charlie as moral guardian of Tom in his downward drift seems more angelic, even feminine, than the hearty masculinity usually associated with the *B.O.P.* Hutchison, in his preface to the book publication, rightly connects Reed's "life-like fidelity" to realistic presentation of how "flesh-and-blood lads" face temptation "in the great hurly-burly of our present-day cities." Reed wrote no further stories in the rather artificial object-narrator genre, but many of the themes from this first serial reemerge in his more conventional novels about postschool life.

Reed's first school novel, *The Fifth Form at St. Dominic's: A School Story* (1887), appeared in the *B.O.P.* in thirty-eight weekly episodes from October 1881 to June 1882. It is still Reed's best-known book, justly praised for its lively pictures of school life and its realistic portrayal of schoolboy psychology. *St. Dominic's* maintained, however, the strong moralistic purpose of the early *B.O.P.* It combines the story of a ten-year-old new boy, Stephen Greenfield, who is first learning to cope at school, with the story of his sixteen-year-old brother Oliver's hard struggle while he is en route to academic (and athletic) success to survive a false accusation of stealing an examination paper. Both brothers are involved, as "fag" (gofer) and scholarship rival respectively, with a counterpoint character, the sixth former Loman, who is the real thief and who is enmeshed in debt to Cripps, the villainous landlord of the Cockchafer Inn. But Reed is not F. W. Farrar, Dean of Canterbury, and the moral contrasts are tempered with understanding and mercy; indeed, after a few purgatorial years in Australia even the wretched Loman can look to a future in his father's law office. All the other boys, too, endure their schoolboy difficulties to go on to respectable upper-class careers. Some of the more dramatic events — Wraysford's rescue of Stephen from a boating accident and Oliver's rescue of the runaway Loman in a storm — are not only exciting incidents, but also parables of moral comradeship.

What gives *St. Dominic's* its continuing appeal, however, is not its meliorist moral plotting, but the liveliness of its dialogue and of its hour-by-hour incidents. The dual point of view allows Reed both sympathy and humorous distance in presenting school life. The conflict in Stephen's younger age-group between the rival protofraternities of Tadpoles and Guineapigs puts into perspective the more serious conflicts between the older Oliver's popular fifth-form friends and the affronted dignity of Loman and the sixth-form monitors. A wonderful minor character, the crippled Tony Pembury, runs a satiric class newspaper, *The Dominican,* from which copious extracts are given, and his sardonic wit balances the occasional priggishness of Oliver and his chum Wraysford. Even the direct lessons of religion, introduced through schoolmasterly and authorial asides, are presented as unintrusive, reassuring interpretations of a complex schoolboy life. Rather than portraying a single, normative view of the public-school ethos, in this novel Reed presents the gradual maturation of his central characters, using the give-and-take of school activity as a background against which Stephen and Oliver can define themselves.

As the most famous of Reed's novels, *The Fifth Form at St. Dominic's* has also attracted by far the most critical attention. Although Loman's story carries echoes of F. W. Farrar's *Eric, or, Little by Little* (1858), as Stephen's does of *Tom Brown, St. Dominic's* was immediately recognized as a landmark in realistic writing for boys. In his 1988 survey of English public-school fiction, Jeffrey Richards claims that *St. Dominic's* "formed the prototype school story, creating a sense of lived school life, with much on games and friendship and rather less on lessons." To its first readers, as Hutchison notes, Reed's boys seemed "very human – neither angels nor monstrosities," or, in Simon Raven's phrase, "ordinary boys in ordinary shades of moral grey." These comments signal how much Reed's achievement rested on bringing into boys' writing a wider change in moral outlook that had entered adult fiction several decades earlier. Isabel Quigly points out how many incidents from this single novel became standard plot items for later writers: "the stolen exam paper, the innocent wrongly accused, his . . . loneliness and final triumph, the boating accident, the runaway lost in a storm, rescued by the boy he has wronged." Edward C. Mack, and by implication many other critics also, blames Reed in that his "very perfection of the formula would eventually spoil the school story." But it is wrong to reduce *St. Dominic's* to its generic imitations. Patrick Howarth, praising Reed's "subtlety in the delineation of character," suggests that the book's literary merits have been underrated. *St. Dominic's* reflects the increasingly dominant athletic ideology of late-Victorian schooling but still has room for individuality and the individual's moral life.

From the editorial standpoint of the Religious Tract Society, however, *St. Dominic's* was, as a public-school novel, slightly off target. The editors wanted stories aimed at more ordinary boys. Hutchison suggested to Reed that his next serial, "commencing with the lower middle-class school, should follow the hero up to London and deal with the trials and temptations incident to breadwinning . . . on the lowest rung of the commercial ladder."

In response, Reed produced *My Friend Smith,* serialized in the *B.O.P.* from October 1882 to June 1883. Unlike *St. Dominic's,* this was a first-person narrative recounting the friendship of the orphaned Fred Batchelor with the mysterious Jack Smith, first at Stonebridge House, an appalling private school for "backward and troublesome" boys, and then as junior clerks together in the city import-export firm of Merrett, Barnacle, and Company.

The school chapters make up less than a quarter of the book, and Reed's description of late-Victorian private-school life, both sadistic and joyless, seems more Dickensian than realistic; signifi-

One of Gordon Browne's illustrations for The Fifth Form at St. Dominic's, *Reed's best-known novel*

cantly, 1882 also saw the publication of F. Anstey's *Vice Versâ,* a humorous treatment of the same kind of school. The boys' rebellion against their oppressors echoes those in earlier nineteenth-century school stories such as Maria Edgeworth's "The Barring Out" or the Dotheboys Hall section of Charles Dickens's *Nicholas Nickleby* (1837–1839), but it is ultimately ineffective.

In the main London episodes, however, Reed is back in form, as the two friends, living in cheap, crowded lodgings and lorded over by the senior clerks, struggle to establish themselves. In the background is always the question of social respectability; Jack's father had been imprisoned for bank fraud, and Jack's loyalty to him after his release interestingly reworks the Pip-Magwitch relationship from Dickens's *Great Expectations* (1861). Most of the temptations that Fred faces in London are economic rather than strictly moral, as he falls in with an extravagant circle of better-off youths led by the pretentious Hawkesbury, a poor clergyman's spendthrift son. One of the best episodes is a holiday outing the group makes by dogcart to Windsor, where allowing a drunk to drive them leads to a symbolic crash and Fred's injury. The two friends also face a moral responsibility for the urban poor when they adopt a cheeky cockney shoeblack, Billy, the streetwise son of an abusive alcoholic mother, who under their patronage eventually makes it to office boy and learns standard English. The concluding episode, in which Fred is falsely accused of stealing a check that Hawkesbury had taken to cover gambling debts, while melodramatic, links directly to the underlying theme of respectability. Moreover, in contrast to the asexuality of the typical public-school story, Fred develops a rather idealized romantic fixation on Jack's younger sister Mary. Though the novel starts in alienated orphanhood, it projects, in a final Christmas dinner, the hope of family renewal. Hutchison's contemporary fears about "young lives . . . engulfed in the nameless blackness of the vortex" of London may have contributed to the novel's melodramatic touches, but he was right to assert that, in *My Friend Smith,* Reed "breaks fresh ground." Once past its derivative private-school opening, the novel raises more difficult issues than any of Reed's school stories, and its dark, urban setting reflects more adequately the underlying social insecurities of British middle-class readers in the 1880s.

In his subsequent serials for boys, Reed followed both aspects of his early success. On the lines of *St. Dominic's* he wrote five more full-scale school stories, four for the *B.O.P.,* updating and refining his formula. *The Willoughby Captains* (1887), serialized from October 1883 to June 1884, reflects the increasing standardization of late-nineteenth-century public-school life, especially in the internal hierarchies of prefects or monitors and the new intramural sporting rivalries among different boarding-houses. The story hinges not only on the conflict between academic attainment and athletic prowess in the appointment of the School Captain, but also on the role of the quieter, more studious boy, Patrick Riddell, in giving moral leadership and reclaiming a boardinghouse that had fallen into a bad state of discipline. *"Follow My Leader": or, The Boys of Templeton* (1885), one of Reed's few boys' books not written for the *B.O.P.* but for Cassell (it was subsequently serialized in Cassell's rival paper, *Chums*), is a conventional treatment of three new boys in their first year at their public school. *The Master of the Shell* (1894), which appeared in the *B.O.P.* from November 1887 to August 1888, centers, as its title implies, on an athletic young schoolmaster, Mark Railsford, who had rowed for Cambridge University against Oxford. Railsford is engaged to Daisy Herapath, older sister of one of his students in the "Shell," or fourth form at Grandcourt. Railsford, through no fault of his own, has quarreled with an unpopular colleague, the aptly named Bickers, who blames him for shielding, or even aiding, the boys

who had tied Bickers up in a boot cupboard. Inevitably, decency wins, and Bickers, not Railsford, has to leave Grandcourt in disgrace. Reed's final comment that it is better to close the novel "amid all the cheery bustle and excitement" than "to linger about talking morality," a backhanded reference to the ending of *Tom Brown,* could stand as a summary of how he had transformed the school-story genre.

The most perfect of Reed's novels in exploiting the school-story formula is probably *The Cock-House at Fellsgarth* (1893), serialized from January to July 1891. As in *St. Dominic's,* there is a dual viewpoint, from the new boy Fisher II and from his older brother Fisher I, treasurer of the School Games Committee. The boys of Fellsgarth are split between two boardinghouses, representing the classical and modern academic tracks, and are rivals for the bragging rights in athletics (the "Cock House"). Rather against Reed's own experience, but in line with the general public-school ethos, the Moderns are noticeably richer and less gentlemanly. The action is limited to a single term (semester) and is almost entirely confined to the school site (unlike earlier school stories). Though there are the inevitable false accusations of theft and dangerous expeditions to mountain and river, it is unobtrusive classical morality rather than heroism that eventually transcends the initial jealousies, and the final football match of the term, in which all the rivals join and achieve cooperative victory, symbolizes the moral resolution of earlier intergroup and interpersonal conflicts. By comparison with that of *St. Dominic's,* the characterization is relatively conventional, but in plotting, Reed's school-story formula had, by the publication of *The Cock-House,* reached a kind of classic unity. In a 1981 essay in *Victorian Newsletter,* Patrick Scott contrasts *The Cock-House* with Kipling's anti-school novel *Stalky & Co.* (1899) to highlight how Reed was inculcating a social ideology of team endeavor free of early Victorian moralistic intrusions.

Reed attempted only one further variation of the school story in *Tom, Dick and Harry* (1894), serialized from October 1892 to March 1893. Again, Reed seems to have been trying to move outside the limits of boarding-school life, starting with Tom's struggle to get a scholarship and depicting a school with both boarding and day students. He makes the boys, including the sympathetic senior boy Tempest, less heroic and morally weaker, and even the masters are a mixed bag. But Reed's reputation for public-school stories had already been fixed by his better-known works, and he could do little to alter it.

As the serialization dates show, however, Reed saw his school stories as only one facet of

Cover for Reed's novel about the trials and eventual triumph of Mark Railsford, an athletic young schoolmaster (Collection of Patrick Scott)

boys' reading. He soon followed up *My Friend Smith* with a second, more closely plotted novel of city life, *Reginald Cruden,* serialized from April to September 1885, in which the two Cruden brothers have to leave their public school, following their father's sudden and debt-ridden death, to support their widowed mother in dismal London lodgings. At the newspaper where they find work, Horace, the younger brother, quickly settles down and is transferred to the subeditors' room, but Reginald, the elder, chafes at the indignity of the print shop. He leaves London to become a clerk in Liverpool and gradually realizes he has been set up as front man for a mail-order scam. Reginald's dilemma, his sense of failure, and his reluctance to contact his family are convincingly portrayed, though his well-meaning attempts to reclaim the street urchin Love are rather sentimentalized. What is apparent, however, is that Reed can offer little solution to the Crudens' plight;

even Horace and his mother cannot make it on his earnings, and Reginald is penniless in a cheap lodging house down by the docks. Reed concludes the novel with a deus ex machina – the exculpation of Reginald, the unexpected restoration of Mr. Cruden's lost investments, and the appearance of an old family friend from India to mentor the boys.

Even bleaker as a depiction of life in the real world is Reed's *A Dog with a Bad Name* (1894), serialized from October 1886 to April 1887. The hero, John Jeffreys, an awkward, gangling nineteen-year-old, half-purposely injures another boy in a rugby match, has to leave school, and is disowned by his guardian. Dogged by this record, he must find employment, first as a private-school master, then as a librarian to a book-loving member of Parliament, as a tutor, as a secretary, and finally as the head of "a great library in the North." With the patronage and support of the M.P., Jeffreys eventually makes a life for himself and even falls in love with and wins the hand of his patron's daughter; indeed, at the end his guardian restores his inheritance. However, the struggles he goes through are daunting, and he lives constantly with the fear that his past will catch up with him. It is a sobering book for Reed to address to his loyal readership of teenaged boys.

In addition to the school and city novels, Reed wrote a sensational schoolboy adventure story, *Roger Ingleton, Minor* (1891), full of disguises and disputed inheritances, which, not surprisingly, was brought out by Low, not the Religious Tract Society. Of his two historical novels, one, *Kilgorman: A Story of Ireland in 1798* (1894), had been started for his wife, who came from the north of Ireland, and was incomplete when Reed died. His Elizabethan novel, *Sir Ludar,* serialized from February to August 1888, follows Charles Kingsley's *Westward Ho!* (1855) in its strong patriotic and anti-Catholic tone. Perhaps writing about the past, such as the English defeat of the Spanish Armada in 1588, allowed Reed greater moral confidence than he could feel about late-Victorian England. Morison, who admires the historical research behind this novel and Reed's bibliographic publications, judges *Sir Ludar* "Reed's most mature work in fiction."

In 1893 Reed developed tuberculosis, exacerbated by overwork. He died before the year was out, aged only forty-one. His subsequent reputation, while well-deserved, has been heavily influenced by the spin Hutchison and the *B.O.P.* put on his work after his death, when Reed's widow transferred most of his copyrights to the Religious Tract Society. Hutchison's memoirs of Reed, published in the *B.O.P.* and various prefaces to collected vol-

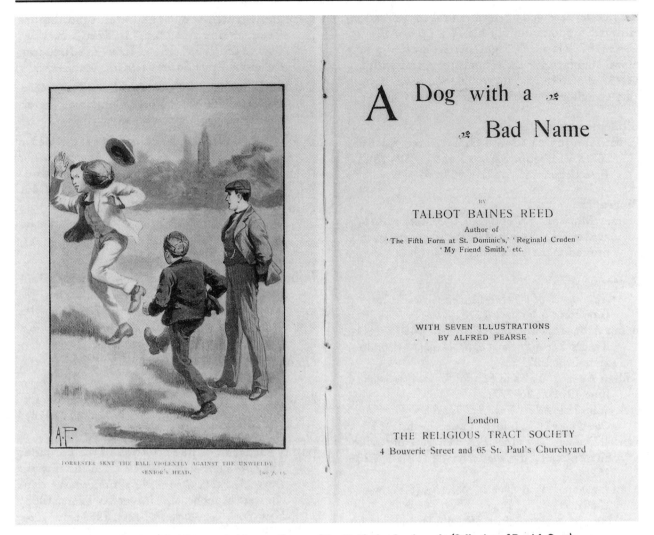

A Dog with a
Bad Name

BY
TALBOT BAINES REED

Author of
'The Fifth Form at St. Dominic's,' 'Reginald Cruden'
'My Friend Smith,' etc.

WITH SEVEN ILLUSTRATIONS
. . BY ALFRED PEARSE . .

London
THE RELIGIOUS TRACT SOCIETY
4 Bouverie Street and 65 St. Paul's Churchyard

FORRESTER SENT THE BALL VIOLENTLY AGAINST THE UNWIELDY
SENIOR'S HEAD.

Frontispiece by Alfred Pease and title page for one of Reed's bleaker boys' novels (Collection of Patrick Scott)

umes, emphasize Reed as "to the last a real boy among boys," and Reed's school novels, in bright pictorial bindings, became standard gift items in the Boy's Own Bookshelf and similar series. Hutchison was proud to have recognized from the start Reed's gift for depicting "healthy flesh-and-blood lads," not the "mere pasteboard figures" of earlier religious writers. Modern critics such as Quigly recognize Reed's pivotal role in altering "the shapeless, long-winded garrulous and moralistic school story," to give it "usable form, the first of its iron conventions."

But the almost exclusive emphasis given to Reed's school stories has in some ways distorted the critical record. Along with lively, nonmoralistic realism, the school novels also show signs of the philistinism of late-Victorian schooling. P. W. Musgrave has drawn particular attention to the short story "The Poetry Club" (in the posthumous

collection *The School Ghost, and Boycotted; With Other Stories*, 1930) as evidence of this aspect. Reed himself seems to have struggled against the "school-story writer" image; he was as concerned with life after school as with school life itself, and his city novels deserve further scrutiny as a response to the economic uncertainties of the 1880s. The near-total absence of fathers from Reed's stories may reflect his own father's death in 1881, but, along with the gender-role issues that Nelson raises, this feature invites a broader psychological criticism of his stories as vehicles of male socialization.

Reed's religious motivation also deserves renewed attention. While the school novels submerge religion in team spirit, his work as a whole reflects not a rejection of traditional religion but a transformation of wide historical importance in Victorian religious discourse, from the transcendent to the moral or ethical. Although much of Reed's work has not yet received modern critical consideration, Howarth's summation in his *Play Up and Play the Game* (1973) is surely right: Reed "created a new moral standard for the school story, and with it a new kind of hero . . . who would impress his personality on schoolboy stories for decades to come."

Bibliography:
P. M. Handover, "Some Uncollected Authors XXXV: Talbot Baines Reed, 1852–1893," *Book Collector,* 12, no. 1 (1963): 62–67.

Biography:
Stanley Morison, *Talbot Baines Reed: Author, Bibliographer, Typefounder* (Cambridge: Privately printed at the University Press, 1960).

References:
"*The Adventures of a Three-Guinea Watch,*" *Observer* (London), 5 January 1975, p. 23;
Brian Alderson, Introduction and postscript to Reed's *The Fifth Form at St. Dominic's* (London: Hamilton, 1971);
Gillian Avery, "Tales in School," *New Statesman* (4 June 1971): 776–777;
Jack Cox, *Take a Cold Tub, Sir! The Story of the "Boy's Own Paper"* (Guildford: Lutterworth, 1982);
Patrick Dunae, "*Boy's Own Paper:* Origins and Editorial Policies," *Private Library,* 9 (1976): 123–158;
Alan Gibson, "T. B. Reed," *Spectator* (6 February 1982): 26–27;
Ian Hay (John Hay Beith), "School Stories," in his *The Lighter Side of School Life* (London & Edinburgh: Foulis, 1914), pp. 151–173;
Patrick Howarth, *Play Up and Play the Game: The Heroes of Popular Fiction* (London: Eyre Methuen, 1973), pp. 49–59;

George A. Hutchison, "The Late Talbot Baines Reed, as Boy and Man," in Reed's *Parkhurst Boys: And Other Stories of School Life* (London: Religious Tract Society [1905]), pp. iii–xx;
Edward C. Mack, *The Public Schools and British Opinion Since 1860* (New York: Columbia University Press, 1941), pp. 148–151;
P. W. Musgrave, "Talbot Baines Reed: the Genre Defined," in his *From Brown to Bunter: the Life and Death of the School Story* (London: Routledge & Kegan Paul, 1985), pp. 112–146;
Claudia Nelson, *Boys Will Be Girls: The Feminine Ethic and British Children's Fiction, 1857–1917* (New Brunswick, N. J.: Rutgers University Press, 1991), pp. 68–71;
Isabel Quigly, "The Central School Story: Talbot Baines Reed and His Followers," in her *The Heirs of Tom Brown: the English School Story* (Oxford: Oxford University Press, 1982), pp. 77–85;
Simon Raven, "*Eric* and *St. Dominic's,*" *Spectator* (14 August 1971): 246–247;
John R. Reed, "The Public Schools in Victorian Literature," *Nineteenth-Century Fiction,* 29 (1974): 58–76;
Jeffrey Richards, "The Perfection of the Formula: *The Fifth Form at St. Dominic's,*" in his *Happiest Days: the Public Schools in English Fiction* (Manchester: Manchester University Press, 1988; New York: St. Martin's Press, 1988), pp. 103–119;
Patrick Scott, "The Schooling of John Bull: Form and Moral in Talbot Baines Reed's Boys' Stories and in Kipling's *Stalky & Co.,*" *Victorian Newsletter,* 60 (Fall 1981): 3–8.

Robert Louis Stevenson

(13 November 1850 – 3 December 1894)

Diana A. Chlebek
University of Akron

See also the Stevenson entries in *DLB 18: Victorian Novelists After 1885* and *DLB 57: Victorian Prose Writers After 1867.*

BOOKS: *The Pentland Rising* (Edinburgh: Privately printed, 1866);

An Appeal to the Clergy (Edinburgh & London: Blackwood, 1875);

An Inland Voyage (London: Kegan Paul, 1878; Boston: Roberts Brothers, 1883);

Edinburgh: Picturesque Notes, with Etchings (London: Seeley, Jackson & Halliday, 1879; New York: Macmillan, 1889);

Travels with a Donkey in the Cévennes (London: Kegan Paul, 1879; Boston: Roberts Brothers, 1879);

Virginibus Puerisque and Other Papers (London: Kegan Paul, 1881; New York: Collier, 1881);

Familiar Studies of Men and Books (London: Chatto & Windus, 1882; New York: Dodd, Mead, 1887);

New Arabian Nights (2 volumes, London: Chatto & Windus, 1882; 1 volume, New York: Holt, 1882);

The Silverado Squatters (London: Chatto & Windus, 1883; New York: Munro, 1884);

Treasure Island (London: Cassell, 1883; Boston: Roberts Brothers, 1884);

A Child's Garden of Verses (London: Longmans, Green, 1885; New York: Scribners, 1885);

More New Arabian Nights: The Dynamiter, by Stevenson and Fanny Van de Grift Stevenson (London: Longmans, Green, 1885; New York: Holt, 1885);

Macaire (Edinburgh: Privately printed, 1885);

Prince Otto: A Romance (London: Chatto & Windus, 1885; Boston: Roberts Brothers, 1886);

The Strange Case of Dr. Jekyll and Mr. Hyde (London: Longmans, Green, 1886; New York: Scribners, 1886);

Kidnapped (London: Cassell, 1886; New York: Scribners, 1886);

Robert Louis Stevenson (photograph by Lloyd Osbourne)

Some College Memories (Edinburgh: University Union Committee, 1886; New York: Mansfield & Wessels, 1899);

The Merry Men and Other Tales and Fables (London: Chatto & Windus, 1887; New York: Scribners, 1887);

Underwoods (London: Chatto & Windus, 1887; New York: Scribners, 1887);

Memories and Portraits (London: Chatto & Windus, 1887; New York: Scribners, 1887);

Memoir of Fleeming Jenkin (London & New York: Longmans, Green, 1887);

The Misadventures of John Nicholson: A Christmas Story (New York: Lovell, 1887);

The Black Arrow: A Tale of the Two Roses (London: Cassell, 1888; New York: Scribners, 1888);

The Master of Ballantrae: A Winter's Tale (London: Cassell, 1889; New York: Scribners, 1889);

The Wrong Box, by Stevenson and Lloyd Osbourne (London: Longmans, Green, 1889; New York: Scribners, 1889);

Ballads (London: Chatto & Windus, 1890; New York: Scribners, 1890);

Father Damien: An Open Letter to the Reverend Dr. Hyde of Honolulu (London: Chatto & Windus, 1890; Portland, Maine: Mosher, 1897);

Across the Plains, With Other Memories and Essays (London: Chatto & Windus, 1892; New York: Scribners, 1892);

A Footnote to History: Eight Years of Trouble in Samoa (London: Cassell, 1892; New York: Scribners, 1892);

Three Plays: Deacon Brodie, Beau Austin, Admiral Guinea, by Stevenson and W. E. Henley (London: Nutt, 1892; New York: Scribners, 1892);

The Wrecker, by Stevenson and Osbourne (London: Cassell, 1892; New York: Scribners, 1892);

Island Nights' Entertainments: Consisting of The Beach of Falesá, The Bottle Imp, The Isle of Voices (London: Cassell, 1893; New York: Scribners, 1893);

Catriona: A Sequel to Kidnapped (London: Cassell 1893); published in the United States as *David Balfour* (New York: Scribners, 1893);

The Ebb-Tide: A Trio and a Quartette, by Stevenson and Osbourne (Chicago: Stone & Kimball, 1894; London: Heinemann, 1894);

The Body-Snatcher (New York: Merriam, 1895);

The Amateur Emigrant from the Clyde to Sandy Hook (Chicago: Stone & Kimball, 1895; New York: Scribners, 1899);

The Strange Case of Dr. Jekyll and Mr. Hyde, with Other Fables (London: Longmans, Green, 1896);

Weir of Hermiston: An Unfinished Romance (London: Chatto & Windus, 1896; New York: Scribners, 1896);

A Mountain Town in France: A Fragment (New York & London: Lane, 1896);

Songs of Travel and Other Verses (London: Chatto & Windus, 1896);

In the South Seas (New York: Scribners, 1896; London: Chatto & Windus, 1900);

St. Ives: Being the Adventures of a French Prisoner in England (New York: Scribners, 1897; London: Heinemann, 1898);

The Morality of the Profession of Letters (Gouverneur, N.Y.: Brothers of the Book, 1899);

A Stevenson Medley, edited by S. Colvin (London: Chatto & Windus, 1899);

Essays and Criticisms (Boston: Turner, 1903);

Prayers Written at Vailima, With an Introduction by Mrs. Stevenson (New York: Scribners, 1904; London: Chatto & Windus, 1905);

The Story of a Lie and Other Tales (Boston: Turner, 1904);

Essays of Travel (London: Chatto & Windus, 1905);

Essays in the Art of Writing (London: Chatto & Windus, 1905);

Essays, edited by W. L. Phelps (New York: Scribners, 1906);

Lay Morals and Other Papers (London: Chatto & Windus, 1911);

Records of a Family of Engineers (London: Chatto & Windus, 1916);

The Waif Woman (London: Chatto & Windus, 1916);

On the Choice of a Profession (London: Chatto & Windus, 1916);

Poems Hitherto Unpublished, edited by G. S. Hellman, 2 volumes (Boston: Bibliophile Society, 1916);

New Poems and Variant Readings (London: Chatto & Windus, 1918);

Robert Louis Stevenson: Hitherto Unpublished Prose Writings, edited by H. H. Harper (Boston: Bibliophile Society, 1921);

When the Devil Was Well, edited by William P. Trent (Boston: Bibliophile Society, 1921);

Confessions of a Unionist: An Unpublished Talk on Things Current, Written in 1888, edited by F. V. Livingston (Cambridge, Mass.: Privately printed, 1921);

The Best Thing in Edinburgh: An Address to the Speculative Society of Edinburgh in March 1873, edited by K. D. Osbourne (San Francisco: Howell, 1923);

Selected Essays, edited by H. G. Rawlinson (London: Oxford University Press, 1923);

Castaways of Soledad: A Manuscript by Stevenson Hitherto Unpublished, edited by Hellman (Buffalo: Privately printed, 1928);

Monmouth: A Tragedy, edited by C. Vale (New York: Rudge, 1928);

The Charity Bazaar: An Allegorical Dialogue (Westport, Conn.: Georgian Press, 1929);

The Essays of Robert Louis Stevenson, edited by M. Elwin (London: Macdonald, 1950);

Salute to R L S, edited by F. Holland (Edinburgh: Cousland, 1950);

Tales and Essays, edited by G. B. Stern (London: Falcon, 1950);

*Dust jacket for a 1911 American edition of Stevenson's classic pirate novel,
illustrated by N. C. Wyeth (Osborne Collection of Early Children's Books,
Toronto Public Libraries)*

Silverado Journal, edited by John E. Jordan (San Francisco: Book Club of California, 1954);

From Scotland to Silverado, edited by James D. Hart (Cambridge, Mass.: Harvard University Press, 1966);

The Amateur Emigrant with Some First Impressions of America, edited by Roger G. Swearingen, 2 volumes (Ashland, Oreg.: Osborne, 1976–1977);

A Newly Discovered Long Story "An Old Song" and a Previously Unpublished Short Story "Edifying Letters of the Rutherford Family," edited by Swearingen (Hamden, Conn.: Archon Books, 1982; Paisley, Scotland: Wilfion, 1982);

Robert Louis Stevenson and "The Beach of Falesá": A Study in Victorian Publishing with the Original Text, edited by Barry Menikoff (Stanford, Cal.: Stanford University Press, 1984).

Collections: *The Works of R. L. Stevenson,* Edinburgh Edition, 28 volumes, edited by Sidney Colvin (London: Chatto & Windus, 1894–1898);

The Works of Robert Louis Stevenson, Vailima Edition, 26 volumes, edited by Lloyd Osbourne and Fanny Van de Grift Stevenson (London: Heinemann, 1922–1923; New York: Scribners, 1922–1923);

The Works of Robert Louis Stevenson, Tusitala Edition, 35 volumes (London: Heinemann, 1924);

The Works of Robert Louis Stevenson, South Seas Edition, 32 volumes (New York: Scribners, 1925).

The life of Robert Louis Stevenson was regarded by his public, his friends, and his biographers to be as thrilling as the adventures in the stories he wrote. He was born in Scotland on 13 November 1850 to a respectable, middle-class family. His father, Thomas Stevenson, a lighthouse engineer and a devout Presbyterian, brought up his son according to the strict principles of mid-Victorian Edinburgh. From his mother, Margaret, Stevenson inherited an optimistic attitude toward life as well as a susceptibility to tuberculosis that kept mother and son in lifelong states of ill health. His early childhood was lonely, dominated by severe bouts of sickness that left him bedridden for weeks at a time. He was devotedly cared for by his mother and by his nanny Alison Cunningham. "Cummy," as he nicknamed his nurse, would read to Stevenson from the Old Testament, from John Bunyan's *The Pilgrim's Progress* (1678), and from verses that depicted the history of Scotland's religious and political battles in order to relieve the monotony of the boy's confinement to bed. Cummy's stories and his father's improvised stories proved to be major sources of literary inspiration for Stevenson. In addition, the novels and travel books he discovered in his father's library stimulated his appetite for adventure.

Because of persistent ill health, Stevenson never remained at one school for very long; however, he enjoyed many childhood games, particularly with his cousin Bob, who lived with the Stevenson family for a short time. He described his intense childhood friendship with Bob as life in a "purely visionary state." The cousins would dress up, invent countries together, and create dramas for the *Skelt* (a toy theater) that his parents had given him. Stevenson emphasized in his essay "A Penny Plain and Two-Pence Coloured" the influence that Skelt had upon his childish imagination and eventually on his literary art by providing "a gallery of scenes and characters with which, in the silent theatre of the brain, I might enact all novels and romances." His grandfather Lewis Balfour's manse at Colinton, with its lavish gardens and wholesome country atmosphere, was the site of family holidays, where Stevenson could play with numerous cousins. The Stevensons would also visit North Berwick, a small seaside town thirty miles from Edinburgh. There Stevenson found companions whom he would lead on seashore excursions that he described as "Crusoeing" – cooking and eating meals on the beach in the open air, playing at pirates and smugglers, hunting for buried treasure, and holding secret meetings at night by lantern light. These games would exercise Stevenson's imagination as rehearsals for the literary adventures that would be the basis of such novels as *Treasure Island* (1883) and *Kidnapped* (1886).

From his earliest days Stevenson was fascinated by the haunts and sights of Edinburgh. He would recall how Cummy would relieve the fears of his long, sleepless nights of childhood illness by pointing out the city lights, especially of houses where other sick children awaited the dawn with their nannies. The strong sense of place which so vividly colors Stevenson's writing originated in his explorations of Edinburgh and the surrounding countryside. During his boyhood and adolescence the city was clearly divided by history and by class. The affluent "New Town" was respectable, socially correct, and characterized by the solid, elegant exteriors of streets like Heriot Row where the Stevenson family took up residence in 1857. Alongside this conventional Edinburgh was the more bohemian "Old Town," notorious for its drinking houses and the brothels of Lothian Road. Beginning in their late teens, Stevenson and his cousin Bob frequented the low haunts of this side of Edinburgh. The juxtaposition of the two faces of the city – the hypocritical facade against the more open, bawdy one – impressed Stevenson as a touchstone of people's dual natures. Interspersed with the adolescent rambles around the town were several tours with his father to inspect lighthouses on the Scottish coast at Fife and Wick and later at Mull. These journeys gave Stevenson a scientific awareness of the sea and the shore, filling his imagination with coastal scenery that he later used in his novels.

When Stevenson entered Edinburgh University in 1867, his parents assumed he would follow in his father's footsteps and become a civil engineer. However, Louis had always had a penchant for writing; as a child of six, he had dictated stories of Joseph and Moses to his mother, and in his school days he had produced homemade magazines singlehandedly. His literary imagination had already been stirred by reading Sir Walter Scott, Alexandre Dumas, and William Makepeace Thackeray and then was broadened by his discovery of Henry David Thoreau, Nathaniel Hawthorne, and Walt Whitman. Under the stimulus of café discussions with new companions from the university, Stevenson soon determined upon writing for his life's vocation. This decision brought him into conflict with his father, but a compromise was struck when Louis switched to the study of law in 1871. Relations with his parents again reached a critical point in 1873 when he disclosed to them that he was an agnostic and a member of a skeptic's club at the university. The motto of the LJR (Liberty, Justice, Reverence) Club, as the group was called, was "Disregard everything our parents have taught us." Exhausted by illness and by the struggles with his family, Stevenson went on a trip to southern France to convalesce and to experiment with his writing. Such voyages abroad, taken to recuperate and to revitalize his literary art, became a constant pattern of his life. He broadened his circle of friends and established important connections with critics and scholars such

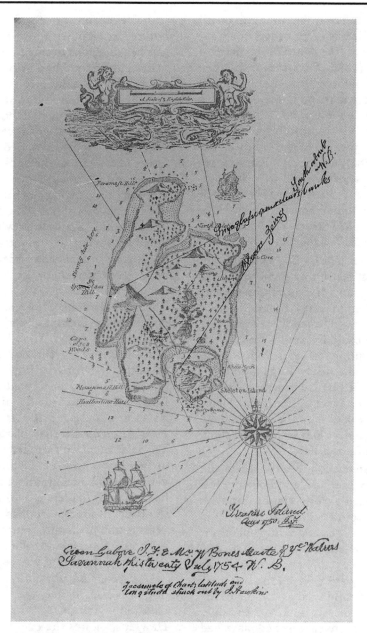

Map in Stevenson's Treasure Island; *based on the map drawn by Stevenson and his stepson Lloyd Osbourne during a holiday in Scotland (Thomas Cooper Library, University of South Carolina)*

as Sidney Colvin, through whom he made contact with the editors of literary magazines. His early published pieces were essays and travel books. His books *An Inland Voyage* (1878) and *Travels with a Donkey in the Cévennes* (1879) describe his excursions in Europe and give a keen sense of how Stevenson pursued adventure for the sake of writing.

In 1875, during a trip to France, he discovered the Barbizon art colony at Fontainebleau and began to reside there intermittently. Its open bohemian lifestyle attracted many foreign visitors, including Fanny Van de Grift Osbourne, an American who

was touring Europe with her children after an estrangement from her husband. Over the course of 1876 and 1877 the tenor of Stevenson's life began to change as he courted Osbourne, who was ten years his senior. The relationship inspired a fertile period of writing for him; he worked intensively at stories and essays that were regularly published in literary journals and that caught the attention of Henry James, Andrew Lang, and Edmund Gosse. In 1878 Fanny and her family left Europe to return to the United States. A year later Stevenson, despondent over her absence, followed her in an arduous voyage across the Atlantic and over the American continent. He recorded the details of his ordeal in a travelogue, published later as *The Amateur Emigrant from the Clyde to Sandy Hook* (1895). Several months after Fanny became legally divorced from her husband, she and Stevenson were married in San Francisco on 19 May 1880. The couple spent their honeymoon in a rustic cabin in the Napa Valley. Stevenson's published journal of the venture, *The Silverado Squatters* (1883), celebrates Fanny's resourcefulness and pioneering spirit. Although Stevenson's parents were initially opposed to his liaison with Fanny, they soon reconciled themselves to the marriage, and in 1880 Stevenson, Fanny, and her son Lloyd returned to Britain.

Thomas Stevenson had by this time guaranteed his son an annual income of £250 to relieve him of financial anxiety, and thus Stevenson and his family had some freedom to travel. From this point onward, the author's life followed a endless quest for a climate where he could live and write without danger to his health. During the years from 1880 to 1887 Stevenson produced a steady output of literary work, including some of his first stories based on Scottish folklore: "Thrawn Janet," "The Merry Men," and "Markheim." These tales show the marked influence of Hawthorne and place Stevenson squarely in the romantic tradition of storytelling.

During his long sojourns at health resorts and residences in France, Switzerland, and England, Stevenson gradually formed a close relationship with his stepson. The two would collaborate on inventing games, creating woodcuts, and writing plays for their toy theater, afterwards publishing their dramas and inventions on a small, handmade printing press. Stevenson had always enjoyed the company of children and valued childhood as a stage of life important in itself, not merely as a step to adulthood. His own childhood inventions and plays had helped him cope with the fears of a solitary life dominated by continual illness. Stevenson outlines his observations of children and their fantasies in "Child's Play," an essay first published in *Cornhill Magazine* in 1878 (collected in *Virginibus Puerisque and Other Papers*, 1881). With particularly keen insight into the young mind, he describes how the child combines fact and imagination by incorporating the real world into his games: "He works with lay figures and stage properties. . . . He can make an abstraction of whatever does not fit into his fable." The phenomena he observed in the games of the young bore a striking similarity to the processes of his own artistic imagination in the act of creating literature.

Stevenson conceived *Treasure Island* during a holiday in 1881 with his parents in Scotland. The tale began almost accidentally from a map that Stevenson and Lloyd had been producing with colors out of a child's paint box. As the map became more embellished with details, a story began to suggest itself in the imaginary landscape. Stevenson described the imaginative process in "My First Book": "as I paused upon my map of 'Treasure Island,' the future characters of the book began to appear there visibly among imaginary woods; and their brown faces and bright weapons peeped out upon me from unexpected quarters." "The Sea Cook," the story's original title, was written with the inspiration provided by Stevenson's nightly readings of the work in progress to family and friends. His father, caught up in the excitement of the tale, collaborated on various narrative details, such as the contents of Billy Bones's sea chest. Stevenson recognized that his novel had the imprint of various authors and stories he had read: Edgar Allan Poe, Daniel Defoe, and Washington Irving. But he had also succeeded in reinventing a genre, the boy's adventure story, and this was quickly perceived by Alexander Japp, a friend who attended the nightly readings of the novel and arranged for its serialization in *Young Folks' Magazine*. *Treasure Island* appeared in the boys' magazine between October 1881 and January 1882 under the pseudonym Captain George North. Stevenson wrote the first part of the book in a white heat, fifteen chapters in two weeks, and then under the stress of illness dropped the project. Later that year he and his family returned to the health resort in Davos, Switzerland, where he finished the novel in a two-week stint of writing.

Treasure Island, his first full-length piece of fiction, was immediately recognized as a landmark of children's literature. The story's narrator, Jim Hawkins, relates the events of his boyhood in the 1740s. His father is the landlord of the Benbow Inn where Billy Bones, an old pirate who once served under Captain Flint, takes up lodgings. After Bones's death a treasure map is found in his sea chest, and Jim, Dr. Livesey, Squire Trelawney, and Captain Smollett set sail on the schooner *Hispaniola* for the Spanish Main to find Treasure Island. Jim's discovery of an attempted mutiny led by the treacherous Long John Silver, the ship's cook, helps save the expedition. The description of the young hero's single-handed recapture of the schooner from a member of the villainous crew is probably the most thrilling episode in the novel. After a prolonged struggle with Jim's company, the mutineers take the boy hostage and then go in search of the

The moon
has a
face like
the
clock in
the hall:

One of Charles Robinson's illustrations for an 1896 edition of A Child's
Garden of Verses

treasure on the island, but they unearth only an empty chest. Jim and Long John are rescued and led to the treasure by Ben Gunn, a sailor marooned on the island many years before. They abandon the mutineers on the island and sail to the West Indies, where Long John escapes the ship. Eventually the *Hispaniola* returns to Bristol where Jim, his friends, and the loyal crew all have an ample share of the treasure.

With *Treasure Island,* Stevenson transforms the physical adventure of a boy's pirate story into a moral quest for the novel's young protagonist. As a narrator relating the past events of his childhood, Jim maintains a point of view that stands between the perceptions of a boy and a man. The tale instantly engages the reader's attention with the opening rush of thrilling events at the Benbow Inn. The nightmarish visits of fearsome pirates and the mys-

teries of disguised characters and puzzling clues needed to discover the treasure are presented from a child's excited perspective. The quest theme expands to several levels of meaning as Jim's acts of discovery become pivotal in deeper ways, from uncovering the mutiny of the crew to reading the duplicity inherent in Long John's complex personality. The boy's ambiguous view of and relation to adults determines the structure of events in the novel. The pirates, representing the underside of civilization, both horrify and fascinate him in the same fashion that he is at once repelled and lured by the quest for the blood-tainted treasure. When Jim and his friends uncover the cash hoard in the cave, the display of all the world's currency seems to epitomize the money myth that has enslaved the adults of the boy's universe. But the gold also represents a tool that Jim must learn to maneuver if he is to grow into manhood in this culture. The game that he and his company play on Treasure Island is that of a very real life-and-death struggle in which not only treasure but also survival itself is at stake.

Much of the artistry of *Treasure Island* stems from Stevenson's genius of description. His literary creativity transformed memories and knowledge of the Scottish coasts and beaches he had explored as a youth into the theater of action that is Treasure Island. In terms of the narrative, a comparable liberating power of the imagination drives Jim's impulsive actions, leading to the rescue of his company from the pirates and eventually to the discovery of the treasure. Ultimately, the success of the novel and its appeal for readers rests in the author's and the hero's abilities to bring to life the topography of a place rooted part in reality, part in fantasy.

Although the serialized form of the novel in *Young Folks' Magazine* was not a great success with readers, many critics of the day recognized that *Treasure Island* had broken new ground in the genre of the romance adventure. James considered the work a real form of insight into the child's consciousness, and Lang perceived the influence of Homer's *Odyssey* and of Mark Twain's *The Adventures of Tom Sawyer* (1876) in the book, particularly in Stevenson's thematic exploration of the individual's dual nature as perceived through the child's perspective. In the genesis of the tale and in his recollection of the elements of his childhood that inspired its creation, Stevenson recognized *Treasure Island* as a touchstone of his literary career, bringing together his art and his life interests in a unique form of storytelling.

After *Treasure Island* was completed, Stevenson remained in Davos with his family to recuperate. He worked on several essays and on *Prince Otto: A Romance* (1885), a fantasy influenced by George Meredith, a contemporary novelist he greatly admired. In 1883, after trying out several residences on the Riviera, the Stevensons settled into a cottage, La Solitude, at Hyères on the Côte d'Azur. This period of Stevenson's life proved to be productive artistically. Later he would write to his close friend and editor Sidney Colvin: "I was only happy once, that was at Hyères." It was here that he completed a project that he cherished deeply – *A Child's Garden of Verses* (1885).

In 1881 Stevenson's mother had shown him a copy of *Kate Greenaway's Birthday Book for Children* (1880), a collection of verses by Mrs. Sale Barker illustrated by Greenaway. Charmed by the collection, Stevenson composed fourteen poems and then developed the project, originally titled "Penny

Whistles," over several years during periods when he felt too ill to write prose. He wrote most of the poems during 1883 and 1884 at Hyères, and the book was published in 1885 without illustrations. Stevenson composed the verses with a very conscious sense of the old nursery-rhyme tradition and also within the context of didactic children's poetry written over the last century, exemplified by Isaac Watts's *Divine Songs for the Use of Children* (1715) and Ann and Jane Taylor's *Original Poems for Infant Minds* (1804). He also most certainly worked under the influence of William Blake's *Songs of Innocence* (1789) and Christina Rossetti's *Goblin Market* (1862). For the most part Stevenson's verses work against the element of didacticism that is so central to the texts of Watts and of the Taylors. Like Blake and Rossetti, however, he re-creates some of the complex dark side of childhood, rendered in deceptively simple forms. Thus like *Treasure Island*, *A Child's Garden of Verses* surpasses the limitations inherent in the traditional genres of children's literature.

Part of the uniqueness of Stevenson's verses lies in the nature of their settings. The narrator recaptures the mythological epoch of the child through a series of snapshots, a collection of landscapes and "innerscapes." The first section of the book, which contains many of the best and most evocative poems, casts the child as an explorer in settings that are exciting, somewhat threatening, and essentially transformations of the familiar. In such poems as "Pirate-story," "Windy Nights," and "North-West Passage," children can play out their fears in the theater of their imagination. The collection of verses as a whole is neatly framed within the gardens where Stevenson spent much of his childhood. The formality and constraint of the well-ordered lawns of Edinburgh's New Town, as well as the idyllic countryside of his grandfather Balfour's manse at Colinton, are mirrored in the poems in the book's section entitled "Garden Days." The contrast between the cozy and the threatening realms of the child's world is a projection of his own emotional state. Thus his bed can be a secure refuge as in "My Bed is a Boat," or in "A Land of Counterpane," an exotic stage for props and games that stimulate a young invalid's imagination, or a distressing prison for a boy bursting to explore his day to the fullest as in "Bed in Summer."

Much of Stevenson's artistry in the design of the book and within the individual poems lies in the balance struck between the simple verse forms and the complex tapestry of moods and images evoked through language and rhythm. The directness of form has a disarming childlike quality that nonetheless reveals an element of control exercised by the adult speaker. The major points in the child's life and vision are derived from Stevenson's own past experience and encompass such contrasting states as fear versus security, illness versus energetic exuberance, or loneliness versus joyful companionship in play.

Like *Treasure Island, A Child's Garden of Verses* presents a topographical survey of landscapes, covering many points in childhood's vision of the adult world. Both the novel and the collection of verse mirror developmental aspects of the child's growth in consciousness. Jim Hawkins's encounter with the adult world through his adventure on Treasure Island transforms the drama of play into an ambiguous and unsettling experience by the end of the narrative. In a similar fashion the adult narrator who evokes his past through poetry recognizes the limitations of the child that must be left behind in the landscape of recollections forming *A Child's Garden of Verses*.

Stevenson's life of travel in search of a more healthful climate imposed a continuous financial strain upon him and his family, and it was his anxiety about money that fueled the writing of *The Black Arrow: A Tale of the Two Roses* (1888). This historical romance was written in two months. It was serialized in *Young Folks' Magazine* and proved to be far more popular with the readers of the children's magazine than *Treasure Island*. Stevenson thought very little of *The Black Arrow*, describing it as a piece of "tushery," that is, an improbable adventure. Set in the reign of Henry VI, during the Wars of the Roses, the novel incorporates many of the elements of Stevenson's childhood reading of British history. The narrative recounts the fortunes of an orphan, Dick Shelton, who is also the ward of Sir Daniel Brockley. When Dick learns that his guardian helped to murder his father and plans to rob him of his inheritance, he tries to flee from Brockley and is imprisoned. With the help of his sweetheart, Joanna Sedley, Dick finally succeeds in escaping and becomes involved in the civil war. The rest of the narrative focuses on the details of Dick's fighting for the House of York and on his relationship with the duke of Gloucester, who knights him for his bravery. The character of Richard III is presented with the same moral ambiguity that colors the portrayal of Long John Silver in *Treasure Island*. Although many reviewers praised the book, they criticized its plot as a mechanical stringing together of historical incidents, incapable of holding the reader's attention. The character of Dick Shelton is a less successful por-

Pencil sketch by Stevenson of his nurse, Alison Cunningham ("Cummy"), to whom he dedicated A Child's Garden of Verses *(Anderson Galleries catalogue, sale number 1171, 22 January 1929)*

trayal of a morally confused hero than that of Jim Hawkins in *Treasure Island*.

From 1884 to 1889 severe illness dominated Stevenson's life. Nevertheless, he wrote continuously during this period and steadily gained a wide reputation, winning critical praise from such important authors as Meredith and James. In the mid 1880s Stevenson and James began a literary debate that influenced the development of the novel over the next several decades. In September 1884 James published "The Art of Fiction" in *Longman's Magazine,* which theorized that the novel, while it could not be reality, should strive to produce an illusion of reality or an "exquisite correspondence with life." Stevenson responded to James's thesis with "A Humble Remonstrance" in the December 1884 issue of *Longman's Magazine*. This challenge to James's concept of fiction, which became a basic document in Stevenson's critical thinking about literature and art, argued that fiction's essential characteristic and art reside in its separate nature, its difference from life. Thus the novelist's aim should be to make stories typical rather than true. The debate inspired James to visit Stevenson in Bournemouth in 1885, and very soon the two authors became close friends and faithful literary correspondents. This contact with one of the century's greatest writers and thinkers impelled Stevenson to clarify his concepts about the role of the imagination in the development of creativity and consciousness, especially in children.

Stevenson's literary achievements and stature grew steadily over the next several years. By 1885 he and his family had established a semipermanent residence in their Skerryvore villa at Bournemouth, and there he wrote one of his most enduring and intriguing works: *The Strange Case of Dr. Jekyll and Mr. Hyde* (1886) originated in a nightmare that Stevenson dreamed sequentially over the course of several evenings. For the next three days he wrote furiously, developing a narrative out of the vision. His wife Fanny, after reading the tale, suggested that he redraft it as an allegory. The book was an immediate success, selling four hundred thousand copies the first six months after it was published in January 1886. The particular circumstances of the novel's conception in a dream seemed to confirm Stevenson's theories about the relationship of art and the imagination. The dual nature of mankind had been an important aspect of his Calvinist upbringing. When these long-repressed thoughts surfaced in the form of a fable, Stevenson felt confirmed in his belief that the power of the subconscious could release a healing self-awareness. Thus the writing of *Dr. Jekyll and Mr. Hyde* reintegrated a divisiveness within the author that had haunted him from earliest childhood.

With another burst of creative energy Stevenson completed *Kidnapped* (1886) a few months later for serialization in *Young Folks' Magazine*. He had begun research for the book in 1881 while investigating Scottish history during the process of applying for a teaching post at Edinburgh University, and he began to incorporate this research into a classical historical romance in 1885. *Kidnapped* was inspired by some records of the Old Bailey trials that Fanny Stevenson had obtained from a London bookseller. The document of a murder in the Scottish highlands at Auchern especially fascinated Stevenson. Set in 1751, six years after the Jacobite Rebellion, the story is narrated by David Balfour, a young Scottish Lowlander who seeks out his uncle

at the House of Shaws to claim his inheritance after his father's death. His uncle Ebenezer tricks the boy and arranges his kidnapping and imprisonment aboard a brig bound for the Carolinas. On board David meets and befriends a Highlander, Alan Breck Stewart, and when the ship is wrecked off the coast of Mull, the two escape and land ashore. Together they journey across Scotland; in the course of the trek David witnesses a murder at Appin and is pursued as a suspect of the crime. After many adventures David and Alan return to restore David's inheritance; Alan then leaves for France.

Several contemporary reviewers recognized a mature artistry in *Kidnapped*. James deemed it on a level with the novels of Thackeray and superior to those of Dumas. He singled out the scenes of interaction between David and Alan as having the "very logic and rhythm of life." Lang praised the book as having more of the spirit of Scott than any other piece of English fiction. In elaborating the relationship between David and other characters who represent father figures for him, Stevenson elevated the story from the realm of pure adventure to that of psychological romance. He had read Twain's *The Adventures of Huckleberry Finn* (1884) a month before he had begun writing *Kidnapped,* and David's trek with Alan across Scotland can be compared to Huck's escape with Jim down the Mississippi – each of these journeys is an odyssey of the soul and of the conscience for the protagonist. In both stories the personal interaction between boy and man recreates the strains of conflict between a son and a surrogate father who represents a diverse ethnic or racial type. In *Kidnapped* the animosity of division between Highlander and Lowlander and David's ability to outgrow his prejudices provide the thematic basis of the novel. Stevenson interweaves the drama of Scottish history with elements of the bildungsroman in tracing the psychological moral growth of his adolescent hero. By achieving a literary success in a work that fuses elements so central to his background and his memories, Stevenson could make a claim to a novelistic style and subject of his own.

In 1887 Thomas Stevenson died, and money from the inheritance gave Stevenson and his family greater freedom to travel. Their thoughts turned to the United States, and in August 1887 they left Britain for good. When they docked in New York a month later, Stevenson was greeted with a tumultuous welcome by journalists and by fans of his books. *Dr. Jekyll and Mr. Hyde* had become a huge success in the United States, and editors clamored for his work. However, Stevenson reacted against

David Balfour; one of W. Hole's illustrations for Stevenson's Kidnapped, *set in the Scottish Highlands during the eighteenth century*

the mercenary nature of American publishing and was embarrassed by the huge sums of money offered to him. Over the course of the next year the Stevensons settled in a remote, quiet residence at a health resort in Saranac Lake, New York. Here the author worked on several essays and on *The Master of Ballantrae: A Winter's Tale* (1889), which recounts a tragic Highland rivalry between brothers during the period of the Jacobite Rebellion. In the spring of 1888 Stevenson decided to accept an offer from Samuel McClure, the newspaper magnate, to write a series of articles for syndication. The Stevensons enthusiastically embraced McClure's suggestion that a cruise in the South Pacific might provide material for the series, and in May 1888 the family, accompanied by Stevenson's mother, set sail from San Francisco for the South Seas. For the next eighteen months they led a nomadic existence, sailing the

schooner *Casco* in the South Pacific with short stops at the islands of the Marquesas, Tahiti, Oahu, the Gilberts, and Samoa. During this itinerant life Stevenson managed to begin several important works of his maturity including *The Wrong Box* (1889), *The Wrecker* (1892), and *The Ebb-Tide* (1894). In 1889 he and his wife purchased a plot of land near Apia on Samoa and began to build an estate they called Vailima.

With the establishment of a more settled existence, Stevenson focused intently on his writing. He began the sequel to *Kidnapped, Catriona* (1893; published in the United States as *David Balfour*) partly to help finance his Vailima estate and partly to tie up the loose ends of the David Balfour story. *Catriona* resumes Balfour's narrative after the point where he reclaims his inheritance from his uncle and parts company from Alan in Edinburgh. An innocent

The last photograph taken of Stevenson

man is arrested and tried for the political assassination that David had witnessed in Appin during his trek across Scotland with Alan. When David attempts to give vital evidence at the trial, he is kidnapped and imprisoned at the Bass Rock. He is allowed to escape after the trial and travels to Holland, where he renews his friendship with Catriona Drummond, a Highlander and the granddaughter of Rob Roy. Despite differences in temperament and upbringing, the two fall in love, and David's adventures are resolved with his marriage to Catriona and his friend Alan's escape to France.

Stevenson considered *Catriona* one of his best literary efforts, deeming it his "high-water mark." Critics of the time agreed; James praised the novel for its artistic construction and the strength of its characterization. Overall, however, the critical consensus has been that *Catriona* is inferior to such enduring classics as *Treasure Island* and *Kidnapped* and comes across as a weak mixture of conventional love story and episodic adventure tale. The ele-

ments of artistry are present, from the topography of memorable Scottish landscapes rendered through striking word pictures to the complex thematic exploration of moral dilemmas that David Balfour faces. However, the love affair between David and Catriona is presented in a wooden fashion, and the intricate pattern of social, political, and personal questions in the novel is not presented as successfully as that in *Kidnapped*.

After completing *Catriona*, Stevenson concentrated on his final major literary effort, *The Weir of Hermiston* (1896), until his death of a cerebral hemorrhage on 3 December 1894. In the years that followed, his literary reputation underwent a cycle of criticism, beginning with eulogistic portrayals adulating him as a saintlike figure whose writings would be enduring classics. In the early twentieth century a critical reaction against Stevenson shattered his mythical stature and relegated him to the canon of minor authors in British literature. More-recent critics such as Robert Kiely, Edwin Eigner, James Pope-Hennessy, and Jenni Calder have written more balanced appraisals of his work. As the author of such children's classics as *Treasure Island, A Child's Garden of Verses,* and *Kidnapped,* Stevenson introduced elements of artistry into a genre that had been derided for its low quality of writing. His explorations of the child's consciousness contributed substantially to concepts of human development, particularly through his emphasis on the importance of play as an activity that stimulates creativity and artistic imagination. Perhaps the highest praise of his books is that they continue to introduce children to the "shock of pleasure" in reading that was such a fabulous discovery in Stevenson's own childhood.

Letters:

The Letters of Robert Louis Stevenson to His Family and Friends, 2 volumes, edited by Sidney Colvin (London: Methuen, 1899; New York: Scribners, 1899).

Bibliography:

W. F. Prideaux, *A Bibliography of the Works of Robert Louis Stevenson,* revised edition, edited and supplemented by Mrs. Luther S. Livingston (London: Hollings, 1918).

Biographies:

Graham Balfour, *The Life of Robert Louis Stevenson* (New York: Scribners, 1901);

Janet Adam Smith, *Robert Louis Stevenson* (London: Duckworth, 1947);

David Daiches, *Robert Louis Stevenson* (Norfolk, Conn.: New Directions, 1947);

J. C. Furnas, *Voyage to Windward: The Life of Robert Louis Stevenson* (New York: Sloane, 1951);

James Pope-Hennessy, *Robert Louis Stevenson* (London: Cape, 1974);

Jenni Calder, *R L S: A Life Study* (London: Hamilton, 1980);

Ian Bell, *Dreams of Exile: Robert Louis Stevenson, a Biography* (New York: Holt, 1993).

References:

Jenni Calder, ed., *Stevenson and Victorian Scotland* (Edinburgh: University of Edinburgh Press, 1981);

G. K. Chesterton, *Robert Louis Stevenson* (London: Hodder & Stoughton, 1927);

David Daiches, *Robert Louis Stevenson and His World* (London: Thames & Hudson, 1973);

Edwin M. Eigner, *Robert Louis Stevenson and Romantic Tradition* (Princeton, N. J.: Princeton University Press, 1966);

Susan Gannon, "Repetition and Meaning in Stevenson's David Balfour Novels," *Studies in the Literary Imagination,* 18 (Fall 1985): 21–33;

Robert Kiely, *Robert Louis Stevenson and the Fiction of Adventure* (Cambridge, Mass.: Harvard University Press, 1965);

Andrew Lang, *Dear Stevenson: Letters from Andrew Lang to Robert Louis Stevenson with Five Letters from Stevenson to Lang,* edited by Marysa Demoor (Leuven, Belgium: Uitgeverij Peeters, 1990);

Paul Maixner, ed., *Robert Louis Stevenson: The Critical Heritage* (London: Routledge & Kegan Paul, 1981);

Irving S. Saposnik, *Robert Louis Stevenson* (New York: Twayne, 1974);

Janet Adam Smith, ed., *Henry James and Robert Louis Stevenson: A Record of Friendship and Criticism* (London: Hart-Davis, 1948);

Robert G. Swearingen, *The Prose Writings of Robert Louis Stevenson: A Guide* (Hamden, Conn.: Archon, 1980).

Papers:

Collections of Stevenson's papers are at the Beinecke Rare Book and Manuscript Library, Yale University; the Pierpont Morgan Library, New York; the Henry E. Huntington Library, San Marino, California; the Harry Elkins Widener Memorial Library, Harvard University; the Edinburgh Public Library; the Silverado Museum, Saint Helena, California; and the Monterey State Historical Monument Stevenson House, Monterey, California.

Bertha Upton
(1849 – 10 July 1912)

and

Florence K. Upton
(22 February 1873 – 16 October 1922)

Greta D. Little
University of South Carolina

BOOKS (by Bertha Upton and Florence K. Upton):
The Adventures of Two Dutch Dolls – and a "Golli-wogg" (London & New York: Longmans, Green, 1895);
The Golliwogg's Bicycle Club (London & New York: Longmans, Green, 1896);
Little Hearts (London: Routledge, 1897);
The Vege-Men's Revenge (London & New York: Longmans, Green, 1897);
The Golliwogg at the Sea-side (London & New York: Longmans, Green, 1898);
The Golliwogg in War! (London & New York: Longmans, Green, 1899);
The Golliwogg's Polar Adventures (London & New York: Longmans, Green, 1900);
The Golliwogg's "Auto-Go-Cart" (London & New York: Longmans, Green, 1901);
The Golliwogg's Air-Ship (London & New York: Longmans, Green, 1902);
The Golliwogg's Circus (London & New York: Longmans, Green, 1903);
The Golliwogg in Holland (London & New York: Longmans, Green, 1904);
The Golliwogg's Fox-Hunt (London & New York: Longmans, Green, 1905);
The Golliwogg's Desert Island (London & New York: Longmans, Green, 1906);
The Golliwogg's Christmas (London & New York: Longmans, Green, 1907);
Golliwogg in the African Jungle (London & New York: Longmans, Green, 1909).

BOOK (by Florence K. Upton): *The Adventures of Borbee and the Wisp* (London & New York: Longmans, Green, 1908).

Few Americans are familiar with the Golli-wogg, though some may know "Golliwog's Cake-walk" from Claude Debussy's *Children's Corner* suite

Florence K. Upton in 1896

(1908). The *Oxford English Dictionary* defines *golliwogg* as a "name invented for a black-faced grotesquely dressed (male) doll with a shock of fuzzy hair." Golliwogg, both the fictional character and the word itself, was first introduced in *The Adventures of Two Dutch Dolls – and a "Golliwog"* (1895), by Bertha Upton and Florence K. Upton. The Uptons, a mother and daughter team, produced thirteen books about a black male rag doll and five wooden

Dutch dolls between 1895 and 1909. The books were published in both the United States and Great Britain, but in Britain they enjoyed their greatest success. However, like Little Black Sambo, the Golliwogg has become a relic of nineteenth-century racism and is no longer respectable.

Bertha Upton, who wrote the verses for these books, was born in 1849 in Great Britain. She came to New York to marry on 2 July 1870 Thomas Harborough Upton, who had immigrated to the United States in 1868. Florence K. Upton, born on 22 February 1873, was the second of four children. The family lived prosperously until Thomas Upton died unexpectedly on 11 June 1889. Supporting the family fell to Bertha and the two older girls; Florence used her artistic talents as an illustrator. By the time the family traveled to London for an extended visit in 1893, Florence was ready for more independence. The children's-book market had established itself as a lucrative one, and Florence chose the fantasy world of toys for her first endeavor. Thus, during this visit to London Florence and Bertha wrote and sold their first book, *The Adventures of Two Dutch Dolls – and a "Golliwogg."* By the time the book was actually published, Bertha and three of her children had returned to the United States. Florence, however, chose to remain in London to pursue her career.

Florence was a skilled artist, determined to create her own books. Preferring to draw from models, she searched for an idea until she came upon some old wooden dolls while cleaning the family attic. In them she found the basis for her story, but she still lacked a hero. An aunt found an old and battered black doll, brought with children from the United States on a previous visit. Florence declared him her hero and called him Golliwogg. Although dictionaries sometimes disagree, she always claimed to have coined the name herself.

This unusual hero – with his funny formal clothes, wide grin, button eyes, and black skin – surprised prospective publishers. His wild shock of fuzzy black hair was reminiscent of Struwwelpeter, the nasty, slovenly character of Heinrich Hoffmann's mid-nineteenth-century cautionary tales in rhyme. Wary publishers thought Golliwogg was ugly, and they were unwilling to take the risk of putting him on the pages of their books. At Longmans, Green and Company, however, J. W. Allen, an experienced editor, took the manuscript and drawings home to his own children for a trial; their enthusiastic response assured the book's publication.

Nevertheless, contemporary critics persisted in labeling Golliwogg unattractive, even ugly, and were unable to understand or accept his popularity among children. One stated he was at a loss to explain how "anything so hideous should please and even fascinate children." The London *Times* (12 December 1898) saw a fashion tending "toward the grotesque" as the reason for Golliwogg's continued success. Yet in comparison to the pallid, staid characters of many Victorian children's books, Golliwogg was healthy, robust, and full of energy. Children were interested in his actions, not his appearance. He was friendly, courageous, and lovable; therefore they embraced him.

The two Dutch dolls of the book's title are sisters, Peggy Deutchland [*sic*] and Sarah Jane. They come to life in a toy shop on Christmas Eve along with all the other dolls. Deciding they need clothes, Peg insists that Sarah Jane secure an American flag flying in the shop so that she can make them dresses. Peg in her red and white stripes and Sarah Jane in the blue and white stars proceed with their adventures through the shop. While enjoying a game of leapfrog with several other dolls, Peg spies the Golliwogg and screams in alarm. He begs them not to be afraid, and soon Peggy and Sarah Jane are chatting away with Golliwogg, charming him with small talk and dancing at a ball. Later Golliwogg suggests they run away, so the dolls embark on an adventure outside the toy shop. Two other Dutch dolls, Meg and Weg, and a miniature wooden doll, Midget, join them. They frolic in the snow. When they want to ice-skate, Golliwogg ventures out to test the ice, falls through, and is rescued by his companions.

These six dolls are the central characters of the series. Peggy is the older sister, a bit vain with a naughty streak, who can be somewhat demanding. Sarah Jane is younger, more modest, and always ready for a new adventure. Meg and Weg play supporting roles to the other, more prominent dolls. Midget is fearless, an eager participant in all their adventures. Golliwogg, a perfect gentleman, becomes the dominant force in the plot. Not until the second book does he become the major player, leading his willing companions as they discover the world.

The Golliwogg's Bicycle Club (1896), next in the series, sets the pattern for subsequent books. The story opens with a busy period of preparation for a new adventure, followed by a series of mishaps, usually including the separation of one or more dolls from the group. Inevitably they overcome the obstacles and head for home, exhausted but satisfied with their exploits. In this book the bored dolls join the latest craze – cycling. After careful planning and hard work building bicycles and tricycles, the

The Golliwogg meets Sarah Jane and Peg, illustration from The Adventures of Two Dutch Dolls – and a "Golliwogg"

group sets off for France. They show off their new vehicles, cycling through the *bois,* and see the Eiffel Tower before departing for the wilds where a lion attacks. Golly protects them by shooting the lion, and the bikers continue on their way to Japan for tea served by a Geisha girl. On the return trip they enter the territory of the dangerous Turks. Golliwogg suggests they wrap their heads in turbans, and they outsmart the bandits, who think they are also Turks. In the book's final adventure, set in a desert, they are attacked by savages who want Golly's scalp. Sarah Jane comes to his aid by offering the chief her stovepipe hat. The chief accepts and treats the group to a feast, and then the dolls head for home.

After three years in London and two highly successful children's books, Florence returned to the United States to study at the Art Students League of New York. She and her mother resumed their collaboration. However, the Uptons may have been affected by charges that Golliwogg was ugly. Despite the success of the Golliwogg books, their third book was a collection of sentimental poetry, *Little Hearts* (1897). Possibly an effort to conform to other children's books of the time, the book had little of the originality and charm of the Golliwogg books and was not successful. The Uptons' fourth book, *The Vege-Men's Revenge* (1897), was a fantasy about Poppy, a little girl spirited away by some vegetables. Motivated by the desire to punish humans, the vegetables plant the girl, harvest her as a new

plant, and prepare a banquet of dishes made with the Poppy plant. In the midst of the reveling Poppy awakes to discover she has been dreaming. The book was no more successful than *Little Hearts*. The public wanted more Golliwogg, and the Uptons' next contract in 1898 stipulated a return of the popular dolls.

To young Victorian and Edwardian readers, Golliwogg was an appealing model of propriety, displaying the virtues of consideration without sacrificing his vitality. In his 1974 autobiography Kenneth Clark calls the Golliwogg books the most influential of his childhood: "I do not think it an exaggeration to say that they influenced my character more fundamentally than anything I have read since. . . . [The Golliwogg] was for me an example of chivalry, far more persuasive than the unconvincing knights of the Arthurian legend. I identified myself with him completely, and have never quite ceased to do so." Clark's reaction apparently is not unique. In his 1946 memoir of his Victorian childhood, Eric Bligh devotes eleven pages to the Golliwogg books and what they meant to him.

In the beginning the Uptons may have shared some of the critics' ambivalence about the strange hero they had created, but their readers' affection for the character must have been infectious. After the first book there is no further mention of his being a frightful, horrid sight; in fact, subsequent comments on his appearance are complimentary: he is "a dear," "a noble man," "a modest, gentle

The Golliwogg and the dolls visit Japan, illustration from The Golliwogg's Bicycle Club

knight." Clark suggests that Golliwogg and his personality grew far beyond the Uptons' original expectation, and Florence's illustrations bear him out. In *The Adventures of Two Dutch Dolls,* the lines of his face and figure are harsh, the nose sharp, and his movements appear stiff. His button eyes have cross-stitch pupils. In later books Golly's appearance is softer, more humanlike: his nose is less prominent, and he seems to move more naturally and smoothly. His eyes cease to be obvious buttons, often becoming oval instead of round; the pupils move about, losing their cross-stitch shape. But the most important change is in the range of his facial expressions. At first Florence used only three basic expressions; she later gave Golly a subtlety suited to the fully developed character he had become. According to Bligh, by the end of *The Golliwogg's Bicycle Club,* Florence had found her touch, creating more elaborate pictures with richer backgrounds of foreign romance and skillfully conveying a wide range of expressions on the dolls' faces.

As Golly's appearance gains dimension, his role also grows. In the later books Golly instigates each new adventure. The other dolls rely on him to provide their entertainment and to insure their safety. In her verses Bertha describes him as "strong," "brave," "patient," "good," and "thoughtful." To the other dolls he is captain, host, and hero, their "dear Golliwogg," always considerate of their comfort and well-being. He plans their trip to the seaside, teaches them to play in the surf, and takes them sailing in the moonlight. Golliwogg even leads them in war, making a cannon and digging trenches. During their search for the North Pole, Golly takes responsibility for feeding the group and for protecting them from polar bears and vicious seabirds. When the dolls are arrested for speeding in a go-cart, Golly loosens a bar in the jail and waits until the girls are safe before he attempts his own escape. His sense of responsibility is keen when the cart blows up, throwing the dolls hither and yon:

> Prone Golliwogg despairing lay,
>   For heart and hope had fled,
> He did not wish to live, because
>   He thought the rest were dead.

Even when he knows they are fine, the "thought of failure tries him sore; / Through him their clothes are spoiled."

Golly is not a benevolent dictator or surrogate father; he is a sensitive and caring hero who leads, but does not dominate, his companion dolls. Sarah Jane is the doll who "has the brains"; it is she who stops the war after shooting the first soldier and wounding him. Although Golliwogg's chivalrous concern for his five lady friends is ever-present, he relies on their judgment and needs their help when things go awry. Sarah Jane knows how to make the boat for their polar adventure. The other dolls support the wounded Golly while Meg binds his arm. When he finds himself set adrift on an ice floe, the dolls send Midget out with a rope to bring him back safely.

After the Uptons' brief experiment with other children's books, their joint efforts produced a Golliwogg book almost every year until 1909. The titles reflect the peripatetic nature of their escapades, not only by the range of destinations – *The Golliwogg at the Seaside* (1898), *The Golliwogg's Polar Adventures* (1900), *The Golliwogg in Holland* (1904), *The Golliwogg's Desert Island* (1906), *Golliwogg in the African Jungle* (1909) – but also by the range of vehicles – *The Golliwogg's Bicycle Club, The Golliwogg's "Auto-Go-Cart"* (1901), *The Golliwogg's Air-Ship* (1902). They also reveal the topical inspiration that guided the Uptons in their creation. *The Golliwogg's Bicycle Club* was prompted by a bicycle craze that brought mobility to the masses in late-Victorian Britain and in the United States. *The Golliwogg's Polar Adventures* was written in response to the public attention in the wake of Robert Edwin Peary's initial polar expedition in 1899. *The Golliwogg's Air-Ship* followed the development of dirigible flights, and *Golliwogg in the African Jungle* reflected the interest in African exploration and the development of photography. *The Golliwogg in War!* (1899) was written in the United States during the Spanish-American War in 1898 and published while Britain was on the brink of war against the Boers in South Africa.

In 1901 the entire Upton family embarked for France, where Florence studied art, and her brother Desmond, architecture. Bertha and Florence continued to collaborate on the Golliwogg books, completing *The Golliwogg's Air-Ship, The Golliwogg's Circus* (1903), and *The Golliwogg in Holland.* In 1906 Florence took a studio in London while Bertha and the rest of the family returned to New York. The collaboration continued across the Atlantic, producing *The Golliwogg's Desert Island* and *The Golliwogg's Christmas* (1907). Florence published her only solo effort, *The Adventures of Borbee and the Wisp,* in 1908. Borbee, the protagonist, is a young boy who, with the help of a fairy-like insect called the Wisp, must rescue a fairy princess from an unhappy marriage that will ban her from Fairy Land. Although the critics liked the book, children were less than enthusiastic. In fact, the Uptons seemed to have lost their magic. Sales of *Golliwogg in the African Jungle* were so slow that Longmans reduced the royalties in an effort to make the book more successful. Ironically, while the books lost favor, the dolls and other commercial products employing the "Gollywog" (spelled with a single *g* to distinguish it from the original) continued to be wildly successful. Because the Uptons held no patent for the Golliwogg, they received no profit from the character's commercial success.

Florence Upton continued her career in London as a respected portrait artist. In 1912 she was called back to New York because her mother was ill. After Bertha Upton died on 10 July 1912, Florence returned to London and her portrait painting. In 1917 she donated the original dolls and 350 drawings from the Golliwogg series to the Red Cross for an auction at Christie's. The dolls and some drawings were for many years displayed at Chequers, the country estate of the British prime minister. They are now housed at the Bethnal Green Museum of Childhood in London.

During the war, Florence worked with the War Refugees Committee and later as a nurse. She also became interested in spiritualism and psychic phenomena. This interest, her portrait painting, and travel filled the rest of her life. She died on 16 October 1922.

The Uptons' Golliwogg lived on, although he was often hard to recognize. The commercialized golliwog came to exemplify racial stigma and exploitation. While the Uptons' Golliwogg may have sometimes appeared silly, even a little ridiculous, there was always something noble about him: he was a chivalrous knight, not a faithful servant; a heroic figure, not a farcical one. Bligh laments the fate of his favorite: "How can I convey any idea of the delight of that book and clearly separate it from later imitations of the Golliwogg . . . a mockery of his original noble-minded self, on those little labels some people stick on their Christmas parcels." Most people today have never seen the Uptons' books. They know the caricature portrayed on commercial products or the thousands of imitation golliwogs found on postcards and in books by Grace Drayton, Ruth Ainsworth, and especially Enid Blyton. Florence K. Upton biographer Norma S. Davis says the doll's personality "changed and diminished drastically in the hands of postcard artists." Other authors saw the golliwog as a bungling, comic figure. For example, Blyton borrowed the character for a book called *The Three Golliwogs* (1944), about three unhappy dolls that nobody ever played with. The dolls, "Gollie," "Wog," and "Nigger," leave the nursery and spread mischief wherever they go. In Blyton's Noddy series, the young Gollie misbehaves, cannot read, and even steals. Modern readers have little knowledge of the character who inspired all these unworthy imitations.

The affection between Golliwogg and his ladies is a major factor in each book. In *The Golliwogg's Desert Island,* a story patterned after Daniel Defoe's *Robinson Crusoe* (1719), the dolls survive a shipwreck and have their wish to be castaways like

Illustration from The Vege-Men's Revenge, *a fantasy about a little girl who is kidnapped and planted by vegetables*

Crusoe. When the storm strikes, Golliwogg launches the lifeboats and sends the ladies down first. Just as he is ready to descend, Sarah Jane realizes that she has dropped their copy of *Robinson Crusoe* on the deck and begs Golliwogg to retrieve it. The patient Golly goes back, gets the book, and then falls into the sea when a big wave moves the lifeboat away. Fortunately, his life preserver keeps him afloat until he reaches an island. Once there, he follows Sarah Jane's idea to live like Crusoe while he waits for the other dolls to find their way to the island in the boat. During the next few days while he waits for the girls to arrive, he hunts, cooks, and lives as Crusoe did. But even after he meets Monday (the Uptons' version of Defoe's Friday), he longs for the company of his friends:

I'm looking for a boat which soon
  This little cove should reach:
It holds the dearest of the dear
  Five little girls I lost at sea
Sometimes I feel I cannot wait
  Until they come to me.

The first to arrive is Midget, who managed to get a ride from a seagull. Golliwogg rescues her from three savage chiefs who are about to roast her.

Then the boat with the other four girls lands safely, and they share a happy reunion. The dolls are pleased to find their plans executed so well by the Golliwogg.

As this story shows, the Dutch dolls are just a bit superficial, even Sarah Jane and the miniature wooden doll, Midget, the most appealing of the five. They love the Golliwogg, but there is little evidence that they recognize the extent of his patience, goodness, and chivalry. It is partially by this contrast that Golly gains depth and stature as a character, becoming the model that he was to Clark. The dolls depend on Golly as the only male in their circle to defend them and keep them from harm. They have complete faith in him. When Midget's balloon drifts away from the airship, she calls through the clouds: "Come! Save poor, tiny me!" Her faith is justified, for time and again Golly brings Midget and the others through safely. He rescues them from a flood in Holland after a dike breaks: " 'Tis he! 'tis he! Our Golliwogg! / We knew he couldn't fail!"

Golliwogg possesses higher virtues as well. In *The Golliwogg's Circus,* when a lion goes berserk and frightens everyone out of the tent, Golly immediately recognizes that they must return all the money they have collected for tickets: "A noble man like Golli-

Illustration from The Adventures of Borbee and the Wisp, *the only book Florence K. Upton wrote without the assistance of her mother*

wogg / And honest to the core, / Must ever do the rightful thing." However, when everyone in the audience refuses to take the money back, Golly accedes, not for personal gain, but to pay the animals.

Honest, selfless, and generous, the Golliwogg also suffers his share of reversals. Over the course of the series he is captured by headhunters eager for his magnificent scalp, blows up the auto cart, gets thrown into the water while foxhunting, and snags his airship on a chimney. These mishaps are not tragedies – the outcome is always positive – nor are they slapstick comedy. They show the mutual affection existing among the dolls, for the dolls are as devoted to their Golliwogg as he is to them. While hunting a seal to feed and clothe them on their polar adventure, Golly gets set adrift on an ice floe moving out to sea. The girls send Midget out to him with a rope to pull him back: "They pull and haul with every nerve / They strain and puff and blow / Until their very finger tips / Like heated carbons glow."

Five female dolls' being squired about and championed by a single male invites interpretation from a feminist perspective, and such readings can, in fact, reveal some interesting and surprising observations. These dolls are not stereotyped helpless females waiting to be taken care of. It is true that Peg often needs protection and that she is the group seamstress, but even she has her assertive moments – as a bullfighter in the circus, for example. Sarah Jane's relationship with Golly is more balanced: she is his helper, contributing significantly to both deciding and executing plans. For instance, when they sail for Holland, she steers the boats while he takes care of the sails. Sarah Jane is capable of independent action to rescue Golly and the rest, as she does in offering the chief her stovepipe hat in *The Golliwogg's Bicycle Club* and in getting the rope before Golliwogg drifts away in *The Golliwogg's Polar Adventures.* Meg and Weg, although they are not especially important in most of the plots, exhibit primarily conventional feminine responses to events. However, in *The Golliwogg's "Auto-Go-Cart,"* Meg unexpectedly and inexplicably wears a man's hat and tie.

Midget, the five-and-one-half-inch miniature doll, proves to be one of the most liberated characters in children's literature: she is independent, fearless, and ready for any adventure. She takes a balloon ride on her own, descends into a fox's hole to flush him out, is washed away in a wooden shoe during a flood, gets lost in the desert, and dances on the jaw of a lion. Occasionally Golly and the other dolls have to rescue her, but whether her balloon goes astray or cannibals capture her, she remains undaunted. She never faints as Peggy sometimes does, and she has no need of a partner as Sarah Jane and the others do. Midget is a truly free spirit.

A Victorian children's book with a black hero also invites critics to look for racist implications. Other books with black and white characters from the turn of the century portray inferior / superior relationships: blacks tended to be lower creatures in need of the superior white's care. In *The Negro in American Fiction* (1933) Sterling A. Brown claims that black children were generally "written of in the same terms as their mothers and fathers, as quaint, living jokes, designed to make white children laugh." Although a doll, Golliwogg is a black character and can be seen as a comment on racial attitudes. Social critics such as David Milner, author of *Children and Race* (1983), see the golliwog as an objectionable representative of racial prejudice and discrimination, describing him as "a ludicrous caricature, . . . the laughing, crying, rubber-lipped, nigger minstrel figure." This hardly resembles the character who taught Clark about chivalry and courtesy; it is more akin to the American "Sambo," a word that came to refer to a black servant or slave, often used as an ethnic slur in the nineteenth century. In *Sambo: The Rise and Demise of an American Jester* (1986), Joseph Boskin describes the Sambo character as "unrivaled in the culture for producing and accepting laughter, for being both the prodder and butt of the joke." Sambo is the American counterpart to the British golliwog, appearing on place mats, kitchen reminders, trays, shoehorns, tea sets, and countless other bric-a-brac. It is the gollie of Blyton and other Upton imitators. According to Boskin, this racist image was designed to achieve social control, its "ultimate objective for whites was to effect mastery: to render the black male powerless as a potential warrior, as a sexual competitor, as an economic adversary."

The image is not a good match for the Uptons' Golliwogg, although they did create other characters that could fit such a role. In *The Adventures of Two Dutch Dolls,* for example, one of the musicians is a minstrel banjo player called Sambo. At the Sandyville Inn in *The Golliwogg at the Sea-side,* the dolls are greeted by a black maître d', who is at first nonplussed by the menagerie of dolls and then, indicating that discrimination is the order of the day, asks if they are at the right hotel. Golliwogg's answer is not specified, but he clearly rises to the occasion, because the man not only accepts him and his party but also recognizes his nobility, naming him "de prince ob Golliwogg." This type of obvious dialect is reserved for such minor characters and is never found in Golliwogg's speech.

There may be some surface similarities between Golly and Sambo the minstrel or the hotel employee, but their social positions are clearly different. Golly is accepted at the best hotels, squires lovely ladies around town, and dances with them at balls. Unfortunately the Golliwogg found in the Uptons' books has been contaminated by the Sambo figure in the United States and by the golliwog figure in Britain. As a result, one of the most original heroes in children's literature remains largely unknown and unappreciated, tainted by his unworthy imitators.

Biographies:

Edith Lyttelton, *Florence Upton: Painter* (London & New York: Longmans, Green, 1926);

Norma S. Davis, *A Lark Ascends: Florence Kate Upton, Artist and Illustrator* (Metuchen, N. J. & London: Scarecrow Press, 1992).

References:

Eric Bligh, *Tooting Corner* (Bloomsbury, U.K.: Secker & Warburg, 1946), pp. 164–174;

Joseph Boskin, *Sambo: The Rise and Demise of an American Jester* (New York: Oxford University Press, 1986);

Sterling A. Brown, *The Negro in American Fiction* (Washington, D.C.: Associates in Negro Folk Education, 1933);

Kenneth Clark, *Another Part of the Wood: A Self-Portrait* (London: Murray, 1974), pp. 6–7;

David Milner, *Children and Race* (London: Sage, 1983);

Edgar Osborne, "Birth of the Golliwogg," *Junior Bookshelf,* 12 (December 1948): 159–165;

Hubert S. Peet, "Birth of the Golliwogg," *John o'London's Weekly* (22 December 1950);

Adaline Piper, "Florence K. Upton, Painter: An Appreciation of Her Work," *American Magazine of Art,* 14 (September 1923): 487–488.

Stanley J. Weyman

(7 August 1855 – 10 April 1928)

Carol Anita Tarr
Illinois State University

BOOKS: *The Other Englishman* (London: Smith, Elder, n.d.);

The Story of a Courtship (New York: Ogilvie, n.d.);

The House of the Wolf: A Romance (London: Longmans, Green, 1890; New York: Burt, 1890; abridged edition, London: Longmans, Green, 1920);

The New Rector (London: Smith, Elder, 1891; New York: American Publishers, [1891]);

The Story of Francis Cludde (London: Cassell, 1891; New York: Cassell, 1891);

The King's Strategem, and Other Stories (New York: Cluett, [1891]);

A Gentleman of France, Being the Memoirs of Gaston de Bonne, Sieur de Marsac, 3 volumes (London: Longmans, Green, 1893; New York: Longmans, Green, 1893; simplified edition, London: Longmans, Green, 1948);

A Little Wizard (New York: Fenno, [1893]);

Under the Red Robe: A Romance (London: Methuen, 1894; New York: Longmans, Green, 1894; abridged edition, London: Murray, 1955);

My Lady Rotha (London: Innes, 1894; New York: Longmans, Green, 1894);

The Man in Black (London: Cassell, 1894; New York: Cassell, 1894);

From the Memoirs of a Minister of France (London: Cassell, 1895; New York: Longmans, Green, 1895);

The Snowball (New York: Merriam, [1895]);

The Red Cockade: A Novel of the French Revolution (London: Longmans, Green, 1895; New York: Harper, 1896);

For the Cause (Chicago: Sergel, [1897]);

Shrewsbury: A Romance of the Time of William and Mary (London: Longmans, Green, 1898; New York: Longmans, Green, 1898);

The Castle Inn: A Romance (London: Smith, Elder, 1898; New York: Longmans, Green, 1898);

When Love Calls (Boston: Brown, 1899);

Sophia: A Romance (London: Longmans, Green, 1899; New York: Longmans, Green, 1900);

Count Hannibal: A Romance of the Court of France (London: Smith, Elder, 1901; New York: Longmans, Green, 1901);

In King's Byways (London: Smith, Elder, 1902; New York: Longmans, Green, 1902);

The Long Night (London: Longmans, Green, 1903; New York: Burt, [1893]);

The Abbess of Vlaye (London: Longmans, Green, 1904; New York: Longmans, Green, 1904);

Starvecrow Farm (London: Hutchinson, 1905; New York: Longmans, Green, 1905);

Chippinge (London: Smith, Elder, 1906); republished as *Chippinge Borough* (New York: Macmillan, 1906);

Laid Up in Lavender (London: Smith, Elder, 1907; New York: Longmans, Green, 1907);

The Wild Geese (London: Hodder & Stoughton, [1908]; New York: Doubleday, Page, 1909);

The Great House: A Story of Quiet Times (London: Murray, 1919; New York: Longmans, Green, 1919);

Historical Romances (New York: Longmans, Green, [1921]) – includes *Under the Red Robe; Count Hannibal; A Gentleman of France;*

Ovington's Bank (London: Murray, 1922; New York: Longmans, Green, 1922);

The Traveller in the Fur Cloak (New York: Longmans, Green, 1924; London: Hutchinson, [1925]);

Queen's Folly (London: Murray, 1925; New York: Longmans, Green, 1925);

The Lively Peggy (London: Murray, 1928; New York: Longmans, Green, 1928).

Collections: *The Works of Stanley J. Weyman,* 20 volumes (London: Smith, Elder, 1911);

The Works of Stanley J. Weyman, 23 volumes (London: Murray, 1922–1929).

Stanley J. Weyman (pronounced *Wyman*), best known as a writer of historical romances, enjoyed his greatest popularity during the decades before and after the turn of the century. Known as "the English Dumas," he carried on the tradition estab-

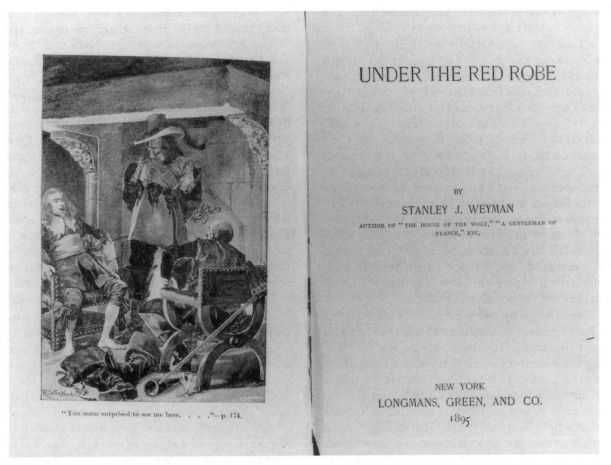

UNDER THE RED ROBE

BY

STANLEY J. WEYMAN

AUTHOR OF "THE HOUSE OF THE WOLF," "A GENTLEMAN OF
FRANCE," ETC.

NEW YORK
LONGMANS, GREEN, AND CO.
1895

"You seem surprised to see me here. . . ."—p. 174.

Frontispiece and title page for an American edition of one of Weyman's historical adventure novels

lished by such novelists as Alexandre Dumas père and Sir Walter Scott. His best novels offer absorbing characterizations and suspense against a backdrop of political and/or religious turmoil in either England or France. For historical accuracy Weyman drew upon the memoirs, letters, and diaries of real personages for much of his material. He was admired not only for his well-planned, exciting plots, but also for the descriptions of individual characters and of mob behavior present in almost every novel. During the 1890s he was immensely popular, producing twelve novels in that decade. At least three of these novels were made into plays and motion pictures, with one transformed into an operetta. Praised by both Robert Louis Stevenson and Andrew Lang, Weyman was not intentionally writing for children, but a few of his novels, especially *The House of the Wolf* (1890) and *The Story of Francis Cludde* (1891), became favorites of young readers.

Stanley John Weyman was born on 7 August 1855, the second son of Thomas Weyman, a solicitor. His formal education began at the local gram-mar school, continued at Shrewsbury School, and ended with his graduating from Christ Church, Oxford, taking a second class in modern history. After teaching history at King's School, Chester, for a year, he began his eight-year career as a barrister, having been called to the bar in 1881 and joining the Oxford circuit. His law career was a lackluster one, for he had a nervous demeanor that angered judges and lost cases. In 1895 he married Charlotte Panting; they had no children. While he was at Oxford, his short story "My Scouts" was published in *Chambers' Journal,* and in 1883, during his ample spare time as a barrister, Weyman returned to writing, eventually contributing twenty pieces, mostly stories, to *Cornhill Magazine.*

With encouragement from James Payn, the editor of *Cornhill,* Weyman wrote his first novel, *The House of the Wolf,* serialized in the *English Illustrated Magazine* in 1888–1889. After submitting the work to six or seven book publishers with no success Weyman sent the manuscript to agents who had just sold a friend's story intended for boys' reading.

The agents sold the novel to Longmans, Green, and Weyman's career as a writer was assured.

The main character is an eighteen-year-old boy oddly named Anne de Caylus (after his famous godfather, Anne de Montmorenci); his two younger brothers also have female names, Marie and Croisette. Their female cousin Catherine has fallen in love with their house prisoner, a Huguenot named Louis de Pavannes, even though their neighbor, the Vidame of Bezers, known as the Wolf, has assumed he will marry her. The Wolf makes it known that he will seek vengeance on Pavannes. In their efforts to help Pavannes, Anne and his two brothers find themselves in the midst of the Saint Bartholomew's Day Massacre in Paris on 24 August 1572, when mobs of fanatical Catholics, urged on by the monarchy, murdered Huguenots in their houses. Even though the brothers are Catholic, they are horrified; they see the uprising as a tocsin.

Anne is young so his judgment is often faulty, but his eagerness and spirit carry him through dangerous situations. His cousin shames him into pursuing the adventure in the first place, admonishing him to be a man and protect her interests. He places all women on pedestals and fails to distinguish between good or bad ones, seeing them all as helpless victims whom he must rescue. Considering himself a knight-errant for the evil Madame d'O, with his "magic ring," talisman, and sword, his innocence is dashed when he discovers the truth about her. Anne de Caylus is a hero of romance, but one who learns the nature of love and honor through experience. In spite of his desire for vengeance, the Wolf saves Pavannes from the mob, and later, when he has the brothers at his mercy, the Wolf inexplicably releases them to return to their home and happiness. Weyman explains in a note that such gallantry was not uncommon in the annals of historical turmoil, for a man's honor was more important than his life.

Weyman's second novel, *The New Rector* (1891), is a quiet story of mistaken identity inspired by the works of Anthony Trollope. Although the protagonist is relatively young and there is a romantic interest, the plot moves slowly, especially in comparison to Weyman's other novels, and is too long to turn on the one plot device of mistaken identity.

The Story of Francis Cludde also achieved its reputation through its appeal to young readers. Recommended in advertisements for both boys and girls, it was fondly remembered by Graham Greene as one of his favorite novels while growing up. Like *The House of the Wolf*, it is told in first person, this time by nineteen-year-old Francis Cludde, disillusioned with his religion and his life, who sets off on his own to build his life anew. He comes to the rescue of two Protestant women, the duchess of Suffolk and Anne Brandon, and helps them escape from the clutches of the vile Clarence, who spies for bloody Queen Mary, the scourge of all English Protestants in the mid 1500s. With the duchess's husband, they flee to the Netherlands, Germany, and then Poland before they return to England just when Queen Mary dies and Elizabeth succeeds to the throne. Eventually they learn their fellow traveler, Anne Brandon, has been spying on them for Clarence and is in fact his wife. They also learn that Clarence is Cludde's real father. Cludde saves his father from death but rejects him nevertheless. Thus the protagonist's search for an identity through Oedipal conflict is a theme readily appreciated by adolescent readers.

Cludde, a nominal Catholic, is converted to Protestantism while in the Netherlands; still, a mob that almost murders them in Germany is made up of ignorant German Protestants, so Weyman's prejudice is as much in favor of nobility as Protestantism. Although acting as a knight-errant for the duchess, Cludde's judgment is as sound as it is quick. When he leaves his home, he relinquishes his noble birthright, but later he is dubbed with a new title as a reward for his bravery by the duke of Cleves; this title is mere confirmation of the noble stature that he has earned and which Weyman requires. The class struggle, too, is somewhat complicated. While in the Netherlands, Cludde sees how the Spanish conquerors take advantage of the Dutch, but since his grandmother was Spanish, he feels some admiration for the soldiers' reckless arrogance. He shows affinity for the persecutors, yet he deliberately casts his lot with the persecuted. His new, self-created identity is an amalgam of the colonizer and the colonized.

A Gentleman of France, Being the Memoirs of Gaston de Bonne, Sieur de Marsac (1893) was praised by Lang and Stevenson, who labeled it a "chivalrous yarn." This novel, set in the late sixteenth century, made Weyman's reputation as a leading historical novelist and went through several editions. The narrator, de Marsac, is a down-on-his-luck, middle-aged Huguenot noble. The king of Navarre, champion of the Huguenots, sends Marsac to rescue Mademoiselle de Vire, who has information for the king of France about the unscrupulous Catholic League. Marsac succeeds, but there follows a series of further captures and rescues until finally Vire delivers her information, and the two are married. The plot moves at a fever pitch, as in the two previous ro-

Cover for Weyman's novel that employs a cowardly narrator,
Nick Price

mances. Weyman's narrator is a master at humbling himself, honorable to a fault but doing the king's or mademoiselle's bidding unthinkingly. The scenes with his mother are cloyingly sentimental. King Henry III of France is portrayed as a fool, while the baron de Rosny and the king of Navarre — both Huguenots — are honorable.

Under the Red Robe (1894), again considered good reading for young people, was popular enough to warrant a stage production (1896) and later a film treatment (1927). Weyman, though somewhat dependent on formula characterizations, did not shun experimentation, and this novel, set in the 1630s, is narrated by de Berault, an admitted rapscallion. To escape capital punishment for illegal dueling, he agrees to spy for Cardinal Richilieu (the owner of the symbolic "red robe") and to arrest a conspirator in the south of France. Instead, Berault falls in love with the conspirator's sister and is con-

verted to proper behavior by her. The first-person narration emphasizes Berault's experience of transformation and his moral turmoil that allows his better side to win.

My Lady Rotha (1894), set in Protestant Germany in 1632, is narrated by the steward to the countess of Heritzburg, a well-educated woman, "gallant of spirit," who refuses to give up her independence until she finds a sympathetic soul in a much older man. Here Weyman's prejudice against Catholics is reversed. During the Thirty Years' War (1618–1648) the resident Calvinists persecute a Catholic family, particularly Marie Wort, who will become the narrator's wife.

A sequel to the popular *A Gentleman of France* was titled *From the Memoirs of a Minister of France* (1895), a collection of twelve stories narrated by Duc de Sully (Baron de Rosny of *A Gentleman of France*). Based on Weyman's reading of Sully's memoirs (1638), the stories reveal the minister as the grand master at checkmating his enemies. Political intrigue at court is softened by Sully's unavoidable involvement in others' love affairs, which he always manages to bring to a fortunate end. The stories reveal how reputations are easily lost and won and how affairs of state commingle with affairs of the heart. Weyman's fascination with French history continues in *The Red Cockade* (1895), a story of the French Revolution.

The Man in Black (1894) is a short novel set in Normandy in 1637 with the titular character being an evil astrologer-magician, apparently the grandson of Nostradamus. He terrifies a beggar boy into servitude, but the boy becomes the magician's nemesis, as he thwarts the plan to make an unhappy noblewoman unwittingly take poison. Since her husband accidentally takes the poison instead, she is brought to trial, but the magician is the one tortured on the rack. The woman's husband, who had bought the poison, is a crude commoner who had married her for her title and estate, so in Weyman's terms, his actions are predictable. The boy, also predictably, turns out to be the woman's lost brother, a male Cinderella who regains his noble status after years of fear and drudgery.

In *Shrewsbury* (1898), set in late-seventeenth-century England, Weyman experiments again, this time with a foolish narrator, Nick Price. An underlying and more sophisticated humor than that of his earlier works is displayed in the ironic relation of the narrator to his adventures. Although its portrayal of King William III is effective, revealing him as asthmatic and weary but determined, Weyman considered this his least successful novel because he failed to balance the cowardly narrator with a strong, heroic one.

Weyman invokes the story of the Trojan War in *The Castle Inn* (1898), set in England in 1767. The protagonist, Sir George Soane, is the Menelaus figure, the would-be husband of the beautiful commoner Julia, who is kidnapped by Lord Dunborough. The work suggests that if Julia had been born a lady, no one would have dared to force himself on her, but as a commoner she is fair game. Her beauty allows her to leap over class barriers, for otherwise, instead of proposing to her Sir George would have left her scrubbing the stoop. Julia is also a kind of Cinderella character, a woman whose appearance makes others assume she is upper class, but only marriage can bring her the reality of that status.

Sophia: A Romance (1899) portrays a high-spirited young woman who is deceived by the Irish rogue Hawkesworth before marrying the older and wiser Sir Henry Coke. Commoners take the brunt of Weyman's class prejudice in this novel, as the Irishman Hawkesworth commits murder and bigamy and Sophia's brother callously takes advantage of an attractive woman because she is only a "chit of a servant."

Count Hannibal: A Romance of the Court of France (1901) reuses the Saint Bartholomew's Day Massacre from *The House of the Wolf*, as well as the May-September formula from *Sophia*. Readers are initially as averse to Count Hannibal as is Clothide Vrillac, the woman of his affections. Hannibal is a cunning adventurer who forces Clothide to reject her fiancé to save herself and others from the murderous clutches of a Catholic mob. Once they are married, Hannibal constantly tests her loyalty, but his carefully laid plans go awry, and he is almost sacrificed to a fanatical priest before Clothide makes up her mind that she in fact does love her husband. The Huguenots are sensible, the Catholics are frenzied, and Hannibal, a nominal Catholic with no spiritual beliefs, triumphs in the love of his equally courageous Huguenot wife. Hannibal is a complex character, and it is fascinating to see how Weyman manipulates readers' changing perceptions of him.

In King's Byways (1902) and the later *Laid Up in Lavender* (1907) are two collections of Weyman's short stories. The former contains adventure stories similar to Weyman's novels of this type, with aristocratic characters set in historical time periods. The latter deals more with quaint scenes of recognition between a man and a woman.

Weyman's only novel with characters entirely of the bourgeoisie is *The Long Night* (1903), set in Geneva in 1602 just after the war with Savoy. There is political intrigue, sorcery, and a love affair between Anne Royanne, accused of being a witch, and Claude Mercier, a young student. Royanne's invalid mother inspires the Genevese to defend their city from the invading Savoyards, and the student proves his courage during the onslaught. Geneva is the heart of Huguenotism, but it is rigidly controlled and its people are subject to fanaticism as much as any other.

The Abbess of Vlaye (1904), set in 1595 in France during the reign of Henry IV, again combines aspects of previous novels: a May-September affair between the shy but courageous Bonne de Villeneuve and the stolid Lieutenant des Ageaux. As in *A Gentleman of France,* des Ageaux is on a mission for the king as a last chance to clear his name, in this case by settling a peasant rebellion; the Abbess of Vlaye is the evil sister of Bonne, a character device

COUNT HANNIBAL

A ROMANCE
OF THE COURT OF FRANCE

BY
STANLEY J. WEYMAN
AUTHOR OF "SOPHIA," "THE CASTLE INN," "A GENTLEMAN OF FRANCE,"
"UNDER THE RED ROBE," ETC.

LONGMANS, GREEN, AND CO.
91 AND 93 FIFTH AVENUE, NEW YORK
1901

". . . IN A PAROXYSM OF SHAME HE SHOOK HIS FIST. . . ."
Page 81

Frontispiece and title page for Weyman's 1901 novel, set during the Saint Bartholomew's Day Massacre of French Protestants in 1572

repeated from *The House of the Wolf*. The chief troublemaker, the Captain of Vlaye, is an upstart commoner who plans to gain status by kidnapping the young countess de Rochechouart for marriage, in spite of his agreement to marry the abbess, whose love for him has distorted her judgment. Vlaye has no claim to his position, and his cruelties provoke the peasants to revolt, but this mob action, though understandable, is nevertheless condemned.

Starvecrow Farm (1905), set in early-nineteenth-century England, involves a young woman, Henrietta Damen, who casts off her fiancé, Capt. Anthony Clyne, and elopes with another man. But before the marriage her lover runs away, and she learns he is both a bigamist and a murderer. Although she now abhors him, Damen refuses to reveal her former lover's whereabouts. Abandoned by her family, her lover, and her fiancé, she is tried and imprisoned, still defiantly refusing to turn informant. After some lost evidence reveals her innocence, she is released and begins a search for Clyne's son, during which she barely escapes rape

and death. Her actions win Clyne's admiration, and they plan once again to marry. Clyne is older, repeating Weyman's formulaic romance, and a few of the kidnappers seem driven to crime by injustices done to them because of their poverty. Furthermore, the worst rake is a parson who uses his position as a cover. Still, the novel's power lies in its suspenseful description of the horrors Damen meets with reckless courage. The kidnappers seem not to care that she is a gentlewoman, and even her own "race" and "class" assume wrongly that she will marry anybody to erase her sin of elopement.

Weyman turned to a new topic in *Chippinge* (1906), dealing with the Reform Bill of 1832 (which tried to provide for fairer representation and voting privileges) and the political and social turmoil surrounding it. The protagonist Arthur Vaughan supports the bill, despite the wishes of his high-born relatives, and gains a seat in the House of Commons. He decides to marry Mary Smith in spite of her low-born heritage. But Weyman avoids such a mixture of classes when he reveals her identity as the daugh-

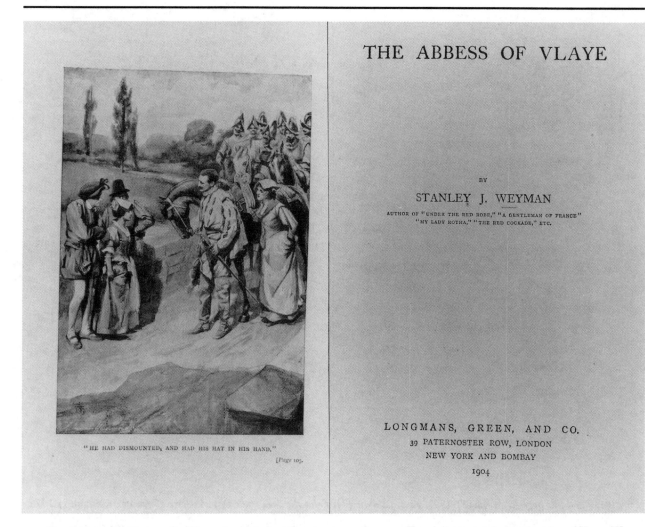

THE ABBESS OF VLAYE

BY

STANLEY J. WEYMAN

AUTHOR OF "UNDER THE RED ROBE," "A GENTLEMAN OF FRANCE"
"MY LADY ROTHA," "THE RED COCKADE," ETC.

LONGMANS, GREEN, AND CO.
39 PATERNOSTER ROW, LONDON
NEW YORK AND BOMBAY
1904

"HE HAD DISMOUNTED, AND HAD HIS HAT IN HIS HAND."
[Page 105.

Frontispiece and title page for Weyman's novel about the adventures of a young French lieutenant during the reign of Henry IV

ter of Lord Robert Vermuyden, Vaughan's sworn enemy. Predictable scenes of mob action and the marriage of Vaughan and Smith ensue. The skeletal framework, dependent upon formulaic romance, lacks enough social commentary to recommend the novel.

Perhaps Weyman tried to rectify his portrait of the Irish rogue in *Sophia* by writing *The Wild Geese* (1908), set in Ireland in the early eighteenth century. The familiar May–September romance is slow to blossom between the shrewish, devout Catholic, Flavia McMurrough, and her Protestant guardian, Col. John Sullivan. He returns home after years as a soldier abroad to ensure his late friend's will is carried out, granting Flavia, rather than her brother James, full ownership. Sullivan suffers the McMurroughs' enmity, but he perseveres in his fair judgment, managing to stop an ill-planned rebellion. While the resident British soldiers see the Irish Catholics as inferior, Sullivan regards them as chil-

dren needing guidance, represented in his tolerant handling of temperamental Flavia.

In 1908 Weyman stopped writing and turned his attention to civic life; he later explained to the *Bookman* that he had preferred to quit while "playing to a full house" than to "go on and tire the audience and ring the curtain down at last on half empty benches." Nevertheless, in 1919 he came out of retirement with renewed energy and returned to the subject of the Reform Bill in *The Great House: A Story of Quiet Times* (1919) and then in *Ovington's Bank* (1922). Some reviewers began to find Weyman's work old-fashioned but continued to praise its accuracy, suspenseful plotting, and believable characterization.

Accusations of old-fashioned adventure might seem valid regarding *The Traveller in the Fur Cloak* (1924), published during a time of widespread literary experimentation. The novel is set during the Napoleonic Wars and is narrated by Cartwright, a

British envoy. He is carrying important papers while traveling with his party from Austria to London. The most perilous part of their journey is through Germany, "a plunge into the unknown." Their German guide knowingly leads them into danger, and Cartwright's chief, Perceval Ellis, is lost during the ensuing adventures, never to be found.

Queen's Folly (1925) is not considered one of Weyman's best works and was condescendingly recommended for young girls. Set in the late-eighteenth century, the story portrays nineteen-year-old Rachel South in her first job as a governess at Queen's Folly, as she attempts to discipline the children and fend off unsolicited male attention. As in *Starvecrow Farm,* the heroine falls in love with a bigamist, a tutor at the house, who tries to kidnap Rachel when she resists his advances. She is repeatedly attacked by Lady Ellingham for what appear to be loose morals, and Capt. George Dunstan, Lady Ellingham's brother, always comes to her defense knowing that Rachel's good intentions can be misinterpreted by her enemies. Eventually Lady Ellingham is reunited with her estranged husband, and Rachel plans to marry Captain Dunstan. The book is unremarkable with a predictable plot and false attempts at suspense.

Weyman's last novel, *The Lively Peggy* (1928), set in the Napoleonic Wars, was published posthumously. It is a better story than *The New Rector* but with some of the same character types. The rector's younger daughter, Peggy, is ostensibly the main character and shares her name with the town's communally owned ship, the *Lively Peggy*. Peggy, against her father's wishes, elopes with Lt. Charles Bligh, who has been drummed out of the service for drunkenness and thus receives no commission in spite of losing an arm in battle. Leaving his pregnant wife, Bligh redeems himself with the command of the *Lively Peggy* in battle, though the ship and crew are feared sunk. Peggy's baby is born dead, and she recovers only when her husband, having been a prisoner of war, is returned and reinstated. The most interesting character is plain-looking, plain-speaking Charlotte Bicester, a member of the nouveau riche, but the only friend to stick by Peggy when all of society and her father have shunned her. Charlotte is finally married to Sir Albery Wyke, Peggy's former lover, an aristocrat with time and money and looking for a good purpose; Charlotte, originally of the middle class, gives Sir Albery a needed direction. Despite good moments the book

is melodramatic, with dialogue such as "You might as well cast yourself over this cliff as come to meet such an outcast as I am! It is folly!"

The three themes most prevalent in Weyman's works can be summed up in one quotation from *Chippinge,* in which Sir Robert Vermuyden clarifies the distinction made between Whigs and Tories: "'We all fear despotism; you, the despotism of the one: I, a worse, a more cruel, a more hopeless despotism, the despotism of the many! That's the real difference between us.'" Weyman's themes of anti-Catholic prejudices, class struggle, and May–September love affairs are all included in this statement. Tyranny (whether that of the Catholic church or political despotism) will be tolerated only so long before the lower classes rebel through destructive mob action. If there is a seasoned, older hand to guide the rising rebellion, then the younger and spirited can infuse the weary rulers with fresh idealism, creating a fairer, more vital system. These thematic overtones are most forcefully presented in Weyman's adult books, including *Count Hannibal, Ovington's Bank, The Red Cockade,* and *The Abbess of Vlaye.*

Whether Weyman intended adults or children as his readers is unknown. His own comments, however, are revealing: writers of romance were those "who never grew up," and he referred to his work as "pleasant fables." Altogether Weyman published several historical studies and literary memorial sketches; many short stories, some of which were collected into book form; and twenty-three novels. These romance novels were certainly appreciated by young readers decades ago. Considering Weyman's old-fashioned style and the difficulty in obtaining his books, a resurgence of popularity or critical appreciation remains unlikely. But because of his probable influence on other writers and his unusual treatment of social issues, his works should be remembered for their popularity in their time.

References:

"The Bookman's Diary," *Bookman,* 74 (May 1928): 121;

Grace Chapman, "Stanley Weyman," *London Mercury,* 27 (April 1933): 530–538;

Leonard Huxley, "In Memoriam: Stanley John Weyman," *Cornhill Magazine,* 64 (June 1928): 752–755;

E. E. Reynolds, "Stanley Weyman," *Fortnightly Review,* 132 (July 1928): 106–115.

Oscar Wilde

(16 October 1854 – 30 November 1900)

Kathy Merlock Jackson
Virginia Wesleyan College

See also the Wilde entries in *DLB 10: Modern British Dramatists, 1900–1945; DLB 19: British Poets, 1880–1914; DLB 34: British Novelists, 1890–1929: Traditionalists;* and *DLB 57: Victorian Prose Writers After 1867.*

BOOKS: *Newdigate Prize Poem: Ravenna, Recited in the Theatre, Oxford 26 June 1878* (Oxford: Shrimpton, 1878);

Vera; or, The Nihilists: A Drama (London: Privately printed, 1880);

Poems (London: Bogue, 1881; Boston: Roberts Brothers, 1881);

The Duchess of Padua: A Tragedy of the XVI Century, Written in Paris in the XIX Century (New York: Privately printed, 1883);

The Happy Prince and Other Tales (London: Nutt, 1888; Boston: Roberts, 1888);

The Picture of Dorian Gray (London, New York & Melbourne: Ward, Lock, 1891);

Intentions (London: Osgood, McIlvaine, 1891; New York: Dodd, Mead, 1891);

Lord Arthur Savile's Crime & Other Stories (London: Osgood, McIlvaine, 1891; New York: Dodd, Mead, 1891);

A House of Pomegranates (London: Osgood, McIlvaine, 1891; New York: Dodd, Mead, 1892);

Salomé: Drame en un acte (Paris: Librairie de l'Art Indépendent / London: Mathews & Lane, Bodley Head, 1893); republished as *Salome: A Tragedy in One Act,* translated into English by Alfred Douglas (London: Mathews & Lane / Boston: Copeland & Day, 1894);

Lady Windermere's Fan: A Play about a Good Woman (London: Mathews & Lane, Bodley Head, 1893);

The Sphinx (London: Mathews & Lane, Bodley Head/ Boston: Copeland & Day, 1894);

A Woman of No Importance (London: Lane, Bodley Head, 1894);

The Soul of Man [first published in the *Fortnightly Review* as "The Soul of Man Under Socialism"] (London: Privately printed, 1895); republished as *The Soul of Man Under Socialism* (London: Arthur L. Humphreys, 1912);

The Ballad of Reading Gaol, as C.3.3. (London: Smithers, 1898);

The Importance of Being Earnest: A Trivial Comedy for Serious People (London: Smithers, 1899);

An Ideal Husband (London: Smithers, 1899);

The Portrait of Mr. W. H. (Portland, Maine: Mosher, 1901); edited by Vyvyan Holland (London: Methuen, 1958);

De Profundis (London: Methuen, 1905; New York & London: Putnam, 1905);

Impressions of America, edited by Stuart Mason (Christopher Millard) (Sunderland, U.K.: Keystone Press, 1906);

The Suppressed Portion of "De Profundis" (New York: Reynolds, 1913);

To M. B. J., edited by Mason (Millard) (London: Privately printed, 1920);

For Love of the King: A Burmese Masque (London: Methuen, 1923);

Essays of Oscar Wilde, edited by Hesketh Pearson (London: Methuen, 1950);

Literary Criticism of Oscar Wilde, edited by Stanley Weintraub (Lincoln: University of Nebraska Press, 1968);

The Artist as Critic: Critical Writings of Oscar Wilde, edited by Richard Ellmann (New York: Random House, 1969).

Collections: *First Collected Edition of the Works of Oscar Wilde,* edited by Robert Ross (volumes 1-11, 13-14, London: Methuen, 1908; Boston: Luce, 1910; volume 12, Paris: Carrington, 1908);

Second Collected Edition of the Works of Oscar Wilde, edited by Ross (volumes 1-12, London:

Oscar Wilde in 1882

Methuen, 1909; volume 13, Paris: Carrington, 1910; volume 14, London: Lane, 1912);

Complete Works of Oscar Wilde, edited by Vyvyan Holland (London: Collins, 1948).

PLAY PRODUCTIONS: *Vera; or, The Nihilists,* New York, Union Square Theatre, 20 August 1883;

Guido Ferranti: A Tragedy of the XVI Century, New York, Broadway Theatre, 26 January 1891;

Lady Windermere's Fan, London, St. James's Theatre, 20 February 1892;

A Woman of No Importance, London, Haymarket Theatre, 19 April 1893;

An Ideal Husband, London, Haymarket Theatre, 3 January 1895;

The Importance of Being Earnest, London, St. James's Theatre, 14 February 1895;

Salomé, Paris, Théâtre de l'Oeuvre, 11 February 1896; London, New Stage Club at Bijou, 10 May 1905;

A Florentine Tragedy, by Wilde, with opening scene by T. Sturge Moore, London, King's Hall, 10 June 1906.

Although Oscar Wilde is best remembered as a dramatist, novelist, essayist, poet, brilliant conver-
sationalist, and flamboyant personality, he was also a writer of fairy tales. Wilde's notoriety — including his arrest and conviction in 1895 for violating the 1885 Criminal Law Amendment Act, which criminalized homosexual activity — led some to regard him as an inappropriate writer for children. However, Wilde's fairy tales reveal themes of morality, Christianity, and beauty and thus reflect the contradiction between Wilde's public persona and his literary works. Collected in two books, *The Happy Prince and Other Tales* (1888) and *A House of Pomegranates* (1891), Wilde's fairy tales were published at the beginning of his most productive literary period. Influenced by the author's association with John Ruskin and Walter Pater, they remain remarkable examples of the literary fairy tale popular in Victorian England and contain themes that dominate Wilde's other, more notable literary works.

Born at Westland Row, Dublin, on 16 October 1854, Oscar Fingal O'Flahertie Wills Wilde was the son of prominent and eccentric parents who possessed an interest in Irish folklore; in fact, his name recalls heroes of Irish legend and literature. Wilde's father, Sir William Wilde, was the foremost eye and ear surgeon of his day and has been called "the father of modern otology." He was knighted in 1864 for his contributions to medical science. In addition to his work as a physician, Sir William Wilde was an avid collector of Irish folktales, legends, and traditions, which he recorded in several published works, among them *Irish Popular Superstitions* (1852).

Oscar Wilde's mother, Lady Jane Francesca Elgee Wilde, was even better known throughout Ireland than her husband and shared his unconventionality as well as his interest in Irish folklore. Lady Wilde, who in her youth adopted the pen name "Speranza," was a voice of Irish nationalism. Writing political articles for a paper called the *Nation,* she drew both criticism and praise for her revolutionary invocation of the Irish to rebel against English authority. She was also a spokesperson for woman's rights and throughout her life adopted causes in which she supported the poor and oppressed, including children. A prolific writer, she was a poet, translator, essayist, and folklorist, who wrote *Ancient Legends, Mystic Charms, and Superstitions of Ireland* (1888) and *Ancient Cures, Charms, and Usages of Ireland* (1890). Fancying herself as a woman of letters who celebrated the arts, Lady Wilde ran a salon in her home, entertaining the most respected writers and artists of the day. Thus Oscar Wilde's concern for the underdog, his predilection for good conversation, and his love of the arts can be traced to his mother.

In his early years Wilde showed a fondness for and facility with language. In 1864 he was sent along with his brother Willie to the Portora Royal School in Enniskillen, Ulster. He excelled in the classics, and in 1871 he won a royal scholarship to Trinity College, Dublin, where he was enrolled until June 1874. Then he received the classical demyship to study at Magdalen College, Oxford.

While at Oxford, Wilde encountered his two most important teachers, Ruskin, then Slade Professor of Art, and Pater, fellow and tutor of Brasenose College. Although earlier influences had instilled in him a passion for art, Ruskin and Pater reinforced it. Ruskin, the moralist, saw art as the cornerstone of a civilization but believed that great art was impossible in a society characterized by materialism and inequality caused by the social upheaval of the Industrial Revolution. He called for social reform. Pater, the epicurean, espoused the doctrine of "art for art's sake." He believed that because life is ephemeral, one should live it to its fullest by inviting new sensations, particularly those aroused by works of art. A disciple of Pater, Wilde came to believe that the only life worth living was one devoted to the pursuit of art and beauty. Thus at Oxford Wilde adopted the life of an aesthete. He decorated his rooms with fashionable blue and white china, grew his hair long, adorned his gawky, oversized body with ostentatious clothing made of the finest fabrics, and sported flowers, thereby differentiating himself from the more austere Victorians of his day. He also became known as a witty conversationalist. Regarding this aspect of Wilde's personality, William Butler Yeats notes in his *Autobiography* (1916) that before he met Wilde, he had "never before heard a man talking with perfect sentences, as if he had written them all overnight with labour and yet all spontaneous." On 10 June 1878 Wilde won the Newdigate Prize at Oxford for his poem *Ravenna,* and the following November he obtained his B.A. degree.

The following year Wilde settled in London and embarked on a writing career. His book *Poems* was published in London in June 1881. In December Wilde sailed to America for a yearlong lecture tour on aesthetics. By this time Wilde's reputation as a wit and a dandy was established, and it has become legendary that upon being asked by a customs official in New York if he had anything to declare, Wilde replied, "I have nothing to declare except my genius." Wilde's tour was successful, and it gave him the opportunity to meet Walt Whitman, whom he admired. Following his lectures in the United States and Canada, Wilde lived in Paris; met Victor Hugo, Paul Verlaine, Stéphane Mallarmé, Emile Zola, Léon Daudet, and Honoré de Balzac; and wrote a play, *Vera; or, The Nihilists: A Drama* (1880). He went to New York for the play's opening, but when it proved to be unsuccessful, he returned to Great Britain, where he resumed his lecturing career, wrote, and from 1887 to 1889 edited a ladies' magazine called *Woman's World.* Wilde's witty epigrams and outrageous personal style made him the toast of English society, and he, painter James Abbott McNeill Whistler, actress Lillie Langtry, and Albert Edward, Prince of Wales, dominated the London social scene in the late Victorian era.

Despite Wilde's social whirlwind, he had become a family man. On 29 May 1884, at the age of twenty-nine, Wilde married Constance Lloyd, a pretty twenty-four-year-old woman from a middle-class Dublin family that was not overly pleased by her rather unorthodox selection of a husband. Their first child, Cyril, was born the following year on 5 June, and a second son, Vyvyan, joined the family on 3 November 1886. According to Vyvyan, Wilde was a loving father who enjoyed playing with his children: "he had so much of the child in his own nature that he delighted in playing our games. He would go down on all fours on the nursery

Wilde's mother, Lady Jane Francesca Elgee Wilde

floor, being in turn a lion, a wolf, a horse, caring nothing for his usually immaculate appearance. And there was nothing half-hearted in his method of play." Vyvyan also describes Wilde's penchant for telling his children stories: "When he grew tired of playing he would keep us quiet by telling us fairy stories, or tales of adventure, of which he had a never-ending supply. He was a great admirer of Jules Verne and Robert Louis Stevenson, and of Rudyard Kipling in his more imaginative vein."

Given Wilde's constant interest in writing as well as his fondness for his sons, it is not surprising that he formulated fairy tales for them, nor that he published the tales for a larger audience. In May 1888 *The Happy Prince and Other Tales* was published in London by David Nutt; it was illustrated by Walter Crane and G. P. Jacomb Hood in the style of ancient Greek art, which delighted Wilde. The book consisted of five tales: "The Happy Prince," "The Selfish Giant," "The Devoted Friend," "The Nightingale and the Rose," and "The Remarkable Rocket." These became part of the tradition of literary fairy tales popular in England during the reign of Queen Victoria from 1837 to 1901. They contain many of the elements of traditional folktales: the triumph of good over evil, the creation of a fantasy world, and the use of the supernatural. However, they were created rather than collected and made use of literary language and ornate descriptions. Most important, these tales provided a vehicle for writers during the Industrial Revolution to speculate on the virtue of Christian goodness at a time when greed, materialism, and division among social classes seemed to dominate; thus, the tales reflected an enhanced social consciousness couched in a fairy-tale setting. In addition to Wilde, other writers drawn to this genre included Charles Dickens, Robert Browning, Lewis Carroll, William Makepeace Thackeray, Christina Rossetti, George MacDonald, and Yeats.

Wilde's collection of literary fairy tales became an immediate success with both the public and the critics. It went into a second printing six months after its initial publication and thrust Wilde, who up to that point had been known primarily as a witty

Walter Crane's illustration for Wilde's "The Happy Prince"

talker and flamboyant aesthete, on a career as a writer. Wilde sent a copy of the book to Ruskin, whose literary fairy tale, *King of the Golden River* (1851), was his only published work of fiction. He also forwarded a copy of the book to Pater, who sent back an immediate reply, "I am confined to my room with gout, but have been consoling myself with *The Happy Prince,* and feel it would be ungrateful not to send a line to tell you how delightful I have found him and his companions." Pater also called "The Selfish Giant" "perfect in its kind." Wilde was heartened by Pater's response and penned a quick note to his publisher saying, "Pater has written me a wonderful letter about my prose, so I am in high spirits."

The literary fairy tales included in *The Happy Prince and Other Tales* embody a storytelling device popularized by Hans Christian Andersen in which any object, natural or man-made, can be personified. They also present a clear moral vision. In them Wilde presents characters with vices – selfishness, greed, vanity, egotism, insensitivity – some of whom overcome them and repent but most of whom do not. In "The Selfish Giant" the title character drives children away from his beautiful garden, proclaiming, "My own garden is my garden . . . anyone can understand that, and I will allow nobody to play in it but myself." After he forbids all trespassers, the Giant learns that spring will not enter his garden either. When the children creep in through a hole and the trees in the garden break into blossom, the Giant realizes the error of his ways. He notices one tree still covered with frost and snow with a child unable to reach its branches. The Giant lifts the tiny child into the tree, which breaks into blossom, and the child kisses the Giant and wins his heart.

Unlike the Selfish Giant, other self-centered characters in *The Happy Prince and Other Tales* do not experience remorse. In "The Devoted Friend" a rich Miller considers little Hans, a gardener, to be his closest friend, and he picks flowers or fruit from Hans's garden each time he passes. Although the Miller claims to be Hans's closest friend, he gives

Illustration by Crane for Wilde's "The Selfish Giant" in The Happy Prince and
Other Tales

nothing in return, nor does he visit in the winter-time when there is no fruit or flowers, believing that people prefer to be left alone with their problems. In the spring the Miller learns that over the winter Hans had to sell his wheelbarrow for food. The Miller promises Hans his old, dilapidated wheelbarrow (which he never gives him) and throughout the summer demands many unreasonable favors from Hans in return, the last of which results in an accident that kills him. Acting as chief mourner at Hans's funeral, the Miller says regarding his now-rusted wheelbarrow that he "will certainly take care not to give away anything again. One always suffers for being generous."

"The Remarkable Rocket" is another tale of selfishness and egoism. A vain, bragging Rocket who considers himself superior to the other fire-crackers earmarked for the prince's wedding celebration remarks, "I am always thinking about myself, and I expect everybody else to do the same." Reflecting upon his own importance, the Rocket convinces himself that the prince and his bride would be forever unhappy if something were to prevent him from going off on their wedding day. Moved to tears by this vision, he is too damp to be used in the wedding festivities, but he believes he is being saved for something even more spectacular. When he finally does explode, he does not realize that no one has noticed, and his vanity remains: "I knew I should create a great sensation."

In the remaining two tales in the volume, virtuous protagonists must endure the selfishness and insensitivity of others. In "The Nightingale and the Rose" the bird vows to help a Student secure a red rose so that he may give it to his love at the prince's ball and win her. The Rose-tree demands that the Nightingale sing all night with its "breast against a thorn . . . and the thorn must pierce your heart, and your life-blood must flow into my veins, and become mine." After a song-filled, painful night, the Nightingale dies, and the Student plucks a perfect crimson rose and gives it to his love. She refuses it, saying that it does not match her dress. Further, the Chamberlain's nephew has sent her jewels, "and everybody knows that jewels cost far more than flowers." The Student, ruminating on "what a silly thing Love is," tosses the flower into the street and returns to his books.

A similar theme of insensitivity prevails in the book's title tale, "The Happy Prince." A beautiful statue of a young prince stands high above the city. From his vantage point the Prince sees the sorrow of the city and is unhappy. He wants to help but cannot because he is securely fastened to his pedestal. He asks a Swallow on his way south to Egypt to help him and on consecutive nights has the Swallow deliver the ruby on his sword hilt and his sapphire eyes and gold gilding to the poor of the city. After completing his task, the Swallow stays with the now-blind, deteriorated statue despite the coming winter. The townspeople notice the now-shabby statue of the Prince, whose heart has broken, with the little Swallow frozen at his feet. Because the statue is no longer beautiful, it is torn down and melted in a furnace, and the bird is tossed on a dust heap.

Just as these tales address human vice, they also portray the opposite: the virtues of compassion, generosity, and love. In "The Devoted Friend" little Hans, not the Miller, best exemplifies true friendship, and in "The Selfish Giant" the Giant learns compassion for the children. In both "The Happy Prince" and "The Nightingale and the Rose" Wilde adopts a theme apparent in the fairy tales of one of his influences, Andersen: sacrificial love. The statue, the Swallow, and the Nightingale willingly suffer and die out of compassion for others, though their efforts go unappreciated. The tales also address another theme popularized by Andersen – the division among social classes. "The Happy Prince," for example, paints in painful detail a picture of the impoverished people of the city. In "The Devoted Friend" the rich Miller remains indifferent to the problems of his poor friend Hans. These tales reflect Wilde's growing awareness of class division and social problems.

Finally, the stories in *The Happy Prince and Other Tales,* with their emphasis on the virtues of charity, tolerance, and love, embody a Christian perspective. In only one of the tales, "The Selfish Giant," does Christ actually appear. At the end of this tale the little boy who kissed the Giant returns to the garden after a long absence. The Giant runs to him and notices that "on the palms of the child's hands were the prints of two nails, and the prints of

two nails were on the little feet." The child tells him, "You let me play once in your garden, to-day you shall come with me to my garden, which is Paradise." When the other children run in the garden that afternoon, they see "the Giant lying dead under the tree, all covered with white blossoms." Ultimately, Christ has forgiven the Giant for his earlier selfish actions and admitted him, with glory, into the kingdom of heaven. "The Happy Prince" also ends with the affirmation of a heavenly reward for the virtuous. God asks one of his angels, "bring me the two most precious things in the city," and the angel brings him the statue's leaden heart and the dead Swallow. God praises the angel's choice and proclaims, "in my garden of Paradise this little bird shall sing for evermore, and in my city of gold the Happy Prince shall praise me."

Wilde followed *The Happy Prince and Other Tales* with a second, more complex book of fairy tales, *A House of Pomegranates.* Illustrated by Charles Ricketts and Charles Shannon, it includes four tales: "The Young King," "The Birthday of the Infanta," "The Fisherman and His Soul," and "The Star-Child." This collection, however, failed to win an audience. An unsigned review in the *Pall Mall Gazette* on 30 November 1891 implored, "Is *A House of Pomegranates* intended for a child's book? We confess that we do not know." The question of Wilde's intended audience for his fairy tales has continued to puzzle critics, and Wilde himself waffled on the subject. Shortly before *The Happy Prince and Other Tales* was published, Wilde told a friend that "it is the duty of every father to write tales for his children" but remarked that "the mind of the child is a great mystery." Later Wilde wrote of the tales in the *Happy Prince* collection, "they are studies in prose, but for Romance's sake into a fanciful form: meant partly for children and partly for those who have kept the child-like faculties of wonder and joy, and who find in simplicity a subtle strangeness." Going even further after publishing *A House of Pomegranates,* Wilde said, "I had about as much intention of pleasing the British child as I had of pleasing the British public."

The four tales in *A House of Pomegranates,* criticized by Yeats as "overly decorated and seldom amusing," are more sophisticated, both stylistically and thematically, than those in Wilde's previous collection. Longer and more reflective of Pater's polished, embellished prose style, they contain classical allusions such as those to the "Bithynian slave of Hadrian" and "silver image of Endymion" in "The Young King." The tales also place greater emphasis on human suffering. In "The Young King,"

Cover and title page designed by C. Ricketts and C. H. Shannon for Wilde's second collection of literary fairy tales, A House of Pomegranates

for example, the king's grandson, who has been raised by peasants, is brought to the palace to be acknowledged as heir. Exhibiting a "strange passion for beauty," he concerns himself with finery and rejects the poor, weak, and oppressed. On the night before his coronation he has three dreams which show him the depths of human suffering, and when he awakes the next morning he rejects his regal robe, scepter, and crown for the simple garments of a beggar. In "The Birthday of the Infanta" a Spanish princess is laughingly entertained by a grotesque Dwarf who thinks that she loves him. When he sees his own horrible reflection in the mirror, he realizes that she was merely mocking him, and in an outburst of revulsion he weeps, kicks, and screams until he dies of a broken heart. The Infanta laughs cruelly and scoffs, "For the future let those who come to play with me have no hearts." The theme of suffering also dominates "The Star Child," in which a beautiful, golden-haired, but also cruel, selfish, and vain foundling child rejects a poor beggar woman who claims him as her son, saying he would rather kiss a toad or an adder than her. As a consequence, his physical appearance is transformed so that he becomes "as foul as the toad, and as loathsome as the adder." Vowing to find his mother and

ask her forgiveness, he embarks upon a long, arduous three-year journey during which he suffers and comes to know the suffering of others. Finally, in "The Fisherman and His Soul" a young Fisherman rejects his soul for the love of a beautiful Mermaid. Wanting to dwell with the Fisherman, the Soul returns for consecutive years offering him wisdom and riches, but the Fisherman refuses until he is offered beauty. He goes with the Soul, which, existing without a heart, has become evil and tempts the Fisherman to steal, strike a child, and kill. The Fisherman attempts to return to the Mermaid but finds only her dead body, at which point he dies of a broken heart. Each of these tales delineates pain and suffering caused by rejection. They underscore Wilde's growing concern for the rejected of society – the poor, the weak, the oppressed – and denounce the indifference of the wealthy ruling class.

Reflective of Wilde's growing social consciousness, the tales in *A House of Pomegranates* attack the insensitivity of the rich and the credo of placing beauty above all else. The Young King, after his dreams of suffering, realizes that his reverence for beauty is misplaced. The Star-Child and the Infanta reject that which is ugly, thereby inflicting pain on others and showing their own character flaws. Ultimately the Star-Child repents for his actions; the Infanta, who remains an unsympathetic character, does not. Finally, the Fisherman is willing to relinquish his Soul for the beauty of the Mermaid and to leave the Mermaid when the Soul promises him greater beauty; his quest destroys both the Mermaid and himself. The message in these tales is that social responsibility to the poor and downtrodden is more important than the acquisition of beauty and wealth, a theme which also dominates "The Happy Prince."

The tales in *A House of Pomegranates* share another similarity with those in the earlier book – a Christian strain, most apparent in their endings. The Young King at his coronation rejects his royal finery, bows his head and prays, and all at once is standing in a robe of golden sunlight and holding a staff of white lilies and red roses. The Bishop kneels in awe and proclaims, "A greater than I hath crowned thee." The Star-Child functions as a Christ figure as well. At the end of the tale he is restored to his original beauty and welcomed into the kingdom by priests who say, "Thou art our lord for whom we have been waiting, and the son of our King." Both the Young King and the Star-Child learn charity and Christian compassion and are thus rewarded with divine intervention. At the end of "The Fisherman and His Soul" the priest orders that the Fisherman, who rejected his Soul, and the Mermaid be buried in a deserted field, whereupon beautiful white flowers grow, reminding the priest of the importance of forgiveness.

Despite their Christian elements, the tales in the collection do not end entirely happily. The Star-Child assumes his throne, but "so great had been his suffering" that he rules for only three years, and "he who came after him ruled evilly." The flowers adorning the Fisherman's and Mermaid's graves are picked and placed on the altar; however, never again "grew flowers of any kind, but the field remained barren even as before." These examples illustrate Wilde's increasing realization of an imperfect, disjointed world in which misery necessarily exists.

Wilde's publication of *The Happy Prince and Other Tales* in 1888 marked the beginning of the seven-year period during which he produced the corpus of the works on which his literary reputation is based. In addition to the fairy tales, Wilde's prolific output during these years includes *The Picture of Dorian Gray* (1891); *Lord Arthur Savile's Crime & Other Stories* (1891); a collection of essays titled *Intentions* (1891); a book of poetry, *The Sphinx* (1894); and five plays, *Salomé: Drame en un acte* (1893), *Lady Winder-*

mere's Fan (1893), *A Woman of No Importance* (1894), *An Ideal Husband* (performed, 1895; published, 1899), and *The Importance of Being Earnest* (performed, 1895; published, 1899), generally regarded as his masterpiece.

During this same period of his life Wilde had his first homosexual encounter and adopted a homosexual way of life. Although in later years Wilde would indicate that he had always been homosexual, the year before *The Happy Prince and Other Tales* appeared, he was first seduced by Robert Ross, who became Wilde's lifelong friend and, upon the author's death, his literary executor. Ross also had the distinction of introducing Wilde to twenty-one-year-old Lord Alfred Douglas, nicknamed "Bosie," the undisciplined, self-centered son of the unstable ninth marquess of Queensberry. Douglas introduced Wilde to male brothels throughout London and became the greatest, and most destructive, love of his life.

The fairy tale has traditionally been a literary form that enables writers to address modern realities in a fantasy setting, and Wilde seems to have invoked this function to address questions of sexual preference. In Wilde's fairy tales heterosexual love, as exemplified by the Fisherman and the Mermaid in "The Fisherman and His Soul" and the Student and his love in "The Nightingale and the Rose," is flawed. The most sympathetic characters are young males – the Happy Prince, the Young King, the Selfish Giant – and the most perfect relationships are those bonding two males, one larger and more dominant than the other, such as the Selfish Giant and the child who kisses him, or the Young King and little Swallow who will not leave him. Wilde also focuses on another issue that stood at the core of his life: aesthetics. Ironically, at a time when Wilde was perceived as an aesthete and a decadent, his fairy tales espoused virtue and social responsibility above hedonism and art.

Wilde's fairy tales, conceived around the same time as his more serious works, bear thematic connections with them, suggesting that Wilde used the fairy-tale form as a testing ground for his ideas. Throughout all of his work a theme of morality pervades. The social consciousness of the fairy tales, for example, finds fruition in the essay "The Soul of Man Under Socialism" (1891), in which Wilde berates the wealthy and privileged for their materialistic concerns and indifference to the poor and suffering. Social commentary, with an emphasis on the role of the rich and the importance of art, is also apparent in *The Picture of Dorian Gray* and in Wilde's social comedies. Wilde's homosexuality, suggested by his fairy tales' portrayals of sympathetic males and male relationships as well as troubled heterosexual relationships, is further explored in *The Picture of Dorian Gray* and the short story "The Portrait of Mr. W. H." (1889). Finally, both "The Birthday of the Infanta" and *The Picture of Dorian Gray* hinge on the characters' horror at seeing their grotesque reflections.

On 28 February 1895 the prolific era of Wilde's literary career came to an abrupt close. On the opening night of *The Importance of Being Earnest* the marquess of Queensberry left Wilde a note accusing him of being a sodomite. Wilde foolishly sued Queensberry for libel, and the case went to trial, revealing damaging evidence against Wilde. Wilde lost and was arrested the same day for "committing indecent acts." After two trials he was found guilty of "gross indecency between males" and sentenced to two years in prison with hard labor, the maximum penalty allowed by law. The sentence was carried out at Pentonville Prison, Wandsworth Prison, and, finally, Reading Gaol.

While in prison Wilde wrote only one work, *De Profundis* (1905), an extended letter to Douglas providing a personal account of his homosexual experiences and trials. After his release he wrote *The Ballad of Reading Gaol* (1898), a poem indicting the British prison system. These later works reflect the themes of homosexuality, morality, and social responsibility – issues already present in his fairy tales.

Wilde's trial and imprisonment had a traumatic effect on his wife and children. Constance Wilde was forced to sell her home and possessions – including all of her children's toys – to pay off her husband's debts, many of which were incurred by Douglas. They left England and went into exile, changing their name to Holland so that they would not be recognized; the children were instructed never to reveal their former identities to anyone. During Wilde's imprisonment Constance visited him once, to inform him of his mother's death on 3 February 1896. Although the couple never divorced, Constance Wilde never saw her husband again, nor would she allow their children to see him. She died on 7 April 1898.

Upon his release from prison on 19 May 1897, Wilde left for France, where he lived under the assumed name of Sebastian Melmoth; he never again returned to England. A broken man, he had lost his money, his career, his family, and most of his friends; like so many of the characters he had written about in his fairy tales, he had suffered. Even after Constance Wilde died, her family made certain that their sons would never be reunited with

their father and told them that he was dead. Thus the boys for whom Wilde wrote his fairy tales never saw him again. On 30 November 1900 Oscar Wilde died at forty-six of cerebral meningitis in Paris. His illness developed from an infection following an operation on his middle ear to correct damage sustained in a prison accident.

Many years after Wilde's death, his younger son, Vyvyan Holland, heard stories of his father's love for him and his brother, and for children in general, which he recorded in his memoir, *Son of Oscar Wilde* (1954). One man wrote to say that when he had been a boy in France, he and his mother often ate lunch at a restaurant frequented by a quiet, refined gentleman known as Monsieur Sébastien. One day the boy clumsily upset something on Sébastien's table, and when his mother began to scold him, the kind man comforted him, kissed him on both cheeks, and with tears in his eyes lamented in English, "Oh, my poor dear boys." Holland relates another story regarding his father in Reading Gaol. Learning that three poor children were in prison for poaching rabbits, for which they could have been hanged, Wilde slipped a secret note to the warders offering to pay their fine and saying, "I must get them out. Think what a thing it would be for me to be able to help three little children. If I can do this by paying the fine, tell the children that they are to be released tomorrow by a friend, and ask them to be happy and not tell anyone." The children were let go.

Wilde's reputation as a writer for children remains solid. His nine fairy tales are still popular in the United States and Europe, although more recent editions generally group the tales in both *The Happy Prince and Other Tales* and *A House of Pomegranates* into a single volume. The tales have been translated into many languages and frequently appear in literary fairy-tale anthologies, particularly those concentrating on the Victorian era. They have been adapted for almost every medium – including motion pictures, radio, theater, and television. Both "The Happy Prince" and "The Nightingale and the Rose," for example, have been made into plays, and "The Birthday of the Infanta" and "The Selfish Giant" into ballets; "The Happy Prince" has also been the subject of an opera.

Despite their popularity, the fairy tales are not considered to be Wilde's major works and thus have received scant critical attention. Traditional research on the fairy tales has centered on four issues: Christian themes, treatment of the poor and downtrodden and Wilde's social commentary, use of language, and authorial motives and intended audience. Some recent critics who see Wilde as an important early spokesperson for homosexuals place the tales in the category of gay fiction. Ultimately critics disagree on the appropriateness of Wilde's fairy tales for children. While some see them as enchanting stories, beautifully written and possessing great charm, others consider their stylized language to be artificially contrived and ornate – hence of little interest to children. Similarly, critics are divided on the morals of the tales. At the end of "The Devoted Friend" Wilde writes that telling a story with a moral "is always a very dangerous thing to do." Nevertheless, his tales are just as frequently criticized for being too moralistic as they are praised for providing valuable lessons for children.

Wilde's life is so compelling that it permeates practically every discussion of his work – even his fairy tales for children. As H. Montgomery Hyde relates, Wilde remarked to André Gide, "Would you like to know the great drama of my life? It's that I've put my genius into my life; I've put only my talents into my works." In light of this, one can see aspects of Wilde in the Remarkable Rocket, who boasts of his own importance; in the Happy Prince, who looks over the city and cries at the suffering he sees; and in the Selfish Giant, who helps a tiny child by lifting him into a tree. However, the fairy-tale character to whom Wilde has most frequently been compared is the Young King, who begins by worshiping beauty and riches and finally, with a greater awareness of human suffering, rejects them, saying, "For on the loom of sorrow, and by the white hands of Pain, has this my robe been woven."

Letters:

The Letters of Oscar Wilde, edited by Rupert Hart-Davis (New York: Harcourt, Brace & World, 1962);

More Letters of Oscar Wilde, edited by Hart-Davis (New York: Vanguard, 1985).

Bibliographies:

Stuart Mason (Christopher Millard), *Bibliography of Oscar Wilde* (London: Laurie, 1914);

Donald L. Lawler, "Oscar Wilde in the *New Cambridge Bibliography of English Literature,*" *Papers of the Bibliographical Society of America,* 67 (1973): 172–188;

E. H. Mikhail, *Oscar Wilde: An Annotated Bibliography of Criticism* (Totowa, N.J.: Rowman & Littlefield, 1978);

Ian Fletcher and John Stokes, "Oscar Wilde," in *Recent Research on Anglo-Irish Writers,* edited by

Richard Finneran (New York: Modern Language Association, 1983), pp. 21–47;

Thomas A. Mikolyzk, *Oscar Wilde: An Annotated Bibliography* (Westport, Ct.: Greenwood, 1993).

Biographies:

Robert H. Sherard, *The Life of Oscar Wilde* (New York: Kennerley, 1907);

Arthur Symons, *A Study of Oscar Wilde* (London: Sawyer, 1930);

Hesketh Pearson, *The Life of Oscar Wilde* (London: Methuen, 1946); republished as *Oscar Wilde: His Life and Wit* (New York: Harper, 1946);

Vyvyan Holland, *Son of Oscar Wilde* (New York: Dutton, 1954);

Lewis Broad, *The Friendships & Follies of Oscar Wilde* (New York: Crowell, 1955);

Rupert Croft-Cooke, *The Unrecorded Life of Oscar Wilde* (New York: McKay, 1972);

H. Montgomery Hyde, *Oscar Wilde: A Biography* (New York: Farrar, Straus & Giroux, 1975);

Richard Ellmann, *Oscar Wilde* (New York: Knopf, 1988).

References:

Karl Beckson, ed., *Oscar Wilde: The Critical Heritage* (New York: Barnes & Noble, 1970);

Joyce Bentley, *The Importance of Being Constance* (London: Hale, 1983);

Patrick Byrne, *The Wildes of Merrion Square* (London: Staples Press, 1953);

J. E. Chamberlin, *Ripe Was the Drowsy Hour: The Age of Oscar Wilde* (New York: Seabury, 1977);

Barbara Charlesworth, *Dark Passages: Decadent Consciousness in Victorian Literature* (Madison: University of Wisconsin Press, 1965);

Philip K. Cohen, *The Moral Vision of Oscar Wilde* (Rutherford, N.J.: Fairleigh Dickinson University Press, 1976);

Richard Ellmann, "The Critic as Artist as Wilde," in his *The Artist as Critic: Critical Writings of Oscar Wilde* (New York: Random House, 1969), pp. ix–xxviii;

Ellmann, ed., *Oscar Wilde: A Collection of Critical Essays* (Englewood Cliffs, N.J.: Prentice-Hall, 1969);

Regina Gagnier, *Idylls of the Marketplace: Oscar Wilde and the Victorian Public* (Stanford, Cal: Stanford University Press, 1986);

H. Montgomery Hyde, ed., *The Trials of Oscar Wilde* (London: Hodge, 1948); republished as *The Three Trials of Oscar Wilde* (New York: University Books, 1956); enlarged as *Famous Trials,* seventh series: *Oscar Wilde* (Baltimore: Penguin, 1963);

Lloyd Lewis and Henry Justin Smith, *Oscar Wilde Discovers America [1882]* (New York: Harcourt, Brace, 1936);

Stuart Mason (Christopher Millard), ed., *Oscar Wilde: Art and Morality* (London: Jacobs, 1907);

E. H. Mikhail, *Oscar Wilde: Interviews and Recollections,* 2 volumes (London: Macmillan, 1979);

Rodney Keith Miller, *Oscar Wilde* (New York: Ungar, 1982);

Christopher S. Nassaar, *Into the Demon Universe, A Literary Exploration of Oscar Wilde* (New Haven, Conn: Yale University Press, 1974);

Arthur Ransome, *Oscar Wilde: A Critical Study* (London: Secker, 1912);

Edouard Roditi, *Oscar Wilde* (Norfolk, Conn.: New Directions, 1947);

Epifanio San Juan, Jr., *The Art of Oscar Wilde* (Princeton, N.J.: Princeton University Press, 1967);

Rodney Shewan, *Oscar Wilde: Art and Egotism* (New York: Barnes & Noble, 1977);

Claude J. Summers, *Gay Fictions: Wilde to Stonewall* (New York: Continuum, 1990), pp. 29–61;

Terence de Vere White, *The Parents of Oscar Wilde: Sir William and Lady Wilde* (London: Hodder & Stoughton, 1967);

Frances Winwar, *Oscar Wilde and the Yellow Nineties* (New York: Harper, 1940);

William Butler Yeats, *Autobiography* (1916).

Papers:

The largest collection of Wilde's papers is at the William Andrews Clark Memorial Library, University of California, Los Angeles. There are additional collections at the New York Public Library; the Pierpont Morgan Library; the Beinecke Library, Yale University; the British Library; the Harry Ransom Humanities Research Center, University of Texas at Austin; the Houghton Library, Harvard University; the University of Edinburgh Library; the Rosenbach Museum, Philadelphia; and Magdalen College, Oxford University.

Minor Illustrators, 1880–1914

Louisa Smith
Mankato State University

The late-Victorian and Edwardian periods provided an atmosphere favorable to the flowering of illustration in children's books. Bursting on the scene were numerous accomplished artists who provided the visualization for a surprising number of authors. A period often called the golden age of children's literature began in the 1860s, principally because the work of Lewis Carroll and John Tenniel established children's literature in its own right. No longer a literature designed solely to teach a moral lesson, children's books exhibited new freedom in design and subject matter.

In some respects the collaboration of artist and author ran parallel to what was being published in adult literature. Many novels of the period were serialized with illustrations in magazines before being published in book form. The public grew accustomed to this combination of text and illustration to the extent that, for example, people purchased a book by Charles Dickens almost as much for the illustrations by Phiz (Hablot K. Browne) as for the text.

As a result of the Education Act of 1870 more children became literate, providing a larger audience for magazines and books catering to young readers. The increase in literacy and a rising middle class resulted in a proliferation of magazines ("papers") published for children — several well-known examples were the *Boy's Own Paper, Chums, Little Folks* – and the family magazines, the *Strand* and *Black and White*. Between 1880 and 1918, 149 new commercial boys' magazines appeared, bringing the total number to 307. Many family magazines that published stories for children also came into existence, and all of these publications included illustrations.

Some illustrators, such as Arthur Rackham, began their careers as magazine illustrators and became well known either for their distinctive style or because their work was associated with a particular author. Many other illustrators entered the field of magazine illustration and remained there until World War I virtually eliminated the market. Another route was taken by Walter Crane, Randolph Caldecott, Kate Greenaway, and Beatrix Potter, who became recognized through their illustrations for picture books, notably enhanced by the pioneering efforts of Edmund Evans with his color-printing advances.

Like those of the 1860s, the 1890s magazines were often the vehicle to book publication. Novels serialized first in magazines such as the *Strand* would appear as books in succeeding years. Frequently the same illustrations would accompany the text. This was true for children's stories as well as adult fiction. Thus illustrators became associated with authors: H. R. Millar with E. Nesbit; Gordon Browne and Leslie Brooke with Mary Molesworth.

The profusion of magazines, those directly published for children and those which featured a children's story, meant that artists could earn a living through illustration. Although only a few were comfortable and such a career meant diligent effort, it was possible. For women it was an alternative to the limited employment options of the day.

Most of these artists received training in state-supported art schools. The National Art School system, founded in 1852 in South Kensington, established branches throughout the country to improve design standards in manufacture. Though many artists rejected their training because of the emphasis placed on classical art, students received instruction and had the opportunity to form alliances with other artists. Outside of London the two best-known schools were the College of Art in Glasgow and the Birmingham School of Design.

Socialism influenced several important art movements during the 1880s and 1890s. The noted leader of the Arts and Crafts movement, William Morris, was a Socialist, and Anthea Callen notes that this movement shares some key ideals with the political orientation: "a missionary concern to improve the condition of man and the quality of life, to make culture and art available to everyone, and

H. R. Millar's portrayal of the fanciful Psammead in E. Nesbit's Five Children and It *(1902)*

to reunite artist and craftsman, designer and artisan." These attitudes extended into the world of children's books and toys.

The Arts and Crafts movement also embraced women artists, though not to the point of supporting suffrage. Women were encouraged to work from their homes, surrounded by their families. That these women often supported their families by their writing or art was overlooked or even concealed. A perfect example of such women is Nesbit, who wrote at home, belonged to the Fabians, and hid the fact that her writings supported her idealistic but wayward husband, his mistress, and a large household.

Working at home was not just the province of women, however. Most of the illustrators of the period did. Many lived in London, close to publishers and often in the southern suburbs. Generally they had studios in their homes or in sheds on their property. Most worked on a freelance basis, and even though some drew almost exclusively for one publisher, they had no guarantee of salary or continued association. Work for these illustrators was

more sporadic after the outbreak of World War I. Photography began to replace illustrations in magazines, and many titles ceased publication during the war. Consequently illustrators such as Norman Ault turned to alternative occupations; others such as Millar had to take what was offered, and often this meant illustrating girls' adventure books, textbook readers, and advertisements.

Prior to 1880 most artwork for newspapers, magazines, and books was reproduced by means of wood engraving, in which an engraver copied the artist's drawing onto a woodblock and then carved it. The success of this alliance depended on the skill of the engraver, and artists often complained of misinterpretation. Evans, however, was one printer who united the best of illustrators with sensitive engraving and color printing. Evans began working with Crane in the 1860s to produce a quality, inexpensive toy book, a genre described by John Barr in *Illustrated Children's Books* (1986) as "six or eight square pages of coloured illustrations, sometimes accompanied by a short text, usually a traditional tale or rhyme. The covers were paper and the price was low. Colour was the important element of the toy book." Evans and Crane took the form to new heights, and Evans continued to improve his color printing, producing the enormously popular and artistically excellent toy books of Caldecott and Greenaway.

However, in the 1880s experiments continued trying to find other ways of reproducing artwork. The engraver could be eliminated by using photography to transfer and acids to etch the artist's drawing onto the block or plate. The new photomechanical methods were called line-block and halftone. The line-block allowed for fewer tonal effects but it could be printed on the same page with typeset text. For the halftone the drawing was photographed through a screen breaking down the lines into many small dots, permitting delicate tonal effects. But halftones required a full-page illustration printed separately from the text on special glossy paper. As Thorpe explains, with these new technologies, newspapers "could print an illustration within a few hours of its delivery," and the print was an accurate rendering of the original drawings. This in turn gave the artist more freedom. "The demand for drawings increased, prices improved, and an increasing number of artists devoted their time and talents entirely to black-and-white illustration." Joyce Whalley and Tessa Chester explain that the introduction of photochemical reproduction met with considerable resistance in Britain "because it put engravers out of work and because now illustrators had to draw for reduction." However, this line-block method gave rise to the new school of black-and-white illustrators who attained new artistic highs. Coupled with the technique was an appreciation for the Japanese use of white space that artists such as Aubrey Beardsley adopted with great effectiveness. By the end of the 1890s artists were working in a new color technology, halftone color printing. This, like black-and-white halftone, had to be printed on special glossy paper. It was the technology used by the lavish gift-book artists such as Rackham and for the delicate watercolors of Potter in the decades leading up to World War I.

Toward the end of the century fantasy literature and fairy tales became dominant modes of writing for children. Stephen Prickett traces the roots of this interest in his book *Victorian Fantasy* (1979), pointing to the convergence of romanticism, Darwinism, expansion of the British Empire, and fascination with the exotic. Fantasy writers George MacDonald and Carroll gave way to new writers Molesworth, Nesbit, and Rudyard Kipling.

The three latter fantasy writers' books were published first in magazines such as the *Strand, Nash's Magazine,* and *Little Folks,* then reissued as books that included some of the same black-and-white illustrations. Occasionally a colored frontispiece was added. Black-and-white illustrators also found a market for fantasy illustration in the field of fairy-tale illustration. These also appeared in magazines for children and were then collected into books. Reissues of fairy tales by Hans Christian Andersen and by Jacob and Wilhelm Grimm and of the *Arabian Nights' Entertainments* were legion, and the buyer often had a choice among several illustrated editions.

H. R. Millar (1869-1939) serves well as the consummate example of the black-and-white illustrator. With the exception of his brilliant *Dreamland Express* (1927), which he wrote and illustrated in color, Millar worked primarily in black and white.

Intending to be a civil engineer, Millar attended the Birmingham School of Art during the late 1880s, where he developed his style and his interest in Russian art. Early work in the student magazine the *Comus* (1889) shows a weaker line than in his mature work, but the architectural elements and perspective that identify Millar's work are already present. Moving to London, he married, took up residency in Chelsea, and began illustrating for the *Strand* magazine. His illustrations for a fairy story by Alexandre Dumas fils appeared in the first issue of the *Strand* in 1891, and his first illustrations published in book form were for an 1890 edition of the popular *Ministering Children* (1854), by Maria Louisa Charlesworth, to which he contributed the frontispiece and five illustrations.

During the 1890s Millar continued work for the *Strand* and illustrated Andersen's fairy tales for the Walter Scott Company; *Untold Tales of the Past* (1897), by Beatrice Harraden for Blackwood; *Aunt Louisa's Book of Fairy Tales* (n.d.), by Laura Valentine for Warne; *Fairy Tales from Far and Near* (1895), collected by Sir Arthur Quiller-Couch for Cassell; and four "gem" fairy tale books, *The Golden Fairy Book* (1894), *The Silver Fairy Book* (1894), *The Diamond Fairy Book* (1897), and *The Ruby Fairy Book* (1898), which were collections of his work in the *Strand,* published by Hutchinson. Although he illustrated realistic work as well, he became noted for his ability to render fantastic landscapes and beings. Perhaps because of this reputation, the *Strand* teamed him with newcomer Nesbit to illustrate eight stories involving dragons, first appearing in 1899. Millar's ability to picture Nesbit's quirky fantasy creations, such as a rusted dragon or a purple dragon with an

Illustration by Gordon Browne for E. Nesbit's The Story of the Treasure Seekers *(1899)*

umbrella, led to a productive partnership. Millar became the standard illustrator for Nesbit's fantasy books while C. E. Brock illustrated her more realistic books about the Bastable family.

In a collaboration that paralleled other illustrator/author partnerships of the 1900–1914 period, Nesbit would send Millar handwritten chapters, and Millar would draw five or six illustrations and send the final product to the *Strand*. Though highly complimentary about each other's work, they never met to discuss what the author wanted illustrated or how the illustrations should appear. Indeed, Nesbit expressed surprise that Millar could draw the Psammead in *Five Children and It* (1902) exactly as she had visualized it. He, in turn, said it was because she had so accurately described the creature. *The Enchanted Castle* (1907) includes a tribute to Millar by Nesbit. At one point in the story Nesbit addresses the reader and says she will forgo description because "Mr. Millar will draw the different kinds of arches for you."

During the time that Millar was working on Nesbit's *The Story of the Amulet* (1906) which appeared in the *Strand*, he began illustrating Kipling's *Puck of Pook's Hill* (1906), also serialized in the *Strand*, followed by its sequel, *Rewards and Fairies* (1910). Macmillan published *Puck of Pook's Hill* with Millar illustrations, but their edition of *Rewards and*

Fairies used new illustrations by Frank Craig. Kipling and Millar never met, but Millar traveled to Sussex to sketch locations for the illustrations.

Millar, in an 1896 interview in the *Idler,* said that he enjoyed studying anatomy, costume, and machines. His particular interests outside of illustration lay with model railroading and trains in general. Perhaps because of his early training as a civil engineer, his drawings of machines, especially train engines, are accurate and detailed. At one point he advertised himself as a consultant on engines. When a story featured an engine such as the one in Nesbit's *The Magic City* (1910), it was selected as a subject by Millar. His drawings of locomotives turn up in issues of *Little Folks* and some of his later books. He contributed an article, "Fifty Years of Model Loco Building," in 1932 to the *Model Engineer and Practical Electrician* and wrote *Dreamland Express* (1927), a wonder book of an adventure on various magical trains.

Little Folks, a monthly magazine for children, was published by Cassell. W. Heath Robinson's first work for children appeared in *Little Folks* in 1896. It was a full-page street scene depicting "The Fairy Pedlar," a poem. In the same year Millar's illustrations accompanied a serialized piece, *The Adventures of a Grecian Hero,* a retelling of Homer's *Odyssey,* and a play of "The Sleeping Beauty." Along

Pages from W. H. Robinson's The Adventures of Uncle Lubin *(1902)*

with others Millar and Rackham contributed illustrations for *Queen Mab's Fairy Realm* (1901), a compilation of fairy tales published by George Newnes. Rackham and Millar illustrations frequently appeared in *Little Folks* and the *Strand* in the 1890–1910 period.

Most illustrators tended not to form into groups. Exceptions were the illustrators for *Punch* magazine, members of the Bloomsbury group, and members of the Arts and Craft movement. Morris's Kelmscott Press brought artisans, writers, and artists together to create each book as a handcrafted work of art. But artists who made their living illustrating, by and large, tended to form more singular friendships, and such was the case with Millar. His close friend Norman Ault (17 December 1880–6 February 1950) illustrated several books and in magazines. The Aults and the Millars appear to have met in Chelsea, although it is possible that both artists were students at the same time in Birmingham.

Ault's and Millar's work appeared alternately on the covers of *Judy,* a humor magazine for adults designed to compete with *Punch* and published from 1867 to 1907. This seems largely to have been the extent of their professional connection, although both illustrated for the *Strand.* Ault and Millar also illustrated

separate volumes of the *Mabinogion* around 1902. Ault wrote and illustrated a full-color fantasy book, *Dreamland Shores* (1920), and illustrated Wilhelm Hauff's *Caravan Tales* (1884) in 1912. When World War I diminished the scope of work for the illustrator, Ault turned to other avenues: first illustrating a book on Roman Britain, and then several editions of Alexander Pope's works.

Illustrators Hugh Thomson (1 June 1860–7 May 1920) and Aubrey Beardsley (1874–16 March 1898) contributed few illustrations to works for children but nonetheless greatly influenced the field. Noted as the successor to Caldecott, Thomson evoked the eighteenth and early nineteenth centuries in his work, an orientation Caldecott had established in his illustrations for children. Caldecott and Thomson both worked on a Macmillan series of classics: Caldecott on an 1875 edition of Washington Irving's *Old Christmas* and an 1877 edition of *Bracebridge Hall;* Thomson on an 1890 edition of Oliver Goldsmith's *The Vicar of Wakefield* (1766) and an 1891 edition of Elizabeth Cleghorn Gaskell's *Cranford* (1891). It was from *Cranford* that the style of illustration harking back to preindustrial rural England took its name, the Cranford school. Brock also adopted this style. Thomson illustrated some fairy picture books for Macmillan in 1898, and later, in 1901, he illustrated "The Witch and the Jewelled Eggs" for *Little Folks*.

Thomson was born in northern Ireland. Largely self-taught, he was apprenticed in the linen trade where his talent was recognized. He was sent to Belfast to work for Marcus Ward, a leader in the color printing of Christmas cards and books. In 1883 Thomson moved to London to seek employment as an illustrator. The *English Illustrated Magazine* made him its chief illustrator, a position he retained for eight years. The photomechanical production method popular at the time suited his fine, graceful lines.

Thomson exhibited his drawings for *The Vicar of Wakefield* at the Fine Art Society at the same time Greenaway was exhibiting. He turned down an opportunity to work for *Punch,* an offer few could refuse, because he claimed he could not illustrate works that did not appeal to him. His most important influence was on perpetuating the fluid, Caldecott line along with the depiction of rural scenes.

While Thomson looked back to the graceful Queen Anne period, Beardsley embraced the aesthetic movement and its interest in the sensual, slightly scandalous art, and he revolutionized black-and-white art by introducing new proportions in the human figure. As a child Beardsley was heavily influenced by Greenaway, and this early impression was probably responsible for his *Under the Hill* (1904), reminiscent of Greenaway's *Under the Window* (1879). Next, he turned to the Pre-Raphaelite Sir Edward Coley Burne-Jones for inspiration, but his introduction to Japanese prints is credited with creating his unique style. Beardsley, who died at age twenty-six in 1898, freed illustration from the confines of well-filled squares through his use of the elaborate borders of the Arts and Crafts movement and the representational art of the Cranford school. He utilized blocks of black and elongated, disproportional figures. Beardsley's designs had a far-reaching influence on other artists, including many who illustrated children's books, such as Rackham. Simon Houfe claims that Beardsley "united book decoration and illustration in [Britain] and gave it credibility with serious artists of the *avant-garde.*" In terms of children's book illustration both Beardsley and Thomson are noted more for their influence than for their contributions.

Gordon Browne (15 April 1858–27 May 1932), like Millar, however, is commonly identified as a prolific illustrator, primarily of children's books. Both contributed to various children's magazines, making their work difficult to catalogue since not all magazines identified illustrators in their indexes. Both Millar and Browne were noted for their interest and accuracy in historical periods, especially military armament and weapons, with Browne concentrating on the 1600s. In collaboration with Lewis Baumer, Browne also illustrated two books for Nesbit: *The Story of the Treasure Seekers* (1899) and *The New Treasure Seekers* (1904). These two books were part of Nesbit's realistic work, so Browne was not called on to present dragons, psammeads, and other fantastic creatures.

The majority of Browne's work, with the exception of *Fairy Tales from Grimm* in 1895 and *Fairy Tales from Hans Andersen* in 1901, was in the realistic vein. Browne was known for taking great care over his interpretation of texts. He read each manuscript twice, first to grasp the plot and then to examine possibilities for illustration. This reputation for care may have been what kept him in demand from his first published work in 1875 well into the 1920s. Like Millar, he executed thousands of black-and-white illustrations and illustrated one hundred books, often at the rate of six or seven a year. In contrast, Thomson took eighteen months to illustrate *The Vicar of Wakefield*.

It has been suggested that Browne's work is not as well known as some other contemporary illustrators because he did not become associated with one particular author as his father, "Phiz," had become associated with Dickens. However, Browne's list of authors is definitely not minor. He illustrated several books by G. A. Henty, Molesworth, and Juliana Ewing besides doing illustrated editions of works by Daniel Defoe, Irving, Sir Walter Scott, Jonathan Swift, and William Makepeace Thackeray.

William Heath Robinson (31 May 1872–13 September 1944) also had family members, his brothers Charles and Tom, working in illustration. All three collaborated on an edition of Andersen's fairy tales for Dent in 1899. William, the youngest Robinson brother, was born in north London in 1872. His son describes his work as prodigious. Like Millar and Browne, Robinson did an astonishing amount of illustration, the publication of which continued until his death in 1950. Robinson worked both in black and white and in color. Unlike Thomson, he found that the cartoon style suited him, and his *The Adventures of Uncle Lubin* (1902, published by Grant Richards) remains a testament to that preference. His cartoons appeared in 1905 in the *Tatler,* the *Sketch,* and the *Bystander.*

From 1896 to 1914 Robinson's work could be found in *Little Folks,* the *Strand,* and the *Quiver.* He experimented with the use of light, sometimes back-

Jessie M. King's illustration of "The Star Child" for a 1915 edition of Oscar
Wilde's A House of Pomegranates

lighting the subjects. Robinson also became known for his use of the circular frame. There are several components to Robinson's artistic endeavors. Like many illustrators of the prewar period, he worked with black-and-white magazine illustration. Some of his work belonged to the art nouveau style such as his illustrations for *Poems of Edgar Allan Poe* (1900). He also illustrated fairy tales and fantasy books beginning with *The Giant Crab and Other Tales from Old India* by W. H. D. Rouse in 1897 and an *Arabian Nights* (for which he did 250 drawings) for Newnes in 1899. Sydney Boot, art director of the *Strand,* selected Robinson to illustrate children's stories, and he and Millar shared that illustrating assignment during 1915 and 1916. In the *Dictionary of British Book Illustrators* Peppin nominates him as "the most versatile of the major British illustrators, as much at home with Rabelais, Shakespeare, Andersen, and de la Mare as with the authors of the comic 'How

to . . . ' series. He was an original and witty draughtsman, with a highly developed eye for nuances of character and detail."

Another artist working in some of the same markets as Robinson was Edmund Dulac (22 October 1882–25 May 1953), principally noted for his color work. The most frequent venue for color illustration was the gift book employing the new three color halftone process. Designed more for adults than for children, gift books often took their text from fairy tales and folktales that could be read and shown to children. Rackham and the Robinson brothers also illustrated gift books.

Dulac was born in France, where he studied law and attended art school. He finally came to London in 1905. His work, which combines British subject matter with distinctly Persian and Indian motifs, came to the attention of gift-book buyers when Heinemann published his illustrations for *Sto-*

WHEN HE HAD FREED WENDY

One of Mabel Lucie Atwell's illustrations for J. M. Barrie's Peter Pan and Wendy *(1921)*

ries from the Arabian Nights (1907). According to Barr, he excelled in "nocturnal or shadowy scenes where figures and forms, lit by pin-points of light, stand out against deep blue or violet backgrounds." He illustrated Nathaniel Hawthorne's retelling of the Greek myths, *Tanglewood Tales* (1853), and in 1911 stories from Andersen. His works evoke art nouveau and art deco, but Dulac was in neither school. He also designed costumes and scenery for the plays of his friend, William Butler Yeats. After World War I Dulac turned to furniture design, medals, bookplates, playing cards, and caricature. He was not alone in these endeavors. Several of the women illustrators of the period also worked in design and jewelry as well as in illustration.

As publishing for children expanded, women began to illustrate for magazines and books. As Callen notes in *Angel in the Studio* (1979), "women were thought to be most able in this field, and it also seems to have been felt that women must know more about children than men, and that they were

therefore better equipped to illustrate children's books." Greenaway's financial success in the 1880s indicated that women could make a living in illustration, although just as for men it was precarious. Many women entered the ranks of illustrators, but surprisingly few are known today.

Jessie M. King (1875–1949) studied at the Glasgow School of Art, where she later taught book decoration. She also worked as a muralist and as a designer of fabric, jewelry, and costume. The College of Art in Glasgow achieved an international reputation and stressed design in everyday accessories. King's background is apparent in her commercial work; as Houfe points out, her illustrations feature "elaborate borders of stylised birds or foliage, suggesting metal-work rather than the printed page." Her work for children was limited, mostly appearing after World War I.

According to Whalley and Chester, in King's use of fine pen lines, "the spirit of Art Nouveau is seen at its purest." They note that King employs

Beardsley's "technique of building texture and shape in shades of grey formed by dots and lines rather than the harsh black masses characteristic of his earlier work." Her illustrations for Kipling's jungle books (1894, 1895) and for a 1915 edition of Oscar Wilde's *A House of Pomegranates* (1891) established her in the field of children's literature. Whereas King married artist E. A. Taylor but was known professionally as Jessie King, Georgina E. Cave was better known by her married name, Mrs. Arthur Gaskin. Both Gaskins illustrated books for children. Arthur Gaskin's (1862–4 June 1928) first book was Andersen's *Stories and Fairy Tales* (1893) and hers was *ABC, an Alphabet* (1895). Both Gaskins attended the Birmingham School of Art and became accomplished in jewelry.

The Gaskins' work is closely tied to the Arts and Crafts movement, showing the connections among design, craft, and illustration. Arthur Gaskin illustrated *The Shepheardes Calender,* by Edmund Spenser, for the Kelmscott Press in 1896. Georgina Gaskin illustrated three other books, *Horn-Book Jingles* (1896–1897), *Little Girls and Little Boys* (1898), and *The Travellers and Other Stories* (1898), which she also wrote. The latter two are illustrated in color. The children in her work look posed and static, and their faces have few features other than round black eyes and mouths. But that does not detract from their charm; rather it weds them to the Arts and Crafts style. The special issue of the *Studio* on children's books in 1897 suggests that the Birmingham artists can be identified as a group. "The idea that links the group together is sufficiently 'similar to impart to all a certain resemblance.' In other words, you can nearly always pick out a 'Birmingham' illustration at a glance, even if it would be impossible to confuse the work of Mrs. Gaskin with that of Miss Levetus." The Gaskins' work in illustration appears to be limited to the 1890s decade. Both King and Georgina Gaskin paved the way for other women artists to enter the field of illustration. Certainly the success of Potter and Greenaway set the standard, but these lesser-known artists showed that there was room for other women in illustration. Women artists who benefited from their pioneering efforts include Anne Anderson, Hilda Cowham, Honor Appleton, and Mabel Lucie Attwell.

Like the other artists mentioned, Attwell (4 June 1879–5 November 1964) began illustrating for magazines such as *Little Folks* in 1890s. She also illustrated a version of the Andersen fairy tales in 1913 and a version of tales of the Brothers Grimm. But her illustrations for a condensed version of Charles Kingsley's *The Water-Babies* (1863) introduced what was to become her trademark: chubby, round-cheeked babies. She was born in London and studied at Heatherley's School of Art. Like King, she married but kept her maiden name. She began a gift-book series, her best work, using half-tone color plates for Raphael Tuck with *Mother Goose* (1909) and *Alice in Wonderland* (1910), an edition of Carroll's 1865 work. These were followed by her Andersen edition, the condensed Kingsley, and J. M. Barrie's *Peter Pan and Wendy* (1921), a republication of *Peter and Wendy* (1911). But as Whalley and Chester suggest, "as her book illustration [later] became less and less successful, so her reputation grew for supplying cute and cuddly children to order: she continued to develop this facility and so achieved a national fame." She became a postcard illustrator until her death in 1964, and as Greenaway had done in the 1890s, she produced yearly almanacs. In these ways she was able to support herself as the demand for her book illustrations disappeared.

The years 1880–1940 constituted a period of opportunity for book illustrators. They trained in public art schools and began work in a time hospitable to design and illustration created by a juncture of the Arts and Crafts movement and the aesthetic movement. Critics and readers alike appreciated illustration for children's works, and the popularity of the fantastic opened a range of subjects for illustration. Printing techniques allowed for invention in black and white and for creative use of color. An expanding middle class created a market for toy and gift books, and literate children read magazines published for them. Consequently, these factors converged to produce a wonderful climate for the illustration of children's literature.

References:

Brian Alderson, *Sing a Song for Sixpence: The English Picture Book Tradition and Randolph Caldecott* (Cambridge: Cambridge University Press, 1986);

John Barr, *Illustrated Children's Books* (London: British Library, 1986);

Geoffrey C. Beare, *The Illustrations of W. Heath Robinson* (London: Werner Shaw, 1983);

Julia Briggs, *A Woman of Passion: The Life of E. Nesbit, 1858–1924* (London: Hutchinson, 1987);

Anthea Callen, *Angel in the Studio: Women in the Arts and Crafts Movement 1870–1914* (London: Astragal, 1979);

Kirsten Drotner, *English Children and Their Magazines 1751–1945* (New Haven: Yale University Press, 1988);

William Feaver, *When We Were Young: Two Centuries of Children's Book Illustration* (New York: Holt, Rinehart & Winston, 1977);

Simon Houfe, *The Dictionary of British Book Illustrators and Caricaturists 1800–1914* (London: Hacker Art Books, 1978; revised edition, Woodbridge, Suffolk: Antique Collector's Club, 1981);

Diana L. Johnson, *Fantastic Illustration and Design in Britain, 1850–1930* (Providence: Rhode Island School of Design, 1979);

Lionel Lambourne, *Utopian Craftsmen: The Arts and Crafts Movement from the Cotswolds to Chicago* (Salt Lake City, Utah: Peregrine Smith, 1980);

Wallace Lawler, "Romance in Black and White: A Chat with Mr. H. R. Millar," *Idler* (1896);

Sally Mitchell, ed., *Victorian Britain: An Encyclopedia* (New York: Garland, 1988);

Brigid Peppin and Lucy Micklethwait, *Dictionary of British Book Illustrators: The Twentieth Century* (London: Murray, 1983);

Stephen Prickett, *Victorian Fantasy* (Bloomington: Indiana University Press, 1979);

R. E. D. Sketchley, *English Book Illustration of Today* (London: Kegan Paul, Trench, Trubner, 1903);

M. H. Spielmann and Walter Jerrold, *Hugh Thomson: His Art, His Letters, His Humour and His Charm* (London: Black, 1931);

James Thorpe, *English Illustration: The Nineties* (London: Faber & Faber, 1935);

Stanley Weintraub, *Beardsley: A Biography* (New York: Braziller, 1967);

Joyce Whalley and Tessa Chester, *A History of Children's Book Illustration* (London: Murray, 1988).

Books for Further Reading

The bibliography below lists suggested historical and critical works as well as studies on dominant literary genres and other relevant topics, such as book illustration, juvenile magazines, imperialism, reading habits, the impact of literature on children, and guides for research. Valuable periodicals for scholarly studies include *Children's Literature, Children's Literature Association Quarterly, Children's Literature in Education, Horn Book, The Lion and the Unicorn,* and *Phaedrus.*

Alderson, Brian. *Sing a Song for Sixpence.* London: Cambridge University Press & the British Library Board, 1986.

Altick, Richard D. *The English Common Reader: A Social History of the Mass-Reading Public, 1800–1900.* Chicago: University of Chicago Press, 1957.

Altick. *Lives and Letters: A History of Literary Biography in England and America.* New York: Knopf, 1965.

Avery, Gillian. *Childhood's Pattern: A Study of the Heroes and Heroines of Children's Fiction, 1770–1950.* London: Hodder & Stoughton, 1975.

Avery. *Nineteenth Century Children: Heroes and Heroines in English Children's Stories, 1780–1900.* London: Hodder & Stoughton, 1965.

Avery, and Julia Briggs. *Children and Their Books: A Celebration of the Work of Iona and Peter Opie.* Oxford: Clarendon Press, 1989.

Bingham, Jane, and Grayce Scholt. *Fifteen Centuries of Children's Literature: An Annotated Chronology of British and American Works in Historical Context.* Westport, Conn.: Greenwood Press, 1980.

Bingham and Scholt. *Writers for Children: Critical Studies of Major Authors Since the Seventeenth Century.* New York: Scribners, 1988.

Blount, Margaret. *Animal Land: The Creatures of Children's Fiction.* London: Hutchinson, 1974.

Bratton, J. S. *The Impact of Victorian Children's Fiction.* London: Croom Helm, 1981.

Cadogan, Mary, and Patricia Craig. *You're a Brick, Angela! The Girls' Story 1839–1985,* revised edition. London: Gollancz, 1986.

Carpenter, Humphrey. *Secret Gardens: A Study of the Golden Age of Children's Literature.* Boston: Houghton Mifflin, 1985.

Carpenter and Mari Prichard, comps. *The Oxford Companion to Children's Literature.* Oxford: Oxford University Press, 1984.

Chambers, Nancy, ed. *The Signal Approach to Children's Books: A Collection.* Metuchen, N.J.: Scarecrow Press, 1981.

Chester, Tessa Rose. *Children's Books Research: A Practical Guide to Techniques and Sources.* South Woodchester, U.K.: Thimble Press, 1989.

Chester. *Sources of Information About Children's Books.* South Woodchester, U.K.: Thimble Press, 1989.

Coveney, Peter. *The Image of Childhood; The Individual and Society: A Study of the Theme in English Literature,* revised edition. Harmondsworth, U.K.: Penguin, 1967.

Crouch, Marcus. *Treasure Seekers and Borrowers: Children's Books in Britain, 1900–1960.* London: Library Association, 1962.

Darton, F. J. Harvey. *Children's Books in England: Five Centuries of Social Life,* third edition, revised by Alderson. Cambridge: Cambridge University Press, 1982.

Drotner, Kirsten. *English Children and Their Magazines, 1751–1945.* New Haven: Yale University Press, 1988.

Dusinberre, Juliet. *Alice to the Lighthouse: Children's Books and Radical Experiments in Art.* New York: St. Martin's Press, 1987.

Egoff, Sheila, G. T. Stubbs, and L. F. Ashley, eds. *Only Connect: Readings on Children's Literature,* second edition. New York: Oxford University Press, 1980.

Field, Carolyn W., ed. *Special Collections in Children's Literature.* Chicago: American Library Association, 1982.

Fisher, Margery. *The Bright Face of Danger: An Exploration of the Adventure Story.* Boston: Horn Book, 1986.

Fox, Geoff, and others, eds. *Writers, Critics, and Children.* London: Heinemann, 1976.

Fraser, James, comp. *Children's Authors and Illustrators: A Guide to Manuscript Collections in United States Research Libraries.* New York: K. G. Saur, 1980.

Green, Martin. *Dreams of Adventure, Deeds of Empire.* London: Routledge & Kegan Paul, 1980.

Harrison, Barbara, and Gregory Maguire. *Innocence & Experience: Essays & Conversations on Children's Literature.* New York: Lothrop, Lee & Shepard, 1987.

Haviland, Virginia, ed. *Children and Literature: Views and Reviews.* Glenview, Ill.: Scott, Foresman, 1973.

Haviland. *Children's Literature: A Guide to Reference Sources.* Washington, D.C.: Library of Congress, 1966; supplements, 1972, 1977, 1982.

Hendrickson, Linnea. *Children's Literature: A Guide to the Criticism.* Boston: G. K. Hall, 1987.

Hollindale, Peter. *Ideology and the Children's Book.* South Woodchester, U.K.: Thimble Press, 1988.

Houfe, Simon. *The Dictionary of British Book Illustrators and Caricaturists, 1800–1914,* revised edition. Woodbridge, Suffolk, U.K.: Antique Collectors' Club, 1981.

Howarth, Patrick. *Play Up and Play the Game: The Heroes of Popular Fiction.* London: Eyre Methuen, 1973.

Hoyle, Karen Nelson, and others, comps. *The Kerlan Collection Manuscripts and Illustrations for Children's Books: A Checklist.* Minneapolis: Kerlan Collection, University of Minnesota Libraries, 1985.

Hunt, Peter, ed. *Children's Literature: The Development of Criticism.* London: Routledge, 1990.

Hunt. *Criticism, Theory, and Children's Literature.* Oxford: Blackwell, 1991.

Hurlimann, Bettina. *Three Centuries of Children's Books in Europe,* translated by Alderson. Cleveland: World, 1968.

Inglis, Fred. *The Promise of Happiness: Value and Meaning in Children's Fiction.* Cambridge: Cambridge University Press, 1981.

Jackson, Rosemary. *Fantasy: The Literature of Subversion.* London: Methuen, 1981.

Lanes, Selma G. *Down the Rabbit Hole: Adventures and Misadventures in the Realm of Children's Literature,* revised edition. New York: Atheneum, 1976.

Lofts, W. O. G., and D. J. Adley. *The Men Behind Boys' Fiction.* London: Baker, 1970.

Lurie, Alison. *Don't Tell the Grown-Ups: Subversive Children's Literature.* Boston: Little, Brown, 1990.

Mack, Edward C. *The Public Schools and British Opinion Since 1860.* New York: Columbia University Press, 1941.

Mangan, J. A. *Athleticism in the Victorian and Edwardian Public School.* Cambridge: Cambridge University Press, 1981.

Meek, Margaret, Aidan Warlow, and Griselda Bareton, eds. *The Cool Web: The Pattern of Children's Reading.* London: Bodley Head, 1978.

Meigs, Cornelia L., and others. *A Critical History of Children's Literature: A Survey of Children's Books in English from the Earliest Times to the Present,* revised edition. New York: Macmillan, 1969.

Muir, Percy. *English Children's Books, 1600 to 1900.* New York: Praeger, 1969.

Musgrave, P. W. *From Brown to Bunter: The Life and Death of the School Story.* London: Routledge, 1985.

Nelson, Claudia. *Boys Will Be Girls: The Feminine Ethic and British Children's Fiction, 1857–1917.* New Brunswick, N.J.: Rutgers University Press, 1991.

Quigly, Isabel. *The Heirs of Tom Brown: The English School Story.* London: Chatto & Windus, 1982.

Rahn, Suzanne. *Children's Literature: An Annotated Bibliography of the History and Criticism.* New York: Garland, 1981.

Richards, Jeffrey, ed. *Happiest Days: The Public Schools in English Fiction.* Manchester: Manchester University Press, 1988.

Richards, ed. *Imperialism and Juvenile Literature.* Studies in Imperialism series. Manchester: Manchester University Press, 1989.

Rose, Jacqueline. *The Case of Peter Pan; or, The Impossibility of Children's Fiction.* London: Macmillan, 1984; Philadelphia: University of Pennsylvania Press, 1993.

Salway, Lance, ed. *A Peculiar Gift: Nineteenth Century Writings on Books for Children.* London: Kestrel, 1976.

Salway. *Reading About Children's Books: An Introductory Guide to Books About Children's Literature.* London: National Book League, 1986.

Sandison, Alan. *The Wheel of Empire: A Study of the Imperial Idea in Some Late Nineteenth and Early Twentieth-Century Fiction.* New York: Macmillan, 1967.

Townsend, John Rowe. *Written for Children: An Outline of English-Language Children's Literature,* third edition. New York: Lippincott, 1987.

Tucker, Nicholas, ed. *Suitable for Children? Controversies in Children's Literature.* Atlanta: Georgia State University Press, 1976.

Turner, E. S. *Boys Will Be Boys: The Story of Sweeney Todd, Deadwood Dick, Sexton Blake, Billy Bunter, Dick Barton et al,* third edition. London: Joseph, 1975.

Warner, Philip. *The Best of British Pluck: The Boy's Own Paper.* London: Macdonald & Jane's, 1976.

Whalley, Joyce Irene, and Chester. *A History of Children's Book Illustration.* London: John Murray, 1988.

Zipes, Jack. *Fairy Tales and the Art of Subversion: The Classical Genre for Children and the Process of Civilization.* New York: Wildman, 1983.

Zipes. *Victorian Fairy Tales: The Revolt of the Fairies and Elves.* London: Methuen, 1987.

Contributors

Diana A. Chlebek ....*University of Akron*
R. J. Dingley ....*University of New England, New South Wales*
Gwyneth Evans................................*Malaspina College, British Columbia*
Lois Rauch Gibson..*Coker College*
Jacqueline L. Gmuca................................*Coastal Carolina University*
Kathy Merlock Jackson ....*Virginia Wesleyan College*
Michael Scott Joseph ....*Rutgers University Libraries*
Greta D. Little................................*University of South Carolina*
Anne H. Lundin ....*University of Wisconsin — Madison*
Ruth K. MacDonald ....*Cheshire, Connecticut*
Corinne McCutchan ....*Lander University*
Claudia Nelson ....*Southwest Texas State University*
Kathy Piehl ....*Mankato State University*
Nicholas Ranson................................*University of Akron*
Mavis Reimer ....*University of Winnipeg*
Lucy Rollin ....*Clemson University*
L. M. Rutherford................................*University of New England, New South Wales*
Patrick Scott ....*University of South Carolina*
Mary E. Shaner................................*University of Massachusetts — Boston*
Louisa Smith................................*Mankato State University*
Jan Susina................................*Illinois State University*
Carol Anita Tarr ....*Illinois State University*
Donna R. White ....*Clemson University*
Harriet P. Williams ....*retired, Durham Academy*

Cumulative Index

Dictionary of Literary Biography, Volumes 1-141
Dictionary of Literary Biography Yearbook, 1980-1993
Dictionary of Literary Biography Documentary Series, Volumes 1-11

Cumulative Index

DLB before number: *Dictionary of Literary Biography,* Volumes 1-141
Y before number: *Dictionary of Literary Biography Yearbook,* 1980-1993
DS before number: *Dictionary of Literary Biography Documentary Series,* Volumes 1-11

A

Abbey Press DLB-49

The Abbey Theatre and Irish Drama,
   1900-1945 ....DLB-10

Abbot, Willis J. 1863-1934 ....DLB-29

Abbott, Jacob 1803-1879 ....DLB-1

Abbott, Lee K. 1947- DLB-130

Abbott, Lyman 1835-1922 ....DLB-79

Abbott, Robert S. 1868-1940 ....DLB-29, 91

Abelard, Peter circa 1079-1142 .....DLB-115

Abelard-Schuman DLB-46

Abell, Arunah S. 1806-1888 ....DLB-43

Abercrombie, Lascelles 1881-1938 ...DLB-19

Aberdeen University Press
   Limited DLB-106

Abish, Walter 1931- DLB-130

Abrahams, Peter 1919- DLB-117

Abrams, M. H. 1912- DLB-67

Abse, Dannie 1923- DLB-27

Academy Chicago Publishers DLB-46

Accrocca, Elio Filippo 1923- DLB-128

Ace Books DLB-46

Achebe, Chinua 1930- DLB-117

Achtenberg, Herbert 1938- DLB-124

Ackerman, Diane 1948- DLB-120

Acorn, Milton 1923-1986 ....DLB-53

Acosta, Oscar Zeta 1935?- DLB-82

Actors Theatre of Louisville DLB-7

Adair, James 1709?-1783? DLB-30

Adam, Graeme Mercer 1839-1912 ...DLB-99

Adame, Leonard 1947- DLB-82

Adamic, Louis 1898-1951 ....DLB-9

Adams, Alice 1926- Y-86

Adams, Brooks 1848-1927 ....DLB-47

Adams, Charles Francis, Jr.
   1835-1915 ....DLB-47

Adams, Douglas 1952- Y-83

Adams, Franklin P. 1881-1960 ...... DLB-29

Adams, Henry 1838-1918 .... DLB-12, 47

Adams, Herbert Baxter 1850-1901 ... DLB-47

Adams, J. S. and C.
   [publishing house] DLB-49

Adams, James Truslow 1878-1949 ... DLB-17

Adams, John 1735-1826 .... DLB-31

Adams, John Quincy 1767-1848 ..... DLB-37

Adams, Léonie 1899-1988 .... DLB-48

Adams, Levi 1802-1832 .... DLB-99

Adams, Samuel 1722-1803 ...... DLB-31, 43

Adams, William Taylor 1822-1897 .. DLB-42

Adamson, Sir John 1867-1950 ...... DLB-98

Adcock, Arthur St. John
   1864-1930 .... DLB-135

Adcock, Betty 1938- DLB-105

Adcock, Betty, Certain Gifts DLB-105

Adcock, Fleur 1934- DLB-40

Addison, Joseph 1672-1719 .... DLB-101

Ade, George 1866-1944 .... DLB-11, 25

Adeler, Max (see Clark, Charles Heber)

Advance Publishing Company DLB-49

AE 1867-1935 .... DLB-19

Aesthetic Poetry (1873), by
   Walter Pater DLB-35

After Dinner Opera Company Y-92

Afro-American Literary Critics:
   An Introduction DLB-33

Agassiz, Jean Louis Rodolphe
   1807-1873 .... DLB-1

Agee, James 1909-1955 .... DLB-2, 26

The Agee Legacy: A Conference at
   the University of Tennessee
   at Knoxville Y-89

Ai 1947- DLB-120

Aichinger, Ilse 1921- DLB-85

Aidoo, Ama Ata 1942- DLB-117

Aiken, Conrad 1889-1973 ....DLB-9, 45, 102

Ainsworth, William Harrison
   1805-1882 ....DLB-21

Aitken, Robert [publishing house] ...DLB-49

Akenside, Mark 1721-1770 ....DLB-109

Akins, Zoë 1886-1958 ....DLB-26

Alabaster, William 1568-1640 ......DLB-132

Alain-Fournier 1886-1914 ....DLB-65

Alarcón, Francisco X. 1954- DLB-122

Alba, Nanina 1915-1968 ....DLB-41

Albee, Edward 1928- DLB-7

Albert the Great circa 1200-1280 ...DLB-115

Alberti, Rafael 1902- DLB-108

Alcott, Amos Bronson 1799-1888 .....DLB-1

Alcott, Louisa May
   1832-1888 ....DLB-1, 42, 79

Alcott, William Andrus 1798-1859 ....DLB-1

Alden, Henry Mills 1836-1919 ......DLB-79

Alden, Isabella 1841-1930 ....DLB-42

Alden, John B. [publishing house] DLB-49

Alden, Beardsley and Company DLB-49

Aldington, Richard
   1892-1962 .... DLB-20, 36, 100

Aldis, Dorothy 1896-1966 ....DLB-22

Aldiss, Brian W. 1925- DLB-14

Aldrich, Thomas Bailey
   1836-1907 .... DLB-42, 71, 74, 79

Alegría, Ciro 1909-1967 ....DLB-113

Aleixandre, Vicente 1898-1984 .....DLB-108

Aleramo, Sibilla 1876-1960 ....DLB-114

Alexander, Charles 1868-1923 ......DLB-91

Alexander, Charles Wesley
   [publishing house] DLB-49

Alexander, James 1691-1756 ....DLB-24

Alexander, Lloyd 1924- DLB-52

Alexander, Sir William, Earl of Stirling
   1577?-1640 ....DLB-121

Alexis, Willibald 1798-1871 ....DLB-133

ISBN 0-8103-5555-8

Documentary Series

Yearbooks